blue
rider
press

UNDISPUTED TRUTH

THREE RIVERS PUBLIC LIBRARY
25207 W CHANNON DRIVE
P O BOX 300
CHANNAHON IL 60410

UNDISPUTED TRUTH
MIKE TYSON

WITH **LARRY SLOMAN**

Blue Rider Press
a member of Penguin Group (USA)
New York

blue
rider
press

Published by the Penguin Group
Penguin Group (USA) LLC
375 Hudson Street
New York, New York 10014

USA · Canada · UK · Ireland · Australia
New Zealand · India · South Africa · China

penguin.com
A Penguin Random House Company

Copyright © 2013 by Tyrannic Literary Company LLC
Penguin supports copyright. Copyright fuels creativity, encourages diverse voices,
promotes free speech, and creates a vibrant culture. Thank you for buying an authorized
edition of this book and for complying with copyright laws by not reproducing, scanning,
or distributing any part of it in any form without permission. You are supporting
writers and allowing Penguin to continue to publish books for every reader.

Library of Congress Cataloging-in-Publication Data

Tyson, Mike.
Undisputed truth / Mike Tyson, Larry Sloman.
p.   cm.
ISBN 978-0-399-16128-5
1. Tyson, Mike.   2. Boxers (Sports)—United States—Biography.
3. African American boxers—Biography.   I. Sloman, Larry.   II. Title.
GV1132.T97A3   2013   2013036115
796.83092—dc23
[B]

Printed in the United States of America
1   3   5   7   9   10   8   6   4   2

BOOK DESIGN BY STEPHANIE HUNTWORK

Penguin is committed to publishing works of quality and integrity.
In that spirit, we are proud to offer this book to our readers; however,
the story, the experiences, and the words are the author's alone.

3 1561 00255 7407

THIS BOOK IS DEDICATED TO ALL THE OUTCASTS—
EVERYONE WHO HAS EVER BEEN MESMERIZED, MARGINALIZED,
TRANQUILIZED, BEATEN DOWN, AND FALSELY ACCUSED.
AND INCAPABLE OF RECEIVING LOVE.

UNDISPUTED TRUTH

PROLOGUE

I SPENT MOST OF THE SIX WEEKS BETWEEN MY CONVICTION FOR RAPE AND sentencing traveling around the country romancing all of my various girlfriends. It was my way of saying good-bye to them. And when I wasn't with them, I was fending off all the women who propositioned me. Everywhere I'd go, there were some women who would come up to me and say, "Come on, I'm not going to say that you raped me. You can come with me. I'll let you film it." I later realized that that was their way of saying "We know you didn't do it." But I didn't take it that way. I'd strike back indignantly with a rude response. Although they were saying what they said out of support, I was in too much pain to realize it. I was an ignorant, mad, bitter guy who had a lot of growing up to do.

But some of my anger was understandable. I was a twenty-five-year-old kid facing sixty years in jail for a crime that I did not commit. Let me repeat here what I said before the grand jury, during the trial, at my sentencing, at my early-release hearing, after I got out of prison, and what I will continue to say until they put me in the ground. I did not rape Desiree Washington. She knows it, God knows it, and the consequences of her actions are something that she's got to live with for the rest of her life.

My promoter, Don King, kept assuring me that I would walk from these charges. He told me he was working behind the scenes to make the case disappear. Plus, he had hired Vince Fuller, the best lawyer that a million-dollar fee could buy. Vince just happened to be Don's tax attorney. And Don probably still owed him money. But I knew from the start that I'd get no justice. I wasn't being tried in New York or Los Angeles; we were in Indianapolis, Indiana, historically one of the strongholds of the Ku Klux Klan. My judge, Patricia Gifford, was a former sex crimes prosecutor and was known as "the Hanging Judge." I had been found guilty by a jury of my "peers," only one of whom was black. The other black jury member had been excused by the judge after a fire in the hotel where the jurors were staying. She dismissed him because of his "state of mind." Yeah, his state of mind was that he didn't like the food he was being served.

But in my mind, I had no peers. I was the youngest heavyweight champion in the history of boxing. I was a titan, the reincarnation of Alexander the Great. My style was impetuous, my defenses were impregnable, and I was ferocious. It's amazing how a low self-esteem and a huge ego can give you delusions of grandeur. But after the trial, this god among men had to get his black ass back in court for his sentencing.

But first I tried some divine intervention. Calvin, my close friend from Chicago, told me about some hoodoo woman who could cast a spell to keep me out of jail.

"You piss in a jar, then put five hundred-dollar bills in there, then put the jar under your bed for three days and then bring it to her and she'll pray over it for you," Calvin told me.

"So the clairvoyant broad is gonna take the pissy pile of hundreds out of the jar, rinse them off, and then go shopping. If somebody gave you a hundred-dollar bill they pissed on, would you care?" I asked

Calvin. I had a reputation for throwing around money but that was too much even for me.

Then some friends tried to set me up with a voodoo priest. But they brought around this guy who had a suit on. The guy didn't even look like a drugstore voodoo guy. This asshole needed to be in the swamp; he needed to have on a dashiki. I knew that guy had nothing. He didn't even have a ceremony planned. He just wrote some shit on a piece of paper and tried to sell me on some bullshit I didn't do. He wanted me to wash in some weird oil and pray and drink some special water. But I was drinking goddamn Hennessy. I wasn't going to water down my Hennessy.

So I settled on getting a Santeria priest to do some witch doctor shit. We went to the courthouse one night with a pigeon and an egg. I dropped the egg on the ground as the bird was released and I yelled, "We're free!" A few days later, I put on my gray pin-striped suit and went to court.

After the verdict had been delivered, my defense team had put together a presentence memorandum on my behalf. It was an impressive document. Dr. Jerome Miller, the clinical director of the Augustus Institute in Virginia and one of the nation's leading experts on adult sex offenders, had examined me and concluded that I was "a sensitive and thoughtful young man with problems more the result of developmental deficits than of pathology." With regular psychotherapy, he was convinced that my long-term prognosis would be quite good. He concluded, "A term in prison will delay the process further and more likely set it back. I would strongly recommend that other options with both deterrent and treatment potential be considered." Of course, the probation officers who put together their sentencing document left that last paragraph out of their summary. But they were eager to include the prosecution's opinion, "An assessment of this offense and this offender leads the chief investigator of this case, an experienced sex crimes detective, to conclude that the defendant is inclined to commit a similar offense in the future."

My lawyers prepared an appendix that contained forty-eight testimonials to my character from such diverse people as my high school principal, my social worker in upstate New York, Sugar Ray Robinson's widow, my adoptive mother, Camille, my boxing hypnotherapist, and six of my girlfriends (and their mothers), who all wrote moving accounts of how I had been a perfect gentleman with them. One of my first girlfriends from Catskill even wrote the judge, "I waited three years before having sexual intercourse with Mr. Tyson and not once did he force me into anything. That is the reason I love him, because he loves and respects women."

But of course, Don being Don, he had to go and overdo it. King had the Reverend William F. Crockett, the Imperial First Ceremonial Master of the Ancient Egyptian Arabic Order Nobles Mystic Shrine of North and South America, write a letter on my behalf. The Reverend wrote, "I beseech you to spare him incarceration. Though I have not spoken to Mike since the day of his trial, my information is that he no longer uses profanity or vulgarity, reads the Bible daily, prays and trains." Of course, that was all bullshit. He didn't even know me.

Then there was Don's personal heartfelt letter to the judge. You would have thought that I had come up with a cure for cancer, had a plan for peace in the Middle East, and nursed sick kittens back to health. He talked about my work with the Make-A-Wish Foundation visiting with sick kids. He informed Judge Gifford that every Thanksgiving we gave away forty thousand turkeys to the needy and the hungry. He recounted the time we met with Simon Wiesenthal and I was so moved that I donated a large sum of money to help him hunt down Nazi war criminals. I guess Don forgot that the Klan hated Jews as much as they hated blacks.

This went on for eight pages, with Don waxing eloquently about me. "It is highly unusual for a person his age to be concerned about his fellow man, let alone with the deep sense of commitment and dedication that he possesses. These are God-like qualities, noble qualities of loving, giving and unselfishness. He is a child of God: one of the most gentle, sensitive, caring, loving, and understanding persons that I have ever met in my twenty years' experience with boxers." Shit, Don should have delivered the closing arguments instead of my lawyer. But John Solberg, Don's public relations man, cut right to the chase in his letter to Judge Gifford. "Mike Tyson is not a scumbag," he wrote.

I might not have been a scumbag, but I was an arrogant prick. I was so arrogant in the courtroom during the trial that there was no way they were going to give me a break. Even in my moment of doom, I was not a humble person. All those things they wrote about in that report—giving people money and turkeys, taking care of people, looking out for the weak and the infirm—I did all those things because I *wanted* to be that humble person, not because I *was* that person. I wanted so desperately to be humble but there wasn't a humble bone in my body.

So, armed with all my character testimonials, we appeared in Judge Patricia Gifford's court on March 26, 1992, for my sentencing. Witnesses were permitted and Vince Fuller began the process by calling to the stand Lloyd Bridges, the executive director of the Riverside Residential Center in Indianapolis. My defense team was arguing that instead of jail time, my sentence should be suspended and I should serve my probation term at a halfway house where I could combine personal therapy with community service. Bridges, an ordained minister, ran just such a program and he testified that I would certainly be a prime candidate for his facility.

But the assistant prosecutor got Bridges to reveal that there had been four escapes recently from his halfway house. And when she got the minister to admit that he had interviewed me in my mansion in Ohio and that we had paid for his airfare, that idea was dead in the water. So now it was only a matter of how much time the Hanging Judge would give me.

Fuller approached the bench. It was time for him to weave his million-dollar magic. Instead, I got his usual two-bit bullshit. "Tyson came in with a lot of excess baggage. The press has vilified him. Not a day goes by that the press doesn't bring up his faults. This is not the Tyson I know. The Tyson I know is a sensitive, thoughtful, caring man. He may be terrifying in the ring, but that ends when he leaves the ring." Now, this was nowhere near Don King hyperbole, but it wasn't bad. Except that Fuller had just spent the whole trial portraying me as a savage animal, a crude bore, bent solely on sexual satisfaction.

Then Fuller changed the subject to my poverty-stricken childhood and my adoption by the legendary boxing trainer Cus D'Amato.

"But there is some tragedy in this," he intoned. "D'Amato only focused on boxing. Tyson, the man, was secondary to Cus D'Amato's quest for Tyson's boxing greatness." Camille, who was Cus's companion for many years, was outraged at his statement. It was like Fuller was pissing on the grave of Cus, my mentor. Fuller went on and on, but he was as disjointed as he had been for the entire trial.

Now it was my time to address the court. I got up and stood behind the podium. I really hadn't been prepared properly and I didn't even have any notes. But I did have that stupid voodoo guy's piece of paper in my hand. And I knew one thing—I wasn't going to apologize for what went on in my hotel room that night. I apologized to the press, the court, and the other contestants of the Miss Black America pageant, where I met Desiree, but not for my actions in my room.

"My conduct was kind of crass. I agree with that. I didn't rape anyone. I didn't attempt to rape anyone. I'm sorry." Then I looked back at Greg Garrison, the prosecutor, or persecutor in my case.

"My personal life has been incarcerated. I've been hurt. This was all one big dream. I didn't come here to beg you for mercy, ma'am. I expect the worst. I've been crucified. I've been humiliated worldwide. I've been humiliated socially. I'm just happy for all my support. I'm prepared to deal with whatever you give me."

I sat back down behind the defense table and the judge asked me a few questions about being a role model for kids. "I was never taught how to handle my celebrity status. I don't tell kids it's right to be Mike Tyson. Parents serve as better role models."

Now the prosecution had their say. Instead of the redneck Garrison, who argued against me during the trial, his boss, Jeffrey Modisett, the Marion County prosecutor, stepped up. He went on for ten minutes saying that males with money and fame shouldn't get special privileges. Then he read from a letter from Desiree Washington. "In the early morning hours of July 19, 1991, an attack on both my body and my mind occurred. I was physically defeated to the point that my innermost person was taken away. In the place of what has been me for eighteen years is now a cold and empty feeling. I am not able to comment on what my future will be. I can only say that each day after being raped has been a struggle to learn to trust again, to smile the way I did and to find the Desiree Lynn Washington who was stolen from me and those who loved me on July 19, 1991. On those occasions when I became angry about the pain that my attacker caused me, God granted me the wisdom to see that he was psychologically ill. Although some days I cry when I see the pain in my own eyes, I am also able to pity my attacker. It has been and still is my wish that he be rehabilitated."

Modisett put the letter down. "From the date of his conviction, Tyson still doesn't get it. The world is watching now to see if there is one system of justice. It is his responsibility to admit his problem. Heal this sick man. Mike Tyson, the rapist, needs to be off the streets." And then he recommended I do eight to ten years of healing behind bars.

It was Jim Voyles's turn to speak on my behalf. Voyles was the local attorney hired by Fuller to act as local counsel. He was a great guy, compassionate, smart, and funny. He was the only attorney from my side that I related to. Besides all that, he was a friend of Judge Gifford's and a down-home guy who could appeal to the Indianapolis jury. "Let's go with this guy," I told Don at the beginning of my trial. Voyles would have gotten me some play. But Don and Fuller made a fool out of him. They didn't let him do anything. They shut him down. Jim was frustrated too. He described his role to one friend as "one of the world's highest-paid pencil carriers." But now he was finally arguing in court. He spoke passionately for rehabilitation instead of incarceration but it fell on deaf ears. Judge Gifford was ready to make her decision.

She began by complimenting me on my community work and my treatment of children and my "sharing" of "assets." But then she went into a rant about "date rape," saying it was a term she detested. "We have managed to imply that it is all right to proceed to do what you want to do if you know or are dating a woman. The law is very clear in its definition of rape. It never mentions anything about whether the defendant and victim are related. The 'date,' in date rape, does not lessen the fact that it is still rape."

My mind was wandering during this lecture. It really had nothing to do with me. We weren't on a date; it was, as the great comedian Bill Bellamy would say, a booty call. Enough said. But then I snapped back to attention.

"I feel he is at risk to do it again because of his attitude," the judge said and stared at me. "You had no prior record. You have been given many gifts. But you have stumbled." She paused.

"On count one, I sentence you to ten years," she said.

"Fucking bitch," I mumbled under my breath. I started to feel numb. That was the rape count. *Shit, maybe I should have drank that special voodoo water,* I thought.

"On count two, I sentence you to ten years." Don King and my friends in the courtroom audibly gasped. That count was for using my fingers. Five years for each finger. "On count three, I sentence you to ten years." That was for using my tongue. For twenty minutes. It was probably a world record, the longest cunnilingus performed during a rape.

"The sentences will run concurrently," she continued. "I fine you the maximum of thirty thousand dollars. I suspend four of those years and place you on probation for four years. During that time you will enter into a psychoanalytic program with Dr. Jerome Miller and perform one hundred hours of community work involving youth delinquency."

Now Fuller jumped up and argued that I should be allowed to be free on bail while Alan Dershowitz, the celebrated defense attorney, prepared my appeal. Dershowitz was there in the courtroom, observing the sentencing. After Fuller finished his plea, Garrison, the redneck cowboy, took the floor. A lot of people would later claim that I was a victim of racism. But I think guys like Modisett and Garrison were just in it for the shine more than anything else. They didn't really care about the ultimate legal outcome; they were just consumed with getting their names in the papers and being big shots.

So Garrison got up and claimed I was a "guilty, violent rapist who may repeat. If you fail to remove the defendant, you depreciate the seriousness of the crime, demean the quality of law enforcement, expose other innocent persons, and allow a guilty man to continue his lifestyle."

Judge Gifford agreed. No bail. Which meant that I was heading straight to prison. Gifford was about to gavel the proceedings to an end when there was a commotion in the courtroom. Dershowitz had bolted up, gathered his briefcase, and loudly rushed out of the courtroom, muttering, "I'm off to see that justice is done." There was some confusion but then the judge banged her gavel on her table. That was it. The county sheriff came over to take me into custody. I stood up, removed my watch, took off my belt and handed them, along with my wallet, to Fuller. Two of my female friends in the first row of spectators were crying uncontrollably. "We love you, Mike," they sobbed. Camille got up and made her way to our defense table. We hugged good-bye. Then Jim Voyles and I were led out of the courtroom through the back door by the sheriff.

They took me downstairs to the booking station. I was searched, fingerprinted, and processed through. There was a mob of reporters waiting outside, surrounding the car that would take me to prison.

"When we leave, remember to keep your coat over your handcuffs," Voyles advised me. Was he for real? Slowly the numbness was leaving me and my rage was kicking in. I should be ashamed to be shown with handcuffs? That's my badge of honor. If I hide the cuffs, then I'm a bitch. Jim thought that hiding my cuffs would stop me from experiencing shame, but *that* would have been the shame. I had to be seen with that steel on me. Fuck everybody else, the people who understand, they have got to see me with that steel on. I was going to warrior school.

We exited the courthouse and made our way to the car, and I proudly held my cuffs up high. And I smirked as if to say, "Do you believe this shit?" That picture of me made the front page of newspapers around the world. I got into the police car and Jim squeezed next to me in the backseat.

"Well, farm boy, it's just you and me," I joked.

They took us to a diagnostic center to determine what level prison I would be sent to. They stripped me naked, made me bend down and did a cavity search. Then they gave me some pajama-type shit and some slippers. And they shipped me off to the Indiana Youth Center in Plainfield, a facility for level-two and -three offenders. By the time I got to my final destination, I was consumed with rage. I was going to show these motherfuckers how to do time. My way. It's funny, but it took me a long time to realize that that little white woman judge who sent me to prison just might have saved my life.

1

WE WERE BEEFING WITH THESE GUYS CALLED THE PUMA BOYS. IT WAS 1976
and I lived in Brownsville, Brooklyn, and these guys were from my
neighborhood. At that time I was running with a Rutland Road crew
called The Cats, a bunch of Caribbean guys from nearby Crown
Heights. We were a burglary team and some of our gangster friends
had an altercation with the Puma Boys, so we were going to the park
to back them up. We normally didn't deal with guns, but these were
our friends so we stole a bunch of shit: some pistols, a .357 Magnum,
and a long M1 rifle with a bayonet attached from World War I. You
never knew what you'd find when you broke into people's houses.

So we're walking through the streets holding our guns and nobody
runs up on us, no cops are around to stop us. We didn't even have a
bag to put the big rifle in, so we just took turns carrying it every few
blocks.

"Yo, there he goes!" my friend Haitian Ron said. "The guy with the
red Pumas and the red mock neck." Ron had spotted the guy we were

after. When we started running, the huge crowd in the park opened up like Moses parting the Red Sea. It was a good thing they did, because, boom, one of my friends opened fire. Everybody scrambled when they heard the gun.

We kept walking, and I realized that some of the Puma Boys had taken cover between the parked cars in the street. I had the M1 rifle and I turned around quickly to see this big guy with his pistol pointed towards me.

"What the fuck are you doing here?" he said to me. It was my older brother, Rodney. "Get the fuck out of here."

I just kept walking and left the park and went home. I was ten years old.

I OFTEN SAY THAT I WAS THE BAD SEED IN THE FAMILY, BUT WHEN I THINK about it, I was really a meek kid for most of my childhood. I was born in Cumberland Hospital in the Fort Greene section of Brooklyn, New York, on June 30, 1966. My earliest memories were of being in the hospital—I was always sick with lung problems. One time, to get some attention, I put my thumb in some Drano and then put it in my mouth. They rushed me to the hospital. I remember my godmother gave me a toy gun while I was there, but I think I broke it right away.

I don't know much about my family background. My mother, Lorna Mae, was a New Yorker but she was born down south in Virginia. My brother once went down to visit the area where my mother grew up and he said there was nothing but trailer parks there. So I'm really a trailer park nigga. My grandmother Bertha and my great-aunt used to work for this white lady back in the thirties at a time when most whites wouldn't have blacks working for them, and Bertha and her sister were so appreciative that they both named their daughters Lorna after the white lady. Then Bertha used the money from her job to send her kids to college.

I may have gotten the family knockout gene from my grandma. My mother's cousin Lorna told me that the husband of the family Bertha worked for kept beating on his wife, and Bertha didn't like it. And she was a big woman.

"Don't you put your hands on her," she told him.

He took it as a joke, and she threw a punch and knocked him on his ass. The next day he saw Bertha and said, "Well, how are you doing, Miss Price?" He stopped hitting on his wife and became a different man.

Everybody liked my mom. When I was born, she was working as a prison matron at the Women's House of Detention in Manhattan, but she was studying to be a teacher. She had completed three years of college when she met my dad. He got sick so she had to drop out of school to care for him. For a person that well educated, she didn't have very good taste in men.

I don't know much about my father's family. In fact, I didn't really know my father much at all. Or the man I was told was my father. On my birth certificate it said my father was Percel Tyson. The only problem was that my brother, my sister, and I never met this guy.

We were all told that our biological father was Jimmy "Curlee" Kirkpatrick Jr. But he was barely in the picture. As time went on I heard rumors that Curlee was a pimp and that he used to extort ladies. Then, all of a sudden, he started calling himself a deacon in the church. That's why every time I hear someone referring to themselves as reverend, I say "Reverend-slash-Pimp." When you really think about it, these religious guys have the charisma of a pimp. They can get anybody in the church to do whatever they want. So to me it's always "Yeah, Bishop-slash-Pimp," "Reverend Ike-slash-Pimp."

Curlee would drive over to where we stayed, periodically. He and my mother never spoke to each other, he'd just beep the horn and we'd just go down and meet him. The kids would pile into his Cadillac and we thought we were going on an excursion to Coney Island or Brighton Beach, but he'd just drive around for a few minutes, pull back up to our apartment building, give us some money, give my sister a kiss, and shake me and my brother's hands and that was it. Maybe I'd see him in another year.

My first neighborhood was Bed-Stuy in Brooklyn. It was a decent working-class neighborhood then. Everybody knew one another. Things were pretty normal, but they weren't calm. Every Friday and Saturday, it was like Vegas in the house. My mom would have a card party and invite all her girlfriends, many of whom were in the vice business. She would send her boyfriend Eddie to buy a case of liquor and they'd water it down and sell shots. Every fourth hand of cards the winner had to throw into the pot so the house made money. My mom would cook some wings. My brother remembers that, besides the hookers, there'd be gangsters, detectives. The whole gamut was there.

When my mother had some money, she'd splurge. She was a great facilitator and she'd always have her girlfriends over and a bunch of men too. Everybody would be drinking, drinking, drinking. She didn't smoke marijuana but all her friends did, so she'd supply them with the drugs. She just smoked cigarettes, Kool 100's. My mother's friends were prostitutes, or at least women who would sleep with men for money. No high-level or even street-level stuff. They would drop off their kids at our house before they went to meet their men. When they'd come to pick up their kids, they might have blood on their clothes, so my mom would help them clean up. I came home one day and there was a white baby in the house. *What the fuck is this shit?* I thought. But that's just what my life was like.

My brother Rodney was five years older than I was so we didn't have much in common. He's a weird dude. We're black guys from the ghetto and he was like a scientist—he had all these test tubes, was always experimenting. He even had coin collections. I was, like, "White people do this stuff."

He once went to the chemistry lab at Pratt Institute, a nearby college, and got some chemicals to do an experiment. A few days later when he went out, I snuck into his room, started adding water to his test tubes, and I blew out the whole back window and started a fire in his room. He had to put a lock on his door after that.

I fought with him a lot, but it was just typical brother stuff. Except for the day that I cut him with a razor. He had beaten me up for some reason and then he had gone to sleep. My sister, Denise, and I were watching one of those doctor-type soap operas and they were doing an operation. "We could do that and Rodney could be the patient. I can be the doctor and you can be the nurse," I told my sister. So we rolled up his sleeve and got to work on his left arm. "Scalpel," I said, and my sister handed me a razor. I cut him a bit and he started bleeding. "We need the alcohol, nurse," I said, and she passed it to me and I poured it onto his cuts. He woke up screaming and yelling and chased us around the house. I hid behind my mom. He still has those slices to this day.

We had some good times together too. Once, my brother and I were walking down Atlantic Avenue and he said, "Let's go to the doughnut factory." He had stolen some doughnuts from that place before and I guess he wanted to show me he could do it again. So we walked by and the gate was open. He went in and got a few boxes of doughnuts, but something happened and the gate closed and he was stuck in there and the security guards started coming. So he handed me the doughnuts and I ran home with them. My sister and I were sitting on our stoop and cramming down those doughnuts and our faces were white with the powder. Our mom was standing next to us, talking to her neighbor.

"My son aced the test to get into Brooklyn Tech," she boasted to her friend. "He is such a remarkable student, he's the best pupil in his class."

Just then a cop car drove up and Rodney was in it. They were going to drop him off at home, but he heard our mother bragging about what a good son he was and he told the cops to keep going. They took him straight to Spofford, a juvenile detention center. My sister and I happily finished off those doughnuts.

I spent most of my time with my sister Denise. She was two years older than me and she was beloved by everybody in the neighborhood. If she was your friend, she was your best friend. But if she was your enemy, go across the street. We made mud pies; we watched wrestling and karate movies and went to the store with our mother. It was a nice existence, but then when I was just seven years old, our world got turned upside down.

There was a recession and my mom lost her job and we got evicted out of our nice apartment in Bed-Stuy. They came and took all our furniture and put it outside on the sidewalk. The three of us kids had to sit down on it and protect it so that nobody took it while my mother went to find a spot for us to stay. I was sitting there, and some kids from the neighborhood came up and said, "Mike, why is your furniture out here, Mike?" We just told them we were moving. Then some neighbors saw us out there and brought some plates of food down for us.

We wound up in Brownsville. You could totally feel the difference. The people were louder, more aggressive. It was a very horrific, tough, and gruesome kind of place. My mother wasn't used to hanging around those particular types of aggressive black people and she appeared to be intimidated, and so were my brother and sister and me. Everything was hostile, there was never a subtle moment there. Cops were always driving by with their sirens on; ambulances always coming to pick up somebody; guns always going off, people getting stabbed, windows being broken. One day my brother and I even got robbed right in front of our apartment building. We used to watch these guys shooting it out with one another. It was like something out of an old Edward G. Robinson movie. We would watch and say, "Wow, this is happening in real life."

The whole neighborhood was also a hotbed of lust. A lot of people there seemed to be uninhibited. It wasn't uncommon to hear people talking on the street: "Suck my dick," "Eat my pussy." It was a different kind of environment from my old neighborhood. One day a guy pulled me off the street, took me into an abandoned building, and tried to molest me. I never really felt safe on those streets. After a while, we weren't even safe in our apartment. My mom's parties ended when we got to Brownsville. My mother made some friends, but she wasn't in the mix like she was in Bed-Stuy. So she started drinking heavily. She never got another job, and I remember waiting in these long lines with my mother down at the welfare center. We'd wait and wait for hours and then we'd be right up front, and it was five o'clock and they'd close the fucking shit on you, just like in the movies.

We kept getting evicted in Brownsville too. That happened quite a few times. Every now and then we'd get a decent spot, crashing for a short time with some friends or a boyfriend of my mother's. But for the most part, each time we moved, the conditions got worse—from being poor to being serious poor to being fucked-up poor. Eventually we lived in condemned buildings, with no heat, no water, maybe some electricity. In the wintertime all four of us slept in the same bed to keep warm. We'd stay there until a guy would come and kick us out. My mother would do whatever she had to do to keep a roof over our heads. That often meant sleeping with someone that she really didn't care for. That was just the way it was.

She'd never take us to a homeless shelter, so we'd just move into another abandoned building. It was so traumatic, but what could you do? This is what I hate about myself, what I learned from my mother—there was nothing you wouldn't do to survive.

One of my earliest memories is of welfare workers coming into the apartment to look for men under the bed. In the summertime, we'd go get the free lunches and free breakfasts. I'd tell them, "I got nine brothers and sisters," so they'd pack more. I'd feel like I just went to war and got a bounty. I was so proud that I got food for the house. Can you imagine that bullshit? I'd open the refrigerator and see the baloney sandwich and the orange and the little carton of milk. Twenty of them. I'd invite people over. "Do you need something to eat, brother? Are you hungry? We have food." We were acting like we paid for this with hard-earned money. It was a free lunch.

I was a momma's boy when I was young. I always slept with my mother. My sister and brother had their own rooms, but I slept with my mother until I was fifteen. One time, my mother slept with a man while I was in the bed with her. She probably thought I was asleep. I'm sure it had an impact on me, but that's just how it was. I got booted to the couch when her boyfriend Eddie Gillison came into the picture. They had a really dysfunctional love affair. I guess that's why my own relationships were so strange. They'd drink, fight, and fuck, break up, then drink, fight, and fuck some more. They were truly in love, even if it was a really sick love.

Eddie was a short, compact guy from South Carolina who was a worker at an industrial Laundromat factory. He didn't get too far in school, and by the time my brother and sister got to fourth grade, he really couldn't help them with their homework. Eddie was a controlling guy, but my mother was a very controlling woman, so all hell would break loose on a routine basis. There was always some kind of fight, and the cops would come, and they'd go, "Hey, buddy, walk around the block." Sometimes we'd all get in on the fighting. One day my mother and Eddie were having a bad argument and they got physical. I jumped in between them trying to defend my mom and I was trying to restrain him and, whop, he slugged me in my stomach and I went down. I was, like, *Oh, man, I can't believe this shit.* I was just a little kid! That's why I've never put my hands on any of my kids. I don't want them thinking I'm a monster when they get old. But back then, beating on a kid was just the way it was. Nobody cared. Now it's murder, you go to jail.

Eddie and my mother fought over anything—other men or women, money, control. Eddie was no angel. When my mother had female friends over and they'd all get drunk and she'd pass out, he'd fuck her friends. And then they'd fight. There was really some barbaric stuff, going at each other with weapons and cursing, "You motherfucker, fuck you" and "You nigga, suck my . . ." We'd be screaming, "Mommy, stop, no!" Once, when I was seven years old, they were fighting and Eddie punched her and knocked her gold tooth out. My mother started boiling up a large pot of water. She told my brother and sister to get under the quilt, but I was so mesmerized watching my wrestling program on the TV that I didn't hear her. My mother was so slick, she walked by and nothing happened, then she came back into the room and by then my sister and brother were prepared, they were hiding under the quilt. Eddie was sitting right next to me, and the next thing I heard was this boom and the pot with the boiling water hit Eddie in the head. A little bit of the water splashed on me. It felt like it weighed a ton.

"Aaggghhh!" Eddie ran screaming out the door into the hallway. I ran right after him. He turned around and grabbed me. "Oh, baby, baby, that bitch got you too?" he said. "Yeah, the bitch got me, ah, ah, the bitch got me!" We brought him back in the room and took his shirt off, and his neck and his back and the side of his face were covered in blistery bubbles. He looked like a reptile. So we put him on the floor in front of the little window air conditioner, and my sister sat down next to him. She took a lighter and sterilized the end of a needle and then burst the blisters, one by one. My sister and I were both crying, and I gave him a quarter to cheer him up.

When I think about it, I always thought of my mother as the victim in most situations, and Eddie did beat on her. I'm sure the lady lib would think that her reaction was great, but I thought, *How could you do that to somebody who is supposed to be your boyfriend?* It made me realize that my mother was no Mother Teresa. She did some serious stuff and he still stayed with her. In fact, he went to the store to buy her some liquor after she burned him. So you see, he rewarded her for it. That's why I was so sexually dysfunctional.

That is the kind of life I grew up in. People in love cracking their heads and bleeding like dogs. They love each other but they're stabbing each other. Holy shit, I was scared to death of my family in the house. I'm growing up around tough women, women who fight men. So I didn't think fighting a woman was taboo because the women I knew would kill you. You had to fight them, because if you didn't, they'd slice you or shoot you. Or else they'd bring some men to take advantage of you and beat you up, because they thought you were a punk.

If I was scared to be in the house, I was also scared to go outside. By then, I was going to public school and that was a nightmare. I was a pudgy kid, very shy, almost effeminate shy, and I spoke with a lisp. The kids used to call me "Little Fairy Boy" because I was always hanging out with my sister, but my mother had told me that I had to stay around Denise because she was older than me and had to watch me. They also called me "Dirty Ike" or "Dirty Motherfucker" because I didn't know about hygiene back then. We didn't have hot water to shower in, and if the gas wasn't on, we couldn't even boil water. My mother tried to teach me about it, but I still didn't do a very good job. She used to take soap and fill a bucket up with hot water and wash me. But when you're a young kid, you don't care about hygiene. Even-

tually I'd learn it in the streets from the older kids. They told me
about Brut and Paco Rabanne and Pierre Cardin.

My school was right around the corner from our apartment, but
sometimes my mother would be passed out from drinking the night
before and wouldn't walk me to school. It was then that the kids would
always hit me and kick me. They were, like, "Get the fuck out of here,
nigga, you, like, nasty motherfucker." I would constantly get abused.
They'd punch me in the face and I would run. We would go to school
and these people would pick on us, then we would go home and they'd
pull out guns and rob us for whatever little change we had. That was
hard-core, young kids robbing us right in our own apartment building.

Having to wear glasses in the first grade was a real turning point
in my life. My mother had me tested and it turned out I was near-
sighted, so she made me get glasses. They were so bad. One day I was
leaving school at lunchtime to go home, and I had some meatballs
from the cafeteria wrapped up in the aluminum to keep them hot.
This guy came up to me and said, "Hey, you got any money?" I said,
"No." He started picking my pockets and searching me, and he tried
to take my fucking meatballs. I was resisting, going, "No, no, no!" I
would let the bullies take my money, but I never let them take my
food. I was hunched over like a human shield, protecting my meatballs. So he started hitting me in the head and then took my glasses
and put them down the gas tank of a truck. I ran home, but he didn't
get my meatballs. I should have clobbered those guys, but I was so
scared because those guys were so brazen and bold that I just figured
they must know something I didn't. "Don't beat me up, leave me alone,
stop!" I'd say. I still feel like a coward to this day because of that bullying. That's a wild feeling, being that helpless. You never ever forget
that feeling. The day that guy took my glasses and put them in that
gas tank was the last day I went to school. That was the end of
my formal education. I was seven years old and I just never went back
to class.

After that, I would go to school to eat breakfast and then leave. I'd
walk around the block for a couple of hours. Then I'd go back for lunch
and leave. When school was out, I'd go home. One day during the

spring of 1974, three guys came towards me on the street and started patting my pockets. "Got any money?" they asked. I told them no. They said, "All the money we find, we keep." So they started turning my pockets out but I didn't have anything. Then they said, "Where are you going? Do you want to fly with us?"

"What's that?" I said.

So we walked over to the school, and they had me climb the fence and throw some plastic milk crates over to them. We started walking a few blocks and then they told me to go into an abandoned building.

"Whoa, I don't know," I hesitated. I was one wimpy little guy against three. But we walked in and then they said, "Go to the roof, Shorty." I didn't know if they were going to kill me. We climbed up to the roof and I saw a little box with some pigeons in it. These guys were building a pigeon coop. So I became their little gofer, their smuck-slave. Soon I found out that when the birds flew, they often landed on some other roof, because they were lazy and in bad condition. I'd have to go downstairs, see which roof they landed on, figure out a way into that building and then go up on that roof and scare the birds off. All day I chased the birds, but I thought that was pretty fun. I liked being around the birds. I even liked going to the pet store to buy their seed. And these guys were tough guys and they kind of liked me for being their gofer. My whole life I had felt like a misfit, but here on the roof I felt like I was home. This was what I was supposed to do.

The next morning I went back to the building. They were on the roof and saw me coming and started throwing bricks at me. "Mother-fucker, what are you doing over here? You trying to steal our fucking birds?" one of the guys said. Whoa, I thought this was my new home.

"No, no, no," I said. "I just wanted to know if you guys need me to go to the store for you or chase your birds."

"Are you serious?" he said. "Get up here, Shorty." And they sent me to the store to buy them cigarettes. They were a bunch of ruthless street guys, but I didn't mind helping them because the birds en-thralled me. It was really cool to see a couple of hundred pigeons fly-ing around in circles in the sky and then coming back down to a roof.

Flying pigeons was a big sport in Brooklyn. Everyone from Mafia dons to little ghetto kids did it. It's unexplainable; it just gets in your blood. I learned how to handle them, learned the characteristics of them. Then it became something that I became somewhat of a master of, and I took pride in being so good at it. Everybody would let their pigeons fly at the same time, and the name of the game was to try and catch the other guys' pigeons. It was like racing horses. Once it's in your blood, you never stop. Wherever I lived from that day on, I always built me a coop and had pigeons.

One day we were on the roof dealing with the pigeons and an older guy came up. His name was Barkim and he was a friend of one of these guys' brothers. When he realized his friend wasn't there, he told us to tell him to meet him at a jam at the rec center in our neighborhood that night. The jams were like teenage dances, except this was no Archie and Veronica shit. At night they even changed the name of the place from the rec center to The Sagittarius. All the players and hustlers would go there, the neighborhood guys who robbed houses, pickpocketed, snatched chains, and perpetrated credit card fraud. It was a den of iniquity.

So that night I went to the center. I was seven years old, and I didn't know anything about dressing up. I didn't know you were supposed to go home and take a shower and change your clothes and dress to impress and then go to the club. That's what the other guys who were handling pigeons did. But I went straight to the center from the pigeon coops, wearing the same stinky clothes with all this bird shit on me. I thought the guys would be there and they'd accept me as one of their own, because I was chasing these fucking birds off of these buildings for them. But I walked in and those guys went, "What's that smell? Look at this dirty, stinking motherfucker." The whole place started laughing and teasing me. I didn't know what to do; it was such a traumatizing experience, everybody picking on me. I was crying, but I was laughing too because I wanted to fit in. I guess Barkim saw the way I was dressed and took pity on me. He came up to me and said, "Yo, Shorty. Get the fuck out of here. Meet me back at the roof eight in the morning tomorrow."

The next morning I was there right on time. Barkim came up and started lecturing me. "You can't be going out looking like a mother-fucking bum in the street. What the fuck are you doing, man? We're moneymakers." He was talking fast and I was trying to comprehend each word. "We're gonna get money out here, Shorty. Are you ready?"

I went with him and we started breaking into people's houses. He told me to go through the windows that were too small for him to fit through, and I went in and opened the door for him. Once we were inside, he went through people's drawers, he broke open the safe, he was just really wiping them out. We got stereos, eight-tracks, jewelry, guns, cash money. After the robberies, he took me to Delancey Street in the city and bought me some nice clothes and sneakers and a sheep-skin coat. That night he took me to a jam and a lot of the same people who laughed at me at the other jam were there. I had on my new coat and leather pants. Nobody even recognized me; it was like I was a different person. It was incredible.

Barkim was the guy who introduced me into the life of crime. Before that, I never stole anything. Not a loaf of bread, not a piece of candy, nothing. I had no antisocial tendencies. I didn't have the nerve. But Barkim explained to me that if you always looked good, people would treat you with respect. If you had the newest fashion, the finest stuff, you were a cool dude. You'd have status.

Barkim took me to a roller-skating rink on Utica Avenue where I met these guys who were called the Rutland Road Crew. They were young, maybe twelve years old, but they dressed like grown men. Trench coats, alligator shoes, rabbit furs, Stetsons with the big brims. They had on designer clothes from Sergio Valente, Jordache, Pierre Cardin. I was impressed. Barkim told me how they did it—these guys were pickpockets, chain snatchers, and robbers. They were just babies. They're in public school and they've got watches and rings and necklaces. They're driving mopeds. People called them thugs but we called them money niggas. That shit was crazy.

Barkim started introducing me to people on the street as his "son." He was only a few years older than me but it was street terminology that warned people not to disrespect me. It meant: "This is my son in the streets, we're family, we rob and steal. This is my little moneymaker. Don't fuck with this nigga." People that respected him *had* to respect me now. He taught me which people to look out for, which people I couldn't trust because they would take my shit right from me. My life reminded me of Oliver Twist, with the older guy Fagin teaching all this stuff. He bought me a lot of clothes, but he never gave me a lot of money. He'd make a couple of thousand from robbing and he'd give me two hundred. But at eight years old, two hundred was a lot of money. Sometimes he'd take out a piece of jewelry that we stole and let me borrow it for a few days.

I took my criminality to another level with the Rutland Road Crew. They were mostly Caribbean guys from Crown Heights. Barkim knew the older set, The Cats. I started hanging out with the RRC, their junior division. I got involved in their little house-robbing heists. We'd go to school, eat breakfast, and then we'd get on the bus and train and start robbing during school hours. That was the beginning of me feeling like I belonged. We were all equal as long as we put in our share of the robbing proceeds.

Some people might read some of the things I'm talking about and judge me as an adult, call me a criminal, but I did these things over thirty-five years ago. I was a little kid looking for love and acceptance and the streets were where I found it. It was the only education I had, and these guys were my teachers. Even the older gangsters said, "You shouldn't do this. Go to school," but I didn't want to listen to them, even though they had respect in the street. They were telling us to stay in school at the same time they were out there robbing. All the guys respected me because I was a little moneymaker. I'd break off some for my friends who needed a little cash. I'd buy us all liquor and food. I started buying pigeons. If you had good birds, people respected you. Plus, it was a rush to steal things and then go out and buy clothes. I saw how everybody treated me when I came around and I was dressed up nice with my shearling coat and my Pumas. I had a ski suit, with the yellow goggles, and I'd never been to a ski slope in my life. I couldn't even spell fucking Adidas but I knew how they made me feel.

One of the Rutland guys taught me how to pick locks. If you get a key that fits the hole, you just keep playing the key and it wears down the cylinder and you can open the door. I was, like, "Fuck!" Man, when we opened some of those doors, you'd see silverware, jewelry, guns, stacks of money. We were so happy we were crying and laughing at the same time. We couldn't get it all. You couldn't walk down the street with that shit, so we just filled up our schoolbags with as much stolen goods we could stuff in them.

One day my friend Curtis and I were robbing a house. The people who lived there were from the Caribbean and so was Curtis. I was in this pitch-black house and I heard "Who's that? Is that you, honey?" I thought it was Curtis playing around, trying to scare me. So I said, "I'm trying to find a gun and the money. Look for the safe, all right?" "What, baby?" I realized then that it wasn't Curtis talking. It was the guy who lived there who was lying on the couch. I rushed to the door. "Curtis, this shit don't look right. Let's get out of here, somebody is in here," I said. But Curtis was a perfectionist. Curtis wanted to lock the door instead of just running away. I ran the fuck out. The owner opened the door and smashed Curtis in the head and knocked him out cold. I thought he was dead. It wasn't until a year later that I saw him again. He was alive, but his face was all shattered, he got hit that hard. Yup, it was the hard-knock life for us.

When we stole silverware or jewelry, we'd go to Sal's, a store on Utica and Sterling.

I was a baby, but they knew me from coming in with older guys. The guys at the store knew I was coming in with stolen stuff, but I knew they couldn't beat me because I knew what shit cost back then. I knew what I wanted.

Sometimes we'd be in the streets and if it was noon and we saw a school, we'd just go into the school, go to the cafeteria, grab a tray, get in line, and start eating. We might see someone we'd want to rob, someone who had their school ring around their neck. So we'd finish the food, put the tray back, get by the door, grab the ring, and run out.

We always wanted to look nice on the streets because normally if you're a little black kid out in the city looking bummy and dirty, people harass you. So we looked nice and nonthreatening. We had the school backpacks and little happy glasses and the Catholic school look with nice pants and white shirts, the whole school outfit.

After about a year, I started doing burglaries by myself. It was pretty lucrative, but hanging in the street and jostling was more exciting than robbing houses. You'd grab some ladies' jewelry and cops would chase you, or what we called heroes would try to come in and rescue the day. It was more risk-taking for less money but we loved the thrill. You normally had to have a partner to be a successful jostler. Sometimes it wouldn't even be planned, but you'd see someone you knew, so you teamed up.

Sometimes you'd find that you had competition for jostling. You'd get on a bus and there might be someone already on the bus waiting to pickpocket some people. But you might be more obvious. That was called "waking the bus." The bus was quiet before you got on, but now that you've come aboard, the bus driver makes an announcement. "Ladies and gentlemen, there are some young men who just got on the bus. Watch your pockets. They will attempt to steal from you." So you get off at the next stop, but the quiet jostler gets off and comes after you.

"Motherfucker, you woke the bus up!" he'll scream. And if he's an older guy, he might start beating on your ass and taking your money or the jewelry that you stole.

People didn't like to go pickpocketing with me because I wasn't as patient or as good as they were. I was never smooth, like, "I'm going to play this nigga, I'm going to do this, right up and close in person." I was much better at blindsiding people.

Any strong guy could blindside someone. But the trick was to be cunning and outsmart them. Most people would think, *They're onto me, I'm going to walk away.* But not me. A lady might have her hand on her wallet all day, and we'd be watching, watching, and she never takes her hand out of her pocket. And we'd follow her and then move away but we'd have one little kid still watching her. And she'd let down her defenses for a few seconds and go do something and he'd get it. Then he'd be gone. And before we got out, we'd hear a gut-wrenching scream, "Aaaaahh, my money, my money!" It was crazy. We didn't give a fuck.

The most primitive move was to snatch somebody's gold chain. I used to do that on the subway. I'd sit by the window. That was when you could open the windows on subway cars. I'd pull a few windows down, and then the car would stop and new people would come on and sit by the window. I would get out and as soon as the train slowly started moving, I'd reach in and snatch their chains. They'd scream and look at me, but they couldn't get off the train. I'd fix the clasp, hold the chain for a couple of days, look good and sport it, and then I'd sell it before the older guys took it from me.

Even though I was starting to look the role, I never could get on with the girls back then. I liked girls, but I didn't know how to tell them I liked them at that age. One time, I was watching these girls jump rope, and I liked them and I wanted to jump rope with them, so I started teasing them and, out of nowhere, these girls in the fifth grade started beating the shit out of me. I was playing with them, but they were serious and I was just taken by surprise. I got serious about fighting back too late. By then, somebody came and broke it up and they'd gotten the best of me. I didn't want to fight them.

It was no surprise to my mother and my sister that I was robbing and doing antisocial things to bring money in. They saw my nice clothes, and I'd bring them food—pizza and Burger King and McDonald's. My mother knew I was up to no good, but by that time she knew it was too late. The streets had me. She thought that I was a criminal and I would die or never turn out to be shit. She'd probably seen it before, kids like me being like that. I would steal anything from anybody. I didn't have any boundaries.

My mother would prefer to beg. She embarrassed me a bit, because she was too honest. She was always asking for money; that's just the way she was. I gave my sister a lot of money for the house to help my mom out. Sometimes I'd give my mother a hundred bucks and she wouldn't pay me back. She didn't respect me like that. I'd say, "You owe me some money, Ma." And she'd just say, "You owe me your life, boy. I'm not paying you back."

The big kids in the neighborhood knew I was stealing, so they would take my money and my jewelry and my shoes, and I would be afraid to tell my mother. I didn't know what to do. They'd beat me up and steal my birds, and they knew that they could get away with bullying me. Barkim didn't teach me how to fight. He just taught me how to dress in nice clothes and wash my ass. Normally when some-one was screaming at me in the street or chasing me, I would just drop my stuff and run. So now I was getting bullied again but I was more of a mark.

Growing up, I always wanted to be the center of attention. I wanted to be the guy talking shit: "I'm the baddest motherfucker out here," "I got the best birds." I wanted to be that street guy, the fly slick-talking guy, but I was just too shy and awkward. When I tried to talk that way, somebody would hit me in the head and say, "Shut the fuck up, nigga." But I got a taste of what it was like to bask in the adulation of an audience when I got into my first street fight.

One day I went into this neighborhood in Crown Heights and I robbed a house with this older guy. We found $2,200 in cash and he cut me in for $600. So I went to a pet store and bought a hundred bucks' worth of birds. They put them in a crate for me, and the owner helped me get them on the subway. When I got off, I had somebody from my neighborhood help me drag the crate to the condemned build-ing where I was hiding my pigeons. But this guy went and told some kids in the neighborhood that I had all these birds. So a guy named Gary Flowers and some friends of his came and started to rob me. My mother saw them messing with the birds and told me, and I ran out into the street and confronted them. They saw me coming and stopped grabbing the birds, but this guy Gary still had one of them under his coat. By then, a large crowd gathered around us.

"Give me my bird back," I protested.

Gary pulled the bird out from under his coat.

"You want the bird? You want the fucking bird?" he said. Then he just twisted the bird's head off and threw it at me, smearing the blood all over my face and shirt.

"Fight him, Mike," one of my friends urged. "Don't be afraid, just fight him."

I had always been too scared to fight anyone before. But there used to be an older guy in the neighborhood named Wise, who had been a Police Athletic League boxer. He used to smoke weed with us, and when he'd get high, he would start shadowboxing. I would watch him and he would say, "Come on, let's go," but I would never even slapbox with him. But I remembered his style.

So I decided. "Fuck it." My friends were shocked. I didn't know what I was doing, but I threw some wild punches and one connected and Gary went down. Wise would skip while he was shadowboxing, so after I dropped Gary, my stupid ass started skipping. It just seemed like the fly thing to do. I had practically the whole block watching my gloryful moment. Everybody started whooping and applauding me. It was an incredible feeling even though my heart was beating out of my chest.

"This nigga is skipping, man," one guy laughed. I was trying to do the Ali shuffle, to no avail. But I felt good about standing up for myself and I liked the rush of everybody applauding me and slapping fives. I guess underneath that shyness, I was always an explosive, entertaining guy.

I started getting a whole new level of respect on the streets. Instead of "Can Mike play with us?" people would ask my mother, "Can Mike Tyson play with us?" Other guys would bring their guys around to fight me and they'd bet money on the outcome. Now I had another source of income. They'd come from other neighborhoods. I would win a lot too. Even if I lost, the guys who beat me would say, "Fuck! You're only eleven?" That's how everybody started knowing me in Brooklyn. I had a reputation that I would fight anyone—grown men, anybody. But we didn't follow the Marquis of Queensberry rules in the street. If you kicked someone's ass it didn't necessarily mean it was over. If he couldn't beat you in the fight, he'd take another route, and sometimes he'd come back with some of his friends and they'd beat me up with bats.

I began to exact some revenge for the beatings I had taken from bullies. I'd be walking with some friends and I might see one of the guys who beat me up and bullied me years earlier. He might have gone into a store shopping and I would drag his ass out of the store and start pummeling him. I didn't even tell my friends why, I'd just say, "I hate that motherfucker over there," and they'd jump in too and rip his fucking clothes and beat his fucking ass. That guy who took my glasses and threw them away? I beat him in the streets like a fucking dog for humiliating me. He may have forgotten about it but I never did.

With this newfound confidence in my ability to stand up for myself, my criminality escalated. I became more and more brazen. I even began to steal in my own neighborhood. I thought that was what people did. I didn't understand the rules of the streets. I thought everybody was fair game because I sure seemed to be fair game to everybody else. I didn't know that there were certain people you just don't fuck with.

I lived in a tenement building and I would rob everybody who lived in my building. They never realized that I was the thief. Some of these people were my mother's friends. They'd cash their welfare checks and maybe buy some liquor, and they would visit my mom, drink some liquor, and have some fun. I'd go into my room and go up the fire escape and break into their apartment and rob everything from their place. Then when the lady would go upstairs, she'd discover it and run back screaming, "Lorna, Lorna, they got everything. They got the babies' food, they got everything!"

After they left, my mother would come into my room.

"I know you did something, didn't you, boy? What did you do?"

I'd say, "Mom, it's not me. Look around," because I would take the food and stuff and leave it on the roof and my friends and I would get it later.

"How could I have done anything? I was in the room right here, I didn't go anywhere."

"Well, if you didn't do it, I'll bet you know who did it, you thief," my mother would scream. "You're nothing but a thief. I've never stole nothing in my life. I don't know where you come from, you thief."

Oh, God. Can you imagine hearing that shit from your own mother? My family had no hope for me, no hope. They thought my life would be a life of crime. Nobody else in my family ever did stuff like that. My sister would constantly be telling me, "What kind of bird don't fly? Jailbird! Jailbird!"

I was with my mother one time visiting her friend Via. Via's husband was one of those big-money showing-off guys. He went to sleep and I took his wallet out of his pocket and took his money. When he woke up, he beat Via up real bad because he thought she had stole the cash. Everybody in the neighborhood started hating my guts. And if they didn't hate me, they were jealous of me. Even the players. I had nerve.

It felt incredible. I didn't care if I grabbed somebody's chain and dragged them down the stairs with their head bouncing, boom, boom, boom. Do I care? No, I need that chain. I didn't know anything about compassion. Why should I? No one ever showed me any compassion. The only compassion I had was when somebody shot or stabbed one of my friends during a robbery. Then I was sad.

But you still fucking do it. You think they're not going to kill you; that it can't happen to you. I just couldn't stop. I knew there was a chance I would get killed but I didn't care. I didn't think I would live to see sixteen anyway so why not go hard? My brother Rodney told someone recently that he thought I was the most courageous guy he knew. But I didn't consider myself courageous. I had brave friends, friends who would get shot over their jewelry or watches or motorcycles. They weren't giving it up when people robbed them. Those guys had the most respect in the neighborhood. I don't know if I had courage, but I witnessed courage. I always thought that I was much more crazy than courageous. I was shooting at people out in the open while my mother looked out the window. I was brainless. Rodney was thinking it was courage but it was a lack of brainpower. I was an extremist.

Everyone I knew was in the life. Even the guys who had jobs were hustling on the side. They sold dope or were robbing. It was like a cyborg world where the cops were the bad guys and the robbers and the hustlers were the good guys. If you didn't hurt nobody, nobody would have talked to you. You would be labeled as square. If you did bad, you were all right. Somebody bothered you, they'd come fight for you. They'd know you were one of the guys. I was so awesome, all these sleazy, smiley scumbags knew my name.

THEN THINGS STARTED TO ESCALATE. I BEGAN TO COME INTO INTIMATE CON-tact with the police. Getting shot at in Brownsville was no big deal. You'd be in the alley gambling, and some guys would come running in shooting at the other guys. You never knew when the shit was going to go down. Other gangs would drive through on their motorcycles and, boom, boom, they'd take a shot at you. We knew where each crew would hang out, so we knew not to go certain places.

But it's something else when the cops start shooting at you. One day a few of us were walking past the jewelry store on Amboy Street and we saw the jeweler carrying a box. I snatched the box and we started running. We got close to our block and we heard car tires screech, and some undercover cops ran out of the car and, boom, boom, they started shooting at us. I ran into an abandoned building that we hung out in and I knew I was free. I knew that building like the back of my hand. I knew how to go into the walls or go to the roof and go through a hole and be in the rafters above the ceiling. So I did that. I got on top of the ceiling and looked through the hole and I could see anyone walking on the floor below.

I saw the cops enter the building. They started walking across the floor, guns drawn, and one of them went right through a hole in the floor.

"Holy shit, these fucking kids are busting my balls bringing me into this building," he said. "I'm going to kill these fucking bastards."

I'd be listening to these white cops talking and laughing to myself. The building was too fucked up for the cops to go up to another floor because the steps were falling apart. But there was a chance that they might look up and see me hiding in the rafters and shoot my ass. I thought about jumping to the next roof because that was my building, but it was a ten-foot jump.

So I made my way to the roof and my friend who lived in my building was on his roof. I was on my knees because I didn't want to stand up and let the cops outside see me, but my friend was giving me the blow-by-blow.

"Just chill out, Mike. They came out of the building. But they're still looking for you. There's a bunch of cop cars down there," he reported.

I was waiting up on that roof for what seemed like an eternity.

"They're down, Mike. They're down," my friend finally said.

So I went down but waited inside a little longer. My friends were looking around the block, making sure the cops weren't hiding there.

"Just wait some more, Mike," my friend said. Finally he told me I could go out. I was blessed to make it out of that situation. The jewelry box we stole had all these expensive watches, medallions, bracelets, diamonds, rubies. It took us two weeks to get rid of all that shit. We had to go sell some there, then go to a different part of town to sell some other pieces.

With all the jostling I did, it's somewhat ironic that my first arrest was over a stolen credit card. I was ten years old. I obviously was too young-looking to have a card, so I'd get some older guy to go into the store and I'd tell him to buy this and this and that and buy something for himself. Then we'd sell the card to another older guy.

But one time we were in a store on Belmont Avenue, a local store, and we tried to use the card. We were dressed clean but we just didn't look old enough to have a credit card. We picked out all these clothes and sneakers and brought them to the counter and gave the cashier the card. She excused herself for a second and made a call. Next thing we knew, she had cut the card in half and in seconds the cops came in and arrested us.

They took me to the local precinct. My mother didn't have a phone, so they picked her up and brought her to the station. She came in yelling at me and proceeded to beat the shit out of me right there. By the time I was twelve, this started to be a common occurrence. I'd have to go to court for these arrests, but I wasn't going to jail because I was a minor.

I used to hate when my mother would get to the precinct and beat my ass. Afterwards, her and her friends would get drunk and she'd talk about how she beat the shit out of me. I'd be curled up in the corner trying to shield myself, and she'd attack me. That was some traumatizing shit. To this day I glance at the corners of any room I'm in and I have to look away because it reminds me of all the beatings my mother gave me. I'd be curled up in the corner, trying to shield myself, and she'd attack me. She didn't think nothing of beating me in a grocery store, in the street, in front of my schoolmates, or in the courtroom. The police certainly didn't care. One time they were supposed to write up a report on me and my mother stormed in and beat my ass so bad they didn't even write me up.

She even beat me up when I was in the right sometimes. Once, when I was eleven, I was shooting dice on the corner. I was up against a guy who was about eighteen. I had a hot hand that day and my friends were betting on the side that I'd hit my numbers. I got down $200, but I hit my number six straight times. I had won $600 of his money.

"Shoot one more time. Shoot for my watch," he said.

Boom, I hit my 4-5-6.

"That's the name of the game," I said. "Gimme the watch."

"As a matter of fact, I ain't giving you nothing," he said and he tried to snatch the money I won from him. I started biting him. I hit him with a rock and we started brawling. Some of my mother's friends saw the commotion and ran to our apartment.

"Your son is fighting with a grown man," one of them said.

My mother came storming over. All the other grown men there were letting us fight because they wanted their money. If this guy didn't pay, nobody else was going to. So I was in the middle of fighting this guy when my mother jumped on me, grabbed my hands, smacked me, and threw me down.

"What are you fighting this man for?" she yelled. "What did you do to this man? I'm sorry, sir," she said to him.

"He tried to take back his money," I protested.

My mother took my money and gave it to the man and smacked my face.

"I'm sorry, sir," she said.

"I'm going to kill you, motherfucker," I yelled as she pulled me away.

I deserved every beating I got. I just wanted to be one of the cool kids, the kid in the street who had jewelry on and money in their pockets, the older kids, the fifteen-year-olds who had girlfriends. I wasn't really into girls that much then but I liked having the clothes and getting all the attention.

By then, my mother was giving up on me. She was well known in the neighborhood and knew how to speak eloquently when she needed to. Her other children had the capacity to learn to get along with others, but then there was me. I was the only one who couldn't read and write. I couldn't grasp that stuff.

"Why can't you do this?" she'd say to me. "What's wrong with you?"

She must have thought I was retarded. She had taken me to all these places on Lee Avenue when I was a baby and I'd undergo psychological evaluations. When I was young, I'd talk out loud to myself. I guess that wasn't normal in the '70s.

Once I got into the court system, I had to go to court-mandated special ed crazy schools. Special ed was like jail. They kept you locked up until it was time to go home. They'd bus in all the antisocial kids and the fucking nuts. You were supposed to do whatever they told you to do but I'd get up and fight with people, spit in people's faces. They gave us tokens to go back and forth to school, and I'd rob the kids for their tokens and gamble with them. I'd even rob the teachers and come to school the next day wearing the new shit I bought with their money. I did a lot of bad shit.

They said I was hyperactive so they started giving me Thorazine. They skipped the Ritalin and went straight to the big T; that's what they gave little bad black motherfuckers in the '70s. Thorazine was a trip. I'd be sitting there looking at something but I couldn't move, couldn't do nothing. Everything was cool; I could hear everything, but I was just zonked out, I was a zombie. I didn't ask for food, they just brought out the food at the right time. They would ask, "Do you need to go to the bathroom?" And I would say, "Oh, yes I do." I didn't even know when I got to go to the bathroom.

When I took that shit, they sent me home from school. I'd stay in the house chilling, watching *Rocky and His Friends*. My mother thought something was wrong with her baby, but I was just a bad-assed fucking kid. They misdiagnosed me, probably fucked me up a little, but I never took it personally when people misdiagnosed me. I always thought that bad stuff happened to me because something was wrong with me.

Besides the zombies and the crazy kids, they sent the criminals to the special ed schools. Now all the criminals from different neighborhoods got to know each other. We'd go to Times Square to jostle and we'd see all the guys from our school, all dressed up in sheepskins and fancy clothes, money in our pocket, doing the same thing. I was in Times Square in 1977 just hanging out when I saw some guys from the old neighborhood in Bed-Stuy. We were talking and the next thing I knew one of them snatched the purse of this prostitute. She was furious and threw a cup of hot coffee at my face. The cops started coming towards us and my friend Bub and I took off. We ran into an XXX-rated theater to hide but the hooker came in shortly after with the cops.

"That's them," she pointed to Bub and I.

"Me? I didn't do shit," I protested, but the cops paraded us out and put us in the backseat of their car.

But this crazy lady wasn't finished. She reached in through the back window and scratched my face with her long hooker nails.

They drove us to the midtown precinct. As we pulled away from Times Square, I saw my friends from Bed-Stuy, the ones who did all this shit, watching from the street. I had been arrested many times so I was used to the formation. But they looked at my rap sheet and I just had too many arrests, so I was going straight to Spofford.

Spofford was a juvenile detention center located in the Hunts Point section of the Bronx. I had heard horror stories about Spofford—people being beaten up by other inmates or by the staff—so I wasn't too thrilled to be going there. They issued me some clothes and gave me a cell by myself and I went to sleep. In the morning, I was terrified. I had no idea what was going to go down in that place. But when

I went to the cafeteria for breakfast, it was like a class reunion. I immediately saw my friend Curtis, the guy that I had robbed the house with who got clobbered by the owner. Then I start seeing all my old partners.

"Chill," I said to myself. "All your boys are here."

After that first time, I was going in and out of Spofford like it was nothing. Spofford became like a time-share for me. During one of my visits there we were all brought to the assembly room where we watched a movie called *The Greatest*, about Muhammad Ali. When it was over, we all applauded and were shocked when Ali himself walked out onto the stage. He looked larger than life. He didn't have to even open his mouth—as soon as I saw him walk out, I thought, *I want to be that guy.* He talked to us and it was inspirational. I had no idea what I was doing with my life, but I knew that I wanted to be like him. It's funny, people don't use that terminology anymore. If they see a great fight, they may say, "I want to be a boxer." But nobody says, "I want to be like him." There are not many Alis. Right then I decided I wanted to be great. I didn't know what it was I'd do but I decided that I wanted people to look at me like I was on show, the same way they did to Ali.

Don't get me wrong. I didn't get out of Spofford and do a three-sixty. I was still a little sewer rat. My situation at home was deteriorating. After all those arrests and special schools and medications, my mother had no hope for me at all. But she had never had any hope for me, going back to my infancy. I just know that one of those medical people, some racist asshole, some guy who said that I was fucked up and developmentally retarded, stole my mother's hope for me right then and there. And they stole any love or security I might have had.

I never saw my mother happy with me or proud of me doing something. I never got a chance to talk to her or know her. Professionally that would have no effect on me, but emotional and psychologically, it was crushing. I would be with my friends and I'd see their mothers kiss them. I never had that. You'd think that if she let me sleep in her bed until I was fifteen, she would have liked me, but she was drunk all the time.

Since I was now in the correctional system, the authorities decided to send me to group homes to get straightened out. They would take a bunch of kids who were down, abused, bad, psycho kids and throw them together in some home where the government paid people to take us in. The whole thing was a hustle. I would never last more than two days. I'd just run away. One time, I was in a group home in Brentwood, Long Island. I called home and bitched and moaned to my mother that I didn't have any weed there, so she made Rodney buy me some and deliver it to me. She was always a facilitator.

Eventually I was sent to Mount Loretto, a facility in Staten Island, but nothing could change me. Now I was pickpocketing guys on the Staten Island ferry. You never know who you're pickpocketing. Sometimes you pickpocket the wrong guy, a bad motherfucker, and he wants his money back. He just starts clocking everyone.

"Who took my motherfucking money?" he screamed.

He started beating on everyone around him, the whole ferry had to jump on the motherfucker. My friend was the one who jostled him, and he kicked my friend in the ass but he didn't know he had gotten the perpetrator. We got off the boat and were all laughing 'cause we got the money. Even my friend was laughing through his tears because he was still in pain. That guy would have thrown us off the boat if he knew we had his money. I get scared now just thinking about the kind of life I was living then. Oh, God, he would have killed us, he was just that fucking fierce.

I was released from the juvie facility on Staten Island at the beginning of 1978, and I went back to Brownsville. I kept hearing that a lot of my friends were getting killed over ridiculous things like jewelry or a couple of hundred dollars. I was getting a little worried but I never stopped robbing and stealing. I watched the guys I looked up to, the older guys, I watched them rise, but I saw their bumps in the road too. I watched them get beat mercilessly because they were always hustling people. But still they never stopped, it was in their blood.

The neighborhood was getting more and more ominous and I was getting more and more hated. I was just eleven years old, but sometimes I'd walk through the neighborhood, minding my own business and a landlord or owner of a store would see me walking by and would pick up a rock or something and throw it at me.

"Motherfucking little thieving bastard," they'd yell.

They'd see me in my nice clothes and they just knew that I was the nigga stealing from them. I was walking past a building one time and I stopped to talk to a friend and this guy Nicky came out with a shotgun and his friend had a pistol. His friend pulled out his pistol and Nicky put the shotgun over my penis.

"Listen, little nigga, if I hear you've been going up on that motherfucking roof again, I'll fuck you up. If I ever see you in this neighborhood again, I am going to blow your balls off," he said.

I didn't even know who the fuck this guy was, but he evidently knew who I was. Can you believe I was just so used to people coming up to me and stepping to me like that?

A few months before I turned thirteen, I got arrested again for possession of stolen property. They had exhausted all the places in the New York City vicinity to keep me. I don't know what kind of scientific diagnostic tests they used, but they decided to send me to the Tryon School for Boys, an upstate New York facility for juvenile offenders about an hour northwest of Albany.

My mother was happy that I was going upstate. By then, a lot of grown men had started coming to the house looking for me.

"Your brother is a dirty motherfucker. I'm going to kill your brother," they'd tell my sister.

"He's just a kid," she'd say. "It's not like he took your wife or something."

Imagine that, grown men coming to your house looking for you, and you're twelve years old. Ain't that some shit? Can you blame my mother for giving up all hope for me?

2

THE FACT THAT THEY WERE SENDING ME UP TO THE STATE REFORMATORY WAS not cool. I was with the big boys now. They were more hard-core than the guys at Spofford. But Tryon wasn't a bad place. There were a lot of cottages there, and you could walk outside, play basketball, walk to the gym. But I got in trouble right away. I was just angry all the time. I had a bad attitude. I'd be confrontational and let everyone know that I was from Brooklyn and I didn't fuck around with any bullshit.

I was going to one of my classes one day when this guy walked by me in the hall. He was acting all tough, like he was a killer, and when he passed by, he saw that I was holding my hat in my hand. So he started pulling on it and kept walking. I didn't know him, but he disrespected me. I sat in the class for the next whole forty-five minutes thinking about how I was going to kill this guy for tugging on my hat. When the class was over, I walked out and saw him and his friends at the door.

That's your man, Mike, I thought. I walked up to him and he had his hands in his pockets, looking at me as if he had no worries in the world; like I forgot that he had pulled my hat forty-five minutes ago. So I attacked him rather ferociously.

They handcuffed me and sent me to Elmwood, which was a lock-down cottage for the incorrigible kids. Elmwood was creepy. They had big tough-ass redneck staff members over there. Every time you saw somebody from there, they were walking in handcuffs with two people escorting them.

On the weekends, all the kids from Elmwood who earned credits would go away for a few hours and then come back with broken noses, cracked teeth, busted mouths, bruised ribs—they were all jacked up. I just thought they were getting beat up by the staff, because back then nobody would call the Health Department or Social Services if the staff were hurting the kids. But the more I talked to these hurt guys, the more I realized they were happy.

"Yeah, man, we almost got him, we almost got him," they laughed. I had no idea what they were talking about and then they told me. They were boxing Mr. Stewart, one of the counselors. Bobby Stewart was a tough Irish guy, around 170 pounds, who had been a professional boxer. He was a national amateur champ. When I was in the hole, staff members told me there was an ex–boxing champ teaching kids how to box. The staff members that told me about him were very nice to me and I wanted to meet him because I thought he'd be nice too.

I was in my room one night when there was a loud, intimidating knock on the door. I opened the door and it was Mr. Stewart.

"Hey, asshole, I heard you want to talk to me," he growled.

"I want to be a fighter," I said.

"So do the rest of the guys. But they don't have the balls to work to be a fighter," he said. "Maybe if you straighten up your act and stop being such an asshole and show some respect around here, I'll work with you."

So I really started to apply myself. I think I'm the stupidest guy in the world when it comes to scholastics, but I got my honor-roll star and I said "Yes, sir" and "No, ma'am" to everyone, just being a model citizen so I could go over to fight with Stewart. It took me a month, but I finally earned enough credits to go. All the other kids came to watch to see if I could kick his ass. I was supremely confident that I was going to demolish him and that everyone would suck up to me.

I immediately started flailing and throwing a bunch of punches and he covered up. I'm punching him and slugging him and then suddenly he slips by me and goes boom and hits me right in the stomach.

"Boosh. Uggghhh, uggghhh." I threw up everything I had eaten for the last two years. *What the fuck was that?* I was thinking. I didn't know anything about boxing then. Now I know that if you get hit in the stomach, you're just going to lose your breath for a couple of seconds, but it comes back. I didn't know that then. I really thought that I wouldn't be able to ever breathe again and I'd die. I was trying desperately to breathe but all I could do was throw up. It was just horrible shit.

"Get up, walk it off," he barked.

After everyone left, I approached him real humble. "Excuse me, sir, can you teach me how to do that?" I asked. I'm thinking that when I go back to Brownsville and hit a motherfucker in the stomach like that, he's going to go down and I'm going to go in his pockets. That's where my mind was at back then. He must have seen something in me that he liked, because after our second session he said to me, "Would you like to do this for real?" So we started training regularly. And after our workouts, I'd go back to my room and shadowbox all night long. I started to get a lot better. I didn't know it at the time, but during one of our sparring sessions I hit Bobby with a jab and broke his nose and almost knocked him down. He had the next week off, so he just let it heal at home.

After a few months of workouts, I called my mother and put Bobby on the phone with her. "Tell her, tell her," I said. I wanted him to tell her how good I was doing. I just wanted her to know I could do something. I figured she might believe me if a white person was telling her it. But she just told him that she had trouble believing that I had changed. She just thought I was incorrigible.

Shortly after that Bobby came to me with an idea. "I want to bring you to see this legendary boxing trainer Cus D'Amato. He can take you to the next level."

"What the heck is going on here?" I asked. I didn't trust anybody but Bobby Stewart at that particular time. Now he was going to transfer me over to another person?

"Just trust this man," he told me.

So one weekend in March of 1980, Bobby and I drove to Catskill, New York. Cus's gym was a converted meeting hall that was above the town police station. There were no windows so they had some old-fashioned lamps to provide light. I noticed there were posters on the walls and clippings of some of the local boys who were doing well.

Cus looked exactly like what you'd envision a hard-boiled boxing trainer to look like. He was short and stout with a bald head and you could see that he was strong. He even talked tough and he was dead serious; there wasn't a happy muscle in his face.

"How you doin', I'm Cus," he introduced himself. He had a strong Bronx accent. He was with a younger trainer named Teddy Atlas.

Bobby and I got in the ring and started sparring. I started out strong, really knocking Bobby around the ring. We would usually do three rounds, but in the middle of the second round Bobby hit me in the nose with a couple of rights and I started bleeding. It didn't really hurt but the blood was all over my face.

"That's enough," Atlas said.

"But, sir, please let me finish this round and go one more round. That's what we normally do," I pleaded. I wanted to impress Cus.

I guess I had. When we got out of the ring, Cus's first words to Bobby were, "That's the heavyweight champion of the world."

Right after that sparring session, we went to Cus's house for lunch. He lived in a big white Victorian house on ten acres. You could see the Hudson River from the porch. There were towering maple trees and large rosebushes on the side of the house. I had never seen a house like that in my life.

We sat down and Cus told me he couldn't believe I was only thirteen years old. And then he told me what my future would be. He had seen me spar for not even six minutes, but he said it in a way that was like law.

"You looked splendid," he said. "You're a great fighter." It was compliment after compliment. "If you listen to me, I can make you the youngest heavyweight champion of all time."

Fuck, how could he know that shit? I thought he was a pervert. In the world I came from, people do shit like that when they want to perv out on you. I didn't know what to say. I had never heard anyone say nice things about me before. I wanted to stay around this old guy because I liked the way he made me feel. I'd later realize that this was Cus's psychology. You give a weak man some strength and he becomes addicted.

I was excited on the ride back to Tryon. I was sitting with a bunch of Cus's roses in my lap. I had never seen roses in person before, only on television, but I wanted some because they looked so exquisite. I wanted to have something nice to take back with me so I asked him if I could take some. Between the smell of the roses and Cus's words ringing in my ears, I felt good, like my whole world had changed. In that one moment, I knew I was going to be somebody.

"I think he likes you," Bobby said. "If you're not a prick and an asshole, this will go well." I could tell Bobby was happy for me.

I got back to my cottage and put the roses in water. Cus had given me a huge boxing encyclopedia to look at and I didn't sleep that whole night, I just read the whole book. I read about Benny Leonard and Harry Greb and Jack Johnson. I got turned out real bad. I wanted to be like those guys; they looked like they had no rules. They worked hard, but on their downtime they just lounged and people came to them like they were gods.

I started going out to Cus's house every weekend to work out. I'd work with Teddy in the gym and then I'd stay over at Cus's house. There were a few other fighters living there with Cus and his companion, a sweet Ukrainian lady named Camille Ewald. When I first got to the house, I would steal money from Teddy's wallet. Hey, that shit doesn't go away just because you got some good shit going on. I had to get money for weed. I would hear Teddy tell Cus, "It has to be him."

"It's not him," Cus said.

I was excited about the boxing, but I became certain that boxing was what I wanted to do with my life after I watched the first

Leonard-Duran fight on TV at Cus's house one weekend. Wow, that fight turned me out, it was so exciting. They were both so stylish and deadly, throwing punches so fast. It looked choreographed, like the two of them were acting. I was just amazed. I've never felt that feeling again.

When I first started going to Cus's, he didn't even let me box. After I finished my workout with Teddy, Cus would sit down with me and we'd talk. He'd talk about my feelings and emotions and about the psychology of boxing. He wanted to reach me at the root. We talked a lot about the spiritual aspects of the game. "If you don't have the spiritual warrior in you, you'll never be a fighter. I don't care how big or strong you are," he told me. We talked about pretty abstract concepts, but he was getting through to me. Cus knew how to talk my language. He had grown up in tough neighborhoods and he had been a street kid too.

The first thing Cus talked about was fear and how to overcome it.

"Fear is the greatest obstacle to learning. But fear is your best friend. Fear is like fire. If you learn to control it, you let it work for you. If you don't learn to control it, it'll destroy you and everything around you. Like a snowball on a hill, you can pick it up and throw it or do anything you want with it before it starts rolling down, but once it rolls down and gets so big, it'll crush you to death. So one must never allow fear to develop and build up without having control over it, because if you don't you won't be able to achieve your objective or save your life.

"Consider a deer crossing an open field. On approaching the forest, suddenly instinct tells it there's danger there, might be a mountain lion there. Once this happens nature begins its survival function where the adrenal glands inject into the bloodstream, causes the heart to beat faster, which in turn enables the body to perform extraordinary feats of agility and strength. Where normally the deer can leap fifteen feet, the adrenaline enables the first leap to be forty or fifty feet, enough to escape from the present danger. The human being is no different. When confronted with a situation of fear of getting hurt or intimidation, the adrenaline speeds up the heart. Under the influence of adrenal glands people can perform extraordinary feats of strength.

"You think you know the difference between a hero and a coward, Mike? Well, there is no difference between a hero and a coward in what they feel. It's what they *do* that makes them different. The hero and the coward feel exactly the same but you have to have the discipline to do what a hero does and to keep yourself from doing what the coward does.

"Your mind is not your friend, Mike. I hope you know that. You have to fight with your mind, control it, put it in its place. You have to control your emotions. Fatigue in the ring is ninety percent psychological. It's just the excuse of a man who wants to quit. The night before a fight, you won't sleep. Don't worry, the other guy didn't either. You'll go to the weigh-in, he'll look much bigger than you and calmer, like ice, but he's burning up with fear inside. Your imagination is going to credit him with abilities he doesn't have. Remember, motion relieves tension. The moment the bell rings, and you come in contact with each other, suddenly your opponent seems like everybody else, because now your imagination has dissipated. The fight itself is the only reality that matters. You have to learn to impose your will and take control over that reality."

I could listen to Cus for hours. And I did. Cus talked to me about the importance of acting intuitively and impersonally and in a relaxed manner so as to keep all my emotions and feelings from blocking what I intuitively knew. He told me that he was talking about that once with the great writer Norman Mailer.

"Cus, you don't know it but you practice Zen," Mailer had told Cus, and then he gave him a book called *Zen in the Art of Archery*. Cus used to read that book to me. He told me that he had actually experienced the ultimate in emotional detachment in his first fight. He was training in a gym in the city because he wanted to be a professional fighter. He had been hitting the heavy bag for a week or two when the manager asked him if he wanted to box with someone. He got in the ring and his heart was beating like a drum, and the bell rang and the other guy charged him and he got knocked around. His nose was swollen, his eye was shut, he was bleeding. The guy asked him if he wanted to go a second round and Cus said he'd try. He went out there and suddenly his mind became detached from his body. He was watching himself from afar. The punches that hit him felt like they were coming from a distance. He was more aware of them than feeling them.

Cus told me that to be a great fighter you had to get out of your head. He would have me sit down and he'd say, "Transcend. Focus. Relax until you see yourself looking at yourself. Tell me when you get there." That was very important for me. I'm way too emotional in general. Later on I realized that if I didn't separate from my feelings inside the ring, I would be sunk. I might hit a guy with a hard punch and then get scared if he didn't go down.

Cus took this out-of-body experience one step further. He would separate his mind from his body and then visualize the future. "Everything gets calm and I'm outside watching myself," he told me. "It's me, but it's not me, as if my mind and my body aren't connected, but they are connected. I get a picture in my mind, what it's going to be. I can actually see the picture, like a screen. I can take a fighter who is just beginning and I can see exactly how he will respond. When that happens, I can watch a guy fight and I know everything there is to know about this guy, I can actually see the wheels in his head. It's as if I'm that guy, I'm inside him."

He even claimed that he could control events using his mind. Cus trained Rocky Graziano when he was an amateur. One time, Cus was in Rocky's corner and Rocky was taking a beating. After being knocked down twice, Rocky came back to the corner and wanted to quit. But Cus pushed him out for the next round, and before Rocky could quit, Cus used his mind to will Rocky's arm to throw a punch and it connected and the guy went down and the ref stopped the fight. This was the heavy dude who was training me.

Cus was a strong believer that in your mind you had to be the entity that you wanted to be. If you wanted to be heavyweight champion of the world, you had to start living the life of a heavyweight champion. I was only fourteen, but I was a true believer in Cus's philosophy. Always training, thinking like a Roman gladiator, being in a perpetual state of war in your mind, yet on the outside seeming calm and relaxed. He was practicing and teaching me the law of attraction without even knowing it.

Cus was also big on affirmations. He had a book called *Self Mastery Through Conscious Autosuggestion* by a French pharmacist/psychologist named Emile Coué. Coué would tell his patients to repeat to themselves, "Every day in every way, I am getting better and better" over and over again. Cus had a bad cataract in one eye, and he would repeat that phrase and he claimed the phrase had made it better.

Cus had us modify the affirmations for our own situation. So he had me saying, "The best fighter in the world. Nobody can beat me. The best fighter in the world. Nobody can beat me" over and over again all day. I loved doing that, I loved hearing myself talk about myself.

The goal of all these techniques was to build confidence in the fighter. Confidence was everything. But in order to possess that confidence, you had to test yourself and put yourself on the line. It doesn't come from osmosis, out of the air. It comes from consistently going over the visualization in your mind to help you develop the confidence that you want to possess.

Cus laid all this out for me in the first few weeks that we were together. He gave me the whole plan. He gave me a mission. I was going to be the youngest heavyweight champion of all time. I didn't know it then, but after one of our first long talks, Cus confided in Camille. "Camille, this is the one I've been waiting for all my life."

I was getting close to being paroled back to Brooklyn when Bobby Stewart came to see me one day.

"I don't want you to go back to Brooklyn. I'm afraid you may do something stupid and get killed or get your ass locked up again. Do you want to move in with Cus?"

I didn't want to go back either. I was looking for change in my life. Plus, I liked the way those people talked and made me feel good, made me feel like I was part of society. So I talked to my mother about staying up there with Cus.

"Ma, I want to go up there and train. I want to be a fighter. I can be the best fighter in the world." Cus had my mind so fucked up. That's all he talked to me about, how great I could become, how to improve myself, day by day, in every way. All that self-help shit.

My mom felt bad about me leaving, but she signed the permission papers. Maybe she thought she'd failed as a mother.

So I moved in with Cus and Camille and the other fighters in the house. I got to know more and more about Cus because we'd have these long talks after I trained. He was so happy when I told him my hard-luck stories about my life. He would light up like a Christmas tree. "Tell me more," he'd say. I was the perfect guy for his mission—broken home, unloved, destitute. I was hard and strong and sneaky, but I was still a blank chalkboard. Cus wanted me to embrace my shortcomings. He didn't make me feel ashamed or inferior because of my upbringing. He loved the fact that I had great enthusiasm. "Enthusiasm"—Cus taught me that word.

Cus could relate to me because he'd had a hard life too. His mother died at a very early age. He'd lost his vision in one eye in a street fight when he was a little kid. His father died in his arms when he was a young man. A cop had murdered his favorite brother.

Cus really only worked a nine-to-five job for one year in his life. And then he left because he got into fights with his coworkers. But he spent a lot of time helping out the people in his neighborhood, solving their problems almost like an unofficial social worker. He derived a lot of pleasure out of assisting other people. Cus helped weed out political corruption in his neighborhood when La Guardia was running for mayor of New York City as a reformer. He did it by standing up to one of the corrupt guys who had pulled a gun on him. He was fearless.

He was also bitter.

"I stood up for the little guy all my life," Cus said. "Lot of my troubles came from standing up for the underdog. Some of the people that I did things for didn't deserve it. Very few people are worth saving."

Cus was totally color-blind. His father's best friend was black. When he was in the army, stationed in the South, he had a boxing team. When they traveled, no hotel would take his black fighters so he slept with them in parks.

He was also a big-time socialist. He was in love with Che and Fidel and the Rosenbergs. He'd tell me about the Rosenberg case and I'd tease him.

"Come on, Cus. That ain't right. They were guilty," I said.

"Oh, yeah," he'd roar. "You're talking now but when they bring slavery back you're not going to be able to say who was guilty or not. They're planning to bring it back too, all right?"

His biggest enemy was Ronald Reagan. Reagan would come on the TV and Cus would scream at the top of his lungs, "LIAR. LIAR. LIAR. LIAR!!!" Cus was a maniac. He would always be talking about who needed to die. "A man dies by the way he lives," he'd tell me.

One day Cus said, "When you make a lot of money, you could really help everybody you ever cared about. You could help the black churches." He thought the black churches were the best grassroots social net for black people. He loved the Reverend Martin Luther King. Cus was always into helping people and that was how he gave all his money away.

"Money is something to throw off the back of trains," he'd tell me. "Money means security, and to me security means death, so I never cared about money. To me all the things that I value I couldn't buy for money. I was never impressed with money. Too many of the wrong people have a lot of money so the association is not good. The truth was, I wasn't careless about money. I gave money to people in trouble. I don't consider that wasting it."

He also didn't believe in paying taxes to a right-wing government. He declared bankruptcy when he owed $200,000 to the IRS.

How Cus got into boxing was itself a mystery. Out of nowhere he popped up and said, "I'm a boxing trainer." Nobody had ever heard of him. He didn't know anything about contracts or fighters, but he claimed to be a manager. He wound up managing and training a promising young heavyweight named Floyd Patterson who was also a poor kid who grew up in Brooklyn. At the time, boxing was ruled by a group called the IBC, the International Boxing Club, owned by rich entrepreneurs who had a stranglehold on the promotion of championship bouts. But Cus guided Floyd to the championship, and then he went after the IBC. Which meant he was going up against the mob, because Frankie Carbo, a soldier in the Lucchese family, was in bed with the IBC. Cus helped break the back of the IBC, and Carbo wound up in jail for conspiracy, extortion, and unlicensed management.

But Cus's heart was broken when Roy Cohn, a right-wing attorney, stole Patterson away from him by wooing the newly converted Catholic boxer with a meeting with New York's Cardinal Spellman. Cus never set foot inside a Catholic church again. He got increasingly paranoid after that. He claimed that someone tried to push him in front of a subway car. He stopped going to bars because he was afraid someone would spike his drink. He actually sewed shut the pockets of his coat jackets so no one could drop drugs into them to set him up. Finally he moved upstate to Catskill.

He was even paranoid in the house. Nobody was allowed into his room, and he would rig up some matches in his door so he could see if anyone had gone in while he was away. If he'd see me anywhere near his room, he'd say, "What are you doing up there?"

"I live up here, Cus. I live here," I'd answer.

One time, me and Tom Patti and Frankie, two other boxers who were living at the house, went out. Cus didn't trust anyone with keys, because we might lose them and then some stranger would have access to the house. When we came home and knocked on the door, there was no answer. I looked in the window and Cus had fallen asleep in his favorite plush chair with the TV blasting because he was half deaf. Tom figured that the time to knock was when the show went to commercial and there were a couple seconds of silence. So at exactly that moment we all banged on the window and yelled, "Cus!! Cus!!" In one-thousandth of a second, Cus did a one-eighty, dropped down, bent over at the waist, with his left hand bracing himself, ready to pop up with the right hand to knock the intruder out. We were all on the floor, laughing hysterically.

Another time, one of the sparring partners who was staying there snuck out during the night to go to town. Tom and I woke up early in the morning and we were going downstairs to get breakfast. We looked in the living room and Cus was on the floor doing an army crawl with his rifle in his hand. The guy had come home and knocked on the window and Cus probably thought it was some IBC guy after him. Tom and I stepped over him and walked into the kitchen to get some cereal.

I could go on and on with Cus stories. He was that unique and colorful a cat. But the best description of Cus I've ever heard was in an interview that the great writer Gay Talese gave to Paul Zuckerman, a young man who was researching a book about Cus.

"He was a Roman warrior two thousand years too late. Warriors like war, need war, that's the atmosphere in which they feel most at home. In times of peace, they are restless and useless men they think. They like to stir up a lot. Cus, like Patton, felt alive when there was confusion, intrigue, a sense of impending battle. He felt most engaged with himself then, his nerve endings, his brainpower was most alive and he felt most fulfilled when he was in a state of agitation. And if it wasn't there, he had to create or heighten it. If it was simmering, he had to turn up the flames to feel fully alive. It gave him a high. He was an activist, he needed action."

Cus was a general and I was his soldier. And we were ready to go to war.

I WAS THIS USELESS THORAZINED-OUT NIGGA WHO WAS DIAGNOSED AS retarded and this old white guy gets ahold of me and gives me an ego. Cus once said to me, "Mike, if you were sitting down with a psychiatrist and they asked you, 'Are you hearing voices?' You're going to say no, but the voices are telling you to say no, aren't they?" Cus was such a deep guy. No one ever made me more conscious of being a black man. He was so cold hard, giving it to me like a bitter black man would. "They think they're better than you, Mike," he'd say. If he saw somebody with a Fiat or a Rolls-Royce, he'd look at me and say, "You could get that. That's not the hardest thing in the world to do, getting wealthy. You're so superior to those people. They can never do what you are capable of doing. You got it in you. You think I would tell you this if you didn't have it in you? I could probably make you a better fighter but I couldn't make you champion."

Whoa. I always thought I was shit. My mother had told me I was crap. Nobody had ever said anything good about me. And here's this dude saying, "I bet you if you try, you could win an Oscar. You'd be just as good an actor as you'd be a boxer. You want to be a race-car driver? I bet you'd be the best race-car driver in the world; you're smarter and tougher than those guys. You could conquer any world. Don't use that word 'can't.' You can't say 'can't.'"

When I got discouraged, as I often did, Cus would massage my mind with thoughts of an exotic world with great treasures. Everything he said was foreign to me, but I liked the sound of it.

"All you have to do is listen to me," he'd say. "People of royal descent will know your name. Do you hear what I'm saying to you, boy? The whole world will know who you are. Your family name will reign. People will respect your mother, your family, your children. When you enter a room, people will stand up and give you an ovation."

Cus wouldn't let me fail. When I felt like quitting and I got discouraged, he just kept on inspiring me. Cus would always say, "My job is to peel off layers and layers of damages that are inhibiting your true ability to grow and fulfill your potential." He was peeling me and it hurt! I was screaming, "Leave me alone. Aarrgghh!" He tortured my mind. He'd see me sparring with an older guy and it was in my mind that I was tired and I wasn't punching back at the guy, the guy was just bullying me, and Cus would talk to me about that, make me confront my fears. He was a perfectionist. I'd be hitting the heavy bag with combinations and Cus would be standing there, watching.

"It's good. It's good. But it's not poifect," he'd say in his thick Bronx accent.

Cus wanted the meanest fighter that God ever created, someone who scared the life out of people before they even entered the ring. He trained me to be totally ferocious, in the ring and out. At the time, I needed that. I was so insecure, so afraid. I was so traumatized from people picking on me when I was younger. I just hated the humiliation of being bullied. That feeling sticks with you for the rest of your life. It's just such a bad, hopeless feeling. That's why I always projected to the world that I was a mean, ferocious motherfucker. But Cus gave me confidence so that I didn't have to worry about being bullied ever again. I knew nobody was ever going to fuck with me physically.

Cus was much more than a boxing trainer. He instilled so many values in me. He was like some guru, always saying things that would make me think.

"No matter what anyone says, no matter the excuse or explanation, whatever a person does in the end is what he intended to do all along."

Or, "I'm not a creator. What I do is discover and uncover. My job is to take the spark and fan it. Feed the fire until it becomes a roaring blaze."

He could impart wisdom in the most mundane situations. Camille was very big on the boys doing their chores around the house. I hated doing chores; I was so focused on my boxing. One day Cus came to me. "You know, Camille really wants you to do your chores. I could care less if you did, but you should do them because it will make you a better boxer."

"How's taking out the trash going to make me a better boxer?" I scoffed.

"Because doing something you hate to do like you love it is good conditioning for someone aspiring towards greatness."

After that, Camille never had to remind me to do my chores again.

One day Cus called me into the room where he was sitting.

"Are you scared of white people?" he said out of the blue. "Are you one of those kinds? You scared of mustaches and beards? I've been around black fighters who were scared to hit white people. You better not be one of them."

It was funny. I had Cus in my face telling me not to be intimidated, but I was intimidated by the way he was telling me not to be intimidated.

Cus was always dead serious, never smiling. He didn't treat me like a teenager. He always made me feel like we had a mission to accomplish. Training day in and day out, thinking about one fucking thing. He gave me a purpose. I had never had that feeling in my life before except when I was thinking about stealing.

Every once in a while, things would happen that made our goal seem much more tangible. One time, Wilfred Benitez came to train at Catskill. I was overwhelmed. I was a groupie. I had seen him fight on television and he was something to watch. It was like he had radar, he'd punch people with his eyes closed. Truly a master. And he brought his championship belt with him. Tom Patti, one of Cus's other boxers, was there with me. Benitez pulled out this little case, and the belt was inside and he let me touch it. It was like looking at the Holy Grail.

"Man, Tommy, look at this, it's the belt, man," I said. "I gotta get one of these now. I'm going to train so hard. If I win this, I'm never going to take the belt off."

I was so happy to be in Benitez's presence. He inspired me, made me want to become more committed and dedicated.

Thanks to Cus, I also got to talk to Ali. In October of 1980, we all drove up to Albany to watch the closed-circuit broadcast of Ali trying to win back his title from Larry Holmes. Ali got the shit kicked out of him. Cus was mad as a motherfucker; I'd never seen him that angry before. After the fight, he was poker-faced because he had to give interviews and shake people's hands, but once we got in the car, we could feel that negative energy. We didn't say a word for the whole forty-five-minute drive home.

The next morning, Ali's aide Gene Kilroy put Ali on the phone with Cus.

"How did you let that bum beat you? He's a bum, Muhammad, he's a bum. No, he's a bum. Don't tell me that, he's a bum. Why did you let that bum hit you like that?"

I was listening to Cus talk and every time he said the word "bum" it was cutting right through me. I started crying. That was a bad day in my life.

Then Cus did a head trip on me.

"I have a young black kid with me. He's just a boy, but he's going to be the heavyweight champion of the world. His name is Mike Tyson. Talk to him for me, please, Muhammad. I want you to tell him to listen to me."

Cus handed me the phone.

"I'm sorry for what happened to you," I said. I was a little dickhead.

"I was sick," Ali told me. "I took some medicine and it made me weak and that's how Holmes beat me. I'm going to get well and come back and beat Holmes."

"Don't worry, champ," I said. "When I get big, I'm going to get him for you."

A lot of people assume that Ali was my favorite boxer. But I have to say it was Roberto Duran. I always looked at Ali as being handsome and articulate. And I was short and ugly and I had a speech impediment. When I saw Duran fight, he was just a street guy. He'd say stuff to his opponents like, "Suck my fucking dick, you motherfucker. Next time you're going to the fucking morgue." After he beat Sugar Ray Leonard in that first fight, he went over to where Wilfred Benitez was sitting and he said, "Fuck you. You don't have the heart or the balls to fight me."

Man, this guy is me, I thought. That was what I wanted to do. He was not ashamed of being who he was. I related to him as a human being. As my career progressed and people started praising me for being a savage, I knew that being called an animal was the highest praise I could receive from someone. When I'd go back to the city, I would go to Victor's Café because I heard Duran hung out there. I'd go and sit at a table by myself and look at the pictures of Duran hanging on the wall. I was living out my dreams.

I was sad when Duran quit during the No Más rematch with Leonard. Cus and I watched that fight in Albany and I was so mad that I cried. But Cus had called it. "He's not going to do it a second time," he predicted.

BY THE TIME I HAD MOVED IN WITH CUS, I WAS ALREADY INTO THE FLOW OF his repertoire. He began to train me hard every day. I never had the privilege of enjoying boxing as a sport or as something to do for fun. Cus was an extremist but I was just as extreme. I wanted to be Achilles right then. I'm the kind of guy they make fun of. "Don't give the nigga a rope, he'll want to be a cowboy." I was the kid who had no hope. But if you give me a glimmer of hope, you're in trouble. I take it to the moon.

Cus normally had to wake the fighters up in the morning, but when he'd get up to do it, I had already come back from running. Cus would usually set the table for breakfast, but I started doing it after my run. He'd get mad. "Who made up my table?" he'd bark. He was upset that I showed more dedication than he did. Then Cus would cook me my breakfast. He'd throw in a whole slab of bacon, twenty or so strips, into the frying pan and then he'd cook the eggs in that bacon grease. I didn't drink coffee so I'd have tea. He did that every morning even if he was angry with me.

I think both of us realized that we were in a race with time. Cus was in his seventies, he was no spring chicken, so he would constantly be shoving all this knowledge into me. Shove, shove, shove all this shit in. If you keep shoving it in, you learn it, unless you're an idiot. I became very adept at boxing but my maturity, my thinking ability as a human being didn't catch up with my boxing ability. It wasn't like I was going to go to school and they were building my character to make me a good, productive member of society. No, I was doing this to become heavyweight champion of the world. Cus was aware of that. "God, I wish I had more time with you," he said. But then he would say, "I've been in the fight game for sixty years and I've never seen anybody with the kind of interest you have. You're always talking about fighting."

I was an extremist. If we got snowed in, Cus trained me in the house. At night, I'd stay up for hours in my room shadowboxing. My life depended on succeeding. If I didn't, I would just be a useless piece of shit. Plus, I was doing it for Cus too. He had a tough life with a lot of disappointments. So I was here to defend this old Italian man's ego and pride. Who the fuck did I think I was?

When I wasn't training, I was watching old fight films for at least ten hours a day. That was my treat on the weekend. I'd watch them alone upstairs, all night long. I'd crank up the volume and the sound would travel through the old house. Then Cus would come up. "What the hell are you doing?"

"Just watching the films," I said.

"Hey, you gotta go to bed. People want to sleep," he said. Then he'd walk down the stairs and I'd hear him muttering, "I never met a kid like this. Watching the films all night, waking up the whole damned house."

Sometimes we'd watch the fight films together and Cus would give me tips on how I could beat Dempsey and Jeffries and Louis.

I was so focused sometimes that I'd actually go to sleep with my gloves on. I was an animal, dreaming about Mike Tyson being a big-time fighter. I sacrificed everything for that goal. No women, no food. I had an eating disorder; I was addicted to food then. And I was going through puberty. I was getting acne, my hormones were raging, all I wanted to do was eat ice cream but I couldn't lose sight of the goal. I'd talk to Cus about girls and he'd pooh-pooh me, telling me that I was going to have all the women I ever wanted. One time, I was morose.

"Cus, I ain't never going to have a girl, huh?"

Cus sent someone out and they came back with one of those minia-ture baseball bats and he presented it to me.

"You're going to have so many girls that you'll need this to beat them off you."

So all I did was jerk off and train, jerk off and train. I thought that after I became champion, I could get as much money and women as I'd need.

In the gym, Cus had some very unusual and unorthodox tech-niques. Some people laughed at the style he taught, but it was because they didn't really understand it. They called it the peek-a-boo style. It was very defense-oriented. You'd keep both your hands in front of your face, almost like you were turtling. Your hands and your elbows move with you, so when the guy throws the punch, you block it as you're coming forward, and then you counter.

Cus's offense started with a good defense. He thought it was of paramount importance for his fighter not to get hit. To learn to slip punches, he used a slipbag, a canvas bag filled with sand, wrapped around a rope. You had to slip around it by moving your head to avoid it hitting you. I got really good at that.

Then he used something called the Willie, named after the fighter

Willie Pastrano. It was a mattress covered in canvas and wrapped around a frame. On the exterior was a sketch of a torso. The body was divided into different zones and each zone had a number associated with it. The odd numbers were left-hand punches, the even numbers were the right-hand ones. Then Cus would play a cassette tape of him calling out the various sequences of numbers. So you'd hear "five, four" and immediately throw a left hook to the body and a right uppercut to the chin. The idea was that the more you repeated these actions in response to numbers they'd become instinctual and robotic and you wouldn't have to consciously think about them. After a while, you could throw punches with your eyes closed.

Cus thought that fighters got hit by right hands because they were stationary and had their gloves too low. So he taught me to weave in a U-shape, not just up and down. He had me on the move constantly, sideways and then forward, sideways and forward. When you were punching, Cus believed that you got the maximum effect from your punches when you made two punches sound like one. The closest you could get to that sound, the higher percentage that barrage would result in a knockout.

Even though he emphasized defense, Cus knew that defensive fighters could be boring.

"Boxing is entertainment, so to be successful a fighter must not only win, but he must win in an exciting manner. He must throw punches with bad intentions," Cus would always say. He wanted me to be an aggressive counterpuncher, forcing my opponents to punch or run. Cus was always trying to manipulate the opponent in the ring. If you kept eluding their punches, they would get frustrated and lose their confidence. And then they were sunk. Slip the punch and counter. Move and hit at the same time. Force the issue. He thought short punches could be harder than long punches. He thought that punching hard had nothing to do with anything physical, it was all emotional. Controlled emotion.

Cus hired the best sparring partners to teach me. My favorite was Marvin Stinson. I believe he was a former Olympian. He had been

Holmes's top sparring partner and then Cus brought him in to work with me. He was an awesome mentor to me, teaching me about movement and throwing punches. When he was finished the first time he came up to spar, he pulled me aside and gave me his running gloves because it was so cold out in the morning when I'd run. He saw that I didn't have any.

My sparring sessions were like all-out war. Before we fought, Cus would take me aside. "You don't take it easy, you go out there and do your best," he said. "You do everything you learned and you do it all full speed. I want you to break these guys' ribs."

Break their ribs? Sparring? He wanted to get me prepared for the guys I'd fight and he certainly wanted me to break the ribs of my opponents in an actual fight. When Cus found a good sparring partner for me, he treated them special because he knew that they gave me good workouts. He always paid the sparring partners top dollar. But that didn't insure that they would stay. Often a guy would come up anticipating sparring for three weeks. But after his first session, we'd go back to the house and he'd be gone. They were so disgusted with getting the shit kicked out of them, they didn't even bother to get their stuff. When that would happen, Tom and I made a beeline for their room and rummaged through their clothes and shoes and jewelry. If we were lucky, we'd find a stash of weed or at least a pair of shoes that fit.

Sometimes Cus would bring up established fighters to spar with me. When I was sixteen, he brought Frank Bruno to Catskill. Bruno was twenty-two at the time. We sparred for two rounds. Before I'd spar with an established fighter, Cus would take them aside.

"Listen, he's just a boy but don't take it easy on him. I'm informing you now, do your best," he said.

"Okay, Cus," they would say. "I'll work with the kid."

"Hey, do you hear me? Don't work with him. Do your best."

We fought to hurt people; we didn't fight just to win. We talked for hours about hurting people. This is what Cus instilled in me. "You'll be sending a message to the champ, Mike," Cus would tell me. "He'll be watching you." But we would also be sending a resounding message to the trainers, the managers, the promoters, and the whole boxing establishment. Cus was back.

Besides watching old fight films, I devoured everything I could read on these great fighters. Soon after I moved in with Cus, I was reading the boxing encyclopedia and I started laughing reading about a champion who only held his title for a year. Cus looked at me with his cold piercing eyes and said, "A one-year championship is worth more than a lifetime of obscurity."

When I started studying the lives of the great old boxers, I saw a lot of similarity to what Cus was preaching. They were all mean motherfuckers. Dempsey, Mickey Walker, even Joe Louis was mean, even though Louis was an introvert. I trained myself to be wicked. I used to walk to school, snapping at everybody. Deep down, I knew I had to be like that because if I failed, Cus would get rid of me and I would starve to death.

Cus had given me a book to read called *In This Corner . . . !* I couldn't put it down. I saw how these fighters dealt with their emotions, how they prepared for fights. That book gave me such superior insight into the psychology of human beings. What struck me was how hard the old-time fighters worked, how hungry they were. I read that John L. Sullivan would train by running five miles and then he'd walk back the five miles and spar for twenty rounds. Ezzard Charles said he only ran three to four miles a day and boxed six rounds. I thought, *Damn, Sullivan trained harder in the 1880s than this guy did in the 1950s.* So I started walking four miles to the gym, did my sparring, and then walked back to the house. I started emulating the old-school guys because they were hard-core. And they had long careers.

I drove Cus nuts asking him questions about these old fighters all the time. I know he wanted to talk about boxing but I think I overdid it sometimes. I read all of Cus's books about boxing, so when we'd sit around the dining room table and Cus would start expounding to the other guys about boxing history and he'd stumble on a name or a date, I'd finish his sentence for him.

"This guy knows everything," he'd say. "He acts like he was there."

I was serious about my history because I learned so much from the old fighters. What did I have to do to be like this guy? What discipline did this other guy possess? Cus would tell me how vicious and mean they were outside the ring but when they're in it, they're relaxed and calm. I got excited hearing him talk about these guys, seeing that he held them in such high esteem. I wanted so much for someone to talk like that about me. I wanted to be part of that world. I would watch the fights on TV and I'd see the boxers punching with grimaces on their faces and their ripped bodies, and I wanted that to be my face and my body.

We talked about all the greats. I fell in love with Jack Johnson. What a courageous guy. He was really the first black-pride guy. And I loved his arrogance. He got pulled over for speeding at the turn of the century and the ticket was for, like, ten dollars and he gave the cop a twenty and said, "Why don't you take this twenty because I'm going to be coming back the same way I'm going."

He was a master of manipulation. When he was training, he'd wrap his penis before he put on his tights to make it look larger and give the white guys an inferiority complex. He'd humiliate his opponents during fights. He was the original trash talker. "I'll give you ten thousand dollars if you can cut my lip," he'd say. He'd laugh in the face of his opponents during a round, talk to his white wife and tell her how much he loved her while he was beating the shit out of the guy he was fighting. He was a guy I would have loved to hang with. He spoke several languages and partied with the royal families of Russia and England. Dempsey was the first million-dollar champion. He brought showbiz and glamour to boxing. I related to him the most because he was a real insecure guy, he was always afraid, but he always overcame those feelings to reach his goals.

Cus loved Henry Armstrong the most. He would constantly attack his opponents and wear them down. "Constant attack, no letup," Cus told me. "Moving his head with a good defense, that's what Armstrong would do. Break his opponent's will, destroy his spirit, make all his causes a lie."

Make all his causes a fucking lie? Whoa. Then Cus would stare at me.

"If you listen to me, you'll reign with the gods. See the way you're interested and talk about all these old fighters? By the time you're champ, if you listen to me, the only reason people would know about these guys was because you'd talk about them. You'll supersede them all. You'll make them forget about everybody. I watched Jack Dempsey as a boy. I've met these guys, shook their hands. They are not what you are. You are a giant; you are a colossus among men."

I ate that shit up. But all this talk about dedication and discipline and hard work wasn't enough to keep me from going back to Brooklyn and doing my jostling and robbing. I was playing two heads of the same coin. I'd be up in Catskill and be the choirboy and then I'd go down to Brooklyn and be the devil. Thank God that I never got arrested for anything. That would have broken Cus's heart.

CUS KNEW HOW TO MAKE ME FEEL LIKE I COULD CONQUER THE WORLD. BUT HE also knew how to make me feel like shit. Sometimes he'd tell me, "You allow your mind to get the better of you." That was his secret, unwritten code way of saying, "You're a weak piece of shit. You don't have enough discipline to be one of the greats." The greats could fight the best fight of their life even if someone had just kidnapped their child or killed their mother. Greats are totally emotionally independent. Performers are like that too, not just boxers. Some of the legendary artists I read about would be high on everything but still be able to go out there and do a record-breaking performance. They couldn't even walk, but they had great discipline and determination. Sometimes they'd go directly from the arena to a hospital. I wanted to be one of those fighters and performers.

From the first night I moved in with Cus, he started to break me down, see how far he could fuck with me for no reason. He'd come to my room and say, "What did you do in school today, what did you do? Well, you had to do something, you were in school all day. What did you learn? Where's your homework? Do you have homework today?" The other guys in the house would always say that Cus favored me but they didn't know what he was saying to me when we were alone.

I was always struggling with my weight. In my mind, I was a fat pig even though nobody would know by looking at me. When I trained, I would put Albolene over my pores and wear a plastic suit for a week or two and only take it off at nighttime when I was taking a hot bath so I could sweat some more weight off. Then I'd go to bed and wake up the next morning and put it on and go run and wear it the whole day.

My weight was another thing that Cus would get on me about. "Your ass is getting fat," he'd say. "You're losing interest, aren't you? You don't want to do this no more, huh, Mike? It's too tough for you, isn't it? You thought that we were playing games up here, didn't you? You thought you were back in Brownsville running around and playing games. Huh?" Imagine hearing that. Just as I was about to enjoy some ice cream that I only allowed myself to have on the weekend, I'd hear that. "Not many people could do this, that's why it's so special. Jeez, I really thought you could."

Sometimes Cus would reprimand me and I'd have no idea why. He would rip into me, put down my character. "You can never reach the apex of what we're aiming for with your infantile behavior and conduct." At times I'd just scream, "I hate everybody here! Agggghhhhh." Cus was tearing me apart.

I would pick up on his positive comments and say things like, "I'm going to do anything I can do to win. I'd give my life to be champion, Cus." And instead of saying, "You'll get it, Mike," he had to just step in my face. "You just be careful what you ask for, you might get it."

He'd even criticize my clothes. On the holidays, they might have some guests over, Camille's sister or someone. I'd put on nice slacks and a shirt and a vest and I'd wear a tie that Camille helped me put on. I'd be sitting there chilling and all the ladies would be saying, "Oh, you look so nice, Mike." And then Cus would come in the room.

"What are you dressed like that for? Your pants are so tight your balls and your ass are all over the place. What is wrong with you?"

Camille would defend me, but Cus had none of it.

"Don't tell me nothing about what you think about this. Camil-lee, please. Okay? There is nothing nice about his clothes."

Cus would never call me bad names like "a son of a bitch." He'd just call me "a tomato can and a bum." That was the boxing equivalent of calling me a dirty, filthy no-good nigga. That would make me cry like a baby. He knew that if he said that to me, it would break my spirit.

I was getting so many mixed messages that I was becoming insecure about how he really felt about me as a boxer. Tom Patti and I once were leaving the gym and Cus was delayed for a second. So I jumped into the backseat and crouched down.

"Tell Cus I walked back home. Because when he gets in the car, I want you to ask him how he really feels about me." Tom agreed. Cus got in the car.

"Where the hell is Mike?" he said.

"I think he's staying in town," Tom said.

"Well, let's go. He can find his way home later." So we started driving and I was lying in the back whispering to Tom because Cus was half deaf and couldn't hear anything.

"Yo, Tom. Ask Cus if he thinks I punch hard," I said.

"Hey, Cus, you think Mike punches hard?" Tom asked.

"Punches hard! Let me tell you something, that guy punches so hard he could knock down a brick wall. Not only does he punch hard, he punches effectively. He can knock a fighter out with either hand," Cus said.

"Ask Cus if he thinks I can really be something in the future," I whispered.

Tom repeated the question.

"Tommy, if Mike keeps his head on straight and focuses on the intended purpose, he'll become one of the greatest fighters, if not *the* greatest fighter in the history of boxing."

I was thrilled to hear that. By now we were at the house. As we got out, Cus saw me lying down in the backseat.

"You knew he was back there, didn't you?" he said to Tom.

Tom pleaded innocence.

"Don't hand me that nonsense. You knew he was back there. You guys are a couple of wise guys right now, let me tell you something."

Cus didn't think it was funny, but we did.

The funny thing is he couldn't control his own emotions. Cus was just a bitter, bitter, bitter man who wanted revenge. Roy Cohn, Cardinal Spellman, those guys haunted him in his sleep. J. Edgar Hoover? "Oh, I wish I could put a bullet in his head, that's what he deserves." He was constantly talking about killing people and some of those guys were dead already! But he hated them. I once said something complimentary about Larry Holmes and Cus went nuts.

"What do you mean? He's nothing. You have to dismantle that man. That's our goal to dismantle this man and relinquish him from the championship. He's nothing to you."

Sometimes Cus would just roar at people on the TV like an animal. You'd never think he was a ferocious old man but he was. If you weren't his slave, he hated your guts. He was always in a state of confrontation. Most of the day he'd walk around, mumbling, "Oh, this son of a bitch. Oh, I can't believe this guy from, you know his name, from such and such. What a son of a bitch."

Poor Camille would say, "Cus, Cus, calm down, calm down, Cus. Your blood pressure is getting too high."

Cus ruled that house with an iron fist, but the funny thing was that it was actually Camille's house. Cus didn't have any money. He never really cared about money and he gave most of his away. Camille wanted to sell the house because it was so expensive to maintain but Cus talked her into keeping it. He told her he'd get a stable of good fighters and things would get better. He was losing hope, but then I came along.

I don't think that Cus thought that in a thousand years he'd get another champion, although he hoped he would. Most of the men who came up there were already established fighters who wanted to get away from the girls and the temptations of the city. Plus, no one liked Cus's boxing style at that time. They thought it was outdated. Then I show up there knowing nothing, a blank chalkboard. Cus was happy. I couldn't understand why this white man was so happy about me. He would look at me and just laugh hysterically. He'd get on the phone and tell people, "Lightning has struck me twice. I have another heavyweight champion." I had never even had an amateur fight in my life. I have no idea how, but somehow he saw it in me.

3

I'LL NEVER FORGET MY FIRST AMATEUR FIGHT. IT WAS AT A SMALL GYM IN THE Bronx owned by a former Cus boxer named Nelson Cuevas. The gym was a hellhole. It was on the second floor of a building that was right next to the elevated subway line. The tracks were so close that you could put your hand out the window and almost touch the train. These fight cards were called "smokers" because the air was so thick with cigarette smoke you could hardly see the guy standing in front of you.

Smokers were unsanctioned bouts, which basically meant they were lawless. There weren't any paramedics or ambulances waiting outside. If the crowd didn't like your performance, they didn't boo, they just fought one another to show you how it was done. Everybody who came was dressed to the nines whether they were gangsters or drug dealers. And everybody bet on the fights. I remember I asked one guy, "Will you buy me a piggy in a blanket if I win?" People who bet and won money on you would usually buy you some food.

Right before my fight, I was so scared that I almost left. I was thinking about all that preparation that I had undergone with Cus. Even after all the sparring, I was still totally intimidated with fighting somebody in the ring. What if I failed and lost? I had been in a million fights on the streets of Brooklyn but this was a whole different kind of feeling. You don't know the guy you're fighting; you have no beef with him. I was there with Teddy Atlas, my trainer, and I told him that I was going down to the store for a second. I went downstairs and sat on the curb by the steps leading up to the subway. For a minute, I thought I should just get on the damn train and go back to Brownsville. But then all of Cus's teachings started to flow into my mind and I started to relax, and my pride and my ego started popping up, and I got up and walked back into the gym. It was on.

I was fighting this big Puerto Rican guy with a huge Afro. He was eighteen, four years older than me. We fought hard for two rounds, but then in the third round I knocked him into the bottom rope and followed with another shot that literally knocked his mouthpiece six rows back into the crowd. He was out cold.

I was ecstatic. It was love at first fight. I didn't know how to celebrate. So I stepped on him. I raised my arms up in the air and stepped on the prone motherfucker.

"Get the hell off him! What the fuck are you doing stepping on this guy?" the ref told me. Cus was up in Catskill waiting by the phone for the report. Teddy called him and told him what happened and Cus was so excited that he made his friend Don, who had driven down with us, give him another account the next morning.

I kept going back to the smokers every week. You'd go into the dressing room and there were a bunch of kids looking at one another. You'd tell them your weight and how many fights you had. I normally told them I was older than fourteen. There weren't many two-hundred-pound fourteen-year-olds around. So I was always fighting older guys.

Those smokers meant so much to me, a lot more to me than the rest of the kids. The way I looked at it, I was born in hell and every time I won a fight, that was one step out of it. The other fighters weren't as mean as I was. If I hadn't had these smokers, I probably would have died in the sewers.

Teddy even got in the action at these fights. We were at Nelson's gym one night and a guy pushed Teddy and Teddy punched the guy in the face and Nelson jumped in. He picked up one of the trophies that were there, solid marble with the tin fighter on top of the base, and he started smashing that guy's head in. If the cops had come they would have charged him with attempted murder. Teddy was always getting into fights. I don't know if he was defending me or if other guys were jealous because he had the best fighter there, but he was never smart enough to back down from anybody. We'd go to Ohio and there was Teddy, fighting with some of the other trainers.

We started driving to smokers all over the Northeast. Before we'd get in the car, Cus would come over.

"I'm going to have some friends watching the fight. I'll be waiting by the phone. I expect that when they call me, they'll be ranting and raving about you," he said. I never forgot that. "Ranting and raving." That would get me fired up, and I'd be pumped for the whole six-hour car ride. I wouldn't rest a minute. I couldn't wait to get into that ring and start beating the motherfuckers. One guy came to the fight with his wife and his little baby and I knocked him out cold.

Cus came to my fifth fight, a smoker in Scranton. I was fighting a guy named Billy O'Rourke at the Scranton Catholic Youth Center. Billy was seventeen and I said I was too because it was a pro-amateur card. Before the fight, Cus went over to O'Rourke.

"My man is a killer," Cus said. "I don't want to see you get hurt."

That was my toughest fight so far. In the first round, I kept knocking this guy down and this crazy psycho white boy kept getting the fuck up. And he didn't just get up, he came up swinging. The more I knocked him down, the more he got up and whipped my ass. I had kicked his ass in the first round, but the second was just a war. We were fighting three rounds and Teddy didn't want to take any chances on a decision going the wrong way.

"Listen, you talk about being great, and all these crazy fighters, and you want to be this great fighter. Now is the time. Get in there and keep jabbing and moving your head."

I got off my stool and went out and dropped O'Rourke twice in

the third round. He was bleeding all over the place. At the end
of the fight, he got me against the ropes. But, boom, boom, boom, I
came back and down he went. The crowd went crazy. It was the fight
of the night.

Cus was pleased with my performance, but he said, "Another round
and he would have worn you down."

In May and June of 1981, I went after my first championship—the
Junior Olympics. I probably had about ten fights at that point. First
you had to win your local tourney, then your region, and then you
competed in Colorado for the national title.

I won all my regionals, so Teddy and I flew to Colorado and Cus
took a train because he had a fear of flying. When I entered the dressing room, I remembered how all my heroes had behaved. The other
kids would come up to me and put out their hand to shake, and I
would just sneer and turn my back on them. I was playing a role.
Someone would be talking and I'd just stare at him. Cus was all about
manipulating your opponent by causing chaos and confusion, but
staying cool under it all. I caused such chaos that a few of the other
fighters took one look at me and lost their bouts so they wouldn't have
to fight me later on. I won all of my fights by knockouts in the first
round. I won the gold by knocking out Joe Cortez in eight seconds, a
record that I believe stands to this day. I was on my way.

I became a local hero after I won that gold medal. Cus loved the
attention I was getting. He loved the spotlights. But I kept thinking
how crazy all this was. I was barely fifteen years old and half of my
friends back in Brownsville were dead, gone, wiped out. I didn't have
many friends in Catskill. I wasn't interested in school. Cus and I had
already established what we wanted to accomplish, so school seemed
to be a distraction from that goal. I didn't care about what they were
teaching me, but I did have an urge to learn. So Cus would encourage
me and I read some of the books from his library. I read books by
Oscar Wilde, Charles Darwin, Machiavelli, Tolstoy, Dumas, and
Adam Smith. I read a book about Alexander the Great. I loved history.
By reading history, I learned about human nature. I learned the
hearts of men.

I didn't get into major trouble in school with the exception of hitting a couple of students and getting suspended. I was just uncomfortable there. Some students would make fun of me, but nobody fucked with me. Cus had told my junior high school principal, Mr. Bordick, that I was special and that "allowances had to be made for him." Mr. Bordick was a beautiful man and whenever there was a problem, Cus would go to the school, do his Italian gesturing shit with his fingers, and I'd be back in school. I'd go home and go to the gym at five p.m. every night for two hours. In the evenings, I'd read boxing books, watch films, or talk to Cus. On the weekends, I'd get up at five, run a few miles, eat, nap, and then be back in the gym at noon. During the week, I ran back and forth from school.

I got some extra running in thanks to my control-freak guardian Cus. I was at a school dance and it was scheduled to end at ten p.m. I told Cus I'd be home at eleven. Everybody was hanging around after the dance, so I called Cus and told him that I'd probably be home a little late because I was waiting for a cab.

"No, run home now. Run. I can't wait up for you," he barked. Cus didn't believe in giving out keys because he feared we'd lose them. I had on a two-piece suit and nice dress shoes, but Cus wanted me home *now*.

"Man, I gotta go," I told my friends. Everyone knew what time it was. If Cus called, I had to go. So I took the fuck off.

One day I was hanging out with some friends and we were drinking and partying, and they were about to drop me off at the house and I saw Cus through the window, sleeping in his chair, waiting for me to come home.

"Turn around. Take me to your house. I don't even want to deal with Cus," I said. Every time I'd come home late he would rip me a new asshole. I'd try to sneak up the stairs, but they were old and rickety, and I'd think, *Shit, I'm busted.* I'd come home from a movie after he gave me permission to go and there was Cus waiting to interrogate me.

"What did you do? Who did you hang out with? Who are they? Where are their families from? What are their last names? You know you've got to box tomorrow."

Cus even tried to marry me off in the ninth grade. I started dating this local girl named Angie. Cus loved her. You would think that he'd discourage a relationship, that it would distract from my training, but Cus thought it would be good for me to settle down with her. I'd be calmer and it would actually help focus me on my boxing. I wasn't serious about Angie. I wanted to live the flamboyant lifestyles of my heroes, boxers like Mickey Walker and Harry Greb. They drank, they had lots of women, and they were living the life. But Camille was on to Cus.

"Don't you dare listen to Cus about marrying anyone," she told me. "You date as many girls as you want and then you select the best."

One day I got into a fight in school and Cus had to go smooth things over. When he got back, he sat me down.

"You're going to have to leave here if you're going to continue to act like that." I just broke down and started crying.

"Please don't let me go," I sobbed. "I want to stay."

I really loved the family environment Cus had given me. And I was madly in love with Cus. He was the first white guy who not only didn't judge me, but who wanted to beat the shit out of someone if they said anything disrespectful about me. Nobody could reach me like that guy. He reached me down in my cortex. Any time I finished talking to him, I had to go and burn energy, shadowboxing or doing sit-ups, I was so pumped. I'd start running and I'd be crying, because I wanted to make him happy and prove that all the good things he was saying were right.

I guess Cus felt bad about threatening to send me away and making me cry that day because he started hugging me. That was the first physical display of affection I'd ever seen from Cus. Ever. But the moment that I cried was when Cus really knew that he had me. From that moment on I became his slave. If he told me to kill someone, I would have killed them. I'm serious. Everybody thought I was up there with this old, sweet Italian guy, but I was there with a warrior. And I loved every minute of it. I was happy to be Cus's soldier; it gave me a purpose in life. I liked being the one to complete the mission.

I started training even harder, if that was possible. When I got home from the gym, I actually had to crawl up the stairs. I'd make my way up to the third-floor bathroom. Cus would run some incredibly hot water into the little porcelain tub and then pour some Epsom salts in.

"Stay in as long as you can," Cus said.

So I'd sit down and get burned, but the next morning my body felt much better and I could go work out again. I never felt so glorious in my life. I had a tunnel-vision mission and I never deterred from it. I can't even explain that feeling to other people.

When all the other fighters would leave the gym and go out with their girlfriends, living their life, Cus and I went back to the house and devised our scheme. We'd talk about having houses in all parts of the world. Cus would say, "'No' will be like a foreign language to you. You won't understand the concept of 'no.'"

I thought that it was unfair for the rest of the fighters trying to win the championship because I was raised by a genius who prepared me. Those other guys wanted to make money and have a good life for their family. But thanks to Cus, I wanted glory and I wanted to get it over their blood. But I was insecure. I wanted glory, I wanted to be famous, I wanted the world to look at me and tell me I'm beautiful. I was a fat fucking stinking kid.

Cus made me believe that the green and gold WBC belt was worth dying for. And not for the money. I used to ask Cus, "What does it mean being the greatest fighter of all time? Most of those guys are dead."

"Listen. They're dead but we're talking about them now. This is all about immortality. This is about your name being known until the end of time," he said.

Cus was so dramatic. He was like a character from *The Three Musketeers*.

"We have to wait for our moment, like crocodiles in the mud. We don't know when the drought will come and the animals will have to migrate across the Sahara. But we'll be waiting. Months, years. But it will come. And the gazelles and the wildebeests will cross the water. And when they come, we are going to bite them. Do you hear me, son? We are going to bite them so hard that when they scream, the whole world is going to hear them."

He was dead serious and so was I. Cus was using me to get back at the boxing establishment. I wanted to be involved with that so badly. It was like *The Count of Monte Cristo*. We were out to get our revenge.

When Cus realized that I was truly with him, he was happy. But then he would just get paranoid. I'd be sitting in the living room reading a book and Cus would be walking around with his robe on and he'd come over to me.

"Yeah, you're gonna leave me too. They'll take you away. You'll leave me just like everybody else," he'd say out of the blue.

I didn't know if he was playing a mind game with me or just feeling sorry for himself.

"Are you crazy, Cus? What are you talking about?"

I would never talk to him like that. That was probably the only time I ever called him crazy.

"You know what I mean. Somebody'll give you some money and you'll just go away. That happened to me all of my life. I put in the time and developed fighters and people stole them away from me."

Go away? I would try to kill somebody who kept him away from me. Floyd Patterson had left him but I was on a different level. I just wanted to be hanging around with him and Camille, my new family. No more hard life.

"You're crazy, Cus," I said, and he walked away.

IN NOVEMBER OF 1981, TEDDY, ME, AND TWO OTHER FIGHTERS GOT IN THE CAR and drove to Rhode Island for a smoker. For the whole ride I was thinking about what I was going to do to the motherfucker when I got there. I had been reading Nietzsche and thought I was a Superman. I could barely spell my name but I was a Superman. So I was visualizing how I was going to electrify the place and how all the people would be applauding me when I kicked this guy's ass. My delusion had me believing that the crowd would be throwing flowers at my feet. I was only fifteen but I would be fighting a guy named Ernie Bennett, the local champ, who was twenty-one. It was going to be his last amateur fight before he turned pro.

We walked into the place and there were a bunch of nasty-looking people in there, packed wall to wall. It was so crowded it felt like I was back in the Brownsville slums. But I didn't give a fuck. I was feeding on all their energy. Teddy said, "Get on the scale." So I took off my shirt and pants. I was only wearing underwear. I was really ripped. I got up on the scale and everyone ran up and surrounded us.

"That's Tyson. That's him," I heard people say.

I was standing on the scale and started getting nervous. These guys were gangsters, legitimate tough guys, and I wasn't from their neighborhood. But then I remembered all those films I watched. Jack Johnson would be on the scale with a crowd around him. I always visualized myself in that position. Then I heard all the whispers and whistling. "That's the guy who knocked out everyone in one round at the juniors," they said.

My Cus thinking kicked in. I was nobility. I was this great gladiator, ready to do battle.

"Hey, champ!" These guys smiled at me. But I'm just looking at them with contempt, like, "Fuck you, what are you looking at?"

I weighed in at around 190.

"Oh, you are too heavy," Bennett's trainer said. He was a deaf-mute but you could make out his words.

"But we'll fight him. We'll fight anybody," the guy said.

"I'm not just anybody," I sneered.

The place was packed. There were at least three thousand people there. We got into the ring and it was nine straight minutes of mayhem. To this day, people still talk about that fight. The crowd never stopped cheering, even during the one-minute rest between rounds they were still applauding. We were like two pit bulls. He was very smooth and elusive and experienced but then, bam, I knocked him through the ropes. I fought this guy hard, right to the end. It was the best performance of my life.

And then they gave him the decision. It was highway robbery. I was distraught. I started crying. I had never lost a fight before. In the dressing room, the deaf-mute trainer came up to me. I was still crying.

"You're just a baby," he said. "My man has had many, many fights.

We were fighting you with everything we got. You're better than my fighter. Don't give up. You're going to be champion one day."

That didn't make me feel any better. I cried during the whole ride home. I wanted to beat that guy so badly. We got back home and I had to get in the shower and go to school. But Teddy must have called Cus because he was waiting for me. I thought Cus was going to be mad at me for letting him down, but he had a big smile on his face.

"I heard you did great. Teddy said the guy was cut and experienced," Cus said. "Hey, take the day off. You don't have to go to school."

There was no way I was not going to school. That guy had given me a black eye and I wanted to show off my badge of courage.

I didn't let that controversial loss get me down. I kept fighting at smokers and knocking out each of my opponents. Cus began coming to more of my fights. He loved it when I would act arrogant and give off an imperious air. Cus was plenty arrogant himself. One time, I was fighting a twenty-four-year-old guy who had been the champion of his region since he was sixteen. No one had ever beaten him.

Before the fight, one of the local boxing officials came over to us.

"Cus, the man you're fighting is big, strong, and scary," he said.

Cus didn't bat an eye.

"My boy's business is to put big, strong, scary men in their place."

I heard that and oh, my heart. Arrrghh. I would turn into fucking hot blue fire. I got so pumped up that I wanted to fight those guys before we got into the ring.

Once, I didn't bathe for three days leading up to a fight. All I thought about was hurting my opponent. I didn't know anything about my opponents in these smokers, there were no videos to watch, no TV appearances by them. So I always imagined that the people I was fighting were the people who had bullied me when I was younger. It was retribution time. No one would ever pick on me again.

Whenever I displayed the slightest bit of humanity at a fight, Cus would be all over me. A guy might try to shake my hand before our fight in a gesture of sportsmanship. If I shook it, Cus went ballistic.

The only display of compassion that he didn't criticize was when I would pick up my opponents after I knocked them out. Dempsey would do that all the time. He would pick up his vanquished opponent, take him back to his corner, hold him, and kiss him. That was right after he tried to eviscerate him. So I'd pick them up and give them a kiss. "Are you okay? I love you, brother." It was almost humiliating for them.

Cus didn't like me to celebrate my knockouts. No high fives, no dance steps.

"You've been practicing this for two years and you're acting like you're surprised this happened?" he'd say.

To Cus, my opponents were food. Nourishment. Something you had to eat to live. If I did good in a fight, Cus would reward me. Nice clothes, shoes. When I won one of my junior championships, he bought me gold teeth. When I got my gold in the '80s, most people would think, "Ugh, criminals wear gold teeth. Be careful." But Cus loved it because all the old-time fighters got gold teeth to celebrate their success.

You'd think with all these knockouts and the junior championship Cus would have had little to criticize. Not Cus. He always treated me like a prima donna in front of people, but behind closed doors it wasn't like that. I'd be alone with him at the house and he'd sit me down.

"You know, you had your hand low. With all due respect, if that gentleman was a bit more professional, a little bit calmer, he would have hit you with that punch."

This was after I had knocked the guy out! Everybody had been congratulating me on my right-hand KO. Cus didn't say I would have gotten knocked out. He said he would have hit me! He would put that idea of getting hit by that punch in my head all day. Then after a couple of days, he'd run that shit again.

"Remember after the fight I told you that guy would have hit you. . . ."

AAAGGGHH.

Cus was all about manipulation, psychological warfare. He believed that 90 percent of boxing was psychological and not physical. Will, not skill. So when I was fifteen, he began taking me to a hypnotherapist

named John Halpin. He had an office on Central Park West in the
city. I'd lie down on the floor of John's office and he'd go through all
the stages of relaxation: your head, your eyes, your arms, your legs,
all getting heavy. Once I was under, he'd tell me whatever Cus wanted
him to say. Cus would write out the suggestions on a piece of paper
and John would recite them out loud.

"You're the world's greatest fighter. I'm not telling you this because
I'm trying to make you believe you are something that you're not, I'm
telling you this because you can actually do this; this is what you were
actually born to do."

Halpin showed us a method by which we could put ourselves into a
hypnotic state anytime we wanted. When we were back up in Catskill,
I'd lie down on the floor or in my bedroom and Cus would be sitting
next to me. I'd start to relax and go into my hypnotic state and Cus
would talk. Sometimes he'd talk in generalities like I was the best
fighter in the world but sometimes it would be specifics.

"Your jab is like a weapon. You throw punches that are ferocious,
with bad intentions. You have a wonderful right hand. You haven't
really believed in it but now you will. You are a scourge from God. The
world will know your name from now until the eons of oblivion."

It was some really deep shit. And I believed it.

Sometimes Cus would wake me up in the middle of the night and
do his suggestions. Sometimes he didn't even have to talk, I could feel
his words coming through my mind telepathically.

I became focused on the hypnosis. I thought this was a secret
method that was going to help me. Some people might think this was
crazy but I believed everything that Cus was telling me. I embraced it
religiously. Cus was my God. And this old white guy was telling me
that I was the apex. Why did I have to be the best that ever existed?

NOW THAT I WAS A GLADIATOR AND A GOD AMONG MEN, IT SEEMED A LITTLE
demeaning that I had to go to high school. Then, in the fall of 1981, I
got in trouble at Catskill High. One of my teachers, a real ignorant
redneck, started arguing with me and threw a book at me. I got up

and smacked the shit out of him in front of all the other students. They suspended me. So Cus grabbed me and we marched into the school and confronted the principal, Mr. Stickler, and the teacher. You would have thought Cus was Clarence Darrow the way he was defending me.

"You maintain that you merely dropped the book and it hit Mike by accident," Cus grilled the teacher. "But if, as you claim, you dropped the book, how could it have been propelled into the air and into Mike's physical person? It would have harmlessly fallen to the floor without causing any injury to anyone."

Cus was pacing the room, making sudden stops and pointing dramatically at my teacher as if he was the guilty party.

They finally compromised and let me stop attending school as long as I got a tutor. Cus was hurt that I was leaving school. He had planned to throw me a big graduation party. On the way home from the meeting at the high school, I looked over at Cus. "Come on. I'm ready to go to the gym."

He just looked back at me. "Come on," he said.

JUNE OF 1982 ROLLED AROUND AND IT WAS TIME FOR ME TO DEFEND MY

Junior Olympics championship. By now my reputation had certainly preceded me. Parents pulled their kids out of the tournament in fear of them fighting me. John Condon, who was part of the Golden Gloves tournaments, wouldn't let me compete. "I've seen you fight. You're too mean. I can't let you fight these kids. You'd rip them apart."

My second Junior Olympics started off well. We were back in Colorado, and in my preliminary matches I knocked out all of my opponents. Then it was time for the finals where I'd defend my title. That's when the pressure got to me. I saw all of the cameras and my insecurities started to kick in. There were all these established boxing officials saying great things about me. I thought that that was wonderful, but that it was all going to end because I was filthy, I was dirty. Even so, I certainly didn't want to let Brownsville down. Cus had told me many times that if I listened to him, "when your mother walks the streets of Brownsville, people will carry her groceries."

I couldn't deal with all that pressure. Before the finals, Cus pulled me aside.

"Mike, this is the real world. You see all these people," and he pointed to all the ring officials and the reporters and the boxing officials in the arena. "When you lose, they don't like you anymore. If you're not spectacular, they don't like you anymore. Everybody used to like me. Believe me, when I was in my fifties, young, beautiful women would chase me all over the place. Now that I'm an old man, no one comes around anymore."

Ten minutes before my fight, I had to go out for some air. Teddy went with me.

"Just relax, Mike, just relax," he said.

I lost it. I started crying hysterically. Teddy put his arms around me.

"It's just another match. You done it in the gym with better fighters than this guy," he tried to console me.

"I'm Mike Tyson . . . ," I sobbed. ". . . everyone likes me."

I couldn't get a coherent sentence out. I was trying to say that if I lost, nobody would ever like me again. Teddy comforted me and told me not to let my feelings get the best of me.

When I walked into the ring, my opponent was waiting for me. He was a 6'6" white guy named Kelton Brown. I composed myself, summoned up my courage. We went to the center of the ring to get the instructions and I got so up into his face with my malevolent stare that the ref had to push me back and give me a warning before the fight even started. The bell rang and I charged him. Within a minute, I was giving him such a masterful beating that his corner threw in the towel. I was now a two-time Junior Olympic champ.

After my hand was raised, the TV commentator interviewed me in the ring.

"Mike, you must be very satisfied with how your career has progressed so far."

"Well, I can say, 'Yes, I am.' I'm in here with kids, but I'm just as old as they are and I am more on the ball than them. I'm more disciplined. I learned first how to deal with my problems mentally, then physically. That's an advantage I have over them mentally."

"How did you feel at the end of the bout after defeating Brown?"

"I went in there to do my job. I don't have nothing bad to say about my opponent. He did a well job. He was just in a little over his head. I commend him on his efforts," I said.

When I got back east, I went back home to Brownsville. Everybody in the neighborhood had seen me on TV knocking out Kelton Brown. A lot of the guys who used to bully me came up to me on the street.

"Hey, Mike, you need anything? Let me know if there's anything I can do for you," they'd say.

They used to kick my ass, now they were kissing it.

But the audience I was really after was my mom. I wanted to share my enthusiasm with her.

"Hey, Mom, I'm the greatest fighter in the world. There ain't a man living who can beat me," I said.

My mom was living in this damp, decrepit, lopsided tenement building and was just staring at me as I talked about myself as if I were a god.

"You remember Joe Louis? There's *always* someone better, son," she said.

I stared back at my mom.

"That is never going to happen to me," I said coldly. "I am the one who is better than everyone else. That's me."

I was dead serious because this was what Cus had brainwashed me into believing. My mother had never seen me like that before. I had always been creepy and looking for an angle. Now I had dignity and pride. Before, I smelt like weed or liquor. Now my body was pumped, I was immaculate. I was ready to take on the world.

"There is not a man in the world that can beat me, Ma. You watch, your boy is going to be champion of the world," I boasted.

"You've got to be humble, son. You're not humble, you're not humble. . . ." She shook her head.

I had my little bag with me and I took out the clippings of me getting my gold medals and handed them to her.

"Here, Mom. Read about me."

"I'll read it later," she said.

The rest of the night she didn't talk to me. She'd just go "um hmm." She just looked at me with concern, like, "What are these white people doing to you?"

So I went back to Catskill and was feeling on top of the world. I was a spoiled upper-middle-class kid there. A few months after that, Cus told me that my mother was sick. He didn't tell me the details, but my social worker had found out that my mother had been diagnosed with terminal cancer. The same day that Cus told me, my sister called me.

"Go visit Mommy," she said. "She's not feeling well."

I had seen my mother a few weeks before my sister called and she had had some kind of stroke and her eye on one side of her face was drooping, but I didn't know she had cancer. The only cancer I knew was my astrological sign. I knew something wasn't right, but I didn't know it had anything to do with dying.

But when I got to the hospital, I got a big shock. My mother was lying in the bed, moaning, but she was pretty catatonic. It was painful just to look at her. Her eyes were sunken; her skin was wrapped tight around her cranium; she had lost all this weight. Her bedsheet had fallen off her and you could see some of her breast exposed. So I kissed her and covered her up. I didn't know what to do. I had never seen anyone with cancer. I'd seen movies, so I expected to see something like "Well, I love you but I'm a goner now, Johnny." I thought I'd have a chance to talk to her and say good-bye before she died, but she wasn't even conscious. So I walked out of that hospital room and never went back again.

Every night I'd go back to the apartment and tell my sister that I had seen Mommy and that she looked good. I just didn't want to deal with the hospital scene, it was too painful. So I went on a house-robbing spree. I ran into Barkim and some other hustlers I knew from the neighborhood and we robbed some houses.

One night before we went out to rob a place, I showed Barkim a photo album I had brought down from Catskill. There were photos of me and Cus and Camille, and me with all these white kids at school.

Barkim couldn't get over those photos.

"Yo, Mike, this is bugging me out. Are they trying you up there? Do they call you 'nigga'?"

"No, this is like my family. Cus would kill you if you said that about me," I told him.

Barkim shook his head.

"What are you doing here, Mike?" he asked. "Go back there with those white people. Shit, man, those white people love you. Can't you see that, nigga? Man, I wish I had some white people that loved me. Go back, man. There ain't shit out here for you."

I thought about what he said. Here I was, a two-time national champ, and I was still robbing houses because you just go back to who you are. Every night I was drinking, smoking angel dust, snorting cocaine, and going to local dances. Anything to get my mind off my mother.

My sister kept telling me, "You came here to see Mommy. Don't get carried away, you're not here to play."

One night Barkim went to pick his girl up and the three of us were walking through one of the Brownsville projects and we saw a couple of my old friends playing dice. Barkim was friends with them too, but he didn't stop to talk to them, he just kept walking. I went over to say hello to them and they said, "What's up, Mike?" but they were acting leery. "We'll talk to you later," they said. I could feel the vibe that something real bad happened, somebody died or somebody got a lot of shit taken from them.

I later found out that there had been some power struggles going on in the neighborhood and when the smoke had cleared, Barkim was on top. He had all of the cars and the girls and the jewelry and the guns, 'cause he had the neighborhood drug enterprise. The whole street scene had changed since I had lived there. Drugs had come in and people were dying. Guys we used to hang out with were killing one another for turf and money.

Then one day my sister came home. I was hungover, but I heard her key in the door, so I opened it and as soon as it swung open, POW, she punched me right in the face.

"Why did you do that?" I said.

"Why didn't you tell me Mommy was dead?" she screamed.

I didn't want to say "I didn't go to the hospital. It was too painful to see Mom a shell of her old self" because my sister would have killed me, so I said, "Well, I didn't want you to be hurt. I didn't want you to know." I was just too weak to deal with this. My sister was the strongest one in my family. She was good at dealing with tragedy. I couldn't even go down with my sister and witness the body. My cousin Eric went with her.

My mom's funeral was pathetic. She had saved up some money for a plot in Linden, New Jersey. There were only eight of us there—me, my brother and sister, my father Jimmy, her boyfriend Eddie, and three of my mother's friends. I wore a suit that I had bought with some of the money that I had stolen. She only had a thin cardboard casket and there wasn't enough money for a headstone. Before we left the grave, I said, "Mom, I promise I'm going to be a good guy. I'm going to be the best fighter ever and everybody is going to know my name. When they think of Tyson, they're not going to think of Tyson Foods or Cicely Tyson, they're going to think of Mike Tyson." I said this to her because this was what Cus had been telling me about the Tyson name. Up until then, our family's only claim to fame was that we shared the same last name as Cicely. My mom loved Cicely Tyson.

After the funeral, I stayed in Brownsville for a few weeks, getting high. One night I saw my friends who had been playing dice a few nights before. They told me that Barkim had been killed.

"Yeah, they got your man," one of them told me. "I thought they got you too, because last time I saw you, you were walking away from the dice game with him and I haven't seen you since."

Barkim's death had a big impact on me. This was the guy who

had first gotten me into robbing, making me his street son. And he had just told me to get out of here and go back with my white family. And it wasn't just him. All my friends in the neighborhood had big hopes for me and Cus. Cus was going to take me places.

"Stick with that white man, Mike. We're nothing, Mike, don't come back here, Mike. I don't want to hear no bullshit, nigga. You're the only hope we have. We ain't going to never go nowhere Mike, we're going to die right here in Brownsville. We've got to tell people before we die that we hung out with you, you were our nigga."

I was hearing variations of that everywhere I went. They took it seriously. To my friends, Brownsville was pure hell. They all wished they had an opportunity to get out like I did. They couldn't understand why I wanted to come back, but I went back because I was trying to figure out who I really was. My two lives were so divergent, yet I felt at home in both worlds for different reasons.

One day there was a knock on my door and it was Mrs. Coleman, my social worker. She had come to take my black ass back upstate because I got caught up robbing and stealing. I was supposed to return to Cus's house three days after my mother's funeral. Mrs. Coleman was a nice lady who drove over two hours from Catskill to get me. She was very supportive of Cus and thought that boxing was a positive direction for me. I was still out of it, so I told her that I wasn't going back to Catskill. She informed me that if I wanted to stay in Brooklyn, then she'd have to do some paperwork and the police would pick me up and she'd place me somewhere in New York. I was sixteen by then, so I knew what she was saying was bullshit. Legally, I didn't have to answer to anybody. But I went back upstate with her. I looked at my apartment and saw how my mother had lived in poverty and chaos and then thought about the way she died. That changed my whole perspective about how I was going to live my life. It might be short, but I was going to make sure it would be glorious.

When I got back to Catskill, Cus really helped get me over my mother's death. He talked to me about the day his father died. Cus was in the house with him and his father was screaming. He couldn't help him because he didn't know what to do. Cus helped me get strong again. During this time there was a white South African boxer named Charlie Weir who was a top contender for the junior middleweight title. He and his team came to Catskill to train with Cus. This was during the apartheid era and Cus told them, "We have a black boy here. He's part of our family. You have to treat him with respect. The same way you treat me and Camille, this is how you treat him."

That was awesome. Nobody ever fought for me like that. Charlie and his team were paying to train with Cus and usually when you pay to train at a fight camp, you run the show. But Cus set them straight. And Cus talked like that at home too.

"Listen, we're your family now, okay?" he told me. "And you're our boy now. And you're going to bring a lot of pride to this family. Pride and glory."

The three of us would be sitting at the dining room table and Cus would say, "Look at your black son, Camille. What do you think about that?"

Camille would get up and come over to me and kiss me.

But our little idyllic scene got disrupted a month later. I fucked up. Cus was having trouble with my trainer Teddy Atlas. They were fighting over money. Teddy had recently married into a family that Cus was really dubious about, so when Teddy needed money, Cus wouldn't give him much. Teddy was struggling, so he wanted me to turn pro so he could collect his share of my purses, but turning pro at that time wasn't in Cus's plan. So it was common knowledge that Teddy was going to leave Cus and that he would try to take me with him. There was no way in the world I would leave Cus.

But then I did something that made Cus get rid of Teddy. I had known Teddy's sisters-in-law before Teddy even did. We had all gone to school together and were friends. The girls would always be flirtatious with me, but I never had a sexual thing with them. I was hanging out with his twelve-year-old sister-in-law one day and I grabbed her butt. I really didn't mean to do anything evil. I was just playing around and I grabbed her butt and I shouldn't have. It was just a stupid thing to do. I didn't think it through. I had no social skills with girls because Cus kept me in the gym all the time. As soon as I did it,

I immediately regretted it. She didn't say anything to me but I knew it must have made her uncomfortable.

Later that evening my sparring partner drove me to the gym to work out with Teddy. I got out of the car and Teddy was waiting for me outside. He looked angry.

"Mike, come here. I want to talk to you," he said.

I went over to him and he pulled out a gun and held it to my head.

"Motherfucker, don't you ever touch my sister-in-law. . . ."

He shot the gun into the air, right next to my ear. The sound was so deafening, I thought that he might have actually shot my ear off. And then Teddy ran. I would have too, because the gym was on top of a police station.

Whenever Teddy talks about this incident now, he makes it sound like he scared me to shit. The truth was, it wasn't the first time someone had held a gun to my head, but it wasn't like I was saying stuff like "C'mon, shoot me, motherfucker." I was nervous. By the way, it took a while for my hearing to come back. But I just felt that I had fucked something up real bad. I really cared about Teddy. I was pissed, though, and I might have told some people that I was going to get back at him, but I would never do anything to hurt Teddy. He taught me how to fight, he was right there from the beginning.

Camille was furious with Teddy. She wanted Cus to press charges and have him arrested but Cus wouldn't do that. He knew that Teddy was on probation for some other issue and that he would have gone right to jail. Teddy and his family eventually moved back to the city.

All this was my fault. I'm just sorry all that went down. After Teddy left, I started working with Kevin Rooney, another boxer who Cus converted into a trainer. Rooney and Teddy were childhood friends and Teddy had introduced Kevin to Cus. You can imagine how high the emotions ran when things played out the way they did.

I FELT PRETTY DEVELOPED BY THE TIME I GOT WITH ROONEY. NORMALLY WHEN guys won tournaments, they'd get choosy about who they'd fight. Not me. I'd fight anybody anywhere: in their hometown, their backyard.

Cus would say to me, "Fight them in their living rooms and their families could even be the judges." I just wanted to fight and I wasn't afraid of anything. I would fight in Chicago, Rhode Island, Boston, anywhere. And people would say, "That's Tyson, he won the Junior Olympics twice."

In December of 1982, I suffered my first loss in a tournament. I was fighting for the U.S. Amateur Championships in Indianapolis and my opponent was Al Evans. I was sixteen then and he was twenty-seven, a hard puncher and a very experienced guy.

I charged him in the first round and threw a ton of punches. I did the same in the second round. I was knocking him from pillar to post. In the third round, I was a little wild and he countered with a left hook and I went down. I got right up and rushed him again. He knocked me down with a right hand this time. I got up and started to charge again and I slipped. That was it, the ref stopped the fight. I wasn't really hurt. I could have gone on. Cus was screaming at the ref from the corner.

I was crushed. I wanted to win every tournament. I liked the way the champion was treated after he won. I wanted that feeling, I was addicted to that feeling.

Cus might have thought that the loss shook my confidence and my desire, because when we got back to Catskill, he gave me a little lecture.

"Look at the champions you've read about in all these books. At some time early in their careers a number of them suffered knockout losses. But they never gave up. They endured. That's why you're reading about them. The ones who lost and quit, well their demons will follow them to their grave because they had a chance to face them and they didn't. You have to face your demons, Mike, or they will follow you to eternity. Remember to always be careful how you fight your fights because the way that you fight your fights will be the way that you live your life."

I won my next six fights, and then I fought for the National Golden Gloves championship against a guy called Craig Payne. I knocked Payne around the ring for three rounds with very little resistance. So

I was confident when the official holding the big trophy walked past me into the ring. Craig and I were on either side of the ref and he was holding our hands waiting for the decision. I started raising my other hand in celebration when I noticed the official holding the trophy giving Craig the thumbs-up sign.

"And the winner in the Super Heavyweight division is . . . Craig Payne."

I was stunned. The audience erupted into boos. Go to YouTube and watch that fight. I was robbed. After the fight, Emanuel Steward, the great trainer from Detroit who had Payne in his program, told me that he definitely thought that I had won. Cus was angry about the decision, but he was happy to see that I could handle that type of competition. He knew that we had won morally, but that didn't make me feel any better. I was crying like a baby for a long time after the fight.

I didn't have time to sulk. I went right back in the gym to train for more tournaments. In August of 1983, I won the gold medal at the CONCACAF Under-19 tournament. I won it again in 1984. That same year I won the gold medal at the National Golden Gloves tournament by knocking out Jonathan Littles in the first round. I had fought Littles in 1982 at the Junior Olympic trials and he was the only opponent who even made it into the second round with me. Now it was time to start getting ready for the Olympic trials.

While I was training for the Olympics, the boxing commentator Alex Wallau came up to Catskill to do a feature on Cus and me. At one point they had us sit in the living room and talk about each other. Cus was dressed in a conservative gray suit and a plaid sports shirt. I was wearing slacks and a shirt and a fly white Kangol cap.

Alex asked Cus about working with me and Cus went off into an interesting stream-of-consciousness rap.

"All my life I've been thinking in terms of developing a fighter who's perfect. To me a person can accomplish this. I recognized the quality of a future champion because he was always able to rise to the level and exceed his sparring partners. Taught him movements like in karate so the body would make adjustments during a fight even if your opponent doesn't make it necessary. He can strike a blow with lightning speed to the complete surprise of his opponents. He had tremendous speed, coordination, and an intuitive sense of timing, which usually comes after ten years of fighting because in the old days they used to box every single day.

"I don't start teaching until I find out if they're receptive. I do a great deal of talking to find out what kind of a person he is. For example we are today a sum total of every act and every deed. So in Mike's case we talk and I try to find out how many layers I have to peel off of him of experience, detrimental and otherwise, until I get down to the man himself and then expose that, so that not only I see but that he can see. The progress begins from that point on more rapidly."

"When you peeled away the layers on Mike Tyson, what did you find?" Alex asked.

Cus hesitated. "I found what I thought I'd find: a person of basically good character, capable of doing the things that are necessary to be done in order to be a great fighter or champion of the world. When I recognized this, then my next job was to make him aware of these qualities because unless he knew them as well as I did, it wouldn't help him very much. The ability to apply the discipline, the ability to do what needs to be done no matter how he feels inside, in my opinion, is the definition of a true professional. I think that Mike is rapidly approaching that status, that important point, which I consider Mike must do in order to become the greatest fighter in the world. And for all we know, barring unforeseen incidents, and if this continues without any interruptions, and if we get the sparring and everything else that goes with it, he may go down in history as one of the greatest we ever had, if not the greatest that ever lived."

I was so happy that Cus was talking about me. Then Alex asked Cus if it was hard for a man his age to work with such a young fighter.

"I often say to him, and I know he doesn't know what I mean but I'm going to tell him now what I mean, because if he weren't here I probably wouldn't be alive today. The fact that he is here and doing what he's doing and doing it so well and improving as he has gives me the motivation and interest in staying alive because I believe that a person dies when he no longer wants to live. Nature is smarter than we think. Little by little we lose our friends that we care about and little by little we lose our interest, until finally we say, 'What the devil am I doing around here? I have no reason to go on.' But I have a reason with Mike here. He gives me the motivation and I will stay alive and I will watch him become a success because I will not leave until that happens because when I leave, he will not only know how to fight, he will not only understand many things, but he will also know how to take care of himself."

Whew. That was just Cus putting this fucking pressure on me again. I know that Cus believed I could handle it, but he also believed that I didn't believe I could.

Then they asked me about my future and my dreams.

"Dreams are just when you're starting off. You have the dream to push the motivation. I just want to be alive ten years from now. People say I'm going to be a million-dollar fighter. Well, I know what I am, and that's what counts more than anything else, because the people don't know what I go through. They think I'm born this way. They don't know what it took to get this way."

"What do you go through?" Alex asked.

"The training. The boxing's the easy part. When you get into the ring to fight, that's the vacation. But when you get in the gym, you have to do things over and over till you're sore and deep in your mind you say, 'I don't want to do this anymore,' I push that out of my mind. At this particular time it's the amateurs and it's all fun, trophies and medals, but I'm like you, I want to make money when it comes to being professional. I like the fancy hairdos and I like to wear fancy clothes, gold, jewelry, and everything. To continue this kind of lifestyle you have to earn the money the right way. You can't take a gun and go into a bank. You might as well do it in a way that you feel good about yourself by doing something you like."

I was bitter about working that hard. I had never endured that kind of deprivation and then I had to get up the next day and do it all over again. I worked hard for those Olympics.

The U.S. team officials wouldn't let me compete at my natural weight, because Cus was feuding with the Olympic boxing guys. It started when they wanted me to fight on the U.S. team at a fight in the Dominican Republic, but Cus wouldn't let me go because we couldn't use Kevin as our trainer. I would have had to use their trainers. He also didn't want me to go because he was afraid that revolutionaries might try to kidnap me.

To get back at Cus, they told him that I would have to fight in the Under-201-pound division. I was fighting at about 215 then so I went on a fast. I put on those vinyl suits again and wore them all day. I loved it; I felt like a real fighter, lose the weight to make the weight. I was so delusional, I thought I was making a great sacrifice.

I had an intense schedule preparing for the Olympic trials. On August 12, 1983, I entered the Ohio State Fair National Tournament. On the first day, I achieved a forty-two-second KO. On the second day, I punched out the front two teeth of my opponent and left him out cold for ten minutes. Then on the third day, the reigning tournament champ withdrew from the fight.

The next day we went to Colorado Springs for the U.S. National Championship. When I got there, four of the six other fighters dropped out of the competition. Both of my victories were first-round KOs.

On June 10, 1984, I finally got a shot at the Olympics. My qualifying fight was against Henry Tillman, an older and more experienced boxer. In the first round, I knocked him almost through the ropes. Then he was up and I stalked him for the next two rounds. But in amateur boxing, aggression isn't rewarded and my knockout counted the same as a light tippy-tap jab. When they announced the decision, I couldn't believe that they gave it to Tillman. Once again, the crowd agreed and they started booing.

I hated these amateur bouts. "We are boxers here," these stuffed shirts would say.

"Well, I am a fighter, sir. My purpose is to fight," I'd answer.

The whole amateur boxing establishment hated me. They didn't like my cocky Brownsville attitude. I was behaving myself but you could still see that New York swagger coming out. And if they didn't like me, they despised Cus. He could be so over-the-top that sometimes he'd embarrass me. I never let him know; I always stood there and listened to him go after these guys, but I was totally embarrassed by the way he would talk to them. He was very vindictive and always out for revenge. He couldn't live without enemies, so he created them. I sometimes thought, *Damn, why couldn't I have been with a nonconfrontational kind of white guy?* I thought I was getting away from that loud life where people screamed at the top of their lungs. But with Cus, it was a constant reminder that I hadn't.

I had a chance to avenge my loss to Tillman a month later at the Olympic Box-Offs. Again I pressed him for three rounds and this time he did even less than in the first fight. Even Howard Cosell, who was doing the announcing for ABC and who had thought Tillman had outpointed me in our first fight, had to admit that I had a much better chance of getting the decision.

I was sure I had won and when the ref lifted Tillman's arm again, I was stunned. I couldn't believe that they'd give him two bullshit decisions. Again the whole audience started booing the judges. Cus was furious. He started cursing and tried to punch out one of the U.S. Olympic officials. Kevin Rooney and some other officials had to hold him back. I was so self-absorbed at the time that I thought all of this stuff with Cus was about me. As I got older, I understood that this was really a story that went back about thirty years. These were his demons and they really had little to do with me.

It was all about Cus being taken advantage of and robbed of his glory. I didn't even know until recently that Cus had sent a friend of ours named Mark, who worked for the FBI, to the U.S. Attorney's office in Albany to investigate the Tillman decisions.

I threw tantrums after the two Tillman decisions. I took the runner-up trophies that they gave me and threw them down and broke them. Cus sent me to the Olympics anyway, to live with the Olympic team. The Olympics were in L.A. that year. He said that I should just go there and enjoy the experience. He got me two tickets to every fight, but I had a pass anyway so I scalped the tickets. And the Olympics weren't a total loss for me. There was this really cute intern who worked for the U.S. Olympic committee. All of the boxers and the coaches were hitting on her, but I was the one who got her. She liked me. After all those years of deprivation, it was nice to finally have sex.

But even getting laid didn't take away the disappointment and pain I felt from having my Olympic dream stolen from me. When the Olympics were over, I flew back to New York, but I didn't go right back to Catskill. I hung around the city. I was really depressed. One afternoon I went to Forty-second Street to see a karate movie. Right before it started, I smoked a joint.

I started getting high and I remembered the time that Cus had caught me with pot. It was right after I had won my second Junior Olympics Championship. One of the other boxers was jealous of me and ratted me out. Before I had a chance to ditch the evidence, Cus had sent Ruth, the German cleaning lady, to my room and she found the weed.

Cus was furious when I came home.

"This must be some good stuff, Mike. I know this must be good because you just let down four hundred years of slaves and peasants to smoke it."

He broke my spirit that day. He made me feel like an Uncle Tom nigga. And he hated those kinds of people. He really knew how to bring me to my nadir.

So I was sitting in the theater, remembering that, and sinking deeper and deeper into my depression. Then I started crying. When the movie was over, I went straight to the train station and went back to Catskill. The whole trip back, I knew I had to immediately throw myself into full-blown training for professional fighting. I had to be spectacular when I turned pro. As we got closer to Catskill, I started talking to myself.

"They're never going to see anyone like Tyson. He will transcend the game. He will be in the pantheon of great fighters alongside John L. Sullivan and Joe Louis and Benny Leonard and Joe Gans and the rest. Tyson is magnificent."

I talked about myself in the third person. Even to myself.

I was completely pumped up when I got off that train and took a cab to Cus's house. The world was about to see a fighter the likes of which it had never been seen before. I was going to transcend the game. With all due respect, and not to be arrogant, but I was conscious of my future prominence as a boxer then. I knew nothing could stop me and I would be the champion as surely as Friday would come after Thursday. I didn't lose a fight for the next six years.

4

COMING OFF OF THOSE TWO LOSSES TO TILLMAN, I WASN'T EXACTLY THE hottest property in the boxing world. Cus had planned for me to win the gold medal at the Olympics and then start my career with a lucrative TV contract. But that didn't work out. No professional promoters were interested in me. Nobody in boxing really believed in Cus's peek-a-boo style. And a lot of people thought that I was too short to be an effective heavyweight.

I guess all that talk got to Cus. One night I was taking the garbage out and Cus was cleaning up the kitchen.

"Man, I wish you had a body like Mike Weaver or Ken Norton," he said out of the blue. "Because then you would be real intimidating. You'd have an ominous aura. They don't have the temperament but they have the physique of an intimidating man. You could paralyze the other boxers with fear just by the way you look."

I got choked up. To this day, when I recount this story, I still choke up. I was offended and hurt but I wouldn't tell Cus that because then he'd say, "Oh, you're crying? What are you, a little baby? How can you handle a big-time fight if you don't have the emotional toughness?"

Any time I showed my emotions, he despised it. So I held back my tears.

"Don't worry, Cus." I made myself sound arrogant. "You watch. One day the whole world is going to be afraid of me. When they mention my name, they'll sweat blood, Cus."

That was the day that I turned into Iron Mike; I became that guy 100 percent. Even though I had been winning almost every one of my fights in an exciting fashion, I wasn't completely emotionally invested in being the savage that Cus wanted me to be. After that talk about me being too small, I became that savage. I even began to fantasize that if I actually killed someone inside the ring, it would certainly intimidate everyone. Cus wanted an antisocial champion, so I drew on the bad guys from the movies, guys like Jack Palance and Richard Widmark. I immersed myself in the role of the arrogant sociopath.

But first I got a Cadillac. Cus couldn't afford to pay for my expenses while we were building up my career, so he got his friend Jimmy Jacobs and his partner, Bill Cayton, to lay out the money. Jimmy was an awesome guy. He was the Babe Ruth of handball and while he traveled around the world on the handball circuit, he began collecting rare fight films. Eventually he met Bill Cayton, who was a collector himself, and the two of them started Big Fights, Inc. They cornered the market on fight footage and Cayton later made a fortune selling those fights to ESPN. Cus had lived with Jimmy for ten years when Cus was still in New York, so they were close friends. In fact, Cus had devised a secret plan to train Jimmy as a fighter and for his first fight ever, amateur or professional, to fight Archie Moore for his light-heavyweight title. Jacobs trained intensely for six months with Cus, but the fight never happened because Archie pulled out.

But Cus never liked Jimmy's partner Cayton. He thought he was too in love with his money. I didn't like him either. Where Jimmy had a great outgoing personality, Cayton was a pompous cold fish. Jimmy and Cayton had been managing boxers for many years and had

Wilfred Benitez and Edwin Rosario in their stable, so despite his dislike of Cayton, Cus promised them a role with me when I turned pro.

I guess Cus saw Jimmy and Bill as investors who wouldn't interfere with my development and would allow Cus to have total control over my upbringing. By now they had invested over $200,000 in me. When I got back from the Olympics, Jimmy told Cus that he wanted to buy me a new car. I think that they might have been worried that I would leave Cus and go with someone else, cutting them out of the picture. Of course, I would never have done that.

Cus was mad because he thought that I didn't deserve it. It wasn't like I had come home with a gold medal. But he took me to a local dealership. Cus was trying to steer me to an Oldsmobile Cutlass because it didn't cost much.

"Nah, I want the Cadillac, Cus," I said.

"Mike, I'm telling you . . ."

"If it's not the Cadillac, I don't want no car." I stood my ground.

I got the car and we drove it back to the house and stored it in the barn. I didn't have a license and I didn't know how to drive, but when Cus got on my case, I'd grab my car keys, run out to the barn, get in the car, lock myself in, and play music.

In September of 1984, I signed two contracts, one with Bill Cayton and one with Jimmy Jacobs. Cayton owned an advertising agency, and he signed me to a seven-year personal management contract representing me for commercials and product endorsements. Instead of the usual 10 or 15 percent, Cayton was taking 33¹/₃ percent. But I didn't know the terms, I just signed it. A few weeks later, I signed a contract with Jimmy and he became my manager. Standard four-year contract, two-thirds for me, one-third for Jimmy. And then they agreed to split the income from the contracts with each other. Cus signed my management contract too. Under his signature it read, "Cus D'Amato, Advisor to Michael Tyson who shall have final approval of all decisions involving Michael Tyson." Now I had an official management team. I knew that Cayton and Jimmy were very savvy guys with the media, and I knew that they knew how to organize shit. And with Cus making all the boxing decisions and handpicking my opponents, I was ready to begin my professional career.

Until about a week into training, when I vanished for four days. Tom Patti finally tracked me down. I was sitting in my Caddy.

"Where have you been, Mike?" Tommy asked.

"I don't need this shit," I vented. "My girlfriend Angie's father is a manager at J.J. Newberry's department store. He can get me a job making a hundred thousand dollars. I got this Caddy. I'm going to split," I said.

The truth was, I was just nervous about fighting as a professional.

"Mike, you're not going to make a hundred grand a year because you're dating his daughter," he said.

"I can do a lot of things," I said.

"Man, you don't have a lot of options. Get back in the gym, win your fight, and move on."

I was back in the gym the next day. Once I got over my nerves, I was proud that I was going to be a professional fighter at just eighteen years old. I had a great team in my corner. Besides Kevin Rooney, there was Matt Baranski. Matt was a wonderful man who was a methodical tactician. Kevin was more "Aarrrgggghhh" in-your-face.

We discussed giving me a nickname. Jimmy and Bill didn't think it was necessary, but Cus wanted to call me the Tan Terror, as an homage to Joe Louis, the Brown Bomber. I thought that was cool, but we never ran with it. But I paid homage to other heroes of mine. I had someone put a bowl over my head and go around it with an electric shaver and give me a Jack Dempsey haircut. Then I decided to go with the Spartan look that all my old heroes had, no socks, no robe. I wanted to bring that look back into the mainstream of boxing.

My first professional bout was on March 6, 1985, in Albany. My opponent was a guy named Hector Mercedes. We didn't know anything about him, so the morning before the fight Cus got on the phone with some trainers and boxing gym owners in Puerto Rico to make sure that Mercedes wasn't a sleeper. The night of the fight, I was nervous, but I knew I could beat the guy as soon as I saw him in the ring.

I knew that Cus would match me up against a weaker opponent for my first few fights to build up my confidence.

I was right. They stopped the fight in the first round when I pummeled Hector to a kneeling position in the corner of the ring. I was excited, but back in the locker room, Cus pointed out all my flaws. "You gotta keep your hands up more. Your hands were playing around," he said.

My next two fights were also in Albany, which was practically my hometown. A month after Mercedes, I fought Trent Singleton. I entered the ring and bowed to all four corners of the arena, then I raised my arms to the crowd like a gladiator. It didn't take long for me to knock him down three times. The referee stopped the fight. Then I sauntered over to his corner, kissed him, and rubbed his head.

I was due to fight again in a month, so in between fights all I did was run, train, and box. That's all Cus wanted me to do. Box, box, box, spar, spar, spar.

I fought Don Halpin on May twenty-third, and he was a much more experienced opponent. He lasted for three rounds while I was switching back and forth from a conventional stance to southpaw, experimenting and getting some ring experience. In the fourth round, I tagged him with a left and a right and he was on his way down when I hit him again with a right hook. He was on the canvas for a good amount of time before they finally got him up. Cus, of course, thought I didn't go to the body enough and I didn't move laterally. But Jacobs and Cayton were thrilled with the way I looked so far.

I started attracting my own following at these fights. They began showing up with little signs like they do at baseball games. One sign read GOODEN IS DOCTOR K BUT MIKE TYSON IS DOCTOR KO. I also started attracting groupies, but I wasn't taking advantage of their advances. I was too in love with myself to think about anybody else. Actually, Cus thought I was going a little bit overboard. He thought I should go out more. So I'd go up to Albany and hang out with some of my friends there.

I hardly made any money from those early fights. My first fight lost money for the promoter, but Jimmy gave me $500. Then he took

$50 from that to give to Kevin and he put $350 in the bank for me, so I walked away with $100. They were more concerned with spreading my name around than making money on these early fights. Jimmy and Cayton were the first fight managers to make highlight reels of all my knockouts and send VHS tapes to every boxing writer in the country. They were very innovative that way.

I was performing sensationally, but it seemed that Cus was getting grumpier and grumpier. Sometimes I thought that Cus thought I was an Uncle Tom. I would try to be polite to the people I'd meet and give them "Yes, ma'ams" and "No, sirs" and Cus would get on my case.

"Why are you talking to them like that? You think they're better than you? All those people are phonies," he'd say. Then when I acted like the god that he kept telling me I was, he'd look at me with disgust.

"You like people looking up to you, huh? Guys like Cayton and them telling you how great you are."

I think he just needed someone to tear into. My day depended on what side of the bed Cus woke up on. By then, I had gotten my license and I would drive him to various meetings and conferences.

On June twentieth, shortly before my nineteenth birthday, I fought Ricky Spain in Atlantic City. This was my first pro fight outside of Albany, but Cus had sent me to watch big fights in cities all over the country to get me acclimated to the arenas.

"Make this your home, know this arena, know this place with your eyes closed," he'd tell me. "You are going to be living here for a long time, so get comfortable." He also took me along when he hung out with big-time fighters. He had me sit with them around a dinner table and get familiar with them so I'd never get intimidated by a fighter.

I was really excited to be fighting in Atlantic City and for it to be broadcast on ESPN. My opponent was unbeaten too, with a 7-0 record with five knockouts. They introduced me as "the Baby Brawler" and I don't know about the "Baby" part, but I floored Spain twice in the first round and the ref stopped the fight.

Jimmy and Cayton were trying to get me a regular slot on ESPN, but Bob Arum, who was promoting the fights, told them that his matchmakers didn't think much of my talent. That really pissed Cus

THREE RIVERS PUBLIC LIBRARY

off. Cus hated Arum's matchmakers and after my next fight, they never worked with Arum again.

But all this political stuff didn't interest me. I couldn't wait for my next fight. It was in Atlantic City again on July eleventh. I was fighting John Alderson, a big country guy from West Virginia who also had a 4-0 record. This fight was on ESPN and I dropped him a few times in the second round and the doctor stopped the fight after he went back to his corner.

I ran my record to 6-0 in my next fight against Larry Sims, but I really pissed Cus off in doing so. Sims was really slick and awkward, one of those cute fighters. So in the third round, I turned lefty and I knocked him out with a resounding punch. In the dressing room later, Cus confronted me.

"Who taught you that southpaw crap? It might be hard to get you fights now," he said. "People don't want to fight southpaws. You're going to ruin everything I created." Cus hated southpaws.

"I'm sorry, Cus." Ain't that a bitch. There I was apologizing for a spectacular knockout.

I was back in the ring a month later and dispatched Lorenzo Canady in one round, and three weeks later I faced Mike Johnson in Atlantic City. When we lined up for the instructions, Johnson looked so arrogant, like he hated my guts. Within seconds he was down from a left hook to the kidneys and then when he got up, I threw a spectacular right hand that hit him so hard his front two teeth were lodged in his mouthpiece. I knew it would be a long time until he came to. Kevin jumped into the ring and we were laughing and high-fiving like two arrogant little kids. I was, like, "Ha, ha. Look at this dead nigga, Kevin."

Now I was 8-0 with eight knockouts and Jimmy and Cus were using all their contacts in the press to get me recognition. I'd go down to New York to go to lunch with Jimmy and his newspaper friends. We really courted the press. I also started getting mentioned in the gossip columns because I started hanging out at the New York City hot spots like the restaurant Columbus on the Upper West Side. I became friendly with the great photographer Brian Hamill, and him and his brother Pete, who was a world-famous writer, started introducing me to all these celebrities. Pete would bring me to the bar and we'd sit with Paulie Herman, one of the owners. Paulie was the man in New York at that time. It seemed to me that he was a bigger celebrity than the celebrities themselves. Everybody wanted to be around Paulie, sit at his table, ask him for favors. I thought that he was a Mafia boss or something.

You never knew who you'd meet at Columbus. Sometimes Pete would leave me there with Paulie. Next thing I knew, David Bowie, Mikhail Baryshnikov, and Drew Barrymore, this little kid, would be sitting at the same table with us. I'd think to myself, *This is deep. You better keep your composure.* Then Robert De Niro and Joe Pesci walked in and sat down. We were sitting and talking and the next thing I knew, Paulie said, "Hey, Mike, we all gotta go somewhere." And, boom, five minutes later I'm at Liza Minnelli's house sitting on the sofa chilling with Raul Julia.

Eventually I met all those New York social scenesters. Being around them, I realized that something special had died right before I had come onto the scene. It was so powerful, you could still feel it in the music of Elton John and Stevie Wonder and Freddie Mercury. You knew they had been to a special place that wasn't around any longer.

But even meeting all these superstars didn't validate my own sense of having made it. That didn't happen until I met the wrestler Bruno Sammartino. I was a huge wrestling fan growing up. I loved Sammartino and Gorilla Monsoon and Billy Graham. One night I went to a party where I met Tom Cruise, who was just starting out. At the same event, I saw Bruno Sammartino. I was totally starstruck. I just stared at him. Someone introduced us and he had no idea who I was, but I started recounting to him all the great matches I had seen him participate in, against people like Killer Kowalski, Nikolai Volkoff, and George "the Animal" Steele. In my sick, megalomaniac mind I was thinking, *This is a sign of my greatness. My hero is here with me. I'm going to be great like him and win the championship.*

Cus wasn't too thrilled that I was spending more and more time in Manhattan. When I went to the city, I'd crash on the couch of Steve

Lott, who was Jimmy Jacobs's right-hand man. Steve was a model junkie and he'd take me to places like the Nautilus Club and other spots where beautiful girls would hang out. At the time I was dedicated to winning that belt so I wasn't really fooling around with the girls yet. I tried to be a nice guy then, not going too far. My weakness was food. Steve was a great cook and when I went out at night clubbing, I'd come back and have Steve heat up some Chinese leftovers for a late-night snack. I'd go back to Catskill after a few days and Cus would be mad.

"Look at your ass. Your ass is getting fatter," he'd shake his head.

My next fight was my first real test. On October ninth, I went up against Donnie Long in Atlantic City. Long had gone the distance with both James Broad, a tough heavyweight, and John Tate, the former WBA heavyweight champ. I knew it would make me look good in the boxing world if I dispatched him promptly. Long was confident going into the fight, telling Al Bernstein of ESPN that he could outpunch me. They called Long "the Master of Disaster," but his night turned disastrous as soon as the opening bell rang. I went after him fast and ferocious and knocked him down seconds into the fight with a lunging left. A little later, a right uppercut dropped him and then I finished him off with a right-uppercut-left-hook combination. It took me under a minute and a half to win.

After the fight, Al Bernstein interviewed me.

"Earlier in the day I really thought that Donnie Long would be a fairly tough opponent for you. He wasn't!" Al said.

"Well, like I told you earlier today, if I knock him out in one or two rounds, would you still consider him that?"

"I thought he was supposed to be, but I guess he wasn't," Al said.

"Oh, *now* he wasn't. . . ." I laughed.

"No, he was a tough man, I'm just saying for you he wasn't tough, apparently, because you beat him."

"I knew from the beginning, but everybody else didn't know that it was no con, it was no con. A lot of people came to look, Jesse Ferguson came to look, the Fraziers came to look. All of you come and get some, because Mike Tyson is out here, he is waiting for you, all come and get some."

I was almost too focused then; I didn't really live in reality. I was interviewed for *Sports Illustrated* and I said, "What bothers me most is being around people who are having a lot of fun, with parties and stuff like that. It makes you soft. People who are only interested in having fun cannot accomplish anything." I thought I was stronger than people who were weak and partying. I wanted to be in that Columbus celebrity world, but I was fighting that temptation to party.

I still wasn't having sex. The last time I had gotten laid was at the Olympics with that intern. It wasn't that I didn't want to have sex, but I was too awkward with women. I didn't know how to access them. "Hey, hi, you want to get laid?" I didn't know how to say that. Around this time, I was supposed to fight on the undercard in Madison Square Garden. My reputation preceded me and my opponent didn't show up. So I left the Garden and went to a whorehouse on Forty-second Street. I had known about the place since I was a kid hanging out in Times Square.

I walked into the joint and sat down in one of the chairs in the outer room. There was a big-screen TV playing porno films. The girls would come up and they'd sit with you, and ask, "Would you like to date?" If you passed on one of them, another one would come over. I was the youngest guy there, so they thought I was kind of cute. I picked out a nice Cuban girl and we went to a room in the back.

Freud would have had a field day with that scenario. Here I was all ready to focus my aggression and beat up my opponent in the ring, but the fight is canceled and I go and get laid. I was actually extremely excited. During our session, her back went out. She said, "Hey, we have to stop. I pulled something in my back." I hadn't finished yet so I asked her for my money back. She changed the subject and asked me for my Edwin Rosario T-shirt that I was wearing. She was too hurt to continue so she said, "Let's talk." We talked for a while and then I left with my T-shirt.

After that, Cus began accelerating my pace. Sixteen days after the Long fight I fought Robert Colay and I threw two left hooks. The first one missed, the second one knocked him out. It was over in thirty-seven seconds. A week later I fought Sterling Benjamin upstate in Latham, New York. I knocked him down with a short left hook and then after the eight count, I swarmed him, throwing devastating body blows and uppercuts. He crumbled to the canvas. The ref stopped the fight. The upstate crowd was going wild and I turned to face them, putting my gloves through the upper ropes, palms up, and saluted them gladiator-style.

But I had more important things on my mind than my eleventh pro victory. Cus was very ill. He had been sick since I moved into the house with him and Camille, he was always coughing, but I knew his condition was getting worse when he didn't travel with us to some of my fights. He stayed home for the Long and the Colay fights, but he made the trip to Latham to see me fight Benjamin. He was too much of an old stubborn Italian man to miss a fight in his backyard. He had no faith in doctors and he was one of the first proponents of vitamins and what we now call "alternative medicine," and nutritional therapy.

I knew Cus was sick but I was just of the mind-set that he was going to make it through to see me become champ because we always talked about it. He was going to stick around to see me become a success. But when we talked in private, sometimes he'd say, "I might not be around, so you've got to listen to me." I just thought he said that to scare me, to make sure I acted right. Cus always said things to make me apprehensive.

He was admitted to a hospital in Albany, but Jimmy Jacobs had him transferred to Mount Sinai in the city. I went with Steve Lott to visit him. Cus was sitting in his bed eating ice cream. We talked for a few minutes and then Cus asked Steve to leave the room so he could talk to me in private.

That's when he told me he was dying from pneumonia. I couldn't believe what he was telling me. He didn't look morbidly ill. He was buffing. He had energy and zest. He was eating ice cream. He was chilling out, but I started freaking out.

"I don't want to do this shit without you," I said, choking back tears. "I'm not going to do it."

"Well, if you don't fight, you'll realize that people can come back from the grave, because I'm going to haunt you for the rest of your life." I told him "Okay," and then he took my hand.

"The world has to see you, Mike. You're going to be champ of the world, the greatest out there," he said.

Then Cus started crying. That was the first time I ever saw him cry. I thought he was crying because he couldn't see me become heavyweight champion of the world after all we had gone through together. But soon I realized he was crying over Camille. I totally forgot that he had another partner who meant more to him than me. He told me he regretted that he had never married Camille because he had tax problems and he didn't want her to take them on.

"Mike, just do me one favor," he said. "Make sure you take care of Camille."

I left the room in shock. I was staying at Steve's apartment, and Jimmy lived in the same building. Later that day, Jimmy came by to get me to go with him to the bank to deposit a check for $120,000 for my last fights. By now my name was in the papers and I was on the cover of *Sports Illustrated* and strangers were stopping me on the street and wishing me well. I was out there, cocky, looking good. I knew all the girls at the bank and normally I'd flirt with them and they'd flirt back.

But right before we walked in the bank, Jimmy stopped.

"Cus is not going to make it through the night, Mike. They say he has a few hours to live."

I just started crying like it was the end of the world. It was. My world was gone. All the girls at the bank were staring at me.

"Is there a problem?" The manager came up to us.

"We just heard that a dear friend of ours is dying and Mike is taking it very hard," Jimmy said. He was cool and collected. Just like that, boom, no emotion, just the way Cus trained him to be. Meanwhile, I was still crying like a lost soldier on a mission without a general. I don't think I ever went back to that bank, I was so embarrassed.

They had Cus's funeral upstate. I was one of Cus's pallbearers. Everybody from the boxing world came. It was so sad. In my sick head all I could think about was to succeed for him. I would have done anything to win that title to insure Cus's legacy. I started feeling sorry for myself, thinking that without Cus, I would have a shitty life. Camille was very composed but when we got back to the house, we cried together.

Shortly after the funeral, Jim Jacobs organized a memorial service for Cus at his old gym, the Gramercy Gym, in the city. All the luminaries were there. Norman Mailer said his influence on boxing was as great as Hemingway's influence on young American writers. Gay Talese said it was an honor to have known Cus.

"He taught me so many things, not just about boxing, which was a craft and could be mastered, but about living and about life, which is not so easily mastered," Pete Hamill said.

Jim Jacobs pretty much nailed Cus in his speech. "Cus D'Amato was violently opposed to ignorance and corruption in boxing. While Cus was unyielding to his enemies, he was understanding, compassionate, and incredibly tolerant with his friends."

I shut down emotionally after Cus died. I got really mean. I was trying to prove myself, show that I was a man, not just a boy. I flew to Texas a week after Cus's funeral to fight Eddie Richardson. Jimmy and Cayton didn't even let me mourn. So I brought along a photo of Cus. I was still talking to Cus, every night.

"I'm going to fight this guy Richardson tomorrow, Cus," I said. "What do you think I should do?"

Even though I was functioning, I'd lost my spirit, my belief in myself. I lost all my energy to do anything good. I don't think I ever did get over his death. I was also mad at him when he died. I was so bitter. If he'd only gone to the doctor's earlier, he could've been alive to protect me. But he wanted to be stubborn, so he didn't get treated and he died and left me out there alone for these animals in the boxing world to take advantage of. After Cus died, I just didn't care about anything anymore. I was basically fighting for the money. I didn't really have a dream. It would be good to win the title, but I just wanted to get some wine, have some fun, party, and get fucked up.

But first I fucked Richardson up. The first punch I threw, a right hand, knocked him down. He hung on for a minute more, but then I hit him with a leaping left and because he was so tall he wound up coming down on the other side of the ring.

Conroy Nelson, who had lost to Trevor Berbick years earlier for the Canadian title, was next. He was still ranked the #2 heavyweight in Canada and was a tough, experienced guy, one of those guys with a big Adonis body. All the announcers thought this was the guy who would finally test me. I just worked over his body in the first round. Two or three times he almost went down from body blows. Then the second started and, boom, boom, boom, to the body and then an over-head right broke his nose and a left hook to the chin drove him to the canvas. When the ref stopped the fight, I paraded around the ring, soaking in the adulation of my hometown fans, arms outstretched.

My next fight was in the Felt Forum at Madison Square Garden on December sixth. All my friends from Brownsville came. But I was too much in the zone to really think about being in New York and having a good time. I couldn't wait to get through these fights and get my shot at the title for Cus. My opponent that night was Sammy Scaff. My postfight interview lasted longer than the fight. Scaff was a lumbering 250-pound Kentucky journeyman and I caught him with two awesome left hooks to the head that left his face a mask of blood and his nose mostly rearranged. After the fight, John Condon, the head of boxing at MSG who was doing the color commentary, asked me what was a typical day in the life of Mike Tyson.

"Mike Tyson is just a hardworking fighter that leads a boring life as an individual. Anyone who says 'I wish I was in your shoes,' the hundreds of people who say that don't know the tenth of it. If they were in my shoes they would cry like babies. They couldn't handle it."

We were back in Latham for my next fight. It was the main event and the arena was packed with my fans. My opponent was Mark Young, a tough-looking guy. When we came to the center of the ring for the instructions, I could feel his energy. You got to stare them down during the instructions, but that doesn't mean anything, that's just window dressing. You feel that energy from their spirit, you feel it from their soul, and then you go back to your corner and you go "Oh shit" or "This guy's a pussy." That night it was "Oh shit, he's coming to fight." Kevin felt it too.

"Hit him with hard jabs and move your head," Kevin said. "Don't forget to move your head, he's coming to fight."

The bell rang and he came out winging. But he was wild and I started throwing hard jabs and moving my head. A little more than a minute in, he threw a wild right, I twisted around him and threw a sneaky vicious right uppercut and, boom, he went up in the air and came down face-first. Ray Mancini was the TV color commentary and he was very complimentary about my skills, but he thought that it was time that my management gave me someone to fight.

But Jimmy stuck to his plan. Two weeks later I was in Albany fighting Dave Jaco. He had a respectable 19-5 record with fourteen KOs including a TKO over Razor Ruddock. He was a tall skinny white guy. He didn't look like much but was really tough. I kept knocking him down and he kept getting up. They stopped it after my third knockdown of the first round.

That night, I celebrated my victory with some friends. About eight o'clock the next morning, I knocked at Camille's door. She opened it and I went inside and sat down. I didn't say anything.

"How did you make out?" Camille asked me.

"I made out good, but I was looking for somebody who wasn't there," I said and tears started rolling down my cheeks. "Cus wasn't there. Everybody tells me I'm doing good, I'm doing good, but nobody tells me if I do bad. It doesn't matter how good I would have done, Cus would have probably seen something I did wrong."

I expanded on the way I was feeling when I was interviewed for *Sports Illustrated* that week.

"I miss Cus terribly. He was my backbone. All the things we worked on, they're starting to come out so well. But when it comes down to it, who really cares? I like doing my job, but I'm not happy being victorious. I fight my heart out, give it my best, but when it's over, there's no Cus to tell me how I did, no mother to show my clippings to."

I put my feelings aside and kept busy. On January 24, 1986, I fought Mike Jameson. He was a big Irishman who had won decisions over Tex Cobb and Michael Dokes. It took me five rounds to stop him because he was a wily veteran and knew when to hold me. It made for a lackluster fight. My next opponent took those tactics to a new level. On February sixteenth, I met Jesse Ferguson in Troy, New York. The fight was on ABC and it was my first national TV appearance. Ferguson had become the ESPN champion when he beat Buster Douglas five months earlier. I was watching him walk around in the arena after he won the championship and I wanted to challenge him for his belt so bad. I fought on the undercard.

I knew it was going to be a tough fight. During the instructions, he didn't even look me in the eye. He had such a humble and submissive posture. But I didn't detect even a drop of fear or intimidation from his energy, so I wasn't going for any of that humble, afraid-to-look-me-in-the-eye shit. I felt that he couldn't wait to slug me.

I had the hometown advantage—in more ways than one. Jimmy had stacked the deck for my first national exposure. He got us to wear eight-ounce gloves, lighter than usual. We were fighting in a smaller ring than normal. And all the officials were in our corner.

I began the fight with a vicious body assault. But Ferguson was shrewd enough to hold on to me. This continued for the first four rounds. But in the fifth, I got him in the corner and connected with a right uppercut and broke his nose. He barely made it through the round and in the sixth he was in trouble again. Then he just blatantly held on to me and totally ignored the referee's command to break. It got so bad that the referee stopped the fight. Ironically enough, a disqualification would have stopped my knockout streak. But the next day the local boxing commission changed the result to a TKO.

When I met with the reporters after the fight, I started a controversy. When they asked me about finishing Ferguson off after I had scored with the uppercut, I said, "I wanted to hit him on the nose one more time, so that the bone of his nose would go up into his brain . . . I would always listen to the doctor's conclusions. They said that any time that the nose goes into the brain, the consequences of him getting up right away are out of the question."

The reporters laughed, but maybe it was just nervous laughter. What I said to the reporters was what Cus used to say to me word for word. I didn't think I said anything wrong. Cus and I always used to talk about the science of hurting people. I wanted to be a cantankerous, malevolent champion. I used to watch these comic book characters on TV, the X-Men and one of my favorites, Apocalypse. Apocalypse would say, "I'm not malevolent, I just am." Cayton and Jacobs wanted me to be friendly with everybody, sociable, but I knew a man who was friendly with everyone was an enemy to himself.

The next day, the shit hit the fan because of my comment. New York papers had big headlines that read, "Is This the Real Tyson, a Thug?" One reporter even called up my old social worker, Mrs. Coleman, and she advised me to be a man, not an animal. But I didn't care. I had a job to do. I wasn't going to be Mike Tyson the heavyweight champion by being a nice guy. I was going to do it in Cus's name. My opponents had to know that they were going to pay with their life or their health if they contested me.

Jimmy and Cayton tried to muzzle me after that. They assigned Steve Lott to tell me what to say after a fight. Jimmy even fired their P.R. guy because he had sent that quote out on the wires. Shortly after that fight Jimmy invited some handpicked reporters to have dinner with us. Ed Schuyler of the Associated Press was there, and he felt that there was a sense of desperation behind Cayton and Jimmy to get me a title before I got into serious trouble. But that wasn't what it was. I think they just wanted to grab the money while they could. They didn't have the respect for the mission I was on.

Cayton and the rest of them wanted to strip me of my history of growing up in Brooklyn and give me a positive image. Cus knew that was bullshit. They were trying to suppress me and make me conform to their standards. I wanted people to see the savage that was within me.

We partied after the Ferguson fight. I was drinking heavily during that time. Not during training, but once the fight was over, it was self-destruction time. I was a full-blown alcoholic. But I drank away from the glare of all the media in the city. We partied in Albany at my friend's bar called September's. That was our stomping ground. Sometimes guys went there from the city or from Boston or L.A. for work-related reasons, and they'd act like big shots, like they were gonna stomp on us little upstate guys, so we'd beat the shit out of them. I didn't want to fight anybody and get sued, but there were people there fighting in place of me. I'd be instigating it, saying shit like, "Just kick that motherfucker. Who does he think he is?" We had a field day with those out-of-towners.

My next fight was against Steve Zouski on March tenth in the Nassau Coliseum. Zouski had never been floored in any of his previous fights, but I scored with several uppercuts in the third round and knocked him out. But I was not impressed with my performance. For one, I had fallen off a ladder in my pigeon coop at Camille's and suffered a cut on my ear. Zouski hit my ear a few times and it blew up during the fight and started to affect my balance. During the interview after the fight, I alluded to my other problem.

"I didn't like my performance," I told Randy Gordon, who had been calling the fight. "I have a lot of personal problems I'm getting over."

Cayton later told the press that I meant girlfriend problems, but that was absurd. I didn't have a girlfriend then. I was just depressed because so many of my friends from Brownsville were getting killed. It was barbaric. Friends were killing other friends over money.

After the fight, one of the officials saw that there was a big bulge on my ear. So the next day Jimmy had a specialist check me out and he realized that my cartilage had gotten severely infected and immediately made me check into Mount Sinai on the Upper East Side. He was worried that I might lose my ear if it went untreated. They had me stay in the hospital for ten days and undergo treatment in a hyperbaric chamber twice a day where they forced antibiotics into the cartilage.

The doctors at Mount Sinai told me that it would be good for me to go out and get some fresh air. So every day after my second treatment at three p.m., Tom Patti and my close childhood friend Duran would pick me up in a limo or we'd walk down to Times Square, where we hung out and took pictures with all the prostitutes and the guys who sold pictures of tourists with pythons coiled around their necks. We were having a blast, partying all night. I'd roll back into the hospital at four a.m. and the nurses would freak. "This isn't a hotel, it's a hospital." When I showed the doctors the pictures of me with the prostitute and the python, they freaked too. "No, no, we didn't mean you should go out all night. We meant go downstairs and sit in Central Park, watch the birds and the squirrels and get some fresh air."

That was almost two months before my fight with James Tillis in upstate New York. When it was time for the fight, I was out of shape because of my illness and also because I had been drinking and partying way too hard. The fight went ten hard rounds and I was just glad to get the decision. I dropped him once, which probably tipped the scales in my favor, but he was the toughest opponent I had ever faced at that point. He gave me such a body beating that I couldn't even walk after the fight. I had to stay in the hotel. I couldn't even drive home. I found out what fighting was really about that night. Several times during the fight I wanted to go down so bad just to get some relief, but I kept grabbing and holding him, trying to get my breath back.

The next day Jimmy Jacobs went into spin mode. He told the press, "The fight was just a hurdle for him. Now we see that he can go the distance." He was a master at manipulating the press, not to mention the public. He and Cayton masterminded a publicity campaign that was unparalleled. No actor in the world ever got that kind of press before. Everybody does it now, but back then, they were true innovators.

Less than three weeks later, I fought Mitch Green at the Garden. He was truly a crazy motherfucker. He tried to get in my head before the fight by telling the *Daily News* that I was nineteen years old but I looked like I was forty. When Marv Albert asked me if Green was get-ting to me, I said, "Mitch Green is a good fighter but he's not on an eloquent level to disturb me. So not at all."

This was my first fight on my new HBO contract that Jimmy and Cayton had negotiated. And it was a thrill to fight for the first time in the big arena in Madison Square Garden. But you wouldn't know it from the prefight interview on HBO. When they asked me if I was enjoying all my newfound attention and wealth, I got morose. "People won't want to be in my position. 'Wow, I can make money,' they say. But if they had to go through some of the things I go through, they would cry. It's so depressing. Everybody wants something. Just as hard as you're working in the gym, people are working that hard try-ing to separate you from your money." That was me being Cus. You'd think I'd be more upbeat since this was my first time headlining the Garden.

Green was a well-respected fighter then. He was a four-time Golden Gloves champion and he had been undefeated until he lost a decision in 1985 to Trevor Berbick for the USBA title. But I knew I was going to beat him as soon as we entered the ring. I didn't get any threaten-ing vibes from him at all. The fight went the distance but that was okay. After the Tillis fight, I wanted to be more comfortable going ten rounds. I knew he couldn't hurt me so I was working on my endur-ance. I won every round and it wasn't a dull fight. At one point I knocked out his mouthpiece and bridge with a couple of teeth in it. He took a lot of punishment. I was so loose that between the eighth and ninth rounds when Kevin was literally in my face jabbering on and on, telling me to punch more, I gave him a little kiss.

After the fight I was back to my usual arrogant self.

"Not to be egotistical, but I won this fight so easy. I refuse to be beaten in there. I refuse to let anybody get in my way," I told the press.

Reggie Gross was my next target. He was a tough fighter they called "the Spoiler" because he had upset some good fighters including Bert Cooper and Jimmy Clark, who was a great American Olympian. The fight almost didn't happen because I was suffering from a bad case of bronchitis that week. I had suffered from bronchitis my entire life and I had gotten used to it, but this was a severe case. They took me to the doctor the day of the fight and he examined me.

"I'm afraid I'm going to have to postpone this fight. He's pretty ill," the doctor said.

"Can I talk to you for a moment, please, sir," Jimmy said. I could see the look in Jimmy's eyes and the next thing I knew I was in the ring fighting. In the first round, I was hitting Gross with a flurry of punches and he was covering up. Suddenly he decided to start trading punches, which was fine with me. He threw a bunch of wild punches that I dodged and then I knocked him down with a vicious left hook and then knocked him down a second time with a succession of punches. The ref stopped the fight because Gross was glassy-eyed, but Reggie complained. "You can't even walk but you want to fight?" the ref said.

My next two opponents seemed to be going down in caliber. Maybe Jimmy and Cayton just wanted me to get some more one-round knockouts after those two decisions. I obliged them with William Hosea, but it took me two rounds to knock out Lorenzo Boyd. But my lightning-fast right to the rib cage followed quickly by a thundering right uppercut left the crowd wowed. Two weeks later I got everyone's attention by demolishing Marvis Frazier, Joe's son, in thirty seconds. I cornered him, set him up with my jab, and then finished him off with my favorite punch, a right uppercut. He looked severely injured so I rushed over to try to help him up. I love Marvis; he's a beautiful person.

I had just turned twenty a few weeks earlier, and the plan was for me to become the youngest heavyweight champ by the end of 1986. While Jimmy and Cayton were negotiating for that, they had me fight Jose Ribalta in Atlantic City on August seventeenth.

Ribalta was a game fighter who, unlike Green and Tillis, actually engaged me. And he seemed to have the will not to be knocked out. I knocked him down in the second, and again in the eighth, but he got up. In the tenth, he went down a third time and when he got up, I swarmed him on the ropes and the referee stopped the fight.

Besides gaining a lot of respect from the crowd and the commentators on his determination, Ribalta also managed to ruin my night. After the fight, I had a date with a beautiful young coed from Penn State University who I had met at the hundredth anniversary of the Statue of Liberty. This young lady accompanied me to my room and she began to touch me but I recoiled in pain.

"Hey! Please don't touch me. It's nothing personal but you have to go now. I just need some peace," I told her. She was very understanding and she drove back to her school, but we made up for it the next time I saw her.

She had been at the fight and had seen all the punishment I had absorbed. I had never been through anything like that before. I felt nauseous from all Ribalta's body blows, even hours after the fight. Ribalta and Tillis were the only two guys who had ever made me feel like that. I never felt that much general pain again. But I remember all the reading I had done chronicling how other great fighters had felt like their heads were halfway off after some of their fights, so I just felt that this was part of my journey.

The negotiations for a title fight were heating up and Jimmy decided that I should fight in Vegas so I could get used to it before I would fight there later in the year to win the title. We stayed at the house of Dr. Bruce Handelman, a friend of Jimmy's. I started training at Johnny Tocco's gym, a wonderfully grungy old-school gym with no amenities, not even air-conditioning. Tocco was an awesome guy who had been friends with Sonny Liston. There were pictures of Johnny and all the old-time greats on the walls.

I was in the locker room one day about to spar when it hit me. I told Kevin that I didn't like it in Vegas and I wanted to go home. I was really just feeling anxious about the fight. If I didn't win the Ratliff fight, I wouldn't qualify to fight Trevor Berbick.

Kevin went out and told Steve Lott. So Steve thought to himself, *WWCD?* or, *What would Cus do?* Steve came into the locker room and tried to be positive. "You're the star of the show. You're going to knock this guy out in two rounds. You'll be fantastic. If you don't like it here, we don't have to come back here ever again, how's that?"

Steve always had a charming way of handling situations. Of

course, I wasn't going anywhere, I was just venting. But he didn't know what Cus would have done. Cus would have looked at me and said, "What? Are you scared of this guy? This guy is a bum. I'm going to fight him for you."

So on September sixth, I squared off against Alfonzo Ratliff, who was a former cruiserweight champion of the world. I didn't think he was a step up from Ribalta, but he certainly wasn't a bum; he was a tough opponent. Apparently, the Vegas oddsmakers didn't agree because they wouldn't take bets on the fight itself, only on the over-under of five rounds. You would think I invented over-under in fight betting. Before me it didn't exist. I took it to a new level of exploitation. The opening bell rang and Ratliff just took off. He made Mitch Green look like one of those power walkers. It was so bad that even the HBO guys were joking. "I wonder if he's going to use his ten- or twelve-speed bike in the second round," Larry Merchant said.

He actually tried to fight in the next round, but he didn't last long. I dropped him with a left hook and then chopped him down with several punches when he got up.

"His bicycle got a flat tire," Merchant cracked. When Jimmy came into the ring after the fight, he commented on Ratliff's running. "I felt his breeze," I said.

Soon it was official. I was to fight Trevor Berbick for his title on November 22, 1986. I had more than two months off between fights and Jimmy and Cayton decided to have me make the talk show circuit to promote the fight and my career. I started out going on David Brenner's *Nightlife*. David was a great guy and he treated me with the utmost respect. He predicted I would be the next heavyweight champ, but as nice as that was, it meant more to me when his other guest, the great former champion Jake LaMotta, made the same prediction.

"Without a doubt, the next heavyweight champ of the world," Jake said when he came out and hugged me. "And if he doesn't do the right thing, I'll give him a beating. You keep it up, pal; you're going to be like Joe Louis, Marciano, maybe even better."

My heart soared when I heard that.

My father, Jimmy "Curlee" Kirkpatrick Jr.

My mother, Lorna Mae.

Me at nine years old.

Cus D'Amato.

Me at thirteen years old.

Dinner with Cus and Camille.

Running while surrounded by trucks as I shoot a Pepsi commercial.

Cus's funeral on November 7, 1985. LEFT TO RIGHT: Jimmy Jacobs, Kevin Rooney, Tom Patti, me, Jay Bright, José Torres, a relative of Cus's, and Floyd Patterson.

At Steve Lott's apartment for my nineteenth birthday party.
LEFT TO RIGHT: Steve Lott, Susan O'Brien, Jimmy Jacobs, Bill Cayton, my first girlfriend Angie, me, Loraine Jacobs, and Doris Cayton.

With my pigeons in Catskill.

Mitch Green and I fight at Madison Square Garden in 1986.
I won in a unanimous decision, running my record to 21–0.

Marvis Frazier and I face off.

Trevor Berbick goes down as I fight him
and become the youngest heavyweight
champion of the world.

Don King and I celebrate my win over James "Bonecrusher" Smith as I claim the WBA belt in my second heavyweight title fight.

I land a vicious punch to the jaw in the seventh round against Tyrell Biggs en route to retaining my heavyweight title in 1987.

The heavyweight title fight between Michael Spinks and me in 1988.
I knocked him out in the first round, defending my three belts.

Wearing my three belts
after my fight with Spinks.

I'm mobbed by a crowd when I return to Brownsville.

Talking with my attorney, Steven Hayes, during the trial to dissolve my contract with Bill Cayton. Sitting at the other end of the table is Jimmy Jacobs's widow, Loraine. Behind us from left to right are Donald Trump, Robin Givens, and Ruth Givens.

I throw a left hook at Larry Holmes during our fight in January 1988.

Meeting some sumo wrestlers during my trip to Tokyo in 1988.

Bill Cayton, me, and Jimmy Jacobs.

With Evander Holyfield.

Al Sharpton and mc.

Walking Kenya,
my pet tiger.

Robin Givens and I get married in 1988.

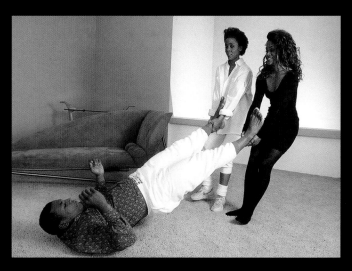

My ex-wife Robin and her mother, Ruth, try to pull me apart.

Then Brenner asked Jake a question and his answer was very prescient.

"Let's say Mike becomes the champ. What advice would you give him?"

"The best advice I could give him is keep yourself busy and make believe you're in jail for a couple of years," Jake said. "Stay away from all the garbage out there. There's a lot of garbage out there."

"Why does it have to be garbage?" I asked.

"Unfortunately, guys like you and I, we attract garbage," he said.

I did *The Joan Rivers Show*. I loved her and her husband, Edgar. They both made me feel so good. I felt their energy was real. That was one of the best times of my life. During our interview Joan asked me if I had an Adrian, like in the movie *Rocky*.

"No girlfriend," I answered.

"When you go into training, do you give up sex?" she asked.

"No."

"See, 'cause my husband always tells me he's in training," Joan cracked.

I did *The Dick Cavett Show* and Dick demonstrated some aikido on me. He asked me to hold him by his wrists.

"The eighty-seven-year-old founder of aikido can get away from the grasp of the world's strongest man," he said and he did a slip move and escaped my grip.

"But no mugger's gonna hold you like this," I protested.

I was so charming on these shows, just the way Jim and Bill wanted me to be. But I didn't want that. I wanted to be a villain. I wanted to model myself on Jim Brown, the football player. When I first started hanging out in bars in the city I'd see older professional football players who played with Jim Brown. They were talking about him like he was mythical.

"Hey, if he came in here and something wasn't cool—the smell of the place, the music that was playing, the volume of the people's conversations—if something just wasn't cool in his mind, he would commence to destroying the place."

I was listening to this thinking, *Fuck, I wish I was a bad mother-*

fucker and had people talking about me like that. If Jim's going to destroy you because he doesn't like the smell of the place, I've got to come in and kill a motherfucker in here.

As the November twenty-second date came closer, I began to train seriously. I trained for a month in Catskill and then we moved to Vegas. Right at the start, Jimmy and Cayton gave me a VHS tape of Berbick's fight versus Pinklon Thomas, the fight he won to become champion. I watched it and reported back to Jimmy.

"Was that tape in slow motion?"

I was arrogant, but I really felt that my time had come. In my sick head, all the great old-time fighters and the gods of war would be descending to watch me join their company. They'd give me their blessing and I'd join their club. I was still hearing Cus in my head, but not in a morbid sense, just supportive.

This is the moment we've been training for since you were fourteen. We went over this over and over again. You can fight this guy with your eyes closed.

I knew Berbick was rough and tough and hard to fight because he was the first man to go fifteen rounds with Larry Holmes in a title defense. Larry had knocked everyone else out. I just wanted to decimate Berbick. Then everybody would take me seriously, because at that time, everybody thought I was fighting tomato cans and fluff; they said this guy's not a real fighter, he's just fighting easy fights, so that's why my main objective was to decimate him. I wanted to take him out in one round—I wanted to hurt him real bad.

Kevin and Matt Baranski were just as confident as me. We were firing on all cylinders. And I was firing on one more. I looked at my underpants a day before the fight and I noticed a discharge. I had the clap. I didn't know if I had contracted it from a prostitute or a very filthy young lady. We were staying at Dr. Handleman's house again so he gave me an antibiotic shot.

Later that day, Steve Lott and I went to rent some VHS tapes.

"Mike, what would Cus say about this guy Berbick?" he asked me.

This was Steve's way of putting me in Cus's shoes, getting me to think like Cus. What Steve didn't know was that I didn't have to think like Cus; I had Cus in my head.

"He'd say that this guy was a tomato can," I answered. "A bum."

I was such a prick at the weigh-in. I was glaring at Berbick every time he was within sight. He'd come over to shake my hand but I'd turn my back on his outstretched hand. When I caught him looking at me, I'd bark, "What the fuck are you looking at?" Then I told him that I was going to knock him out in two rounds. He'd pose with the belt and I'd yell out, "Enjoy holding the belt. You won't have it too much longer. It's going to be on a real champion's waist." I was so disrespectful and offensive. For some reason I just didn't like Berbick at that time. Plus, I wanted that belt. That green-eyed monster set in.

I was also mad that Berbick's trainer Angelo Dundee was bragging that Berbick would beat me. Cus was always so jealous of Dundee, who had trained Ali, because he got all the media attention. Cus didn't think he deserved it.

"Berbick has the style to do a number on Tyson," he told the press. "Trevor is licking his chops at the thought that for once, he won't have to chase, that Tyson will be right there in his face. Trevor is a good body puncher and he has twenty-three KOs to his credit. He's confident and so am I. I think he'll stop Tyson in a late round."

I couldn't sleep the night before the fight. I was on the phone a lot, talking with girls who I liked but never had sex with. I tried to take my mind off the fight by asking them what they were doing but all they wanted to talk about was the fight. Then I got up and started shadowboxing in my room.

The day of the fight I had some pasta at one o'clock. At four, I had a steak. Then some more pasta at five. In the dressing room I had a Snickers bar and some orange juice.

Then Kevin wrapped my hands and put on my gloves. It was time to walk to the ring. It was chilly in the arena so Kevin cut a towel and draped it over my neck. I was wearing the black trunks that I had changed to a few fights ago. I had to pay a $5,000 fine since Berbick was wearing black, but I didn't care. I wanted that ominous look.

I was the challenger so I had to go out first. They were playing a
Toto song for my entrance but all I could hear in my head was that
Phil Collins song "In the Air Tonight": "I can feel it coming in the air
tonight, oh Lord / And I've been waiting for this moment for all of my
life, oh Lord."

I went through the ropes and I started pacing around the ring. I
looked out at the crowd and I saw Kirk Douglas, Eddie Murphy, and
Sly Stallone. A few minutes later, Berbick entered wearing a black
robe with a black hood. He was projecting cockiness and confidence,
but I could feel that was all a façade, an illusion. I knew that this guy
was not going to die for his belt.

Ali was introduced to the crowd and he came over to me.

"Kick his ass for me," Ali told me.

Five years earlier, Ali had been beaten by Berbick and retired
after the fight, so I was more than happy to comply.

"That's going to be easy," I assured Muhammad.

Finally it was time to fight. The bell rang and referee Mills Lane
motioned us into action. I charged Berbick and began peppering him
with hard shots. I couldn't believe that he wasn't moving and he
wasn't jabbing; he was standing right there in front of me. I threw a
right hand near the beginning of the fight square on his left ear,
trying to bust his eardrum. About halfway through the round, I
staggered him with a hard right. I swarmed him and by the end of
the first, Berbick seemed dazed. He had taken some really, really
good shots.

I went back to my corner and sat down. Because of the antibiotic
shot, I was dripping like a Good Humor bar in July. But I didn't care;
I was in there to nail Berbick. Besides, one of my heroes, Kid Choco-
late, fought with syphilis all the time.

"Move your head, don't forget to jab," Kevin said. "You're head-
hunting. Go to the body first."

Ten seconds into the second round, I hit him with a right and
Berbick went down. He sprang up immediately and came right back
at me. He was trying to fight back but his punches were ineffective.

With about a half a minute or so left in the round, I hit him with a right to the body instead of an uppercut and then I shot the uppercut but I missed him. But I threw a left and hit him in the temple. It was a delayed reaction but he went down. I didn't even feel the punch, but it was very effective. He tried to get up but then he fell back down and I noticed that his ankle was all bent.

No way he's gonna get up and beat the count, I thought.

I was right. He tried to get up a second time and he lurched across the canvas and flopped down again. He finally got up but Mills Lane hugged him and waved him off. That was it. I was the youngest heavyweight champion in history.

"It's over, that's all, and we have a new era in boxing," Barry Watkins, the HBO announcer, said.

"Mike Tyson did what Mike Tyson normally does. And that's fight," Sugar Ray Leonard added.

"That's with a capital *F*," Watkins said.

I was just numb. I couldn't feel anything. I was conscious of what was going on around me but I was just numb. Kevin hugged me. José Torres came over.

"I can't believe this, man. I'm the fucking champion of the world at twenty," I said to him. "This fucking shit is unreal. Champion of the world at twenty. I'm a kid, a fucking kid."

Jimmy came into the ring and gave me a kiss.

"Do you think Cus would have liked that?" I asked. Jimmy smiled.

Don King, whose son managed Berbick, came over to congratulate me. Then I looked out over the audience and started to feel arrogant. *Yeah, we did it,* I thought. *Me and Cus did it.* Then I started talking to Cus.

"We did it, we proved all those guys wrong. I bet Berbick don't think I'm too short, does he?" Then I realized that Cus would have hated the way I fought.

"Everything else you did in the ring was garbage," I heard him say in my head. "But the ending was so resounding that it's all people will remember."

It was time for the postfight interviews. I had to acknowledge Cus. I was the best fighter in the world at that time, and I was his creation. Cus needed to be there. He would have loved to have told off those people who wrote him off as a kook. He would have said, "Nobody can beat my boy here. He's only twenty but nobody in the world can beat him."

"This is the moment I waited for all my life since I started boxing," I said when the press conference started. "Berbick was very strong. I never expected him to be as strong as me . . . every punch I threw was with bad intentions. My record will last for immortality, it'll never be broken. I want to live forever . . . I refused to lose . . . I would have had to be carried out dead to lose. I was coming to destroy and win the Heavyweight Championship of the World, which I've done. I'd like to dedicate my fight to my great guardian Cus D'Amato. I'm sure he's up there and he's looking down and he's talking to all the great fighters and he's saying his boy did it. I thought he was a crazy white dude . . . he was a genius. Everything he said would happen happened."

Someone asked me who my next opponent would be.

"I don't care who I fight next," I said. "If I'm going to be great, then I'm going to have to fight everybody. I want to fight everybody."

Even Dundee praised me after the fight.

"Tyson throws combinations I never saw before. I was stunned. I worked with Ali and Sugar Ray Leonard, but I'm seeing from Tyson a three-punch combination second to none. When have you seen a guy throw a right hand to the kidney, come up the middle with an uppercut, then throw a left hook?"

I didn't take that belt off that whole night. I wore it around the lobby of the hotel. I wore it to the after-party, and I wore it when I went out drinking later with Jay Bright, my roommate at Cus's house; Bobby Stewart's son; and Matthew Hilton, the fighter. We went to a dive bar in Vegas called The Landmark, across the street from the Hilton. Nobody was in there, but we just sat and drank all night. I was drinking vodka straight and I got truly smashed. At the end of the night, Matthew passed out and I went around to different girls' houses, showing them my championship belt. I didn't have sex with them, I just hung out with them for a while, and then I'd leave and call another girl and go over to her house and hang out. It was crazy. You have to understand that I was still only twenty years old. And when you think about it, a lot of my friends were only fifteen or sixteen. That wasn't a big difference at that age. Now all of a sudden, because I'm champion of the world, everyone expected me to be a totally together guy because of the title and what it represents. But I was just a little kid having fun.

And I was lost. By the time I won the belt I was truly a wrecked soul because I didn't have any guidance. I didn't have Cus. I had to win the belt for Cus. We were going to do that or else we were going to die. There wasn't any way I was leaving that ring without that belt. All that sacrifice, suffering, dedication, sacrifice, suffering. Day by day in every way. When I finally got back to my hotel room early that morning, I looked at myself in the mirror wearing that belt, and I realized that I had accomplished our mission. And now I was free.

But then I remembered reading something Lenin wrote in one of Cus's books. "Freedom is a very dangerous thing. We ration it very closely." That was a statement I should have taken into consideration in the years that followed.

5

"MY NAME IS MIKE TYSON. I'M A PROFESSIONAL FIGHTER. BOXING IS A LONELY sport. The sparring, the training, and especially the roadwork, give me plenty of time to think. One of the things I think about most is how bad drugs are and how much they hurt people. Well, we can get rid of drugs if each of us, one by one, decides to say 'No.' It's a small word with a big meaning. Say it, SAY NO TO DRUGS!"

That was a public service announcement I did for the Drug Enforcement Administration to be broadcast right before my first title defense in 1987. I also did PSAs for New York State. They showed me hitting a heavy bag and then turning to the camera. "That's right, stay off crack, so you can win."

The irony of all this is that while I was filming these spots, I was financing my friend Albert in his crack enterprise back in Brownsville. Right around the time that Cus died, I started giving Albert five thousand dollars here, twenty thousand there, just so that he didn't have to work for someone else. I wasn't a partner and I never wanted any return from my investment. I was just worried about his safety. Albert and I had grown up and robbed and stolen together. I didn't want him to worry if one of the dealers he was working for said, "Where's my shit?" The drug business in Brownsville in the '80s was like 1820s slavery. When you're working for these guys, your life meant nothing. If you had that man's package, you couldn't quit when you wanted to. Once you held that hand and made that deal, you were his property.

I thought about getting Albert to come to work with me. But guys like him were just too antisocial. They didn't believe in hanging out, carrying no bag, being a yes-man, kissing ass because I was champ. Nobody was going to be bossing him around. The only thing we knew was violence in Brownsville, even with people we love. Albert was much too hard-core to be part of my entourage. He wasn't going to do a Mike Tyson "Yes, ma'am, how are you doing? May I help you?" Guys like him would get angry and they'd have no control over their emotions. So rather I said, "Here. You take this money."

But my plan didn't work. A young Turk ready to get his meat shot Albert and a couple of my other friends in 1989. They were only twenty at that time and there was also a sixteen-year-old who wanted a piece of the dream. The Benz, the girls, and the status killed them. There was a lot of dying then. I paid for a lot of funerals.

I DID TWO THINGS RIGHT AWAY WHEN I WENT BACK TO NEW YORK AFTER WIN-ning the title. I went up to Catskill and showed my belt off everywhere. I wore it outside for three weeks, sometimes even sleeping with it on. One day I walked into the kitchen and told Jay Bright to come with me for a ride. There was one more person I wanted to show the belt to. I told Jay to drive to the liquor store and I gave him some money to buy a large magnum of Dom Pérignon champagne. Then I had him drive to Cus's grave. When we got to his stone, we were both crying. We both said a little prayer and then I popped the cork and we both took a big swig and then I poured the rest of the bottle on Cus's grave, left the empty bottle on the grass, and left.

The second thing I did was to go down to New Jersey and deal with my mom's grave. Her boyfriend Eddie had been hit by a car and died right before the Berbick fight, and he was buried next to my mother. So I had both of them exhumed and put into nice bronze caskets, and then I bought a massive seven-foot-tall headstone for her, so every time people came to the cemetery, they'd know that that was *the* Mike Tyson's mother there.

By that point, I had moved into my own apartment in Jimmy and Steve Lott's building. Probably so they could spy on me because I was their cash cow. I really wanted to enjoy being the champion. It was the first time we had ever set a goal and gone through all the blood, sweat, and tears to accomplish it. Now I could be mentioned in the same breath as Joe Louis and Ali. I wanted to bask in that, but I felt guilty and empty. Cus wasn't there to enjoy it with me or to give me direction. For the first time in years, I didn't have a goal or a desire to do anything. It might have been different if I had a companion or a child. All of my friends had kids by then. But I had been too busy fighting.

I also felt like a fake. Jimmy and Bill were intent on stripping away all the Brownsville from me and giving me a positive image. But Brownsville was who I was, my personality and my barometer. That was the important essence that Cus wanted me to keep. They had me doing those anti-drug messages and posing for posters for the NYPD but everyone knew I was a criminal. I had come from a detention home. Now all of a sudden I was a good guy? No, I was a fake fucking Uncle Tom nigga.

I felt like a trained monkey. Everything I did now was critiqued, everything had to be premeditated. I'd go on a talk show and they didn't want me to wear nice jewelry. Steve actually asked me to take off my matching gold bracelets. I didn't want to live with restrictions like that. I didn't become the heavyweight champ of the world to be a submissive nice guy.

Jimmy and Cayton wanted me to be another Joe Louis, not Ali or Sonny Liston. They wanted me to be a hero, but I wanted to be a villain. The villain is always remembered, even when he doesn't outshine the hero. Even though the hero kills him, he makes the hero the hero. The villain is immortal. Besides, I knew that Joe Louis's hero image was manufactured. In real life he liked to snort cocaine and screw lots of girls.

I wanted people bowing at my feet; I wanted people catering to me; I wanted to be chasing the women away from me. This was what Cus told me I would be doing, but I was not getting it. But it was supposed to be my time in the ring now. I was still sitting in the bleachers; they were not letting me in the ring.

When I moved into my apartment, Steve hooked me up with a great stereo system that cost about twelve grand, and he got shit from Jimmy for spending that much of my money on it. Later that year, we were walking through the Forum shops in Caesar's and I saw a watch.

"Use your card, get me that watch," I said.

"No fucking way," Steve said.

"Why not? You know I'll pay you back," I protested.

"No way, Jim will fucking kill me," he said.

It was then that my demons would tell me, "These white guys don't care about you like Cus."

I loved Jimmy, but he was always trying to keep me in line.

"Mike, you have to do this because if you don't, this multimillion-dollar company will sue us." So we had to do this fight or that commercial. I was still an immature kid. In the middle of shooting a commercial I'd say, "I don't want to do this shit. I want to go to Brownsville and hang out with my friends."

I went back to Brownsville almost every night that I wasn't in training. I got the royal treatment there. Literally. When my Jamaican friends would see my limo roll up, they'd take out their guns.

"They're shooting for you, Mike, twenty-one guns, nigga!" one of them would say.

And they'd give me a twenty-one-gun salute. Boom, boom, boom.

Sometimes I'd be walking down the street with a few friends and I'd see some guy who had bullied me years before. My friends didn't know I had a beef with this guy, but they could tell just by the way the cat was looking at me that there was no love between us.

"You know this motherfucker looking at you? Who's this bitch?" one of my friends would ask me.

I didn't have to answer.

"Who the fuck are you looking at, motherfucker?" my friend said. And it's on. They'd just crack him. I'd have to tell them to leave him alone.

Once I began making a lot of money boxing, I got a reputation as being a Robin Hood in the hood. People who didn't know me would make a big deal about me going back to Brownsville and giving my money away. But it wasn't like that. People who came from where I had come from had a responsibility to take care of their friends even if it was twenty years later. So if I went away and made this money and I went back I had to break off some for my friends who weren't doing as well. I would pick up cash from Cayton's office and divide the hundred-dollar bills into packets of a thousand dollars. I'd usually carry about twenty-five thousand in cash with me and would go around and distribute it to my friends when I'd see them. I'd tell them to go buy a tailored suit and then we'd go out that night.

I didn't even have to know the people who I gave money to. I'd stop my car and give out hundred-dollar bills to bums and homeless people. I'd gather up a bunch of street urchins and take them to Lester's Sporting Goods store and buy them all new sneakers. I later found out that Harry Houdini did the same thing when he started to make it. I guess that's what poor people who get rich real quick do. They don't feel like they deserve it. I felt that way sometimes, because I forgot how much hard work I had put into my career.

This was a really fucking downtrodden, drug-infested, gang-infested, sex-infested, filth-infested neighborhood. And you're from this cesspool, you know? Just giving them money and helping these people, it doesn't solve their problems, but it makes them happy.

Whenever I was handing out money, I'd be sure to go and track down all the old ladies who were my mother's friends. I'd be with a friend in the car and I'd drive to a certain project where I knew this one old lady lived and my friend would wait in the car and I'd get out and knock on her door and give her some cash. Then I'd do the same thing again and again. I didn't think that I was noble doing all this. That's what you're supposed to do. Maybe I believed that that was how

I could clean my sins and buy my way back to heaven. I guess I was looking for redemption.

I got down on myself a lot, but I always had friends in Brownsville who wouldn't let me go there. I'd sit there and complain how hard life was and this one guy, who I prefer not to name, would look at me.

"Oh, it's hard? Who did you kill lately, Mike? What house did you go into and tie everybody up, huh, Mike?"

Whenever I had something negative to say about myself, he'd say, "There's nothing bad about you, Mike. You're a good man. You don't escape where you come from because you have money now. If you weren't a good man, we would all have you in the trunk, Mike."

A lot of my friends from Brownsville wound up incarcerated in Coxsackie, which was not too far from Catskill. I had gone to school with most of the people who worked at the prison there, so when I'd go up there to visit my friends who were in jail, I wasn't going to the visiting room, I would hang out with them in their cells, because I knew the warden and all the guards. I gave my friends the shoes off my feet, the jewelry off my neck, and the guards were all looking the other way. One time, I was walking through the range, where the cells were, and I saw Little Spike from the Bronx who had been locked up with me in Spofford. Now he's not so little, he's a monster.

"Yo, Mike. What's up, man? What are you doing?" he shouted.

He thought I had been busted again and they were taking me to a cell.

I was living this crazy dual life. One day visiting friends in their prison cells, the next day hanging out with Rick James. I had met him a few times before but the first time we really spoke to each other was at an after-party for some new movie. We were at a big club, maybe a thousand people were there, but you're going to notice Rick James. He called me over.

"Hey Mike, get in this picture with us."

He was posing with Eddie Murphy and Sylvester Stallone. Right around then he had made a lot of money from Hammer sampling him on "U Can't Touch This," so Rick was back in business.

Next time I saw him I was in the lobby of a hotel on Sunset Boulevard. I was sitting outside with Ricky Schroder and Alfonso Ribeiro from *The Fresh Prince of Bel-Air*, just chilling. Ricky was probably seventeen then and Alfonso was maybe sixteen. But we're sitting there drinking, and I looked up and I saw a convertible Corniche Rolls-Royce pull up and Rick get out. He was wearing a loud shirt with a tie, but the tie wasn't tied and the shirt was unbuttoned. He came over to us, slapped me five, and then he looked at Alfonso, and then, boom, he hit him hard in the chest.

"Gimme that fucking beer," he said and grabbed Alfonso's beer.

"Rick, this is a kid, you can't hit this guy like that," I protested.

He just took that bottle and swigged from it.

"What's up, nigga?" he said to me.

Rick just didn't give a fuck. Eddie Murphy and his brother Charles told me a great Rick James story. He once was working on some music with Eddie and he was over at Eddie's house. I went in and Eddie came up to me.

"Mike, this nigga's put his feet on my chairs," Eddie said. He was complaining about Rick. Eddie had an immaculate house; everything had to be just right. And Rick was putting his smelly feet up on the chairs and they had asked him to stop, but Rick didn't give a shit.

"Fuck this. I can do what I want," he said.

So Charlie, Eddie's brother, went over to Rick.

"Motherfucker, this ain't no joke up here," he said and started choking Rick to restrain him.

That didn't go over too well with Rick. He got up and dusted himself off. And when Charlie turned his back to him, Rick called out.

"Hey, Charlie."

Charlie turned around and, POW, Rick hit him so hard that you could see the impression "RJ" from Rick's big diamond ring on Charlie's face.

The next day, I went back to Eddie's house and Eddie and Charlie were marveling over the fact that Prince and his guys had kicked their ass playing basketball. Prince had on his high-heel shoes and he was still hitting every bucket. Swoosh. Swoosh.

But if I had to credit one person for mentoring me in the ways of celebrityhood it has to be Anthony Michael Hall, of all people. When I was coming up in fame, before I became champ, I'd hang with him a lot. He was the man. He was the first guy I knew who had celeb money. And he was burning it up, man, with limos everywhere. He was so generous. So when I crashed my Caddy, I went out and bought a limo because I had seen how cool it was when we'd ride around in Michael's.

I used that limo to go to Eddie Murphy's New Year's Eve party in 1987 at his New Jersey mansion. It was a star-studded party with Al B. Sure!, Bobby Brown, Run-DMC, and Heavy D. I was cocky but I was still a little shy. But not too shy to pile three girls in the back of the limo and take them back to my apartment in Manhattan.

My days of abstinence were over. I was an extremist at everything I did, including sex. Once I started banging women, the floodgates opened. Short, tall, sophisticated, ugly, high-society, street girls, my criteria was breathing. But I still had no line and for the most part didn't know how to approach women.

When I went to Brownsville, I'd visit a childhood friend of mine who had become a pimp. We'd be sitting in his brand-new limo just talking and he'd suddenly stop and get out of the car.

"Go get the motherfucking trick," he'd yell at one of the girls congregating on the street. "You see that motherfucker on the corner? What are you doing bullshitting with these bitches?"

Then he'd get back in the car.

"These bitches need direction, Ike," he'd say. "They get distracted real quick. I need to get a seeing-eye dog to guide these bitches."

One time, I came to see him at four in the morning.

"What the fuck are you doing here, Mike?" he said.

I had never told him that I wanted to fuck some of his girls before, but he didn't even let me get it out of my mouth.

"Get the fuck out of here, Mike, all right? You are Mike Tyson. Don't be fucking these hos and nasty bitches."

Sometimes I'd be with my friends that I used to stick up places with. By then, they had their Mercedeses and were looking just as good as me. We were laughing, hanging out in a club, and a beautiful woman would walk by with a guy. I started talking to her and my guys would stand all around and block her man off. Oh, I ain't worth a damn. Stupid, ignorant, distinguished gorillas with guns. They're looking at this guy, like, *What the fuck are you doing, nigga?* Meanwhile, another guy is saying to the girl, "You'd better be nice to my motherfucking man or I'm gonna kill your fucking husband." That was the eighties. That's how people rolled back then in Brownsville.

I never talked to girls in Brownsville. They were scared of me because I was real crude when I was young and I had a nasty attitude back then. The girls in my neighborhood could always see through me. I didn't have enough game for them. So my friends would go, "Come here, baby, let me talk to you." It was easier to meet girls back in my white world. I'd meet them at photo shoots or when they'd interview me, or they'd be the model working with you on the shoot. Being the champ made me slightly more confident around women, but it also made the women a lot more aggressive. So that made me feel it was okay to do things. Like if they were hugging me, it made me feel that it was okay to grab their ass and kiss them because at twenty I still didn't know any better. I really believed that every women who approached me wanted to have sex with me. Before I was "Mike Tyson" nobody wanted anything to do with me. Since I wasn't particularly adept with women, if I slept with someone once, I'd try to see them again.

I still didn't have the tools to decipher women's intentions. Beautiful women would hit on me but I was such a smuck. Instead of saying, "Hey, let's go to my car" or "Let's go hook up in my apartment," I'd make plans to go to a movie with her the next day. Then I'd go home and jerk off thinking about her. I could have had her right there in the room. I should have just said, "Why don't you come over right now." I once was talking to a girl for hours and finally she said, "Hey, listen, I'm just going to get in this car and come over to your apartment." In my head I was going, *Thank God. Oh, thank God.* And I sprayed the deodorant thing even though my house looked good and I got my condoms and some porn movies out. Everything was ready. I was just so happy.

I'd be hanging out with older celebrities at Columbus and they'd see that girls would like me and they'd say, "Why don't you bring her over to my hotel and we'll have dinner?" They could see that I wasn't too cool with the girls. When girls started coming on to me at Columbus, I'd take them downstairs to where the bathrooms were. The place would be packed and they'd see us go down. And then when we came back up, the girl's back would be all dirty from the bathroom floor. And Paulie would go, "Yo, Mike. They're all coming up dirty."

Once I started, I couldn't stop. I got too self-indulgent. I'd have ten women hanging out in my hotel room in Vegas. When I had to go down for the press conference, I'd bring one and leave the rest in the room for when I was finished. Sometimes I'd get naked and put the championship belt on and have sex with a girl. Whenever there was a willing partner, I wanted to do it. The crazy part was that I was trying to satisfy each one of them. That was impossible; these ladies were nuts. After a while, I put together a Rolodex of girls in different cities. I had my Vegas girls, my L.A. girls, my Florida girls, my Detroit girls. Oh, man, why would I want to do that?

I just went totally off the track. I was burning the candle at both ends, training hard and partying just as hard as I was training— drinking, fucking, and fighting with these women all night. Just stupid selfish shit that you do when you're a young kid with some loot.

Around this time, I met a girl who was more than my match. I had been introduced to some people who were at the top of the fashion world. This wasn't Columbus, this was the real international jet-setting dining-with-royalty scene. I was going out with a model at the time but my friend Q got angry with her over some money. "Forget her, Mike. I am going to put you in touch with perhaps the most beautiful woman in the world. She's just a teenager now but she will be the highest-paid model soon. You better get with her now because she won't talk to anyone in a few years."

Q invited me to a party that this girl would be attending. It was at an exquisite apartment on Fifth Avenue. We're chilling and Q brings this model over to meet me. She was everything Q said she was, plus she had an amazing English accent. You could tell she was on top of her game. We started talking and she knew who I was and she seemed intrigued with me.

We had exchanged numbers, so the next day I looked for the piece of paper she gave me. I found it. She had written "Naomi Campbell" on it along with her number.

The next thing I knew, we were dating. We couldn't keep away from each other. She was a very passionate, physical kind of person. We actually had a lot in common. She was raised by a single parent. Her mother broke her ass to save enough money to send her to private schools in England. Naomi was a privileged little young lady all her life.

We fought a lot. I was always with other girls and she didn't like that. I don't think we were meant to be in a great love affair but we were two people who really liked being around each other. She was so focused on her career. She was just an awesome strong-willed person. And she'd fight for you. If I'd get in a scrap she'd be right alongside me, she wasn't afraid to fight. She wouldn't let anyone talk back about me either. She was just a little girl trying to find her way back then, both of us were really, and the world was devouring us. We didn't know anything about life then, or at least I didn't. But in a few years, she was on top of the world and no one could withstand her. She could have any man on the planet. Her presence was too strong. They had to give in.

But I wasn't ready to settle down with one woman. So besides the young ladies that I'd have casual sex with, I also started seeing Suzette Charles. Suzette was a runner-up to Miss America, who had stepped in and assumed the crown when Vanessa Williams had to give up her title when nude photographs of her were published in *Penthouse* magazine. Suzette was a very nice, mature girl, a few years older than me.

But what was I doing juggling all these women? I couldn't imagine doing that today. Go to somebody's house and by the time you get bored with them, you go to somebody else's house to spend time. And then at the end of the night, after visiting two or three women, you go home and you call somebody else to spend the night with you. That's a crazy lifestyle, but everyone I was around then was telling me it was normal, because I was hanging around celebrities who were doing the same thing as I was.

So in a short time I had gone from famine to feast with women. And then I added one more to the buffet. I met Robin Givens. I was in England in bed with this British chick and we had the television on in the background. They were showing *Soul Train* and I turned to look at the screen and there was this beautiful black girl on the show.

"Who's that girl?" I asked the British chick.

She didn't know, so I started watching closely and they said that the guest stars were the cast of *Head of the Class*. So I called my friend John Horne in L.A. and he called Robin's agent and we set up a dinner in L.A. when I got back to the States. I went with my friend Rory Holloway, an old friend from Catskill. We met at Le Dome, a nice restaurant on Sunset Boulevard. I was always late then, I thought that everybody should wait for me, but I should have known something was up when I walked into the restaurant and Robin was sitting there with her sister, her mother, and her publicist.

I also didn't know that Robin and her mother, Ruth, had been on the prowl for a big black celebrity for Robin since she graduated from college. I felt a strong sexual vibe from her, some sort of chemistry. She says that later that night the two of us were alone and that I fell asleep on her lap and drooled on her. I guess that's the way to win a woman over, drool on her.

After I saw her and her mother in operation mode, it struck me that her mother was a prolific stage mom, investing in her daughter so that she could be, or at least marry, somebody big. They somehow finagled their way onto Cosby's show and then wormed their way into staying at his house in L.A.

I certainly didn't want to put any money in her pocket, but to read Robin's account of our time together is like reading the worst romance/horror novel imaginable. In her description of the first days we spent together in L.A., she talks about a time when her mother and her sister had to go to Japan, and Robin and I would be alone.

"I don't know what you're trying to do or what this boy is all about,

I don't know who you are trying to hurt," her mother told her. "Sometimes I believe it's me, because you think I demand too much and other times I feel it's you yourself, because of your word, you can't live up to what I demand. But I do know one thing, when you play with fire, you're going to get burned, and mark my words, some things are just too dangerous to play with."

This shit sounds like a bad Lifetime movie. What her mother probably said was, "Let's get our hooks in this guy. This is what I've been training you to do for years. It didn't work with Eddie Murphy or Michael Jordan, so let's try this big black buck."

"Mom, what are you talking about?"

"I've worked too hard to have you throw it away on some . . ."

"Mom, we're just having fun. Don't you think I deserve to have some fun?"

Ruth the Ruthless was acting like I was some freeloader trying to get my hands on some of that *Head of the Class* money, which couldn't pay a month's worth of my rent. They had nothing until I came on the scene. They were two broke charlatans. They didn't own anything. They were just one big illusion.

In her book, Robin implied that we hadn't slept together, but I actually nailed her the first or second night when she came to my hotel. Instead she claimed that we strolled through the mall and played with puppies at pet shops for hours. Can you see me in a motherfucking mall, the heavyweight champ of the world? What the fuck am I doing in a mall?

The truth is I wasn't petting puppies with her, I was introducing her to heroin dealers. One night a few months later, we were walking in Manhattan on Sixth Avenue and Forty-first Street and we passed by Bryant Park and I saw this dope dealer who I knew from Brownsville. I walked over to him and slapped him five and Robin was blown away that I knew this guy. I'm sure she was mortified to be around someone like that, she was so artificial. At that time, she just wasn't comfortable being around normal everyday folk. But to me, the neighborhood heroin dealer was normal everyday people.

I had been out of action for over three months, the longest layoff in my career at that point. Action in the ring, that is. Now it was time to grab another belt. James "Bonecrusher" Smith was the WBA champion and I took him on in Vegas on March seventh.

I didn't go into the fight at 100 percent. I was suffering from a pinched nerve in my neck that would haunt me for years, so I was in a bit of pain. But I walked into the ring like I owned that place. I thought that the ring was my home and it was where I lived and I was totally comfortable in its circumference. But I still wasn't a seasoned fighter.

My ego was so out of whack then. I felt like John McEnroe. *Fuck you, who cares?* I had so much respect for him. He was a beast, and that was just how I felt. I felt entitled to anything concerning the boxing world, and if I wasn't getting it, then you were going to hear from me.

I went into the ring first. When Bonecrusher came in and we faced off, I didn't feel any threat at all. I knew I'd be too elusive and he wouldn't be able to hit me. He was a good strong fighter. He knocked out a lot of guys, but it was difficult for him to get to me.

The fight began and by the second round, Bonecrusher's strategy was obvious. He was going to hold me or backpedal away from me. The crowd started booing as early as the second round and at the end of that round, referee Mills Lane deducted a point from him for holding. I was happy that he was holding me because I was in such tremendous pain from my pinched nerve that it could have been an ugly night. I just couldn't get comfortable and I kept twitching from the pain the whole fight. My equilibrium was all messed up. He pretty much gave me an easy night off. The only time he connected was about ten seconds before the fight was over. I won every round.

I was criticized after that Bonecrusher fight, but what could I have done? He just didn't want to fight. When I was on the BBC shortly after the fight, I had to defend myself.

"We are all disappointed with the Bonecrusher fight and I guess you were too," the host said.

"I was fighting a very strong man but he just didn't come to fight. He held me so tight it was almost impossible for me to get loose. I couldn't believe it. He was fighting for the heavyweight championship of the world; this is the time to go all out and expose yourself," I said.

"We're impressed with your dignity in and out of the ring, but once or twice at the Bonecrusher fight you let that slip a bit between rounds," he said. He was referring to some scrums between the rounds.

"No, no, on the contrary. I was trying to pull him in to fight. I would have done anything. I would have tap-danced in the middle of the ring. I said, 'Come on, fight.' People were paying a thousand dollars for ringside tickets. You must entertain the public, give them their money's worth."

After the fight, I got a $750,000 advance from Nintendo to use my likeness for a boxing video game called *Mike Tyson's Punch-Out!!* I was never a video game kid so that didn't really excite me. I just wanted to fight, all that other stuff was foreign to me.

I started to feel alienated from everything with all this celebrity bullshit. And I had no one to talk with about it since Cus was gone. Alex Wallau interviewed me for ABC's *Wide World of Sports* and I said, "I used to keep a lot of things inside and Cus and I would talk about them. Now when those things come up, I just keep them inside." That's a sign of getting ready to lose it, right there.

I was coy when he asked me about the girl situation but he wouldn't let it go.

"Come on, you mean there aren't a ton of girls after the heavyweight champ of the world?"

"They don't want me, they want the cash. I look in the mirror every day and I know I'm not Clark Gable. I wish I could find a girl who knew me when I was broke and thought I was a nice guy. Cus never told me it would be like this, he told me I'd make a lot of money and I'd have a lot of girls and I was going to be happy. But he never told me life would be like this."

I was a misfit from Brownsville and all of a sudden I was getting all this adulation. It was crazy. And it was about to get crazier. I was falling in love with Robin. I remember the exact moment too.

We were walking down Wilshire Boulevard in Westwood. Robin

was teasing me about something and she hit me and took off. I ran after her and just as I was about to catch up to her, she made a quick lateral move, and I just kept on and I fell down and I literally slid across the street like I was sliding into home plate. There were cars coming but I was going so fast it looked like I was shot out of a sling-shot. As my slide came to an end, I maneuvered myself into my best B-boy pose. I had on these really expensive clothes and they were completely shredded from that slide. I was so embarrassed but I kept the pose. I lay there talking to her for a few seconds as if nothing had just happened. Robin was standing there laughing. She thought it was the funniest thing she had ever seen. Then I fell in love with her. Later I realized that this little incident was a metaphor for our whole rela-tionship. She teased me, she made an elusive move, and I played right into her hands. It was chess and I was her pawn.

But how could I have expected to be sophisticated in these matters of the heart? Robin was my first real relationship, except for Naomi who, by the way, was pissed when she found out about Robin. Before that, it was just juggling a lot of girls I was fucking and telling a lot of lies. That's why I don't lie anymore—because I was so good at it. It's probably also why I used to work so hard to degrade myself. I couldn't take being the big fish and having everyone talk nice about me. That made me feel uncomfortable because of my low self-esteem. It got to be overbearing and I had to berate myself and cut myself down. Every-body was saying so many good things about me that it fucked my head up. Hey, let's get some balance. It's not like I was a fucking saint. I shot at people. My social skills consisted of putting a guy in a coma. If I did that, I might get a good pasta meal. That's how Cus programmed me. Every time you fight and win, you get rewarded.

So maybe Robin was just what the doctor ordered. A manipulative shrew who could bring me to my knees. I was like a fucking trained puppy dog around her. "That's okay, please, please, you can steal my money, but don't take the pussy away, please, please." Don't get me wrong. It wasn't just about sex. I think I got off most on the intimacy. I don't even think I was very good sexually then. I heard her once say that I was good in bed but I don't agree. I was just a young guy in love. I had never had that feeling before.

I was back in the ring in May. My next opponent was Pinklon Thomas, who was a great fighter. We had a press conference before the fight. I was up on the stage and I saw Robin come in with some of her fellow actors from her sitcom and I was ecstatic. I was flossing, posing for pictures, just happy. Now, that was a departure for me because I was never happy at these press conferences, I always had that ugly look on my face. The press was confused.

"What happened to Tyson?" one of the reporters said. And then they turned around and saw Robin there and put two and two together.

"No wonder why he's so happy," somebody else said.

Once they said that, it was on. Pinklon came over to shake my hand and I went into Iron Mike mode. "Suck my dick," I told him.

"Oh, you're going to be like that? To hell with you," he said.

"You dumb ignorant nigga. Don't you know I'm a god? You should be on your knees sucking my dick right now for me giving you this opportunity to fight me," I came back. Today I'm just so embarrassed that I ever said something like that to a grown man.

I was hoping that Robin didn't hear that. Holy shit, the minute she came into that room, she had taken me off my square. There I was, jumping off the stage, going over to her and the cast in my cool hip nonthreatening black man persona.

"Hi, guys. How are you all doing?"

That's the phony shit that Cus was talking about. So I had to go back and forth between my megalomaniac shit and my nonthreatening shit and it was confusing even me. It's hard trying to be two motherfuckers at once in one place.

"You motherfucker, I'm going to kill you, nigga." "So how are you doing, my love?"

I was defending my two belts that night, so I was psyched but I wasn't overconfident. Pinklon was a former champion only beaten once by Trevor Berbick and that was a fluke. I got off good that night and almost knocked him out in the first round. But in the second, third, fourth, and fifth he was coming back. He probably won a few of those rounds. He had a masterful, hard jab, but he was just tap, tap, tapping, and getting points.

Between the fifth and sixth rounds, Kevin got on me in the corner.

"Are we going to fight or are we going to bullshit, huh? Fight or bullshit."

I told Kevin that Thomas was getting tired right before the sixth round.

In the sixth I got off a devastating left hook that exploded on his chin, but he was such a disciplined and composed fighter that he acted like it didn't faze him. But I had watched all the great fighters, Robinson, Marciano, I knew that if I hit you right, you're hurt. I don't care how much of a poker face you have on. So I just threw everything I had at him, maybe a fifteen-punch barrage, and I came up with that resounding knockout. He was knocked-out cold and once he fell onto the floor, he was so gutsy he tried to get up. But I saw the pain on his face and I knew he wouldn't make it. That might have been the most vicious knockout of my career. It was like hitting the heavy bag, I wasn't worried about anything incoming. Just think about how much character he exhibited. All that pain on his face and he's still trying to get up. I thought, *Damn. You want some more?*

Even though I won the fight with a masterful knockout, I wasn't pleased with my overall performance, and I began questioning the fights that Jimmy and Cayton were lining up for me. Cus wanted to work with me on certain things before he died. But these guys didn't care, they just threw me in with anyone. Cus might have thought that the Pinklon match was too soon and he might have put me in with someone else. I didn't look good that fight even though the knockout was resounding. Cus would have been angry with me. But I didn't have that anymore. I didn't have to worry about somebody ripping my fucking ass out in the dressing room if he didn't like what I was doing. I didn't have to listen to anybody. You know how easy it is to relax when you don't have to give a fuck?

After the Thomas fight, I had more time to spend with Robin. We had sex, but it wasn't passionate. She's not the type to be sucking on your toes and all that shit. She's pragmatic. But I just thought she was an adorable girl. Until she caught me cheating. I was constantly cheating on her and constantly getting caught. I wasn't too suave. She'd see lipstick on the crotch of my sweatpants.

Then it was on.

"Fuck you. How could you do this? Aggghh," she'd scream and charge me, throwing punches and trying to kick me in the balls. She was relentless. I'd get frustrated and I'd slap her and figure that would end things, but it didn't. She'd fight back harder. She wasn't a Brownsville girl, she was a suburban girl, but don't underestimate her. She had been in a few fights. These moments reminded me of my mother's dysfunctional relationships with men.

The truth is I was sick of fighting. I was sick of fighting with Robin and I was sick of fighting in the ring. The stress of being the world's champ and having to prove myself over and over just got to me. I had been doing that shit since I was thirteen. And it wasn't just the time I spent in the ring. Whether it was during a fight or in camp sparring, I had always fought guys who were more experienced than me. Normally when you see a champion sparring somebody or even fighting someone, he's fighting somebody who is inferior to him who he can handle with ease. But my sparring partners were constantly trying to hurt me. That was their instruction. If they didn't do that, they'd be sent home. When you start training, you're scared. You ain't going to go out and play and party because you know you have to fight this guy and the last time he gave you a fucking headache. You're not going to go outside to the bar around the corner and visit no girl. You're going home, you go in the tub, you're going to concentrate on how you are going to box this guy the next day. That was my life and I was tired of it.

I've always been a depressed kind of person, but this stress was just making it worse. I was moody all the time. I had to go right back into the ring the first day of August, so I had to start training with hardly a break. I got to camp in Vegas and I got homesick. I missed hanging out and partying in Albany with Rory and my other friends. It came to a head a little more than a month before the Tony Tucker fight. This was going to be the biggest fight of my career, the fight to unify all three titles.

I pulled Steve Lott aside one day in the gym.

"I'm going to retire," I said.

The pressure was getting to me. Big clumps of my hair were falling out from alopecia, a nervous condition. I didn't even care if I got a third belt. Robin wasn't exactly an anchor of stability for me; we were always fighting and temporarily breaking up. I was stressed out just from walking down the street. Guys would come up to me and say that they had bet their lives on me and I had to win or else they'd lose their house and their wife would leave them. I didn't want to let those people down.

I guess I just never thought I was good enough for the job. I was too insecure to be that dominant person. Between fights I was going to these really bucket-of-blood places, in the middle of Bumfuck, Florida, and I'm strutting in there and all these motherfuckers got their guns up. And I'm talking shit and starting fights. I've got all these diamonds on me, they should have beaten my ass and robbed me. They could have killed my fucking ass. Praise be to Allah that these people never killed me. You could put me in any city in any country and I'd gravitate to the darkest cesspool. Sometimes I'd go alone with no security. But I never got shot, never got stuck up. I always felt safest when I was in the hood. People would always ask me, "Mike, you ain't scared down there?" I'd say, "Shit, I'm scared on the Vegas strip." I was just so at home there. I'd see a lady and her kids out late at night in the freezing cold and it reminded me of my mother and me.

So about a month before the Tucker fight I disappeared from camp and went to Albany and started partying. I partied for two weeks straight. I told my friends at a nightclub that I was retiring. But Jimmy got me on the phone and started threatening me. Everyone would sue us if I didn't make the fight. I should have retired then, but I didn't have control of my own life. What did those guys know about my life? Jimmy thought that Robin might be good for me, that she'd settle me down. I guess that Robin was a better deceiver than Jim was.

I got back to training about two weeks before the fight. I had been partying hard in Albany and I never got into real tip-top shape. In the first round, Tucker hit me with an uppercut that backed me up. Everybody made a big deal about it, but I didn't feel it at all. It was just me making a mistake. In the fourth round, I took control of the fight and I won almost every round after. The fight went the distance. While we were waiting for the decision, Tucker came over to Rooney and me.

"You're a damned good fighter. Don't worry, I'll give you a chance to fight me again," he said.

"You think you won?" Rooney said. "Get the fuck out of here."

Then Tony started praising Jesus. But it didn't help. I won a unanimous decision but I didn't feel good about it. I didn't feel good about anything at that point in my life. Larry Merchant must have picked up on that while he was interviewing me on HBO after the fight.

"For a guy who just won the undisputed championship of the world, you'd think you'd be a little happier."

"As long as you make mistakes, you don't have the means to be happy," I said. "I'm a perfectionist and I want to be perfect."

After the fight, Don King threw a hokey "coronation" to celebrate me winning the unified title. I didn't even want to go to it, but Jimmy told me it was part of doing business so I attended. I felt like I was a piece of a freak show. Chuck Hull, the ring announcer, had changed into a medieval English costume. He was surrounded by six mock Beefeater trumpeters wearing Elizabethan blue-velvet costumes with feathered caps. They paraded my two "victims" down a red carpet, "Sir Bonecrusher" and "Sir Pinky." Then Hull spoke.

"Hear ye, hear ye! By order of the people of the world of boxing, in this glorious year of nineteen hundred and eighty-seven, it is hereby proclaimed that in lands near and far, one man above all others shall stand triumphant in the four-corner-square ring of battle, hereby trumpeted as the ultimate world heavyweight champion."

Then Don King gave one of his typical wild shit speeches. He just wanted to be more famous than the fighters. Then they paraded all the HBO executives and the fight promoters down the red carpet. A children's choir sang. They got celebs like Dennis Hopper and Philip Michael Thomas to hand out trophies to every minor functionary there. When it was my friend Eddie Murphy's turn to hand out a trophy, he ad-libbed, "The man whipped everyone's butt and he ain't got a trophy. All the white men got trophies. I don't understand."

They were saving the best for last. They put a chinchilla robe from Le Nobel furriers around me, then they had Ali place a jeweled crown on my head, studded with "baubles, rubies, and fabulous doodads," King said. They gave me a jeweled necklace and a jeweled scepter from Felix the Jeweler.

"Long live the heavyweight king!" Don screamed. I felt like a circus clown. Then they asked me to give a speech. What the fuck could I say?

"Does this mean I'm going to get paid bigger purses?" I cracked. "Pleasure to be here. I came a long way. I look forward to defending the title as long as I can." I felt like such a smuck.

I had extra motivation for my next fight. I was going to fight Tyrell Biggs in Atlantic City on October sixteenth. I was still jealous of him having a gold medal from the Olympics when I was shut out. Now the boxing writers started turning on me. They were writing shit about Biggs being able to beat me. Wally Matthews of Long Island's *Newsday* wrote, "There are doubts about how good Mike Tyson really is." They thought that my extracurricular activities outside of the ring might be stunting my growth.

A week before the fight, I got interviewed about it.

"I never really hated anybody. I think I hate Tyrell Biggs," I said. "I want to give him a good lesson, I want to hurt him real bad." What I really meant was that I wanted to fuck up the darling of America. I wanted to be the villain, but that didn't mean I didn't want my gold medal. Plus, Biggs had dissed me at an airport once. We were flying together to the Olympics in L.A. He was going to fight and I was just going to observe and have a good time. Some fan came up to us. "Good luck at the Olympics," he told us both.

"What? You mean on this flight, not his fight. He's not fighting at the Olympics," Biggs said.

Shit like that stayed with me then. I trained so hard. I was motivated to kick his ass. I don't even like talking about this fight. It was seven rounds of heartless punishment. I elbowed him, low-blowed him, punched him after the round was over. That was my dark, stupid, ignorant side, my side that I'm ashamed of, coming out. I prolonged the punishment over seven rounds. I was a young, insecure kid and I wanted to be special at someone else's expense.

"I could have knocked him out in the third round, but I did it very slowly. I wanted him to remember it for a long time," I told the reporters after the fight. "When I was hitting him in the body, he was making noises like a woman screaming."

I was just being a jerk. I did hear him make some hurt noises but he wasn't screaming.

I had a personal stake in the fight after that too. Cus and I had been talking since I was fourteen about beating Larry Holmes. He had given me a blueprint—hit him with the right, behind my jab. I thought I would become part of boxing history by taking Holmes out and avenging my hero Ali's defeat, like Sugar Ray Robinson avenged Henry Armstrong by beating Fritzie Zivic.

Three weeks before the fight, Kevin gave me a warning.

"Holmes is a better fighter than Biggs and you trained harder for Biggs than you're training for this," he told me. "You better step it up."

So I did.

I went to the prefight press conference but I was bored. I always hated those things. Sometimes I'd even fall asleep at them. There was nothing I wanted to hear. I just wanted to fight; I didn't want to go through all of that stuff. Don King would be talking all this bullshit and gibberish, making up these fake fucking words. "The matrimony of fisticufftis and delishmushnisifice of illumination, critation and emancipation." Who wanted to hear that shit?

But at this press conference, I decided to snub Holmes. I was very offensive. So Holmes got arrogant.

"I'm going down in history, not Mike Tyson, he's going down in history as a son of a bitch. If he do happen to win the fight, down the line he'll destroy himself." I guess he was Nostradamus that day.

We broke all records for ticket sales. All the celebs were there—Jack Nicholson, Barbra Streisand, Don Johnson, Kirk Douglas.

I got so wound up warming up in my dressing room that I literally punched a hole in the wall. I'm just an animal sometimes. I turn from a rational to an irrational person in a tenth of a second. I think about being bullied as a kid and having my money taken from me. I didn't intend to put my hand through the wall, but I hit it a good shot. I had been warming up and I knew the wall was pretty solid. I was hitting it, pow, pow, pow, and then, boom! My hand went right through it.

I had quite a few girlfriends at the fight. Robin was there and so was Suzette Charles. But I was sneaky enough to get other girls in too without my management even knowing. I'd get two tickets for this dude, but his daughter was my girl. Another one came with her brother. I was devious.

I made my entrance without music. I was all business. They brought Ali into the ring to wave to the audience. He came over to my corner. "Get him," he said.

The bell rang and we went at it. I was beating Holmes every round. He hadn't trained enough, so he was scared to throw a punch. In the fourth round, I was on the ropes and the referee said, "Break." As soon as he said that, I threw that two-punch combination that Cus used to talk about. POW, POW, and he went down. He got back up but he was hurt. All I had to do was touch him, I didn't even have to hit him on the chin, he was going down. I was going full speed ahead and he was avoiding most of the punches. He was very difficult to hit because his arms were so long he could catch your punches in the air. But then he made the mistake of throwing an uppercut and he got caught in the rope and, BAM, I knocked him out. I tried to help him up but his corner wouldn't let me near him.

So I leaned in and said, "You're a great fighter. Thank you."

"You're a great fighter too, but fuck you," he said back to me.

"Fuck you too, motherfucker," I said.

At the post press conference I was very modest.

"If he was at his best, I couldn't have stood a chance," I said. I hadn't turned over a new leaf and become humble overnight. I was quoting Fritzie Zivic, the great champion, who said that after he beat Henry Armstrong. You'll notice that I'm always quoting my heroes, it's never me talking.

After the fight I was honored to have Barbra Streisand and Don Johnson visit me in my dressing room. I loved Barbra. She was from Brooklyn too.

"I think your nose is very sexy, Barbra," I told her.

"Thank you, Mike," she said.

Can you imagine me, a twenty-one-year-old kid, living my dreams like this? Barbra Fucking Streisand coming to my dressing room to see me? Cus always told me that anything I ever saw on TV I could have. And that included women. Robin wasn't the only girl I met like that. If I wanted some exotic car I could call any place in the world and they'd custom design it for me and put it on a boat and ship it to me.

That's the way I started getting my clothes. Besides the great old fighters, I used to use the tough Jewish gangsters as role models. Guys like me who had no core identity would emulate other people's lives. If I read that Joe Louis loved champagne, I started drinking champagne.

I was enjoying the perks of fame. I'd see a beautiful girl and I'd say, "Hey, come here, talk to me, do you like this car?" It might have been a Mercedes. And she would say something like, "Wow, this is a beautiful car."

"Do you really believe this is a beautiful car?"

"Oh, man, I would love to have a car like that," she'd say.

"And I would love to have you. I think a fair exchange is operative, right? Come with me."

It worked every time.

When I wasn't training, I'd wake up and open up a bottle of champagne and order up some caviar, some lox, some egg whites. I'd have one or two beautiful women in the bed and I'd put some Billie Holiday on the stereo. I was living in a fantasy world. I never had to wait in line to get into a restaurant or a club. I'd date beautiful models, hang out with the jet-setters. This was the world Cus wanted me to be part of. But he also wanted me to hate the people in that world. No wonder I was so confused.

After a while, the perks of fame began receding and the magnitude of my renown became a burden. I'll never forget one time when I was just starting my professional career, I was hanging out with Pete Hamill and José Torres. Pete said, "Let's go for a walk."

So we bought some ice cream and walked up Columbus Avenue.

"Enjoy this now, Mike," Pete said. "Because soon you're not going to be able to do this anymore."

Now I couldn't go out without getting mobbed. I might sneak out to a club before one of my fights and the people in the club would start busting me.

"What the fuck are you doing here, Mike?" they'd say. "We're going to see you next week, motherfucker. You'd better win. I can't believe your ass is not in training."

I might see a pretty girl there and I'd ask some guy, "Who is that girl?"

"Fuck that bitch, Mike," the guy said. "I don't know who she is, but I'll bring her to the fight. Just go train, nigga."

It was worse when I'd be on the streets of Brownsville. A lot of guys there had no control over their emotions and they took the notion of disrespect very seriously. I'd be standing there with some guys and some stranger would come up to me.

"Hey, what's up, man?" he'd say all friendly.

I'd do that white shit, "Hey, how are you doing?" but one of my friends would freak.

"Hey, Mike, you know him?"

"Nah."

"What the fuck you talking to him for?"

They didn't like to see no man suck up to another man. They'd tell someone who came up to us, "Get the fuck away from him. Leave him alone."

People in Brownsville didn't like their space being invaded. That's bad news in the hood, but that's par for the course when you're a celebrity. So I was at war with myself, my own instincts. I was uncomfortable in my skin, as the rehab people say. Sometimes it got ugly too. More than once, I'd be in a bad mood and an obsessive fan would follow me around.

"I love you, Mike. Can I get an autograph?" he'd say.

"Get the fuck away from me you fucking freak," I'd say and kick his ass. To be honest, I wasn't meant to be a famous guy.

When I recount these stories, I can't believe what a disrespectful ignorant monster I was then. All that fame shit just makes you feel hollow if you're not grounded. Add to that the boozing and the girls and it all began to affect my performance. Guys who I should have been able to knock out in one round would go five, six, sometimes the distance. There was no way that someone could be a sexual Tyrannosaurus and the world's champion. You have to willingly surrender one of them. You could have sex at any age, but you can't always be a world-class athlete. But I stuck with the sex.

I was just a miserable person then. I couldn't understand why anyone would want to be with me. *I* didn't want to be with me. I think that my mother handed down her depression to me. I didn't know what I was doing when I was the champion. I just wanted to be like my old heroes. I didn't care if I was going to die tomorrow. I had read a book about Alexander the Great when I was younger. He would rather have a few years of glory than a lifetime of obscurity. So what did I care if I died? I never had no fucking life, what did I have to look forward to?

I had everything I wanted, but I wasn't happy within myself. The outside world wasn't making me happy anymore. I didn't know how to get it from the inside, because happiness, as I realized later, is an inside job. So in this state of despair I did the last thing I should have done. I got married.

I got married to Robin because she was pregnant and I was thrilled to become a father. That's the only reason. The problem was that Robin didn't tell me she was pregnant. Jimmy Jacobs did. And he found out when Ruth, Robin's mother, called him to tell him. I didn't know it at the time, of course, but it was all bullshit. Robin was never pregnant. It should have been a tip-off that the woman I was sleeping with didn't even tell me herself. Everything about these two women was fugazi. Robin told the world that she had dropped out of Harvard Medical School to pursue an acting career, but when some reporters actually went to check, they found that her name never showed up in their records. I don't care how much you claim to love someone, when you lie it will always come back to haunt you. That's what Robin and her mother were. Confidence people, con artists, borderline prostitutes. Ruth publicly sued the great Yankee Dave Winfield for giving her herpes. And you know something ain't right when you get up at your own college graduation and get booed by all of your 129 classmates like Robin did.

I didn't know nothing about lying about being pregnant. I didn't know that kind of stuff went on. I tried to do the honorable thing, but it was the smuck thing. I was El Smucko. Maybe I should have been a dick, like the rest of the black men. No way, Jose. You remember the old *Maury Povich Show* when the ladies accuse the guy and say, "You are the father of this child"? I should have said, "Naw, see you on Maury." But I wasn't that guy. I was the guy who put diamonds under her pillow, but even that wasn't enough to satisfy her. So when we were at the NBA All-Star game in Chicago in February of 1988, I took her to the house of this priest I knew and had him marry us on the spot. I didn't even ask her if she wanted to get married, it was just an impulsive thing. She played coy and I had to give her a little light-weight intimidation, at least that's what I thought, and then she agreed and Father Clements married us in the hallway of his house and then we went to my friend's club to celebrate.

When we got back to New York, Ruth had already called Jimmy and threatened that she was going to fly us to Vegas to get married unless we were immediately legally married in New York. Jimmy wanted to delay it so we could sign a prenup but I was so smitten that I didn't care about any prenup. So we went to City Hall, got a license, and got legally married. Right away, Ruth started talking about finding a suitable mansion for the three of us to live in. Robin had always told me that she and her mother came as a package, but there was always something really strange about her relationship with her mother. It was too bizarre for even the Freud people to contemplate. They didn't have a word for it. Robin wasn't the right sex to have an Oedipus complex. I just think she had a Herdipus complex.

6

AROUND THIS TIME I MET THE LEGENDARY WORLD-FAMOUS PIMP/AUTHOR
Iceberg Slim. I wish I had met him before I married Robin. He would
have set my ass straight. I was out in L.A. one night at a club and I
ran into Leon Isaac Kennedy. We were talking and he nonchalantly
mentioned that Iceberg had told him something.

"Excuse me, do you mean Iceberg Slim the writer?" I said.

Leon told me he was his friend, and I couldn't believe it. I thought
Iceberg was a mythical character. He had gotten his name because he
was sitting in his favorite bar, high on cocaine, when someone shot at
the guy next to him. The bullet grazed his friend and then went right
through Slim's hat. But he didn't flinch, he just took his hat off and
inspected the entry and exit holes. His friends thought that he was so
cool he should be named Iceberg.

So I told Leon that I wanted to meet him and he picked me up the
next day and we drove to Iceberg's apartment. He was living in a
shitty little pad in the rough part of Crenshaw. He was in his seven-

ties and he was living alone. I sat down and talked with him for seven hours straight. We talked about his life and his books. I thought that he would talk like a crude street guy but he was very erudite and spoke nobly. He enunciated each syllable precisely. I was thinking that he became a self-educated man when he was in prison, that he just learned these words from a dictionary. But I later learned that he had gone to college first before he went into the life. He showed me his baby and childhood pictures and he was just a cute, lovable little kid. Berg was an extremely interesting character. You never would have thought you were talking to someone so steeped in the world of vice.

The first thing that I asked him was if he was the best pimp out there.

"No, I was nowhere near the best pimp. It's just that I was educated and I knew how to read and write and put these stories together. And that's all probably that I had. Those other guys were monsters," he said.

He told me a lot of stories of his escapades, but he was at a point in his life where he wasn't proud of them. When he got older, he had daughters, so he didn't play the game anymore. But when he had been in the life, he was brutal to his girls. I found out later that he had used the pimp stick that his mentor had invented. He'd bend a clothes hanger and put it on a hot stove and beat his hos with it. He was the guy who, if it was raining out, told his girls, "Bitch, you had better walk between the raindrops and get my money. And don't get wet."

Berg wasn't a happy, smiley kind of guy, and he wasn't even excited that I had come to see him. I think that he thought that was the way it was supposed to be. He was the Mack. When you look at these pimps with their high heels and their funny-colored suits and stuff, we think they're clowns, but their confidence is sky-high. We don't understand how they get these girls to do what they do, but it's all in the confidence. We laugh at these guys, but we envy them. How do these guys get this kind of control, to make these women do this stuff and then get money for doing it?

I kept making pilgrimages out to see Iceberg. I even invited him to see me fight but that would have been too much for him. Back in the day he was an immaculate dresser. He was one of the first guys to wear the ascots. He was the first nigga with French cuffs. But if he was to show up at one of my fights, he told me that he would have had to get his old leather suit out and he didn't want to bother with that. He was very much into his brand. People expected him to look a certain way. "I got to be in my leather pants and I don't feel like doing that," he said. I respectfully told him that I would buy him whatever he wanted, but he was a classy guy and he refused my offer.

I once brought Don King, Rory, and John Horne to see Iceberg. Slim was in his pajamas in bed and we sat like little schoolkids at his feet on a raggedy old couch. We were paying homage to Berg, so if we wanted to talk we had to raise our hands. "Excuse me, Mr. Berg," and then we'd ask him a question. That must have been killing Don's arrogant ass to have to raise his hand and get called on.

One time, I raised my hand.

"Mr. Berg, what's this macking shit? Does that mean if I can control a girl and make her do what I want her to do, that's macking?"

"No, that's not macking," Berg replied slowly. "Macking is when you're in control of all your elements, like right here. I know everything that is happening. Macking has nothing to do with the woman. The macking pulls in the woman, attracts the woman, then she knows what to do. In order for the macking to attract her, she has to be in the life. They're magnetized; it's magnetizing macking. It ain't about no making girls do what you want them to do, she knows what to do. They're automatically in the life, they're attracted to the magnetizing of the macking and then that's just it, everything is just opening up for you. They're bringing you money, everything is happening. All this you hear about these young guys saying what they're doing and who they're beating. That's not right. The woman chooses; this is by choice, not by force."

We're listening to this and thinking, *What the fuck?* I had to ask Don if this was the real guy. I was just taking Leon's word. But Don was in the same demographic so he confirmed that that was the real Iceberg.

Even in his pajamas, you could sense his charisma. He knew that we were there to pay homage to him and get an education. We had thousands and thousands of dollars' worth of custom-made clothing on, carrying our finest leather bags, and he wasn't impressed by us in the smallest bit. He expected us to be there.

It used to be that before we would go out to a club to hang out and get some girls, we'd go visit Berg and get his blessings.

"What's up, Berg? We're going out tonight," I'd say.

"Well, just be careful, young man. Don't be out there letting these girls touch you. I know you're famous and it's hard for you, you'll probably let these girls touch you. You can't do that, son. You tell them, 'Hey, hey, get your hands off me. What's your pedigree, baby? Where's your man at? Don't handle me like that, baby, please.' You got them all touching you and you're laughing and smiling, Mike, that's not the way to go. I understand you're in that beautiful-people life, Mike, but you can't have these women handling you like that. What's wrong with you man, are you a freak? You should be telling them, 'I could choose you, but I want to see your man first.' Is he of the top caliber? You have to see her pedigree. If she's with a knuckleheaded two-dollar sneaker pimp, you can't mess with her."

Berg seemed content in his situation. There was nothing about him that made me feel that he was insecure. He lived in a dilapidated apartment building that was worth maybe fifty thousand dollars and I was a millionaire. I was carrying more cash in my bag than Berg's whole building was worth. But we were paying homage to him. Before we left that day, I told Don to give Berg some money. He broke off about 10K.

Another day Iceberg began lecturing me.

"Mike, you're a very dangerous kind of guy. You're going to leave here and have women problems all your life, because you'll just fuck anything. And then you want to give them all full speed ahead, you want to give them all everything you got. You just will always have women problems, boy. I see you're into satisfying every woman and you're going to lose at that every time. You let them invade your mind. You're not a lovey-dovey guy, you've got to stick and move since you're too emotional with women. You're going to always have some kind of connection with them or they're going to have some connection with you, because you have to satisfy that feeling. And that's very dangerous. Dangerous to yourself. You put that pressure on yourself, you don't feel good, you don't satisfy the woman. That's a problem with your mother. There's some connection that you had with your mother."

Berg was getting sick and he was getting ready to die. He told me that he wanted one of those coffins that goes in the wall, above the ground, so that the bugs and the roaches wouldn't get him.

"Now listen, Mike, I don't want to be in the ground, I want to be in the wall. I don't want the roaches and bugs eating me up. I'm beautiful, Mike. I don't want them eating my eyes. I gave too much to the world, Mike."

That's just how arrogant pimps are. A pimp wants to be able to go to his own funeral to see who came. He don't care that he's dead, he just wants to know that the whole world came.

So I gave him twenty-five thousand dollars in cash from my bag and politely said, "Bergie, man, don't worry about it. This is for the walls." Iceberg took the money and said, "Wow, man." But he never once said "Thank you." That's why I loved him. He kept it real until the end. I think he expected me to say "Thank you" for giving him my money. Most pimps don't care about anyone but I knew he did. If I didn't think he was a good person I would never have given him the cash.

ABOUT A WEEK AFTER ROBIN AND I GOT MARRIED, I WAS ASLEEP IN CATSKILL. When I woke up, I saw there was some snow on the ground, so I called Bill Cayton to tell him that I couldn't make it into the city. He had wanted me to sign a new managerial contract that had been changed to state that if either Jim or Bill died, their wives would get their share of the proceeds. That seemed innocuous enough but alarms should have gone off in my head when Bill got the police commissioner of Albany to send a marked police car to drive me to the city. They wanted that thing signed awfully bad.

Jimmy and Bill were there along with José Torres. José was getting canned as the commissioner of boxing in New York, but I guess he was there to help out his friends Jimmy and Bill.

My next fight was with Tony Tubbs in Japan. If I thought I was getting the celebrity treatment in the States, Japan was totally over the top. There was mass hysteria when my plane landed and I was engulfed by thousands of screaming fans. We were the first attraction at the Tokyo Dome, a new stadium that held sixty-five thousand fans and within an hour of the tickets going on sale, we had sold 80 percent of them. The Japanese promoter, Mr. Honda, had handpicked Tony Tubbs as my opponent because he thought that he had the best shot at prolonging the fight into the later rounds and satisfying the audience. Don King had even promised Tony a $50,000 bonus if he came in at under 235 pounds. But Tony was battling some demons then and he couldn't make weight.

Robin joined me in Tokyo and Larry Merchant interviewed her right before the fight.

"Inquiring minds want to know: How does a woman who went to Sarah Lawrence College and Harvard Medical School wind up falling in love with a guy who's a graduate of the school of hard knocks?" he asked.

"God, I want to know too. We have a lot in common. Traditional families. It was sort of love at first sight. It was hard at the beginning but we got through it and we got married."

Traditional families? Yeah, traditional for Iceberg Slim, maybe. But Robin loved the attention.

The fight didn't last long. I felt Tubbs out in the first round and I was pleased to see that he wasn't trying to clinch. It would have been hard for him to run at that weight. In the second round we actually traded punches and I stunned him with a left to the temple. Then I unloaded some vicious blows to the body and when he came off the ropes, I knocked him out with a left hook.

When Larry Merchant interviewed me after the fight, I was my usual megalomaniac self.

"I refuse to be hurt, to be knocked down. I refuse to lose!"

On the plane ride back to New York, Robin began throwing her weight around. She cornered Bill Cayton and according to him said, "I'm Mrs. Mike Tyson and I'm taking over." She demanded to see all the paperwork concerning my agreements with Bill and Jim. If she wanted to see the books, it was fine with me. If Jimmy had been there, I'm sure the situation would have been handled more smoothly. He was much more of a people person than Bill. But Jimmy had to miss the fight because he was in a hospital in New York. He had lied to me and told me that he couldn't attend the fight because he was trying to locate some rare film footage of black boxers from the turn of the century.

Nobody had told me that Jim was seriously ill, so when I got a phone call in my limo from Robin a few days after getting back to New York, it threw me for a loop.

"Michael, Jimmy is dead," she said.

I was messed up. I had known Jimmy for a long time. I had felt that Cus had entrusted me to Jimmy, who was very close to Cus. If Cus was like a father to me, Jimmy was like a brother. So you can imagine how my grief was compounded when I found out that Jimmy had been suffering from chronic lymphocytic leukemia for over nine years and had hidden his condition from me. What's worse, everyone had lied to me and told me that Jimmy wasn't that sick. Maybe that was why Bill was so insistent on giving me a police escort to sign the contract before I left to fight Tubbs.

I flew to L.A. the next day for Jim's funeral. With Jim gone the vultures were circling around for the fresh meat: me. Don King was there and he and I wound up being two of the pallbearers for Jim's coffin. I was surprised that Bill chose Don because Bill was trying to cut Don out of promoting my fights. I bet that Don hustled Bill and told him that he'd help him handle me. I wasn't exactly close to Cayton. During the funeral ceremony, Don and José Torres were in the back of the chapel, probably doing business. I'm sure that José was angling to get in on managing me. He was going to be out of work soon after that.

While I was attending the funeral, Robin and her mother were making a scene at the Merrill Lynch office in New York that handled my finances. Bert Sugar, the great boxing writer, happened to be in the office at the time and saw Robin and her mother screaming at the Lynch people.

"Give me my money," they demanded. When my account executive refused, Robin called him a "motherfucker." They wanted to withdraw five million cash to buy us a mansion in New Jersey that Robin's mother had picked out. Before I flew to L.A., Ruth had me sign a paper giving Robin power of attorney over me so she could withdraw the money. The morning of the funeral, Robin called me from the Lynch offices and put the executive on the phone. He explained that my money was in short-term investments, triple tax free, that were coming due on April fourteenth. The interest from those would have paid most of my 1988 tax bill, so that's why he didn't want to pull the money out. I listened and then told him to give them the money. I was in love. I was El Smucko.

Ruth had found us a nice house. It was in Bernardsville, New Jersey, thirty miles west of New York, but in traffic it felt more like three hundred miles from the city. It was a sprawling stone house that had once belonged to the undersecretary of state for FDR. I worked with a Spanish lady to decorate it and we picked out really high-end opulent furniture. Each room had a different theme to it—one was Mediterranean, one was Victorian. I didn't know it at the time, but Ruth was going around suggesting to my friends that if they wanted to get us a wedding present, we needed furniture. Now do you see what kind of hustlers we were dealing with here?

I didn't spend much time in that house. When Robin was working, we'd go to L.A. to her place there. But every once in a while, we'd plan a party. Ruth and Robin hated my friends from Brownsville. They were such wannabes they didn't want to stoop to hanging out with people from the hood. Robin even once hired Porta Potties for a party we had because she didn't want my friends to go inside the house to piss.

The same day that they stormed the Merrill Lynch offices, they served notice on Cayton's office, demanding to see all their financial records concerning me. Once we got married it was like a switch went off. Robin became more demanding. Nothing could please her. She and her mother wanted more and more control over me. I just got tired of that and started fucking more and more other girls.

One day Robin and Ruth and I were in downtown Manhattan at a soul food restaurant and Robin put her hands in my pocket to get money for the bill and she came up with some condoms. Robin got really mad but Ruth didn't seem that disturbed. "No, Robin, it's okay, these things happen early in the marriage," she said. I guess she didn't want to upset the Golden Goose. So we left and Robin was still mad and she got behind the wheel and started driving down Varick Street to go back to New Jersey through the Holland Tunnel. She never drove well to begin with, but she was so angry that she rammed the Bentley into the car in front of us.

The driver of that car came out and yelled at us that his hand was messed up so I gave him twenty thousand dollars in cash. He ran, and I mean ran, straight to the off-track betting office a block away. Then two Port Authority cops came onto the scene. I didn't want to get Robin in trouble so I took the rap and told them that I was driving the car. I was so in love with her at the time. One of the cops seemed really happy to see me. I could see the larceny in his eyes. He was giving me too many compliments on how beautiful my car was, so my brain started moving and I knew then that he would probably take a bribe. So I offered him the car if he wouldn't report the accident.

"I can't do that," he said.

"Yes, you can," I said. "You work too hard. You put your life on the line every day. You deserve it."

"What am I going to do with a Bentley?" he said.

"Sell the parts," I suggested.

"Man, don't tell me that," he said, as if he was already contemplating that.

By this time Robin and her mother had already fled from the scene in a cab. As the cop was considering my offer, a second man came on the scene, claiming that his hand was broken in the accident. The cop immediately jumped on him.

"I'm not gonna tell you no more. Get the fuck out of here!" he told the guy.

So I left the car there and took a cab over to Cayton's office. I called the cops. "They fucking took my Bentley. Get my fucking car back!" We got it back that day.

After a few months with Robin and her mother, I was going crazy. I called Gene Kilroy, Ali's right-hand man.

"The women are driving me crazy. They're treating me like I'm a slave. The mother talks to me like I'm her husband," I moaned.

It wasn't just Robin and her mother. Everybody was vying to get control over me with Jimmy out of the picture. The women had a meeting with me and Bill and their attorney, Michael Winston. They got all the financial records but they couldn't understand any of it so we showed the records to Don King. That was just the wedge he needed, and he began poisoning Robin and Ruth's mind about Cayton because Cayton was trying to cut Don out of my future promotions.

The truth is I was pretty oblivious to all this intrigue swirling around me. I had one of the biggest fights of my career in June, a showdown with Michael Spinks, who in some people's minds was the people's heavyweight champ. He had to forfeit his IBC belt when he had pulled out of the unification tournament. I was training for that. I wasn't interested in going over any goddamn contracts line by line. El Smucko.

We all went down to the Merrill Lynch offices and moved ten million dollars to another bank so they could have full check-writing privileges with that money. This was after I spent over a half million dollars on jewelry, clothes, and furs for both of them and $85,000 on a BMW for Robin.

Right before I was about to shoot a Diet Pepsi commercial, Ruth stopped the cameras and did some extortion stuff on Cayton. He agreed to drop his cut of the earnings from one-third to 25 percent. Which was actually a good thing. Most managers got just 10 or 15 percent and he was gouging me for one-third of my commercial work.

By the end of May, Ruth had her attack dog Winston file a civil suit to get rid of Cayton as my manager. I wasn't really against that. After they had all lied to me about Jimmy's condition, I couldn't trust those guys. I really felt I needed a fresh start. The idea that they could just hand me off like chattel from Jimmy to Bill made me sick. I didn't know which way was up. I still was conflicted about fighting. When I had a fight, I thought about retiring. But when I didn't fight, I wanted to fight. My head was so far up my ass.

Robin claimed that she had had a miscarriage. She was supposedly three months pregnant when we got married. Now it was June and she hadn't gained a pound, so the next thing I knew she was in bed and she claimed she had miscarried our baby. Now I'm glad that we didn't have a kid together but back then part of me wanted a child. She didn't want my baby anyway. She would have died if she had a nappy-head black baby like me.

All this pressure was getting to me. I had a press session with some boxing reporters and I started losing it.

"You ruin people's lives; I'm a sucker to even be talking to you guys. I should be ready to rip your heads off. My wife, my mother-in-law, they're being cut to pieces. When I'm in that ring, I don't have no more problems. It's easy to forget problems when people are throwing punches at your head. The people in the fight business are so bad. I thought people where I came from were criminals, but these guys are bigger crooks than the guys in my neighborhood could ever be. They're not out for my best interests, they tell me they are, but they're not. They say 'I did this for you and that for you' but it's not true. Whatever they did, they did for themselves. Whatever I get, they get a bigger percentage of it."

Around that time I called up Shelly Finkel, one of the few human beings in the boxing business.

"Shelly, I feel like I'm going to kill either Robin or Cayton."

Shelly immediately called Cayton and told him to talk to me and Robin, but Cayton told Shelly that I should come to him. He couldn't even be a friend to me when I needed him.

Robin and her mother had me set up from the beginning. They had me down, but they just couldn't hang in and stay married long enough. I was probably just too overbearing for them. They were probably thinking, *If we just stay a little bit longer, we'll get the money, but God, this guy's too fucking crazy.*

So that's when they started to implement Plan B.

On June thirteenth, two weeks before my big fight with Spinks, Wally Matthews from *Newsday* got a call from an Olga. Olga was Ruth's assistant, her slave girl, but she claimed to be a vice president at Ruth's alleged company. Well, she had an office, let's put it that way. An office paid for by the major investor in her company. Dave Winfield. She got that money before she sued him for allegedly giving her herpes. Olga told Matthews that Ruth and Robin were getting crucified in the press and she wanted to set the record straight. I physically abused both Ruth and Robin, Olga claimed. But she said it wasn't my fault. I just wasn't socialized.

Now, being a good reporter, Wally told her that he needed someone to go on the record. Olga said she'd get back to him. The next day she said Ruth and Robin wouldn't go on the record but that it was all right with them to print it. Wally said that wasn't good enough, he needed someone to quote. That night Olga called back and gave him Robin's sister's number in Portugal where she was attending a tennis tournament. He called Stephanie and she confirmed everything. She said I showed up to Robin's sitcom set in L.A. drunk, that I broke lights and cursed and hit Robin in the head with a closed fist. "He knows how to hit her, and where to hit her, without causing any real damage." Yeah, like I'm some kung fu master. But Stephanie added that it wasn't my fault because I JUST WASN'T SOCIALIZED.

Now Wally felt like he was being played. It was like Olga and Stephanie had been reading from the same script. So Ruthless invited him to her "office." Wally went there and it was all dark and spooky like a witches' coven. Even the walls were dark. Winston, their attorney/lapdog, was there and he told Wally that he couldn't use his tape recorder. But my man was a sly, slick dog. Wally reached into his pocket and turned on his hidden tape recorder. Ruth said that she was going public with all this because of Cayton. She wanted to make me understand the business end of things so that Robin and our children and I would be well provided for.

"Truly I've grown to love Mike," she told Wally. "Clearly he loves Robin and he loves me."

But Cayton had poisoned the press against her, and she had received death threats and obscene phone calls, she claimed. She went on for an hour. And then, surprise, surprise, Robin showed up at the office/coven.

"Oh, Mom, I didn't know you had company," she gushed. "I didn't know the press was here!"

Within seconds Robin was crying. Yes, she sobbed, Mike had hit her.

"So that is true?" Wally asked.

"You can't quote me, it must be off the record," Robin said.

But then she said, "Mike has changed tremendously in the year and five months I've known him. I really feel Michael has NOT BEEN SOCIALIZED. He's only twenty-one and he's a young twenty-one."

The next day, Wally called me in A.C., where I was training, to get my reaction to my wife and mother-in-law's story. He left a message and I called him back.

"What's the problem? What's so urgent? Am I in trouble?"

I listened as Wally told me of the charges that I physically abused Ruth and Robin. Of course I denied all that bullshit. But then he asked me how I felt about my family's revelations.

"I feel great. You opened my eyes to a lot of things here. You can't say bad things about a person, call them an asshole, and then say you love them. What they're saying basically is that I'm useless. I can't understand it. Maybe I'm not the man for them. You know what I mean? Maybe I'm not man enough for them. I'll get by somehow. I always find a way to get by."

Robin also went on a local New York station's five o'clock news show and claimed that she found that twenty million dollars was missing from my accounts. She also claimed that private detectives were following her mother and that Cayton had offered Father Clements fifty grand to help us get a divorce. And then, incredibly, she said, "Michael has orchestrated everything."

What the fuck did I do? These were dirty, filthy scoundrels. Besides being after my money, I think these people were so into themselves and wanted to be bigger than they were. They wanted to be the face of the product, the face of me.

Wally's article was due to hit stands in the Sunday paper, so on Saturday the two women came down to my training camp. They didn't want me to read the story before they could prep me. They just claimed that they were misquoted. And El Smucko believed them.

"Bill will be dead and gone in ten years, but I'll still be with my wife," I told the press. "He's trying to embarrass us, he's trying to make it look like I can't control my wife and that they're gold diggers." Robin was there and she got her two cents in. "They're trying to destroy us; they want to say who I slept with, instead of asking about Mike's business. This is the day we decided about Cayton."

"He's a snake, a ruthless guy," I said.

"Bill is finished," Robin vowed.

Meanwhile, Ruthless was quoted in another article. "I'm his surrogate mother, not his manager. I'm the glue that holds my family together. If I fall apart, we all do."

These were some delusional hos. Meanwhile, Don was lurking behind the scenes, waiting for the women to do the heavy lifting of getting rid of Cayton so he could swoop in. He actually told me that the women would overplay their hand. While all this was going on, José Torres was still trying to worm his way into the picture and manage me. I truly was the Golden Goose. Michael Fuchs from HBO called me "a cash register in short pants." I squelched the idea of José managing me in the *New York Post*, so he went out and got a book deal with Time Warner with a $350,000 advance, which was big bucks then. Four years earlier José had promised Cus that he would write a book on how I had been molded into a champ. José was supposed to share the money from the book with Camille, but now he was selling the book to the publisher as an authorized biography of me.

So this was the shit I was dealing with going into the Spinks fight. A day before the fight I was asked about the circus going on around me.

"I hate them all; writers, promoters, managers, closed-circuit, everybody. They don't give a fuck about me, they don't give a fuck about my wife, they don't give a fuck about my trainer, my mother-in-law, my stepmother, my stepbrother, my pigeons. Nothing concerns them but the dollar, so I don't want to hear anything. We're friends, that's bullshit, I don't want no friends, there's no such thing as personal friendships. I can go in the street and fight, I don't need anybody to manage me. It's too late for that stage, I'm too mature. All I need is a trainer. I'll go in the street and make a million dollars in a street fight."

God, I was lost. I talked about moving to Monaco, anyplace that was far away where I could go and be welcome. I did an interview with Jerry Izenberg, a veteran reporter from the Newark *Star-Ledger*. He saw how much distress I was in. He asked me what I thought about when I did my morning runs.

"I think about Cus and some of the things he told me and how right he was about some things. And how he's not here anymore to help me. And then I think about certain things and it occurs to me how much more fun it used to be. It wasn't about money then so much. We were all like a family. We were together but then suddenly he died and everything became money, money and I don't have anyone to talk to."

And then I grabbed Izenberg and buried my head in his chest and started crying hysterically. I cried so much that Jerry had to go to his room and change his shirt.

But all these distractions made me more focused in the ring, where I could escape this bullshit. I was knocking out guys right and left during sparring. Right before the fight I was back to my usual self. I told the reporter for the *Boston Globe* that "I'll break Spinks. I'll break them all. When I fight someone, I want to break his will. I want to take his manhood. I want to rip out his heart and show it to him.

People say that's primitive, that I'm an animal. But then they pay five hundred dollars to see it. I'm a warrior. If I wasn't into boxing, I'd be breaking the law. That's my nature."

I guess I was getting to Spinks with all this bravado.

"A little terror in your life is good," he told the press at the final prefight press conference.

I was totally confident going into the Spinks fight. But I still didn't get the respect I deserved from the people in the street, who had followed Spink's boxing accomplishments longer than mine. I'd be walking around in New York or L.A. before the fight and guys would come up to me.

"Spinks is going to knock you out, nigga. He's going to whoop your ass."

"Are you on drugs?" I said. "You have to be an extraterrestrial to believe that shit."

They were just haters.

I heard that Roberto Duran wanted to come to the fight and I got very excited. I told Don to give him two tickets if he would come to my dressing room so I could meet him. He did one better. He came to my hotel room the day of the fight. I was so happy to meet my hero that I just knew that I was going to win after that. He was with his friend Luis de Cubas. De Cubas started giving me all this advice like, "Go right out and fuck him up from the opening bell."

"Shut the fuck up," Duran said. "You take your time, boy. Use your jab. Just go behind your jab."

The night of the fight, the Spinks camp tried to fuck with my head. Butch Lewis, his manager, came in to observe my gloves being taped.

"No, no, you gotta take that glove off and retape it," Lewis said after Kevin was finished. "There's a bump in the tape."

"I'm not doing nothing. Fuck you," I said.

"I'm not afraid of you," Lewis said. "Retape that glove."

"I'm God, I don't have to do nothing," I sneered.

"Well, you're gonna do this, God," Butch said.

"Fuck you," Rooney said.

We finally called in Larry Hazzard, the New Jersey boxing commissioner, and Eddie Futch, Spinks's trainer, and they okayed the
tape job.

But I was pissed.

Spinks entered the ring first. I decided I'd work on his mind a little
bit, so I entered the arena to the sound of funeral music. I walked
slowly up to the ring. I looked at the audience like I wanted to kill
them. I just wanted to create this whole ominous atmosphere of fear.
I was one-hundred-percent aware of the audience when I was moving.
My every thought was to project my killer image. But I also wanted to
be one with the audience. I started doing my out-of-body stuff so I
could be one with them, so when I got into the ring I could just lift my
arms and the audience would go nuts. Then I would see my opponent's
energy leaving him slowly.

Robin had Winston serve Cayton with a lawsuit at ringside. She
was wearing an electric red low-cut dress and she sat next to Don. Of
course he was delighted when she told him about the lawsuit. Norman
Mailer was at the fight. He wrote something interesting later: "Tyson
looked drawn, not afraid, not worried, but used up in one small part
of himself, as if a problem still existed that he had not been able to
solve." Norman was right, but I had more than one problem.

As soon as I entered that ring and looked over at Spinks, I knew
that I had to hit him. He wouldn't look at me during the ring instructions. As we were waiting for the bell to ring, Kevin told me that he
had bet his share of the purse that I would knock Spinks out in the
first round. When the bell rang, I went right at him. I stalked him for
a while and we traded blows and I knew he couldn't hurt me, I couldn't
even feel any of his punches. About a minute in, I got him on the ropes
and hit him with a left uppercut and knocked him down with a right
to the body. That was the first time that Spinks had ever been to the
canvas in his whole career. I knew the fight was over then because I
had been dropping my sparring partners all week with body punches.
And he had gone down from a punch that I didn't even think was that
solid. He got right up and took the standing eight-count and we resumed. Three seconds later he threw a wild punch and I unleashed a

right uppercut and it was over. I walked back to my corner with my hands outstretched, palms up. All the great old fighters did that, it was a gesture to demonstrate humbleness, but in my mind I was still the greatest.

At the postfight press conference, I said that I could beat any man in the world and that, as far as I knew, this might be my last fight. I meant both those statements. I certainly didn't want to fight again until I had everything in my life situated. By then, I pretty much knew I had to get rid of the women and my management team. I needed a fresh new start.

We had an after-party and all the celebrities showed up—Stallone and Bruce Willis and Brigitte Nielsen. I was walking around the room when I saw my sister Denise holding court at one table. *Uh, oh, I better leave because somehow I know I'm going to be embarrassed,* I thought. I tried to sneak away, but then I heard her booming voice, "Mike!" I kept walking, pretending I didn't hear her. "Mike! Mike, you motherfucker, you'd better get here right now." I went back to the table. "Mike, get me a Diet Coke. And hurry it up!" my sister said.

"Yes, Niecey," I said. Some things never changed.

My sister was an awesome person. She was always worried about me. She probably wanted to beat up Robin and Ruthless but I didn't want her to do that. Niecey was a simple woman. She was so happy to meet entertainers like Oprah and Natalie Cole. And she loved putting me in check in front of them like she did ordering me to get her a Diet Coke. People would be saying, "Look, there's Iron Mike," and she'd be bossing me around.

I'd be in Los Angeles and my sister would call. "Hey, Mike, I need to get me a mattress."

"Okay, I'll send someone over to get you one," I'd say.

"Well, I don't know those people. Mike, you've got to come and get it."

My friend Shorty Black had a little rinky-dink bar in Queens, but my sister made it sound like the biggest thing in the world. "I'm going to Shorty's tonight," she'd tell me.

I offered to get her into Bentley's or the China Club or any of the happening clubs in the city but she was content to go to Shorty's.

I had dedicated the fight to Jimmy Jacobs. Afterwards I had to make my usual stop at Cus's grave. After every defense of my title, I'd go up there with the big bottle of champagne and celebrate with Cus. Cus loved champagne. Rooney always loved to get after me about that.

"Stop putting the damned bottle on Cus's gravesite," he'd tell me. Every time he saw a Dom Pérignon bottle by the grave, he knew it was mine.

Things got crazier after the Spinks fight. Cayton was indignant because he got sued, but nobody in the press thought it was wrong for Jim and Bill to hand me over like I was a piece of property. If anyone was betrayed it was me. With Jim gone, there was no way that I would have wanted Cayton to be my manager. And if Cus had still been around, Cayton would have been long gone. Cus never liked Cayton because he had done some work with the IBC, Cus's mortal enemies.

The women had enlisted Donald Trump in their camp as a consultant to advise them, but that turned out to be a bad move. He wasn't a boxing guy. He didn't know anything about negotiating purses, ancillary rights, foreign rights, TV deals. There were too many people who were making money off of me to let this bickering continue for long. In July, Bill renegotiated his contract and went down to 20 percent for his managerial fee and 16 percent on endorsements and commercials. One of the reasons that everyone settled was that my purse from the Spinks fight had been held up by the lawsuits. So now I got my check for ten million dollars and Bill got his five million.

Everyone was pressuring me to get back in the ring, but I was in no hurry. I was supposed to fight Frank Bruno in London but at the press conference to announce the settlement with Cayton, I stunned everyone.

"I think I'm going to pass on the Bruno fight and take six to eight weeks off to relax. I just don't feel like fighting now," I said.

I was spending more and more time with Don King by that point.

I had gone to Cleveland in May and stayed at his house for a few days. Don had gotten me to sign a promotional agreement with him, but we kept it hushed up until after the Spinks fight. He had played all of us perfectly.

Sometime that year Don had taken me to see Michael Jackson perform. Don had done promotions for Michael and his father, so he took me backstage after the show. I had met Joe Jackson at some of my fights because he was a player. So we were backstage and Michael was by himself, standing in the corner, waiting for his car to come. Nobody could get near him. But he saw that I was surrounded by people wanting my autograph. I wanted to shake his hand before he got in that car, so I walked over to him.

"How are you doing, Mr. Jackson? It's a pleasure to meet you," I said.

He paused for a second and looked me over.

"I know you from somewhere, don't I?" he said.

He shat on me that night. He knew who I was. But I couldn't be mad, I thought it was beautiful. I couldn't wait to try that line on someone.

When Don King came to New York on August sixteenth, he dropped the bomb that I had signed an exclusive promotional contract with him. Bill went ballistic and threatened to sue. The women were pretty much out of the picture by now. They had lost their bid to take over my business. So they were continuing their Plan B—paint me out as some kind of monster and get a great divorce settlement. Throughout the summer, Robin kept giving interviews claiming that I was violent with her. But when the reporters would ask for documentation, they couldn't back up her bullshit claims. I really don't like to talk bad about people, and for all I know they both could have changed now, but back then they were the lowest serpenty bitches in the galaxy.

The women's next plan was to get me committed to a psychiatric ward so they could take control of my finances. Ruthless kept trying to get me to see this shrink she knew, Dr. Henry McCurtis. I refused to see him. So they talked to him on the phone and got him to write out prescriptions for lithium and Thorazine for me. He told them I was suffering from manic depression. Ruthless enlisted her brother Michael to give me the medicine. But he thought it was bullshit. At first, he'd say, "Mike, you want this medicine?" Eventually he'd just tell me, "Mike, don't take this shit. I wouldn't." Then Ruth tried to get my friend Rory to make sure I took the meds. Ruthless would call every day to make sure I had taken them. Rory didn't give a shit so he'd just tell Ruth that we were out of pills and he told me she would send more out overnight by FedEx.

I was on alcohol not pills when I got into a little street scuffle with Mitch Green. Since I beat him, he had hit the skids. He had been busted for drugs, and was arrested for refusing to pay bridge tolls and for robbing a gas station. Supposedly the nigga had held up the station, tied up the attendant, put him under the cash register, and then collected the money from people coming in for gas.

So I had been clubbing one night at the end of August and decided to drop by Dapper Dan's to pick up some clothing they were making for me. It was a white leather jacket that had DON'T BELIEVE THE HYPE, the name of that Public Enemy song, across the back. I also had some white leather Daisy Duke–type short-shorts to go with it. Hey, I was in shape back then, I wanted to show off my muscular thighs. Every hip hop artist/drug dealer was getting their threads from Dapper then and they would stay open late. So I rolled in there about four in the morning. I'm not a hip hop or drug guy, but I'm a street guy and we all hung out at Dapper Dan's.

Buying shit always made me happy, so I was feeling good. But my mood was severely altered when this crazy motherfucker Mitch Green came storming into the store, bare-chested.

"What the fuck are you doing here, you faggot? You and your motherfucker girlfriend Don King fucked me over in that fight. You're all a bunch of faggots," he started ranting. "Look how you talk! You're a faggot!"

Now I was living in that bullshit "Hey, guys" white world at the time, still trying to get corporate endorsements, but deep down inside

I was a bloodthirsty killer. I decided to try and channel my eloquent Jewish side that I picked up from businessmen like Jimmy Jacobs.

"Now, Mitch, you must consider what you are doing. I do not think that this course of action is in the long run advantageous for your health. You'll remember that I already vanquished you when we met in the ring," I said. "You need to proceed to the nearest exit immediately."

"You didn't beat me!" he screamed. "I had no food. That motherfucker Don King didn't give me no food."

I didn't want to keep arguing with him because I really didn't want to kill this chump. So I took my clothes and started walking out. I got to the sidewalk but the crazy nigga followed me out there still ranting and raving. Then I had an epiphany. *I was Mike Tyson, the undisputed heavyweight champion of the world. I didn't have to take this shit.*

He got in my face and started clawing at me and I looked down and he had ripped my shirt pocket. That was it. I just walloped him right in his eye. I was drunk and didn't realize that he was high on angel dust so he really wasn't going to hit me back. It was like fighting a ten-year-old. I would drag him all up the street and he was screaming. He fought me better in the ring than he did that night.

I was throwing punches and crunching this guy and he was weaving and wobbling from side to side like he was going to fall but he didn't go down. So I did a Bruce Lee *Enter the Dragon* roundhouse kick on his ass and he went down. My friend Tom, who often drove me around when I was drunk, tried to get me away from him.

"Yo, Mike, I think you killed this nigga," he said.

"Well, maybe he shouldn't have fucked with me," I said. And as we turned to go to the car, the *Night of the Living Dead* zombie pops back up like Jason from *Friday the* Fucking *13th* and kicks me in my balls.

"Fuck you, faggot!"

That was not good. So I jumped on his neck and started punching him to the ground where I proceeded to smash his head into the pavement until he was out cold. Now I was tired so I went over to my car. I was driving a canary yellow Corniche Rolls-Royce. $350,000 back in 1988. I got in and waited for Tom to get behind the wheel. Tom got in.

"Just drive, let's get out of here," I said.

"No way. That crazy nigga is under the wheel," Tom said.

I looked out my window and up popped Mitch again. He was screaming and yelling and banging on the window. Then he just ripped my sideview mirror right off. That's fifty grand right there. Now I was as mad as a motherfucker.

I pulled open my door and grabbed his head and then I hit him with my signature punch, the right uppercut. Boom! Mitch went flying up in the air and came down like a ragdoll, right on his head. Anyone who's familiar with street fights knows that when your head hits the ground twice, the first bounce knocks you out and the second one wakes you up. Well, Mitch only bounced once and then this gnarly white shit started oozing out of his mouth. By then, there was a big crowd of pimps and hos and crackheads and they were all going, "Oooooooooo." I was scared. I really thought he was dead. I had crushed his eye socket, broken his nose, cracked some ribs, and one of his eyes was closed for the season, but I still wasn't satisfied. Thank God there was a big audience there because if there hadn't been, I would have snapped his neck and killed the motherfucker. I'm not a nice drunk.

This is the last I'll have to worry about Mitch, I thought. Wrong. A few days later, I was on a date with some exotic hot Afrocentric chick named Egypt or Somalia or some country like that. You know, the ones with the turban and the flowing dresses. We were sitting having lunch at a sidewalk café that made you think you were in some Black Paris. I was looking out to the street and I saw a huge man on a ten-speed bike.

That can't be Mitch Green because I know the motherfucker is a zombie and he don't come out in the daytime, I thought to myself. Just as he was about to turn the corner, he looked back and caught my eye. Oh shit. He turned that bullshit bike around and went over to the hostess, who looked like Queen Latifah in the movie *Jungle Fever*.

"Is that Mike Tyson over there?" he asked.

"Yeah, that's Mike Tyson," she told Mitch. "Hey, champ," she yelled to me and pointed at Mitch. She looked at me as if to say "You handle this."

Why did that girl do that? Why? Now Mitch charged over to my table.

"You bitch faggot. You didn't kick my ass. You snuck one sucker punch in," he said.

"Oh, I hit you one time and fucked you up, crushed the side of your face, broke your teeth, broke your ribs, all that shit with one punch?"

We were getting ready to go again when Sister Egypt/Somalia put her hand over my arm. The one that was holding my steak knife. I wasn't a vegan then.

"Be cool. Don't play yourself, brother. You're worth too much to us. That's just the white man's trap. You don't want to be in that white man's cage."

If I had already slept with her, I would have jumped up and carved that nigga up with my knife. But I hadn't so I just let it go and turned away from Mitch. He got back on his bike, but word had spread and some of my friends in the neighborhood followed his ass and shot at him to scare him away. And I never did get any from Egypt/Somalia.

But I certainly got a lot of publicity from that fight. I had to appear in court the next day to answer a summons for simple assault, a misdemeanor. Plus, I had fractured my hand on that solid uppercut, so my next fight with Bruno had to be postponed. Now the media were all turning on me. First they build you up and then they tear you down. That's the name of the game. It didn't matter that I had been assaulted and challenged by an out-of-control angel duster. Now everyone wanted to know why I was in Harlem at four in the morning. They were going back and trying to dig up shit on my years in Catskill, making up crazy stories about how my violent episodes had been hushed up. Even my man Wally Matthews took me on in *Newsday*.

"As Undisputed Heavyweight Champion of the World, a millionaire, and an important athlete, who strives to be a role model for youth, especially underprivileged black youth, Tyson should know better. It's another blotch on Tyson's increasingly besmirched personal image."

Violent. Monster. Antisocial. What was next, mental patient? That's just what the Ruthless Two were up to. On September fourth, I was up in Catskill with Camille. I hadn't been seeing much of Robin and Ruthless, but I had been taking those damn pills that McCurtis had prescribed, from time to time. Camille was against me taking them; she thought they made me dopey and withdrawn. I kind of liked that dopey feeling but she was urging me to get a second opinion. While I was there, Robin called me all the time. "Why are you up there? Why aren't you with us?" all that bullshit.

"Fuck you, I don't want to talk to you anymore. I want to divorce you. I want to kill myself," I answered one day and hung up. I was really mad and I got into my car to go to town to get some stuff. It had been raining out and the dirt driveway was all muddy. To get to the main road you had to drive up the driveway about fifty feet at a ten-degree angle. I started my big BMW and gave it gas, but my wheels were spinning in the mud so I gave it more gas and I skidded out and headed for a big tree. I had intentionally planned to hit the tree to get attention but I never tried to kill myself. I knew the car would protect me. But my head hit the steering wheel and the next thing I knew Camille was standing over me, slapping my face, and attempting to give me mouth-to-mouth resuscitation so I'd come to.

Oh great, my staged "suicide attempt" backfired on me. I didn't want to die or even injure myself. I just wanted attention. I still loved Robin and I wanted to make her feel bad for all the pain she caused me. Even then, I had an addict mentality. I take the poison and then wait for my enemy to die.

Because I had lost consciousness for a while, Camille called an ambulance and they took me to the local Catskill hospital. Somebody must have called Robin because while I was settling into my hospital room, eating some take-out Chinese food that I had Jay bring me, Robin rushed in, followed by camera crews and another ambulance. She was going to save the day—in time for the five o'clock news.

"See what the fuck you made me do?" I snarled at her.

The doctors told me I had a chest concussion and blunt head trauma, so I decided to get transferred to New York–Presbyterian Hospital in the city. Of course, Robin was right next to my gurney, dramatically trying to move the photographers away but staying right in the center of their frames. When we got to the city, Robin and her mother gave the hospital an approved list of visitors. On the list was Donald and Ivana Trump, Howard Rubenstein, the P.R. man, and their attorneys. They weren't my friends, but my friends weren't coming around when I was with the Terrible Two anyway.

I did have one unwelcome visitor though. My window was open and I heard a commotion down on the sidewalk outside. I looked out and I couldn't believe my fucking eyes. It was Mitch Green, surrounded by the media. Mitch had his shirt off and he was shadowboxing and screaming, "Cicely Tyson is a faggot! I'm going to beat his mother-fucking ass." I couldn't escape this fool. If there was ever a black guy who resembled the Frankenstein monster it would be Mitch Green.

I realized why the P.R. guy was on my approved guest list when I picked up the next morning's *Daily News*. There was this big article by some feature writer named McAlary, a guy I didn't know, not a boxing man. He said that my accident was a serious suicide attempt.

"I'm going to go out and kill myself. I'm going to go out and crash my car," he claimed that I had told Robin. Then he wrote that a week earlier I had threatened to kill Robin. Unnamed "friends" of mine were quoted as saying that I had bought two shotguns in Catskill to kill myself with. He had a grieving Givens sitting worried at my bedside while I said, "I told you I'd do it. And as soon as I get out of here I'll do it again." McAlary wrote that the women were pleading with me to go see Dr. McCurtis and "sources contended that McCurtis wanted to commit Tyson for psychiatric evaluation."

BINGO. It didn't take a Harvard Medical School student to see that these two women were building a case that I was an out-of-control psycho that should be committed and that my wealth should be under their control.

McAlary went on to say that I had been sick all these years and I had been on medication, but Cus took me off it because he just cared about me fighting. Total bullshit. McAlary wrote that only Trump, Rubenstein, and Parcher, their lawyer, really understood my needs and were more interested in my well-being than in my next fight. Robin's camp must have leaked this shit to the papers. And Ruthless must have dragged out that old bullshit that I knew how to hit Robin without leaving marks because there it was in the article. Yeah, I'm a sophisticated black Fu Manchu motherfucker. So me, Iron Mike Tyson, I'm supposed to know how to beat people up without leaving a mark. Yeah right, when my whole career was built on me being a bonebreaker. The more you read of this article, the more you realized that the Ruthless Two's fingerprints were all over this. I guess they were trying to get their mental-cruelty divorce papers in before mine.

McCurtis kept calling Camille at the house, urging her to make sure that I took my drugs. A few days later, I flew to Moscow with Robin and her mother and her publicist because her sitcom was filming there. I was always fascinated by Russian history, so I decided to take the trip there. I used to hear Cus and Norman Mailer talk about Tolstoy, so I became a great fan of Russian culture and their prize-fighters.

Before we left we had to answer reporter's questions. I ridiculed the attempted suicide story.

"I love my wife, I don't beat my wife, I'm never going to leave my wife and my wife is never going to leave me." I was in my El Smucko mode.

"Nobody, but nobody is busting up our marriage," Robin said. "I'm still in this, I love Michael and will take care of him. Michael loves me too much to kill himself and leave me alone."

Yeah, she was still in it until she got the money.

When we got back from Moscow, all these stories of me being out of control started getting leaked to the press. Supposedly I was running around the hotel screaming, hanging from a high ledge, threatening to kill myself. I guess they forgot that we were in Russia and the Russian cops would have beat my ass if I did anything like that. The women even tried to get me arrested in Russia, but it didn't work. We were in the lobby of our hotel and Robin and her mother started screaming and telling the security guard to arrest me. He came over to me.

"Come here," he said to me. "This is nothing. These women are bullshit."

He pulled out a bottle of vodka and we had a drink together.

When the U.S. reporters actually fact-checked Robin's wild stories, they interviewed one of the producers of her show who said, "Mike was a perfect gentleman in Russia."

One of the makeup people on the show told her friend that the stories of me beating up Robin were a big joke.

"I read all the papers where Robin's being quoted as saying how much he hits her and beats up on her. I do the makeup on her, I see her. There were no bruises on this girl. I just don't understand how she's getting away with it."

A few days after we got back from Russia, Ruth and Robin finally dragged me to see Dr. McCurtis. After about an hour of him telling me how sick I was, I started believing him. He had the degrees on the wall. If I told him he was a shitty fighter, was he going to dispute me? Now they had me thinking that I was manic-depressive. That's what he kept on drumming in. Look, I knew I had always been a depressed kind of guy, and sometimes I'd have manic energy and stay up for days. I've been like that all my life. So they convinced me to take the drugs and then they paraded me in front of the cameras.

"I was born with this disease, I can't help it. Maybe that's why I am successful at what I do. It's like going through a metamorphosis, changing from very, very depressed to very, very high-strung and the high-strung period is so overwhelming. You know, like I'm anti-drugs, but it's like being high and not being able to sleep for three or four days and always being on the run. You're just paranoid, it's abnormal," I said.

"He's been like this for many years and they've been ignoring it,"

Robin chimed in. "Michael takes a great deal of protecting. You can't put a Band-Aid on it. Who cares if he fights again, this guy's got to live the rest of his life. We'll be in treatment together."

Now that I was a zombie again, taking these pills, the Ruthless Two decided that Camille had to be out of the equation. I had just started paying for Camille's expenses after Jimmy died. Both Ruth and Robin told Camille that if I was going to pay all the house bills, the house should be put in my name. When they told me that, I flipped out. "Are you fucking crazy, bitch?" I told Robin. The next day Robin called Camille again and she ordered Camille to stay out of my life. I never knew that at the time.

Everybody asks me about that infamous *20/20* show. Barbara Walters even recently worried that she broke up our marriage. If that was true, I wish she had interviewed us sooner. The funny thing about that show was that I recently found out that Robin wasn't even supposed to be on it. There was a segment with Cayton shot at his office. Then the crew came to our house to film me and Ruthless individually. Just as the crew was about to pack up, Robin pulled Barbara aside and told her that she still didn't have the truth.

I guess Robin knew that Barbara would take the bait.

I had no idea what she was about to say when they positioned me behind her on the couch. They started rolling the cameras again. It started innocuously enough.

"You are a college graduate, well educated, actress. This is a man who is a high school dropout, who went to reform school. You are very different, at least on the surface. Why do you love him?" Barbara asked Robin.

"Because he is smart and because he is gentle, he's got this incredibly gentle side. Because Michael loves me more than anything in the world. I feel like he needs me, which I like, I like that," she gushed.

"That's why I love her, she really feels that she can protect me," I added. I could just hear Cus yelling, "Phony bastard!"

"There was no prenuptial agreement?" Barbara said.

"Why should there be?" Robin said. "We got married to be together forever. Not to plan for divorce."

Then Barbara asked me what I thought about what Robin said.

"If you are going to marry somebody, you trust them, and that's what marriage is all about, being together for the rest of your life. I do have many of millions, my wife would just have to ask for it and she has everything I have. If she wants it right now, take it, she can leave right now, take everything I have and just leave. She has the right to do it; she has the power to do that. She is still here, she tolerates my shit, and I love my wife."

Then the temperature changed.

"Robin, some of the things that we've read; that he has hit you, that he has chased you and your mother around in Russia. That Mike has a very volatile temper. True?" Barbara asked.

"Extremely volatile temper. He has got a side to him that is scary. Michael is intimidating, to say the least. I think that there is a time when he cannot control his temper and that is frightening to me, or to my mother and to anyone around, it's scary."

I wasn't on drugs right then but it felt like it. I couldn't believe the shit she was saying.

"What happens?" Barbara prodded.

"He gets out of control, throwing, screaming . . ."

"Does he hit you?"

"He shakes, he pushes, he swings. Sometimes I think he is trying to scare me. There were times when it happened that I thought I could handle it, and just recently I have become afraid. I mean very, very much afraid. Michael is a manic-depressive, he is, that is just a fact."

Can you imagine sitting there hearing this shit from your wife, knowing that an audience of millions would see it? Saying our marriage has been "torture, it's been pure hell, it's been worse than anything I could possibly imagine." I was fuming, but trying to keep cool. This was the ultimate betrayal.

"I don't know what Mike Tyson would be without my mother. She's been the glue that kept us together," Robin went on. "If we left Michael, and I do come with a package, my mom, my sister, that's how I am, he would undoubtedly be alone and I don't want that to happen. He would have gotten so, so bad that I think maybe one day he would have been more deliberate and killed himself or hurt someone else. That undoubtedly, unquestionably would have happened."

I didn't know what to say. I'd never dealt with anything of that particular magnitude before. When I look back at it now, I can't believe I sat there and didn't say anything. But then again, if I would've started smashing her fucking face and going crazy in front of the cameras, that's what they would have wanted. So I stayed cool. I know they expected me to go crazy on television and start ranting and raving. That was the whole plan I think. But it backfired on them.

My friends were indignant at what Robin did on that show. I was getting hundreds of irate calls. I was still angry a few days later. Robin and Ruth and I were in the New Jersey house when I got so angry that I started breaking glasses and plates and throwing and shattering empty champagne bottles. Olga was there and she called the police. The cops came and I met with them at the front door. I was polite and told them everything was all right, I just wanted to be left alone. Then the cops split up and one stayed with me and the other one went with Robin. She showed him the damage in the kitchen. The cop who was with me told me that Robin was concerned about me because of the damage I had done to the kitchen.

"I own this house and everything in it," I started yelling. "I can do anything I want to my property. If I want to break something, nobody can stop me." Then I picked up a large brass fireplace ornament and threw it through the glass window next to the front door. Right then, their pal McCurtis called.

"Do you want to talk to your doctor?" the cop asked me.

I ignored him and kept walking into the next room. The good doctor told the cop that Robin and her crew should leave the house and I should be committed for a psychiatric exam. The cops then rounded up the women and they moved to the driveway to go to their car so Robin could go to the police station and file a report. I stormed into the driveway.

"Fuck you all. You're scum. Get off my property and fuck off," I screamed. Then I got into my Rolls-Royce and started driving through the dense backwoods of my property. I wasn't even on a paved road. I just wanted to get away from all of them.

The next day Robin and her mother left for L.A. My friend Mark Breland, the boxer, wanted me to make up with Bill Cayton and shake his hand. Shelly Finkel and Cayton had brainwashed Mark. They told him I was really messed up and they convinced him to come talk to me. We went up there and Cayton was very concerned about the manic-depressive label so he set up an appointment for me with Dr. Abraham Halpern, the director of psychiatry at the New York United Hospital Medical Center in Port Chester, one of the top psychiatrists in the world.

Halpern saw me for an hour. Then he called and spoke to Camille, Steve Lott, and Bill Cayton. He was certain that I didn't suffer from manic depression. He tried to call the Ruthless Two, but they had disconnected their phone. When Halpern called McCurtis to see why he had diagnosed me as a manic-depressive, McCurtis started backpedaling. He said I wasn't a full-fledged manic-depressive, I merely had a mood disorder, something he called "Boxer Syndrome." That was a new one for Freud.

I was relieved that a much more prominent shrink had cleared me of manic depression, but I wondered why Bill made such a big deal about seeing me to Mark. He really had nothing to say. I went there under the pretense that something big was going to happen and then I got there and he was real ambiguous on what he was trying to say. My relationship with Bill had run its course.

So when all the dust cleared, there was Don still standing. I had no illusions about him. When Robin used to ask me about Don, I'd say, "Look, I know how to control a snake. This guy is a snake, but I know how to control a snake." Don did have his good points. Two days after the women split for the coast, Don took me around to each and every one of my bank and brokerage accounts. He had them take Robin's name off of each account and switch them back to me. That was fifteen million right there. We got there right in time to stop payment on a check for $581,812.60 that Robin had just written out to Robin Givens Productions.

The people in the banks hated those women's guts so much that they were thrilled to help us. We were up there partying with the bank president and all the bank workers—popping champagne and ordering in pizzas. "Fuck them bitches," we all shouted and downed our bubbly.

7

THAT *20/20* SHOW REALLY BACKFIRED ON ROBIN AND HER MOTHER. AFTER WE split up, I went to a wrestling show in Chicago and when I walked in and sat down, I got a standing ovation from the audience. People were coming up to me, telling me what ugly shit they had done to me on the Barbara Walters show. I also got tons of sympathy pussy. Women would approach me and say, "Oh, God, I can't believe what the horrible woman did to you. Please let me hold you, let me suck your dick, let me take care of you." I'd say, "No, ma'am, it's all right, no. Okay, well just suck it a little, ma'am, not much." That whole year was crazy.

I was severely traumatized by that relationship. Those were cold broads. It was my first relationship and I wanted to just cancel it out, but love leaves a black mark on your heart. It really scars you. But you have to take chances to keep growing as an individual. That's what life is all about. And I always had the newspapers to vent to. A guy from the *Chicago Sun-Times* asked me about Robin and her mother.

"They use them but they don't like or respect black people. The way they talk about black people, you'd think you were living with the Ku Klux Klan," I said. "They thought they were royalty. She and her mother wanted so much to be white, it's a shame. And they were trying to take me away from the people I grew up with and throw me into their kind of high-class world."

I was making changes in my life on all fronts. Bill was still technically managing me, but he was out of the picture. Maybe things would have been different if Jimmy was still alive, but after he died nobody could stop me from doing what I wanted to do. Looking back on it, I don't think Jimmy and Bill were evil. I think they were businessmen and they were more seasoned than I was. But I was in way over my head and they took advantage of that too. But they were control freaks. As I got older I wanted my liberation, I wanted to do my own thing. If I failed or succeeded, it didn't matter, I just wanted to do it on my own.

And then I got caught up with this other piece of shit, Don King. Don is a wretched, slimy reptilian motherfucker. He was supposed to be my black brother, but he was just a bad man. He was going to mentor me, but all he wanted was money. He was a real greedy man. I thought I could handle somebody like King, but he outsmarted me. I was totally out of my league with that guy.

I met Don through Jimmy and Cayton. So if I got involved with Don it was mostly their fault. When you really think about it, Jimmy and those guys let Don see how weak they were with me. They involved him in our business and he saw an opening. Without sounding egotistical, the whole Tyson thing was too big for Jimmy and Bill; it was probably even too big for Cus. They never saw anything like me. Nobody in the entire history of boxing had made as much money in such a short period of time as I did. I don't know how he would have handled this thing. I was like some really hot, pretty bitch who everybody wanted to fuck, you know what I mean? It was just that Don got to me, but if it hadn't been Don, it would have been Bob Arum or somebody else.

With Cus and Jim gone I didn't care about any of those people. So

I thought, *Whoever gives me the highest bid, whatever I wanted, I'll go with them.* It became a game to me. Everybody was thinking about themselves, so I might as well think about myself. All my friends from my neighborhood were dying and dead anyway, so I was trying to have some fun. I had no anticipation of having a long life. I was too much of an irritant. You catch me in one of my irritating moods and you might get shot. I was living a fantasy life, going from country to country, sleeping with beautiful strangers. That shit began to take a toll on me.

Don gave me the freedom to do what I wanted. He was handling the business and making deals behind my back, but I wasn't his bitch. He was very smart in instilling in me the auspices that it was me and him against the world. "Black man, white man, black man, white man." He was always spouting some bullshit that the white mother-fuckers were no good and that they were out to kill us all. I actually started believing some of his shit. I played into that stuff. He contaminated my whole barometer.

Anybody could have looked at Don with his hair and his big mouth and his ghetto-fabulous flamboyant style and seen that he was a sick motherfucker. But I was confused back then. All joking aside, if Cus had been alive, he would have gone with King to promote me. Cus hated Bob Arum, King's rival. I don't know why. I didn't think Arum was worse than Don but Cus told me, "Nobody could be worse than Arum."

I got a lot of flak for going with Don. I was with my friend Brian Hamill at Columbus one night. De Niro was there, sitting at a table, and Brian and I were standing near him. Brian was going off on me signing with King.

"What the fuck are you doing getting involved with Don King?" he was almost yelling. He wasn't saying it for De Niro's benefit, but Bobby could hear every word.

"Do you know how many black fighters he's robbed? You know the history."

"Brian, I've got so much money, I don't give a fuck," I said.

And I didn't then. I didn't know how long that ride was going to last. I was just living my life day by day. But I knew that I loved being champ and I felt that nobody could do that job better than me. I would destroy anything in front of me. If you were in the same occupation and we weighed the same, you would be dead. My whole job was to hurt people. Jim and Bill tried to tone that down, but Don was with the program. So when I started hanging out with Don, boom, the whole public perception of me changed. Now I was a bad guy.

In October of 1988, Don took me to Venezuela for the WBA convention. Then we went to Mexico for the christening of Julio Chavez's son. That trip was a real revelation for me. We took a day trip to the pyramids and this little kid came up to me, begging. The guides we were with said, "No, Mike, don't give them money." But how couldn't I? A hundred dollars was nothing to me, but it meant everything to the kid. So I gave him some money and he was so appreciative. I was thinking, *Wow, this is a good kid,* and I went to touch his hair and it felt as hard as a rock. It felt like he hadn't washed his hair in years. You could have hurt someone with his hair. Then we went to Culiacán and I saw more kids begging. I bought clothes for this one kid and next thing I knew he was bringing around three more friends and then twenty more of his cousins were coming by for clothes. That's why I liked that one kid, he never came by himself; he always brought his friends and relatives, and every time I bought them all stuff.

It was just like in Brooklyn when I bought sneakers for those street kids. These Mexican kids had never left Culiacán and I dressed them and we were all hanging out. I had so much money and the clothes that I was buying were so cheap. You just knew you were going to hell if you didn't spend money on those children. By the time I left we had a crew of over fifty kids that were dressed up sharp.

Before I went to Mexico, I had such a big chip on my shoulder. I had never known anyone poorer than me. I couldn't imagine anyone in the world being poorer than I had been. I was blown away by the poverty in Mexico. I was actually mad at them for being poorer than I had been because I couldn't feel sorry for myself anymore. More than anything else, my success stemmed from my shame about being poor. That shame of being poor gave me more pain than anything in my life.

So many of my problems stemmed from thinking I deserved shit after being so poverty-stricken growing up. Cus was always trying to get me to transcend myself and separate myself from my ego, get out of my own head. But it was hard. Hey, I deserved that car, I deserved that mansion, I deserved a bad bitch. When I got with Don, I had to have the top-of-the-line cars and lots of them. I was getting the best Lamborghinis and a bulletproof Hummer that had been owned by some Saudi prince. I was going to Bristol to the Rolls-Royce factory and they were designing my custom Rolls for me.

Cus wouldn't have approved of all that. If a guy had a convertible, Cus thought he was a selfish pig. We'd see a nice car and I'd say, "Wow, that's a cool car, Cus."

"Nah, that guy is selfish," Cus said.

"Why is he selfish?" I'd ask.

"He drives that two-seater so he doesn't have to drive more than him and his friends around."

Cus had an old beat-up van that could hold twelve people. That's just the way he was.

We would have had a great reality show back in 1988. I say this with all modesty, I started the whole bling-bling look with my customized stretch limos and collection of Rolls and Lamborghinis. P. Diddy and them were trying their best to get in our camp, but we set the tone. I started the trends that were followed by today's hip hop moguls. I was the first to buy Rolls-Royces and Ferraris. In 1985 what other black guy in his twenties was buying these kinds of cars— legally? And I didn't have just one. I had a fleet of them. These up-and-coming hip hop stars used to throw after-parties for our fights. They didn't even know what Bentleys were. They thought those were old man's cars. And back in the '80s, I was gutting them out and putting Gucci and refrigerators in them. I even put a hot tub in one of my limousines. I know I was the first to put a fax machine in a car.

"You got the contract. Okay, we're in the car. Fax it to me."

We used to buy pieces of jewelry that cost two, three million. I'd buy a girlfriend a piece of jewelry for a million five. After every fight, my crew would go out in fur coats and stretch Rolls-Royces. When I bought that house in Bernardsville, New Jersey, I invited my friend EB over and said, "Nobody's macking like this." Everybody was always jealous of me because I used to throw my wealth in their faces. Yet I did share. If I ate, everybody around me ate. But they were still jealous. In all of my houses, everything was Versace, from the furniture to the walls to the comforters to the sheets to the towels to the ashtrays to the glasses and the plates.

I met Versace through an Italian journalist who came to interview me in Catskill. She was a very attractive woman who was a few years older than me, and I took her upstairs and we had sex and I saw that she was wearing Versace underwear.

"I model for him," she told me. "I can get you all the clothes you want. I'll introduce you."

Versace was the coolest. He offered to send me clothes but I was too impatient.

"If you just wait, I'll send you everything for free," he'd tell me.

"Send me what you can and I'm going to buy what I can, okay?" I told him.

I was living out the fantasy. I'd go to London or Paris to get some clothes and all the salespeople would run out of their stores.

"Champion! Champion!" they'd shout, trying to get me to go into their place. I was taking the Concorde to see a girl, and we'd walk down the street and the whole city stopped. They literally had to drag us into the stores, we were so mobbed.

In Vegas it was worse. I'd go to the Versace store in Caesars and the whole mall would shut down. I was flourishing with all that attention. I was looking around at the clothes and I didn't think, *Thank you very much,* I was looking mean at the people in the store. I didn't even bother trying on clothes in the dressing rooms. I'd just strip down to my underwear in the middle of the store. I was ripped to a shred back then and hundreds of people would be watching me try on clothes through the store window. I'd see a girl in the crowd that I liked and I'd say to one of the salespeople, "Let her in, please."

She'd come in.

"Do you want to stay here and help me pick out things? Do you need anything?" I'd ask her. When I'd finish shopping, I would have dropped $300,000 cash money that visit. Versace got mad at me.

"This guy spends too much money," he'd tell whoever we were with. But he was no one to talk. That guy spent more money than I did.

It's funny that they make a big deal about Kanye West dressing up his women. I did the same thing. I always liked to dress my girls. I think it went back to my childhood. I used to watch my mother dress the prostitutes who came over. She'd try various wigs on them and then different outfits. So that's what I did. Not because I was such a fly guy but because I used to see my mother do it with the girls. I even taught Don how to dress. He was dressing like he came right out of the movie *Super Fly* back then.

"Nigga, you can't be with us, you dressing like this. We have an image to uphold, Don, we are fly niggas. You are a bum," I told him. "You're a big man, you should dress different. Versace is the future, Don."

That whole gangsta rap image formed around me. I was bringing that attitude to the world. I represented that era. Even Don got freaked out by the image I was portraying at that time. Near the end of 1988, Don tried to soften my image by having Jesse Jackson baptize me in Chicago. That was all bullshit. After the baptism, I took one of the choirgirls back to the hotel and fucked her.

They had me saying I was born-again in *Jet* magazine. "Remember this: Reach for God, don't reach for the stars, you might get a cloud and nothing is in the clouds. Reach for God, reach to shake God's hands." That was all bullshit. The only spirituality I had back then was in my dick.

I spent a lot of time in L.A. in the late '80s. I had an apartment in Century City off Wilshire. A friend of mine was christening his boat and he had a party where I met this beautiful girl named Hope. She was with a girlfriend of hers and they arrived near the end of the party when the food had run out. I was sitting at a table with a big plate of food in front of me, so Hope walked up to me out of the blue and went into a great Andrew Dice Clay imitation.

"Look, my friend will blow you if you buy dinner. Me and my friend are starving."

I thought she was hilarious. I invited them to pull up a seat and I shared my food with them. I didn't get any feeling that she wanted to be intimate with me so we just became running dogs. She had a lot of girlfriends and I would say, "Hope, I really like that girl a lot." So she hooked me up. I became a big brother to her. She was always having problems with men. I would take one look at a guy and tell her, "Hope, that guy's gay," or, "This guy will never care about you." I was really good at seeing through people's bullshit. Except for the women in my life.

We became close. Hope was going to college then and she didn't have much money, so I let her stay in the spare bedroom in my apartment. But we were just platonic friends. No one could believe it because Hope was so hot.

"Mike, you're fucking her. I know you are," all of my friends would say. "I saw you fuck that ugly fat bitch, you got to be fucking this one."

I became super protective of Hope. One of our favorite places to go was this club called RnB Live. That was where Hope bumped into Wesley Snipes. She started dating him while I was out of town. When I got back to L.A., she came to me crying. Wesley had broken her heart; he didn't want to see her anymore.

"See, Hope, this is what happens when you mess with those kinds of guys in your life. You need a straight guy," I told her.

But Hope didn't want to hear that. She wanted to hear "Why are you crying, Hope? I'm going to kick his ass."

Hope didn't get what she wanted from me, so she said to me, "Oh, and Wesley didn't get why I was, with you. He said, 'What are you doing with a guy like Tyson?' to me."

I knew that was bullshit.

A few days later I made plans to meet Hope at RnB. I sat next to her and asked her how school was, when we saw Wesley Snipes walk in. I excused myself and walked over to him. Wesley looked up, saw me, and panicked.

"Mike, please don't hit me in my face, that's how I make my living," he said.

"Man, don't worry about that thing with Hope. She's just hurt." We both laughed about it.

But I had been drinking a lot of champagne that night, so when I saw Keenen Ivory Wayans, I had to tell him something. He had been doing an impersonation of me on his show *In Living Color*.

"Yo, Keenen, can I talk to you for a minute?" I asked.

"Yeah, Mike, what's up?"

"Did I do something to you or your family?" I said.

"No, why?"

"Because these motherfucking jokes about me have got to stop."

He got all apologetic. And the jokes about me stopped. All those comedian guys talk shit on stage or in front of the cameras, but when they see me, they want to slap five.

The same time I was running with Hope, I started hanging out with this incredible guy named Kevin Sawyer. He had a pager company in L.A. and his store had become a hangout spot for all the players, hustlers, and pimps. Jamie Foxx and Joe Torry worked there before they were famous. It was a business place. People would go in to buy pagers and I would be there shooting dice in my Versace clothes with my big diamond watches and my Rolls parked outside.

Kevin was an incredible ladies' man. He was very charismatic and the women loved him, even though he stuttered. Me and Kevin and my friend Craig Boogie would have competitions to see how many women we could get in a day. The sex scene was crazy then. I'd meet girls on the street, say, "Come, let's go," and we'd go. I'd be in a club and I'd be touching girls, putting my tongue on their backs, licking their skin, and I didn't even know them. But I'd take them home and let my friends have sex with them too. My reputation began to spread. I was the guy who might take you shopping, but then we would go home to have sex.

One time, Boogie was driving me around Philadelphia. I was there training for the Buster Mathis Jr. fight. I saw a beautiful girl walking down the street. I didn't even have to say anything to her; the girl just hopped right in the back of the car.

"Where are we going?" she said.

Another time I was in a cab in New York with this girl I had met. She started taking off her clothes in the cab and having sex with me. It wasn't even a limo; it was a regular yellow cab. I was, like, "Whoa. Okay, let's go."

In my mind I was ordained to do this. All my heroes had had all these women. Someone should have said to me, "This is going to have an ugly ending." But there was nobody there to do that.

I started making sex videos at home. Boogie would direct the scene, place the camera in the right spot, and then he'd hide in the closet and watch. They started calling me "the Womb Shifter" or "the Pelvis Pulverizer." I'd show the tapes to my friends and then I'd destroy them. Man, if one of them had gotten out, it would have made the Kardashian tape look PG-13.

I was drinking a lot in those days and partying wherever I found myself. I had a girlfriend in Chicago named Carmen. She was a nice Catholic girl from a solid family—too nice to be hanging around us. I was in a nightclub in Chicago one night with her and Eric Brown, who everyone called EB. They had a sexy-lady contest and some guy disrespected Carmen during it. I didn't say anything, but I was fuming. I guess the guy thought that he had punked Mike Tyson, but I followed him, sneaky-like, downstairs to the bathroom.

"Listen, man, I don't care about no pussy. But you don't ever fuck with me like that, man. This championship shit don't mean nothing. We can get it on right here."

The guy looked terrified. Just then EB and some of the club security guys barged into the bathroom and pulled me away from the guy. I was pretty drunk, so I bolted out of the club and jumped into my car. I had my long stretch limo with the hot tub in the back that night. I told the driver to drive me over to the south side. EB was frantic when he realized I was gone, so he called the limo driver's car phone.

"Where are you?"

"We're on Sixty-seventh and . . ." the driver said.

"What! *I* don't even go over there," EB worried.

"What do you want me to do?" the driver asked.

"Meet me back at the Ritz-Carlton," EB said.

We headed back to the hotel. Little did I know, but about thirty cars were following my limo, all filled with women. They had been on our tail since I left the club. When I got out of the limo in front of the Ritz, EB was waiting for me. But first, I walked over to each of the cars that followed us, pulled out my roll of cash, and threw hundred-dollar bills on each car.

"What the hell are you doin', Mike?" EB said.

"That's all they want. Money," I said.

I walked into the hotel, EB beside me.

"What are you doing here?" I said to him.

"I'm waiting on you," EB answered.

"I don't need nobody waiting on me. I came into this world by myself and I'm going to leave by myself," I said.

"Well, I got to stay with you for the night, so you've just got to get mad at me," EB said.

We got into the elevator to go up to the room.

By then, I was hungry, so we got off the elevator and went to the restaurant. This little white dude came up to us and said, "Sorry, Mr. Tyson, the restaurant is closed."

I grabbed the guy around the neck, picked him up and said, "Feed me, don't treat me like no nigga."

Fifteen minutes later, we had an amazing spread before us. I ate all my food, then started in on EB's too. Suddenly I broke down.

"Man, why'd she do me like that?"

I still hadn't gotten over Robin.

"Man, take it easy," EB said.

"That bitch. I loved her. She didn't have to do me like that," I moaned.

My mood was spiraling downward, so EB pulled out his phone and called Isaiah Thomas's mother, Mary. She was a beautiful lady. Mary started consoling me and after a few minutes, I felt better.

It seemed that every time I went out, trouble was following in my wake. Sometimes it wasn't even my fault. I once was in New York and picked up this Spanish girl. She was a transit cop in one of the city projects, but I knew that with a little sprucing up, she'd be stunning. So I got her a whole makeover and some nice new clothes and she was gorgeous. That night I invited her and a few of my female friends to the China Club, a hot club at that time, and we got a table. Just me and eight girls. I looked like a Mack. So naturally some guy was going to come over to the table to talk to the girls. I didn't act like it was a big thing, I was cool. The guy wasn't even talking to my girl, the cop, but the next thing I knew, she jumped up with both of her hands up. "Halt! Do not advance any further. These ladies do not want your attention," she said to the guy.

I was looking at this, thinking, *What the fuck is going on?*

The guy was with a bunch of his friends and they were at the next table laughing at this lady. The next thing I knew, she went over to the guy laughing the loudest, grabbed him upright, and, ba-boom, kicked the guy in the head. She was in full-on combat mode.

You would have thought that the girls at the table would be happy she was defending them, but they were all afraid of her.

"You have to tell this bitch to get out of here, Mike," one of my female friends said. "What if the press hears about this, Mike?"

"Baby, everybody is scared," I told the cop. "You got to go."

I couldn't believe it. She smacked and kicked a big man and he and his friends had done nothing wrong. Oh, my God.

One of the reasons that I didn't think I was going to live long was because I thought I was the baddest man in the world, both in the arena and out on the streets. When you add the alcohol to that giant ego, anything could happen. It felt like I was always on a mission, but what was I looking for, what was the problem? I was always mad at the world. I always felt empty. Even after Mexico, I had a chip on my shoulder about being poor, my mother dying, that I had no family life. Being champ of the world just accelerated and intensified those feelings.

Then I created that Iron Mike persona, that monster, and the media picked up on it and the whole world was afraid of that guy, the guy who could make women leave their husbands for a night and cheat. That image of being the big bad motherfucker was really intoxicating but inside I was still just a little pussy—this scared kid who didn't want to get picked on.

But I had to play that role, I didn't know what else to do. One night I was at Bentley's, the New York club. I was drunk and thinking I was a tough guy. I was hitting on some girl and the girl's husband didn't like it and he pulled out a gun and aimed it at me.

"Go ahead and shoot, motherfucker. You bitch nigga. I'm going to fuck your wife," I said.

I was talking stupid, un-fucking-legible English. Allah is my witness, I'm just grateful the guy didn't have the guts to kill me. He was just talking shit but he wasn't working no fingers, just working that tongue.

When I started working with Don, I had two of my friends from Albany, Rory Holloway and John Horne, come to work with me. They were always trying to get me to stay away from the gangster rap crowd, but I loved those rappers. Back then those guys helped me, they understood my pain. One time, I was at a club in L.A. with John Horne and James Anderson, my bodyguard at the time. We were with Felipe, who ran the club. I had a room with Felipe's cousin Michael. As we walked in someone yelled out, "Yo, Mike, when you want a real bodyguard, come get some Long Beach Crips."

Horne thought he was some kind of stand-up comedian and he made some crack about being in a Crip neighborhood once with his wife wearing a red jumpsuit. He thought the guys would laugh. But the guy didn't even let him finish his sentence.

"You're lying. You were never in my motherfucking hood with red on." Once he said this, it was on.

He went all left field and he and all his friends pulled out their guns.

"Get your man, Mike, get your man," the guy said.

I didn't know what to do. I just started talking some slick bullshit and I put out my hand.

"Nigga, slap my hand," I said. "My friend thinks he's a comedian."

And I defused it. That guy, Tracy Brown, became one of my best friends. He was a cold cat. He did fifteen years and then came home and got killed. He was a beautiful brother.

I always had to save Horne's ass. He was an arrogant guy. We went to a Bulls game in Chicago one night. Walter Payton came with us and I had EB and John along. We had the long limo with the hot tub in the back and we were wearing our white mink coats. John and I had gone to the bathroom and this little guy came up and wanted to shake my hand. John just said, "Get out of the way," and pushed on by. He really dissed him. The guy turned real cold.

"Just say sorry right now and it's over. If you don't, it's gonna be a problem."

I immediately read the situation. A bitty guy fronting like that, he's got to be in a gang.

John finally picked up on it and he apologized and shook the guy's hand.

"Thank you, sir," the little guy said. Then he shook my hand and kissed me. When we left the bathroom, the little guy had about fifty guys around him.

"We love you, champ," the guys yelled at me.

I told Horne I was tired of stepping in and protecting him, tired of squashing things. I was the guy going out there with guns in my face, the one who cools the shit down, when these guys were supposed to be protecting me.

At the beginning, I was my own bodyguard. But that didn't turn out so good. I couldn't be beating up people because they wanted an autograph and I happened to be in a shitty mood. So I went out and got some real bodyguards. Not to protect me from the public, but to protect the public from me. I had a friend named Anthony Pitts. We would hang out together in L.A. I knew that Anthony could be good bodyguard material because one night we were courtside at a Lakers game and this disrespectful, out-of-control fan stumbled and knocked into Anthony and didn't apologize. Anthony got up and knocked this motherfucker out right onto the court. I said, "Oh shit!" The game was playing and this guy was laid out cold right out on the court. The police came to get the guy and we had to walk over his body because the game was still on!

Anthony decided I needed a real bodyguard one night when we were at a club in downtown L.A. I was there with Anthony and my friend Johnny, a white dude. We were outside talking to some girls. I had drawn quite a crowd of attractive young women when I heard someone say, "Fuck Mike Tyson!" All of a sudden the whole club was running into the street. So I grabbed this girl I had been talking to and we started running to my limo and I heard, boom. The guy had a gun and had shot at me, but he missed me and hit the girl in the leg. I was such a selfish pig that I still tried to get the wounded girl into my car to take her home. Her girlfriend was screaming, "They shot her because of you, Mike. They wanted to get you." I wanted to get out of there, but my chauffeur wasn't behind the wheel. I looked in the back window and he was curled up hiding in the back. That's when Anthony decided to be my bodyguard. We took off and I left the girl behind. I felt bad that she got shot. Needless to say, she never talked to me again.

With all this drinking and partying, my weight shot up to 255 that December. My next fight was with Frank Bruno, but that wasn't until the end of February 1989. Then I found myself without a trainer. Kevin was always in the papers talking negative bullshit, saying I didn't know what I was doing. He was very anti-Don, always pro-Cayton. I think that his hatred for Don was blinding him. Kevin really fired himself. He didn't want to be with us. He wanted the whole Cayton team back. We were going to hire him back at the same price, but he didn't want it. And then he sued me.

I hired my Catskill roommate Jay Bright to be my new trainer. I wanted Jay to get some money because he was part of Cus's family upstate. We also hired Aaron Snowell, who claimed he had trained Tim Witherspoon. Tim later told me that Snowell was just his running partner who had carried the bucket into the ring, but I didn't care. I was a pugilistic god. My opponents should die with fright at the thought of fighting me. Oh, God!

Before we started training, I had some legal matters to resolve. In January a girl filed a million-dollar suit against me for grabbing her buttocks at Bentley's, a nightclub just blocks from my apartment in Manhattan. Anthony was with me then and he told me to say that I didn't grab her buttocks but that I was behind her and fell into her as I tried to break my fall. Anthony always came up with plausible deniability. And he would often take the fall for me. Another time we were at Bentley's and I grabbed some girl's ass and when she turned around Anthony piped in.

"No, no, that was me, baby. I'm sorry. I thought you were my ex-girl," he told the girl. He defused that one.

But the first girl was taking me to court and she planned on having her friend who was there with her testify against me. I had seen the friend in court the day before she was supposed to testify against me, so I went looking for her and, amazingly enough, I found her out that night with a friend of mine.

"Hey, you're the girl from the case," I approached her.

"Don't you get in my face," she said.

"Hey, I don't want to get in your face," I said calmly. "I'm not mad at you. I'm mad at your friend. I didn't do anything to her."

I figured that if I fucked this girl, she couldn't testify against me the next day.

"Hey, it's no problem, sister. Why don't you and me go for a ride in the Rolls?" My strategy worked. The girl didn't testify.

In January I also had to appear in court for a deposition in connection with Cayton's suit versus Don King. Thomas Puccio, a famous attorney, was Cayton's man. He asked me about the Spinks fight payment and I told him that I couldn't recall if I had been paid. When Puccio showed him that I had been paid my full twelve million dollars, I couldn't recall what I did with the money. I didn't even have my own accountant at the time; I was just using Don's. I didn't have anyone to tell me how to protect myself. All my friends were dependent on me. I had the biggest loser friends in the history of loser friends.

But the deposition got interesting when Puccio asked me about Jimmy and the revised managerial contract I had signed right before he died.

"I had total trust, implicitly, totally, with every soul of my body, in Jim," I testified. "I signed that agreement because Jimmy asked me to sign it. I always trusted Jimmy, I never believed my listening to Jimmy would all come down to this, and being here facing you. I didn't understand Cayton was my manager, because Jimmy, by some means, I can't understand why, Jimmy had me sign this. Like I said, I trusted him and I signed it. I wanted to fight in the glory of Jim, I loved Jim," I said. "He could have informed me about Mr. Cayton being my manager, which he didn't."

But Puccio kept pressing me. He grilled me about the specific terms of my contract with King. I had no idea what was in the contract. Do you think I read that shit?

"You're stressing me out," I told Puccio.

The truth was, I was more interested in putting the moves on Puccio's hot young assistant lawyer, Joanna Crispi. I told her she had a nice ass and I kept trying to get her attention. I'm sorry you have to read about this. What was I thinking? You can't do shit like that. But I did.

My own litigation with Robin was still in the courts, but that didn't keep us from seeing each other. Whenever I was in L.A., I'd stop by for a booty call. I once drove up to her house in my Lamborghini Countach. I knocked on the door and there was no one there. That was odd. So I went back to my car, when I spotted Robin pulling up in her nice white BMW convertible. I should have recognized it, I bought the motherfucker. *Great, I can still get my quickie in,* I thought, but then I spotted a white silhouette with flowing blond hair in the passenger's seat. Shit, it was probably one of her girlfriends from *Head of the Class.* But I looked closer and saw that it was a dude. Someone she was probably giving head to. They pulled up and got out of the car and I saw that the guy was Brad Pitt. When Brad saw me standing there in front of the house, you had to see the look on his face. He looked like he was ready to receive his last rites. Plus, he looked stoned out of his gourd. Then he went all pre-*Matrix* on me. "Dude, don't strike me, don't strike me. We were just going over some lines. She was talking about you the whole time."

"Please, Michael, please, Michael don't do anything," Robin was crying. She was scared to death. But I wasn't going to beat no one up. I wasn't trying to go to jail for her, I was just trying to get in some humps before the divorce.

"Come back later, Mike," she said. "I'll be home, come back later."

It was what it was. Brad beat me to the punch that day so I went back the next day.

That wasn't the last time I saw Robin. While I was training for the Bruno fight, Robin was shooting some B movie up in Vancouver. She kept calling me for help, saying she was being stalked. I wanted to be by her side to protect her. I ditched my security team and immediately flew up there. I was grateful to get out of town because I was tired of training anyway. I was in full romantic mode, so I walked up to the hotel carrying a big bottle of Dom Pérignon. Suddenly I was surrounded by a swarm of reporters and camera crews. Robin had set me up. She had told the media that I was the one stalking her. They were swarming me, asking why I was stalking her, so I acted on instinct. I transformed my champagne bottle into a bludgeon to escape with. Of course, I scared a few reporters and broke a really expensive camera in doing so, which set me back a few pennies. I spent the night with Robin, but I was so disgusted by her behavior that I left the next morning. That was the official end of my relationship with her.

Our divorce was finalized on February fourteenth. Ironic, huh? Robin got some cash money and got to keep all the jewelry I had bought her, which was worth a fortune. Ruthless took some of Robin's booty and opened up an indie film production company in New York called Never Blue Productions. My friend Jeff Wald, the Hollywood producer, had recommended that Howard Weitzman represent me. He was a beast. At one point in the case, Robin had argued that a big check to herself was valid because it said on the bottom line "Mike Tyson gift." What she didn't know was that the bank microfilmed every check. So Howard had blown up the original microfilmed check and put it on a large piece of cardboard to show the court that Robin had written that shit on it after the check had cleared.

Robin also tried to keep my Lamborghini. She took that car and put it in her garage and then had someone put cement blocks into the ground in front of the garage door so we couldn't get it out. But that was no problem for Howard. He hired some private investigators who were ex-Mossad agents and they had the car out in twenty minutes without waking up anyone.

I was free of Robin officially, but instead of being elated, I was really down. I didn't want to be married to her anymore but I felt humiliated by the whole process. I felt like half a person. I had endured the dark side of love—betrayal—and I was ashamed because it had played out in front of millions of people. This was the first time I had made myself vulnerable to someone else. Here was someone I would have died for and now I didn't even care if she died. How does love change like that? Now that I'm a more conscious person, when I think about those times, I realize that Robin and Ruthless were really deplorable people. There was nothing they wouldn't do for money, nothing. They would fuck a rat. They had no boundaries—money was like paper blood to them. They were evil people.

But it was time to go back to fighting. The entire boxing industry was waiting for my next fight. We had brought the whole entertainment base back to the sport. My fights were sold out the minute they were announced. Everybody was going to Vegas to hang out at the MGM Grand. The place was packed like sardines when we were there. The word was out that I'd go to the mall at the MGM Grand and spend two hundred and fifty thousand the night before the fight, so there were all these Mike Tyson look-alikes there. They'd do my walk. I'd be in the room sleeping and there were all these Tyson sightings. Every high roller from around the world was there. Billionaires, actors, actresses, hustlers, they were all there. There'd be whores sitting next to U.S. senators ringside.

But I was in no shape, especially mental, to fight. Bruno should have kicked my ass. I just didn't care anymore. I was tired of fighting. I didn't have Cus's system in my head. But I put up a good front. At one of the first press conferences before the fight I tried to sound upbeat.

"I'm happy to be back. I've gone through a lot of distractions recently, but I really think it's good for someone to go through something like this. Actually, I've been through this pain before but this time it was publicized," I said. "I know I learned a great deal about myself and had to deal with adversity. My main objective now is to get back on top. It doesn't matter if I'm famous, or recognizable. You can't be on top if you don't perform and I plan on performing again and getting back on top."

But the reporters just wanted to know about my storybook romance with Robin and what happened.

"Hey, I went through a stage, fell in love, and I might fall in love again, but not the same way."

I showed a little more bravado as the fight approached.

"People say 'poor guy' about me. That insults me. I despise sympathy. So I screwed up and made some mistakes. 'Poor guy' sounds like I'm a victim. There's nothing poor about me."

We put Rory and John Horne up at the Hilton a few weeks before the fight. A few days later, they were wearing gold watches and jewelry from the hotel shops, which were charged to my bill. I was told that they were even stealing towels from the hotel.

I didn't train particularly hard for the fight. I had sparred with Bruno when I was sixteen at Cus's and had gotten the best of him then. I had no strategy to fight him. I knew I could pick off his jab and he couldn't hurt me with his power punches. At the weigh-in, Bruno attempted to stare me down, so I pulled my shorts down and showed him my pubic hair.

When the fight began, I felt a little rusty but I was punching pretty hard. I dropped him with the first punch. Then I got a little reckless trying to finish him off and I misanticipated his speed and he hit me with a left hook and a short right. People made a big deal that I was wobbled with the punches, but that wasn't so. It was just za-bang and then I was back in charge. I almost finished him off at the very end of the second round. After that, he held me after every punishing blow I got off. With a minute to go in the fifth, I wobbled him and then spent the next forty seconds stalking him. He was ready to go and I got him against the ropes and landed a devastating right uppercut, and Richard Steele stopped the fight. He was out on his feet.

In the postfight interview, I lorded over my opponents.

"How dare they challenge me with their primitive skills?" I sneered.

I was quoting Apocalypse from the X-Men. I was just a big kid, quoting a comic book.

I was scheduled to fight again in July, but HBO wanted to sign me to a lifetime contract. I was constantly the slave nigga. They needed me just like the head slave on a plantation. Just imagine that shit; these suits were fighting over me to rip my soul apart.

I started training for the fight in Ohio. I had bought a house right near Don's. On May thirty-first, the HBO guys went out to Don's to talk about the proposed deal. I didn't show up. I had been partying the night before.

King met with the press and painted a rosy picture of our relationship.

"It's a family affair, where togetherness, solidarity, and unity prevail. Mike understands he has to be better than he is. My job is to be honest with him. He's the man, to allow him to make his own mistakes," he said. "He has to grow up like everyone else, it's all about Mike growing up and I can't wait to make him independent of me."

Now the motherfucker was just copying Cus.

"I do not try to emasculate him, decide what is right and wrong for him. He decides, I'm not his father, but the heart of the father, that many kids in the ghetto don't have. I could relate to what Mike Tyson is suffering."

What can I say about this guy? He wouldn't know the truth if it hit him. He tells the truth by accident.

I hadn't shown up by lunchtime so they started the meeting without me. I rolled in about four in the afternoon, wearing black-and-white-striped lederhosen that Dapper Dan had made for me.

I didn't give a shit about that meeting. I was so bored in Ohio. Sometimes I would get a gun and shoot up the cars on Don's estate. One of the reasons that I was out in Ohio was that I had been banned from a lot of clubs in the city. I even got Paulie Herman kicked out of his own club. He was an investor in the China Club and Paulie and I were there one day and something happened with me and a woman. I think I bossed around a waitress and got mad because she was slow bringing us our champagne. She ratted me out to the boss and he came back to our table and threw us out. So we went to Columbus and Paulie opened the place and we drank there.

Hope spent a lot of time in Ohio with me. I'd have girls come in and out, but it was nice to have someone nurturing like Hope when the other girls left. I'd wake her up in the middle of the night and she'd make us some sandwiches and we'd just talk. I remember telling Hope, "A lot of people don't know this about me, but I can't even make myself a sandwich." I always had people there to do things for me. It was a lonely and depressed time for me.

Then another one of my so-called friends stabbed me. José Torres's book about me finally came out. It originally was supposed to be an authorized biography, but when I got with Don, we withdrew my cooperation. Next thing I knew it was a tell-all book filled with dirt and lies and distortions about me. He had a scene in the book where we were supposedly walking and talking about women and sex and he had me say, "I like to hear them scream with pain, to see them bleed. It gives me pleasure." I never said that about women. I said that about my opponents in the ring. Torres was just a pervert. The book was filled with inaccuracies like that.

I didn't bother to deny the stories when the book first came out, but I did comment on Torres's betrayal. "He's your friend, he's hugging you, tells you how much he loves you and he'll die for you but now I have to make some money so I'm going to cut your throat and leave you to bleed to death."

While we're on the subject of blood, I became preoccupied with AIDS at this time. My next fight was in Atlantic City on July twenty-first. Part of the preparation for the fight was to take an AIDS test. Because boxers often bleed, they were trying to protect the referees, the cornermen, and the other boxer. I was scared to take the test. I was always sleeping with nasty girls so I thought I had AIDS. They came to test me and I just refused.

"Take the fucking test, Mike," Don would plead. "You don't got that shit."

"How do you know? What symptoms show that I don't have it?"

What Don didn't know was that a childhood friend of mine had died of AIDS. My friend and I both had unprotected sex with the same girl. And then the girl died of AIDS too. We all used to go to this one club and the bouncer knew that I was close to the girl, and whenever I'd show up at the club, he'd just look at me.

"Yo, Mike. How you doin'? You look like you been losing weight."

I just knew that behind my back he was telling people I was sick with AIDS.

AIDS was everywhere in our lives then. One of my childhood role models had contracted it. We called him Pop, we didn't even know his real name. He was a flamboyant gay guy, about five years older than me. He was a big-time moneymaker because he dressed immaculately with big furs and rings and diamonds so nobody in the stores would think he was stealing anything. Pop would only hang out with women when he was getting down. He didn't like bringing us around because we would wake the place up. But he was always generous and would break us off some.

My next fight was against Carl "the Truth" Williams. He was a 12-1 underdog and I didn't think he posed any real threat to me. To stir up some interest in the fight and to make some quick cash, Don had set up a 900 phone line. When you called in, you were supposed to get exclusive information about me for your money. It was really just a tape recording of Don interviewing me.

"If you beat Carl Williams, who will you fight next?"

"I don't know," I answered.

And people paid for that shit.

The fight itself didn't last as long as that 900 phone call.

Williams kept throwing his left jab and I pinched to the side and simultaneously threw a left hook that landed square on his jaw. He went down and got up, leaning against the ropes for balance. The ref asked him a question and didn't like what he heard and stopped the fight. The fight had lasted two seconds longer than the Spinks fight. I was surprised that the ref stopped it. I didn't think Williams was hurt that bad. But as I told Larry Merchant after the fight, I would have been all over him. I was always the most dangerous when I had someone hurt.

Merchant asked me who I would fight next and he threw out a whole list of names including Holyfield, Douglas, and Dokes.

"Come one, come all. No one can get close to me. I'm the best fighter in the world," I said.

"Don told me if I knock this guy out, he's paying me a hundred thousand dollars," I told Larry. Don squeezed his way into the camera frame. "When is this going to happen?"

"At the post press conference," he said.

"Oh, yes. Oh, yes." I got so excited. "My church can use that money," I said.

We collected that cash and put it in our bag and Craig Boogie and I went to Mount Vernon directly after the fight to hang out with Heavy D and Al B. Sure! We hung out at Heavy's house with his parents for a few hours and then we went to the city to spend that money at the churches of our choice—first Columbus and then every club from Harlem to downtown. I stayed in New York partying for a month after that fight.

Of course, I went right back to Brownsville and spread some of the wealth in my hood. And sometimes Brownsville came uptown to us. I was riding up Madison Avenue in my limo with my old friend Gordy. I looked out the window and saw this man and woman in long expensive fur coats walking quickly down the street chased by a manager from one of the expensive stores on Madison Avenue.

"Hey, come back here! Come back here!" the manager was yelling.

Then I looked closer and I realized it was Pop and his friend Karen. Gordy and I laughed our asses off that even though he had AIDS Pop was still doing his thing.

I REALLY WENT OVER THE TOP IN THE YEARS WE HAD TEAM TYSON. I WASN'T operating on a logical basis in my mind. I truly thought I was a barbarian champion. "If you don't like what I say, I will destroy you, tear your soul apart." I was Clovis, I was Charlemagne, I was one mean son of a bitch. One of my bodyguards actually began to think that his name was "Motherfucker" because all he'd hear was "Motherfucker, get me this" or "Let's go, motherfucker."

That was a wild camp in Ohio. Everybody was getting their ass kicked around. I was that kind of ruler. Nobody was getting fired, we were just kicking ass. I remember kicking Don King in the head so hard that EB said it looked like dust came out of his Afro.

One Sunday I told Don, "Man, I ain't never seen a million dollars in cash. You better go get me a million dollars."

"But the bank is closed, Mike!" Don said.

"You got connections. Go open the bank and get my million dollars! I want to see it in cash," I warned. Man, I was fucked up. I was just making shit up, finding a reason to kick Don in the head.

"Don't do that, Mike. Don's going to get you killed, Don gets people killed," everybody would say.

"You all afraid of him?" I said. Bam! I kicked him in the head.

One day Ali and a few other people were at Don's house in Vegas. I used to hear stories that Ali and Larry Holmes and a lot of other boxers were scared of Don because they thought Don could get them killed. I respected them and wanted them to know that Don was nobody to be scared of. I would say deplorable things about him in front of everyone just to prove how worthless he was. I don't know if that was the real motivation for me whupping his ass. I was a young immature kid then and I just felt like doing it.

Rory and John would come to me. "Mike, listen, the man's sixty-something years old. You keep hitting him, you're going to give him brain damage. He told us to call you and let you know he ain't going to come around if you keep hitting him, so just chill out." So I had to chill out.

They all thought I was crazy. I wasn't training. I was partying too much. And then having barely trained, I'd go fight a guy and still knock him out. You know, I might have for that moment of time been crazy. I'm so far away from that person now. I'm, like, *Whoa, fuck, I was crazy.*

I really believed that I was the baddest man on the planet. I was kicking Don's ass thinking I was fucking John Gotti over here. Don used to try to get me to go see a doctor. He'd say, "Mike, you need to go see a psychiatrist, brother. Something ain't right here." He actually got me to see Dr. Alvin Poussaint, Bill Cosby's guy, a distinguished professor of psychiatry at Harvard Medical School. He was a real erudite didactic guy. Poussaint asked me what my problem was and I started saying crazy shit to him. "Fuck it. I don't care about living and dying, I don't give a fuck." That guy was so bourgeois and regal he made me sick to my stomach. He got the fuck away though. He ran out of the house and never came back.

When I think about all the horrific things that Don has done to me over the years, I still feel like killing him. He's such a liar and betrayer. He's not a tough guy. He's never been a tough guy. All the tough-guy things he's done have been through him paying someone to do it for him.

I didn't care what anybody thought about me then. I was just living every day the way I wanted to. I was like a cowboy gambling with life. I wanted to be the villain and I had become that person. *Boxing Illustrated* magazine published an article, "Is Mike Tyson Becoming the Most Unpopular Heavyweight in History?" Dave Anderson from the *New York Times* wrote a column, "Who Is Out There to Stop Tyson?" The press was turning on me and I loved it. I was such an irritant. I needed more people to fight.

The press despised me by then. I'd spit at them, yell at them; that was just who I was. I'd tell them, "You just say something back. You could sue me but you're going to have to use that money to buy yourself a fucking wheelchair with the fancy motors and toilet because that's what you'll be going around in."

"How dare you talk to me? You never fought a day in your life and you're here judging people. Who are you? You've never even put on a pair of gloves. You got your job from your brother. The only things you can do is drink and cheat on your wife. You're just some fucking derelict that writes for a newspaper."

Don signed me to fight Razor Ruddock next. The hotels in the States weren't interested in paying big fees for that fight. Trump felt burnt by my last quick KO over Williams. So King found some guys in Edmonton, Canada, to pay a $2.6 million site fee. We were scheduled to fight on November eighteenth. But after hanging out in New York, I went out to L.A. and resumed nonstop partying there. I wasn't too interested in fighting Ruddock. I had seen him fight Michael Weaver and he boxed brilliantly against him. But he never fought like that again. He turned into a knockout artist. In his fight before he was scheduled to fight me, he had been floored in the second round by Bonecrusher Smith and then he got up to knock him out impressively in the seventh.

I started training for the fight in Vegas in September but my heart wasn't in it. I didn't want to fight anymore. We moved camp to Edmonton in mid-October. I wasn't in training. I was just sleeping with women. I didn't even want to leave my room. I got my friends to grab a random girl and bring her back to my room. I didn't care how she looked or what her name was. When we were done, she'd leave and another random girl would come. I finally told Don to make some excuse and postpone the fight. We used my bronchitis. I could have easily fought with it but when a doctor would see my X-rays he'd get alarmed. We called the fight off on October twenty-sixth and flew back to Vegas. Don had found some doctor to certify that I had contracted pleurisy. Pleurisy? What the fuck is pleurisy? I was worried that it was a venereal disease.

Don started looking for an easier matchup for me. He decided to take me to Japan in January to fight Buster Douglas, who he thought would be a pushover. Then he struck a deal with Evander Holyfield's people and set up a match with him in June 1990 at the Trump Plaza. I'd walk away with $25 million for that fight. Cayton, who was still my manager of record, was happy to hear that.

So I threw myself back into partying. In November I got to meet some of the greatest celebrities imaginable when I participated in a celebration of the sixtieth anniversary of Sammy Davis Jr.'s showbiz career. I had such a great time. I talked to George Burns and Milton Berle about Fanny Brice and Ruby Keeler and Al Jolson. George was so old he had actually worked with Fanny. I hung out with the whole Rat Pack. Those guys really liked me a lot.

But meeting these guys couldn't hold a candle to meeting my boxing idols. Of any celebrity I met around that time I was most in awe meeting Max Schmeling. He was in his mideighties when I met him. It was fascinating to talk to him about boxing. We talked about Dempsey and Mickey Walker. He told me that Joe Louis was the greatest fighter and also the greatest man. When he heard that Joe Louis was bankrupt, he left Germany and went to Harlem to look for Joe. Can you imagine an older white guy going to all the clubs in Harlem looking for Joe Louis? By the time I met him, Schmeling had become a billionaire, he owned all the rights to Pepsi in Germany. But what was so fascinating about him was that he still loved boxing. Everywhere he went, he'd take copies of his old fight films with him.

I loved old fighters. When I learned that Joey Maxim, the former light heavyweight champ, was working as a greeter at a Vegas hotel, I'd go visit him every other week and talk to him about his career. He was so mad that he was never introduced at ringside at any of the big fights at the Hilton, so I made sure they did that from then on. I never looked at guys like him as being bums or down on their luck. I looked at him as being bigger than me. It wasn't like I was some big shot doing him a favor coming in; I was in awe to be there with him. I was just so happy to see him and touch him. When I went home that first night, I cried.

ON JANUARY 8, 1990, I GOT ABOARD A PLANE TO FLY TO TOKYO. KICKING AND
screaming. I didn't want to fight; all I was interested in then was
partying and fucking women. By the time we left, I had put on thirty
pounds. King was so worried about my weight that he offered me a
bonus if I would make my usual weight when we fought in a month.

I didn't consider Buster Douglas much of a challenge. I didn't even
bother watching any of his fights on video. I had easily beaten everybody who had knocked him out. I saw him fight for the ESPN championship when I was on the undercard and he got beat by Jesse
Ferguson, who I had knocked out in my first fight on ABC. I felt like
my heroes Mickey Walker and Harry Greb. I read that Greb was so
arrogant he'd tell his opponents that he hadn't trained because "you
are not worth me sweating for." So I followed his lead. I didn't train at
all for the fight. Anthony Pitts was there with me and he would get up
early in the morning and run with my sparring partner Greg Page.
But I didn't feel like it. Anthony would tell me that he'd see Buster out
there, digging in with his army boots on, snotsicles hanging off his
nose, getting in his run.

I couldn't eat since I was overweight and I wanted to lose the
weight and win the bonus from Don, so I drank the soup that was supposed to burn off fat. And then I had the cleaning ladies for the main
course. It was ironic, because you go to Japan and the women seem so
shy and introverted, but fortunately I ran into some unconventional
Japanese ladies. People would ask me if I learned any sexual tips from
the Japanese women, but I didn't have time to learn. This was no sex
education course; this was a guy trying to get his rocks off.

I didn't even have to pay the maids to screw them. But I did tip
them heavily because I had a lot of that Monopoly-looking money they
had over there. They must have been appreciative because they'd come
back and sometimes bring friends.

"My friend would like to meet you, Mr. Tyson, sir. She would like
to accompany us, sir."

Besides having sex with the maids, I was seeing this young Japanese girl who I had had sex with the last time I was in Japan for the Tony Tubbs fight. Robin would go out shopping and I would go upstairs in the stairwell with her.

I had her do the same thing this time. There were too many people on my floor and I didn't want Don or Rory or John or Anthony to know my business. They might have scared her; she was very shy around people. In the two years since I had seen her, she had matured a great deal.

So that was my training for Douglas. Every once in a while, I did show up to work out and spar. I was sparring with Greg Page ten days before the fight and I walked right into a right hook and went down.

"What the fuck are you doing?" Greg asked me later.

A few days later, Don opened up one of my sparring sessions to the public for $60 a head. I never saw any of that money, of course. At the time, I didn't even know he was charging people. We were supposed to spar for two rounds but I looked so bad that Aaron Snowell and Jay stopped it after one and closed the session. Don was pissed off. He wanted to make a buck. He had no idea I was so out of shape. Don knew nothing about fighting. He couldn't tell the difference between a guy in shape or out of shape. He didn't even know how to tie a boxing glove.

The day before the fight I weighed in at 220½ pounds, my heaviest fighting weight to date. But I still got my bonus. The day before the fight I also had two maids at the same time. And then two more girls, one at a time, the night before the fight.

I wasn't following the story but apparently Douglas had a lot of motivation to do well in this fight. In July of 1989, he had been born-again. And then his wife left him, his baby momma got a terminal disease, and early in January while he was in camp his mother died. I didn't know any of that and I didn't care. HBO was making a big deal about Douglas fighting for his mother, but my arrogance at the time was such that I would have said that he was going to join her that night.

We fought at nine a.m. because of the time difference back in the

United States. Half of the arena's sixty-three thousand seats were empty. Don was a lousy promoter. As soon as I got with him, everything just sunk. He was a dark cloud.

It wasn't the usual Tyson going into the ring. It was obvious to anyone who was watching that I really didn't want to be there. The fight started and I fought horribly. I was punching as hard as shit because I knew if I caught him right he wasn't going to get up, I didn't care how big he was. But I was hardly throwing. It was the least amount of punches I'd ever thrown in a fight. He used his jab and his reach to throw me off my game and then when I tried to throw body shots, he just held me. He fought very well that night. But I was an easy target for him. I wasn't moving my head at all.

He wasn't intimidated by me. In fact, he was the one punching after the bell and on breaks. He was fighting dirty but that's just part of boxing, everyone did that. After the third round, I went back to my corner and it was obvious that Aaron and Jay were in over their heads.

"You're not closing the gap," Aaron said. "You've got to get inside, you're flat-footed in there."

No fucking shit. Why don't *you* try to get inside? The guy had a twelve-inch reach advantage on me.

"Get back to what you know," Jay said. "Do it. Let it go."

Easy to say when you're not getting punched. I kept staring at the floor.

Douglas rocked me in the fourth and the fifth. During the fifth round, my eye began to swell, but when I went back to the corner, they didn't even have the End-Swell to keep my eye open. I couldn't believe it when they filled what looked like an extra-large condom with ice water and held it to my eye.

I was exhausted by the sixth round. My left eye was totally shut. But Buster looked tired too, especially when the seventh round began. But I couldn't get to him. In the eighth he wobbled me and had me against the ropes in the last twenty seconds. I was looking for one punch by then. I was still rocked by his punches, I couldn't focus but I saw an opening. For the whole fight he had eluded me whenever I saw openings and I couldn't bridge the gap, but by then he was tired too and he couldn't move. So I threw my trademark right uppercut and down he went.

Then I got screwed. The timekeeper was Japanese and the referee was Mexican and they spoke different languages and couldn't coordinate the count. When the ref was saying "five," Douglas had actually been on the canvas for eight seconds. So he got a long count. I had to take the short end of the stick. That's just part of boxing but I think I was really screwed. The WBA was supposed to be on our side. I knew I was going to win because the guys I fought were fighting me and the officials too, basically. Don always paid off the officials. At least that's what he told me. Maybe he forgot to pay off the ref that night.

But I don't want to take anything away from Buster. He had so much courage and guts that night. I had hit him with an awesome shot. Anybody else's head would have been sent to the space shuttle if they had experienced that punch. I was so spent that I couldn't follow up on the knockdown the next round. He came back strong. When the tenth began, I hit him with a straight right to the jaw but then he unleashed a barrage of punches at my head, starting with a right uppercut. I was so numb that I didn't even feel the punches, but I could hear them. My equilibrium was shot. Then I went down.

When I hit the canvas, my mouthpiece came out and as the ref was counting, I was trying to stumble to my feet and grab the mouthpiece at the same time. I was operating on pure instinct. I was totally out of it. The ref hugged me after he counted to ten. I walked back to my corner totally dazed. I was chewing on my mouthpiece but I didn't even know what it was.

"What happened?" I asked my corner.

"The ref counted you out, champ," Aaron said.

I knew it was inevitable. I was fucked from early on that fight. I didn't do the postfight interview with HBO, my head was still ringing. I must have had at least one concussion.

Within minutes Don had organized a meeting with the WBC and WBA officials. Then he called his own press conference.

"The first knockout obliterated the second knockout," he ranted. Jose Sulaiman, the president of the WBC, suspended recognition of anyone as champion because the ref had failed to take the count from the timekeeper. The referee admitted that he had made a mistake. Sulaiman immediately called for a rematch. By then, I was conscious enough to join the press conference. I was wearing sunglasses to hide my mangled eye and holding a white compress to my swollen face.

"You guys know me for years, I never gripe or bitch. I knocked him out before he had me knocked out. I want to be champ of the world. That's what all young boys want," I said.

I went back to my hotel room. There was no maid there. It was weird not being the heavyweight champion of the world any longer. But in my mind it was a fluke. I knew that God didn't pick on any small animals, that lightning only struck the biggest animals, that those are the only ones that vex God. Minor animals don't get God upset. God has to keep the big animals in check so they won't get lofty on their thrones. I just lay on my bed and thought that I had become so big that God was jealous of me.

8

IT WAS A LONG FLIGHT BACK FROM TOKYO. MY EYE WAS STILL FUCKED UP SO I was wearing these big dark sunglasses that Anthony Pitts gave me. During the flight I talked to Anthony.

"So I guess you're going to leave me now," I said. The addict in me was saying "I'm doomed. My world is over."

"Mike, I'll never leave you," he said. "You can't fire me and I can't quit so we're stuck together. You watch, you'll be all right when the swelling goes down."

We went straight to Camille's house when we landed. I'm a weird dude, I go right back to the basics. Home to my moms. The next morning Anthony got up at seven a.m., and when he went downstairs I was already doing sit-ups and push-ups.

"Oh, now you want to train? After the motherfucking fight," he said.

"Man, I'm just trying to stay focused," I said.

I talked to Camille later. She had been at the fight watching from the front row and she thought that I looked like I was in a daze.

"You didn't throw any vicious punches," she said. "You looked like you wanted to lose. Maybe you just got tired of it."

She was probably right. I believed in the Cus theory that the only thing wrong with defeat is if nothing is learned from it. Cus always used to tell me that fighting is a metaphor for life. It doesn't matter if you're losing; it's what you do after you lose. Are you going to stay down or get back up and try it again? Later I would tell people that my best fight ever was the Douglas fight because it proved that I could take my beating like a man and rebound.

So I hung out in Catskill and played with my pigeons and read about my heroes. How Tony Zale had come back from Rocky Graziano. How Joe Louis came back to demolish Max Schmeling. How Ali came back from exile. How Sugar Ray Robinson just bridled at seeing the word "former" in conjunction with his name. My narcissism started working again and I started thinking that I was from these guys' bloodline. I knew that it was inevitable that I would get back those belts. I was going to go away to some destitute place and learn this masterful trade and come back and be better, like in all those great Shaw Brothers karate movies. Ain't that some bullshit? I was just a sewage rat with delusions of grandeur.

Meanwhile, the whole boxing world was in turmoil. The day after the fight, every major newspaper abhorred the idea that Douglas wouldn't be recognized as the new champ. As soon as he got back to the States, Jose Sulaiman recanted. And Don was reduced to begging for an immediate rematch. He was banking that Evander Holyfield, who was the mandatory challenger, would take a nice sum to step aside to let me fight a rematch. But Holyfield's people knew that if Evander beat Buster, Don would be on the outside of the heavyweight picture looking in.

Then there were the reporters who couldn't contain their glee that I had lost. That little slimy coward Mike Lupica from the New York *Daily News* saw me as some Satan figure.

"Someone who bounces women around and gives it in the back to his friends and turns his back on people who helped make him champion, making it seem as if dogs have more loyalty than he does . . . Tyson was some kind of savage, on whom the culture bestows all that is normal, only for him to reject the gifts and the givers, and revert to life on the instinctual level. The only end for such a man is death."

Woooo! I loved that shit.

I picked up on that sentiment in an interview I did with ESPN. They asked me why everyone was so fascinated with my life.

"I believe a lot of people want to see me self-destruct. They want to see me one day with handcuffs and walking in the police car or else going to jail. Like you've seen Marlon Brando's son. People love saying, 'This is what I told you, I told you he was heading for that.' But I'm not in jail and I'm not in Brownsville anymore and I beat all the odds."

Don had me do a few press conferences and I tried to put on the best face I could but my honesty kept getting in the way.

"Nobody's invincible," I told them. "Sometimes the guy just breaks your will in a way. Buster kicked my butt. I didn't train for that fight. I didn't take the fight serious. I was fucking those Japanese girls like I was eating grapes. You'd thought I was Caligula when I was out there in Japan."

In L.A., I cracked up the press when I told them how I watched the fight on tape back home.

"I sit there and I tell myself, 'Hey, man, duck!' But on the screen, I don't duck. I scream, 'Duck, you dummy!' But the dummy don't listen to me."

A reporter asked me if I felt suicidal after losing the belt.

"Hey! I got lots of money to spend before I kill myself. You have to deal with things like this every day. Did I cry? I wish I could cry! The last time I cried was when I got my divorce. That's when you cry. Actually, can I tell you something? It was a relief, is what it was. It was a relief of a lot of pressure."

The divorce really fucked me up. I wouldn't want to ever tell anybody that now, so for me to say that then means I must have still been fucked up about it.

People were trying to make excuses for me, but I wasn't buying it.

Even Larry Merchant, who was not always respectful to me, tried to blame the loss on my eye closing up when he interviewed me for an HBO special a week after the fight.

"You have another eye. Use that one. You fight to the finish," I said. "My heart was still beating."

When I got back from L.A., I went straight to my refuge in Catskill. Except now half the world was going up there looking to interview me. You'd see reporters from Brazil, England, Scandinavia, Japan hanging out in Catskill and Albany, going to the places I frequented like September's. They'd ring Camille's door and she'd fight with them.

"You don't come here anymore, you leave him alone, he's just a little baby!" she yelled. "You should feel ashamed of yourself."

Buster Douglas won the fight but no one was paying any attention to him, people were looking for me. They even made a dance video of my knockout and me fumbling for my mouthpiece. It was ironic. I subconsciously wanted to lose to get out of that pressure cooker but not even that worked.

"Now I can't quit, I'm a whore to the game," I told one reporter. "Now I have to prove something. In fact, now I wonder sometimes if I'm not bigger than I was before because I lost."

In the midst of all this confusion, my sister died. She was the only person who wasn't afraid to put me in deep check. She was always my protector, even right until she died. She was pretty obese and her husband told me that she had been doing cocaine the night before. I really hope that she wasn't doing it because she was depressed about me. I had a long phone conversation with her the night before she died.

"Go talk to your father," she said. "And please get your eye checked out."

She was always close to Jimmy, our biological dad. She wanted us to start having a relationship. My sister was something. I'd try to give her money but she didn't like to take my money. She was really comfortable with her ghetto life. She never sweated me for anything.

I was sad when she died, but by then I had become accustomed to death and understood it implicitly. We had her funeral in Brooklyn and the Reverend Al Sharpton presided over it. We would make fun of Reverend Al and tease him about being fat and his big hairdo but he was a giant hero in our community. We were proud of him. You saw where he came from and you knew where he was then and you'd have to say it was a miracle. I saw a documentary on PBS the other night about the history of Broadway and they had Milton Berle talking about growing up poor in Brooklyn. He said that having a humble shitty-paying job wasn't failing. Going back to Williamsburg and Brownsville, that was failing. That cut me right to my soul.

I had to go visit my friends in Brownsville after I lost the title. I really didn't want to go back with my tail between my legs but my friends were wonderful. It was all love. I hung out a lot with my friend Jackie Rowe. She and I used to hustle together when I was a kid. Me and my friends would rob a place and then go to Jackie's house to split the money up. Jackie was a big, brash, in-your-face person, kind of like my sister. In fact, after Niecey died she began to call herself my sister.

Despite thinking that the gods wanted me to get my belt back, I was sad and embarrassed and doubting myself after my loss. Jackie was always upbeat.

"Are you crazy, motherfucker?" she'd yell at me. "Do you know who you are? It was one fight, Mike. You lost. Big deal. Let's move on. You're the best."

"Do you think so?" I'd say.

"Yes, I know so. You just didn't follow protocol; you just didn't do what you were supposed to do."

"You're right, you're right," I said.

I'd visit Jackie and park outside her apartment, which was in one of the city housing projects. I'd just chill at her house and Jackie would go out and get me my favorite food. I'd hang out her window calling to girls. They'd look up and do a double take.

"That can't be Mike Tyson. Is that Mike Tyson? Mike! Mike!"

When the word got out, so many people rushed out that they had to put police tape around my Ferrari and cordon off the whole block.

Sometimes Jackie took me up to Harlem and people would go crazy.

"You're still the greatest, champ," they'd yell out. "You can do it again!"

I definitely got some reassurance by being around all these people and seeing that I was still loved.

Don had signed me to make my comeback in Vegas on June 16, 1990, fighting Henry Tillman. I started training in New York before we went out to Vegas. My buttocks-grabbing case was winding down and I'd go to court and then go train. Emile Griffith, the former world champion, was working with some fighters at the gym I was training at. One day he said something that just rocked me to my bones and made me finally forget about my loss to Douglas.

I was talking to him about that Douglas fight.

"Yeah, I really didn't do that well, huh?" I said.

"I know the great Mike Tyson is not going to let something like this discourage him," Mr. Griffith said.

Oh, man. Those few words completely changed my opinion of myself and my comeback. Isn't that crazy? Just hearing those words made me forget about the loss and think I was champion again. Once he said that, I was back.

We had two new additions to Team Tyson. Don had hired Richie Giachetti as my new head trainer. And I had my first child with this woman Natalie Fears, a son that I named D'Amato.

In mid-April we relocated to Vegas to train. I jumped into it like a maniac. Up at four a.m. to run, working out at the gym, sparring in the afternoon, then riding a bike for two hours at the Las Vegas Athletic Club. George Foreman was fighting on my undercard and he had an interesting thing to say about losing a title.

"You are ashamed to see everybody, especially the skycaps at the airport. You don't want to see the taxi drivers because everybody is going to say something, in your mind. And you have to build yourself up, so you start spending billions of dollars on cars, suits, anything you can to make yourself look like the best in the world. Mike Tyson will never sleep again until he gets a chance to fight for the title again and win it. He'll never sleep again until he redeems himself. I hate to see a young man go through that, but that is the way that it is."

I didn't necessarily agree with George then. I was such a megalomaniac that I knew that it was foreordained that I'd win the belt back. I just knew that I had to train.

The night of the Tillman fight I was primed. I'm fighting the guy who beat me in the amateurs. It was a great comeback story. The guy goes down and I'd get revamped.

Even though he was an Olympic gold medalist and had a respectable 20-4 record, the odds were 1–2 for a first-round knockout.

I obliged the oddsmakers. At the very beginning of the fight, I took a heavy right from him and it didn't even faze me. I slowed him up with a huge right to the body and then finally caught him with an overhead right to his temple with twenty-four seconds left in the round. He was out on his back. I really didn't want to hurt Henry. I wanted to get it over with real quick. I liked him a lot and I was just glad he got a nice payday. Tillman was one of those fighters who was really great but just didn't have confidence in himself. If he had believed in himself, he would have been a legendary fighter; he would have been in the Hall of Fame.

At the postfight press conference Don was being Don.

"He's back, he is Mighty Mike Tyson," he yelled.

I yanked his arm and told him to shut up.

"You know you are back," Don said.

I talked a little bit about the fight and gave Henry some props but I wanted to talk about my baby boy.

"He's so gorgeous. He's six weeks old and twelve pounds. He can already sit up! I live for my son."

A few months after the fight, my buttocks case finally came to a conclusion. I was convicted of battery and, to assess damages, her attorneys made us file a statement of my assets. Don's attorney filed it and we found out that Don still owed me $2 million from the Tokyo fight. According to what was filed I had assets of $2.3 million in cash, the Jersey house that was worth $6.2 million, my Ohio house, and about a million and a half in cars and jewelry. My assets totaled $15 million but with all my purses I should have had a lot more. I didn't know if they were cooking the books for the trial or if I was getting ripped off. Either way the damages the jury awarded to that woman were a bit short of the million dollars they were asking for. They gave her $100. When I heard that verdict, I stood up in court, pulled a hundred-dollar bill out of my pocket, licked it, and pasted it to my forehead. I guess she didn't want to take cash.

My next comeback fight was supposed to have taken place in Atlantic City on September twenty-second. I was going to fight Alex Stewart. Stewart was a former Jamaican Olympiad who started his career with twenty-four straight knockouts. His only loss was an eighth-round TKO by Evander Holyfield, a fight that he was dominating until he got cut and Holyfield went to work on that cut. During camp, I got a cut over my eye and I needed forty-eight stitches to close it so the fight was postponed until December eighth.

Meanwhile, HBO was pressing to re-sign me. Seth Abraham thought he had reached a deal with Don for a ten-fight extension for $85 million but then Don backed out of it. He claimed that the reason he backed out was because he didn't want Larry Merchant doing my fights, because Merchant would always talk shit about me. After the Stewart fight Don used that excuse to move to Showtime. I thought that the Showtime deal was better, but later I would learn that it was better for Don not me.

While I waited to fight Stewart, Buster Douglas defended his title against Evander Holyfield. I knew Holyfield would win. Douglas went in way overweight and Holyfield was the better fighter. Douglas just quit. He got hit a little and laid down. He was a whore for his $17 million. He didn't go into the fight with any dignity or pride to defend his belt. He made his payday but he lost his honor. You can't win honor, you can only lose it. Guys like him who only fight for money can never become legends. I can tell that it still affects Buster to this day. Years later, I ran into him again at an autograph session we both attended. No one wanted his autograph. This was the guy who made history for beating me but now his legacy had been reduced to nothing.

The next night after his win, Holyfield announced that he would defend his title against George Foreman. That pissed me off. Everybody wanted to put me down, overshadow me, but they couldn't. I was still the biggest star in the boxing world, bigger than any of them without a belt.

Stewart and I finally squared off on December eighth in Atlantic City. HBO was so intent on re-signing me that they even hired Spike Lee to do the prefight introduction film segment just to placate me. I decided to talk some shit on film with Spike and make people mad.

"Everything is totally against us," I said. "Don and I are two black guys from the ghetto and we hustle and they don't like what we're saying. We're not like prejudiced anti-white, we are just pro-black."

I didn't take that shit seriously. I was just having fun fucking around.

"They're always changing rules when black folks come into success, black success is unacceptable," Don said. When HBO screened the segment for reporters, they were disgusted. Mission accomplished.

But I was paying a price for my association with Don. Hugh McIlvanney, a famous Scottish sportswriter, had blamed my losing to Douglas on my relationship with King.

"Of all the contributing factors in Tyson's downfall, most damaging of all, perhaps, has been his alliance with Don King, who has precipitated decay in practically every fighter with whom he has been associated."

He was absolutely right. Don was very toxic. His presence was offensive. He did it on purpose. Everybody blackballed me once I got involved with him. He gave me free reign to indulge my childish behavior and people saw that I wasn't trying to get away from him, so they blocked everything I tried to do.

At the prefight press conference, I sounded crazy.

"I am a champion. Being a champion is a frame of mind. I'm always going to be champion. Being happy is just a feeling like when you are hungry or thirsty. When people say that you are happy, that's just a word somebody gave you to describe a feeling. When I decided to accomplish my goals, I gave up all means of even thinking of being happy."

I am not a happy camper. I just wasn't built that way.

I must have liked fighting at Trump's casino in Atlantic City. That was my third fight there and my third first-round knockout. I hit Stewart four seconds into the fight with my right hand and he went down. Then I stalked him around the ring and floored him again with a right. I was pretty wild and at one point I even missed and fell to the canvas. But I finally cornered him and knocked him down with a left with thirty-three seconds left in the round. The three-knockdown rule was in effect, so they stopped the fight.

When they finished examining Stewart, I went out to him and hugged him.

"Don't be discouraged. You're a good fighter. Remember I got beat by a bum."

On my way out of the ring, Jim Lampley, the play-by-play announcer for HBO, asked me a few questions. The last two fights, I had refused to talk to Larry Merchant when the fight was over.

"I'd like to thank all my fans watching on HBO for supporting me all these years," I interjected. "This is my last fight for HBO because I think that they'd rather see Holyfield than me."

The new sensation in the heavyweight ranks was a Canadian boxer named Razor Ruddock. He had fought Michael Dokes in April of 1990 and the tapes of that knockout were circulating throughout the boxing world. I finally saw the tape when Alex Wallau of ABC Sports showed me a copy.

Dokes was ahead during the fight and then, boom, Ruddock hit him with one punch and knocked him cold. It was a very frightening, gut-wrenching, breathtaking KO.

"What do you think?" Alex asked me.

Since I was a palooka in the art of manipulation, I laid back and stayed cool.

"What about it? I'm not Michael Dokes. He's going to be a quick knockout, he's nothing."

But with Holyfield signed to fight Foreman, I had to keep busy. So Don signed me to fight Ruddock in Vegas on March 18, 1991.

Fuck, these people are trying to kill me out here. They're sending the big guns out to get me, I thought.

I started training hard in early January. I had Tom Patti, my old housemate when Cus was around, in my camp. We were watching TV one night and one of Ruddock's fights came on and I saw a flaw in Ruddock.

"I'm going to kill this guy," I told Tom.

I knew that Ruddock was a dangerous puncher, but I also saw that I'd be too elusive for him. He wouldn't be able to hit me solidly.

We almost started the fight a few days before it was scheduled at the prefight press conference at the Century Plaza Hotel in Los Angeles. We were doing the face-off for the photographers and I told Ruddock that I was going to make him my bitch. Razor tried to approach me like a tough guy and Anthony Pitts pushed him back. I said, "No, no. Let him come closer to express himself better." I knew I could beat him in a street fight. Razor's bodyguards wanted to step up but it was squashed.

So we went to the airport for the plane back to Vegas. Turned out that Razor and his crew were on the same flight. When we got there, Rory forgot his phone in the car so Anthony went to get it from Isadore, our driver. When Anthony was on his way back, he started walking down the steps and Ruddock's people were walking up the steps and they blocked off Ant.

Ruddock had twin bodyguards and one of them, Kevin Ali, said, "Oh, you think you're bad?" He showed Anthony his walkie-talkie. "You see what these are for?" So he stepped up on Anthony and Anthony popped him. But Isadore saw there was a fracas and he ran up the stairs and grabbed Anthony.

"Isadore, why are you grabbing me?" Anthony said. "Grab one of these motherfuckers."

By then, airport security had broken up the fight. When Anthony returned to the waiting area, he told me what had gone down. When we got on the plane, I saw that they were supposed to be sitting behind us, so I moved my guys to the back of the plane. The whole flight I was flinging grapes at Ruddock. Just to be safe, we called ahead and had our whole crew, the training camp, the sparring partners, everyone, meet us at the airport in case something went down. But nothing happened.

When we got to the Mirage the night of the fight, they had us in facing dressing rooms and Kevin Ali started trash-talking Anthony.

"Yo, man, let me tell you something," Anthony said. "I don't smoke, but I will smoke your whole fucking family, you, your brother, your mother, I'll kill all you motherfuckers, I don't give a fuck."

John Horne heard Anthony hollering and he pulled him aside.

"Yo, man, you don't go inside the ring tonight," he said. "You stay outside the ring. Because if Mike wins this fight, I know these motherfuckers are going to start something, so you be aware."

It was a chilly night in Vegas and we were fighting outdoors in front of a huge crowd of sixteen thousand people. I wore a green-and-white-striped sweat suit and a ski cap into the ring. I was the first boxer to wear urban clothes into the ring.

Ruddock looked nervous and was hyperventilating. He was in with the big boys now. I knew he was going to come right at me, he was so nervous. A few seconds into the fight, I rocked him with a right hand. He came back with some hard punches but I was just too elusive for him. In the second, he went down from a left but it was a glancing blow, it looked like his leg got tangled up with mine, but my vicious body attack had slowed him to a standstill. He couldn't hit me with hard punches, and by the third round he was pretty much holding on for dear life. I managed to get in a vicious left-hook counterpunch with ten seconds to go in the round and he went down.

I was winning every round. In the sixth, he suddenly seemed to wake up and hit me with a flurry of hard punches. I shook my head at him. He hit me with a right to the jaw and I tapped my jaw and dared him to throw again. Me taking those punches with impunity must have demoralized him because I came out in the seventh and stunned him with a left hook to the jaw. Four more punches and he was stumbling back into the ropes. But Richard Steele jumped in and stopped the fight without Ruddock even going down. I thought the stoppage was premature, although one more punch and he would have been down.

Before I knew it, I was in the middle of a riot. Murad Muhammad, Razor's manager, got my trainer Richie on the floor and was kicking him in the head. Jay Bright pulled me over to a corner and we watched the rumble. By then, Anthony Pitts had come into the ring and he saw Kevin Ali charging across the ring and Ant cracked him with a right. Then Razor's brother Delroy tried to hit Anthony, but Anthony grabbed him and was about to throw him over the ropes out of the ring but security grabbed his arm. So Delroy was up in the air, pushed up against the rope, and he had his arm hanging down, trying to catch himself. While this was happening, my friend Greg snatched Kevin Ali's Rolex and then went into his pocket to see what else he could get. It was a crazy scene.

There was a lot of controversy about the quick ending, so we decided to give Ruddock a rematch. We were at Don's office on East Sixty-ninth Street in Manhattan, working out the details of the second fight. Don and Rory and John were upstairs, but I was chilling downstairs with Anthony because I was chatting with Don's cute little receptionist who I was sleeping with. All of a sudden, Kevin Ali walked in. Kevin was a good Muslim brother but some Muslim brothers take their Muslim thing and bring it with them everywhere they go, fighting, eating, everywhere. So Kevin looked at me and said, "Oh, most beautiful champion. Great fight. I have to give you much respect. You're a true warrior." Then he pointed towards Anthony and said, "But I'm gonna kill him."

"Yo, man, I'm standing right here, motherfucker," Anthony said. "Don't send no messages to nobody for me. If you've got something to say, say it."

"We're going to have to do this and what we do is, do or die. We could do this shit right now," Kevin said.

"That was just work, that's over, let that shit go." I tried to defuse the situation.

"No, champ, I can't let that go, I gotta do this," Ali said.

So he put his briefcase and his coat down and, boom, Anthony cracked him with one punch. They were fighting by the stairs and Don had a wall divider that blocked off the stairs, so I didn't actually see Kevin go down, but it was like in a cartoon, you heard him go boom, boom, boom, down each step. Then he flew back up like he was a superhero and they went at it again. My friend Greg walked in drinking a bottle of soda and he saw Anthony and Kevin going at it so he clocked Kevin in the head with his bottle. Kevin went down and Greg started going through his pockets.

"No, Greg, we can't do that shit here," I said. "You need some money, nigga? We can't rob motherfuckers."

All this commotion made Don and John and Rory come down the stairs to see what was happening. Ali had gotten up and he claimed that Anthony had sucker-punched him.

"That's bullshit," I said. "Ant was just in there chilling, this motherfucker came in threatening Anthony. Ant just defended himself."

Don kicked Kevin Ali out of the office and Kevin went outside and started pacing up and down in front of the townhouse. When we left, we saw Ali there. Our driver at the time was Captain Joe, a forefather in the Nation of Islam. He knew the Ali twins. Ali wanted to resume the fight but I told him that it was Ramadan and it was a time of peace.

"Mike, this is a man thing," Captain Joe said. "He can't be in peace with Ramadan until he has peace with himself. He has to settle this."

"Do you want to do this?" Ali asked Anthony.

"Hell, yeah. You said do or die."

The two went at it outside on the sidewalk like Rock 'Em Sock 'Em Robots. Anthony finally connected and dropped Ali. He hit the ground and Anthony drop-kicked him twice to the head. He was about to do it a third time when Rory grabbed him.

"You're going to kill him, man," Rory said.

"That's the whole motherfucking idea," Ant said. "He said 'do or die.'"

It was time to go to the movie. Anthony stepped over Kevin and we got in the car and split. Just then, Al Braverman, a legendary trainer who worked for Don, walked up to the office entrance. He saw Ali lying there unconscious and ran into the office and got some paper towels and water and cleaned him up and revived him. They called for an ambulance and that was the end of that.

The rematch was set for June twenty-eighth. I had some time off before we went to camp, so I drove my black Lamborghini Diablo from New York to Ohio and did some sightseeing. Then it was back to Vegas to train. Richie had put me on a strict regimen that included a seven p.m. curfew so I was rested for my six-mile run at five a.m. I was so bored. Most of the time when I wasn't training, I would watch cartoons. Then Don would come storming into the room.

"God dammit, Mike, you are going to watch something else besides these fucking cartoons," he said, and he put on documentaries about Nazi Germany. Don was obsessed with the Nazis. It was Hitler this and Hitler that. He thought that the Jews were the niggas of Germany and that fascism could happen here so we should learn from history.

We had a new chef in camp. Chef Early, who had been with us for a long time, was fired by Don for supposedly sneaking out the back door with meat. That seemed like bullshit to me. One of my bodyguards, Rudy Gonzalez, ran into Chef Early's nephew a few years later and he told him that Chef Early had been fired by Don because he wouldn't put that "magic powder" in my food. He claimed that John Horne had given Chef Early a powder that was supposed to be some "endurance vitamins" that I had refused to take. Chef Early looked at the powder and found a tiny piece of orange capsule with a "5" or an "S" on it. Rudy looked it up in a PDR and it looked like a section of a Thorazine pill. I guess Don was so afraid of me, he was trying to medicate me without me knowing it.

Richie's regimen was driving me crazy. One night I woke Rudy up at eight p.m. and we snuck out in my Ferrari and drove to L.A. so I could have a booty call. Rudy gunned that mother up to 190 mph and we made it to L.A. in two and a half hours. So I began doing that regularly and it started to show in the gym. I was operating on only two hours of sleep. Giachetti had no idea why I looked so lackluster, but he finally busted me when he looked at the mufflers on the Ferrari and saw that they looked like burnt marshmallows.

So they made Rudy put alarms on all the doors to prevent me from sneaking out at night.

One night Rudy woke up when he heard a loud thump. He got up, turned on the light, and walked outside and found me tangled up in a thorny bush. I had fallen from a second-story window trying to sneak out of the house. My plan was to silently roll the Ferrari down the driveway and then take off for L.A.

I was so desperate all my life to get out and have some fun. I should have said, "Fuck you all, I'm going out," but instead I snuck out. I'd be in Nicky Blair's, my favorite restaurant in Las Vegas, holding court, surrounded by girls, and Don would storm in.

"What the fuck are you doing, Mike?" he'd bellow. "We've got a fight coming up."

"Excuse me, Don," I'd say. "I would appreciate it if you would just leave. Oh, by the way, girls, this is Don King."

When my nocturnal speed races to L.A. ended, I had Rudy ship the car to my Ohio house, where they knocked a hole in the exterior wall of my game room and had the car mounted on a platform in the middle of the room so me and my friends could hang out in it.

I went after Ruddock before the fight began. We were doing a taping for Showtime and I wore dark glasses and looked pretty surly.

"I will make you my girlfriend," I told Ruddock.

"I'm not going to come down to your level," he said.

"Make sure you kiss me good with your big lips," I countered.

I was pretty offensive but I knew he was a macho, testosteroned guy. I knew that would get to his psyche. That was one of Cus's tactics of mind control. Confuse the enemy.

Another reason I kept going to L.A. was because my friend Kevin Sawyer who had the beeper shop would beep me and tell me he had some girls lined up for us. He'd get a half a dozen girls and we'd get a room and have an orgy.

I loved hanging out with Kevin. I was mean and nasty to girls then. So before I got there, he would tell the girls, "Mike is really a nice guy. He just never had a good upbringing. He was abandoned as a kid and he has trust issues." That shit would work like a charm. I'd call them bitches and sluts and they'd say, "I understand your situation. My parents also abandoned me." Kevin would tell me, "Just go along with this shit, okay?" Don and John and Rory would get so furious when I'd get beeped. They wound up taking my beeper and putting it in the freezer and then they threatened to kill Kevin.

My second fight with Ruddock was epic. He went into that fight ten pounds heavier. I actually weighed one pound less, but I was weak because I had lost thirty-five pounds in less then a month. I was out of control before the fight, drinking, gorging on food, fucking women. I would get up and sneak out to Roscoe's in L.A. for fried chicken. So I took fat-burning water pills, and I didn't eat anything after dark. I'd work out morning, afternoon, and night.

In the second and the fourth round of the fight, I knocked Ruddock down and had him in trouble a number of times, but I just couldn't finish him off, I was too weak. He was hitting me hard, like a mule, but I was focused. We both got points taken off for hitting after the bell; I had two more points deducted for low blows. It was a war. But I still won an easy unanimous decision.

IN JULY I WAS HANGING OUT IN D.C. WHEN I GOT A CALL FROM MY FRIEND OUIE back in New York. An old friend of ours had been shot in D.C. and Ouie was worried that if the wrong people saw me, they might go after me too. I wanted to get off the streets and wait until all the heat had cooled down, so I went to see Whitney Houston perform that night and stayed backstage and hung out with her after the concert.

On my way back to New York, I was passing through Philadelphia and they had the Budweiser Superfest going on at the Spectrum. Craig Boogie was working the show and I was hanging out backstage with him when B Angie B, one of Hammer's backup singers who was performing there, came up to me and grabbed me. We were hanging out and we slept together that night. Angie then told me that she was going to Indianapolis to perform at the Black Expo. Earlier that day I had received a call from Reverend Charles Williams, who ran the Black Expo, inviting me to make an appearance, so I decided to go and meet her in Indiana.

I was trying to ditch my bodyguards. Anthony was out in L.A.

getting ready to get married that week. I told Rudy not to come with me. Rudy called Ant and then Anthony called John Horne and they decided that Dale Edwards should meet me in Indianapolis. Dale was a nephew, either by blood or by marriage, of Don's. He was a Cleveland police officer.

Dale and I checked into our hotel. Then I had my limo driver drive me over to B Angie B's aunt's house. That night we hung out at a nightclub and had three bottles of Dom Pérignon. We walked out on the bill when the house photographer asked me to take a picture. We got back to my hotel at about 2:30 in the morning. Angie and I had sex that night and then again a few times the next morning. Then Angie left to get ready for her performance.

A little bit later, Reverend Williams came to bring us to the Expo. He asked me if I wanted to say hello to some of the girls in the Miss Black America pageant. When we entered the ballroom at the Omni Hotel, the girls went crazy.

"Look—it's Mike Tyson!" they all screamed.

I walked towards them and they surrounded me, hugging me, kissing me. They were filming a little promotional video, so while the contestants twirled and danced I walked down the line, checking them out, doing some awkward dancing and impromptu singing. "I'm in a dream, day after day, beautiful women in such an array." I must have looked like a real schmuck.

As the girls surrounded me, I'd say shit to them like, "Hey, I want to see you tonight. Is that possible? Oh, boy, this is going to be fun if you decide to come to my room." I was being a pig, but they were going for it. I hugged Desiree Washington, one of the contestants, in the middle of the first take of that video and told her that I wanted to get with her later. She was very flirty with me and friendly and she wanted to hang out. I explained to her that I would do some other things and go to the concert with my friends, but I would see her later that night. I even told her to bring her roommate so we could have a ménage à trois in my room. When I left, it was clear to me that she knew we were going to have sex later that night. I even saw her later that afternoon at the opening of the Black Expo. She was with her roommate, Pasha, the one I was trying to get to come along with Desiree.

"There's the two look-alike twins," I said when I saw them.

Desiree took out some photos of them taken during the swimsuit competition. She seemed anxious for me to see them. And she confirmed that we were on for later that night.

I was being chauffeured around town by this middle-aged black lady who owned the limo company. Dale and I were total assholes to her. We kept calling her a dumb, ugly bitch. I made her stop the limo and I got out and pissed right in the street. I was being a total arrogant dick, and it would come back to bite me when she testified against me.

After the concert, Dale and I got back in the car and called Desiree, who was in her hotel room. I told her to wear some loose clothing and I was surprised that when she got into the car, she was wearing a loose bustier and her short pajama bottoms. She looked ready for action. We started making out in the backseat. It was only a block from her hotel to mine. We got out of the limo and she and I went to my suite and Dale went to his room.

Later after all the shit had gone down, Anthony was furious with Dale. He blamed him for everything that happened to me in Indianapolis. It was pretty common practice for my bodyguards to stay in the living room of my suites when I had a girl in bed, especially a girl we didn't know. Many times I'd open up my door after having sex and Anthony would be sitting there. He wanted to be right there, listening to what was going on, in case there was a problem. Sometimes I'd even invite the bodyguards into the room and we'd fuck the same girl.

Desiree came into my room and we went straight to my bedroom. She was sitting in somewhat of a Buddha position and we talked a little bit. She seemed to know all about my pigeon hobby. She talked a little bit about Rhode Island. We even discussed seeing each other again when I was back east.

Nowadays I don't normally like to be graphic in my descriptions of sexual congress, but I think in this case I must be because of the ramifications of what went down. After we talked awhile, I started kissing her. She got up and went to the bathroom, and I later learned that her visit there was to remove her panty shield. Then she came back to bed and I started performing cunnilingus on her. I normally do that because I make it a practice to make sure that a woman is satisfied when we have sex. I had no idea I was gargling blood because she didn't tell me she was on her period.

We must have had oral sex for about twenty minutes and then we started fornicating. She seemed to be really into everything. At one point she seemed to be getting uncomfortable and complained that I was too big, so I asked her if she wanted to be on top and she did. I wasn't wearing a condom, so before I came, I withdrew from her and ejaculated outside of her.

Now it was really late and I was going to have to get up in an hour or so to catch the first flight to New York. I told her that she could stay in my room because she was telling me how small her room was at the Omni and she had to share it with some other girls, but she then asked me to take her back to her hotel.

Now, this is where it gets crazy. I told her I was too tired, but I'd drop her off at her hotel when I had to go to the airport.

"No, take me down." She got all prissy on me.

"Fuck you, then," I said. "Get the fuck out." I was just a rude, spoiled twenty-five-year-old.

She got up, got dressed, and walked out of the room. Dale, my bodyguard, who was supposed to be in the other room of the suite, was outside his room next door getting a hamburger delivered from room service. She passed by him on her way out. Then she got into my limo and told the driver to take her back to her hotel.

On the way back to her hotel, the only thing she said to the limo driver was, "I don't believe him. I don't believe him. Who does he think he is?"

About a week later, I was in the car with my friend Ouie who was driving. He got a call and his face dropped.

"Fuck, Mike! Our summer is fucked up. Someone said you raped her," Ouie said with disgust and he threw his phone down.

"What? Who the fuck did I rape?" I said. I was thinking to myself that maybe I had disrespected one of my street girlfriends and they were playing me.

"Where did this happen?" I asked Ouie.

"Indiana," he said. "What the fuck happened in Indiana?"

I told him how this girl Desiree had come to my room at two in the morning and how I had dissed her. I was told that she had called my house in Ohio the day after we were together, but I never responded.

The next day it was on the front cover of every newspaper. Now all these non-talented comedians were doing "Mike Tyson the rapist" jokes. When I saw Don, he was worried.

"Now you need my help, nigga. Your dick got you in trouble now. God dammit, Mike, now you need me."

When he calmed down, I explained to him what happened. He knew I didn't do it. How do you rape someone when they come to your hotel room at two in the morning? There's nothing open that late but legs.

Don's first strategy was to bribe her.

"We could pay the bitch," he said.

He actually tried that later by having a friend of his, Reverend T. J. Jemison, talk to her family and offer them money to drop the charges, but the holy man wound up getting indicted. I wasn't aware that Don had done that but it wasn't the first time that Don had paid a member of the clergy for a favor.

We knew that we were facing something serious, so Don went about getting me a lawyer. I really didn't have any input into the selection of the lawyer or my defense in general. I was used to other people deciding my destiny, whether it was the juvenile court system, Cus, Jimmy, or Don. Don wound up hiring Vince Fuller. Fuller had been Don's tax attorney and he had gotten him off on a tax evasion charge. Fuller also represented John Hinckley and used the insanity plea to get him an acquittal after he tried to assassinate President Reagan. I later found out that Fuller was handling Don's suit against Cayton at the same time. I wouldn't put it past Don that he owed Fuller money and he was letting Fuller bill me so that I'd pay for both my and Don's cases. All I know is that Fuller made over a million dollars to defend me.

I didn't get along with Fuller from the get-go. Don told Fuller that I was an ignorant nigga. He was a real Waspy arrogant guy, not my type at all. Anybody could see he was a cold fish. He had never tried a criminal case in a county court, and there was no way in the world that he was going to relate to an Indianapolis jury. In fact, no one on his team had ever tried a criminal case that was not in a federal court. I still don't know why they didn't let the local homeboy Jim Voyles do more of the work in that trial. I really think that I would have been acquitted if he had handled the case.

Some people think that just because someone is convicted of a crime, especially one as heinous as rape, that that automatically means that the convicted person did it. All I can say is, if you don't take my word that I was not guilty of this crime, then I suggest that you read two books that came out after I was in jail. One is by Mark Shaw who is a writer and a former criminal defense attorney and was the legal analyst for my trial for CNN, *USA Today*, and ESPN. The other book is the self-congratulatory-attempt-to-grab-some-headlines book written by the prosecutor in my case, Gregory Garrison. I didn't pay much attention to my trial as it happened; I was an arrogant young man who couldn't be bothered with these kinds of proceedings. I didn't understand them. That's what I paid those suits for. But if you read these books then I think that you'll agree that the last thing that was served in Indianapolis back in 1992 was justice.

There was a lot of interesting insight into the prosecution's case, reading Garrison's book. In fact, up until they reached the verdict, key members of the prosecution team didn't even think they had a case against me. Jeff Modisett, the elected prosecutor of Marion County, won his office by just 285 votes out of 180,000. The only district he carried was the black district. He was no schmuck. He didn't want to alienate his base, so he decided not to charge me with a crime; instead he would send my case to a grand jury to let the "people" decide if a crime had been committed. If I wasn't indicted, he could care less. He even told some of his colleagues that he would "just as soon see the case go away."

Tommy Kuzmik, the sex crimes investigator for the police, told Modisett that they would have a problem with physical evidence because there wasn't any. But he said that Desiree would make a great witness because she was "intelligent, articulate, attractive—easy to look at, easy to understand, easy to believe." But most importantly, she wasn't a victim who "talked street." You figure out the code there.

Garrison also said that because people who could help the case were scattered around the country, "the FBI located and interviewed potential witnesses." Hmm. Is this standard operating procedure for every rape allegation in the country? Somehow I don't think so.

So a special grand jury was appointed on August 13, 1991. Modisett assigned the presentation of evidence to the grand jury to his deputy prosecutor David Dreyer. Now, Dreyer was an interesting individual. According to Garrison, Dreyer was always a little put off by Desiree's act. When she testified before the grand jury on August sixteenth, Dreyer thought that the major problem she had was her "lack of emotion. She seemed too much the beauty queen, detached, maybe even a bit cold." Dreyer thought that the chances of getting an indictment from the grand jury were at best fifty-fifty. In fact, Dreyer had so many reservations about Desiree that Garrison quoted him as saying, "As matter of fact, when the jury began its deliberations, I wasn't sure in my own mind if there had been a rape or not!" And that's the deputy prosecutor talking. That sounds like the very definition of reasonable doubt to me.

I had to testify before the grand jury on the thirtieth. Well, I didn't have to. In fact, Jim Voyles was begging Vince Fuller NOT to have me testify. There was no upside to my testifying. The only thing it could do was give the prosecution ammunition to come after me with during the trial. But somehow Fuller and Don convinced themselves that I should go before the grand jury.

"This man is innocent. Mike Tyson says he's innocent. He's testifying because I think that's what we're supposed to do," Don bellowed on the courtroom steps in front of all the media that day. "I'm going to let due process take its course. I'm not an attorney, I'm just a promoter of the greatest fighter in the world, and he's going to win the championship in the fall."

I was facing a long stretch in jail and he was promoting my damn fight with Holyfield that was scheduled for November. Only in America.

They had me dress in a very conservative dark blue double-breasted suit. We were brought to a small room with a noisy window air conditioner. There were six jurors there. Five of them were white. They asked me questions and I answered very softly and the court reporter made over a hundred errors in her transcription.

At one point they asked me if Dale Edwards had been in the parlor of my suite. I said he was. Dale had testified he was. That's where he was supposed to be. I couldn't know for sure because the bedroom door was closed.

To indict me they needed five out of six votes. We took a recess at one point and I had been eyeing this large candy bowl that was in the middle of the table that the jurors had been eating from.

"Could I have a piece of candy, please?" I asked.

"Sure," they said. And the one black lady handed me the candy.

On September ninth, the grand jury began deliberations. The vote was 5–1 to indict me for rape. You do the math. I was indicted on one count of rape, two counts of criminal deviate conduct (using my fingers and using my tongue), and one count of confinement. I faced sixty years in jail. My trial was scheduled to start on January ninth.

We held a press conference after the jury came back with their vote. Don rattled on and on about famous celebrities who had gotten into trouble—Elvis, James Dean, Marilyn, Judy Garland. Then I gave my statement.

"I know what happened. I know I'm innocent. I didn't hurt anyone. I didn't do anything. I love women—I mean, my mother's a woman. I respect them as well."

From September until the start of the trial, I ate a lot. I was nervous. I was training to fight Holyfield, but my heart wasn't into fighting. A few weeks into training, I tore cartilage in my ribs. The doctors recommended that I postpone the fight. I actually could have fought, but I was happy to postpone it. I had too much on my mind.

While I was stressing and eating, the prosecution assembled their team. Modisett's gamble failed. The grand jury didn't make my case go away, so he did the next-best thing: He hired an independent Republican special prosecutor to try my case. Greg Garrison was a former deputy prosecutor who had been making money recently by prosecuting drug dealers on RICO charges and getting a cut of everything that was confiscated from the dealers. Garrison was making so much money from those cases that Modisett assigned those drug cases in-house once he was elected. What a sleazeball.

Modisett only paid Garrison $20,000 to take on the case, but this wasn't about money—he was doing this for the glory and to get his name out in front of the world. If you read his book, you'd think that he took this case to help defend Indiana from the ravaging Hun. "I am a product of rural Indiana, a land of conservative Republicans and hardworking, decent people who tend their own fields, respect the law, and help their friends when needed. . . . Make no mistake, Tyson picked the wrong place to commit his crime. Indiana is different from Palm Beach or D.C. or L.A."

Garrison started investigating the case. The first place he looked was at Desiree's panties. He was concerned about the lack of any physical injury to Desiree, so he went to the grand jury room and examined the clothing she wore that night. "It seemed like a risqué costume when you just looked at it lying on the table," he wrote. Damn straight. She was wearing long shorts, a bustier that "would have stopped traffic on the right woman," and her panties. He didn't think the panties were "consistent with the image of a young gold digger heading out to get into the pants and pocketbook of the former heavyweight champ of the world." I guess he didn't understand the concept of a booty call.

"I opened the panties and looked down at them as if I were going to put them on." Now, this is some perverted shit. He lined up the bloodstains on the panties and then decided that Desiree had jerked her panties on after we had sex and blotted them with the bleeding from the injuries I had inflicted on her. And then it all fit in his mind. She was telling the truth and I had raped her. The smoking gun was her panties.

He thought, *Hell, I'm forty-four years old and have had sex a few times in my life. And you don't hurt a woman that way. Not and keep it up. If it hurts, you get told to stop.*

Garrison also couldn't believe that we had oral sex for twenty minutes or so.

"Again, his description of the event veered wildly counter to everything I knew about sex." Maybe he should have read a little of Dr. Kinsey instead of all those law books. He was convinced that Desiree wouldn't have had the two small abrasions in her vagina if we had consensual sex and she was lubricated. But it wasn't an issue of lubrication. It was an issue of size and intensity. This could happen to anyone during sex.

Of course, this issue came up during the trial. My man Voyles wanted to address the issue of my size and get a doctor to testify that it could have caused her vaginal abrasions, but Fuller didn't want to hear about it. He was squeamish about any of the sexual aspects of the case.

Even after his CSI investigation of the panties, Garrison still had no idea about my motivation to rape someone. "I admitted I had no idea why Tyson would have chosen to rape Desiree when he could have had any one of a score of women." He was still asking himself that question after I had been convicted.

Then Garrison and his assistant, Barbara Trathen, took a little road trip. In November they went to Rhode Island to meet with Desiree and her family. They were struck by how "polite and genteel" her family was. Of course, appearances could be deceiving. By the time the prosecution had gotten to Rhode Island, Desiree and her mother had accused her father of abusing them and he had moved out.

Desiree and her family were met at the airport by Edward Gerstein. Now, Mr. Gerstein is a very interesting and important player in this case. Shortly after the rape investigation, a Rhode Island lawyer named Walter Stone approached the Washington family. He was a counsel to the International Boxing Federation, so he told them it would be a conflict of interest for him to represent Desiree but that his partner Edward Gerstein could do so. So Gerstein became Desiree's civil attorney. He was the one they had hired to sue me for civil damages and negotiate big fees for movie and book rights. Gerstein's involvement with the Washington family freaked Garrison out.

"This news was a live wire. If there were even a hint of pending litigation out of the Washington family, the case would be hurt. It would be impossible to refute the gold digger charge."

So what did the prosecution do? Keep this information from my defense team. After the trial was over, Star Jones, who was then NBC's legal correspondent, criticized the prosecution for not revealing the fact that Desiree had a retainer with a civil lawyer. "That's sleazy. A prosecutor has the duty to turn over all the evidence," she said.

Garrison and his deputy started questioning Desiree. Apparently, the whole issue of Desiree going to the bathroom in my room and taking off her panty shield was a little troubling to him. According to Desiree, I had suddenly turned mean and lustful and she was freaked out. So she went to the bathroom and took off her panty shield and went back to bed. When Garrison asked Desiree why she had gone to the bathroom, she answered, "It was the first thing I could think of doing after he turned mean."

Well if that was true, the second thing she could have thought of doing was to keep on walking right out the door. If she sensed danger, like she claimed she did, it would have been easy for her to just leave. Voyles even re-created a model of the hotel room that cost $6,000 to demonstrate that fact. But of course Fuller shut him down and never used it during the trial.

Garrison didn't think much of the whole panty shield dilemma the prosecution faced. He was eager to believe Desiree when she said that she discarded her soiled panty shield "out of habit" and that when she realized that she had left her purse in the bedroom, she thought that she could pick up another panty shield "at one of the parties she wanted to attend." WTF? Nobody ever talked about going to parties that night. Where was she going to get another panty shield?

Garrison also heard about my deposition in the Cayton case where I propositioned Thomas Puccio's female assistant, Joanna Crispi. He was shocked that I simulated intercourse using my fingers, and then told her, "I want to fuck you," but somehow he couldn't believe that I had said the exact same thing to Desiree Washington. Right there was proof of my crude m.o. at that time with women.

Garrison flew to D.C. and met with the U.S. Attorney to get dirt on Fuller. The fed told Garrison that everyone in Washington legal circles was baffled as to why Fuller had accepted the case. It didn't fit his blue-blood firm's profile. "They just don't do street crimes. Never. Not even in the D.C. area."

While he was in D.C., Garrison stopped at the BET studios to talk with Charlie Neal, who was the announcer for the Miss Black America Pageant. Charlie told Garrison that he saw no change at all in Desiree after the alleged rape. Plus, I could have had my pick of the women there. Why did I need to rape one? I guess Garrison didn't like what he had heard from Charlie.

"What he [Charlie] had to say boiled down to *I didn't see nothin', I didn't hear nothin', I don't know nothin'*. It was clear to me that he must be thinking that these honkies weren't going to get a thing from him against a brother," Garrison wrote. What a lowlife racist asshole.

But I was most upset when I read that my old friend José Torres had met with Garrison. He went into his usual bullshit that boxing is lying for a living and that the best boxers were the best liars. And he told Garrison that no other boxer lied like I did. Then Torres repeated his bullshit stories about me and women and sex that he had put into his book. Torres told Garrison that I had bragged to him about hitting Robin so hard that she "hit every fucking wall in the room." According to him, I said it was the greatest punch I had ever thrown.

Torres had explained to Garrison that he was on the outs with me, so Garrison should have taken most of this with a grain of salt. The worst betrayal was when Garrison asked Torres if I was capable of rape.

"Oh, yes. Absolutely," he said, and then he went into his pseudo Freudian bullshit about how I couldn't control my libido because my id was too strong. "He takes what he wants. He always has," Torres said. I couldn't believe what I was reading. What a disgrace of a human being. Garrison finished his interview by asking Torres what he could expect if I took the witness stand.

"He'll try to outthink you and give the jurors what they want. Remember, boxers are liars. And Tyson's the best."

Before the trial started, Desiree went to Indianapolis for her deposition. Fuller decided not to do it, so he had his co-counsel Kathleen Beggs do it. Garrison was shocked at Beggs's strategy. She tore Desiree a new asshole. Beggs was "accusatory, arrogant, unkind, and mean-spirited," according to Garrison. Instead of being sweet and finessing out some information that my defense could use, she reduced Desiree to tears. It was a major blunder. But not the last that my million-dollar defense team would commit.

My trial began on January 27, 1992. My judge was a lady named Patricia Gifford. She had overseen the grand jury, so she was automatically assigned to the case. She was a former deputy prosecutor in that county's office who had specialized in rape cases. She helped initiate the rape shield legislation that shielded rape victims from any evidence of their sexual history being introduced. Later this would play a big role in my case. She was a card-carrying Republican who could trace her ancestry back so far she was a member of the Daughters of the American Revolution. Her father was an army colonel. Just my kind of girl. Judge Gifford could have easily recused herself from my case. In fact, after my conviction, the Supreme Court of Indiana wrote a new Tyson Rule. They ordered rotation so that the same judge who presided over the grand jury wouldn't get the actual case.

It was time to select a jury of my peers. The only problem was that back then, Indiana used voter registration rolls to get their jury poll, which meant that since a lot of black folk didn't vote, they couldn't be included as potential jurors. That's another Tyson Rule that was changed after my case. So out of 179 people called as potential jurors, 160 were white. Fuller and his team even had problems picking the jury. They had no experience doing that. In federal court, the judge picks the jury, and Garrison was a master at that. He could interview the potential jurors and bullshit with them, ask them if they lived near that big Walmart out by the interstate. Fuller couldn't even begin to connect with the Midwestern jurors.

Fuller was too stubborn to even hire a jury selection expert. As a result, he let this former Marine named Tim onto the jury. Later one of the other jurors would say that Tim was "much more conservative than the rest of us, more straight, a real redneck." This guy would become the foreman of my jury and have more of a role in getting me convicted than anybody else.

If, as some people think, 90 percent of cases were decided in the opening statements, then we weren't going to do so good in this court. Garrison's opening lasted for forty-five minutes. You would have thought he was reading from that book *Fifty Shades of Grey*.

"He's grinning at her. His voice is low, different than before. And he pulls her legs apart and sticks his fingers into her. She cries out in pain. The medical, anatomical, physiological miracle of human sexuality that causes the female of the species to become lubricated when she's sexually excited ain't working, and she's terrified. So when these big fingers go into her, it hurts a lot, and she cries out, 'Don't!'"

"She hops up from the bed and puts her clothes on fast, wiping her tears, getting her clothes on, trying to find her dignity along with her clothes, and says, 'Is the limo still down there?' He says, 'Oh, you can stay if you want.' She says, 'Why? So you can do that again?'"

Fuller was a dry twit compared to this Garrison guy. He tried to paint a portrait of Desiree as sophisticated beyond her years, not the sweet, innocent girly girl the prosecution presented, but Garrison kept objecting during Fuller's presentation. Fuller did point out some key inconsistencies between what Desiree told the various other girls. She told some people she screamed, told others she didn't. She said that I attacked her in the bed to one person and that we'd had sex on the floor to someone else. It sounded like she was making up her story as she went along. But Fuller made a major error during his opening statement. He promised that the jury would hear from me. You don't do that in a major case like this. There were some people who thought that the state's case was so weak that we could have called no witnesses, just rested, and still have won an acquittal. But he promised them me, so I would have to testify. What's worse, during his whole opening argument, Fuller not once came near me. Not one pat on the shoulder, not one glance in my direction, not one display of bonding between the defense lawyer and his client. That was first-year law school shit.

"Jurors weren't seeing a defense team at work, only a foghorn barrister from another state who had made a cold-fish first impression." I didn't say that, Mark Shaw did.

After calling her roommate to the stand, Garrison brought on Desiree. Using the rape shield law, they made her out to be some shy, naïve college student who was a Sunday school teacher and an usher in her church. She claimed that when I asked her to go down to the limo, she was reluctant until I told her we'd go out "sightseeing." Yeah, there's a lot to see in Indianapolis at two in the morning. I was there recently doing my one-man show and the only thing you could see around the Canterbury Hotel area was ambulatory schizophrenics, homeless people, and a washed-out hooker if you were lucky.

Desiree repeated her story that we didn't kiss or hold hands and that I didn't display any signs of affection until I got her on the bed and I turned weird and mean. She repeated that she then went to the bathroom and took off her panty shield and threw it away. "I had a pad in my purse but I figured I could put it on later."

When she got back, she claimed, I pinned her down, took off her top, and slid her shorts off and her panties down and then inserted two fingers into her vagina. Then I penetrated her. She said that she told her mother what had happened the next night and then they called 911.

Garrison thought that she had testified spectacularly. Others weren't so sure. Some reporters thought that she was too "stoical" and one even wrote that she seemed "a little prissy" and "almost too perfect." Before the trial, Garrison had brought in another attorney, Robert Hammerle, to do a mock cross-examination of her so they could see how she would respond to pressure.

Hammerle began to ask her about the improbabilities that he saw about the case.

"Look, you met Mike Tyson, and you saw him making all of these passes at girls . . . and then you gave him a picture of you in a bathing suit, and you still didn't think he had sex on his mind?" he asked Desiree.

"No," she said.

"He called you in the middle of the night, and you went down to his limousine and when you got in, he kissed you, and it still never crossed your mind that he had sex on his mind?"

"No."

"Then you went to the hotel, and you went to his room, and you sat on his bed, and it never crossed your mind that he wanted to have sex with you?"

"No."

"And then he said, 'You're turning me on,' and you didn't think he had sex on his mind?"

"No."

He kept going on and on, asking her about the panty shield.

"It didn't make sense," Hammerle told Garrison, "but that was her story and she stuck to it. My overall impression was that she did battle with me. I had heard that there was this eighteen-year-old naïve lady but I came away with the feeling that while it could have happened, I was dealing with someone much stronger who wouldn't let me run over her. I couldn't figure out how this all fit with all the naïve mistakes she was supposed to have made."

Hammerle told his wife about the panty shield incident. His wife said that any woman who goes to the bathroom to remove her panty shield is expecting to have sex. And he agreed with his wife. When Hammerle ran into Garrison the next day in the City-County Building, he told him, "You, my friend, are in a world of shit!"

I wish that Hammerle had been my attorney. When it came time for Fuller to cross-examine Desiree, he didn't even seem to want to be doing it. Mark Shaw agreed with me.

"Fuller's polite and less than forceful cross-examination was difficult to understand, especially when Garrison's direct examination gave him so many opportunities to probe Washington about what specifically happened in the hotel room between her and Tyson," he wrote.

He couldn't understand why Fuller didn't take advantage of her defensiveness. She would have given him a lot more information than was requested. He never followed up on the specifics of the agreement her family had with her civil attorney. In fact, she lied about the purpose of having one. She knew full well she was going to sue my ass and collect lots of money when this criminal case was over. And she did.

Fuller never fired rapid questions at her like Hammerle had in his mock cross-exam. He never put her on the defensive. If he had, the jury might have seen that she wasn't as naïve as she projected herself to be. When Fuller had noted that Desiree had been reprimanded for acting like a groupie when she was backstage that night at Johnny Gill's concert, she actually told the jury that she didn't know what the word "groupie" meant!

He didn't even ask her any questions about her removing her panty shield! He didn't wonder how I could have been giving her oral sex and still be pinning her to the bed. Where were the bruises if I had physically overpowered her? If she had screamed, why didn't anyone in the hotel hear her? C'mon, we were in a hotel room in the middle of the night where the walls echo because it's so quiet and she screamed? If anybody ever attacked me, I would have been gone. I'd have lost it as soon as I got in the hallway. I'd be in the Twilight Zone, knocking on people's doors, "Help me, come, this guy's right in here." You don't have to be F. Lee Bailey to decipher her bullshit.

The other state witness who hurt me was the emergency room doctor, Stephen Richardson. He testified that he had examined Desiree the night after the alleged attack. He found no bruises or abrasions on her arms or legs, no signs that she had been hit or squeezed. There was no trauma to her labia majora or labia minora. But he did find two very small abrasions, an eighth of an inch wide and three-eighths long on her introitus, the opening to her vagina. He said that 10 to 20 percent of rape victims have injuries there. And he said that in twenty years of practice, he had seen those injuries only twice from consensual sex.

To hear him talk, these were very small abrasions, but Garrison had blown up a huge picture of Desiree's privates, mounted it, and displayed it in the courtroom. You'd look at that picture and you'd think that somebody had taken a mallet and beat her vagina.

Fuller had nothing to counteract Dr. Richardson's testimony. He could have. Voyles had a urologist lined up to examine my member and testify how those little abrasions could have been caused by penetration, but Fuller didn't want to go there. He should have. Instead of the urologist, Fuller got some lame doctor who was so confused that she started scoring points for the prosecution! My million-dollar defense team.

Before the prosecution finished putting forward their case, my lawyers attempted to get three witnesses added for the defense. My defense team was getting a lot of crazy calls during the trial, so they were a little skeptical when they got a call from a girl who said that she and two of her friends had seen me and Desiree hugging and kissing in the back of the limo and holding hands on the way into the hotel! Now this would have been huge and it would have shown Desiree to be the sophisticated liar that she was. So Voyles got permission to take the limo out of evidence. He put it in front of the hotel at nighttime and you could see through those tinted windows like it was day.

They checked the girls out and they were all credible, so they tried to get them admitted as witnesses but Judge Gifford nearly had a fit. She wanted to know why the prosecution hadn't been told about these witnesses immediately. Because they had to be checked out, shown not to be nuts. She didn't care. It was like she took it personally.

"I am of the opinion that not excluding the witnesses would result in substantial prejudice to the State of Indiana, and I believe that the State of Indiana is entitled to a fair trial the same as the Defendant in any case," she said, and excluded probably my most important witnesses from testifying.

Then the state wrapped up their case. They called Mrs. Washington to the stand and she poured it on thick.

"Desiree is gone, and she's not going to come back. I just want my daughter back."

Even some of the jurors started crying.

Then they played an edited version of her 911 tape. This was like calling Desiree to the stand again and without letting us cross-examine her.

"I went out with this person in a limousine that night and the person told me that he had to go in to get his bodyguards and he asked me if I wanted to come in for a second and I said, 'Oh, okay, fine.' You know, thinking this was a nice person. And we went in and the person started attacking me. I just came out of the bathroom and this person was in his underwear and he just basically kind of did what he wanted to do and kept saying, 'Don't fight me, don't fight me.' And I was like saying, 'No, no, get off me, get off me, please, get off of me.' And he was going, 'Don't fight me, don't fight me.' And the person is a lot stronger than I was and he just did what he wanted to and I was saying, 'Stop, please, stop, please.' And he just didn't stop."

Later in that tape, the dispatcher kept telling Desiree that she was the victim, she was the victim, and then Desiree slipped something very interesting in.

"I'm not trying to tell you what to do but don't be scared," the dispatcher told her. She was pushing Desiree to report the rape.

"But someone nationally known against someone just like me, a regular person, I mean, people like just kind of naturally think that I'm going for the money or something," Desiree said out of nowhere.

Allowing that tape to be entered in evidence was very prejudicial to my case.

Many legal scholars thought that it should have been inadmissible, but that didn't stop that little lady judge.

It was time for us to put forward our case. By then, Voyles and I were totally disheartened. I never really had any faith in the system. The Kennedy kid had been found innocent of rape in Palm Beach just a month before my trial started, but I knew I was supposed to be convicted, that was just how the system worked. I'm a descendant of slaves. That people can respect me as a human being, to this day, is something that I have doubts about. I was the nigga and that cowboy prosecutor was going to put his spurred cowboy boots in my face. None of those people were going to help me. I was fucked the day I got indicted. They were going to get me one way or another.

Fuller and Beggs didn't help. Kathleen Beggs was about as warm as a table. She got into it a few times with Judge Gifford and you could see that the judge just hated her. When Voyles tried to tell Fuller that Beggs should warm up a bit, Fuller told him, "We don't need that kind of advice from you."

The genius Fuller's whole defense of me was that Desiree should have known what she was getting into because I was a boorish, vulgar, unredeemable sexual animal. That was my lawyer's characterization of me. Even Garrison couldn't believe Fuller's strategy. He knew that by painting me as a sex machine it would raze my reputation and alienate me from the jury. I would be "so insensitive and crude that no right-minded person could have any sympathy for him." What's worse, Garrison called Fuller's defense strategy racist. "The defense robbed Tyson of his individuality and turned him into a cardboard figure from a racist X-rated cartoon," Garrison wrote in his book.

I had to laugh when one girl who we called as a defense witness told the court that she overheard me telling another contestant, "I want to fuck you, and bring your roommate too, because I'm a celebrity and you know, we do that kind of thing."

I didn't help my case myself. When I was called to testify, I was so arrogant and was a hostile witness for my own case. By then, the writing was on the wall. There had been a fire in the place where the jurors were staying and one of the black jurors told the judge that he was too badly shaken to continue. He was the guy who always complained about the food and the lodging. When the judge let him leave, Garrison was thrilled. He was convinced that that guy would have hung the jury. There was new only one black left on the jury.

We put on a lot of witnesses who contradicted Desiree's image. One of the contestants testified that Washington told her that "she wanted money, wanted to be like Robin Givens." She also said Desiree used foul language and made sexual innuendos. According to her, I said,

"Do you want to come to my room? I know I'm not gonna get nothin' but I'll ask anyway." That sounded like me.

Another girl testified that when she saw me, she said to Desiree, "Here comes your husband. He doesn't speak very well."

"Mike doesn't have to speak. He'll make the money and I'll do the talking," Desiree said. Both girls said they saw no change in Desiree after the alleged rape.

Another girl said Desiree and I were cuddling like a couple at the pageant. Still another girl said Desiree gave me a "look that could kill" when I patted another girl's behind. Caroline Jones testified that Desiree told her, "There's twenty million dollars," when she saw me at the rehearsal.

On February seventh, I took the stand. I basically told the same story that you've already read. Except that when I said that I told Desiree that I just wanted to fuck her, it was like the jury had been hit with a bolt of lightning, as if they had never heard the F word before. Fuller did a lousy job of preparing me and leading me through my testimony, and when he was finished, Judge Gifford called for a recess until the next day, which gave the prosecution the whole night to review my testimony and prepare their traps.

When we resumed the next day, Garrison made a big deal out of the fact that when I said, "I want to fuck you," an eighteen-year-old would never answer, "Fine, call me." I guess he was living in the dark ages, but then again this was the same man who, after hearing that I claimed that I had oral sex with Desiree for twenty or so minutes, wrote, "His description of the event veered wildly counter to everything I knew about sex."

He also spent a lot of time getting me to confess that my success in the ring was the result of my cunning, my ability to feint, and that, of course, meant I was a liar.

After I was finished testifying, they brought Johnny Gill on to say that when I told Desiree that I wanted to fuck her, she didn't even flinch. Fuller called some more contestants to say that Desiree said that I was "really built" and "had a butt to hold on to." The whole defense was so scattershot that even I could see that there was no cohesion to the case he was building. The major flaw was that Fuller and Beggs were too prudish to get into the nitty-gritty details of the sexual encounter. They didn't give the jurors the actual facts to base their judgment on.

Fuller was so boring during his final argument that one juror actually interrupted him and asked to go to the bathroom. That wasn't such a good sign. When was he going to get to the crucial point that when I supposedly said that Desiree was turning me on, she responded not by leaving the hotel room but by going to the bathroom and taking off her panty shield and then coming back to the bed? I was waiting, but he never did.

Garrison then gave his final argument. It was the same old same old, but he fed those jurors his corn-fed bullshit in a way that Fuller never could have. "The world's eyes are upon us. People everywhere want to know if the citizens of Marion County have got the courage to do a hard thing. I don't want this man convicted because the world watches. I want him convicted if you believe the evidence proves beyond a reasonable doubt that this beautiful, honest kid came to town, got deceived by a professional deceiver, got lied to, schmoozed and romanced, isolated and defeated, raped and made the subject of deviant behavior. If that's what you believe, and the evidence is so, then that must be your judgment. That's all."

The final nail in my coffin came right before the jury went out to deliberate. Fuller made a motion that the judge should include an instruction on implied consent when she instructed the jury before they left to discuss the case. That meant that I couldn't be guilty of rape if the "conduct of the complainant under all the circumstances should reasonably be viewed as indicating consent to the acts in question." But the former rape prosecutor shut Fuller down and the jury never knew about this established legal precedent.

On February tenth at 1:15 p.m., the jury of eight men and four women started deliberating my case. Not surprisingly, the former Marine and now IBM salesman Tim was elected foreman. After fifteen minutes of deliberation, without discussing the evidence, they took a poll. It was a six to six vote. Less than nine hours later, they had reached a unanimous verdict.

We all went back to the courtroom. When the jury filed in, they couldn't even look at the defense table. That was it. When I heard "guilty" on the first count, I felt like I had been punched. "Oh, man," I whispered. But I wasn't at all surprised.

We had to face the press outside. I was allowed out on bail until my sentencing.

"No way I got a fair shot," I said. "I knew I was innocent but I knew the verdict was going to be quick because of the mentality of the court and the prosecutor. The prosecutor was a racist, weak, publicity-happy little weak man. I was nervous because I knew this was going to take me away from people I loved but I was prepared for that."

Tim, my ex-Marine nemesis, told the press that "when we put it together the issue of consent was clearly not given."

Mark Shaw got it right in his book. "To his dismay [the criminal justice system] hit Tyson with a pro-prosecution judge, prosecutors who may have withheld critical evidence, a borderline incompetent trial defense attorney whose bumbling defense may have been more responsible for the guilty verdict than everything else combined and a jury that paid more attention to Tyson's bad-boy public image than to the incompleteness of the case's facts. Garrison's best achievement at trial was his strategy in successfully presenting Desiree Washington as the shy, inexperienced, naïve, prim and proper college student that they in fact knew her not to be. Utilizing the full protection of the rape shield law, and fully aware that Washington had in fact signed an agreement to sue Tyson and sell her movie and book rights, the prosecutors, who were also aware of Washington's questionable sexual past, and her need for therapy, made certain that the jury never saw any indication that Washington was anything other than a church-going goody two-shoes."

Some karma came back on Garrison during the trial. He lost his wife. She had just had a baby and she ran off with the policeman who had been assigned to guard her during the trial.

9

I SPENT SOME TIME IN MY NEW YORK APARTMENT BETWEEN MY CONVICTION and my sentencing. One day I was walking back from a girl's house and was about to enter my building when I saw a man standing outside. I walked right by him but I heard him speak.

"Hey, how are you doing, son?"

I looked at him and immediately recognized that it was my father. I hadn't seen him since my mother's funeral ten years earlier.

"Hey, how are you doing?" I said. He had scared me at first, but I wasn't tripping. I had had a pretty good life so I wasn't bitter at him. He looked pretty timid and a little intimidated. I'm sure that he had heard some bad things about my street personality. But when I smiled and hugged him, it eased the tension.

"Come on upstairs," I said and led him into my lobby.

"Hello, Mr. Tyson," the doorman and the building's valet both said.

"Wow, you're a big man, huh?" my father said.

"No, I'm not big at all, it's just an illusion," I told him.

My father had wanted to see me years earlier. In October of 1988, the *New York Post* sent a reporter to my father's housing project in Brooklyn and interviewed him.

"I'm not going to Mike with my hands out," he told the reporter. "I don't want Mike's money. It's not that I wouldn't take it, that I couldn't use it, but I'd take it only if Mike wanted to give it out."

At that time I was just too focused on my fighting to reach out to him. But over the years I had heard many stories about my father from people back in Brooklyn. He was a real shrewd street guy—a hustler, gambler, and a pimp/deacon. My father was one of those Jesus freaks who would kill you for Jesus. He was from Charlotte, North Carolina, right smack in that Bible Belt. When he was younger, he sang in a gospel group. He always stayed with Jesus his whole life, but he was doing the dirt too. He was the real deal. He'd dress very well and get control over all the women in his church when they came to him for advice. When I was growing up in Brooklyn, women would stop me on the street and tell me, "Your father and his brother were pimps and we worked for them." He had a reputation as the baddest hustler and pimp in Brooklyn.

I was nowhere as tough as my father. I always wanted to imagine I was as tough as he was, but I just wasn't that guy. I had heard that my father had to leave North Carolina after getting into some dispute with a white guy. His uncle, who was an Uncle Tom–type guy, mediated the dispute and saved my father's life by promising that he would leave town. So he came to New York. When he got here, he went to some bar and started talking with a nice-looking woman. Then this guy with a nice big hat came in, one of those cool black guys, and smacked my father off the barstool and started talking to the girl.

"This motherfucker is a country-assed nigga," the guy told the girl. "Don't waste your time with him."

My father got on a bus, went all the way back to Charlotte, got his rifle, came back to New York, and found the guy and shot him. If he had a beef with the police in Brooklyn, he and his brother would just shoot it out with the cops. My father had a lot of respect in the Brooklyn community.

My mother met my father back in Charlotte. She was in school in Winston-Salem and she met my father's sister, who was basically a recruiter for my father. She would pick up drugs for him or find cute women. So she brought my mother to meet my father. When I was growing up, my father wasn't much of a presence, but he came around periodically. We didn't give him much credit because my mom was pretty bitter towards him, but I believe he did the best he could with the family skills he had. It wasn't easy being a black man with a family back then.

So we went upstairs and he liked my place. We ordered some food up and just started talking. He seemed surprised that I had reacted so positively to him. I could see that he could use some money so I gave him some. I really wanted to know more about him so I invited him to come out to my Ohio house. I offered to buy him a car to drive out there and I suggested I get him a Mercedes-Benz.

"Oh, God, no, son, please don't," he protested. "The only thing I can do is drive a Cadillac, I don't know how to drive a Mercedes." He really had that pimp/preacher mentality about Cadillacs.

My dad drove out to Ohio a few weeks later with my sister's two kids. He was a very interesting man at that stage of his life. He'd stay in church all day. He'd be there from nine in the morning until five at night, then come home and eat something and then go back to church until eleven.

He seemed to like my lifestyle. After a few days he got comfy and invited one of his preacher friends over—another guy who dressed real sharp. They'd be sitting around talking shit. I would just watch him, study his characteristics. I saw that he loved candy. He was a sixty-eight-year-old man and he was just loving eating his candy. I thought, *Wow! I'm a candy guy. That's where I'm getting it from.*

In a way, I envied the way he had all these relationships with women. I was just miserable with relationships, but he had to beat women away. My father was a very successful pimp, but I couldn't get two dogs to fornicate. My father had seventeen kids and they all became awesome people. Later on I met some of them and none of them were crazy like me.

At one point I sat my father down and said, "Teach me something. What do you know about life? What can you pass down to me? Be my father."

"I can't teach you anything, son," he said. "All I know is the Bible and pimping. And that's not for you. I know, I saw you with your women."

I had been trying to impress him with all my glamorous women.

"You're a sucker, son. It's nothing bad, some people are just like that when it comes to women," he said. "Some men never reach that level in life where they can handle them. You're just one of those guys. You don't know how to talk to women. You're just not good. You're kissing them in your mouth. Fuck, do you know what they're doing when they're not here with you? They're fucking sucking my dick, or somebody's pissing in their mouth. And you're kissing them, putting your tongue in their mouth, son."

When my father first came to visit, he had been very humble. But once he saw that I was open to him and giving him money he started to get cocky.

"I don't know if you are really my son, to be honest. You got one woman going out and one coming in and they're almost meeting each other," he told me near the end of his stay. "You've got to tell them to come together. I had five or six girls in the house with your mama. . . ."

Whoa. He was getting way too pimpish and giving me way too much information. I wasn't strong enough to handle it.

"Hey, chill, man," I said. "I love my mother. You're my father, I love you. Let's not talk about you and her. Let's just work on our relationship as father and son."

I HAD SOME THINGS TO TIE UP BEFORE I WENT BACK FOR SENTENCING. I WAS convinced that I was going to prison, so I called Natalie, the mother of my son D'Amato.

"Listen, I'm going to send you a hundred thousand dollars now. Then when I'm in there I'll have them send you something every month."

As soon as she got that money, she went out and got a lawyer and sued me for millions. Which was great because years later, as the case progressed, my lawyer had the court order a paternity test and it turned out that the kid wasn't even mine. I deserved that. That's what happens when you fuck with hos. It was another harsh betrayal. I was crushed when that first test came back. I really thought he was my kid. I had spent a lot of time with him. I even proudly posed with him on the cover of *Jet* magazine. That woman tormented and stalked me for years after that paternity test. I don't think anything good will ever come out of her life. I wouldn't be surprised if someone involved with her was caught dead in the house or something.

After I was sentenced and processed, they sent me to the Indiana Youth Center. It was a medium-level security prison that had been designed in the 1960s for rich, white nonviolent youthful offenders. By 1992, the Indiana prison system was so overcrowded that they began sending adult offenders there, mostly people convicted of sex and drug crimes who were too weak to handle the really tough prisons. But as time went on, they began sending some murderers and other violent offenders there. When I arrived, there were about 1,500 prisoners, over 95 percent of them white.

They assigned me to the M dorm, one of the newer units. We were housed in two-man rooms that had reinforced doors and a small window instead of bars. When you walked into the room, there'd be two bunks to your left and a toilet and a cabinet where you could store stuff to your right. There was also a desk where you could study. The whole room was only eight by nine feet.

At the time, I didn't realize that being in jail, even for a crime that I didn't commit, was a blessing in disguise. If I had stayed out, God knows what would have happened to me. Being locked up was the first time in my life that I could actually catch my breath and be still, but I don't want it to sound like I instantly gained enlightenment or that I was singing "Kumbaya" all day. I was angry as fuck when I first got put in. I knew that I would be in for at least three years. If it had been a white girl, I would have been in for three hundred years.

The first few weeks I was in jail, I was just waiting for someone to try me, to mistake me for weak. I couldn't wait to prove to these psychopaths that I was just as homicidal as they were, if not more so. I had to let all of them animals know not to ever go near my cell or touch my shit. I was aggressive and ready to go to war.

One day shortly after I got there, I was walking around and one guy yelled at me, "Hey, Tyson, you fucking tree jumper." I had no idea what he was talking about. I thought that was a compliment, that I was some great athlete who could perform amazing acts of physical prowess, even jump over trees. But then I asked someone.

"A tree jumper is a rapist, Mike," the guy told me. "You know, a guy who waits behind a tree for a little kid to walk by and then jumps out and grabs them."

"Oh, Christ," I said.

But days after that, I was sitting in the rec room and this really nice, wonderful inmate sat down with me. He was one of those ultra-polite Christian brothers with the beautiful smile all the time, the most well-liked and respected guy in the jail.

"Mike, you are not no rapist," he said, staring directly in my eyes. "I've been around you. You're a big silly kid that likes to have some fun, but you didn't rape nobody. I know because I *am* a rapist. That's what I did. I brutally raped and abused a woman. You ever see that white woman who comes to visit me? That's not my girlfriend, that's my victim."

"What?"

"I got the Lord now, Mike. I done wrote her, and we've been communicating and she comes and visits me. So I know a rapist, Mike, because I am one."

While I was getting acclimated to prison, there was controversy on the outside. Most opinion polls found that a large number of people were questioning my verdict, even ones that polled mostly women. A vast majority of black people thought that I didn't receive a fair trial. Even one of my jurors told a reporter that none of the black jurors in the jury pool wanted to touch my case because they were scared. Every day I'd talk to Don on the phone and he assured me that he was working on getting me out immediately. So you can imagine how I felt

when on March thirty-first, six days after I went to jail, a judge denied my appeal bond. I immediately stopped eating any solid food and
just drank liquids. Then I started getting write-ups. I was disciplined
for giving my autograph to a couple of inmates. I became belligerent
and got infractions for threatening guards and other inmates.

I got into a scrap with a big young light-skinned black guy named
Bob. We were fooling around, but then it got serious and he wanted to
go and I put a big knot on the top of his head. One of the other inmates
named Wayno came over and told me to chill out.

"You've got nothing to prove to these dudes," Wayno told me. "These
guys are going to be here for a long time, but you're trying to go home,
brother."

He was right. Fortunately for me when the guard came over, Bob
didn't give me up. He said that he had tripped. That could have earned
me another few months in jail.

It was hard to maintain my humanity in a place like that. I saw
things that I couldn't understand one human being doing to another.
I watched people get cut fighting over a cigarette. Somebody might
throw some gasoline in another man's cell and try to light it and burn
him up. Or somebody would grab a lady guard and throw her in the
bathroom and rape her. I saw guards run out with half their heads
sliced open with a razor or because someone beat them with a stapler.
The people doing that shit didn't care. They were facing forty, fifty, a
hundred years already. They couldn't give them any more time than
they already had. So you'd be walking a tightrope messing with these
borderline sociopaths. These people needed to be in hospitals more
than prisons.

I was very paranoid the first few months there. I thought that
somebody, either an inmate or a guard, was going to set me up and
put some dope in my room or provoke me to hit them so I'd get more
time tacked on to my sentence. I just wanted to survive. So I'd stay in
my room all the time, I didn't want to see anybody. Sometimes I would
walk over to Warden Trigg's office.

"Listen, I'm ready to go home. Don't you think it's time for me to
leave?" I'd say.

"No, I think it's time for you to go back to your cell," he'd answer and then he'd call the guards and they'd escort me back. Then one day I went into my cell and closed the door. A white inmate yelled out to me, "Get out here. You got nothing to be ashamed of. I did your time ten times already. You got to get in shape and get right. You're going to fight again. You only got wino time."

One time, I got into a shouting match with a white racist guard and all the other inmates started jumping in trying to get involved. The Aryan supremacists from another quad came rushing over because they thought one of their boys was involved. So the guard called out a whole goon squad and there was total chaos. People were yelling, "Fuck 'em up, Mike! Kill that fucking pig!" It was a real riot. They had to lock the dorm down and they shipped my ass down to the hole.

The hole was a trip. They threw me in a six-foot-by-nine-foot room with just a mattress on the floor and a toilet. During the day they would remove the mattress and make me sleep on the concrete floor because they didn't want me to be comfortable.

It was pretty inhumane to be in a room twenty-three hours a day with the light always on, but you get used to it. You become your own best company. In a weird way, you get your freedom in the hole. Nobody was controlling your every move like they did in the general population. The hole was the worst situation you could be in and that became my element.

I was such a troublemaker my first year in prison. I kept getting written up for not moving fast enough, being rude, threatening the guards, pushing people. I was being so disruptive that they almost sent me to the P dorm. That's where they sent all the really dangerous inmates who didn't want to work or follow orders. They were segregated from the rest of the prison population. I was thinking that I was one of those crazy motherfuckers, so I began acting like them. They'd be locked in a room all day and the guards would watch them constantly.

"Fuck you, you fucking pussies," the P dorm guys would yell at the guards.

They had screens on the windows and when we'd walk by, they'd yell at us too.

"Hey, champ, chill out, champ. I hear you're getting wild out there. You don't want to come over here, champ. You don't want to fuck with us," they'd yell.

"Hey, when you get some etiquette, you can come amongst the rest of the people," I yelled back.

"Fuck you, you arrogant pigeon-loving motherfucker," the guy answered.

I chilled out after that. I didn't want to be living like some animal. It got so bad that they actually took the screens off the P dorm and put up solid glass so they couldn't spit on the people walking by.

I settled for the hole. Why not? I grew up in places where it smelled like raw sewage.

I came from a cesspool.

IN DECEMBER WE FOUND OUT THAT DESIREE HAD DISCUSSED BOOK AND FILM deals with civil lawyers before the rape trial. Now some of the jurors were worried that they had made the wrong decision.

"I cannot see her as a credible witness from what I know now," Dave Vahle, one of the jurors, told the press. "We felt that a man raped a woman. In hindsight, it looks like a woman raped a man."

Both he and Rose Pride, another juror, sent letters to the Indiana Court of Appeals requesting that I be given a new trial. Desiree tried to do damage control by going on *20/20* and giving *People* magazine an interview. Then in July, she finally sued me in civil court. Her father said that the suit was instituted because she was sick of being called names by Don King and my appeals lawyer, Alan Dershowitz. Desiree had a new lawyer named Deval Patrick. You may recognize that name. He's the governor of Massachusetts now. He's also the guy who sued me for unspecified damages to Desiree Washington, for both emotional and physical distress—he claimed that I had given Desiree not one, but two venereal diseases.

Shortly after that, Ed Gerstein, Desiree's original ambulance chaser, got an opinion from the suit he filed with the Rhode Island Supreme Court over his original retainer agreement with the Washington family. Among other things, the court issued a public opinion saying that they believed that the State of Indiana should look into this matter because Desiree may have committed perjury in addressing the issue of the retainer during her cross-examination at my trial. Dershowitz was immediately all over this information, calling it a "smoking gun" that would get my conviction overturned. He also called Desiree "a money-grubbing gold digger who is a liar to boot."

On July ninth, five hundred people showed up at a rally to support me in downtown Indianapolis. A city councilwoman from Compton came all the way to address the crowd.

"We will not let Desiree get away with using us as a tool to destroy one of the greatest men we've ever known."

But about a month later, Judge Gifford dashed my hopes again. She denied me a new trial and affirmed an earlier ruling that Dershowitz couldn't depose Desiree about her retainer agreement with her civil lawyer. She made it personal, saying that she was shocked by Dershowitz's "attempt to perpetrate a fraud upon the Court."

In October of 1992, my father died. I wanted to go to the funeral but they wouldn't let me. They were really trying to break me in there. I was still getting penalized heavily for marginal offenses, racking up more and more time. I actually paid for two funerals for him, one up north, and then we sent him down to North Carolina. My nephew told me that my father's common-law wife was so mad because all of his ex-prostitutes were sitting in the front row to pay him homage.

After the New Year, there were major developments in my case. On January twelfth, *Globe* magazine broke the story that Desiree was not as innocent as the prosecution portrayed her. They interviewed friends of hers who all said she was sophisticated when it came to sex. One friend even said that Desiree only cried rape when her father found out that she'd had sex with me and he was furious.

At the end of January, *Hard Copy* produced a one-hour special called "Reasonable Doubt" about my case. When Desiree had gone on *20/20* earlier, she had told Barbara Walters that she would have dropped the charges against me if I only would have apologized to her. Dershowitz was all over that.

"Can you imagine anyone saying they'd accept an apology for being raped?" he asked.

On February fifteenth, the Indiana Court of Appeals heard arguments on my appeal. Prior to the hearing, the justices had finally released the retainer agreement with Desiree's civil attorney. Dershowitz had four major issues that he felt could warrant a reversal— the witnesses who were excluded who saw Desiree and I necking, the exclusion of the implied consent instruction to the jury, the admission of the 911 tape, and the Gerstein retainer for a civil case against me. Many legal experts, including Mark Shaw, thought that Gifford had made enough errors to warrant a new trial.

After the arguments on that appeal, another bombshell hit, this one concerning Desiree's prior claims of being raped. Wayne Walker, a high school friend of Desiree's, alleged that Desiree told her father that he had raped her and then told Wayne that she had done it "to cover myself . . . or I would have been in big trouble." Walker told ESPN Radio that when he heard about Desiree accusing me of rape, "the first thing that came to my mind was 'she's doing it again.'"

Later that same month, the *New York Post* reported that in October 1989, Mary Washington had Donald arrested and charged with assault and battery against Desiree. Desiree told police that her father had "hit me and pushed me under the sink . . . he continued slamming my head into the wall and the floor. I freed myself and reached for a knife to protect myself."

What could have caused her father to assault Desiree? Well, when we look at her mother's deposition for my trial, she claimed that her husband "flew off the handle" when Desiree told him that she had lost her virginity. Her mother was so concerned that she arranged for Desiree to undergo "psychotherapy because of severe depression and suicide threats."

So Desiree's mother was confirming that Desiree had lost her virginity in October of 1989, which was exactly when her friend Wayne said they had sex and she had falsely accused him of rape. Desiree, of course, swore in an affidavit in response to my lawyer's amended appeal that she never had sex with that boy.

"I categorically and unconditionally deny that Wayne and I ever had sexual intercourse with penetration. I also categorically and unconditionally deny that I ever accused Wayne of having raped me."

There was only one problem. Dershowitz had uncovered another boy, Marc Colvin, a friend of Desiree's, who came forth and stated that what Desiree swore to was a lie.

"I am very reluctant to come forward with this information because I still consider Desiree Washington to be a friend. She called me on the telephone towards the end of 1989 and confided in me that she had sexual intercourse with Wayne Walker. . . . She also said that after it happened, she went into the bathroom and cried."

Oh, what a tangled web we weave! Fast-forward two years. I can only wonder what her father would have said and done if Desiree told him that she had had consensual sex with me. We're obviously not dealing with the most stable family unit here.

I was feeling pretty confident about my appeals with Dershowitz heading the case. So I was stunned when I lost the appeal before the Indiana Court of Appeals on August seventh. In a 2–1 decision, two of the justices felt that Gifford didn't abuse her discretion in blocking the testimony of my most important witnesses. One judge saw it my way. Judge Patrick Sullivan wrote, "My review of the entire record leads me to the inescapable conclusion that he [Tyson] did not receive the requisite fairness which is essential to our system of criminal justice." In other words, this nigga got fucked. I finally lost whatever little confidence I had left in our system. This was crooked business as usual. So I wasn't surprised at all when, six weeks later, the Indiana Supreme Court refused to even hear my appeal.

But check out why they didn't. To consider my case, they would have had to have a 3–2 majority vote. I would have gotten that vote except for the fact that Judge Randall Shepard, a liberal member of the court, had withdrawn from the case because of a conflict of interest. It seemed that the judge and his wife had gone to the twentieth reunion of his Yale Law School class. The judge's wife went to the ladies' room and on her return bumped into Dershowitz.

"She said she had told Dershowitz that she had seen him argue the bail request before the Indiana Court of Appeals and that he needed to be better attuned to the Indiana way of approaching things as this appeal progressed. . . . I agree . . . that this conversation was improper. My wife is not a lawyer and she did not fully appreciate the reasons why such conversations are considered improper. . . . She regrets very much having initiated this colloquy and feels a deep sense of embarrassment about it. My own decision not to disclose the reasons for my disqualification was motivated by a desire to protect my wife from the embarrassment she would feel about public disclosure and debate concerning her conduct," Judge Shepard later wrote.

It seemed that Shepard's wife was giving Dershowitz some pointers on how he could win my appeal. But the judge didn't want to make it appear that his vote was dictated by his wife's opinions. So in saving his wife's face, he fried my black ass. The final vote without Shepard was 2–2, and that was enough to shut me down.

Now I had no hope of getting right out of prison. It took me about thirteen months to figure out the right way to do my time. My whole first year was hell, getting months and months added to my sentence. I was suspicious of everyone there. They had put me in a cell with a guy named Earl who was a model prisoner. Earl was in there for thirty years for selling drugs, which meant that he had to do at least fifteen years. The administration thought that he would be the best guy to mentor me and keep me out of trouble.

The first night that we were together, I took a pencil and held it menacingly.

"I'll fucking kill you if you touch my shit, motherfucker. Better nothing be missing," I said. "And I'm not cleaning no room. Just don't talk to me."

Earl just looked at me.

"What the fuck? Yo, Mike, I'm not that guy," he said. "I'm with you, brother. I'm here to help you. Don't get caught up in that bullshit. It's just gonna get you a whole asshole full of extra time. I knew guys who came here with a year, three years, and they wound up doing life for the same bullshit. You just don't know how to move yet, young brother.

You need me to teach you how to move and it's gonna be easy sailing from here on in."

Little by little Earl schooled me. It took me some time to realize it, but Earl was awesome. We'd walk around the dorm and Earl would point things out.

"Stay away from these motherfuckers over there, Mike. And don't ever talk to those cops there. Don't even say 'Good morning' to them. Just keep your mouth shut at all times, Mike. Listen, if you see me sucking somebody's dick or fucking his ass, don't be surprised. I would never do that, but if you saw it don't be surprised. Don't ever be surprised at anything you see here, all right? And don't comment on nothing, just keep your mouth shut. If you see a bunch of niggas stabbing someone, just keep moving. Don't look at them, don't let them see you look at them. Whatever you see here, you don't see. Somebody is fucking someone, just mind your business. Don't make no jokes or comments about it because that's his wife, nigga. Just like if you disrespect somebody's wife in the street they're gonna kick your ass, it's the same if you disrespect their wife in here."

He was right. You couldn't apply your outside standards to what was going on in there. You think about homosexuality in the outside world and you might think of a meek person who could easily be taken advantage of. But these people were warriors. They'd kill you in a second. You'd see two big strong guys walking in the yard, holding hands. You respected those people because if you didn't, you'd have a very serious problem. In prison, anybody is capable of murder. It doesn't matter how big or small they are.

After a while in prison, I began to see the humanity in everyone, even the racist guards. I don't care if it's black gang members, Nazis, Mexican gangbangers, you started to get familiar with them when they told you that someone in their family died or that they had problems with their wife.

Once I really saw how the system worked, I began to manipulate things to my advantage. This inmate named Buck helped me in that process. Buck was a lifer from Detroit who had done about fifteen years. I used to get a ton of letters a day from people all over the world. One day he was in my room reading through some letters.

"Hmm, Mike. I can tell that you don't know how to read your letters," he said.

"What do you mean, nigga?" I said. "I can read."

"You can read, but you don't know how to *subliminally* read. There are messages here. People don't want to hurt your feelings because you're a famous fighter and they think you have lots of money, but they're using words that you're not aware of because you haven't been to school a lot, Mike," he said.

He was telling me this shit, but it wasn't offensive.

"Look, this one broad says, 'If there is ever anything you need, anything that I could do, please let me know.' See, that doesn't mean 'If I could do anything for you,' that means 'I want to do something for you, you just need to tell me.' Or take this other letter. 'I would love to get to know you and cultivate a relationship with you as human beings.' Listen, that means that she wants to elevate your status in life, your health, and well-being. That means if you need anything, she would help you out.

"We are in a unique situation here, Mike. We're on the edge of making a lot of money. Times aren't so good for you. You spent a ton of money on lawyers. You'll probably have to spend a ton more on that bitch who's suing you. You need commissary money. How are you going to eat well? You can't eat this food in the cafeteria."

"You're right, I do need commissary money," I agreed.

So I went with Buck. He started taking my letters and writing replies to these people and the money started flowing in. We were getting cash, we were getting jewelry, there was foreign currency coming, we were drowning in money. Around that time, Voyles got a phone call from one of the wardens.

"We have a problem with Mike's commissary," Warden Slaven told Jim.

"What's the problem?"

"He's got one hundred thousand dollars in his account," Slaven said.

But soon I started to get scared because some of these people wanted to come and visit me. What do I do? I had no idea what Buck had told these people in the letters. I was thinking that he had me ready to marry some of these women. I was starting to think it was a setup.

I knew I needed to break off Buck for doing this, so I told him to have the people send money to my "sister" or my "aunt" and then Buck could arrange to get the money from the people they were sending it to. Buck left prison so I had a young gangbanger named Red write the letters. All of a sudden, Red was sporting a nice new watch and was looking like a pimp with diamond rings and chains.

One day this girl from England showed up wanting to see me. She was a girl that Red had been corresponding with. He was in the hole then and he told me to go out and see her. But he didn't tell me that they had a tumultuous relationship and they were beefing. So I went out there thinking, *This is going to be great.*

We sat down in the visiting room and this girl started in on me. She was holding a baby.

"Where's my diamond chain? Where's the watch I gave you? I want them back, you motherfucker!" she screamed.

Whoa! I didn't have to take this shit from some crazy lady I didn't even know. I called out to the guard, "I'm ready to leave," and I walked away.

I guess she complained to the administration and they started an investigation. The guy handling the case came to me and said, "You don't know this girl, do you? She never gave you any jewelry, right?" He knew I had something to do with it, but they didn't want any heat from Internal Affairs.

"No, sir, I don't know anything about any of that. I never wrote that girl," I said. The prison was very concerned that they might get sued since I was a ward of the state. But they did some more investigation and caught Red and shipped him out.

By now you're probably wondering what a young, virile man like me was doing for sex in jail? Well, I was getting some in jail thanks to this little white inmate. I would see this guy get a visit from this girl

who came in all pregnant. I was thinking she had somebody else's baby and was coming in to break the news to him, but it wasn't like that. They were kissing and he was tonguing her. The administration went crazy and confronted him.

"You don't care that your wife is having someone else's baby?" they said.

"Hey, this is my personal business. Why are you up in my business?" he answered.

So I asked him what the real deal was.

"They're my babies, Mike. I've had two of them since I was in here. This is how you do it. You get your lady to come in wearing crotchless underwear and one of those loose summer dresses with the buttons down the front. But you have her wear it backwards so the buttons are in the back. Then you request an outside visit and you go to the yard where they have the picnic tables set up. And she sits on your lap facing away from you and you just give it to her right there. There's no cameras out there, you just have to watch out for the one guard who's monitoring the inmates."

That guy never should have told me that shit. Since I was falsely imprisoned, I thought, *Why do I have to stop my sexual activities? I didn't commit that crime. Why do I have to stop having sex?* That was my mind-set. I'd go through my fan mail and pick out the girls who I liked the most. I'd write them back, "Hey, would you be interested in visiting me? I'll send you a ticket." I'd give them all the instructions about the loose dress and the crotchless underwear. They were probably thinking that we were going to do the cheap-feel shit.

So when the first girl came, I was already sitting in the outside yard. I couldn't go up and greet her because I was sitting there thinking nasty stuff so that I'd be ready for her. She came over and kissed me and I turned her around and, boom!

She could have had AIDS or anything. I was just reckless. I just flopped her on top of me without a condom on.

Lord, I didn't even know this girl and we were doing it in broad daylight.

After a while, I had it down to a science. As soon as the girl got

on my lap, I'd hold her hand and start stroking so that they couldn't even see that she was moving. Because if you're doing it too hard she's up in the fucking air like she's on a trampoline and that wasn't going to work.

It was going great until I got stupid. One day I couldn't control myself and I was just laying it down and going for it. What happened was that the guard had left his post and he had circled around and snuck up on me from behind and saw what was going on. Somebody probably ratted me out because the guards never left their position in the window. I got sucker-punched.

Around this same time, one of the girls who had visited me from Atlanta came out with an article in *Star* magazine. She claimed that I had got her pregnant in jail and they showed this picture of her with a big belly. Thank God it was just a fake belly that they rigged up so she could sell the story to the rag. I was really relieved, but that was the end of my little sexual escapades. They canceled all outside visits for the whole prison. Everybody was so pissed off at me. They even called it the Tyson Rule.

By now Earl was getting ready to get out. Before he left, he sat me down.

"When I leave, I want you to go with Wayno. He's the only good guy here. Be careful of all those other guys, Mike. You're an inmate, but those guys are convicts. They're gonna do this until the day they die. Just stay with Wayno, he's not going to run you up into some bullshit."

I knew Wayno by then, but I wasn't close to him. We became close as soon as he moved into the cell with me. In fact, we became so close that he's still working with me to this day. Wayno practically ran that prison. He was in for dealing coke, but he had an IT background, so he worked processing the Inmate Tracking System. He was the president of our dorm, the assistant coach of the varsity basketball team, and a leading member of the Islamic community in there. Plus, he was from Indianapolis, so he had gone to school with a lot of the guards. Shit, he had probably sold them coke.

I was supposed to be working in the rec department. I guess they gave me that job so that I could be in the gym and train out. But most of the time I was on the phone. I was a real phone hog. As soon as the count was cleared after breakfast and everyone was accounted for I'd get on the phone. Each dorm had its own phone and it was on a first-come, first-served basis with a sign-in sheet. I'd have someone sign up and then trade them a couple of packs of cigarettes for their slot.

I would always say that I had legal shit to handle and that I was on with my lawyers, but most of the time I was talking to my friends and girls.

"Tyson, you've been on the phone for an hour," another inmate would say.

"This is fucking legal business, okay? Go talk to the warden," I'd answer.

I was treating that phone like it was an umbilical cord to the outside. But that was a big lesson I learned in prison. Wayno explained to me that sometimes when you're trying to keep connections out there, it could only make your time in prison harder. I learned that you had to check all your cars and your money, your boxing gloves, your belts, your women, your rings, your cell phone, all that shit, just check it at the gate. They didn't exist anymore until you got back out. But I was such a spoiled brat, I didn't want to follow the rules, because I thought that I could change them even though they had been etched in stone. It didn't work that way.

I had my close party friends all over the country who would talk to me at any time. One of them even had a dedicated phone line for me. He'd go out to parties and take his cell phone and I'd call him and he'd put some girls on the line.

When I wasn't on the phone, I was in my room reading. The judge really wanted me to get my GED, so I started to study for that with Muhammad Siddeeq, who had become my spiritual advisor. I didn't have any desire to do math or shit like that, so I started studying Chinese with a teacher that Siddeeq brought in. I learned enough Chinese so that when I went to China years later, I could actually carry on a conversation.

I was totally into reading though. There's nothing that'll pass time more than reading a whole book. Wayno and I would read to each other in our room every night. One guy would have the book and the other would have a thesaurus or a dictionary so that when we came across a word we didn't know, we could look it up. We'd even use the words in sentences so we really got them down.

I really enjoyed Will Durant's *The Story of Civilization*. I read Mao's book, I read Che. I read Machiavelli, Tolstoy, Dostoyevsky, Marx, Shakespeare, you name it. I read Hemingway, but he was too much of a downer. I gravitated to reading rebellious, revolutionary books. My favorite was Alexandre Dumas's *The Count of Monte Cristo*. I really identified with the main character Edmond Dantes. He had been framed by his enemies and sent to jail too. But he didn't just sit there and brood; he prepared for his eventual success and revenge. Whenever I felt lost in prison, I'd read some Dumas.

I was angry at society to begin with, and I began to see myself as a martyr. I always used to say that a tyrant dies when his reign ends, but when a martyr dies his reign begins. So when I read Mao and Che I became even more anti-establishment. I dug Mao so much that I had his face tattooed on my body. Arthur Ashe too. I really liked his autobiography, I had no idea he was so sound and adept.

I was right there next to Mao on the long fucking march. My objective became to manipulate the system every way I could. I'd look for the weakest, newest guard or just a guard who was impressed with who I am.

Once Wayno and I started to room together, we were unstoppable. Wayno had a store in his room. He would barter commissary items to the other inmates at a rate of two to one. If you wanted a bag of chips but didn't have money in your commissary, you'd go to Wayno. He'd give you a bag and mark your name down and then you'd pay him back with two bags. So before I moved in with him, I told him, "Brother, if there's anything in here now you need, take it. Take some soup."

"Mike, I don't need any of that, because if you give me anything, I'm just going to flip it and make some money for it, that's all," he said. So I gave him a bunch of stuff and by the time I moved in with him, our store was so big that he had to keep our merchandise in a few other people's rooms.

We'd sell the usual commissary items—cookies, cigarettes, chips— but I decided to use my celebrity to our advantage. Maya Angelou had just visited me and we took a picture together. One night I was hungry and this other guy had some doughnuts that I really wanted.

"Hey, brother, I have the Queen of Intellect of our people here, Maya Angelou. Look at that picture. That's worth at least fifty bucks," I said.

That guy was crying he was so touched by that photo. He went and put ten bucks in my commissary each time, and little by little he paid that $50 off. I did that a number of times whenever someone famous came to visit me.

Some of the female fans who wrote to me would send me dirty pictures of themselves, so I sold the pictures and the letters separately. Either someone wanted some jerk-off material or they wanted a relationship. Sometimes I'd give them the picture and the letter together. Depending on the girl's picture, I'd figure out what demographic would be attracted to that particular girl. If I had a picture from a Midwestern woodsy type of girl, I'd go to one of the redneck guys and say, "Check her out." It's funny, but some of those guys wrote those women and ended up getting married to them.

Then we progressed from nasty pictures to phone sex. When it was seven a.m. in Indianapolis, it was four a.m. in L.A. The clubs were just getting out and I'd call my friend collect. He'd have a few girls up at his pad ready for action.

"Let the games begin!" he'd say after accepting the collect call. We'd charge guys for listening to him and the girls having sex. Sometimes I'd find out the guy's name and then tell the girl to tailor her conversation to him.

"Oh, John, you turn me on. I'm getting so wet now," she'd say. John paid through the nose for that shit.

I was even getting my friends on the outside laid. I had a friend in Chicago who owned the hot club in town, and I'd send girls who wrote me from Chicago to his club so he could check them out, see if they were good stuff. That was an investment in my future. If they were nice, I'd see them when I got out.

Wayno and I were wheeling and dealing like crazy. We expanded our store to something like seven or eight rooms. Wayno kept the records and if someone was reluctant to pay us back, I was the enforcer.

"Motherfucker, give me my money, man." I'd pay them a little visit. Needless to say, even if they had to borrow from someone else, we got paid.

We were living like kings. Wayno had all these connections to the Aryan guys who worked in the kitchen and to some of the corrupt guards who'd smuggle shit in for the inmates, so you'd never find me in the chow hall unless they were serving ice cream.

Most nights we'd just chill in our room and the guards would deliver whatever food we ordered—pizza, Chinese food, Kentucky Fried, White Castle, whatever. Sometimes we even ate lobster and barbecue. I think that Wayno had shrimp fried rice for the first time while he was in prison. He would read aloud some book about Cleopatra and we'd have discussions like we were in a college dorm while we ate. When we wanted an authentic home-cooked meal, I'd just tell Siddeeq to have his wife cook us some delicious red salmon steaks and salad.

I did want a bigger room. Wayno and I visited our friend Derrick and he was in a corner room, which was much bigger than the regular rooms. I needed more space. Shit, my mail alone almost ran us out.

"Wayno, I can't take this shit, we need a bigger room," I said. "Get us an appointment."

He arranged for us to meet with Mr. Turner, who was our dorm counselor and worked under Mr. Dalton, who was in charge of all the dorms. We sat down and Wayno started making the case for us having a larger room. He was good at that because he used to represent other inmates when they had their hearings with the administration. So he was talking diplomatically and most articulately to Turner about our "legitimate needs" and if the administration could "consider our respectful request." But I was getting frustrated with all the red tape.

"Mr. Turner, sir, do you think when you and Mr. Dalton are out there hunting deer and burning crosses over the weekend you could think about me and my brother here moving up to a bigger room?"

Turner turned whiter than he already was.

"Yes, Mr. Tyson, we'll look into that right away."

Needless to say, we didn't get the larger room.

We had the basketball coach on the payroll. He was a guard, but he was smuggling us in food and my favorite wave hair grease. I knew that greed reached into the core of human beings. I knew that you could always give people some money to do shit for you. You can buy people pretty cheap. The last part I didn't fully understand. I was always overpaying.

One day I said, "Yo, can you get me any bitches?" He didn't flinch. He stood there, like, "How many you want to get?"

"Listen, it don't even have to be all that deep, right? Can I fuck that fucking guard right there? Do you think she's down? I'll give her a thousand bucks."

Now he was thinking about his kickback.

"Mike, are you serious? Because I will talk to this bitch right now. I know this bitch from the clubs, Mike. This bitch will fuck you."

This is a guard talking. I thought he'd say something like "Don't worry about it. I'll try to drop it by her later," but he was all gung ho, so I got a little nervous that I was going to get in trouble.

"Brother, brother, you're conducting yourself like a savage," Wayno told me. "Go in the room and wash your face, brother. Conduct yourself like a businessman."

So I dropped the idea.

They just kept trying to break your spirit in that place. If they saw you having a friend who was helping you do your time, they would take him away and ship him out. They did that to Wayno in the middle of the night. They sent him to Wabash, a brand-new level-four facility with a super max. Wayno was frantically writing down the phone numbers for his sister and his friends so I could call them and let them know where they had taken him.

That really made me hate Warden Trigg. I had to figure out a way to get back at him. He was pretty well disliked there. Every time he would walk the yard the inmates would yell, "You fucking George Jefferson–looking nigga. You're just an Uncle Tom." I remembered that he really liked this girlfriend of mine who would visit. She was a beautiful mulatto girl and he would let her come in even if she wasn't on the approved list. Trigg had a house on the grounds, so I told her, "Go over to his house and chill with him. Let him have a feel and then we can say that he molested you." I was real dark and bitter, but my mood changed and we never implemented that plan.

I was getting along well by then with my fellow inmates. I was feeling that I was a big motherfucker in prison, maybe even bigger than I was out in the world. My ego was that crazed. But everybody did know that I was a good guy at heart, as far as prison standards went. Whether you were white, black, whatever, if you needed something and Mike had it, you got it. It wasn't about owing me anything.

By the time Wayno left, I was a straight-A prisoner. I never drank the whole time I was in and I didn't smoke any pot. Nobody would have sold me any even if I wanted some. Everyone just wanted me to get into shape so I could come out strong and start fighting again.

But I couldn't give up my sex, so I started getting it from the inside. It started when they made me go into the drug counseling program, because if you passed the test, you'd get time taken off your sentence, so everyone from the superintendent to Don to the inmates was encouraging me to take the class. Even the drug counselor approached me and said, "I can help you get six months taken off your time." I didn't want to because I wasn't fucking with no drugs then, but it could get me time off, so I went to the class that was taught by this nice lady. She was a little big, but beggars can't be choosers. I was in class for a few days when she came over to check on my work. I don't know what came over me, but I started whispering in her ear.

"How are you doing?"

I so desperately wanted to get her. But she turned around on me and started talking street.

"Boy, anybody else say this to me, I'd have them shipped right out of here to Pendleton. You come in here and sexually harass me? Murderers wouldn't even come to me with that bullshit."

"Well, I am not one of those people," I said. "I am just a man seeing somebody that needs some help, like myself. We are both in a situation where we need help. I'm sorry, I didn't mean to say that, but I just saw you come in the other day with your son. I know you guys aren't doing so well, so if I can help you please just let me know. I'm sorry."

"Motherfucker, I should write your ass up."

"Really, I'm for real."

Then she told me some shit about her roof caving in during the last storm and I was thinking, *Yes!*

"So you've got a caved-in roof and you've got the baby in there? Wild dogs could come in there and bite him. Anything could happen to you. You can't defend yourself, you're a single mother."

"Yeah, and you're going to send somebody to fix it?" she said. "How are you gonna do this shit?"

"Just give me your address and there will be a package there tomorrow," I promised. I ran right to the phone and called a friend in Chicago and told him to get her ten grand by the morning.

The next day she came in wearing a pretty dress and nice makeup and a big smile. I thought, *OHHHHH shit!!!*

"How are you doing today, Mr. Tyson?"

I guess she got the package. I got so nervous. I didn't know what we were going to do. We were in the room by ourselves.

"You just go over to your usual desk over in the corner. Nobody can see it from the window. I am going to bend over to correct your work and you just stand behind me, all right?"

"Cool, cool," I said.

I was so nervous, I couldn't get hard. I was worried that it might be a setup. While we were trying to do it, I was looking around to see if there was a hidden camera somewhere. I was scared that any minute they were going to kick in the door and say that this was a rape.

So I tried to put that out of my mind, but I couldn't get hard. I was thinking of nasty things, I was touching her, I was licking on her, but it wasn't working. I even tried to stuff it in, but no luck.

"This is just not going to work. Let's just try this some other time."

I went back to my dorm and she called me back later that day and it worked out that time. Once we started we couldn't get enough. She kept calling me back to the room.

"Tyson to the school," I'd hear on the loudspeaker.

She'd be calling me back three times a day. She called me when I was doing my roadwork. I had to tell her, "No, you can't call me when I'm running, baby. It's the only time I've got to run." If anyone asked why I was putting so much time into the class, she'd just say, "He needs to finish his preparation for his test."

She was a heavy girl too. I had to pick her up and put her against the wall. Thank God I had been lifting weights. After a while, we did it on the desk, we did it on the floor. I was having so much sex that I was too tired to even go to the gym and work out. I'd just stay in my cell all day.

By then, Wayno had been transferred back and we were together again.

"How come you're not working out, brother? You're normally out here running ten miles a day," he asked me.

"I'm hitting the drug counselor. I got me a girlfriend in here," I said.

"You've got to stop this shit, Mike," he said. "You'll get into trouble. You've got to train."

It turned out that Wayno knew this woman from the outside. She was a little upset at first that I told Wayno about us, but soon he was standing outside the classroom door as a lookout.

Then one day I found out that she was pregnant. I called my friend from Chicago and he came down and took her to the abortion clinic. He was so pissed off.

"Pussy is pussy when you're in jail, but I'm the one who's got everybody staring at me when I'm walking into the clinic with this big chick," he complained to me.

After a couple of years, I really got used to being in prison. If I had a bad day because I saw something on television I didn't like or if I had received a bad phone call and I didn't want to talk to anybody, I'd tell Wayno to tell the administration that I wanted to check myself into the hole for a few days. Wayno would pack up my stuff—my glasses, a couple of books—and I would go and chill out in segregation deten- tion. I even had a guard smuggle me in a Walkman. They didn't allow inmates to possess Walkmans because the crazy-assed inmates would turn their Walkmans into walkie-talkies and spy on the whole fuck- ing prison administration. But once you were in the hole, they didn't check your cell, so I'd get my Walkman and listen to Tevin Campbell. His was the only cassette tape I had. I'd be running in place and doing my sit-ups butt-ass naked. I would run in place so much that when I left prison my imprints were in the cement. I broke that floor down.

I even got ahold of a cell phone down there. I'd be calling up friends at two in the morning and they'd freak out when the call didn't come up collect. They had great reception down there too.

YOU REALLY KNOW WHO YOUR FRIENDS ARE WHEN YOU FACE ADVERSITY. SO many people ran from me like the plague after my rape conviction. I was blessed to have so many good people in my life who supported me through thick and thin. My spirits would be boosted by everything I'd get and by visits from people who meant something to me.

My mom Camille came to visit me three times. I never wanted her to see me in there but I couldn't keep her away. It was a tough trip for her; she was in her eighties, but she did it. Jay would come with her and we'd talk about comic book heroes. I'd be worked up after reading one of the comic books that Stan Lee, the creator of Marvel Comics, had sent me. He also had a drawing done of me posing with some of his Marvel Comics superheroes like I was one of them. One time, Jay and I got into a debate about which cartoon character was the toughest. He picked Galactus and I had my man Apocalypse. We went round and round on that topic until Jay said, "Mike, Galactus eats planets. How can you beat that?"

My little daughter Mikey, my firstborn child, came to visit me a few times with her mom. She was only three years old then, but to this day she remembers those plane rides from New York to Indiana and posing for pictures with me in front of the brick walls.

Don King showed up a few times. Every time he came, he had a contract for me to sign, which was totally illegal, but he didn't care. I was happy he came because I knew it was about making money. Rory and John Horne would come with him, but they'd visit me more often too. They put in some time.

I was also thrilled to get a visit from Betty Shabazz, Malcolm X's widow. That tripped me out. I was so surprised and intimidated that she came to see me, I was on my best behavior. I didn't want to say anything crude. She was an awesome lady.

James Brown, the Godfather of Soul, stopped in to see me. Brother Siddeeq brought him in. He was wearing a purple suit, purple shoes, and a red tie with his hair all processed. He was telling me how he was going to whip Jackie Wilson's ass because Jackie tried to mess with James by running his fingers through his hair.

"I'm no boxer, I'm from Georgia," he said. "People were scared of Jackie. I wasn't. Feel this."

He showed me his bicep.

"Hard as a rock."

I asked James about Otis Redding, who was a good friend of his. James said that his plane was better than Otis's plane, which had been overloaded and crashed, killing Otis. It was awesome to hear James boast like that. He had the ego of a fighter.

He went on and on about his various enterprises like the radio stations he owned. He pitched me on letting him manage me, so I told him to stay in touch with Siddeeq. He sent Siddeeq a letter shortly afterwards. He would manage me and he'd take 70 percent and I would get 30 percent. And I thought Don King was bad.

I'll never forget the time that Tupac came to visit me in prison. Of all my celebrity friends, I've gotten more questions about Tupac than anybody else. All over the world when people see me, even before they ask me about boxing, they invariably go, "What was Tupac like?"

Tupac was everything. He was fucking Huey Newton, he was Mao

Zedong, he was Karl Marx, he was just everything. I can quote Marx and Hegel, but Tupac was really prolific talking revolutionary theory. When you talked to him and got to know him, he was much more of a didactic cat than a thug. He had a fascinating mind.

I met him in 1990 at an industry party at a club on Sunset Boulevard in L.A. The promoter of the party was my friend and we were standing around outside shooting the shit. Everybody was dressed natty for this event and I saw a small black street kid lingering near the door.

"What's up, Shorty? How are you doing?" I said to the kid. He reminded me of myself when I was a young kid on the streets, hanging out in front of clubs that I couldn't get in.

"Nah. What's up?" he replied.

I could see he wanted to go to the party, so I told my friend to let him in. But the little kid said, "One second," and ran off and came back with fifty guys, one of whom was Tupac.

"Whoa," my friend said. We walked all those kids around to the back door and let them in. I stayed outside talking for a while, but when I went back inside, I saw Tupac onstage with a mic rocking the party. I couldn't believe it. He came offstage and we hugged and laughed together. When he smiled his beautiful smile, he lit up the whole goddamned club. I could see that this kid was someone special.

Fast-forward to prison. I got a letter from Tupac's mom. I knew who he was, he was exploding overnight, but I didn't realize that he had been the kid rocking that club back in 1990. His mother said in the letter that Tupac was going to be in Indianapolis for a show and wanted to come see me. As soon as he walked into the visiting room, it was bedlam. He maybe weighed 130 pounds, had on these clothes that were bigger than he was. Blacks, whites, Latinos, Martians, everybody started going crazy. Even the guards were cheering. I had no idea he was that famous. When I saw him, I realized he was one of the kids I let into that party in L.A. years earlier.

We went out to the picnic tables in the yard.

"We need to throw a concert right here for you," he said and jumped up on the picnic table. "My nigga, I love you," he screamed at me.

I was sitting at the table, begging him, "Get down, please. Please come down. They'll lock you up with me. Please stop."

He was bent on doing an impromptu concert, but I was getting nervous. Everything was peaceful and then all of a sudden Tupac was up on the table, and everyone was cheering. *Oh shit, this little motherfucker is going to get me in trouble,* I thought.

"Mike, don't let them get you, brother, don't let them get you, man."

I finally got him down off the table. I started busting his chops. I had just become a Muslim and I was playing Mr. Righteous Guy.

"Listen, man, you need to stop eating that pork," I said.

"How do you know I eat pork?" he said.

I was teasing him but he took it serious.

He calmed down and we started talking. He told me that he never forgot our first meeting.

"Nobody never done that—let a bunch of street niggas into a nice club like that. You kept it real," he said.

"No, no, that's crazy, nigga," I said. "We've all got to enjoy this world. It's nothing man, we're just the same."

Tupac was an immovable force as a personality. He'd seen so much pain and hardship. Sometimes the adversity we live through traumatizes us and gives us baggage, and we bring our baggage everywhere we go. I bring my baggage into my religion, I bring it into my relationships sometimes, I bring my baggage into my fucking fights. I don't care how much we succeed, our baggage still comes with us. For Tupac, being born in prison, seeing his mother's friends killed or sent to prison forever, that just put him in a state of nonism where he felt no one was listening to him or cared. So he went on autopilot and did the best that he could. Tupac was really a freedom fighter.

I would talk to Tupac about the Black Panthers. I knew about his mother's involvement with them. She was a strong woman. By this time I had become pretty radicalized from reading all those militant books.

We got close after that, and he came out to visit me a few times. I would hear shit that he was in the paper for shooting cops, fighting with people.

"Hey, listen, if you're not careful, you're going to be coming in by the time I'm coming out."

Then he got shot and he was locked up. I'd arrange with a friend on the outside to set up a three-way call with Tupac. He told me that a friend of mine had shot him, but I didn't know that for certain.

Once I had gotten acclimated to prison, I started seriously plotting my comeback. It was depressing to hear the news about who was winning the heavyweight championship. The belt was being passed around like a volleyball. I was intent on getting out and reclaiming it and showing everybody that I wasn't the loser that they thought I was. No, I would be a god reclaiming my throne. In my sick mind, I was an ancient noble character and if I lost my quest to get the belt back, civilization as we knew it was done for. I was taking my little narcissistic quest and putting it on the whole world.

I needed that vision, though. I needed that drive for accomplishment or I would have rotted away in prison, so I made my plan. I knew what I had to do; I knew how to discipline my mind with the right things. The last thing I wanted to be was docile. The administration had assigned me to the gym because they wanted me to keep in shape, but then they locked me out because they thought I was involved in the drug trade in prison. But I wasn't. I was only smuggling in my hair grease. I wanted to get high in prison but I didn't because I was on a mission to get the belt back.

So I mainly did running and calisthenics to get into shape. I'd run in the yard in the morning, then do a lot of cardio work, jumping rope and push-ups and sit-ups. I had gotten letters from two former boxers who were in prison—Rubin "Hurricane" Carter and James Scott, who actually fought the majority of his fights while he was in Rahway State Prison. Scott wrote to me that I wouldn't be shit until I could do "a hundred push-ups in the clip." That was street-gang talk, a gun clip that could hold a hundred bullets. I couldn't do it at first, but I practiced and practiced and finally I wrote him back, "I got a hundred in the clip."

At night I'd have Wayno hold my legs down and I'd do five hundred sit-ups at a clip. I did them until my butt would bleed. We had a wall radio in the cell where you could plug your headphones in and listen to music so you didn't disturb your roommate, and I would get up at two in the morning, put on my shorts and my headphones, and jog in the room for hours. When Wayno would wake up, all the walls were sweating and steamed up from my exertions. Sometimes I'd jog in place in my room during the day and all the guards and inmates would come by and watch me through the little window for hours.

It was worse when I'd shadowbox. I'd be surrounded by inmates, guards, administration people, and every one of them was a fucking trainer.

"Move, nigga. Duck, duck," they'd say. Everyone had comments to make.

"I'm the pro, goddamnit," I'd say. "You just watch."

When I went in, I was 272 pounds, but in six months I had gone down to 216. I went from a little gorilla to some chiseled Adonis.

I began studying Islam while I was in prison. I had actually been introduced in Islam way before I had even gone to jail. Captain Yusuf Shah, Don's cook, was a Muslim brother who had been Malcolm X's teacher and Elijah Muhammad's right-hand man. Captain Joe, as we called him, was very highly respected. He had become my chauffeur, but he should have been my bodyguard; there was no problem that he couldn't solve.

Don had fired him because he had stomped on Don's pork chop. Don would routinely humiliate Captain Joe into cooking pork. Captain Joe used to actually wear iron gloves to prepare them. One day I saw Captain Joe crying and he was beating on the pork chop.

I was in L.A. when I heard that Don had fired Captain Joe, but when I landed back in New York, Captain Joe was there to pick me up at the airport.

"I heard you were fired," I said.

"No, no, good champion brother, nothing happened," the Captain said. "It was a misunderstanding. I upset Mr. King. It was my fault, I shouldn't have done it because it's his food. I'm just a silly man. Allah has blessed me with the privilege of working with Mr. King again."

"Captain Joe, if you don't tell me what happened, *I'm* going to fire you," I said. "I heard some people came up to see Don. What happened? How many people came up?"

"Seventy-five, all strapped," Captain Joe said humbly, but with a sinister strength that showed he still had power.

Apparently when he went back to Harlem and told his brothers in the Nation of Islam that Don had laid him off, seventy-five armed men went to Don's office, roughed up a few people, and made Don hire Captain Joe back, from what I was told.

"You don't fire Captain Joe, Captain Joe fires you," they told Don's staff.

So he went back and made Don assign him to me as my chauffeur. He still had a lot of pull. He was an old, harmless-looking man, but with one call he could get you what you needed. It was an honor for me to have him work for me. Captain Joe was an awesome mentor to me—kind, considerate, generous, a precious man. We would talk about spirituality all the time. He thought all spirituality was good. He was so happy when I got baptized; he thought it was wonderful that I took it seriously. I never had the heart to tell him that I took the choirgirl right back to my hotel room after the ceremony.

So I was already receptive to Islam when I went to prison. There was this convict from Detroit we called Chuck who had grown up as a Muslim. I met him at the mosque. Don't get me wrong, you didn't go to the mosque just to pray. Everybody transacted business in there. It was a place to meet up with other inmates from the various dorms. I was learning my prayers, but I would go and get my messages there too. I was praying to God, but I got a .45 too. It's just what it was. I love Allah, but I'm Mike too, and he made me this way—a manipulator and a hustler.

So Chuck started teaching me the prayers. He was a horrible teacher. He was hyperactive and rude and not very friendly. But he spoke Arabic. We'd go over the prayers and he'd yell, "Did you get it yet?"

"You just told it to me once, what are you talking about?" I'd say.

He had said the prayer like a speed freak. He could have used some Ritalin.

So he'd slow down a little and go over the prayer, but then they'd yell, "Chow," and it was lunchtime and he'd take off.

So I learned that opening prayer and then I started going to classes with Wayno. His Islamic name was Farid. At first I was rude and obnoxious. Brother Siddeeq would sit me down and talk about Islam, but I was so irritable I didn't want to hear about it. But once we got to know each other, Siddeeq asked me if I would join with the others in prayer and I chilled out. I got in the habit of praying and then I started reading the Koran with Farid. I didn't have any one moment of revelation. It was just like, this is who I am now.

I wasn't getting the spiritual side of Islam. That came much later. I wasn't really ready for religion then. Back then, I used Islam to subsidize my time and it helped me a great deal. I had something to believe in, but I did all of the right things for the wrong reasons. But it was definitely part of my growing up and learning about love and forgiveness. That was my first encounter with true love and forgiveness.

A year before I was scheduled to be released, there was talk that I would be granted an early release. A lot of national press people like Greta Van Susteren were questioning my conviction. My lawyers were talking to the court and to the Washingtons. Apparently, they had reached an agreement. I would pay the Washingtons $1.5 million and I would apologize to Desiree and I would get out of jail immediately. I didn't even have to admit to raping her, just apologize for it. Some of my friends like Jeff Wald were pushing for the apology.

"Mike, I'd admit to raping Mother Teresa to get the fuck out of jail," he told me.

"If I apologize, the prison in my head would be worse than the prison I'm in now," I told him.

So they brought me to Judge Gifford's courtroom in June of 1994 for a sentence reduction hearing. I was dressed in denim pants, a light blue work shirt, and work boots. The new prosecutor asked me if I had anything to say.

"I've committed no crime. I'm going to stick with that to my grave. I never violated anyone's chastity."

That wasn't what anyone wanted to hear. They sent me right back to jail. Everyone was hugging and kissing me when I got back.

"Fuck them motherfuckers," they all said.

"Chill out," I said. "I'm cool. Another year. Let's just do this shit."

I knew that this wasn't going to be the end of Mike. I was only twenty-eight by then, but I knew that there was going to be some good reward for me after I did my time. More press came out to interview me. I was reading a lot and I was sharp and very politically focused then.

Larry King came and did a two-part interview with me from jail. He really wanted to get a picture of what it was like for me to go from the top of the world to being behind bars.

"Romantic love, you miss romantic love?" he asked.

I couldn't tell him about my teacher.

"Maybe, but what is love? Love is like a game, love is competition. Most people who are gorgeous, a guy or a woman maybe, love comes to them all of the time because they attract love. But they never fought for love, what are they prepared to do for love? Love is a situation where you must be prepared to do something, because if you have something lovely, somebody is going to want to challenge you for it, and if you've never been competitive enough, the slightest struggle and you are going to give in."

"Obviously, you gained better control of your own total environment here. What about food? Do you miss certain foods, no?"

I couldn't tell him about the lobster and the Chinese food and all the menus we had in our room.

"I'm just me," I answered.

"I'm just trying to put the audience into what would it be like to not have the things they have every day," Larry said.

"I'm going to tell you something, there are people that have been to prison, and perhaps a lot worse than the situation I am in. But you just become very much attached to yourself. I believe there is a playwright by the name of Tennessee Williams who said, 'We must distrust one another because that is the only way to protect each other from betrayal.' And I am a great believer in that, I'm a great believer.

I believe everyone that is involved in my life, one day or the other will betray me. I totally believe that. And a lot of people say no, no, no. But that is what I believe."

"If you believe that, you must be unhappy," Larry said.

"No, I am not unhappy, I am just aware of my circumstances."

"I'll give you a human thing you must miss. Cheering," Larry said. "You must miss that."

"Can I tell you something now? Praise be to Allah, I cheer for myself a hundred million times a day in my mind. To me I am my biggest fan, there is nothing in the world better than me. So I don't think about that, those guys really don't know what they're cheering for. I know the total me and I know why they should be cheering, but they don't know, they cheer for the knockout. That's all they cheer for, the knockout and the performance. I cheer because I know who I am."

Everything was going fine in prison until someone ratted out me and the drug counselor. I was going to get out in one week if I passed the last test, but suddenly this guy from Internal Affairs came to see me. Someone had told them that I had been in the room for hours with this teacher, so they sent an investigator from outside the prison to interview me. I was sweating like a pimp with one ho.

"You're supposed to be getting out in a few weeks but that will change if you're found guilty," he said calmly.

Holy shit. The air left me in a second.

"But I didn't do anything, sir. Anybody can tell you that I'm a good student," I said. I was so scared of this little white guy, I was Tomming it all up. "Yes, sir. No, sir."

"There have been inmates saying that you have been in that room with the counselor for inordinately long amounts of time," he said.

"I don't know anything about that. I'm just doing my work. I have some counseling needs. I've used drugs and alcohol excessively and there are many temptations that I must battle every day. . . ." I was freelancing it.

"You know, I think you got a real bum deal in your case, Mike, but this is a very different and very serious matter," he said.

I was scared to death when I left that guy. I went out to the visiting area because I had this girl on her way to visit me. I was tripping out. And then I saw the white guy who had just interrogated me going to talk to my counselor.

"Are you looking for me, motherfucker?" she started yelling at the guy.

Holy moly. My balls were in my sneakers by then. I couldn't believe she was screaming at this white guy. I was thinking, *Oh, God, we're fucked now.*

"What the hell do you want to know about me? I've been here for seventeen years doing my job."

She ripped into this guy and pulled out her ghetto card and totally intimidated him. Then she came over to where I was sitting in the visiting room. She started talking to me and she touched my dick through my pants and it started getting hard and then she wrote her name right on my pants where my dick was.

"Holy shit, how could you do that?" I said.

She just smiled.

I never heard anything about that investigation again. At the end of the drug course, I passed my test, even though I shouldn't have. On one of the tests they asked me to name the "three basic needs." I answered—sex, food, and water in that order. No air, just sex, food, and water.

It was a matter of days before I'd be released. I was going out with millions and millions of dollars guaranteed to me from Showtime and the MGM Grand, thanks to deals that Don had made. I had been courted by everyone, but Don seemed to be the best move. He was offering the most money. And I was also leaving with a new girlfriend waiting for me.

I had met Monica Turner years earlier. She was a friend of Beth's, one of my lady friends. Beth wanted to set me up with Monica because she thought we'd be a good match. So Monica sent me a letter at Camille's house and enclosed a photo. I didn't follow up with her until two weeks before my trial. I was in D.C. and I showed up in front of her house with two stretch limos. I had her number in my head because I have a photographic memory, so I figured I'd go over there and see her because we had never met in person.

"Where you at?" she said.

"I'm at your front door."

I met her at the door and tried to talk my way in, telling her that we should go upstairs, but she wasn't going for it. Craig Boogie was there with me.

"Can I use your bathroom?" he asked.

And she let him right in.

"Why are you letting him in the house? You don't even know him," I said.

"Because you want to come in and do something else, but he just wants to go to the bathroom."

So I just gave her a kiss and I left and I didn't talk to her again. Then one day when I was in prison, I got a letter from Monica.

"Oh, God, please call me, please," she wrote. She was very concerned and caring. So I called her collect.

"Hey, you want to be my girl?" I asked her right off the bat. That's how I lived my life, right in the moment.

"Yeah! I do," she said.

I was glad. She was a nice, smart girl. She'd been through a lot; she'd been abused, been through some hard times. She was going with one of the New York Knicks then but she dumped him.

I sent her some plane tickets and she came right out to Indiana. She wasn't making much then; she was a student studying to be a doctor.

She saw me in the visiting room and started crying.

"I can't believe you're in here," she said.

We hit it off and she kept coming to see me every opportunity she had, sometimes even twice a week. We never had sex while I was in prison. We might have fooled around a little, but I didn't want to risk having her banned from visiting me. More than anyone else, I really looked forward to seeing Monica when I was in there.

When she first started visiting me, she was a little overweight. I was really shallow then so I told her she needed to lose a few pounds. I put her on a workout plan and started training her over the phone. She was really motivated and lost the weight.

I had been there for three years, and I was finally getting out. I got up really early that morning and packed all my stuff. Farid had been discharged earlier, so I didn't have any really close friends there, but I said my good-byes to the inmates. I was being processed and was waiting to go out and greet the hundreds and hundreds of reporters and cameramen who had been waiting outside since the middle of the night. Right before I was set to go, this little white female guard came up to me.

"I'm proud of you, man," she told me. "I didn't think you could handle this, but you did. You didn't let them break you. Congratulations."

I thought about what she said for a second. My megalomania kicked in and I thought, *Didn't think I could handle this? Does she know where the fuck I came from? I was born in the institutional system. Who the fuck does she think I am?*

But that wasn't what she was talking about. She was talking about taking that long fall from grace and adapting to a society where I didn't look at myself as being bigger than everyone else. We were all equals. What that guard said went right over my head—the head that, despite my best efforts, was getting bigger and bigger with each step I took towards the outside world.

10

I couldn't sleep the night before I was going to be released from prison. At four a.m. I started hearing the helicopters whirring outside in the sky. They were from the news stations who were getting their live feed ready. Outside the facility, the parking lot was jammed with satellite dishes and the cars of print reporters. Across from the lot, a huge crowd had gathered in a cornfield in the dark, waiting to get a glimpse of me leaving. At six a.m., Don and Rory and John Horne arrived in a black stretch limo and went into the facility.

I was waiting for them, but I really didn't want to leave the prison. I had gotten used to being in jail. I enjoyed just being able to chill and get visits from celebrities and TV journalists. It was a rest well deserved, but then I had to go out into the world again.

I took a deep breath and then we left. It was only a short walk to the limo, but it seemed like an eternity. The cameras were flashing, the four helicopters were whirring, and the people in the cornfield cheered. It was sensory overload. I was wearing a simple black coat

with a white linen shirt and a white knit kufi on my head. I was trying to be a humble brother, but it was hard.

Before we flew to Ohio, I wanted to stop at a local mosque and pray
as a heartfelt gesture of appreciation and gratitude, but even that
became magnified into a circus show. Siddeeq had enlisted Muhammad Ali to pray with me and he was waiting at the mosque when we
got there. There was a mob of people and everyone was jockeying for a
position so they could be seen with me in the camera shot. I was always the vehicle to get someone on television or have them mentioned
in the papers. That was the devil at his best, right there.

After we prayed, we flew to my house in Ohio. It was ironic that
the same team that had seen me into prison was now ushering me
out. Don was already pissing me off and I was only hours out of prison.
He had stocked the limo with Dom Pérignon. Along the way to my
house there were yellow ribbons tied around the trees and big ban-
ners that read MIKE WELCOME BACK TO YOUR FAMILY and CHAMP WE
MISSED YOU.

When we got to my house, I saw that Don had planned a big
welcome-home party. He had invited all these people who I had no
connection to and he catered the event with lobster, shrimp, and pork,
and champagne—real appetizing stuff for a Muslim. I kicked everyone out of the house, including Don, and then Monica and I consummated our relationship.

When Don came over the next day, I fired him. We were supposed
to have a big press conference announcing our deals with the MGM
Grand and Showtime, but I didn't give a shit. I scratched his name off
the press release.

"Mike, please don't do this, please," Don started begging. "Don't do
what these white devils are doing to me." I could give a shit about his
pleas. But then he opened up an attaché case filled with a million dollars in cash and that caught my attention. No other promoter could
come up with that much cash, so I changed my mind again. I put his
name back in the release and a few days later we held a press conference to announce our new deals.

I had no time to adjust to the world. I had so many people in my face because I had $200 million in fights lined up. It was worse than when I went in. Everybody was around me saying, "Mike's the man. He's the man." But now I had a different frame of mind. I was afraid of everybody. Prison doesn't rehabilitate anyone; it dehabilitates you. I don't care how much money you earn when you get out, you're still a lesser person than when you went in. I was paranoid. I thought everybody was gonna hurt me. I'd panic every time I'd hear an ambulance siren. One time, Monica and I were in bed and I woke up and looked at her and grabbed her. For some reason I thought somebody had come into the bed and was trying to stab me. I was so scared.

I wasn't the same guy; I had become hard. Prison basically took the whole life out of me. I never again trusted anyone—not even myself around certain people. I never wanted to be in any kind of situation around women. It had been brewing over my head for so many years that I wasn't able to let it go; it even really bothers me to this day. All my friends say, "Let that die, let that die," but they're not the one who has to deal with it. That's a hard pillow to sleep with.

I had signed those two contracts that advanced us a lot of money, so no one wanted to hear that I needed some time to get my mind and my life together. Everybody expected so much out of me. I was conflicted. As scared as I was, I was also starting to get arrogant again. I wanted everything. I thought I was owed a lot from my time in prison. I wanted to fuck the best girls, buy the best cars, own the best houses. I was the Count of Monte Cristo. I was a gladiator. God himself couldn't produce a better fighter. And here I was, afraid of ambulance sirens.

I wanted to perform up to the most impeccable standards, but I didn't know if I could. I was twenty-nine years old, but I felt a lot slower. I didn't have the same hunger I had before I went to jail. And, more than anything else, I felt ashamed that I had been in prison. Every time I went to a new city, I had to go and register as a sex offender. If I forgot, I'd get pulled aside at the airport by the police.

"Excuse me, can I talk to you?" the cop would ask. "I see that you haven't registered when you came here, so if you would be so kind as to register in your destination city that would be much appreciated. I could arrest you right now so I think it would be prudent to register as soon as you arrive."

Oh, God. That shit still goes on to this day when I travel.

Even though everyone was expecting me to decimate the whole heavyweight division, it wasn't going to be that easy. Nobody in boxing history had ever been robbed of three years of their life and then come back like nothing had happened. Ali had been stripped of his title, but he hadn't been in jail for three years, unable to train, so that just added to the pressure I was under.

I really tried to be a good brother when I got out, but I got swept into the material world. There were too many people throwing themselves at me and my consciousness wasn't fully developed then. I was still praying but all these distractions were permeating my head and pushing me back to that pre-prison Mike.

It's easy to blame Don for pulling me right back into that sick world of garish consumption and booze and women. Maybe he was genuinely concerned that I might begin to follow some Muslim creep and get rid of his ass. But you can't blame anyone but me. I wanted to prove to everybody that I was still the man, even though I had been locked up for three years. Underneath that chiseled body, I was still a glutton. If it was up to me, I'd eat cakes and ice cream all day. So I had to suppress that part of me.

But it wasn't that easy to suppress my sex drive. Monica wanted to surround me with a family and a stable home life, but I didn't want that back then. I was totally out of my league trying to be a family man; I was still much too immature. My idea of being a family dude was "Just shut up and take the money." I was a selfish pig.

Shortly after I got out of jail, I was in New York with Craig Boogie. We were walking down the street and I saw this beautiful black girl and I started following her. I was trying to stop her to get her to talk to me, but she ducked into a Banana Republic store. I followed her in and saw her go into a dressing room to try something on. We were waiting outside the door when she came out of the store.

She just kept running away, she didn't want to talk to me.

A week later, I was doing a photo session in my house in Ohio for some magazine and this girl showed up. She was the stylist on the shoot.

"Hey, I know you," I said. "I guess our meeting was just fate. You were delivered to my house."

She was so hot that the photographer was hitting on her the whole time too. But I kept up with that prisony pseudo intellectual modern mack rap and she went for it. She told me her name was Tuesday, and from that day on we would be together for many, many Tuesdays to come.

Now that the money was rolling in, it was time to buy some really luxe properties. I needed a place in Vegas since I would be fighting there, so I bought a beautiful six-acre spread next door to Wayne Newton's mansion. I had a great time decorating that house. Everything was Versace, from the toilet paper holders to the blankets and the pillows. When you entered the house through these giant wooden doors with crystal handles, you immediately saw a giant waterfall with two lion figurines on either side of it. There were vaulted ceilings so the trickling of the water would cascade throughout the house and create a feeling of tranquility.

I liked to watch karate movies, so I set up several different home theaters there. My bedroom was tricked-out with the latest in high-tech sound equipment. I loved my sounds so much that sometimes I would put sound systems in my cars that cost more than the car itself. For the foyer upstairs, I commissioned a two-thousand-square-foot mural of all the greatest fighters in history. That set me back $100,000.

When you went out to the backyard, you'd think you were in Italy. Or at least the Bellagio Hotel. I had a moat put in, as well as a huge pool. The pool was ringed with seven-foot statues of fierce warriors like Alexander the Great, Hannibal, Genghis Khan, and Jean-Jacques Dessalines, the Haitian revolutionary. You can't just go out and buy a giant statue of Hannibal, so I called the guy who did the lions at the MGM Grand, and he worked from pictures I supplied and then got a crane to place the statues. Ringing the entire yard were exotic trees that cost $30,000 each. The maintenance on the trees came to almost $200,000 a year.

Of course I had to have an East Coast mansion as well, so I went out and bought the largest house in the state of Connecticut. It was over fifty thousand square feet and had thirteen kitchens and nineteen bedrooms. My goal was to fill each bedroom with a different girl at the same time. It was quite a spread. Thirty wooded acres, an indoor and outdoor pool, a lighthouse, a racquetball court, and an actual nightclub that I called Club TKO.

I felt like Scarface in that house. My master bedroom was five thousand square feet. I had a walk-in closet that was so big and filled with elaborate clothing and shoes and cologne that you would have thought you were in an actual Versace store. When Monica was there, she had her own walk-in closet that was over a thousand square feet. There was a huge balcony off the bedroom that looked out over the main floor of the house. I could get to the bedroom by walking up these twin circular marble stairs or I could take a glass elevator. It was a great house, but in the six years I owned it, you could count the number of times I was actually there on two hands.

I still owned the Ohio mansion, and then I bought a fourth house for Monica, a nice place on the golf course of the Congressional Country Club in Maryland, the same course Tiger Woods often played on. But I wasn't just spending my money on houses. I started indulging again in my car obsession. When I had been in jail, I was down to six cars, but I started building my collection again with Vipers, Spyders, Ferraris, and Lamborghinis. We'd drag race them up and down the street outside my Vegas house.

I'd supply all my guys with fine cars. Me and Rory and John Horne once were walking by a Rolls-Royce dealership in Vegas and we looked in the window. The salesmen inside didn't think much of three black guys in sneakers and jeans peering through the glass at the expensive cars, and when we walked in the place, they didn't recognize me so they had some junior flunkie take care of us.

"That Rolls there, how many do you have on the lot?" I asked the guy.

"Do you want to test-drive it?" the young salesman asked.

"No, I'll just take all you have in stock," I said.

That kid got promoted to general manager after I left the place.

AFTER EACH OF MY FIGHTS, BOOGIE AND I WOULD GO TO L.A. AND SPEND THE entire day shopping on Rodeo Drive. Then we'd have a nice dinner, pick up some girls, and hit the clubs. I'd still hit the Versace store at Caesars from time to time, dropping $100,000 at a time. We'd leave the place and it looked like a scene out of *Coming to America* with all these people carrying bags and bags just loaded with stuff. The ironic part is that most of the clothing stayed in my closets. I would usually just wear my sneakers and my jeans or some sweats. Johnny Versace used to send me invitations to all his parties when I was in prison. He knew I couldn't come but it was his way of letting me know he was thinking about me. He was an awesome guy.

I had so much money that I couldn't even keep track of it. One time, Latondia, Rory's assistant, was hanging out in New Jersey at Rory's house. She didn't have time to pack a bag, so when she got there, she went to a guest room where there was a Louis Vuitton duffel bag. She assumed it was either mine or Rory's, and figuring she could find a clean T-shirt in there, she opened the bag and was shocked. There was a million dollars in cash in the bag. She immediately called Rory into the room and showed him her discovery.

"Man, Mike forgot where he left that bag," Rory said. "I'm going to call him right now and ask him to loan me two hundred thousand dollars."

That bag had been there for over a week. I had had a rough night in the city and had forgotten where I had left it. Every time Latondia would bring my clothes to the cleaners in Vegas, she would come back with plastic sealed envelopes containing priceless bracelets or $20,000 in cash that I would have left in my pockets before the clothes were sent out. When it came to money, I wasn't such a big details guy.

But my most over-the-top spending was when I decided that I should buy some tiger and lion cubs. I was still in jail when I was talk-

ing to my car dealer, Tony. I was anxious to find out what new cars
were coming out when Tony told me that he was thinking about getting a tiger or a lion and drive around with it in his Ferrari.

"Hey, I want a tiger," I said.

Tony got the word out and Anthony Pitts heard about it and the
next thing I knew as soon as I got home to Ohio from prison there
were four cubs on my lawn. I was fascinated with them. I played with
them a lot and I soon realized that they didn't have the same personality as our common cat house pets. They'd get finicky and pissed off
when you played with them too much. You had to learn their behavioral characteristics because in a few short years they'd be seven feet
tall, weigh over four hundred pounds, and could stand up on their
hind legs and break the top of my skull off with a swipe of their paw.

I got closest to the white tiger cub that I named Kenya. She went
everywhere with me and even stayed with me in bed. People in the
wild-animal world couldn't believe the relationship I had with her.
They said that in thirty years they had never seen a white tiger follow
somebody around like she did with me. She would walk through the
house crying like a baby, looking for me. If I had a girl in the house, I
would lock her outside in her sanctuary and she'd cry. Hot summer
nights when she was in heat, she'd cry until I would go out and rub
her belly.

Kenya pretty much had the run of the house. When she was outside, she'd sit on top of the pool ledge and look over the fence at Wayne
Newton's horses. She could have easily jumped that fence but she
never did. We had this trainer named Keith working with her, and
I paid him $2,500 a week to train her. My assistant Darryl and
the people who cleaned the house helped raise her, but they didn't
want to go near her. She'd nip at them sometimes, so they didn't really
trust her.

When you have cubs, you have to have them around you all the
time because if you leave them alone and then come back, they don't
know who you are and then you've got a problem. So I got licenses for
my animals and got two eighteen-wheel vans to transport them

around the country. By then, I had only the two tiger cubs. The lions kept going up on two paws and were too intimidating. One of them actually bit me on the arm and I had to go to the hospital and get six stitches to close the wound. At the emergency room, they said, "Hey, what happened to you?" and I told them that I had gotten bit by a dog. I wanted to kill that motherfucking lion, but I realized that it was my fault, so I got a tetanus shot to be safe and then I gave him away.

After a few months of getting acclimated back to society, I began to train for my comeback fight. I had added a new member to my team. I had met Steve "Crocodile" Fitch years earlier in the bathroom of Madison Square Garden that night my opponent never showed up. He had asked me if I was fighting that night and I said, "Yeah, if my opponent shows up." When I was in jail, I was talking to Rory, and Crocodile had been working with the boxer Oba Carr, who Rory managed and Don promoted, so Rory put him on the phone with me. We were talking about some friends of mine who he had met when he was in jail and we just clicked. So when I got out, I told him to hang out with us. He was my kind of guy—a street guy.

After I got out of jail, Don didn't come around too much. I think he was still scared that I'd get physical with him. So he used John Horne to deal with me on business matters and Rory was my point man for anything personal. They were splitting the 20 percent manager's fee, but even then they were making more money than they could have ever dreamed. Besides Rory and John, I had my same security team headed up by Anthony Pitts. I also had Farid, my old cellmate, around until the authorities told us that we couldn't associate with each other because we were both felons.

By now Team Tyson had gone high tech. Instead of using phones, we each had a walkie-talkie so we could all communicate about what was going on. Everybody had their own handles. Rory was L1 and John was L2. Ant was T1. My friend Gordie was called Groove. Don was called Frederick Douglass because of his hair. I had a few different handles. Sometimes they called me Mad Max. Sometimes it was Arnold, after Arnold Rothstein. Most of the time it was Deebo. They called me Deebo after the bully in that movie *Friday* because I was always, "Give me this, give me that," housing other people's stuff, eating their food, changing the TV programs they were watching.

I didn't really like that whole walkie-talkie setup because it meant that I could be tracked down much more easily. I was trying to be disciplined in camp, but sometimes the smell of a French fry would knock me off track and I'd sneak out and go eat. And I was always trying to ditch my security and get down with some woman. As the fight on August nineteenth with Peter McNeeley approached, I'd get more and more surly. I had been confident about it at first because I was in such great shape coming out of jail, but when we started sparring in camp in Ohio, I got hit with some punches from an amateur young kid and it hurt like hell. I wasn't accustomed to getting hit. I was supposed to box five rounds but after two I said, "That's enough for today. I'll be back tomorrow." Fuck, I couldn't believe that this little amateur kid had hurt me so bad. Taking punches was definitely different from being in shape. I thought, *How could I beat McNeeley when that amateur nearly stopped me?*

I eventually got my rhythm back and I was ready to go when August rolled around. I was my usual ornery self when we got together for the prefight press conference. I strolled in wearing a black suit and a white Panama hat. Nobody in boxing was taking McNeeley serious as an opponent. This guy was a club fighter at best.

I named the McNeeley fight "King Richard—The Return of the King." I used to name my fights after warriors. Even though Cus was long dead, I'd talk to him. "Don't worry, Cus, the King is coming back. King Richard is going to return triumphant."

If I had any doubts, they were all dispelled when I got in the ring and stared at McNeeley. We came together for the instructions and he wouldn't look at me. A year after the fight, he told some reporter what was going through his mind.

"Tyson came into the ring with this thuggy song and I wasn't prepared to be scared. I was checking him out at the press conferences and he wasn't that big in street clothes. I stood in my corner with my back to him, that's not where you want to get beat, staring at your opponent. I was just going to look at his belly button when we got to the middle of the ring. Well, Pandora's box, I have to take a peek. He's all pumped up. He's so wide! His lats are gigantic. His neck, his cranium. He's a fierce-looking individual. I winked and blew him a kiss, but I was scared."

I was just thinking this guy was crazy! I wanted to say, "You're really a fucking asshole," but I couldn't break my tough-guy image. When the bell rang, he swarmed me and got me in my corner. I countered with a short right and he went down, but then he jumped right up like a jack-in-the-box. Before Mills Lane could even begin a mandatory eight-count, this guy was skipping around the ring and then charging back at me. I couldn't believe this shit. After the eight-count, he came at me again and I hit him with a left hook and a right and he went down again. He got up and could have continued, but his trainer jumped in the ring and stopped the bout while Mills Lane was taking me to a neutral corner. It was a disaster. People started booing. The ring announcers kept saying, "What a letdown." We were fighting before fans in ninety countries, the biggest audience in history, and the guy's corner wouldn't let him fight.

At the press conference after the fight, I tried to be humble and praise Allah. "I've got a lot to learn. I have to continue to cultivate my skills," I told the reporters. When they asked me about his corner stopping the fight, I said, "You know me. I'm a blood man. I'm glad they stopped it. Look, fighting to me is what theory was to Einstein and what words were to Hemingway. Fighting is aggression. Aggression is my nature. I don't want to talk about boxing."

Afterwards McNeeley said, "Look at the films! I came to fight. I talked the talk and walked the walk."

"He also swooned the swoon," the *New York Post* wrote.

The Nevada Athletic Commission decided to withhold his manager's share of the purse. But the manager turned out to be a genius. He got McNeeley two national commercials—$40,000 from AOL to reenact the fight and $110,000 from Pizza Hut where he was knocked out by the pizza crust.

I guess Don was embarrassed by the fight because he had lined it up for me, and he decided that my fans could save their $50 and watch my next fight on free TV. I was set to fight Buster Mathis Jr. on Fox on November fourth. I'm sure Don picked that date because it was the same night as the pay-per-view of the third fight between Riddick Bowe and Evander Holyfield, but it became a moot point when the fight was postponed because I fractured my right thumb. Immediately, the press jumped all over me. The *New York Post* had a headline that read: "Prove It, Mike."

They actually had a point. I had postponed several fights in the past as a tactic to psychologically mess with my opponent's head. My opponent would be all ready to fight, all pump, pump, pump, and then I'd postpone it and they'd never come back like that again. They would think that I was working out hard because I was in the gym all day, but I wasn't actually doing anything. Then I'd bust my ass before the rescheduled date and they'd have already peaked. That was a trick that Cus taught me.

Part of the problem was that the pressure mounting on me to win the title back was escalating.

"The public isn't going to put up with me fighting ten or fifteen nobodies before I fight for the real title," I told a reporter. "There is a great deal of pressure on me to get some things done right now. People want to see Mike Tyson in big-time fights. And I have exclusive contracts I have to honor. Those contracts pay too much money for me to come back slow and easy. It's business, big business. All those people care about is that I'm in the ring and making them money."

We rescheduled the fight for December sixteenth in Philadelphia. I guess the oddsmakers saw something in my McNeeley fight. He was only a 15–1 underdog, but they had Mathis at 25–1. Mathis was a much better fighter than McNeeley, but he did come in a little overweight. At the weigh-in, I took off my PROPERTY OF ALLAH sweatshirt to reveal chiseled abs.

"Cut in stone! Adonis!" Don King kept bellowing.

But when it was Buster's turn, he kept his T-shirt on and he weighed a flabby 224.

When the fight began, Buster tried to do what McNeeley had done and charged me. Buster and I fought in close for two rounds and then in the third he tried to smother me against the ropes, but I moved to my left and got my leverage and peppered him with two right uppercuts and he went down. When I was asked at the press conference why I had missed so many punches, I said that I was "lullabying" Mathis and that the missed punches were "all a plot, all a setup. Just like this society." In truth, Mathis was just really hard to hit. If you look at his whole career, nobody had done what I had to him.

Mathis was a little lighter.

"Mike Tyson dropped me and when I looked up the count was at five. I said to myself, 'Damn, whatever happened to one to four.'"

Frank Bruno, one of the reigning heavyweight champs, was ringside and Crocodile and I went to work on his head. As we left the ring, Croc yelled at Bruno.

"There he is, Mike. There goes your meat right there. We're coming for you, son."

I pointed at my pecs.

"I'm number one," I told Bruno.

The fight with Buster drew a twenty-nine share of the audience, the highest rating ever for Fox TV, but I wasn't pleased with my performances coming out of jail.

I brought Kenya to that fight. By now Monica had a girl we named Rayna and I had a stepdaughter named Gena, along with my own daughter Mikey I had with a woman from New York. Monica or the kids couldn't get close to me when Kenya was around. If they'd get affectionate with me, Kenya was ready to attack. I left her in the hotel room during the fight and when I got back to the suite it was totally demolished. The blinds were ripped, she had shit on the floor, the big couch in the living room was torn to shreds.

She did the same thing to Don King's townhouse in Manhattan when I stayed there after the fight. I left her and went out to a club and she was mad. When she was through with that townhouse, they had to close it down and fumigate it, she messed it up so much. You'd think we would have learned a lesson. We were in Ohio and Rory locked her up in my garage. When he came for her later, she had literally torn the roof off of one of my Maseratis.

I HAD ONLY BEEN OUT OF JAIL FOR A YEAR, AND DON ALREADY HAD ME FIGHT-ing Frank Bruno for his belt, but I wasn't really in shape either physically or emotionally for that sort of pressure again. I was interviewed by *The Ring* magazine and you could feel my anguish.

"I find myself more nervous now than in the beginning of my career or when I was champion. Maybe it's a slight insecurity. Even in training, I find myself taking that last breath. I don't know if it's good or not. I know what to do, but you have those doubts. I guess that's what pisses you off—you have those doubts about yourself even though you've been successful for so many years."

When the interviewer asked me about my loss to Douglas, I started ranting.

"People say, 'Look how much money you have.' But I've been through a bunch of dysfunctional evaluations. I just can't imagine anybody being jealous of my life. If they had to go through what I went through, they'd probably kill themselves. I almost died. My hair started turning gray and falling out because I was thinking of those things. I could've snapped then but instead I just got out and just went and ran all day in place in my room. I'd get in the shower and then, boom, it just hits you again. I just expect the worst of things to happen now. If good things happen, I enjoy them. But I expect the worst things to happen. I expect to be dumped on all my life. I just need to get my confidence back. After I have that fight with Bruno and I have the belt around my waist, there's nobody who could beat me. My confidence will rise to the sky, to the stars."

But for every sympathetic interviewer with whom I could share my pain there were others who wanted to destroy me. I was doing a national media conference call for the fight and one guy asked, "Mike, is there any truth to the rumors that you've got some eye injury and, if so, is that from the effects of all those years of Mace during sex?"

Sometimes I just didn't know how to shut my big mouth. At one of the press conferences to promote the fight, it was revealed that I had donated fifty thousand dollars for a Martin Luther King Youth Center in Vegas.

"It doesn't make me a nice guy. Everything is more of a burden now. I don't know if I should use the word 'burden' but I'm just not a happy type of guy. I try to do my best but I always fall short of the mark," I said. Then when a reporter asked me about my new daughter, I gave Monica a little left-handed compliment.

"Her mother is beautiful but Rayna is so beautiful and gorgeous that she makes her mother look like a yard dog." What was I thinking?

We had a crazy camp for the Bruno fight. Crocodile kept getting in fights with my sparring partners. Then he'd tell them that I'd bust their heads if they keep disrespecting him. He would put the first guy in the ring and then he would come over to me.

"You know, Mike, all them guys are saying that they're going to kick your ass. That they should be fighting for the title, not you."

He had me in the middle of it. These guys were now trying to kill me. I was in a fucking life-or-death situation with my sparring partners. What the fuck?

One day close to the fight, I was jumping rope and Crocodile came over.

"You're back, champ. When Ali was in exile, he came back and fought for the world title," he said.

"Yeah, Ali didn't get his, but I'm not fighting Joe Frazier. I'm fighting Frank Bruno. Ali had to fight animals when he came back. But I'm going to get mine," I said. "I'm going to get this guy."

I took that confidence into the ring with me. I was led in by Crocodile who was wearing a black vest with white lettering on the back that read, LOVED BY FEW, HATED BY MANY, RESPECTED BY ALL. I was booed for the first time in my career going into the ring because thousands of Bruno's rabid English fans had flown to Vegas for the fight, but I didn't hear shit.

"*Tyson is a rapist, la la la, la la la,*" they chanted. I didn't hear that either.

When Bruno entered the ring, I smelled the fear on him. His own promoter noted later that as soon as Bruno's dressing room door opened for his ring walk, "it was as if someone had put a pin to Bruno and all the air rushed out." He must have crossed himself a dozen times while they played the British national anthem. Him being scared gave me a real confidence boost. He gave me a good fight the first time we squared off. He had beaten my sparring partner Oliver McCall for the title and he also knocked out Lennox Lewis.

I knew that Bruno really didn't want to be in there, so all I had to do was be tough and hit him with some good shots and it would be a wrap. At the end of the first round, I stunned him with a right that opened up a bad cut over his left eye. He was holding me so much in the second round that Mills Lane had to deduct a point from him. It didn't matter. About a half a minute into the third round Bruno turned southpaw for a second and I rocked him with two left hooks. He tried to hold me but I got in two vicious right uppercuts, the second one almost knocked him up off his feet. He collapsed against the ropes and then I finished him off. I had gotten in twelve uncontested punches. Mills Lane stopped the fight and I was the new WBC heavyweight champion.

I turned around and raised my arms in triumph, soaking all that adulation up, but then I gained some kind of respect and self-dignity and fell to my knees and put my forehead on the canvas and paid homage to Allah and made a short prayer.

In the back of my mind I knew that if Bruno had fought me in this fight with the same spirit he did in the first fight, there was no way I would have beat him. So I got up and I went right to his corner where he was sitting on a stool being consoled by his wife. I stroked his head and kissed him on the cheek.

That night I had a party in my hotel suite. My friend Zip and a bunch of his L.A. boys came up. Zip loved champagne, so I ordered a hundred bottles of Dom Pérignon and we drank all night.

My humility wore off six days after the fight. I was supposed to fight Bruce Seldon next for his belt.

"I think I deserve a lot more than thirty mil and I don't think I've been getting what I'm entitled," I told the press. "I have children to take care of. Nobody cares if my children are starving or on welfare. Nobody's gonna give me no handouts and say, 'You are a great champion, we owe you this.'"

I was the champion again, which meant that I would be an even bigger target for scamsters, cheap hustlers, conniving women, and every con artist around. I couldn't even count the massive amount of money that my management team paid out to keep the gold diggers and the ambulance chasers away. Rory and John Horne used to actually leave Johnny Tocco's gym before I would and approach the girls who were waiting for me. They knew that if I caught a glimpse of one of them, I would say, "Let's go," and my training regimen would be shot.

"What do you want from Mike?" Rory would ask the girls. "If you cared about him, you wouldn't be here."

Then they'd give the girls some cash to leave so I could train.

My assistant Latondia handled the brunt of all the psychos and scam artists who were after my money. She paid out money right and left to people who would come up to the office in wheelchairs with casts and doctors' bills and claim I was responsible for them somehow. Workers at my house would "fall" off ladders and sue. Women would drive up in limousines wearing mink coats and wait for hours in the hope that I'd show up at the office.

Some of the time I did have altercations when I'd go out and drink heavily when I wasn't in camp. So some of the money might have gone to the Unanticipated Consequences of Getting Shitfaced Fund.

A prime example of all this happened a few weeks after the Bruno fight. I was in Chicago hanging out at my friend Leonard's nightclub. I was chilling in Leonard's office right off the VIP area with Anthony and a couple of other friends when a crazy lady in a micro skirt and big knockers wanted to meet me. They brought her up to the office. We necked a little bit.

"You know I want you," I told her. That was my one line. I was a regular black Rudolph Valentino, aka El Schmucko.

She started heating it up, so Anthony and the other guys left the room and went outside to the VIP area. I gave her a little love nip on the neck, but when I found out she was from Indiana, I gave her the boot. Literally. I think I kicked her in her butt. Then I walked her out of the office and she left. Anthony noticed that she wasn't flustered or anything because that was his job.

The next day, Leonard got a call from this woman's boyfriend.

"My girlfriend said that Mike Tyson accosted her in your club last night," he said. "And she just filed a police report."

Not good. I was still on probation from Indiana. If I as much pinched a girl on her ass, Judge Gifford could haul my ass back into jail for nine more years.

So Leonard and a friend of his, who was a big entrepreneur dealing in illicit consciousness-altering substances, drove to Indiana to see the girl.

She told them that I had bitten her neck and tried to touch her privates.

Leonard sensed immediately that we didn't want another "he said, she said" situation. And he knew she was only in this to separate me from a large chunk of my money.

"Tell me what you need, because we don't need any adversity," he said.

"Here, here's ten grand," his friend the entrepreneur offered.

"Ten grand! I want ten million," the girl said.

"Ten million!" Leonard roared. "What did he do, rip your pussy out and take it so it's no longer there? We'll talk more about this."

By the time Leonard got back on the expressway to Chicago, the story was all over the news. She called the press as soon as they left.

So they turned around and drove back to her house. Now she had some two-bit lawyer there, some guy in a cheap suit and sleeves up to his forearms. He was adamant about wanting ten million.

Leonard and his friend drove back to Chicago. He was trying to figure out a strategy when this woman's friend, who Leonard knew, called him.

"Let me tell you, nothing happened to that woman," her friend said. "We drove all the way back that night and she wasn't mad about anything Mike did."

So Leonard took one for the team. Her friend was a big fat chick, so he had a limousine pick her up and brought her to Chicago to tell her story at a press conference that Leonard called. Leonard met the car halfway to the press conference and he talked a little while to the girl and then he fucked her in the backseat of the limo.

The next day two police officers came to investigate the claims. Leonard told them that he and two other women, his niece and a girl he was banging, were in the room with us the entire time. Leonard had to drive over to my house in Ohio, where I was forced to remain until these charges against me were substantiated, to get my story straight. My house was already surrounded with press cars, so Leonard took the license plates off his car and drove through my gates. He told Rory and John what I should say to the police officers when they interviewed me the next day.

Before I was remanded to stay at home I had gone back to Leonard's club one Sunday night when he had gangster night. Two thousand gangsters and their posses packed the club every Sunday. I was sitting at Leonard's table in the VIP area when a bunch of these young gangster guys came up to me. I was really stressing about this case, thinking this liar could send me back to jail.

"Yo, Mike, what about that bitch," one of the young guys said. "Where does she live at, man?"

I kept my mouth shut. I was thinking that this guy might have been an undercover cop trying to set me up.

This lady was not the most credible person for the cops to believe. She was a twenty-five-year-old beautician and liquor store owner from Gary, Indiana, whose husband had been murdered weeks earlier while he was facing charges of selling rock cocaine. Plus, days before the incident with me, she had reached a settlement in a personal injury suit she had filed after being in a 1994 traffic accident, where the investigating cop filed a report that no one had been injured.

When the cops refused to file charges, the woman sued Leonard's club in federal court, saying that he had allowed her to be accosted. She got her money when his insurance company settled out of court.

Even my probation counselor tried to get in on the action. The Indiana court had appointed a Cleveland-based psychologist named Dr. Keith J. Smedi to supervise my probation. Everything I did had to go through this guy. I couldn't even be intimate with Monica without getting permission from him. This guy was both stupid and corrupt. He had the IQ of a fucking lit candle. He must have gotten his Ph.D. from his uncle.

While he was working for the state supervising me, he was telling all my friends to persuade me to go into business with his father. I knew I could work with a guy like that because if I got in trouble, he'd never violate me, he'd just hold it over my head. I knew that, as time went on, he'd reveal himself to be dirty so I just played him.

At first he was all strict, saying I couldn't hang out with any of my high-profile friends. But then he tried to extort me. He saw this Chicago case as his ticket to the big time. A few weeks after the dust had cleared and the cops had declined to press charges, Smedi sent my office a bill for his services.

On April 7th, while in Chicago for Muslim Easter services, Mr. Tyson entered a nightclub and caused by Mr. Tyson's poor judgment and possible parole violation behavior, a major setback in the "trust" and "positive direction" his program towards, was experienced and handled by Dr. Smedi. Mr. Tyson's recovery from his incarceration also experienced a serious setback! There were five choices to levy upon Mr. Tyson. Dr. Smedi had the responsibility to make this recommendation!

1. Dr. Smedi chose NOT to have Mr. Tyson returned to
   Indianapolis, Indiana as initially requested to possibly face the
   judge and the charges of this young woman who accused Tyson
   of biting her face while in the nightclub.

2. Dr. Smedi chose NOT to have Mr. Tyson returned
   to Chicago and face extensive interrogation by the Chicago
   authority.

3. Dr. Smedi chose NOT to have Mr. Tyson immediately
   re-incarcerated pending the Chicago investigation this
   April 7th episode.

4. Dr. Smedi chose NOT to add time onto Mr. Tyson's
   present term of parole and offender therapy program.

5. Dr. Smedi chose to consider a large "Monetary charge"
   in order to reach the thinking and feeling levels of this offender
   Mike Tyson.

Dr. Smedi therefore levied a seven million dollar (behavioral modifi-
cation thinking impact charge based on Tyson's earning potential
of Tyson) for this act of extremely poor judgment which was observed
as potential risk to relapse behavior and parole violation behavior
in lieu of the above alternate options. This monetary charge is aimed
at impacting (ie shocking) Mr. Tyson were [sic] it will cause the
most "memory" in order to make him to rethink his actions and apply
in real life this "thinking insight" while in nightclubs and other
areas were [sic] "Young women are in abundance in his long term
future and especially after parole is terminated. **Of course this
could be levied only once in the course of a sex offender's
parole. Any further acts of poor judgment parole violation
behavior will result in possible extension of parole and
possible recommendations for re-incarceration.** (This is not
expected, due to Mike's good efforts so far, lets keep it up!) **This
seven million dollar amount is discounted** to two million dollars, due to Mr. Tyson's overall positive effort to this point in time,
aside from the April 7th mishap. *Remember this charge is in
lieu of extending the parole time and to eliminate severe, negative media reports if Tyson had been forced to face Indiana
and the Chicago authorities and to restrain from having to
"add more time" to Tyson's parole restrictions. Most of these
immediate restrictions after Chicago have been removed at
this date.*

Total breakdown: April through August 1996 expenses: $182,862.00
April 7th: Offender's poor judgment/potential offender parole
violation behavior setback charge: $2,000,000.00

Total due Dr. Smedi: $2,182,862.00

Payment in full expected by September 15th, 1996

Respectfully submitted K.J. Smedi. PhD.

Wow, I got a five-million-dollar discount for good behavior. We
never paid this poor schmuck, and as soon as my probation was over
we fired his ass.

Now that I had my belt back, my grandiosity began to stomp all
over my humbleness. I threw myself a thirtieth-birthday party at my
Connecticut estate and spent a fortune flying in friends from all over
the country and putting them all up in a nearby hotel that we took
over. We had thirteen different chefs, each one cooking in their own
kitchen. Everyone from Oprah to Donald Trump to Jay Z to street
pimps and their hos were there. There was a guy hand-rolling cigars.
Frankie Beverly and Maze performed. You entered the house on an
actual red carpet. Once you got past the forty big Fruit of Islam bodyguards stationed outside.

I was so egomaniacal that I reserved the nineteen bedrooms in my
house for girls who I wanted to sleep with. I actually told Crocodile,
"See all these girls? They're mine." Hope was pissed at me. She had
been staying at the house, but I moved her out and put her up at the
hotel so the room would be available for one of my lady suitors. She
was hurt. Hope was an extremely attractive woman and the girls I
was sleeping with were nowhere near her stature.

"Mike, this woman you're bringing in is just so atrocious and un-
clean, she's going to dirty my bed. You're gonna have to burn the mattress if she sleeps on the bed," Hope told me.

I didn't even bother to invite Monica. I hardly saw her much by then. She was always trying to make it work out, but I was a cad. I was definitely not marriage material.

THE NEXT STEP IN UNIFYING THE TITLE WAS TO GET THE WBA BELT. IT WAS around the waist of Bruce Seldon, but it wouldn't be for long. I didn't think much of Seldon as an opponent; he wasn't much of a competitor. I hardly trained for the fight. Crocodile came with me to the prefight press conference and we both got under his skin so much that he started doing push-ups off a chair in the hallway at our weigh-in. He looked terrified. Seldon's manager had bragged about what a great athlete Seldon was—he could run a fifty-second quarter mile, jump forty inches off the ground.

"What's he gonna do when he gets in the ring?" I said. "Is he going to pole-vault out of there?"

I regained my WBA belt in less than two minutes. I hit Seldon on the top of his head with a right. Although it wasn't a hard punch, my elbow hit him in the follow-through and he went down. As soon as he got up, I threw a left hook that put him down on his stomach. He got up but then he started wobbling and Richard Steele ended the fight. I didn't think that either of those punches was enough to knock out a guy, but his trainer later said that Seldon had had a nervous breakdown in the ring he was so scared.

"Cus, you got two down and one to go," I told Ferdie Pacheco when he interviewed me after the fight.

I had fought eight rounds since getting out of jail and I had earned $80 million. That was all that people focused on. Nobody ever gave me any credit for coming out of jail after three years behind bars and winning two championship belts. That hurt my heart a lot not to get that recognition.

After the Seldon fight, Tupac came to my dressing room. I was so happy to see him. Tupac represented where all of us black people came from and what we're trying to hide. I have Jewish friends who might look at a Jewish guy and say, "He's too Jewish." That's what some blacks thought about Tupac. He was that bitterness, that frustration that was in all of us and that we were all trying to hide and not let people know we possess. We want to front that we have it all together, but it's not like that. If you're black, it's constantly a struggle. I don't care how rich you are or how much power you have, they're still going to come after you. Tupac would talk about black people who were tired of being beaten down and who had nothing. Tupac put our slave heritage in our face and most black people respected his strength in doing that. He let us know why we should be angry.

I made plans to see Tupac later that night at Suge Knight's Club 662. But I wanted to go home and hang out with my daughter, Rayna. I had a few drinks at home and I passed out. Someone woke me.

"Mike, they just shot Tupac."

I couldn't believe it. He had been in a car driven by Suge and they stopped at an intersection and someone in the next car started shooting at them. It had to be a setup. Especially since Tupac had had an altercation with a gang guy in the casino after the fight and stomped him in his face. He didn't kill the guy, but his senses had to be on high alert after that. When I come out of the ring after fighting, my senses are at their zenith. I can see everything, smell everything, hear everything in the audience. You'd think that Tupac's were like that too after his altercation. So he had to have been assassinated.

Being a street guy, it just didn't seem right to me. Normally these guys have forty guys shielding them in their entourage. He doesn't have cars around him blocking him off in the traffic? If Tupac was their general and had just been in a fight, they should have put a shield around him. Where was that shield? That was just a really nasty night. Tupac was only twenty-five, but he had such determination and will. Where did he get that stuff from? Such a big heart, such a caring man, but still a warrior. He was a beautiful person and I really enjoyed the time I spent with him.

So now I had two belts and tons of money and I should have been a happy camper. But that was not who I was. I was always a depressed, wretched person. I'd been on medication since I was a kid and I was probably still getting medicated after I got out of jail. But then I began to self-medicate. I'd been dying to smoke pot the whole time I was in jail, but I didn't dare do it because they'd do random piss tests. But now I had the quack doctor, Dr. Smedi, and I knew he'd make sure my piss was clean.

I even began to do coke again. It was right after the Seldon fight and I was with a friend who had some and I told him to give me the bag. Out of the blue. That's what addicts do. I hadn't done those kinds of drugs in fifteen years and, boom, it just snapped right back.

I know that good Muslims didn't smoke weed or snort coke or drink champagne but I was going through an awful lot of shit. I'm sure Allah knew that my shit was just overwhelming and that I wasn't strong enough then to deal with it.

Because of some bullshit lawsuit by Lennox Lewis, I had to relinquish my WBC belt right after the Seldon fight. Lewis was the mandatory challenger, but I wanted to unify the titles. So now I just had the WBA belt and my next opponent was Evander Holyfield.

If I would've fought Holyfield in 1991 when I was supposed to fight him originally, I would have knocked him out. He knows that, everybody in his camp knows that. The best thing that ever happened to him was that I went to prison. That's when I lost all my timing. I couldn't be the tough eight-round fighter I had been. I told everybody that I wasn't ready to fight major-league fights, but Don was pushing me and I wanted the money. I was being greedy, so I took the fight.

Holyfield hadn't looked very good in his fights leading up to ours. He lost a couple of them but at least he was active. I watched him fight Bobby Czyz, a puffed-up light heavyweight and Czyz beat the shit out of him before he lost in the tenth round, so I didn't really train all that much for the first fight with Holyfield. I looked at some of his fights, but I didn't really have any particular strategy going into my fights at that time, usually it was just go in and hit them. The odds opened up at 25–1 in my favor.

Later I found out that Crocodile was getting reports from slick guys around who were supposed to know the boxing game. Holyfield had been training in the mountains for seventeen weeks like a dog, but Croc was hearing some bullshit disinformation that he wasn't even in shape.

"Mike, you're gonna kill this guy," he kept telling me.

Holyfield and I go back a long way. We were both together at the Junior Olympics and we were always friendly with each other. He was always on my side, rooting for me while I was fighting, and vice versa. He got a lot of bad breaks in the amateurs. He lost some fights that he should have won, and then they screwed him big-time in the Olympics. When we were younger, we never thought we would ever fight and make that much money together later on.

Actually, that's why I was fighting. My heart wasn't into boxing but I needed the money. There was no fun in getting into the ring for me anymore. Once I left prison, the fun really died. That's why I had a guy like Crocodile around me then. He was a good guy and he always motivated me, got me psyched to fight. He was also a training nut and I needed somebody like that pushing me then.

The first fight started well enough. I landed a good body shot on him in the first round and he screamed. I was thinking that I was going to win. But from the second round on, I really blacked out. I didn't know what was happening at the time, but during the second fight, I finally realized he had been using his head to butt me senseless. From the second round of that first fight on, I was fighting on pure instinct; I didn't remember anything. In the sixth round, one of his head butts opened up a cut. The next round I was almost knocked out by a butt. In the tenth round, he connected with twenty-three power punches, and I never felt a thing, I only heard the sound of them whooshing around my head. I was only staying up because of adrenaline. When I'd go back to my corner between rounds, I didn't hear a fucking thing my trainers were saying to me. I don't remember going into the ring, or getting up to fight; I just remember being there. After the fight was over, I was still so out of it that I asked my cornermen which round I knocked Holyfield out in.

In the dressing room afterwards, Crocodile was enraged.

"Look at your head, Mike," he told me. I had six knots as big as a fist all over my head from Holyfield's head butts. Plus, Croc was con-vinced that Holyfield had been using steroids. One of the guys in his camp, Lee Haney, was a former Mr. Olympiad and a suspected steroid guy. He said that Holyfield seemed normal at the weigh-in but when he entered the ring he looked like Goliath.

I wanted to fight Holyfield right again, I was so mad. I was really sore and beat-up, but I started training the next night.

I was angry that I lost my title, but I never looked back at fights or was, like, "Aw, fuck it." It just happened and I would start my day over. Losing is very traumatic for some people. Floyd Patterson would put on fake beards and wear dark glasses when he went out in public after he lost his title. When Foreman lost to Ali and then to Jimmy Young, the press asked him what it was like to lose and he said, "It's like being in a deep dark nothing, like out at sea, with noth-ing over your head or under your feet, just nothing, nothing but noth-ing. A horrible smell came with it, a smell I hadn't forgotten, a smell of sorrow. You multiply every sad thought you ever had it wouldn't come close to this and then I looked around and I was dead. That was it. I thought of everything I worked for, I hadn't said good-bye to my mother, my children, all the money I hid in safe-deposit boxes, you know how paper burns when you touch it, it just crumbles. That was my life. I looked back and I saw it crumble, like I'd fallen for a big joke."

I never had a reaction like that. I know who I am, I know I'm a man. A guy like Holyfield based his whole existence around boxing, that's why he continued to fight for so long. I was raised with Cus D'Amato. He'd always say that boxing is not your life, it's what you do for a living; it's what you do to make a life, but it is not your life. He said, "Losing, winning, never take it personal." Every time I lost, I just dealt with it, because it never became my life. That's what I was taught.

By that time, Monica was pregnant with our second child. I was getting a lot of shit from the Imam in my Vegas mosque about the fact that we hadn't gotten married yet. The truth was I hardly saw Monica and the kids. I was in training and when I wasn't in training I was seeing one of my multiple girlfriends. In fact, the day that I proposed to Monica, Hope had been staying with us, since she was going to school in D.C., and I dropped her off at her school and then went to hit some new girl I had been seeing in D.C.

Hope was ragging on me about getting a prenup. I probably should have, but I was an impulsive smuck. Monica and I would fight all the time. Of course, a lot of the time it was over my cheating.

I had Brother Siddeeq fly to Maryland and he performed the ceremony and then he brought the papers to a local D.C. Imam who could certify them. Being married didn't change anything with Monica. I was still seeing my girls on the side and now I had to go into training for the second Holyfield fight.

When I began to get ready for our rematch, I told the press that I had had a bad night but that I would fight Holyfield like I knocked him out the first time. I got that attitude from the Mexican fighters. When you fight an American fighter and knock him out, invariably the next time you fight, their fighting is tentative. But with a Mexican fighter, even if you knocked him out the first time, he's going to fight the next fight like he knocked *you* out. Those guys don't feel intimidated. They come back uninhibited and just go for it.

I made some changes for the second fight though. My old roommate Jay Bright had been my trainer but I replaced him with Richie Giachetti. Firing Jay was easy. He was family and family is always the first to go. I trained twice as hard for the second fight.

Three days before the fight, there was some controversy over the referee. Mitch Halpern was supposed to ref the fight again, but he had been drunk as a skunk during the first Holyfield fight. As soon as I went out for the instructions and he went to touch my glove, I smelled it. His eyes were red. I'm an addict, I could tell right away. No referee would have let me take that kind of punishment that Holyfield was giving me, but he let me take it all the way to the eleventh round because he was so drunk and out of it.

Some people in my camp tried to get Halpern off the second fight. I don't know much about it, I never objected to anybody. My job was to fight and not worry about the referee or the timekeeper. But John

Horne went before the commission and said that Halpern was too lenient in allowing Holyfield to hold me and butt me.

"If it wasn't for Mike Tyson you wouldn't be here," he told the commissioners.

That was smart. The commission voted 4–1 to retain Halpern. But after the issue was raised, Halpern took himself off the fight. Holyfield's camp had gotten Joe Cortez and Richard Steele, two referees that they thought might favor me, excluded from the fight, so the commission wound up using Mills Lane. Mills Lane was a former district attorney and district judge who had been quoted extensively saying that I was a "vicious criminal" who shouldn't be allowed to box. How could I possibly get a fair shake when the ref was saying stuff like that against me? What I didn't know at the time of the second Holyfield fight was that Lane and Holyfield had a close relationship. Holyfield's own trainer, Tommy Brooks, was quoted as saying that Mills Lane "cried tears" the night Holyfield lost to Riddick Bowe. I didn't know that Mills was in love with Evander.

Holyfield and I were originally supposed to fight for the second time on May 3, 1997, but I got head-butted in training and the fight was postponed to June twenty-eighth. I was the challenger, so I had to enter the ring first. On my walk in we played a song by Tupac. People think that I would use gangster rap to solidify my image, but that wasn't the case. I was just listening to good music going in.

The fight started and I was feeling pretty good. I was confident, my body felt good, my movement was fluid. I was pretty elusive, moving around, not throwing anything big, just boxing. Then Holyfield butted me again. It was obvious to anyone watching that Holyfield's tactic was to wait for me to throw a punch and then burrow in with his head. So the head butts were no accidents, they were a strategy.

It got worse in the second round. I started winging some punches at Holyfield and he dove in again and, boom! A big gash opened up over my eye. I immediately turned to Mills Lane.

"He butted me!"

Lane didn't even say anything, but he ruled it an accident.

Now Holyfield started looking at the cut on top of my eye. He was charging at me with his head. He was taller than me, so what was his head doing underneath my head? I was getting frustrated.

When the third round began, I was furious. I was so anxious to start fighting that I left the corner without my mouthpiece, but Richie called me back and put it in. We started the round and I hit Holyfield with a couple of hard punches. The crowd started going crazy. They could feel that the fight had really shifted. And that's when he butted me again. I started feeling weary, like I was blacking out a little, but my anger and adrenaline jolted me back. I just wanted to kill him. Anybody watching could see that the head butts were so overt. I was furious, I was an undisciplined soldier and I lost my composure. So I bit him in the ear.

People think that I spit my mouthpiece out to bite him, but I didn't. From that point on, I don't remember too much because I was so enraged. When I looked at the tape, I must have spit the piece of his earlobe on the canvas because I was pointing to it. It was, like, "Yeah, you take that." They actually found that piece after the fight and tried to sew it back on but it didn't take.

Holyfield leapt up in the air in pain and then he turned to go to his corner, but I followed him and pushed him from behind. I wanted to kick him right in his groin, but I just pushed him. It was a street fight now. The doctor took a look at him and allowed him to continue and then Mills Lane took two points away from me, but in my mind, it didn't matter. They were all against me anyway. So the fight resumed and he butted me again. And the ref, of course, did nothing. So we clinched and I bit him again on the other ear, but we kept on fighting till the end of the round.

Then all hell broke loose. Holyfield's corner complained to Mills Lane that I had bitten him again and Lane stopped the fight. I was too enraged to even hear the ring announcer say, "Referee Mills Lane has disqualified Mike Tyson for biting Evander Holyfield on both of his ears." Holyfield was in his corner. He didn't want any part of this shit, but I was still trying to get a hand on him. I wanted to destroy everything and everybody in his corner. People were pulling me and blocking me and he was standing in his corner, huddled up. Everyone was protecting him. He looked frightened. I was still trying to get at him. I had fifty people on me and I was still fighting the cops. Oh lord! They should have tased me. I vote for being tased that night.

Somehow they got me out of the ring. On the way back to the dressing room, someone tossed a full bottle of water at me and someone else gave me the finger. I climbed over the railing and tried to get at them, but my cornermen pulled me back. Then more people were throwing their sodas and beers on us. Anthony Pitts's $2,500 tailor-made suit was ruined.

Mills Lane was interviewed in the ring and he claimed that all the butting Holyfield had done was accidental. Holyfield was interviewed and he praised Mills Lane.

"I'm grateful we have a referee like Mills Lane to see the situation that this thing is intentioned."

I was still going crazy in the dressing room. I had my gloves on and I was punching the walls. John Horne went out to talk to Jim Gray, the Showtime announcer.

"All I know is that Mike got a cut over his eye three inches long and Evander got a little nip on his ear that don't mean nothing. He jumped around like a little bitch. The head-butting was going on so long. Come on, one head butt may be accidental, fifteen is not," John said.

I barely remember being interviewed after the fight. My face was a grotesque mask, all cut up and swollen. I looked like a monster. Jim Gray caught up to me outside my dressing room as I was leaving.

"The head butt in the second round, which opened the gash in your eye, tell us about that firstly," he said.

"He butted me in the first round, but then he butted me again in the second round, then as soon as he butted me I watched him, he had held me and he looked right at me, and I saw him and he kept going, trying to butt me again. He kept going down and coming up and then he charged into me. And no one warned him, no one took any points from him. What am I to do? This is my career. I can't continue getting butted like that. I've got children to raise and this guy keeps butting me, trying to cut me and get me stopped on cuts. I've got to retaliate."

"Now, immediately you stopped fighting right there and you turned to Mills Lane and you said what, and as a result of which he did nothing, but what did you say to Mills right at that time?"

"I don't remember, I told him that he butted me. I know I complained about being butted and we complained about it the first fight. Listen, Holyfield is not the tough warrior everyone says he is. He got a little nick on his ear and he quit. I got one eye, he's not impaired, he's got ears, I got one, if he takes one, I got another one. I'm ready to fight. He didn't want to fight. I'm ready to fight him right now."

"Mills Lane stopped the fight, it wasn't Holyfield who stopped the fight," Jim said.

"Oh, he didn't want to fight. . . ."

"Mills said he stopped the fight. You bit him, was that a retaliation for the eye, when you bit him in his ear?"

"Regardless of what I did, he's been butting me for two fights," I said.

"But you've got to address it, Mike."

"I did address it! I addressed it in the ring!"

"Why did you do that though, Mike, I mean was that the proper response?"

I was getting exasperated.

"Look at me, look at me, look at me, look at me!" I screamed. "I've got to go home and my kids are going to be scared of me, look at me, man!"

Then I stormed off. We drove straight to my house where all the women were waiting. For some reason, none of the wives had gone to the fight, they just watched it on TV.

There were angry protestors outside my gates. People were blowing their horns and screaming, "Fixed fight!" and "Move out of the neighborhood!" and someone even threw a fish head onto my property. They kept it up until some of my security guys shot some BBs in their direction.

A doctor came and stitched up my cut. Then I started pacing around the dining room.

"I shouldn't have done that," I said. I was regretful but reluctantly regretful. I was an undisciplined soldier.

"My fans are going to hate me," I worried.

Monica was very understanding and comforting. She told me that everybody makes mistakes. After a while, I smoked some weed and drank some liquor and went to sleep.

Back at the MGM Grand, people were fighting one another in the casino, being sent to the hospital. Gaming tables were knocked over and people were grabbing the chips. They had to close it down. And then they looked at the surveillance videos and tracked down and arrested the people who stole the chips. It was mayhem.

The next day I was feeling really down. I had no idea that what had happened would become such an international incident. My whole life's been like that. I say or do something I think is small but the whole world thinks it's big. I didn't think that people would use my reaction to define my career. Maybe I should have thought about how things will affect me in posterity, but that's not the way I think.

People said I thought I was gonna get beaten, so I did the biting routine. That's bullshit. If that was the case, I would have done that in the first fight. In any fight anybody ever saw me lose, I took my beating like a man, I never sat down. No one could ever call me a dog. I was angry, I was mad, I lost my composure. I bit Evander Holyfield's ear because at that moment I was enraged, and I didn't care about fighting no more by the Marquis of Queensberry rules.

But there was no escaping the story. *Sports Illustrated* put it on the cover under the huge headline "MADMAN!" President Clinton said that he had been "horrified." They were making jokes about it on Letterman and Leno. I was nominated for Sportsman of the Ear. They said it was a good fight for Pay Per Chew. The press called for a lifetime ban. I was called "dirty," "disgusting," "repellent," "bestial," "loathsome," "vile," and "cannibalistic." But I didn't care about any of that. I already felt that things were stacked against me anyway.

Part of the problem was that people were responding to images, not reality. If you watched a tape of the fight you'd see that Holyfield was clearly fighting a dirty fight, but he had the good-guy image. He was the one who strolled to the ring singing gospel songs. It didn't make huge headlines when he was later implicated in a steroid ring out of Mobile, Alabama.

The crazy part was, there were a lot of people out there who were defending what I had done. I got a lot of love from the overseas press. Tony Sewell, an English writer, published an article called "Why Iron Mike Was Right to Take an Earful." He wrote, "As the world rises in moral indignation and demands that Tyson be banned for going berserk, I smell a distinct waft of hypocrisy. Tyson was a gladiator who broke the rules. The real savages are the audience who now want to feed him to the lions."

I reached the darkest place that's in each and every human being— the place where you say, "Oh, this is fucked, I shouldn't do this, but this is who I am." After a few days, I went out and there would be crowds of people applauding me for biting that guy. Everybody thought it was cool.

"Yeah, champ, I'd bite that motherfucker too," they'd scream.

I felt much better when people were condemning me for biting that ear than when they praised me for it.

Shortly after the fight, the lawsuits rolled in. One guy started a class action suit to get his ticket money refunded. Another woman who was serving drinks at a temporary bar in the arena said she was injured when a security guard threw her over a table when the riots broke out. All of those suits were dismissed.

Holyfield's wife was also threatening to sue Crocodile. During the fight, Crocodile was screaming out instructions and exhortations to me.

"Bite, bite, Mike!" he yelled.

But she didn't know that when you say "bite" it just means to fight harder.

Don was worried about me being banned for life, so he convinced me to do some damage control. He hired Sig Rogich, my great public relations specialist, to write a statement that I read that following Monday at a press conference at the MGM Grand.

"I snapped. Saturday night was the worst night of my professional career. I'm here today to apologize, to ask the people who expected more from Mike Tyson to forgive me for snapping in the ring and for doing something I have never done before and will never do again." I apologized to Holyfield and then continued to read the words that were written for me. "I thought I might lose because of the severity of the cut above my eye and I just snapped. I can only say that I'm just thirty-one years old, in the prime of my career, and I have made it this far because I had no other way. I grew up in the streets, I fought my way out and I'll not go back again. I learned the hard way from the past, because I didn't have the luxury of schools or people to help me at a time when I needed it the most, and I expect punishment and would pay the price like a man. I reached out to the medical professionals for help to tell me why I did what I did, and I will have that help, now I will attempt to train not just my body, but my mind too."

I was reciting those words, but I wasn't buying into them. I felt shitty and embarrassed for saying all that because it wasn't what was in my heart at the time. I was just going through the motions. I knew that they would hold it against me anyway and frankly, I really didn't care if I got suspended. I was in New York buying a Ferrari when the Nevada State Athletic Commission met to decide my fate. I was represented by Oscar Goodman, who would go on to become the most famous mayor in Las Vegas history. Writers had been calling for a lifetime ban. Oscar put up a good defense, but in the end, those commissioners wanted some more blood. On July ninth, they called me a "discredit to boxing" and fined me 10 percent of my purse, which was $3 million, and then suspended me for at least a year. I really felt betrayed after all the money I'd made for that city. Nobody else even approached the revenue I brought into Vegas.

It was another Tyson Rule. A fine and suspension like that was unprecedented in organized sports. In 1977, Kermit Washington of the Lakers fractured the Houston Rockets' Rudy Tomjanovich's jaw and skull during a game. He almost killed Rudy and he ended Rudy's career with that punch, but he was only fined $10,000 and suspended for sixty days. A hockey player named Dale Hunter viciously cross-checked Pierre Turgeon from behind after Turgeon stole the puck from him and scored a goal that put the game away. The hit effectively ended Turgeon's play-offs that year. Hunter only got a twenty-one game suspension and lost $150,000 in salary. But even better, in the famous ice hockey Summit Series of 1972 between Russia and Canada, Bobby Clarke took his stick and gave Valeri Kharlamov, the Russian's best player, a vicious two-hander to the ankle. Kharlamov's ankle was broken and the Canadians went on to win the series. Clarke wasn't even fined or suspended. He became a Canadian hero.

"I don't know what I was thinking at all. It was an awful thing to do," he'd say later. "But it sure felt good."

I know that Evander knew that feeling too. When he was eighteen, he was competing in the semifinals of the Georgia Golden Gloves, fighting this guy named Jakey Winters. Winters dropped Holyfield with a left hook to the body and a left to the head. Holyfield got up, dazed and in danger of getting knocked out. So he clinched Winters, spit out his mouthpiece and took a bite out of his shoulder, drawing blood. Winters pulled back in pain and screamed. And then the bell rang. The referee took a point away from Holyfield and the fight continued. Winters won a unanimous decision. The only consequence Holyfield faced from his bite was a bruised ego and a unanimous decision against him.

11

I TRIED TO STAY OUT OF THE SPOTLIGHT DURING MY SUSPENSION FROM BOX-
ing. At first I was hardly seen out in public. One reason for that was
that I spent a lot of time indoors at strip clubs. Whenever I'd meet a
new girl, I'd take her to a strip club on the first date. It got so bad that
Latondia had to bring the checks I needed to sign to the club and I'd
autograph them while a girl was dancing on a pole ten feet away from
me. I was really living a fantasy life.

In October of 1997, that Mitch Green lawsuit finally came to judgment. Mitch was suing me for $3 million in compensatory damages
and $20 million in punitive damages. I was scared that my image had
deteriorated so much that I'd be on the hook big-time with the jury,
so I almost offered Mitch a quarter of a million dollars to settle the
suit. Thank God I didn't. The jury ruled that I was provoked into the
fight. They awarded him $100,000 but found him 55 percent respon-
sible for the injuries, so I only had to pay him $45,000.

But I was running real low on cash. Even though I had made about

$114 million from 1995 to 1997, I had spent almost all of that, plus I had a tax bill of $10 million due. I had about $6 million left and Don offered to advance me $4 million to take care of the taxes. But I wanted to use that money to set up trusts for all my kids. So I didn't pay the taxes and gave the money to the children. In retrospect that was a stupid decision but I was arrogant at the time. So arrogant that I thought I could get high, drink all night, and then drive home to Connecticut from New York doing 130 miles per hour on my motorcycle.

The ironic part was that I was only going 10 miles per hour when I crashed my bike. Just minutes earlier, the police had pulled me and some of my motorcycle friends over because we were speeding, and I didn't even have a license or anything but they let us go with a warning. We kept heading to my house but I kept dozing off and I slowed down to a crawl. I nodded out for a second and when I woke up, I saw my friend right in front of me. I didn't want to hit him and fuck him up, so I slammed on my brakes and went flying over the handlebars.

Latondia was working out of the Connecticut house during my suspension and she got a call from the highway patrol that I had been in a motorcycle accident and had refused medical help. I was so messed up that a lady pulled over and wanted to take me to the hospital but I had her drive me home instead. When I got home, I just wanted to go to sleep I was so out of it. But Latondia had called Monica and Monica jumped on the first flight from Maryland, but in the meantime she urged Latondia not to let me fall asleep under any circumstances. My ribs were killing me and I couldn't even talk without gasping for air because I had punctured one of my lungs but I didn't realize that then.

I kept trying to nod off, but all I heard was, "Don't go to sleep, Mike." Eventually Farid and Latondia got me into a hot tub to soak because I was in so much pain, but that didn't even help. We finally drove to the hospital emergency room. I had a broken rib, a broken shoulder, and a punctured lung. The nurses were amazed that I hadn't broken my legs because the fall had shredded my pants. I was overweight then. I really believe that the excess weight had cushioned some of the fall. They filled me up with morphine and I kept ringing the bell for more. I threw up and all this pasty white shit came out of my lungs. But I did enjoy that morphine.

I started feeling better a few days later and I threw everyone out of the house. Monica, her mother, my daughter Rayna, Rory, my security, I just told everyone to leave. Farid and Latondia were getting ready to go when I called them back in and told them to stay. A few days later Latondia was in her office and I went in.

"Latondia, talk to Shawnee. I want you guys to get along and I want everybody to work together. Things are going to change. Are you with me?"

"Of course. You know I am," she said.

I don't think she took me too seriously, but I had been talking a lot recently to this woman named Shawnee Simms. Craig Boogie had found her and introduced me to her. Boogie was always surfing to find people who would bring deals to me. Shawnee was living in Atlanta and she was a fast talker who talked up a big game. She claimed she could bring in all these revenue streams for me, and she wanted to start a foundation to clean up my image and get the Shrivers and the Kennedys on board. I was up for anything that would bring in money because I was broke and didn't see Don going out of his way to get me any deals.

I had a deal on the table with the WWF to make a *WrestleMania* appearance in March of 1998. So I invited Shawnee up to Connecticut for the meeting. We had been talking to her on the phone every day for weeks, but this was the first time that we had met her.

During the meeting, Shawnee put her hand on my shoulder. When we left the building, I took her aside.

"Don't you ever fucking touch me in public again. Don't touch me when I'm talking to businesspeople," I said.

I got all Arnold Rothstein on her ass.

But Shawnee hung in there. Some of my friends had warned me about her from the beginning. They thought that Shawnee had picked their brains for information about me. They figured that Shawnee had just studied up on me and the boxing scene on the computer all day so she knew the names of all the players. They were convinced that Shawnee wasn't a great businessperson; she just had a lot of game. But I was willing to give her a shot. She was always in my ear. "Mike, you should have some endorsements. You should be making sixty million a fight. Blah blah blah."

On one of her trips up from Atlanta, I wound up sleeping with Shawnee. Not because I was attracted to her; I was just high. I don't think she was trying to seduce me. We never slept together again. I was just a pig that one time.

My contract with the WWF was finalized at the end of December. Don King Productions would be paid my fee of $3.5 million for me being guest referee at the main event of *WrestleMania XIV.* I would also get 25 percent of the revenue from all pay-per-view buys in excess of six hundred thousand. That seemed good but then I found out that Don had signed another contract where he would get $300,000 for providing my likeness for the WWF to use in their promotional campaign. Plus, he would get 10 percent of the revenue from the pay-per-view buys in excess of six hundred thousand. How the fuck did Don get to make money off my likeness?

I turned to an entertainment industry friend of mine. I had met Jeff Wald through Don when I was getting myself away from Cayton. He had helped me in the Robin divorce and he was generally a cool guy. I respected Jeff because, like Don and I, he had come up from nothing. He told me that his father had died when he was a kid and his mother would beat his ass all the time.

I was in L.A. at the end of January with a lot of questions about how my business was being handled. So I had Shawnee call Jeff. It was 6:30 in the morning and she told Jeff that I was standing outside his home/office. Jeff was pissed because it was his birthday, but he let me in.

"Who owns my likeness?" I said as soon as we sat down.

I told him about the three hundred grand Don was getting for the use of my likeness. He thought that was outrageous so he got on the phone with Don.

"You can't make that money off Mike's image," he told Don.

"Is Mike sitting there?" Don asked.

"Yes," he said.

"Okay, I'll give him the pictures, but you shouldn't be meeting with Mike without me, motherfucker," Don yelled.

He got off the phone and then I handed Jeff eight typewritten pages filled with the details of my most recent financial statement. Jeff started skimming the pages and he freaked out.

"Why are you being charged eight grand a week for the house you stay in during camp? And you're getting charged thousands of dollars for towels. Who the fuck is your accountant?"

I told him it was Muhammad Khan.

"That's Don's accountant," he said. "Who are your lawyers?"

I told him about my business managers from Sidley Austin.

"Those are Don's lawyers. I've dealt with them many times," he said.

I was getting angry. Jeff told me to come back the next day when he had a chance to look over the documents thoroughly. I went back to my room at the Hotel Bel-Air.

After I had left Jeff's house, King called Jeff and he threatened that he was going to fly out to L.A. and shove a shotgun up his ass. Well, he did fly out to L.A. He came to the Hotel Bel-Air to beg me to come to my senses. I was getting into my limo outside the hotel when Don tried to squeeze in with me.

"Mike, we got to talk," he said. "Why are you doing me like this when these white motherfuckers have me in court again?" The government was prosecuting him a second time for insurance fraud.

I kicked him in the head and he flew out of the car. Then I got out and stomped on him some more. I think I shocked all the people waiting for their cars.

"You want to meet, meet me over at Jeff Wald's office," I said and got into the car.

I was sitting in the conference room with Jeff and his partner Irving when Don showed up.

Jeff was all over Don from the beginning.

"Look at all this shit you did to him, man," he said, holding the financials. "This isn't right."

"You mind your own business, Judas," Don said. "You ate my food, you sat in the seats that I gave you. . . ."

They screamed at each other for a little while and then Don took a conciliatory approach.

"Look, I'm going to fire Rory and John, and you and Irving can have their twenty percent," Don said.

"Wait a minute," Jeff said. "Mike is sitting right here. That's his twenty percent. It's his choice who is going to manage or not manage him. Besides, you're giving us twenty percent of what? The guy has no license and you ain't done shit to get it back. Fuck you!"

They started screaming at each other again. I was getting tired of all the words; I wanted action. So I grabbed a fork and I went after Don. Jeff threw all 5'6" of himself between us.

"Motherfuckers! Don't you dare do this in my house!" he screamed. In the hallway, his secretary was freaking out and she ran right out of the house. Meanwhile, Don left the conference room and went down the hall to my private office and called Monica and tried to get her to calm me down.

Things cooled down and Don came back into the room.

"Don, look at all this fucking money you took from Mike," Jeff said.

"But look how much money I made him," Don answered.

"That doesn't give you the right to fucking steal," Jeff said. "I don't care what you made him. You didn't protect him. You were supposed to be the guy who protected him from the white devils. First of all, you don't have a black person working for you. The only white devil in this room is you."

I cracked up.

Don left the office.

"You guys take over this stuff," I told Jeff and Irving. Jeff went right to work. He brought in an accountant who demanded all the files from my old accountant. Then he brought in John Branca and his law firm to go through all of my contracts. Branca was one of the top lawyers in the country.

Meanwhile, Don started blasting Jeff every chance he got. He was interviewed on Showtime during one of the fights and he told Jim Gray, "That Jeff Wald is a Judas and a racist." Jeff was watching with his wife and she was not happy. The next time Jeff went to New York, he hired a big off-duty police lieutenant as his bodyguard.

On February second, I fired John Horne and Rory as my managers. Branca sent them a letter terminating their services. I loved Rory but I had no choice but to fire him along with John. The more we dug, the more we found out that Don was using these guys to get me to sign contracts that screwed me right and left. Meanwhile, they were making millions and millions of dollars. By then, I was almost numb from all this betrayal and all the drugs I was taking. Maybe it was better that I was numb. If I wasn't, I just might have taken a gun and blown their fucking brains out. That's what I might have done when I was younger. But I was happy that I didn't have those guts by now.

On February fourth, Jeff Wald's office released a formal statement from me.

> At the present time, I have taken control of my own affairs both personal and business. I have hired new attorneys and accountants who report directly to me. I have formed Mike Tyson Enterprises and I am in the process of moving forward with my life. I appreciate the support I have always gotten from the American public and look forward to a bright new future with great anticipation.
>
> At the present time, I am not answering any questions—but stay tuned.

The next day I was in New York at a press conference at the All Star Cafe to promote *WrestleMania*. All the reporters wanted to ask me about was my relationship with Don and John and Rory. I confirmed that I had fired John and Rory and that I was trying to extricate myself from Don. And then I extended an olive branch to Rory.

"I hope Rory doesn't take the firing personally. Rory is still part of my life. It's up to him what role he wants to play in my life."

I got my answer when Don and John and Rory issued their own statements.

"I love Mike and he knows it, but there are often outside forces and individuals that will try to capitalize on Mike's frustration that comes from his layoff as a result of the suspension," Don said.

John and Rory seemed to be in denial. "I think there is sometimes a frustration and misunderstanding that can occur in the best of friendships and business relationships, and that's how we categorize this," they said in their joint statement.

There was my answer. Rory had cast his lot with two scumbags. I had been let down and betrayed by someone I would have died for. But I'd been betrayed before and it was time to move on. I never talked to Rory and John again.

We began to untangle the webs that Don had created. One of them was with Showtime. We found huge payments that were given to Don "on behalf of Mike Tyson" that I never saw a penny of. Showtime took the position that I owed them that money. Jeff called up the Showtime guys and screamed and yelled and got them to come out to a meeting in California with our legal team.

"You guys are worse criminals than Don King," he told them. "You guys are fucking executives."

All they cared about was getting their bonuses at the end of the year. But there was nothing we could do; we had a valid contract with Showtime.

I was a little less polite to the Showtime execs. I wouldn't kowtow to them. I didn't think of them as big executives. I'd get on the phone with them and just threaten to kick Jay Larkin's ass. They'd be saying, "You can expect a letter from our lawyer."

"Fuck your lawyer in the ass, motherfucker," I'd scream.

We were finding so much shit that Don and them had pulled that Jeff reached out to Dale Kinsella, Howard Weitzman's partner. Dale was a great litigator. I met with him a few times. Dale remembered that meeting when he was interviewed for a documentary film about me.

Maya Angelou visits me in prison.

Leaving the Marion County Courthouse in Indianapolis with my attorney
Jim Voyles after my sentence-reduction hearing, where I refused to apologize.

Don King and my team usher me into the limo waiting outside of the Indiana Youth Center.

Muhammad Ali congratulates me after the Nevada State
Athletic Commission decides to reinstate my boxing license.

I throw a left at Lennox Lewis during the first round of our bout for the heavyweight title in 2002.

Referee Eddie Cotton counts me out in the eighth round of my fight with Lewis.

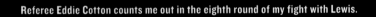

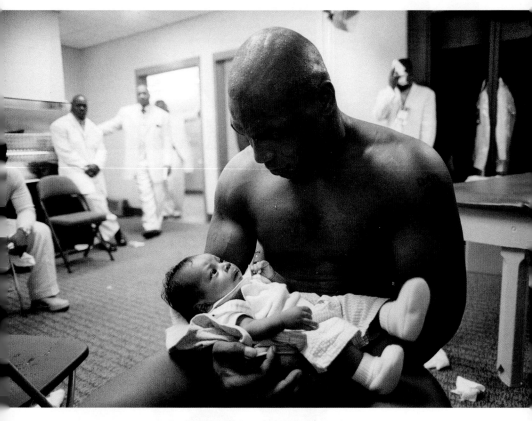

Sitting in my dressing room with my two-month-old son Miguel before the Lewis fight.

Revisiting the *WrestleMania* crew in 2010 with my son Amir. Standing with us are Triple H and Hornswoggle.

With my brother Rodney and nephew Lorenzo.

FROM TOP TO BOTTOM:
Milan, me, Kiki, Morocco.

With the cast of *The Hangover* after we won a Golden Globe Award.
FROM LEFT TO RIGHT: Ed Helms, Justin Bartha, Heather Graham, me, and Bradley Cooper.

While on my hajj to Mecca, I visited with these Saudi officials during a stop in Medina.

With the therapist who introduced me
to the twelve-step program, Marilyn Murray.

My son Miguel with my daughter Mikey.

Exodus poses with Miguel.

Gena and me with Rayna.

With my daughter Milan.

With my kids. FROM LEFT TO RIGHT, BACK: Milan, Amir, and Mikey;
FRONT: Rayna, me, MIguel, and Gena.

With my beautiful wife Kiki.

Talking about my life, family, and career in 2012.

"Mike's future was well planned out by Don King prior to getting out of prison. He gave trust to him in many areas and Don managed to insure that Mike had no lawyers, no financial advisors, and no accountants. I was walking him through some of the legal documents, just one of which managed to take 43.5 million dollars out of Mike's pocket and put it into Don's pocket."

That was just the tip of the iceberg.

It was a good thing that I had been seeing a shrink since December. Monica had set me up with Dr. Richard Goldberg, the chairman of the psychiatric department at Georgetown Medical School. At first I was a little reluctant to open myself up to a middle-aged Jewish man, but he was really a terrific guy and I benefited a lot from my visits with him. Goldberg diagnosed me as suffering from "dysthymic disorder," which was basically chronic depression. He got that right. He put me on Zoloft and I was doing well, considering the circumstances. Of course, I was supplementing his drug regimen with some of my own extracurricular drugs too.

I'm sure that the Zoloft had some bearing on me not going postal when I got into a weird confrontation at an all-night restaurant in Maryland. I had been hanging out and getting high at this club DC Live in Washington. When the club closed, I went to get a bite with this woman Adoria, who was the director of VIP relations at the club, and her coworker and Jeffrey Robinson, a mutual friend of Adoria's and mine. We got to the restaurant at about five a.m. and were seated at a table. Then Michael Colyar, some comedian we had met at the club, came in with his "bodyguard" and two black women in their thirties. They wanted to sit with us, so the manager moved us all to a bigger table in the main room. These women had an attitude from the start, so I tried to ignore them. But when a pretty young European woman came over to our table and asked to take a picture with me, the black chick in the red dress started going off on me.

"I hope you're enjoying your Mike Tyson 'celebrity' bullshit," she said.

Meanwhile, the hot European chick was putting her arms around me and posing.

"My own sisters don't show me love like this," I told Adoria's co-worker.

Now the woman in the red dress went berserk.

"You're not going to praise white women and disrespect black women while there are two black queens here," she said.

"Yeah, you're not going to disrespect all black women while you have that white bitch in your arms," her friend in the black dress said.

I tried to ignore them but the woman in red just kept going.

"You ain't nothing. You're just a ghetto nigga who managed to get some money," she said. "I'm a correctional officer and if you had been in my prison, I would've had your ass in lockdown."

"Fuck you, you bitch." I couldn't take her shit any longer. She was bringing me down from my high.

Adoria got up and told the comedian to get those bitches out of the restaurant. He started escorting the one in red out, but she still had to get in some bullshit.

"You ain't nothing, nigga," she said.

"Yeah? I'll jump over ten lying black bitches like you, to get to one dead white ho," I said.

That made her go postal. She grabbed a cup of coffee from a nearby table and threw it on me, ruining my zebra-striped shirt. I jumped up and accidentally knocked a section of the table to the side and some glasses and dishes fell to the floor. I was so irate that my friend Jeffrey had to hold me back.

I threw some money on the table and we left. I heard later that the comedian and the two women sat and ate for another hour, laughing and making fun of me. When a guy from the next table asked her what had happened, she told him, "I called Tyson an ignorant motherfucker. I will not tolerate him being disrespectful to black women. I just don't appreciate Tyson talking and laughing with these whities while he has sisters at his table."

I knew all this because when I got home that night, I called Jeff Wald and he immediately called the owner of the restaurant and tracked down the customers and the staff and got depositions from all of them. Those two harlots wanted to harass me and goad me into a lawsuit. That didn't work but that didn't stop them. First their attorney contacted my attorney and asked for $20 million. Nine days later, the two shrews filed a $7.5 million lawsuit against me claiming that I verbally and physically abused them after my sexual advances towards one of them was spurned. They were claiming assault, battery, defamation, and emotional distress. They were so traumatized that they couldn't even speak to the reporters at the press conference. But their ambulance chaser could.

"These women were put through a horrendous ordeal, cursed, verbally abused in a situation in front of a fully packed restaurant."

He changed his tune a bit when he got all the depositions we had collected. By the end of the year, they offered to settle for $2 million, then they went down to $850,000. Eventually we paid the woman in red $75,000 and the other one $50,000. We had to settle. My name was mud. I was the arrogant nigga who nobody liked, especially upper-middle-class people. It was a bad time for me. I'm sure that if someone had killed me, they would have gone free.

By the end of February I had new management in place. I hired Jeff Wald, Irving Azoff, and Shelly Finkel, an old friend of mine who used to manage Evander Holyfield, to be my advisors. They would split the standard manager's fee of 20 percent three ways. I would be taking home a lot more money because one of the things we uncovered when we went through Don's contracts was that in addition to his fees as promoter of my fights, he was also taking 30 percent of my purse money, which was illegal. So when I fought Holyfield and my purse was $30 million, I wound up with only $15 million because Don was taking $9 million and John and Rory were splitting $6 million. Don was also helping himself to 30 percent of the bonus money from Showtime and the MGM Grand.

But it got worse. King was getting all the income from the site fees and from foreign telecasts. When he made my deal with the MGM Grand, he was given a $15 million loan from the MGM Grand to purchase MGM stock that was guaranteed by MGM to be worth at least double the value at the end of the term of the contract. I never saw any of that $15 million. Don also had all these side deals with Showtime that were predicated on bringing me to the table. So they paid him to promote non–Mike Tyson events because of my name. The Show-time deal also allowed either Showtime or Don to audit the books, but barred me from doing so!

As if screwing me out of all that money wasn't enough, Don was nickel-and-diming me too. He was paying exorbitant purses to the other boxers on my cards and that money wound up coming out of my pocket. He paid $100,000-a-night consultant's fees to his wife, and $50,000 fees to his two sons. Don's daughter was pulling in $52,000 a year from being the president of the Mike Tyson Fan Club, a club that never met. His daughter didn't even bother to open up the stacks of letters sent to the club.

I was charged huge fees for work allegedly done to my Ohio man-sion. I was billed for maid service, legal fees, and pool maintenance at King's Las Vegas mansion. I paid $100,000 for a WBC "title sanc-tioning fee" for my 1991 fight with Razor Ruddock. But it wasn't even a title fight. He also charged me for the $2 million fee to get promo-tional rights to Ruddock in the future. All my travel was arranged and billed through a travel agency owned by Don's wife. I was paying ridiculously high fees. Oh yeah, I was paying through the nose for my towels too.

On March fifth, we sued Don in U.S. District Court in New York for at least $100 million. That same day, my lawyer John Branca sent me a pep-talk memo. "This will give you an opportunity to establish your **PLACE** in **HISTORY**—to be a leader in seeking to redress the wrong-doings and injustices perpetrated by Don King, not only on you but on many other fighters during the last two decades. As such, you would secure your place not only in boxing but also in social and cul-tural history in the manner of an Arthur Ashe or Curt Flood. The success of what we are doing depends entirely on your **STRENGTH** and your conviction. Don King will look for and exploit any weakness in you. This will require **DEDICATION** and **PATIENCE** and could take three years in court with Don King but if you stay committed, you will win." Branca and Jeff Wald also mapped out a strategy to boost my income with a clothing line, a record label, merchandising deals for posters, and an autobiography.

Four days later, we sued John Horne and Rory Holloway for another $100 million. By inducing me to sign the deal with Don while I was in prison, which was illegal to begin with, they made $22 million each on my fights after I got out. If they had been real managers, they would never have allowed me to sign off on any of the deals that Don brought to me, especially the revised deal that gave him 30 percent of my purses and bonuses. Instead of being locked into Don for four years, I would have been a free agent and could have worked on a fight-to-fight basis with the promoter who offered me the most money. But it was my fault for hiring a failed stand-up comedian and my wingman to steer my career. Cus once told me, "Hey, there's animals disguised as human beings out here and you're not sophisticated enough to decipher the two."

I didn't expect to hear anything from Rory, but I was amused to read what John Horne had to say after we sued his ass.

"Mike Tyson could never appreciate what we were trying to do. Mike Tyson is a convicted rapist, a felon, and we made him the biggest deal in boxing. If he lives for a long time maybe he'll understand what an achievement that was. Mike, I am not your bitch. I stood by you out of love and loyalty only."

And he also said this, "Don King is a great man. When you hear people ripping him, they've never had lunch with him. Don King respects my ability and I respect him."

Even though I had my advisors working on my career, three women—Shawnee, Jackie Rowe, and Monica—were doing a lot of the day-to-day work. I didn't want Monica to get involved in the boxing world. She shouldn't have to get infected by that bug. I attracted scumbags. They may have been sophisticated and good at what they did, but they were still scumbags because big money was involved. Monica just wanted to protect me. I see that now, even if I didn't understand that at the time.

Shawnee and Jackie were something else. They were both big,

brash women. Jackie was totally street. We were cut from the same cloth. Instead of talking all political to executives like, "Mike is the biggest attraction out there and MGM should be more than happy to . . ." she'd say stuff like, "You motherfuckers should be licking this man's ass." Shawnee wasn't as crude as Jackie, but she could be cruel. Dealing with Shawnee and Jackie was more than Latondia could handle. She got sick of being bullied around and quit. I was still barely involved in my own shit then. I was just out there getting high, throwing my life away.

I was hurting for money, so I sold off sixty-two of my vehicles, including some sports cars, six Ducatis, and four Honda trucks, and realized $3.3 million from the sale. My new team had gotten involved in the WWF deal and we renegotiated that now that Don wasn't in the picture. Instead of a $3.5 million fee, I wound up with $6 million and 35 percent of the pay-per-view buys in excess of one million. I was really looking forward to working for the WWF. When I was a kid, I'd watch wrestling all the time on WNJU, Channel 47, the Spanish UHF station.

I got a lot of criticism for appearing at *WrestleMania,* but it was really one of the highlights of my life. People were saying that their wrestling was bullshit, but that $6 million check wasn't bullshit. I was supposed to have reffed for the WWF at a Hulk Hogan match back in 1990, but they used Buster Douglas instead after he knocked me out.

I had so much fun promoting this event.

The WWF wanted me to do *MAD TV* and the writers even wrote up some suggested sketches. One had me hosting a Martha Stewart–type show on the new Lifetime channel, which had branched into sports.

"I find simple flower arrangements bring a little touch of spring in the middle of winter," they had me say. "See, here I've taken these lovely irises and added a touch of pansies."

One of the wrestlers would correct me and say that you can't mix irises and pansies and then we'd get into a fight.

Another proposed skit was a fake commercial where a guy at a party tries to tell an interesting story but he just can't. Everyone leaves him sitting alone and then the voice-over comes in.

"Has this ever happened to you? Well, not anymore. Because Mike Tyson will come to your house and punch you in the face!"

Then I punch the guy in the face. They cut to the party again and the guy is fucked up, swollen face, bandages all over, black eye, and he can barely talk. But as he struggles to speak, he's the center of attention.

"So if your life is really boring, just call us and Mike Tyson will come over and punch you in the face!"

Jeff and Irving and Shelly put the kibosh on doing that program. I would never have gotten my license back if I'd done it.

We went to a few different cities to do live events to promote the show on March twenty-seventh. In Boston we held a huge outdoor rally in City Hall Plaza. It was awesome. The crowd went crazy screaming and cursing at me and Shawn Michaels and Steve Austin. They held up signs like TYSON BITES and EARS FEAR TYSON. Austin had called me out and pushed me at an earlier appearance, so now I jumped into the ring while Michaels and two of his comrades in D-Generation X had Austin against the ropes. I kicked him in the shins a few times and then planted a big wet kiss on his forehead.

The night of the event, I entered the Fleet Center wearing a D-Generation X T-shirt. During the match I was openly rooting for Michaels from ringside. When Austin got knocked out of the ring, I threw him back in. Then the referee in the ring got knocked out. I got into the ring and dragged him out. It was back and forth between Michaels and Austin, but finally Austin pummeled Michaels to the canvas. The ref was still unconscious. So I jumped into the ring and instead of attacking Austin, I counted Michaels out, making Austin the new champ. We celebrated together and he gave me an Austin 3:16 T-shirt. Michaels regained consciousness and confronted me for my betrayal. I floored him with one punch and then draped the Austin T-shirt over his body and Steve and I walked out with our arms around each other.

At the press conference after the match, I was asked about Don and John and Rory cheating me out of millions of dollars.

"I did a little screwing too," I said. "I guess what goes around comes around."

Someone asked me about the way I pulled the unconscious referee out of the ring.

"I'm on parole. For the record, I didn't slam the referee. I politely took him out of the ring and put him on the mat."

Austin and I told the press that we had been secretly working together all along, but I kind of undermined the credibility of that by continually referring to him as Cold Stone instead of Stone Cold. I was so high that I had the munchies.

In May, we announced that I was forming my own record label, Iron Mike Records. With the help of Irving Azoff and John Branca we would find a major label to distribute our artists' work. In the meantime I had Jackie Rowe handling the business end. We also added my former lawyers and financial managers at Sidley Austin to our lawsuit. I was hoping to get something from these lawsuits soon because I was paying out lots of money to defend myself from all the lawsuits that were coming in against me. Besides the two women in the restaurant, I was being sued by my former tiger trainer, the company that owned a house in L.A. that I backed out of buying, my jeweler in Vegas, my Vegas house contractor, that quack Dr. Smedi, and even Kevin Rooney, my old trainer.

The craziest lawsuit was filed by Ladywautausa A. Je, a wacky black broad who would have her assistant photograph her with unsuspecting celebrities on Hollywood Boulevard. I had come out of a meeting with a filmmaker when she lifted her leg up against me and had her guy take a picture. Next thing we knew, she was filing a suit for sexual battery claiming that I pressed my body against hers, "pulling up her body suit saying, 'Take a picture of this.'" As soon as we produced a few witnesses she dropped the case. But it got publicity.

I did great with the Smedi suit. He sued me for the original $7 million he claimed I owed him, so we countersued and he wound up paying me $50,000. I didn't do as well with Rooney. Despite the fact that he claimed to have an oral agreement in which he was to be my "trainer for life" and despite the testimony from many friends of Cus's who said that Cus had become disenchanted with Rooney and wanted to replace him, the second U.S. Circuit Court of Appeals reinstated a $4.4 million award that a jury had given him years earlier.

So it was time to get back in the ring. I had sat out a year by then. Jeff had been talking with Dr. Elias Ghanem, who was the head of the Nevada boxing commission. I loved Dr. Ghanem. He was an Israeli-born Lebanese man who came to the States with nothing and built up an amazing medical practice because he was a throwback—a doctor who really cared about his patients. Elvis, Michael Jackson, Wayne Newton, Ann-Margret—he treated all the Vegas stars. He loved boxing too. He assured Jeff that I would be able to get my license back because my punishment was "a little over the top." After the Holyfield thing, he took me aside.

"You fucked up, but it's going to be all right," he told me.

Shelly had decided that we should get a license in New Jersey. He was unaware of Jeff's maneuverings and Shelly and I had good relationships with Larry Hazzard, who was a former referee and the current New Jersey boxing commissioner. Jeff was against going to New Jersey but he was in no shape to intervene. So on July twenty-ninth I appeared before the New Jersey Athletic Control Board for a hearing. You would have thought Saddam Hussein was testifying. I walked into the building holding hands with Monica and we were cheered by most of the spectators but booed by the six protestors from the National Organization for Women who protested me pretty much everywhere I went.

Inside the hearing room, there were enough cops lined up to stop a full-scale riot. They must have been pretty scared of me. The hearing went well at first. Monica testified that "boxing is his passion and he really, really, really misses it. He needs boxing and I think boxing needs him." Then it was former heavyweight contender Chuck Wepner's turn. He cracked up the whole room when he recalled referee Tony Perez's instructions before Wepner fought Muhammad Ali in 1975.

"He didn't want me to choke or rabbit punch. Those were my two best punches."

Bobby Czyz testified that even though I had snapped in the ring, I should be allowed to continue fighting.

"A piece of the street came out in him," he said. "If I hit a guy and his eye fell out, I would eat it before I gave it back. That's the kind of mind-set you have to have as a boxer. Mike is not anywhere as bad as all them people say. He made a mistake. I also know he has changed considerably. Mike Tyson has gone out of his way to cut out the evil forces from his life."

They even showed a video that Camille, who was ninety-three by that time, had made, up in Catskill. She said that I continued to support her and call her my "white mother."

My own testimony started out on the right foot. I told them that I was foggy from the repeated head butts by Holyfield.

"I just snapped. Nothing mattered anymore at that particular point." I got all choked up and had to compose myself. "I'm sorry for what I did. I wish it never happened. It will haunt me for the rest of my life."

But then at the end of my testimony, the assistant attorney general, Michael Haas, kept battering away at me, wondering why I had bitten Holyfield. He kept asking me over and over again if I could do something like that again.

"This ordeal ruined my life internally," I said, trying to contain my anger. "You think I want to do it again?"

I was supposed to read a closing statement, but that creep had gotten under my skin.

"I don't want to say it now because I'm angry," I told my lawyer, Anthony Fusco Jr. "You know what I mean, man? Fuck it. Why do I got to go through this shit all the time?"

"Relax, relax." Fusco tried to calm me down.

Fuck them. I just felt like being like a prick. I was tired of suppressing my rebellious side. I thought about Bobby Seale and the Chicago Seven, who didn't take any shit from their judge.

Despite my outburst, we were sure that Jersey would grant me my license even though New York State Attorney General Dennis Vacco tried to butt in. Vacco was part of a group that included Senator John McCain who were trying to clean up boxing. They had held hearings in Washington and I had even submitted a statement blasting Don.

"My financial career was placed in the hands of a promoter and manager who were allowed to run amok. The opportunity for abuse is gigantic. Fighters can wind up like slaves."

McCain had introduced a bill to create national regulations over boxing. So Vacco was complaining that Jersey shouldn't license me until Vegas did.

"I would be very offended if they actually licensed him or permitted him to box in New Jersey," Vacco told the press. Then he told the reporters that he would personally deliver that message to the Jersey attorney general.

All this controversy worried Jeff and the others, so on August thirteenth, on the eve of the New Jersey Control Board meeting to decide my fate, my advisors withdrew my application.

I was mad at the world and I was getting high every chance I got. At the end of August, Monica and I were driving near her house and someone rear-ended her Mercedes because the guy behind him rear-ended him. The guy got out of his car and came around to our driver's side and started mouthing off at Monica, then he started shouting at the guy who hit him. I just got of the car and started beating the shit out of everyone involved. I kicked the first guy in the balls and then I slugged the guy who hit the first guy. Monica was yelling and I had to be restrained by my bodyguard who was in the car in front of us. I feel so bad about this now, but I was going through a real depressive phase of my life. Can you imagine that? I had a wife and kids, but I felt hopeless.

We got back in the car and Monica drove away. Someone had called the police and they pulled us over a few miles from the scene. I was as high as a kite and I started complaining about chest pains and then I told them that I was a victim of racial profiling. They offered to take me to a hospital, but I told them that Monica was a doctor so they let us go. I actually did go and get checked out in a local hospital but I was fine. Since the cops weren't on the scene of the accident, all they could eventually charge me with if the other guys decided to press charges was misdemeanor assault.

They did. On September second, Richard Hardick, the guy that rear-ended us, filed an assault charge against me for kicking him in the groin. The next day the other guy, Abmielec Saucedo, filed for getting punched in the face by me.

Everyone working with me was worried about this case. We were getting ready to try to get our license back in Vegas, but how would the commissioners react to my road rage? What's worse, I was still on probation in Indiana. If she wanted to, Judge Gifford could haul my ass back to the IYC to serve another four years.

I appeared before the Vegas commission on September nineteenth. I drove up to the hearing on one of my motorcycles, wearing blue jeans and a black T-shirt. All my lawyers in their suits were waiting for me outside and when I got off my bike, I threw my helmet down on the ground. The lawyers ran off, they were scared shitless of me. Jeff Wald and I cracked up.

It was a very contentious hearing. My lawyer Dale Kinsella was pounding on the enormous fine they had levied on me and how much my financial situation was fucked. I pretty much let my lawyers and character witnesses do the talking. When I did answer some questions, I'd look over to Dr. Ghanem, and if I was about to say the wrong answer, he'd subtly shake his head as if to say, "No, don't say that, don't say that." The hearing lasted six hours and after it was over Dr. Ghanem met the press.

"In six hours Tyson did not blow up," he said. As if that was a major accomplishment for me.

The commission didn't rule on my application that day. In fact, they passed a motion that I had to submit to a detailed psychiatric evaluation before they would even vote on reinstatement. They gave me the choice of going to the Mayo Clinic, the Menninger Clinic, or the Massachusetts General Hospital. The decision was a no-brainer. One of Irving Azoff's fraternity brothers was the head of psychiatry at Mass General.

So I called up two of my L.A. girlfriends and had them fly out and meet me in Boston. I was staying in a hotel and then I'd go to the clinic at Mass General every day and get tested. The night before I was to start my treatment, I picked the girls up at the airport in my limo, then I had my limo driver score some coke. We partied like crazy every night I was there.

I went to the hospital that first morning in a pissed-off mood. I was directed to meet my doctors in what looked like an upscale waiting room or even someone's living room. I figured I was getting the VIP treatment.

"Man, this is bullshit," I said. "I don't deserve to be here with all these motherfuckers." Everyone else in the room looked a little wary of me.

Just then, a white woman, about twenty-nine, came up to me. She reminded me of Velma from *Scooby-Doo*. She was wearing a turtleneck sweater and had that bowl haircut and big horn-rimmed glasses. She sat down next to me and looked concerned. I figured she was one of the professors from the psychiatric ward.

"What's wrong? You seem down," she said.

"They think I'm crazy because I bit this nigga's ear, but they don't know. The only reason I bit him is because he kept head-butting me and the referee wasn't calling it and I felt desperate and I had no choice."

She thought for a minute.

"You were in a fight," she said calmly.

I was high as a kite but those words penetrated to my core like some ancient Zen wisdom.

Fuck, I *was* in a fight. I felt cured immediately. She said it so authoritatively. I was amazed that she totally understood me, after just a few seconds with me. *That's why they must pay these shrinks the big bucks,* I thought.

Just then my euphoria was interrupted by a nurse.

"It's time for your meds, Nancy," the nurse said to the woman I was talking to.

"Shove 'em up your ass," she snarled and she knocked the medication

out of the nurse's hand. The nurse then gestured and two big atten-
dants came out and put the lady into a straitjacket. She was fighting
these two guys until they finally overpowered her.

Then I looked around the room. There was a guy drooling in
the corner, talking to himself. I realized that I wasn't in an upscale
waiting room, I was in the psychiatric unit and everybody in there,
including the Velma lookalike from *Scooby-Doo*, was as crazy as a
motherfucker.

The Vegas commissioners were due to rule on my reinstatement on
October nineteenth, so my lawyers were working overtime to reach a
settlement with the two guys from the road rage incident. I wound up
paying each guy $250,000 on signing the settlement agreement and
they'd each get an additional $150,000 from Showtime following my
first fight after the suspension. They also each signed an affidavit
that affirmed that although it was their belief that I was the person
who struck them, because of their "disorientation and the confusion
that surrounded the events that occurred that day" they couldn't "be
absolutely certain that it was Mr. Tyson who struck me."

Before my hearing on October nineteenth, one of the commissioners insisted that my psychiatric records be made public. This was a
load of bullshit and my lawyers fought it tooth and nail, but there was
some obscure law and there was no way they could vote me back unless we released the findings. Now everyone in the world could see just
how low my self-esteem was. Even though I was chronically depressed,
the doctors said, "Mr. Tyson is mentally fit to return to boxing, to
comply with the rules and regulations, and to do so without repetition
of the events of June 28, 1997. While we take note of the impulsivity,
emotional problems, and cognitive problems outlined above, it is our
opinion that none of these, alone or in combination, render Mr. Tyson
mentally unfit in this regard."

In other words, I was a sick motherfucker, but I could still get in
the ring and try to beat the shit out of somebody.

I had Magic Johnson with me at the next hearing. He was interested in getting into boxing promotion and he was certainly a very

nonthreatening black man to these commissioners. But when he got into how he would handle me, I started to get irritated.

"Mike knows money, but he doesn't understand it and I hope to teach him to understand it. He needs to become a businessman. Mike is the only guy I know who can make one hundred or two hundred million dollars but would rather not have it. He would rather give it away. He has to get a money manager and that is what I would bring to the Mike Tyson team."

But I kept my cool. And that same day the commission voted 4–1 to restore my license.

Now I could get back in the ring and make some money. I was $13 million in the hole to the IRS by now. That might freak out a lot of people, but I was used to getting multimillion-dollar payouts, so I knew I could rebound. It's funny, right around this time my new accountants discovered an IRA account in my name that over the years had appreciated to over a quarter of a million dollars.

The accountants began to dig around and found out that Cus had set up that account for me back in Catskill. When they told me it was Cus, I cried like a baby. For the first time in my life, I understood what "It's the thought that counts" meant. Cus must have known I'd screw up my money. I never thought anyone loved my black ass. It restored some kind of faith in mankind for me at that point.

On December first, we pleaded no contest to the Maryland road rage misdemeanor charges. Since we had settled with the two guys, my lawyers were convinced that I would get a slap on the wrist at my sentencing, which would be sometime in February of 1999.

My first comeback fight was scheduled for January sixteenth against the South African fighter Frans Botha. He was nicknamed the White Buffalo and he was no tomato can. He had actually won the IBF title in 1995, but he later tested positive for steroids and they stripped him. Then he fought on the undercard of my first fight with Holyfield and put up a great fight for Michael Moorer's IBF belt until he was stopped in the last round, so I wasn't taking him lightly.

Four days before the fight I sat down in Vegas for a series of satellite TV and radio interviews. My first interview was with Russ Salzberg with Channel 9 back in New York.

"Mike, Botha's a 6 to 1 underdog. Any concerns on your part?" he asked.

"I don't know nothing about numbers. I just know what I can do. I'm going to kill this motherfucker."

"Okay," he said, a little taken aback. "You take into the ring a lot of rage. Does that work for you, or does it work against you at times?"

"Who cares? We're going to fight anyway. What does it matter?"

"Well, for example, rage against Evander Holyfield worked against you."

"Fuck it! It's a fight! So whatever happens, happens."

"Mike, you gotta talk like that?"

"I'm talking to you the way I want to talk to you. If you have a problem, turn off your station."

"You know what? I think we'll end this discussion right now," Russ said.

"Good! Fuck you!"

"You got it. Have a nice fight, Mike."

"Fuck off! Asshole!"

"You're a class act, buddy."

"So's your mother."

Part of the reason I was so belligerent was that I had been taken off my daily dose of Zoloft a week before the fight.

I was so rusty for that fight. It was a horrible night for me. Botha was holding me continually. He clinched me in the corner at the end of the first round and I leveraged his left arm with my right arm and I tried to snap it off. I'm a real dirty fighter. I shouldn't say this, but it's true. I think I really wanted people to talk about how dirty and vicious I was. When they asked me after the fight whether I was trying to intentionally break his arm, I just said, "Correct."

I won only one round of the first four and in that round Richard Steele deduced a point from me. The Showtime guys—Kenny Albert, Ferdie Pacheco, and Bobby Czyz—all thought that Botha was getting to me with his holding and was turning it into a street fight. But after the fourth round, I told Crocodile and my new trainer Tommy Brooks that he was getting tired and I could get to him. Apparently, Ferdie Pacheco didn't believe that.

"Tyson looks like he's in slow motion. He can't get off two punches. That's the mark of a shot fighter, he can't get off punches. Oh!"

I didn't need two punches. Just as Ferdie was saying that, I hit Botha with a right hand square on his jaw. He crumpled to the canvas. He tried to get up but he couldn't beat the count. Then he careened into the ropes and collapsed back on the canvas. It was an ugly fight, but I redeemed it with a resounding one-punch knockout. Botha went down like he had been shot with an elephant gun. The White Buffalo just got poached.

There was intrigue with my team now too. Shelly and Shawnee had gotten together and ganged up on Jeff and Irving. Jeff was still recuperating from his surgery and had to go back to L.A. to coproduce Roseanne Barr's new show, so he pretty much left the picture. My career was in the hands of Shelly, Shawnee, and Jackie Rowe.

And the Maryland judicial system. I showed up in a small court in Rockville on February 5, 1999. I was wearing a charcoal gray suit and a black vest. Monica was there with me, along with at least a dozen of my lawyers and advisors. I had pleaded no contest to the charges and my attorneys had worked out a deal that would avoid jail time. I'd just pay a fine, be put on probation, and be ordered to do community service. But then I got fucked again.

The new district attorney, Doug Gansler, and his assistant prosecutor, Carol Crawford, showed up in court with an eleven-page document that made me sound like I was a Nazi war criminal. Crawford especially seemed to loathe me. She was a very masculine-looking woman with a severe short haircut. She seemed hell-bent on taking out her anger towards all men on me. I was her showpiece.

Instead of keeping up their end of the deal, these two liars trotted out every derogatory thing they could pin on me, including quotes from Teddy Atlas saying that Cus had spoiled me as a kid. They quoted from my own interviews, including the *Playboy* interview from 1998 where I told Mark Kram, the writer, that I was "a very hateful motherfucker" who would "blow one day." Then they cited Kram himself when he wrote that I was "the darkest figure in sports" that he had ever encountered.

"This comment is noteworthy from a man who met with the reviled boxing legend Sonny Liston, an ex-con who died of a drug overdose in suspicious circumstances, and, coincidentally, one boxer the defendant has expressed an affinity for," Gansler and Crawford wrote in their memo in aid of sentencing.

They even turned around my psychiatric report from Mass General that, except for the depression, gave me a clean bill of health.

"Perhaps we can't find something 'wrong' with the defendant beyond that which one might find 'wrong' with any neighborhood bully. For this bully, however, the world is his playground. One commentator, clinical psychologist Robert Butterworth, Ph.D., may have provided the greatest direction for the court. After reviewing the Kram interview comments by the defendant, Mr. Butterworth commented, 'If he's telling us all he's going to do this, we'd be idiots not to see it coming.' Although we do not punish prospectively in this jurisdiction, the Court must always consider the safety of the defendant, as well as the public, in sentencing appropriately. The defendant is nothing less than the time bomb buried in our own backyard."

Can you believe this shit? What was this, Stalinist Russia? These two liars wanted to use an interview where I blew off steam and a diagnosis from this Dr. Butterworth who never laid eyes on me to put me behind bars before this "time bomb" blew up. Anybody could see that these people were just out to abuse me, but no one cared because they probably thought I deserved this.

"Although we do not punish prospectively in this state"—but that's exactly what they were arguing for—"executed incarceration, as a starting point, will address the twin goals of punishment and deterrence. Rehabilitation, through the fine programs of this jurisdiction, may be commenced while incarcerated and followed during any probationary period. Given the defendant's denial of responsibility, his defiance, his comments on his character, and his predictions of future conduct, the goals of deterrence and rehabilitation may never be achieved. However, for at least the period of incarceration, the public at large will be protected from his potential for violence."

Judge Johnson agreed. He sentenced me to two years in jail, with one year suspended, and fined me $5,000, and ordered me to serve two years probation and perform two thousand hours of community service. He also denied me bail if I appealed the decision.

The standing-room-only courtroom filled with shocked gasps. I was stunned. Monica started crying hysterically. They slapped handcuffs on me and took me right to jail.

Gansler was getting his fifteen minutes of fame. People actually were outraged that I could be sent to jail for a year after we had reached a plea deal for no time with the old state attorney.

"Any prosecutor would do what I did," Gansler told an AP writer. "People are going to say what they're going to say."

They threw me in a five-and-a-half-foot-by-eight-foot cell in Cellblock Two, which was their version of protective custody. That meant that I was separated from the inmate population who were mostly white privileged kids from Montgomery County. My unit was isolated with just a few people who were either too weak to be in population or too aggressive. I begged them to put me in population. I needed to be out there to work the system to get my privileges. I was raised that way. Instead I was in protective custody and the guards were coming around and taking pictures of me and selling them to the papers.

I was in for two weeks when I got sent to their version of the hole. It started when they sent some prison shrink to see me. I was seeing Dr. Goldberg, one of the best psychiatrists in the country, so I refused to even talk to this fool. He cut my normal dose of Zoloft in half. When they came with a different-looking pill, I refused to take it. Two days later, I was in the dayroom, on the phone, when a particularly sadistic guard came in and hung up the phone in the middle of my conversation. I was a different person in jail; I was more fastidious than I was at home. One little thing went wrong and I was ready to go off the hinges and tear it up.

I got enraged and pulled the TV set off its metal bracket, threw it on the floor, then picked it up and chucked it at the bars of the cell where the warden and two guards were observing me from behind. A small piece of plastic broke off and went through the bar and hit one of the guards. The guards immediately sent me to "administrative segregation." I was locked up for twenty-three hours of the day and wasn't allowed to buy snacks from the canteen or have visits or telephone calls, except from my lawyers or doctors. Doctor Goldberg visited me the next night and got me back on my regular dose of Zoloft.

After the TV incident, the jail administration charged me with disorderly conduct, destruction of property, and assault on a corrections officer because the little plastic shard hit him. They threw me in the hole, and I wasn't a happy camper. I thought I was one of those Baader-Meinhof German political prisoners who would go crazy when they were put in jail. They'd kill guards, they'd kill themselves. I even started wearing a little Spanish bandanna on my head and was butt naked, throwing things at the guards.

They sentenced me to twenty-five days in isolation, but my lawyer appealed and I got out after five days. I really didn't like this prison. I wanted to be sent back to Indiana. I had nobody to work with in this jail, nobody to bring me stuff and get me girls. I was still on probation there so they could have easily yanked me back. The problem was that they could make me serve the last four years of my previous sentence. Jim Voyles, my Indiana lawyer, made about twenty trips back and forth from Maryland and finally reached a deal where I would serve an extra sixty days in jail at Maryland, and Indiana would wash their hands of me forever. Judge Gifford was more than happy to sign off on that. Nobody wanted me back in Indiana.

I was pissed. I wanted to sue the judge's ass to get back there. But when I settled into jail in Maryland, it turned out not to be too bad. Monica started cooking for me and I was allowed to have the food sent in. After a few months, I started gaining so much weight that I asked them if I could bring in my treadmill and a stationary bike and they let me. I was always the privileged prick in prison.

We even shot a cover for *Esquire* while I was in there. Monica brought my new baby boy, Amir, to the prison and we posed for pictures to accompany an article about me.

I started mingling with the other guys in protective custody. There were a number of young kids who were in there for murder. Two of them even hung themselves while I was in there—one guy was a wealthy Israeli kid and the other a black kid. I paid for the black kid's funeral because his parents didn't have much money. It broke my heart to see these young beautiful kids from privileged families getting caught up in drugs and then doing something like murdering someone over a hundred bucks. When I left that jail, there must have been $12,000 on my books, so I had the prison split that money up among the five guys who were in isolation with me. They weren't no tough guys. They were little kids who had no money who were never going to go home.

I sort of became the protective custody Don at that place. The other guys would send messages to me through the guards and ask me to talk to them about their problems. Some of the guards would come to me and tell me about a kid who might be having a problem and I'd send him a message and tell him to chill out.

I didn't get many visitors in jail in Maryland. Monica came, Craig Boogie came, some other friends dropped in. My Jamaican girlfriend, Lisa, came. She had written her name in the visitors' log and Monica came a few hours later and saw her name and threw a shit fit. Thank God they had that little glass window separating us.

But the visitor who got the most attention when he came was John F. Kennedy Jr. He came to visit me one night. When the word got out, ten news teams showed up and waited outside for hours. Inside, it was pandemonium. I had John say hello to all the other inmates in isolation with me. "Yeah, hug their mom. Give the kid a kiss." I was the big Don.

John and I were friends from New York. I met him on the street one day and he invited me up to see him at his *George* magazine office. He was such a beautiful, down-to-earth cat, riding his bike around

Manhattan, taking public transportation sometimes. The first thing he told me when he came to see me was, "My whole family told me not to come to see you. So when you see them and they're all saying 'Hi' to you, you get the picture."

Right before he came, one of his cousins got in trouble for screwing his babysitter or something like that.

"Yeah, my cousin is the poster boy for bad behavior," John said.

"Whatever you do, don't disrespect your family in public. Don't do that because that's what society wants. People want to break you and make you like you're nothing," I told him. "Just call them an asshole in private. Don't ever do it in front of the public."

We talked about the Kennedy family a lot, especially his grandfather, but he didn't seem to know that much about him, other than he didn't teach any of his sons anything about business. "Nobody in my family knows how to run a business, that's why they all went into politics. He wanted us to be pampered guys."

I guess that's why he was doing his magazine, to learn the business end. He felt that he had no accomplishments in life and that was one thing that he could point to.

We talked about my case a little bit.

"Look, I know that the only reason you're in here is because you're black," he told me. He was letting me know that he knew what time it was.

At one point, I just flat out said to him, "You know you've got to run for political office."

"What?" He seemed a little taken aback. "Do you think so?"

"You'd be letting my mother down, my mother's people down. They saw you under that desk. You can't let a lost generation that believed so much in your family down. Not me, fuck me, I'm going to do what I do, but you can't let those people down. Your father and your uncle were their hope and you're the bloodline to that hope," I said.

He didn't say anything. Maybe he thought I was crazy.

"No, nigga, you've got to do this shit. Are you crazy? What's the purpose of you even living? That's what you were born to do. People's dreams are riding on you, man. That's a heavy burden but you shouldn't have had that mother and father you did."

He would have made a great politician. He really cared about people; you could tell it wasn't some phony-baloney shit. Just the way he really engaged with people, really catching the eyes of people he didn't even know. He wasn't scared to be seen out in public; he was out there looking to engage. *Whoa,* I'd think, *this is one interesting guy.*

He looked tired that night. He told me he had to get some coffee because he was going to fly back to New York that night. He had flown down with his flight instructor.

"No, man. Go over to the house. Stay with Monica and the kids," I told him. "You're fucking crazy to fly that plane anyway."

"You don't know how I feel up there, man. I feel so free," he told me.

"You must feel stupid, you up there and you don't really know what you're doing. If you have to fly, fly by yourself. Please don't take somebody you love up there."

He didn't say anything, but he went to see Monica that night and she told me that he said, "Well, Mike said I was stupid for flying my plane. He's the one who got in the motorcycle accident."

We also talked about hanging out when I got out of jail. He was talking about other women and I got a sense that he was going through a lot of shit with his wife.

"When you get out, give me a little time to handle some stuff with my wife. Then you and I have got to hang. You need to come with me to Aspen."

"Aspen?" I said. "They got no niggas in Aspen. I'm not gonna get no love up there."

"Uh-huh. There's Lynn Swann," John said.

"Lynn Swann ain't no nigga," I said.

"Yeah, you're right," he conceded.

Of course, I made the pitch to get out right then. I had been in jail for almost four months already. That was enough time I thought. One of John's cousins, Kathleen Kennedy Townsend, RFK's oldest daughter, was the lieutenant governor of Maryland at the time.

"Get me out of here," I begged. "Ask your fucking cousin."

"Mike, I don't really know her," he said.

Maybe he was sophisticated enough not to say anything in that visiting room.

"You don't know her? What the fuck do you mean? You all play football together up there in Hyannis Port."

He smiled and then he left. The media surrounded him when he got out.

"I'm here in support of my friend," John said. "Mike's a much different man than his public image would suggest. He's a man who was really putting his life back together and has an opportunity to do so in the future. I hope perhaps coming here and telling folks that, people might start to believe it, because he's had a difficult life."

Then he got into his limo and drove to my house to get some coffee. Shortly after John-John was there, boom, I got out of jail.

12

AS SOON AS I GOT OUT OF JAIL, THE VERY FIRST DAY, I WENT HOME, PACKED A bag, and went to New York. I didn't hang out and spend time with my family like I should have. Boom, I got in the car and drove to New York to see one of my girlfriends. I just didn't have the skills or tools to be a responsible person. Or the desire. You can't have one foot in a marriage and the other foot in the gutter. Having all those girlfriends while I was married was like a drug in itself. And if I needed some more, I'd just walk down the street and women would throw themselves at me. I was a slave addicted to the chaos of celebrity. I wished I could stop it but I couldn't.

Nothing in my life was pretty then. My new business guys had negotiated new deals with Showtime and the MGM Grand because Don wasn't in the picture, but I was still on the hook for all those millions that Showtime had advanced me and that wound up in Don's pocket. And the IRS was still on my back.

I had moved to Phoenix to start training for my next fight, and at the beginning of June I started doing community service at the infamous Sheriff Joe Arpaio's jail in Phoenix. He was thrilled to have me there. I would walk around his tent city and talk to the prisoners and tell them to stay out of trouble. Meanwhile, my probation officers were treating me like I was John Gotti. They'd try to write me up every chance they got. If they heard a rumor that I was out at a club, they'd call my lawyer and we'd have to get witnesses to dispute it. Then the lawyer would write them: "As I indicated to you, Mike did not visit the Amazon nightclub on Tuesday, June 29th, as Monica confirmed. Mike was in his room asleep."

My lawyer even started telling my bodyguards to be on the alert.

"As you know the Maricopa County Adult Probation Department is intensifying its surveillance of Mike. Accordingly, as Anthony has already begun to do, I'd like to establish the following procedures. If Mike leaves the hotel after ten p.m. you should page both Paul and his surveillance officer, Chad. Anthony has these numbers. Additionally, please telephone my voice mail and leave me an identical message as to where Mike is going. If Mike leaves to go to another club, or even to a restaurant, it's important that you make telephone calls to both probation officers and myself informing all parties of the itinerary. As I discussed with Anthony, it's important that Mike remain calm, no matter what probation does. In the event that a confrontation occurs with a probation department, or is about to occur, please call me immediately."

I'm Al Capone! I'm a bad nigga, the scariest man alive. You know my megalomaniacal ego was eating this shit up. They were treating me like I was the Godfather.

And I was still a huge target for cheap shots. One day in August I was doing my service at Sheriff Arpaio's tent and he called me into his office.

"Mike, one of my sheriffs is pressing charges against you. She said you struck her and knocked her down. I don't know why it took her a week to file these charges," he said.

"You were with me all the time. You know this is bullshit," I said.

"I don't see how you could have done this," he agreed.

Of course, it was all bullshit. But this was the shit I had to go through. Getting charged for things while I was doing community service? They found video and pictures taken of the scene when the incident was supposed to have taken place and the sheriff was there with me and she was all smiles, so they dropped the case but I could have been sent back to jail in Maryland. I think they were really out to embarrass Arpaio. His sheriffs didn't like him too much.

I got back in the ring in Vegas on October 23, 1999. My opponent was Orlin Norris. Back when I was champ, I didn't know who this guy was, but he used to show up at my press conferences and just stare all crazy at me. He fought on some of my undercards, but I didn't recognize him. I was thinking, *This nigga might have a gun. Who is this guy? Did I talk shit to him or win all his money at a dice game?* I was scared. Nobody had ever had the balls to do that to me. He'd just stare at me, not say nothing. I thought he was probably someone I had wronged in the streets.

He had been the WBA cruiserweight champion, so he did know how to fight. We felt each other out the first round and, right at the bell, I hit him with a left uppercut that sent him down. Richard Steele deducted two points from me for hitting after the bell, but it didn't matter. Norris went back to his corner and sat on his stool and didn't get up. He claimed that he had injured his right knee when he went down and he couldn't continue. The crowd started booing and throwing things and next thing you knew, there were fifty uniformed cops in the ring. Here we go again. I was really in good shape and I would have applied the heat and knocked him out in the next round, but he wouldn't get off his stool. It's funny when you watch the video; he got up and strolled back to his corner, fine, and listened to his trainer tell him what he was doing wrong. But he quit and that was another black mark on my name in Vegas. They ruled it a no contest. I didn't realize it at the time, but that was the last time I'd ever be in a ring in Las Vegas.

Shelly Finkel thought that it might be better for me to fight outside the United States for a while and let Vegas calm down after the Norris fiasco. So he set up a fight for me in Manchester, England, on

January 29, 2000. I was going to meet Julius Francis, the British heavyweight champion. England was a trip. I was mobbed everywhere I went. When I visited the ghetto in Brixton, there were so many adoring fans swarming me that I had to take refuge in a police station. I think it might have been the first time in my life that I entered a police station voluntarily.

A week before the fight, I did an interview with Sky TV.

"Do you think you are getting fair treatment here?" the interviewer asked.

"Your guys treat me with kid gloves compared to what they do in the United States. They make you not even want to come outside sometimes, but I am strong and there is nothing that can stop me. I refuse to be beaten down anymore or be stomped on emotionally anymore. Whatever comes at me I am just going to put my head up and face it."

"Twenty-one thousand people snapped up all of the tickets to see you in two days. What do you think is your magnetism for fight fans?" he wondered.

"I don't know, but I do know there's another sixty thousand that couldn't get tickets and I think they should just crash the gate and come in, that's what I believe."

"Don't give them ideas, Mike." He sounded terrified.

"That's what they need, they need ideas. They're supposed to see me fight. I was a fan of Duran and I rounded up a bunch of guys from the street. 'Come on, man, come on! They can't stop us!' And we just crashed right through the gate."

"A couple more questions about Julius Francis. Tell us your prediction of what is going to happen?"

"I don't know. I think I am going to kill Julius Francis," I said, deadpan.

"You don't mean to kill him really, do you? I just said that because the people will pounce on the quote and say, 'Oh, Mike Tyson wants to kill Julius Francis.'"

"That's okay. Listen, can I tell you something? It doesn't faze me what anyone says about me. Michael and Tyson are two different people. To my children and my wife I am Mike and Daddy. But I am Tyson here. Tyson is just a freak, somebody who generates a ton of money. No one knows me, no one has any kind of consideration for my feelings, my pain, anything I've ever been through in my life. You have no iota who I am or what I am. They don't even know why they cheer for me. Why, because I'm a good fighter? Because I stand up for myself? Tyson is not who I am. I become that person, but I am Mike and Daddy, and that is more important to me."

"And the only time you are that other person is when you are in the ring, yeah?"

"Right now! I am Tyson right now."

"The guy?"

"Yeah, I'm the guy that's gonna make the whole freak show happen on the twenty-ninth. Everyone is going to come and watch me kill somebody, or beat somebody up, or knock somebody out. Tyson is the ticket, Tyson is the moneymaker. Not too many people care about Michael personally, because Michael is just some nigga out of Brownsville, Brooklyn, that just happened to make it one day, or was lucky. Where I come from, I am the piece of gum on the bottom of your shoe. God has blessed me, I don't know, he put me in this situation to be around, I don't know, I guess you guys are supposed to be decent people, right?"

I couldn't walk the streets of London because we'd start a riot, so we went shopping by car. One time, we stopped for a light and when people saw I was in the car, they started rocking it. Other people were diving headfirst into the car. It was like a scene out of a third-world country where the dictator was trying to leave and the crowd was doing everything to block the car, even tear the roof off. But these people were showing love.

"We love you, Mike! We love you!" they were screaming.

It was like Beatlemania. A lady friend was with me and it looked like she was going to take a heart attack.

"Damn," she said, turning around to look at me. "Who the fuck are you?"

We got back to our hotel, but the crowd just swarmed under the window and started chanting. They wouldn't leave until I went out on the balcony and gave them the thumbs-up and saluted them. I thought I was fucking Charlemagne.

I had some vocal detractors too. I got no support from the ladies' groups. They would boycott my appearances. I was invited to visit Britain's parliament, but all the lady M.P.s protested. Maybe it was because when I visited Madame Tussauds wax museum, I called the statue of Winston Churchill "another damn limey."

But I enjoyed fighting the protest groups. I relished being an international fucking pig. I felt like Dillinger. Because I had such a disgusting reputation, the gangsters in any country I went to would open up their clubs for me to hang out in.

"Fuck them motherfuckers, Mike," they'd say. "We're with you."

I had met an awesome Russian girl at my hotel who saw my jewelry and told me to visit her at Graff Diamonds, the highest-end jewelry store in the world. She worked there translating for the Russian oligarchs and their wives when they visited the store. I went there with my fight promoter, Frank Warren, who was the Don King of Europe. She waited on me and she started flirting. She asked me what I was like as a boy and I told her, "I used to rob people and steal."

"Stop playing!" she said.

"No, really. I broke into houses and robbed people at gunpoint."

She showed me two amazing jewel-encrusted watches that cost about $800,000 U.S. each. Warren tried to be a big shot.

"I'm going to buy these for him," he told the girl. He had a relationship with the owners of the store. So I took the two watches along with a pair of diamond musical pocket watches and a diamond bracelet. The total bill was around $865,000.

I also picked up the girl and slept with her a few times before I had to go to Manchester to fight. I wasn't really worried about the fight. You could see that Francis wasn't training seriously; he came in at 243 pounds. He had gone to some army camp to get in shape and he got fatter. I don't think that the English press thought much of his chances. The London *Daily Mirror* gave him $50,000 to put an ad for their paper on the bottom of his boxing shoes. They got their money's worth. I knocked Francis down five times in the first four minutes of the fight before the ref stopped it.

When I got back to London, I called up my Russian girlfriend. While I was talking to her, I could hear some guy in the background saying, "Who is that, Tyson?" She hung up and came right to see me at my hotel. I started getting nervous. She had told me when I first met her that she was seeing this Chinese arms dealer named Michael.

Oh shit, I thought. *I am fucking dead.*

I was convinced he was going to follow her to my hotel. When she got there, I immediately barraged her with questions.

"Will Michael get mad? Is Michael the jealous type?"

"To hell with him," she said. "I don't care anymore. He's just a pain in the ass. But he does have a lot of money and he takes good care of me."

Jackie Rowe was in the room and she put some street shit on this naïve girl. The Russian girl was so overwhelmingly beautiful that she had never learned how to play games. But this time she had to because she was going to lose her sugar daddy if she did anything rash. I was going back to America the next day. I wish she could have come with me but that was impossible.

"No, no, no, no," Jackie told her. "You have to go back to him and tell him that everything is all right. Don't pull your head out of the lion's mouth abruptly. You've got to pull it easily out. Look, you need that money. Mike is going home. Don't lose that guy."

She took care of it. I knew that the guy was going to take her back. She was really an awesome lady.

I went back to the States, but it wasn't long before I got in trouble again. On May eighteenth, I was with my barber friend Mack chilling at Cheetahs strip club in Vegas. Back then when I wanted to get my head clear, I went to a strip club. That's just what people did back in the early 2000s.

So I was sitting on a couch at the back of the club next to the DJ booth, talking to my friend Lonnie who was one of the managers. This stripper, whose real name was Victoria but went by the stripper name of Flower, came up to me and asked me if I wanted a lap dance. I didn't want anything from her, but she was persistent. She kept insisting she give me a lap dance. She approached me a number of times, then she tried to sit down on my lap. I put up a hand to stop her and she teetered on her high heels and fell on her backside. I think I also called her a "skank" and a "dirty whore." She went back to her dressing room, embarrassed.

From the dressing room she called her husband and told him what had happened. He called the police and claimed that me and my entourage were at Cheetahs right that moment manhandling the strippers and throwing them around the club. The Vegas police dispatched eight cars to the scene. I talked to one of the cops who told me that when he was working the Vice division, strippers wouldn't take no for an answer. They were just hustlers trying to milk men dry. The cops took Flower aside and grilled her and she admitted that I never struck her and that she was fine, she was just embarrassed. She told the cops that her pride was hurt and she told me that if I had thrown her $500 this never would have happened. "After all this embarrassment I should be able to get something out of this," she told them. The cops then left and because there was no incident, they didn't charge me with anything. She finished her shift, doing lap dances and pole dances.

I guess she went home to her scam artist husband and he got to her because the next day she changed her story and filed a police report that claimed that "Tyson reached out with his open hand and punched/shoved her in the chest area causing her to literally fly across the room and land on the floor. She stated she was stunned and Tyson proceeded to call her a 'skanky whore' and 'a bitch.' She said she received bruises from the incident." The police then reopened the investigation and again found no merit to her claim, calling her allegations "completely unfounded."

But that didn't stop her. She sued me a few months later. In the suit she said, "Tyson's violent and painful blow sent Victoria several feet across the floor and caused her to fall on her tailbone, with the heel of her shoe sharply striking her leg as she landed on the floor." She claimed emotional distress, bodily injury, and stress in the marital relationship that curtailed their marital activities.

The case dragged on. The following April I had to give a deposition. I was not amused having to sit there and listen to her lawyer's bullshit questions. He was asking me to recount the situation when she approached me.

"You're sitting, if I understand it, and I'll try to make this short, you were sitting on, I guess, the couch area next to the deejay booth?"

"Yes."

"And how did she come at you?"

"She's a tramp. She insisted on giving me a lap dance. I said, 'No.' I didn't want a lap dance. She went away and came back and she was insisting. She tried to thrust herself upon me. I put my hand out."

"Did your hand come in contact with Miss Bianca?"

"Yeah, it could have, but from her being aggressive. My hand was out there for her to keep her distance away from me, not from me being aggressive, no."

He kept badgering me. I called him a piece of shit and a fucking dick. He called for a recess and huddled with my lawyer. We had offered him ten grand to settle the case, they were asking for forty. When they came back from recess, he told me he wasn't going to keep me anymore.

"I don't need to be here anymore, because your client is a liar. You don't want to keep me here, I've done nothing wrong," I said.

The case went to arbitration when their attorney claimed that we had accepted the forty-grand settlement. The arbitration judge ruled against her. They appealed. We arbitrated again and she got $8,800, plus I had to pay the arbitrator $1,615. And my attorney charged me $25,000. That was the most expensive lap dance I never had.

By June, I was back in Phoenix training for my next fight. I was in a really bad mood and I was taking it out on my probation officer who was a really nice woman. But I didn't get my ass thrown back in jail thanks to one of the greatest lawyers I ever came across. His name was Darrow Soll and he was a Jewish cat, a former Green Beret. He didn't look like a badass; he was big but not muscular big. He was solid. We really bonded. Darrow was a really smart lefty, ACLU-type guy. He told me his father had been killed by one of those white Aryan supremacists, but he would still defend Aryan Nation guys. Darrow would take up the cases of the black guys who were on death row unjustly and not even charge them, even though he was broke to the teeth half the time. He was a wonderful man.

He was connected in the Phoenix law scene and helped smooth out a lot of shit for me over the years. My probation officer Erika was trying to get me to do more community service, but two different places refused to take me, so I yelled at her a couple of times on the phone. But Darrow chilled her out and told her that "medication" problems were causing my bad behavior.

"Good news. After much discussion Erika agreed to omit Mike's verbal outbursts from her reports to her supervisor. She did this in large part because Mike was apologetic in his last meeting with her," he wrote in a memo to my team.

Now my English promoters were worried about that bullshit lawsuit from the Cheetah girl. If I had had a bad probation report I might not have been allowed back into the U.K. to fight Lou Savarese. I was due to leave on June sixteenth, but I was back in New York because one of my best friends Darryl Baum got murdered on June tenth. People called him "Homicide" but I still called him by his original street name, "Shorty Love." He hated that name because he hated anything that would make him seem soft and vulnerable. Shorty Love was from my neighborhood and he had a really notorious street rep for hurting people. I would always see him hanging around with the tough guys in the neighborhood. These guys were damn-near grown and he was just a little kid, but it was like he was the leader.

They called him Homicide because he was a knockout artist when he was twelve years old. He'd go up to someone on the street and knock them out with one punch and rob their jewelry or their sheepskin coat. In 1986, he went to jail on a two-to-six-year sentence for robbery. He was so violent in jail that he wound up serving twice his time. He finally got out on December 31, 1999. When he got out, I broke him off some money and bought him a nice Rolex and a chain and a Mercedes-Benz. I also offered to give him a job as one of my security men. I just wanted him to get off the streets and straighten out his life.

"Hang out with me," I told him. "Don't do that shit no more, we could get some money."

"I ain't going to take no fucking money from you, Mike," he said. "Too many people took money from you."

Shorty Love was gangster to the core. He wanted to be in that life. He got involved in a drug dispute between two rival gangs and they shot him dead six months after he got out of jail. Isn't it crazy? All of my old friends, they all got murdered or they killed somebody. They were good people just caught up in drugs, sex, and death. That's what my life was all about, being reckless.

I paid for Shorty's funeral. I rented out this big luxurious Italian funeral home in Brooklyn and we had to add three other rooms because so many people showed up to pay their respects to him.

So I reluctantly got on that plane to England to make my fight. As soon as I got to London I looked up my Russian girl, but she had gotten fired from Graff Diamonds. Frank Warren, my promoter, had never paid them the money for the jewelry he bought me when I was in London for the Francis fight. What was worse, Graff said they were going to sue me. I was furious. I'm a spoiled narcissistic little brat, so Mr. Warren was going to have to pay.

I told Tommy Brooks, my trainer, to tell Warren to come up to my hotel room.

Warren supposedly had the same gangster reputation that Don King had. He had all the European fighters scared and intimidated of him, so he came into the room oozing arrogance.

"You never paid for that jewelry you were going to buy for me," I said. "Isn't Don King your friend?"

"Yeah," he said with an attitude.

"Didn't Don tell you what happened when he disrespected me?"

"Yeah, he told me that you smacked him around."

"That didn't alarm you, when he told you that? You didn't get frightened?"

"No," he said with disdain.

Today I'm pretty much a wimpy guy, but back then if someone openly dissed me, there had to be violence involved. There was no diplomatic way it could be handled. The way he confronted me when I asked him those questions was not acceptable. He was looking at my face and telling me "No," but what he was really saying was, "You're not in America. You're just a fucking pussy, nigga."

Whack! I just started beating his ass. I broke his jaw with one punch. He fell down and I stomped him and broke his ribs. I picked up a paperweight off my dresser and I hit him in the face with it and broke his eye socket. Then I dragged him over to the window and almost threw him out onto the street. He was begging for his life.

"Oh, you're not such a tough guy now, huh, motherfucker?"

I threw him back down on the floor.

"You have the balls to talk to me like that and do what you did to me?" I screamed at him. "Take your motherfucking clothes off. Get naked."

"No," he pleaded.

I kicked him in the head.

"You've beaten me, isn't that enough?" he pleaded.

"You weren't thinking that when you didn't pay that bill, huh? Take your clothes off now."

He recovered enough to get to his feet and he sprinted out the door. I started chasing him down the hallway but I was in my socks and I kept slipping and he got away. I was furious.

Once I got to Scotland my mood lifted. The fight was in Glasgow and the reception for me there was overwhelming. I was doing some blow before the fight and I smoked some pot. There was no problem with the blow because that leaves your system right away, but for the pot, which stays in your system, I had to use my whizzer, which was a fake penis where you put in someone's clean urine to pass your drug test. Jeff Wald's assistant Steve Thomas used to travel with me and contribute.

I was high as a kite the day before the fight. They dressed me up in a kilt and I saluted the crowd from the top of a Mercedes-Benz. I was jumping up and down on the roof of the car screaming, "Champion! Champion!" and the people went crazy. A German man came up to me and told me it was a German car, trying to impress me that it was expensive.

"Big fucking deal," I said. "Oh, so this is what you did with the money that you stole from the Jews? You bought cars?" I shouldn't have said it; that was just me being political and disgusting.

Savarese was an interesting opponent for me. He was no tomato can. He had gone the distance and lost a split decision to George Foreman in 1997. In 1998 he knocked out Buster Douglas in one round. He had thirty-two KOs in forty-two bouts, but I didn't think he would pose any problem for me.

The bell rang and he went down from my first punch, a looping left hook that hit him up on the temple. He got up and I was all over him. He was on his way down again when the ref got in between us. I didn't realize that the ref was actually stopping the fight, so I kept punching and I accidentally hit him with a left hook and knocked him down. The British broadcasters later joked that that particular ref could never take a punch.

I was one of those spoiled-brat fighters. I thought I could get away with things like hitting the ref and not getting in trouble. But this particular time I really wasn't trying to hit the ref. I was just being mean until I hurt Savarese. I was really psyched up when Jim Gray from Showtime interviewed me after the fight.

"Mike, was that your shortest fight ever?"

"I bear witness there is only one God and Mohammed blesses and peace be upon him as his prophet. I dedicate this fight to my brother Darryl Baum, who died. I'll be there to see you, I love you with all of my heart. All praise be to my children, I love you, oh God, oh man, what?!"

"Is this your shortest fight ever, in any time? Amateur, professional, ever?"

"Assalamu alaikum Maida. I don't know man, yeah, Lennox Lewis, Lennox I am coming for you."

"Is it frustrating to train like you did and then have this over in seven or eight seconds?"

"I only trained probably two weeks or three weeks for this fight. I had to bury my best friend and I wasn't going to fight, but I dedicated this fight to him. I was going to rip his heart out, I am the best ever, I am the most brutal and the most vicious and most ruthless champion there has ever been, there is no one could stop me. Lennox is a conqueror? No! I am Alexander, he is no Alexander. I am the best ever, there has never been anybody as ruthless. I am Sonny Liston, I am Jack Dempsey, there is no one like me, I am from their cloth. There is no one that can match me, my style is impetuous, my defense is impregnable and I am just ferocious, I want your heart, I want to eat his children, praise be to Allah!"

With that, I stormed away. I was doing all this ranting because I was losing my mind. I was getting so high, my brain was getting fried. I was taking phrases from the Shaw Brothers karate movies like *Five Deadly Venoms*. I was quoting from Apocalypse, my favorite cartoon character. He was just a black badass and he always spoke so nobly. "Watch me and tremble as I bring the purity of oblivion to your world." I was a little guy but I talked big like that. I was talking that WWE wrestling patter, eating his babies. I thought I was a tough badass but I was really just a showman in my blood.

When I got back to London, there was a controversy brewing. I was still ready to kill Frank Warren. You can watch that fight and see how enraged I was. I was looking for him after the fight because he had no shame. He had a broken eye socket, cheekbone, and jaw, and still showed up at the fight. But back in London he went into hiding. The *Daily Record* newspaper had a front-page article saying that I attacked him in my hotel suite over $630,000 still owed for the jewelry. Warren told them that the story was "total rubbish." I had to hold a news conference to address the issue because back in the States my probation officer had some questions for me.

"Did you hit him?" a reporter asked me.

"No, sir."

"Did you try to throw him out a window?"

"No, sir. I love Frank Warren."

Back in the States my parole officer worried about my comments after the Savarese fight and about the alleged confrontation with Warren. Darrow smoothed it all out. I was even allowed to associate with Ouie.

One of the conditions of my parole was to see a psychiatrist, so I met with Dr. Barksdale and his associate in Tempe, Arizona. The meeting didn't go so well. But once again, Darrow came to the rescue.

"It is my understanding that the initial meeting with you and your partner may have been rough," he wrote Barksdale. "Notably, however, Mike telephoned me last night on an unrelated issue and explicitly asked whether he could see you and your partner again. I must tell you that, based upon my experience with Mike, this was quite encouraging."

I was back in Vegas. One of the reasons why I was in such great shape for the two fights in the U.K. was that I had taken to walking thirty miles a day, sometimes in 105-degree weather. I usually walked alone, but I had some foolish friends who thought that it might be a joyride to walk with me and pick up girls along the way, but it wasn't like that. There was no talking, no stopping, I was just zoning out. One friend of mine had a heart attack walking with me.

I started these long walks when I was reading a book about Alexander the Great and his army. They were walking sixty miles a day back then so I just said, "Fuck this, I can do this." I got to ten miles a day and my feet felt like someone had taken a blowtorch to them. I had great sneakers on too, New Balance, and they still felt like someone set them on fire. I did a little more reading and I found out that all these great warriors would do these marches high. The history of war is the history of drugs. Every great general and warrior from the beginning of time was high.

So I started incorporating weed and alcohol into my walking regimen. I was pissed off in general but walking high in over 100-degree heat took my bipolar shit to a new level. Liquor, the weed, and the heat didn't go together. I'd be walking bare-chested with my shirt tied around my head. My pants were falling off because I had lost so much weight. The sun had fried me, so I was as black as tar. I looked like a crackhead. People would see me and they didn't know if it was me or not. One guy came up to me for an autograph and, pow, I smacked him. I saw a girl I had slept with one time who worked at Versace. She was concerned about me.

"Mike, are you all right?" she asked me.

"Fuck you, bitch," I yelled at her. "I hate your guts. I never liked you."

The sun had really fried my brains, I was losing my mind.

I didn't carry any money on me and I'd get so dehydrated that I'd stumble into stores and the guys in there gave me water. Sometimes the local news choppers would be overhead following me around like I was O.J. in the Bronco.

All this walking was driving my security crazy. They nicknamed me Gump after Forrest Gump. Anthony Pitts would try to follow me at a discrete distance, but sometimes I'd lose him. Sometimes I didn't even know he was around. I'd walk over to Cheetahs from my gym and Anthony had the managers primed to call him when I got there. Then Anthony and my other guys would take turns sitting in the parking lot watching for me.

One time, I walked all the way over to my friend Mack's barbershop from my house. It was a particularly hot day and I had a big bag of weed with me. I was hanging out with Mack at his house, but then he had to go pick up some clothes from the dry cleaner so I started walking home. I was so out of it that I was talking to myself. I got a few blocks when I saw Anthony following me in his Suburban. I was high and I just snapped. I didn't care if I lived or died. I'd go through spurts like that. In my stoned paranoid mind, Anthony was spying on me. Why did he want to go everywhere I fucking went? It slipped my mind that I was paying him to do this.

So I turned down an alleyway that led to a police station. By the time Anthony followed me, I was complaining to the cops and pointing him out. Anthony got out of his truck.

"I'm hired to look after you and now you need to get in the truck," Anthony said. "Come on, we're going back home."

"I'm not getting in," I said. "This guy is bothering me. I want this man arrested. He's been following me." I was screaming, and all the time I had a huge bag of weed on me.

The cops then started questioning Anthony and I took off. I was a few blocks away but Anthony caught up with me again. I was so pissed off that I picked up a brick that was lying in the gutter and threw it right through the windshield of his Suburban. Shawnee sent him the money to replace his window the next day.

On August twenty-second I was fined $187,500 for accidentally hitting that ref in Glasgow. It was the largest fine in U.K. history. I looked at it as a value-added tax. Besides, I was getting ready to make $20 million fighting Andrew Golota, the Foul Pole. Golota, a huge gentleman of Polish descent, had the reputation of being the dirtiest fighter in boxing. He was ahead in two fights with Riddick Bowe when he was disqualified for repeated low blows. I had gone to the same special ed school as Bowe so I was really psyched to win a fight for him.

We held a press conference in L.A. on September fourteenth to hype the fight and I was my vintage self.

"I'm a convicted rapist! I'm an animal! I'm the stupidest person in boxing! I gotta get outta here or I'm gonna kill somebody," I mock screamed.

"I'm on this Zoloft thing, right? But I'm on that to keep me from killing y'all. That's why I'm on that. Listen, now I'm out here fighting, right? They got me on some shit that got my dick fucked up, they got me on all type of shit, right? I'm just keeping it real here, right? I don't want to be taking the Zoloft, but they are concerned about the fact that I'm a violent person, almost an animal. And they only want me to be an animal in the ring."

I was on a roll. Or at least on some deep weed.

"You report on boxing, but you all have never fought, never been the champion and don't know our pain, our sweat. Don't know it's so fucking lonely. Boxing's the loneliest sport in the world. You know what I'm saying? I didn't fuck my wife in a year. Do you think I give a damn about Andrew Golota? I haven't seen my kids in months."

"Why?" one of the reporters interrupted my monologue.

"None of your damned business, white boy, but I haven't seen them in months. And you think I give a damn about you and any of y'all? I don't care if I'm living or dying. I'm a dysfunctional motherfucker. Bring Andrew Golota on, bring those guys, they can keep their title, I don't want their title, I want to strip them of their fucking health. Because I'm in pain, I want them to see pain, I want their kids to see pain. Lennox Lewis, I want his kids to go, 'Ooo Daddy, are you okay, Daddy?' Yeah, I don't care about them, because they don't care about me and my kids."

When I got back to my house in Vegas, I was playing with two new cub cats that I smuggled in. By then, I had to get rid of Kenya. We were keeping her in Texas and my trainer was showing her to some animal enthusiasts who supposedly worked with tigers. I don't know what happened but I heard that the lady enthusiast climbed over the fence to get Kenya and things went terribly wrong. They're no good after tasting that blood, so I had to get rid of Kenya. We donated her to a zoo in California. I got sued, of course, but I won the case. I didn't have to give the lady any money but I felt bad, so I gave her $250,000. She deserved something, I thought.

The Golota fight was in Detroit on October twentieth. The night before the fight I was really nervous. When I saw Golota in person at the weigh-in, I freaked out. He was really big and crazy and he had all those big red bumps over his back from taking steroids. He looked like a fucking leper. *What the fuck am I doing here fighting this big crazy guy,* I kept thinking while I was lying in bed trying to sleep. So I lit up a joint and as soon as I took that first toke my whole mood changed. *Fuck that nigga,* I thought. Whoa, I needed that joint.

The night of the fight I refused to take a urine test before I went out. I figured I'd just get the whizzer from Steve Thomas afterwards. Puffy and Lil Wayne were there and we had some rappers from the Cash Money crew rap me into the ring. I had my best game face on when we met in the center of the ring. I felt bad for that little ref. Between me and Golota, one of us might clock his ass.

The first round, I went to Golota's body a lot and I could sense him breaking down. I was moving pretty fluidly and I was working off my jab. Jab in the face, boom, boom, then some punches to the body. He was keeping his left hand low. He threw a weak jab and I went under him and, boom, I cut his left eye with a punch. With about ten seconds to go in the round, I got in a solid straight right hand and down he went.

I went after him at the beginning of the second round. I was swinging wild punches that were missing, but I got in some punishment to his body. By the end of the round, he was retreating and just slapping his punches at me.

I was up and ready for round three to start when I couldn't believe my eyes. Golota was fighting with his corner. I watched the Showtime feed later and Golota didn't want to go out for another round, but his cornerman, this small, old Italian guy, Al Certo, was screaming at him.

"Throw your right fucking hand," Certo said.

"I'm stopping the fight," Golota said.

"Don't you dare, you cocksucker. You're gonna win this fight."

"Stop it," Golota said.

"Don't talk like that. C'mon, you fuck you. You're gonna win this."

"I quit," Golota said. And got up and pushed Certo to the side and started pacing around the ring. I didn't know what the fuck this lunatic was doing.

"No, no," Certo screamed at him.

Golota walked over to the ref.

"I quit," he said. And the ref waved the fight off.

But Certo wasn't finished. When Golota got back to his corner, Certo tried to stuff his mouthpiece in and push him back out. But Golota had had enough. He put his robe on and rushed out of the ring. On the way to the dressing room, he was pelted with all kinds of shit and someone threw an orange soda and hit him and his whole body turned orange.

Afterwards, Golota tried to blame his quitting on getting dizzy from head butts but he just quit on his stool. He was one of those guys who went nuts from the pressure of fighting. But the next day, Golota's wife took him to a hospital in Chicago and the doctor diagnosed him with a concussion and a fractured left cheekbone, the one that was the target of the right hand that floored him.

As soon as I got back to my dressing room, the Michigan officials rushed in to give me my urine test. Because of Golota, they probably were testing for steroids, so I didn't have time to get the whizzer from Steve Thomas. I had to give them my own urine. Of course, they found the weed in my system. They should have given me a bonus for fighting under pot because it dulls your aggression. They suspended me for ninety days, which didn't matter because I wasn't going to fight anyway, but they also fined me $5,000 and made me donate $200,000 to a Michigan-based charity. And they took away my TKO and changed it to a no-decision.

Even with that $20 million from that fight, I was fucked financially. It got so bad that I started hustling some Malaysian promoters who wanted me to fight over there. They sent this lady named Rose Chu to convince me and she spent weeks at my house. They offered me a site fee of $16 million and they gave me a million-dollar advance and I even got them to spend $200,000 on renovations to my house and a down payment for a new Rolls-Royce.

At the beginning of 2001 my accountants sent me a cash flow breakdown for the year 2000. I had started the year $3.3 million in the hole. I earned $65.7 million in 2000, including a $20 million settlement from Sidley, my former business manager. They knew what they had done with Don was highway robbery, so they were happy to settle. The problem was that I spent $62 million that year—$8 million for taxes, $5.1 million for legal fees, $5 million to Monica, $4.1 million to repay a loan from one of my promoters, $3.9 million to Rooney for his suit, $3.4 million in payroll, $2.1 million for cars, $1.8 million infusion into Iron Mike Records, the shit added up.

Of course, my new management team had no answers. They were at one another's throats. Jackie was telling me that Shawnee was ripping me off royally.

"Mike, she's stealing money. Whenever you fight and you get a new car, she buys the same car you've got. She's a player. She don't play checkers, she plays chess," Jackie said. I got them on a three-way call but Shawnee started crying and said, "I told you she don't like me."

Shawnee had visited the seventy-five-thousand-square-foot office that Jackie had opened in Brooklyn for Iron Mike Records and Shawnee decided she needed the same luxurious offices in Atlanta where she lived. Like an idiot I agreed. I never once stepped foot in those offices.

The truth was I couldn't give a shit about my business. I wanted to deal with my vices and nothing else. My attitude was, *I don't give a fuck*. Why would I think like that when I was at the top of my game? The sad truth is that no one ever had my best interests at heart except for Cus. I still can't believe that he put that money aside for me in an IRA. When I think about that, I cry to this very day.

Things didn't get better in June of 2001 when Camille died. I plunged deeper into depression and took more drugs. But I had to start training for my next fight, which was going to be in Denmark, so we set up camp at Big Bear City in San Bernardino County, California.

Monica and the kids came to stay with me for a few days. The day after they left, Rick Bowers, one of my security guys, and I went to the local Kmart because that was the only place in town to get certain provisions. There was an older woman, maybe fifty or so, at one of the cash registers. She was far from a looker but she had a dynamite body. She asked me for an autograph when we were checking out and then slipped me her phone number. Dog that I am, I called her and she came over to the house that Rick and I were staying in.

We had sex on the couch in the living room. The next morning Rick took Crocodile to the emergency room because Croc wanted to have something looked at. The Kmart woman was there and she told Rick that she "did something I shouldn't have done." I had told her the night before that we shouldn't be having sex because I was in training. She also told Rick that I had hurt her during the sex and that she needed treatment. Then she asked him how I felt about her since we had sex. Later she called Rick and arranged to meet him at the local Denny's. She told Rick that she liked me and that she was disappointed that I hadn't come with him. She kept bugging Rick to call me and tell me to come down because she wanted to go out with me again.

Then she started calling Rick on his cell and warned us to leave town because the D.A. wanted her to press charges. She also said she was going to the tabloids. Rick said, "How do we fix this?" and she said, "I just need a new car," because she had some run-down piece of shit.

Rick came back to the house.

"What's up with that Kmart lady? She says you hurt her," Rick said.

"Huh?" I had no idea what he was talking about.

We decided to go and confront her at her job. We met her in the parking lot and she was just nuts. She started talking about going to the tabloids with the story and that she needed a new car. I listened for a few seconds and then I turned to Rick.

"Let's get out of here, I told you she was crazy," I said.

Now she really got pissed. There were people around us in that parking lot and she felt disrespected.

The next day, July eighteenth, we opened the papers to see that this lunatic was saying that I had raped her. I went to the gym and there were hordes of media trying to get me to make a statement.

Within hours, Darrow was on the case. He went to the gym, told Rick to go back to the house and pack all our shit, and in a half hour we were all on a small prop jet heading to L.A. Then Darrow went back to Big Bear City and went to work.

It's amazing how similar this claim was to Desiree Washington's. Both of them were trying to get in touch with me after sex and I wasn't returning calls. Both of them flipped out when I treated them like a cad after. The difference was that this time I had a genius of a lawyer who actually did something proactive to defend me. He began by interviewing some of the Kmart lady's coworkers. He found a close friend who worked with her who told him that the alleged victim had approached her at work the day after and told her that she had "made love" with me. She described me as being "sweet" and "nice" and how she "liked" my kisses and sweet talk. She also drew a picture of a large penis on a piece of paper and told her friend that I was that big and that she actually was hurt after having sex with me. She asked her friend to drive her to my house so she could get an apology from me for disrespecting her. She was disappointed because she expected "red carpet" treatment from me and I didn't even serve her any refreshments. She also told her friend that she wanted things to "go a little farther" to get revenge against me because I didn't apologize to her.

Darrow didn't stop there. He got a call from the Kmart lady's nephew, Kermit, and set up a meeting at Kermit's apartment. Kermit told Darrow that he rented his apartment and that "I sure wish I had the two million dollars to afford the entire building." Darrow then asked Kermit if he could record their conversation and Kermit said, "That's not the way I do business. I guess you don't want to do business."

Darrow found the manager of Kmart, who told him, "You can't believe anything she says." Her manager also told Darrow that the woman was openly discussing her rape allegations with anyone who would listen, including her customers at Kmart. She was enjoying all the attention from the tabloids. Darrow also talked to the lady's landlord who told him that she wasn't "a very credible individual." He even found a customer of the lady who ran a computer business who gave Darrow a tape of a conversation between the lady and himself because the woman wanted to meet him after work. She told the computer guy that she was frustrated with her situation at home with her husband and that she sought out physical companionship elsewhere. When the computer guy told her he didn't want to have an affair, she started harassing him with phone calls.

Last but not least, Darrow even got affidavits from two prominent doctors who said that pain and/or bleeding is often a consequence of consensual sex.

Darrow put all of these interviews into a hundred fifty pages that he presented to the D.A. of San Bernardino County. He told the D.A. that under the California penal code the D.A. was "obligated to inform the grand jury of evidence that reasonably tends to negate guilt" and that his investigation had uncovered a wealth of evidence that

strongly supports "Mr. Tyson's unwavering contention that he has engaged in *absolutely no criminal wrongdoing whatsoever.*"

Meanwhile, the Kmart lady got that ambulance chaser Gloria
Allred to represent her in a civil claims case. And Showtime was concerned that the allegations had received press around the world that
could "seriously impede Showtime's ability to conduct its preparations
for Tyson's next bout in Copenhagen." They wanted a resolution to see
if the D.A. would press charges. They got it. After receiving the amazing document Darrow had prepared, the San Bernardino D.A. refused
to return an indictment against me. I guess sometimes justice does
prevail.

Then they tried to screw me again. A few weeks later, I was lying
down in the television room at my Vegas house, watching ESPN
SportsCenter. I could smell the fried chicken that Chef Drew was
whipping up in the kitchen for lunch. Just a typical Vegas morning.
Until my assistant Darryl rushed into the room. "Yo, Mike. I think
the Taliban is here." He seemed hysterical.

"Darryl, shut the fuck up," I said. It was about ten days after the
terrible attacks on 9/11.

"No, really, I think the Taliban are on the property." Darryl didn't
crack a smile.

"What are you talking about?" I said.

"Mike, come here, please," he said. So we walked outside.

There were about a hundred guys with green camouflage outfits
on, assault weapons in their hands, and hand grenades dangling off
their belts. They each held a big clear protective shield in their other
hand. They were slowly advancing on the house, periodically hiding
behind my massive palm trees. On top of that, there were two huge
battering ram tanks coming through each of the big wrought-iron
gates of my property that had the word SWAT stenciled on their side.
We heard a buzzing sound and looked up. There were helicopters in
the sky. My house was being invaded.

By now the whole battalion were getting ready to go through the
front door. They had their clear shields in front of them and their guns

in their hands and their blouse pants over their boots. Then they drew down in front of us.

"Freeze! Stop moving!" one of them barked.

I stood still.

Click, click, click, the sound of cocked rifles wafted through the air.

"Bin Laden is not here. We don't have anything to do with that nine-eleven stuff," Darryl said. He had probably been watching too much CNN. They did look like military guys on an exercise in the desert. The only problem was this desert was my property.

They finally identified themselves. They weren't the Taliban, they were the Vegas police. I'd never seen so many police in one spot in Vegas in my life. They said they were there to investigate a charge that I had held a young woman hostage in the house for three days and had raped her. I had some armed guards on the property who Darryl had set up in a guard shack. I guess this young lady had told the authorities that we had guns on the property so they came overly prepared. We had just changed the work policy and the guards were working from dusk to dawn. It was about eleven a.m. when the police stormed in, so the guards were already gone for the day and the gates were open.

As soon as Rick saw the troops invading us, he was on the phone with my lawyer Darrow Soll. Darrow told him to get me out of the house and to say nothing, not a word, to the police. Sounded right to me. They searched us and then they ordered us all off the premises. They made Darryl stay because he was the property manager and could give them access to everywhere they wanted to go. For some reason they let Chef Drew stay too. But while they had him on the ground, the smell of burning chicken came from the kitchen. They let him up so he could go back to the kitchen and stop the house from burning down.

With only Darryl and Drew there, they began to tear my house apart—room by room, box by box, paper by paper. They lifted box springs and mattresses off the beds. They went through every video. They were there from eleven in the morning until one in the morning the next day. Hell, at one point they even ordered pizza in and had a dinner break. They were nice enough to offer Darryl a slice but he refused.

They wound up confiscating a bunch of stuff including my personal sex tapes. I kept calling in through the day. "Darryl, are they still there?"

"Yeah, Mike, they're tearing the house apart."

I had gone to the gym and then had my bodyguard Rick drop me off at another girlfriend's house. I was confused as to why these guys were raiding my house. It turns out, I had met the girl who called the police at Mack's barbershop. I brought her back to the house and she basically moved in for about a week. I'd leave her when I went to train and she'd be going into the kitchen wearing only one of my T-shirts and have Chef Drew whip up some food for her. She knew all the security codes to the house and the gate, so she could come and go as she pleased. So how was she kidnapped? When she finally left the house, Rick drove her home. She left happy. So what could have compelled her to say all that shit about me so my ass got raided?

I found out when a record producer friend of mine called me from Houston. He told me that the girl was seeing another very prominent boxer. When she got back to him after being with me, he was furious. And he beat the shit out of her. Then he told her to go to the police and report that I had kidnapped her and held her against her will.

I was really pissed off. I couldn't be certain that this other boxer was behind all this shit, but if he was, he was as good as dead. But I'm a strong believer in karma—that bad things happen to bad people. I contemplated laying him down and he must have figured I would because he increased his security. But his bodyguards would have meant nothing. I knew a little gangbanging guy from the hood who used to take me to my community service. He told me to just say the word and he would make a call and I'd have two hundred people, all strapped, standing with me. I appreciated the offer but I turned him down. I never did pursue revenge. I even got high with that boxer a few years later. I really wanted to fuck him up then. But I let it slide.

After the raid on my house, the girl's identity got out, and reporters would come down to the barbershop to try and interview me. Mack would hide me in the back room and deny seeing me that day. Mack even called Stewart Bell, the district attorney, and told him that he had introduced the girl to me. He said that she was no prisoner; she was even driving my car all around town. Mack told him that he was concerned because I was supposed to leave soon for Copenhagen for my next fight.

"Don't worry about that," Bell told Mack. "Mike can go fight there. We have more investigating to do and if anything happens it will be after the fight."

We had a little drama on the flight to Copenhagen for the Brian Nielsen fight. Crocodile started throwing up and then he passed out. He had OD'd. They rushed him to the hospital. Three days went by and we actually thought that Crocodile had died, but when we went to the weigh-in, he showed up like nothing had happened. Crocodile was one of those guys who could do drugs night and day and then stop cold turkey and go train a fighter for six weeks. Then he'd come back and get high like nothing happened.

"Yo, man, what you been doing?" I'd ask him.

"I haven't got high since the last time I saw you," he said.

"Listen, I haven't stopped since the last time I saw you," I said. "Fuck, how do you do that?"

When I get high, I have to be arrested to stop. We had Darrow along with us on that trip. Shortly after we got there one of those big Danish biker types said something to Anthony Pitts's wife and Darrow just turned around and, wop, knocked the guy out cold with one punch. He actually beat Anthony to that punch.

"This is the best," I said. "I've got my lawyer and my fucking bodyguard with me at the same time."

Denmark went crazy over us. They sold out the huge arena in no time. I hadn't fought in over a year and I figured that I could get some rounds in with Nielsen. He was the IBC champ at the time but it was pretty meaningless. They called him Super Brian and his record was 62-1, but he really hadn't fought any high-caliber fighters in their prime. He had beaten Bonecrusher Smith, Tim Witherspoon, and

Larry Holmes, but they were on the way down when he met them. But he was a big boy, 6'4" and 260 pounds, so I had a big target to aim at. I punished him with body blows in the first round and with seconds to go in the third, I knocked him down with a series of devastating combinations. He went down like a redwood tree. If the ropes hadn't cushioned his fall I think he would have split the ring in two. It was only the second time in his long career that he had been down. I was having a good time in the ring. I had put on some weight, ostensibly because he was so heavy, but in reality, I hadn't trained much for the fight. I came in at 239 pounds, my heaviest fighting weight ever, so I wanted to get some rounds in.

I battered him around the ring for six rounds. At the beginning of the seventh, he just stayed on his stool. He had a cut over his left eye and I had been working it all night. He told the ref he couldn't see out of the eye, but he really was just worn out. But he was a nice guy. Nobody liked him because he was really arrogant, but I related to him.

Once the fight was over, we went into full party mode. I had a big suite and Croc and I got some weed and some booze and we had girls come up. They were normal, straight girls, not hookers or dancers, just nine-to-five corporate types. There was a big sex scene in Denmark with all these sex clubs, but that was a little too crazy for me even. Their concept of sex over there and Germany and the Balkan states was too aggressive.

Crocodile was going crazy over there. He was fucking the promoter's daughter. Then he got a Palestinian girl in the bathroom of my suite and I walked in on them.

"Hey . . . Hey, brother." I tapped him on the shoulder and we started tag-teaming her. We went back in the room and there were all these other girls there and we started having sex with them. I was on one side of the room and Croc was on the other and I heard one of the girls say, "I love you, Crocodile."

"How do you love him?" I shouted from across the room. "You've only been knowing him for a week."

I even nailed the tough female bodyguard that was the head of the security team that the Danish promoter had hired. She looked real tough and had her hair up in a bun, but Crocodile was amazed when he walked into my room and she was in the bed with her hair down, wearing one of my T-shirts, looking all feminine. She really fell for me. She even followed me back to the States, but I didn't pursue the relationship.

After a few days of partying in Copenhagen, everyone went back home, but Crocodile and I stayed and partied all over Europe for the next two months. We went to Amsterdam, of course, and smoked the whole time. That was where I finally learned how to roll a blunt. I was so high and still tired from the fight, so we just got some girls up to our massive suites in the hotel and stayed in for most of the time.

From Amsterdam we went to Barcelona. We were all over the place. But then one of my trainers started calling Crocodile, telling him to get me back home, so we eventually went back.

I hung around New York for a while, and I took Crocodile to Brownsville to see my old neighborhood. Crocodile was driving one of my Rollses and it was midnight and we pulled over to a corner. About a hundred guys came up to the car and they were losing it. They were so happy to see me. I broke them off some money. Later that night, I went to Jackie's house to sleep and told Crocodile to get himself a hotel room. When I woke up in the morning, I looked out the window and there were thirty guys standing around my car watching Crocodile sleep.

"Why didn't you sleep in a hotel?" I asked him.

"Man, I just wanted to sleep in the car," he told me. But later I found out that he thought the hotels around there were like flophouses.

While I was waiting for Shelly Finkel to negotiate a fight for the heavyweight crown, I had a warm-up fight. I was at the Sugar Hill Disco in Brooklyn in the early hours of December sixteenth. I was chilling with my childhood friend Dave Malone and a bunch of girls when this broad, tall guy came in. He was wearing a big mink coat and a nice hat. I thought that for sure this guy was a gangster.

"Mike, have a drink with me. C'mon, you can't fuck with the little people anymore?" he asked.

I gave him some respect and we had a few glasses of champagne and we smoked a little weed. He told me his name was Mitchell Rose and that he was the first person to beat Butterbean.

"Mike, if me and you would have fought, you would attack and I would counter," he bragged.

"Brother, can you be kind enough to say that again?" I said. "I thought you said something, but I wasn't sure."

"If me and you would have had a fight, you would attack and I would lean back and counter," he said, as he hit on a joint.

"Pass me the joint," I said.

He passed it to me and I tore off the end where his lips had touched the joint before taking a hit.

"Pass me my champagne," I said.

He gave me the flute. I threw the glass on the floor.

"Get the fuck out of here, nigga," I snarled.

I got up and I was going to go for him right there in the club but David defused it. Eventually Mitchell left.

A short time later, me and David and about four girls left the club. And right there on the sidewalk was Mitchell Rose.

"Hey, Mike, go on home with those chicken heads," he said, referring to the girls. That was it. I jolted after him, and his mink coat came off. I started throwing vicious lefts and rights, but he slid away from my drunken swings and took off. So I picked up the mink coat, pulled down my pants, and wiped my ass with his mink. By now the sun had come up and there were a lot of people going to work and the buses were driving past and the whole club had spilled out onto the sidewalk and everyone was watching me wipe my ass with his coat. Oh, God! Can you imagine if it was today with all the video cameras in the phones?

Nobody can make a better fool out of me than myself. I'm so much like my mother in that respect. Once my mother started up, she'd rant and tell people to "suck her pussy" and to "fuck off." Then later, we'd both feel bad about what we had done.

Four months later, Rose filed a $66 million lawsuit against me. He wanted money for attempted assault on him and actual assault on his mink coat. He also wanted $50 million for punitive damages. This guy still haunts me to this day, trying to piggyback me for notoriety. He even wrote a self-published pamphlet called *Mike Tyson Tried to Kill My Daddy.*

The negotiations to fight Lennox Lewis were in their final stages and we were set to meet in April, so I decided to party a little bit more before I started to train. Less than a week after the Mitchell Rose street fight, I took two young female street girls on vacation to Jamaica. They were my hangout partners. I would go to Versace and dress them. We had sex and got high together and if I wanted other girls they would get me some awesome chicks. I always had girls who would get me other girls. So if you saw me with a beautiful girl, you might have thought I was having sex with her but most likely she was gay or bisexual and it wasn't me she was interested in. And I'd get girls too, so we'd both help each other out.

When Shelly heard that I was going to Jamaica, he flipped out. He knew I'd be wearing the most expensive jewelry and back then people were getting robbed and killed in Jamaica right and left. So he sent the great Jamaican fighter Michael McCallum, who was a world champion in three weight divisions, to get my jewelry.

"McCallum, nice to see you," I said. "What are you doing here?"

"They sent me to come and get your stuff," he said.

"Come hang with us, bro. It's going to be a blast," I said.

"All right. But first you've got to take your jewelry off. These people are poor, Mike, if they see it they'll take it," he said.

"Fuck that shit," I said. "They don't want to take it; they want to see me with it. They ain't gonna respect me if I go down there without my jewelry," I said.

He was reluctant but I wouldn't budge. And we went all over the worst parts of Jamaica and nobody tried anything. All we got was love. I got the highest I had ever been in my life at Damian Marley's house, which had belonged to his dad. We were getting so high, we were sweating. And that wasn't no down weed, that was weed that kept you numb. It was exotic, intense yet still relaxed.

One night McCallum took me to, of all places, a strip club. I was looking at all of these awesome Jamaican girls.

"Hey, Mike, I would like to get some of them to accompany me back to the hotel. How much do you think it would cost?" I asked him.

"You could probably get that one there for forty thousand," he said.

"Forty thousand dollars for her?" I couldn't believe it.

"No, no, that's Jamaican money. Twenty dollars U.S.," he explained.

"Fuck, let's get them all. Tell the place to close down," I said.

"They can't do that, Mike," he said. "Pick three of them."

So I picked three hot ones and we all went back to my room and partied.

When it was almost New Year's Eve, I decided to leave the girls behind in Jamaica and bring in the New Year in Cuba for a few days. Rick, my security guy, insisted that he go with me. He was holding my passport. I didn't know it but Shelly was nervous that if the Cuban government stamped my passport, the Americans wouldn't let me back in the country.

As soon as I got off the plane, I felt like I was in heaven. Being in Cuba is like being in a time capsule set for 1950. They've restored all these old-school American cars from the '50s and the houses all look like they're from that era. As soon as we checked into our hotel, I ditched Rick. I wanted to check out the people. That was actually the second thing I did. The first thing I did was snort some coke. I had brought my drugs along from Jamaica.

The Cuban people were wonderful. I walked around and nobody bothered me. No one said anything to me except for maybe coming up to me and asking me for a hug or seeing if I needed anything. Everyone was so hospitable and protective. It wasn't a crazy mob scene like in Scotland or England or Japan. The Cubans were pretty hands-off. Maybe they thought I was crazy. But a good crazy, because they were all smiling and laughing.

I had been walking around Havana through the ghettos and the alleyways for a couple of hours when this guy came up to me. He spoke perfect English.

"Mr. Tyson! Mr. Tyson! I saw you walking, I couldn't believe it was you. You can't be walking by yourself in these streets. You need family. Yo, Poppy, you stay with me, in my house."

"All right, cool," I said. I'm that kind of guy.

He took me to his house and now I had to line up a woman.

"So what is happening here?" I asked. "Show me the ladies. I'd like to go to a nightclub."

"Oh, no, you don't go to nightclub for that. You need a wife? Stay right here."

And this guy ran out, jumped a fence, ducked into an alleyway and minutes later, out of nowhere, he came back with this beautiful young lady wearing a summer dress.

"I have your wife," he said. "Is this one okay?"

I couldn't believe I could possibly do any better. I didn't want to mess this up and make this girl feel I didn't like her. How could he possibly top this girl?

"This one is just fine," I said.

I thought this was some pimp/ho shit, so I reached into my pocket.

"How much do I owe you? How many dineros?"

"No, no, no," he said. "You are family now. This is your wife."

This woman was wonderful. If I needed anything, she'd get it for me. She was so attentive. We walked around a bit and then we went back to this guy's house because he wanted to make us a nice dinner.

His wife cooked some nice lobsters and then the guy brought a couple of bottles of wine to the table. I couldn't believe my eyes. One of them was a bottle of Lafite Rothschild. That was a $2,000 bottle, but these people didn't have money like that. They were living in what was basically a run-down tenement building. I thought that maybe somebody in this guy's family had worked at one of the hotels that Meyer Lansky owned and when the revolution came, they took off with this bottle. He was trying to be hospitable, bringing out his nicest bottle of wine, but I didn't have the heart to drink it. So I suggested that we open the cheaper bottle.

My host planned a big night out for us. We were all going to go to the spectacular stage show they put on in the Copa Room at the old

Hotel Habana Riviera, which used to be owned by Lansky. The only problem was that on the way to the Riviera, I had to lean my head out of the cab and projectile vomit. I didn't realize it at the time, but the lobsters had been boiled in unpurified water and I must have gotten a bad case of Montezuma's revenge.

I tried to make it through the show but I couldn't. I was as sick as a motherfucker, but that didn't stop me from being my pervy self. I wanted to get my girl back to my hotel room. I was thinking that this vomiting shit was going to go away and my dick was going to get hard.

So I got my wife and I thanked my host by giving him a beautiful expensive ruby bracelet I had on, and then we got a cab back to my hotel. My girl had never been in a nice hotel because the Cuban government doesn't allow locals to go into tourist hotels. They claim that they do that to protect the tourists from prostitutes who might slip them a Mickey and rob them but I think they just don't want the Cuban people to get a taste of the luxury life.

Before I could get to my room, there were Cuban TV film crews set up in the lobby. I guess the news that I was there had spread. I was bare-chested and I didn't have any underwear on and my pants were loose from all the vomiting and you could see my plumber's crack, so the last thing I wanted was the paparazzi to film me. I went berserk. I picked up some of their equipment and threw it at them, then I grabbed three glass Christmas ornaments off the tree and chucked them at the press. I punched one of the photographers in the head. I went crazy, but the paparazzi picked up their cameras and split.

When we got to the check-in desk, I thought that I'd have to finesse my girl inside, but the receptionist told me that government officials had called the hotel and that it would be okay for me to bring any guests to my room. We went to bed and the girl was on me, but I was so sick I couldn't do anything. I felt better in the morning, and Rick and I were flying back to Jamaica on an early flight. I had sex with the girl before we left and she was sad that I was leaving. I had given away all my money and most of my jewelry except for this diamond chain I was wearing that was worth fifty or sixty thousand. To me that was like buying a candy bar. She was hesitant to take it, but I forced her to. I was hoping that she'd sell it and make enough money to support her whole family for a few years at least.

I left my girl in the hotel room and I met Rick in the lobby. We went to the airport to wait for our plane and we were both ravenously hungry, but Rick didn't have any money on him either. I was surrounded by tourists asking me for my autograph, so I started bartering the autographs for food.

"Please, if you would be kind enough to buy us some food for the autograph?" I asked. In case they didn't speak English, I demonstrated by pointing to the food stand and making believe I was eating.

When I got to Cuba, I must have weighed 270, but when I got back to Jamaica, I had lost about thirty pounds. I hadn't considered that I had food poisoning or some parasite. In fact, it wasn't until one of the girls I had brought from New York saw me that she triggered a huge alarm in my head.

"Mike, you lost so much weight, even though you haven't been training. You look good," she said.

Oh shit, I thought.

I was convinced I had AIDS. When I had taken those strippers home that night before I had gone to Cuba, I was fucking one of them and my rubber just popped. And as soon as the woman realized what had happened she had a really strange look on her face. I was convinced that she had given me AIDS. But maybe she thought that I had given it to her.

13

I WAS WORRYING THE WHOLE FLIGHT BACK TO NEW YORK. I WAS ALSO STILL A
little high from the last of the coke I had in Jamaica. Usually I just
breezed through customs with the royal treatment, but this time I
was met by people from Homeland Security. And these guys were all
hard-asses.

"What were you doing in Cuba?" one of them asked.

How did they know I was in Cuba? It wasn't on my passport. Then
I remembered the fight I had with the paparazzi in the lobby of the
hotel. It was all over the news.

"I was just hanging out for New Year's," I said.

"So you figured you'd just take off and go to Cuba for a New Year's
vacation for a day, disregarding the laws we have in place that pro-
hibit travel to Cuba," the official said.

"I did it from Jamaica," I said, as if that was any better.

"Did you spend any American funds?" he asked.

"I had Cuban currency but nobody took it. They only take U.S. dollars over there," I told him. I bought Cuban money because I thought they would take it, but I got scammed.

This was not the best time to be caught sneaking into Cuba. Bush had just been elected and he said that he was going to crack down on any relations with the Castro government, so I played the religion card.

"Am I being held here because I'm Muslim?" I asked the lead interrogator. "This ain't no Muslim shit. I'm just trying to have a good time, brother."

They all laughed. Once I get a laugh out of people, I'm a ham. So I gave them a little shtick and they said, "Go ahead, you can go."

I was still sick and losing weight when I got back to the States, so the first thing I did was to make an appointment to see a doctor. I just knew I had AIDS. I started calling all my friends to say good-bye to them. I even called Monica and told her that I had AIDS and that I was going to die. That might not have been the smartest move.

I went to see a Spanish doctor and he did the AIDS test. It came back negative.

"Nah, doctor. I have it. You're not doing this shit right. Get me another doctor," I said. He started laughing.

"Mike, you're HIV negative," he said.

"Did someone pay you to say I don't have it?" I said. He finally convinced me that I was AIDS-free.

I was also worry-free. I had a huge fight in a few months with Lennox Lewis for the heavyweight title, and I was fucking around in Jamaica and Cuba not even training, just living a crazy drug-fueled life. I had to be nuts.

Then I started getting fallout from the Cuba trip. Darrow was seriously concerned that the Bush administration was going to make an example out of me.

He sent out a memo to my whole boxing and legal team.

"As you are no doubt aware, Mike is alleged to have traveled to Cuba and to have committed an assault on a Cuban journalist while there. I am less troubled by the assault (it is unlikely the Cuban government would be able to extradite Mike given the current status of Cuban-American diplomatic relations), than by the fact that the Cuban American National Foundation (CANF) has petitioned the Department of Justice and the Department of the Treasury to investigate Mike for criminal violations of the Cuban Assets Control Regulations and the Trading With the Enemy Act. It is difficult to determine how seriously the Bush administration will take this matter. Unfortunately the Bush administration, in order to repair the damage caused by the Clinton administration's handling of the Elian Gonzalez matter, has pledged to organizations such as the CANF to enforce strenuously travel and trade restrictions.

"Obviously, I was unaware of Mike's visit to Cuba. To the extent that Mike was there for a statutorily exempt purpose, or to the extent that Mike's Cuba-related expenses were covered by a person not subject to U.S. jurisdiction, and that Mike provided no service to Cuba or a Cuban national, we should attempt to confirm this as soon as possible.

"Lastly, it is my strong advice that Mike cease from making any additional statements regarding his travel to Cuba. Specifically, I was contacted by Tom Farrey of ESPN who purported to have numerous photos and quotes related to Mike's travels. Apparently, Mike is alleged to have stated that he was there as a tourist and to support the 'people' of Cuba. We refused to confirm that Mike was in Cuba. The bottom line is that Mike should not travel to a foreign country without first consulting legal counsel. This is particularly true given his status as a felon and a registered sex offender."

Darrow was always there for me. Nothing ever came out of that Cuba trip.

But right after I got back, Monica filed for divorce. I guess she had had enough of my fooling around, because I sure did a lot of it. Calling to tell her that I had AIDS probably didn't help either. And the fact that I had just had a baby boy with this stripper in Phoenix was icing on the cake. I couldn't blame Monica. What kind of marriage was it where I could fuck five different girls a night and then just send her money? I don't know if we were ever in love.

I had met my baby momma Shelley at a strip club in Phoenix. I really liked Shelley. She kept her house immaculate and she did a lot of stuff with me. She was a fitness freak, so when I'd work out and go run, she'd run with me. I'd run five miles, she'd run ten. She'd always one-up me. One time, my assistant Darryl and I were throwing around a fifteen-pound medicine ball and Shelley got in on the action. She and I threw the ball two hundred fifty times and I got sore, but she kept on throwing it with Darryl. This ninety-pound Mexican chick must have done five hundred throws. She wore our asses down.

Shelley tried to work on our relationship. She'd talk to Hope and get tips from her on how to keep me happy. When she got pregnant with Miguel, I had no idea how I could take care of another kid. I was broke and in debt by then. She kept saying she was going to get an abortion, but she didn't.

The Lewis fight was scheduled for April so I didn't have much time to stop doing coke and weed and start training in earnest. I was still high on coke when I flew to New York to do a big press conference with Lennox on January twenty-second. They had us facing each other on slightly elevated platforms on one big stage at the Hudson Theatre. The Showtime announcer Jimmy Lennon Jr. introduced each of us like it was a real fight. As soon as Lewis was announced, I lost my mind. I looked over at him and wanted to hit the motherfucker. So I got off my platform and went up in his face. I guess Lewis was expecting trouble because he had about ten huge forest-tree-looking motherfuckers hiding in the wings, so as soon as I did that, they all came rushing out. I was only there with a few of my bodyguards, Anthony and Rick and my trainers and also Shelly Finkel. The Lewis camp must have thought that we'd see these big guys and run.

I moved up to get in Lewis's face and one of his bodyguards pushed me back, so I threw a left hook at him. Lewis then threw a right at me and Anthony threw one back at Lennox and all hell broke loose. I found myself down on the ground with Lennox, but he was so tall that when we went down, I didn't fall by his head; I was down by his leg. So I bit him on the thigh. He said that he had my teeth imprints for a while after that.

They pulled us apart and I couldn't get near him but I saw his bodyguard who pushed me so I spit right in his face. Anthony told me that I was so filled with rage that I picked up a fire extinguisher and threatened to hit Ant with it.

"Mike, you ain't going to hit me with that," he said to me. "I ain't even worried because I love you, you love me. Put the fire extinguisher down and let's get the fuck out of here," he told me.

But first I had to preen in front of the stage where all the reporters were assembled. I put my arms in the air to show off my biceps and then I grabbed my crotch.

"Put him in a straitjacket," someone yelled out.

"Put your mother in a straitjacket you punk-assed white boy. Come here and tell me that. I'll fuck you in your ass you punk white boy," I screamed.

"You faggot. You can't touch me, you're not man enough. I'll eat your asshole alive, you bitch. Nobody in here can fuck with me. This is the ultimate man. Fuck you, you ho."

Shelly Finkel was trying to restrain me, but I shrugged him off.

"Come and say it in my face. I'll fuck you in your ass in front of everybody. Come on, you bitch, you scared coward. You are not man enough to fuck with me. You can't last two minutes in my world, bitch. Look at you scared now, you ho. Scared like a little white pussy. Scared of the real man. I'll fuck you until you love me, faggot!"

That was the audacity that Cus had instilled in me. But it was also me talking like my momma. She would curse just like that. I feel bad now about saying that to that writer. I was out of my mind coming down off my high.

After the press conference I went out to see my pigeons in Brooklyn with a friend of mine named Zip. He was really concerned.

"What the fuck are you doing, Mike? You're going to blow all this fucking money," he told me. "You're up there acting like a nigga. They could arrest you."

"What did I do? They attacked me first," I said.

"Not Lewis. I heard you threaten somebody's life. If that reporter gets scared, they can put charges on you, man. Are you fucking crazy?

That's almost a terrorist threat. You're a scary motherfucker, Mike. You may not be to us, but to them you're scary."

Then we flew some birds and smoked some weed and I did some coke.

"You're fucking up, Mike," he told me again. "Why are you doing this shit? Why are you out here fucking with these pigeons? Go back and train, man. We should be out near a beach on a yacht. Just train and fight, Mike."

On January twenty-second, the same day that I was in New York for the Lewis press conference, the Las Vegas Police Department said that they found evidence in the raid on my house supporting the woman's claim that she was raped and held hostage. Now they could only wait to see if the D.A. would bring charges against me.

Meantime, Darrow Soll had gone to work. He got affidavits from all the people who had seen this woman in the house. He called up all the maids, the landscapers, the plant waterers, everybody who had seen her. They all testified that the young lady was more than pleased to be there, walking around the place of her own free will with nothing on but a T-shirt.

By then, the girl had recanted and she went to my friend Mack and told him that she had been pressured by both the police and her boyfriend to file charges. Her stepfather had also told Mack that she had lied.

I was at the barbershop one day when a black lady who worked for the FBI came in for some work on her eyebrows.

When she saw me, she said, "I've watched your work on tape and you look very good."

It took me a second to realize that she was referring to my private sex tapes that the cops had confiscated from my house.

"Umm, mmm, mmm," she said. "You are something else, boy."

Thanks to Darrow, the whole thing was shut down. The D.A.'s office stood up to the cops and after seeing the so-called evidence the cops presented, they decided not to bring charges against me. Meanwhile, my name had been dragged through the mud again for no reason.

Because of the fracas at the Lewis press conference, the Nevada officials voted 4–1 to deny me a license to fight there. Why was everything my fault? At Lewis's last press conference, during an interview segment for ESPN, he and Hasim Rahman had a knockdown brawl on the air that was much worse than the little scuffle we had in New York. But now they had to find a new venue and the fight was postponed until June. Which gave me more time to get high.

In February, a state senator in Texas said that I should be arrested if I went back to Texas because I didn't register as a sex offender when I trained in San Antonio in 2001.

It was bullshit; I had registered, but why let facts get in the way? When we announced that the fight would be held in Memphis, officials in both Tennessee and Mississippi announced that I had to register as a sex offender before the fight. Why was I such a pariah in my own country? Overseas, the people knew what time it was. Whenever I went abroad, especially in former Communist countries, I was treated like a hero.

I went to Hawaii for my training camp. That should give you some indication of how much I was motivated for this fight. The epicenter of some of the baddest weed in the world was there. I was smoking my brains out. Even the prospect of getting the belt back didn't mean much to me by then. I just wasn't focused at all.

I was obviously fucked up then, big-time. That's why I was doing weed. And the residue of coke doesn't leave your system right away, especially psychologically. All that Maui Wowie made for some interesting press conferences. In one of the most serene places in the world, I met with the press and started ranting about hypocrisy in society.

"I'm just like you. I enjoy the forbidden fruits in life too. I think its un-American not to go out with a woman, not to be with a beautiful woman, not to get my dick sucked. . . . It's just what I said before, everybody in this country is a big fucking liar. The media tells people . . . that this person did this and this person did that and then we find out that we're just human and we find out that Michael Jordan cheats on his wife just like everybody else. We all cheat on our fucking wife in one way or another, either emotionally, physically, or sexually. There's no one perfect. We're always gonna do that. Jimmy Swaggart is lascivious, Tyson is lascivious, but we're not criminally, at least I'm not, criminally lascivious. I may like to fornicate more than other people—it's just who I am. I sacrificed so much of my life, can I at least get laid? I mean, I been robbed of most of my money, can I at least get head without the people wanting to harass me and wanting to throw me in jail?

"I'm a big strong nigga that knocks out people and rapes people and rips off people. I don't know nothing about being the heavyweight champion, the only thing I know is how to fight. I am a nigga, right? No, really, really, really, I'm not saying like I'm a black person, I am a street person. I don't even want to be a street person, I don't even like typical street people. But that is just who I became and what happened to my life and the tragedies in life that made me that way. The pimps, the hos, the players, the people who have been cast aside, the people who have been lied to, the people who have been falsely accused, the people who were on death row and killed for crimes they never committed. Those are my people. I know it sounds disgusting. Those are the only people who showed me love.

"But I'm Mike, I'm not malevolent or anything, I just am. And I just want to live my life and I know you guys talk some bad stigma out there about me, but you know I'm going to make sure you talk about me, and your grandkids and kids after that are going to know about me. I am going to make sure of that. They are never going to forget about me. Your great-grandkids are going to say, 'Wow, wasn't that a bizarre individual?'

"I feel sometimes that I was not meant for this society because everyone here is a fucking hypocrite. Everybody says they believe in God but they don't do God's work. Everybody counteracts what God is really about. If Jesus was here, do you think Jesus would show me any love? I'm a Muslim, but do you think Jesus would love me? I think Jesus would have a drink with me and discuss 'Why are you acting like that?' Now, he would be cool. He would talk to me. No Christian ever did that. They'd throw me in jail and write bad articles about me and then go to church on Sunday and say Jesus is a wonderful man and he's coming back to save us. But they don't understand that when he comes back, these crazy, greedy capitalistic men are gonna kill him again."

What was I, Lenny Bruce now? These reporters were sitting there taking all this down, parsing every word to get to the true essence of me, but what was so obvious was that this was the Maui weed talking. I was stoned out of my mind. End of story.

I did a ton of crazy interviews, and they culminated with my appearance on *The O'Reilly Factor* on Fox. Rita Cosby interviewed me. She was combative, asking me the most outrageous questions just to get me to say something crazy so that O'Reilly could go ballistic and take something I said out of context and put me down.

"Are you an animal?" Cosby asked me during the interview.

"If necessary. It depends on what situation am I in to be an animal . . . If I'm fighting because I'm constantly being assailed against by your cohorts or people in the street because they feel that they have the right to assail me because of what people write in the papers, because of the courts, then you're correct and you're right." I told her that I would tell my kids that they were niggas and that "this society will treat you like a second-class citizen for the rest of your life, so there are certain things that you must not get upset for. But, you must fight."

"Are you evil?" she asked.

"I think I'm capable of evil like everyone else."

She also seemed to enjoy asking me about my financial state.

"I do need the money. That's why it's called 'money'—because we all need it. It's our god. It's what we worship, and, if anybody tells me anything different, they're a liar. Stop working, just live on the street and show me how much God's going to take care of you."

"Where does the rage come from?" she finally asked me.

"You're so white. Where does *that* rage come from?" I replied.

Lennox and I fought in Memphis on June eighth. Wherever that rage had come from, by then it was gone, even despite the fact that on the day of the fight, Monica served me with more divorce papers. Besides getting served, I was being sued up the ass by everybody. I had my little baby boy there with me because his mother had flipped on me so I was taking care of him. I was a mess. But still, my dressing room before the fight had a party atmosphere. It was packed with people. I'd never kissed babies or laughed or posed for pictures before a fight when Cus was around, but that was what was going on that night.

Shelly had gotten rid of Crocodile and Tommy Brooks and they had brought in a new trainer, Ronnie Shields. Crocodile came to the fight and stopped in to see me before it began. I grabbed him tight and hugged him.

"Croc, I'm so tired," I said. "I'm so tired."

When they were making the introductions in the ring, they cut it in half with twenty yellow-shirted security guards who formed a wall between me and Lennox. The fight started and I was aggressive in the first round, stalking him around the ring and making him hold me so much that the referee had to warn him. But after that round, something strange happened. I just stopped fighting. It was as if my mind had shut down. Ronnie Shields and my other trainer Stacy McKinley were shouting instructions at the same time, but I didn't hear a word either of them said.

It was very hot in the arena and I got dehydrated. I couldn't seem to start. As the rounds progressed, I stood there in front of him and got hit. I knew I wasn't in any condition to beat anybody, especially a fighter of Lennox's superb skill level. I had only fought nineteen rounds in the past five years. All those years of snorting coke and drinking and smoking weed and screwing around with massive amounts of women had finally taken their toll.

A lot of my close friends and associates thought that I had been drugged during the fight, I seemed so passive. I was in a fucked-up mood and it was hard for me to throw punches. It was as if all those heroes, those boxing gods, those old-time fighters had deserted me. Or I had deserted them. All of my heroes were truly miserable bastards, and I emulated them my whole career, a hundred percent, but I was never really one of those guys. I wish I was, but I wasn't.

By then I had spent years in therapy with different psychiatrists and the whole purpose of my therapy was to curb all my appetites, including my appetite for destruction, the one that had made me Iron Mike. Iron Mike had brought me too much pain, too many lawsuits, too much hate from the public, the stigma that I was a rapist, that I was public enemy #1. Each punch I took from Lewis in the later rounds chipped away at that pose, that persona. And I was a willing participant in its destruction.

It went eight rounds and I got tagged with a solid right hand and I went down. I was bleeding from cuts over both of my eyes and from my nose. The ref counted me out. Jim Gray interviewed both of us at the same time after the fight. During the interview, Emanuel Steward, Lennox's trainer, interrupted Gray.

"I'm still one of Mike's biggest fans," he said. "He's given me so many thrills, going back to Roderick Moore. You've given all of us a lot of excitement. He's the most exciting heavyweight in the last fifty years."

"How sorry are you guys that this fight didn't occur many years ago when you, Mike, were at your best and you, Lennox, weren't quite as old either?" Gray asked.

Lennox was starting to answer and I wiped some of the blood off his cheek.

He said, "Heavyweights mature at different times. Mike Tyson was a natural at nineteen. Nothing stood in his way and he ruled the planet at that time. But I'm like fine wine. I came along later and I took my time and I'm ruling now."

"Mike, are you sorry that this fight didn't take place years ago?"

"It wasn't meant to be. I've known Lennox since he was sixteen. I have mad respect for him. Everything I said was to promote the fight. He knows that I love him and his mother. And if he thinks that I don't love and respect him then he's crazy."

"So you're saying that a lot of the behavior was just to sell tickets and that doesn't represent your true feelings?" Gray seemed shocked.

"He knows who I am and he knows that I'm not disrespectful. I respect this man as a brother. He's a magnificent, prolific fighter."

The little gesture of me wiping the blood off Lennox's cheek was seized on by all the boxing writers. They thought that I had been heroic in defeat. And for the first time, a lot of them seemed to see the human behind my façade. Almost.

"Tyson is a despicable character. A rapist, a thug you would not want within an area code of your daughter. But it's going to be just a little harder to despise him now," a nemesis from *Sports Illustrated* wrote.

As soon as the fight was over, I got right back into my vices. I had met an attractive Dominican girl named Luz. She had come to the Lewis fight with some other guys and we started hanging out. She lived in Spanish Harlem in New York and I moved in with her that fall. And I was right back in my environment. Abandoned buildings, the dope man on the street, people were OD'ing, a fat lady was pushing an addicted newborn down an alley, niggas with beers shooting at one another. That's my element, sorry.

It was bad for me to be in my element, but once I was there my senses sharpened. I was paranoid, on the move, I was in survival mode. Once I moved into Spanish Harlem, I became Brownsville Mike again. People were feeding me. My drugs were free. I started hanging out in the drug dens.

How did I get from slapping a motherfucker five and letting him take a picture with me to being right there in the dope den where the naked women are packing the bags of coke? How did I get there, sniffing the coke and the man is going, "No, that shit is for the dumb crack niggas. This is the flakes. You've got to try the flakes, Poppy." I took one hit of that shit and my eyeballs froze.

I'd go down to the restaurant that was on the corner and they'd give me free food. I'd be eating all the rice and beans and they were plying me with liquor and it was still early in the morning. Some of my gangster friends would come to visit me. They'd be in their Rollses and fancy cars.

"What the fuck are you doing up here with these bitches?" one of them asked me. "Come live in my house."

"No, I'm good right here, nigga," I said. "This is my woman, I'm good."

"Mike, you got to watch these niggas up here," he said.

"Nah, man. These people are good," I told him.

I was hanging with those people and deep in my heart I knew I belonged there at that moment because that was how I felt about myself. Because in the hood it was different—people might feed me for free and give me drugs and take care of me, but if something went down, I was there with them. I had my vices and the people in the neighborhood understood my barometer.

I was juggling at least twenty girls at that time. Sometimes their worlds collided and I bore the brunt of it. Someone I was dating heard that I had been with someone else. Now, you would think a girl would be out of her mind to put her hands on Mike Tyson. But when they got mad they didn't give a shit. They'd hit me and scratch at my face. Then when you thought that it was all over and they'd cooled down, the next thing you know, a rock hits you in the head and she was mad as a motherfucker all over again.

ON JANUARY 13, 2003, MY DIVORCE WAS FINALIZED. MONICA GOT THE CON-necticut house, her house, and $6.5 million from my future earnings. Eventually she would get a lien on my Vegas house. She was pretty hostile towards me at this point, but I didn't care about giving her the money. I'm a street guy; I was going to be out in the streets hustling.

Even though my heart wasn't in boxing anymore, I still had to make some money. I had Shelly get me a fight on February twenty-second against Clifford Etienne. A week before the fight, I went to get a tattoo that became my most notorious tattoo. I told the artist, S. Victor Whitmill, aka Paradox, that I wanted a tattoo on my face. I hated my face and I literally wanted to deface myself. I suggested tiny little hearts all over it. It wasn't some ploy to make me more attractive to women; I just wanted to cover up my face. But Victor refused to do that; he said that I had a good face. He came up with that Maori tribal design and I told him I'd think about it. The more I thought, the more I liked the idea of putting a tattoo that was used by warriors to scare their opponents in battle on my face. So I went with it.

I trained much harder for this fight than the Lewis fight. I came in under 225 pounds, nine pounds lighter than for Lewis. Etienne had a good record and he was in the top ten of both conferences, but he had a weak chin. He'd been knocked down ten times in twenty-six fights.

There was a documentary crew trailing me around for a film. They filmed me as I gulped down my prefight meal.

"I hate Mike Tyson. I mostly wish the worst for Mike Tyson. That's why I don't like my friends or myself. I'm going to extremes. Maybe in my next life, I'll have a better life. That's why I'm looking forward to go to the other world—I hate the way I live now. I hate my life now."

I didn't know why I was more focused for this fight than for the fight with Lewis. I didn't know if I was coming or going. The bell rang and I charged Etienne and we came together on the ropes and I pulled him down on me. I think that I had hurt him with one of my first punches. We got up and I ducked one of his punches and threw a counter that landed square on his jaw and down he went. I thought that he could have gotten up. I didn't think it was a great punch that could knock someone cold, but I don't really know because it was really precise. After he was counted out, I helped him get up and we hugged. Clifford whispered something in my ear.

Jim Gray came into the ring to do the interview.

"He said something to you in your ear that nobody could hear, what exactly was it that he said?"

"To be honest, he said, 'You need to stop bullshitting and be serious, you're not serious, that's why you are out here playing around.' He said the truth."

"And he is right, isn't he?" Jim asked.

"Yeah, he is. I am just happy to be back in Memphis and give a decent show and I am glad brother Clifford gave me a fight and people don't understand the business when you show your love and respect, when you fight one another, because that is how we elevate our lifestyle."

"Mike, were you really sick this week? What was the problem?"

"I broke my back."

"What do you mean by that, you broke your back?"

"My back is broken."

"A vertebrae or a portion . . . ?"

"Spinal."

"You did that in sparring?"

"No, I did it by a motorcycle accident. The doctor discovered, I was doing my sit-ups, 2,500 a day with my twenty-pound weight, and one day I couldn't move anymore. And I just asked the doctor, 'What is wrong?' And he said, 'Believe it or not your back is broken slightly.'"

"Are you in pain right now? Did you take some type of injection? How did you make it to this fight?"

"I can't take injections; you know they're going to test me. But all praise be to Allah, I don't know. I'm just happy that I'm fighting and I'm punching well and accurate."

"Were you ready for this fight, Mike, I mean your trainer Freddie Roach advised you four days before the fight, not to fight. Were you ready?"

"No, but I'm obligated, I've got to be a man and fight. I canceled too many fights in my career, and I don't want anybody to think I was afraid. And I needed the money, I am always in need of money, and I am glad the both of us did it. I have so much respect for him as a man, he is a friend of mine."

Gray started asking me whether I was going to fight Lewis again. That was the speculation: another big Lewis fight to make a lot of money.

"I'm not ready to fight him now. I'm not interested in getting beat up again. I don't know if I want to fight anymore if I have to fight Lewis next fight. I want to get my shit together. I'm so messed up; I just want to get my life together."

I carried that morose attitude with me back to my hotel suite, trailed by my documentary film crew. I did a video conference call with my kids to see if they had seen their daddy win. Then I kicked the camera crew out of my room and started partying with my pimp/ gangster friend. He had brought some of his girls with him along with another girl who was a friend of a friend. I had a few snorts of coke and smoked some weed and my mood lifted. We had a few bottles of Dom Pérignon open. My friend was telling one of his war stories and we were all laughing and the girl who was a friend of my friend joked and said, "Oh, you're full of shit, nigga."

BOOM! My friend grabbed that Dom bottle and clocked her on the head with it. I tried to stop him, but he was too fast. The blood was bursting out of her head like an oil geyser.

I was thinking that my life was ruined. We were in the South. The girl was screaming like crazy, and she was married to a very well-known celebrity. My friend was going to have to kill these people and I would be associated with all this. Then all of a sudden, my friend and the girl were talking all pleasant with each other. That was just how that pimp-ho shit goes.

I had picked up another $5 million from the Etienne fight, but I was still in massive debt. My lawsuit against Don King was still making its way through the court system and Don was getting nervous about me having my day in court. So he started reaching out to me. I didn't have any long-standing contract with Shelly, so I was a free agent of sorts at the time. Don figured he could woo me and show me a little cash and I'd come back to him and drop the lawsuit.

I was consumed with getting money. I couldn't wait years for the lawsuit to play out; I needed money right then. Instant gratification wasn't quick enough for me. So I reached out to Jackie Rowe to help me deal with Don. Jackie was like a pit bull. I'd say, "Baby, get me this," and she'd go out and get it done. And then I'd go get high.

In April of that year, I had Jackie talk Don into buying me three Mercedes-Benzes. I had him put one of them in Jackie's name, one in Luz's name, and the other in my friend Zip's name. We were playing Don, telling him that if he'd come through with cash and cars, maybe I'd drop the lawsuit. So Don would set up a meeting thinking he could fool me into signing some new agreement to settle the case for peanuts and I'd wind up robbing or beating him each time.

One time, I brought two childhood friends of mine to a hotel room where Don was staying. When we got there, Don started threatening my guys and talking smack. "I got three bodies, two on record," Don bragged. He looked over at my friend but my friend didn't say anything. He was supposed to scare Don, but Don had him all shook up. I was looking at my guys like, *What the fuck, you're supposed to be tough guys.* So all of a sudden I got up and smacked the shit out of Don.

"Just shut the fuck up, motherfucker," I said.

And my guys, the guys I brought up to deal with Don, started jumping on me to restrain me.

Meanwhile, I kept meeting with Don whenever he reached out to me. I'm so happy that at that stage in my life, I didn't have the guts that I had back when I was younger or I really would have done a number on Don. Don once called me and said that he was going to come over to my office in Vegas and drop off $100,000 for me. My friend Zip was in town, so the two of us were there waiting for Don to show up.

Don arrived with a bag full of cash.

"I've got to pay some people off," he said and began counting out $100,000. Zip walked over to him, calmly took the whole bag, and brought it over to me.

"Thank you very much. Please escort Don to the door," I said.

Zip grabbed Don's arm and walked him out.

"Me and the champ are going to work out now," Zip said.

"Hey, man, I need that money. I've got to pay some people off. I told you that," Don said.

"See you later, Don, it was a pleasure meeting you. I've always been a big fan," Zip said and closed the door in his face. We started counting the money. There was sure a lot of gwap in the bag.

My lawyer Dale Kinsella heard about these meetings with Don and drafted a letter to Don's attorney at the end of May.

I am appalled about what is going on with the participation of your office in the last thirty days.

1. Jerry Bernstein and I are Mike's counsel of record. To work so perilously to exclude us from what is going on should cause anybody, let alone Judge Daniels, to have serious reservations about any proposed settlement.

2. Don appears to have learned absolutely nothing from this litigation. It is Don's persistence in getting Mike sequestered, whether in an office or in a hotel room, and having him execute documents *without the benefit of any independent legal or financial advice, which is a core fact of this litigation.* I truly do not understand what anybody on your side of the table is thinking.

3. Mike's propensity to sign agreements, let alone settlement agreements, under the influence of people that he trusts, respects, and/or whom he believes he can trust (even if momentarily) is well documented. His recent decision to settle his divorce with Monica without counsel or financial advice (which had to be undone on the grounds of undue influence) is a prime example of what I am talking about.

4. If and when Mike is served with process, and if and when Jerry and you and I are called upon to address the court, these matters as well as others will undoubtedly be raised. I agree with the court that Mike's case is his case and not his lawyer's, but for everybody's sake any settlement consummated between Mike and Don should (and probably must) be reviewed by someone who is independently representing Mike.

In this context, I would appreciate it if Don and/or your office would see fit to advise Jerry and me to what in the world is going on.

What Dale didn't know was that a few weeks before he sent that letter, I had Jackie negotiating with Don behind their backs. My assistant Darryl had called Jackie to tell her that we were down to our last $5,000. We had no money to pay the house bills or the maintenance workers or anything. Jackie came out to Vegas and saw how dire my financial situation was.

"I want my fucking money from Don," I told her.

Don was thrilled to hear from Jackie. He was desperate to settle the case because we finally had gotten a trial date the coming September. As soon as we heard that, Jeff Wald told me that Don was going to do his magic and we'd see why he was Don King. Jeff didn't know that I had Jackie talking directly with Don, trying to get some money from him. Don was offering me a $20 million settlement in exchange for him getting to promote my fights again. I told Jackie that before we could talk about working together and settling, I wanted three things of mine that Don still had—a green Rolls-Royce, a painting that the Italian prime minister Silvio Berlusconi had given me that was supposed to be worth a lot, and the thing I was worried the most about: a drawing of me in the middle of a bunch of X-Men that Stan Lee had done.

Don called Jackie and told her that he would fly us down to Florida and put us up in the Delano Hotel so we could work out a settlement. Jackie, her son, my girlfriend Luz, and I got on Don's private jet and flew down. I packed a big block of coke and a duffel bag with a half-pound of reefer. I was doing my coke and smoking my blunts and listening to my Discman and I was higher than the plane was when an epiphany hit me.

"This is my motherfucking plane. I paid for this plane. And this motherfucker is acting like he's doing me a favor sending me down on my own fucking plane. This nigga is playing me."

The drugs were playing with my head and I was freaking out and getting jealous.

Don picked us up at the private airport in his Rolls and he had Isadore Bolton, his chauffeur, who used to be my chauffeur before he stole him from me, driving some of Don's associates in the lead car. We were driving down to Miami from Fort Lauderdale on I-95, the main highway, and Jackie was in the front seat and I was in the back with Luz and Jackie's son. Don said some innocuous thing, and all that jealousy and rage spilled out of me and I kicked him in his fucking head. Boom! You don't turn your back on a jealous cokehead.

Don swerved off onto the side median and I started choking him from the backseat.

"No, no, let him go, Mike," Jackie screamed.

"Jackie, you hold this nigga up, I'm coming to the front," I said.

She said, "Okay, I got him."

I got out of the car to get into the front seat and kick his ass some more, but Jackie couldn't hold him, she was in shock, and Don took off down the median.

Now I was on the side of the fucking highway by myself. Don drove a little bit down the road and then let Jackie and her son and Luz out of the car. They came up to me carrying my bag with the half-pound of reefer. I had the coke stash on me when I got out of the car.

"Why did you let him go, Jackie?" I screamed. "Now we're out here on the fucking highway."

The cars and the trucks were whizzing by us. All of a sudden, Isadore pulled up. He was there to pick us up because he lost our car and when he called Don, Don told him to turn around and get us.

He pulled up alongside me and rolled his window down and told me to get in the car.

"Fuck you, motherfucker," I screamed.

Isadore got out of his driver's door and I was right on him. I punched him in the face twice, shattering his left orbital bone. The force of the blows knocked him across the driver's seat and I reached in and grabbed his leg and bit it. Isadore managed to kick me off him and close his door, so I punched the outer panel of his door and bent the steel. I was about to break his window when he managed to drive away.

His shoes were still on the side of the road and he was driving barefoot.

Then the cops came. They were talking to us and I had the half brick of coke and Luz was holding the duffel bag with the half-pound of weed. These cops were so excited to see me that the motherfuckers didn't even ask me what the four of us were doing on the side of the highway. They'd have put anybody else's ass on that grass, and they'd be locked up for life for having all that coke. I'm an extremist. Why couldn't I just buy an eight ball? No, I had to have a half a brick. The guys who sold it to me said, "Mike, this is sales weight. Police are not going to hear that you're getting high with a half a brick of blow." And I had this as my personal stash.

The cops offered to drive us to our destination and we piled into one of the cars and they took us to South Beach. Don had reserved half of a floor for us, so we started living it up. Jackie talked Don into giving us some money, and he sent a guy over with a couple hundred grand.

We partied every night for a month and then a friend of mine came by with his tour bus and we picked up a couple of girls and drove all around the East Coast.

In June, I got hit with another bullshit paternity case. This lying wench Wonda Graves claimed that I had raped her in 1990 and that I had fathered a boy. That piece-of-shit lawyer Raoul Felder, who represented Robin Givens, took on the case and bragged that he would "defeat Mike Tyson in the ring again." They both crawled back into the gutter when the DNA test came back and showed a zero percent chance that I was the father.

But I was no angel then either. Later that month I was visiting my childhood friend Dave Malone and we were flying our pigeons in Brownsville. That night Dave drove me back to the Marriott Hotel where I was staying. Outside the hotel, two guys who were returning to their rooms and they were pretty drunk and came up to me and asked me for an autograph. I was high on cocaine. Let me tell you something about me. When I was getting high and it was nighttime or early in the morning, I was not a good person to meet. I was just nasty, looking for trouble. I could have these Herculean fucking mood swings, almost Jekyll and Hyde shit.

So these two Puerto Rican guys approached me and asked me for my autograph. I told them to fuck off.

"You ain't all that, anyway," one of them said. "We got guns and you only got your fists."

If I wasn't on coke probably nothing would have happened. But I was, so I chased them into the lobby and up the escalator. We got to the top of the escalator and I knocked one of them out with one punch. The other guy was hiding behind the front desk and I pulled him out and hit him. He was spared when hotel security came.

The fight was my fault. They were going to charge me with misde-

meanor assault and them with menacing and harassment. I had to go
to court the next day and when I got back I showed my friends Dave
and Zip the thick rap sheet that was part of the court record.

"They're born troublemakers," Dave said. "Look at their records."

"Hey, that's my rap sheet," I corrected him.

"Man, we hang around you because we think you're a celebrity and
you're gonna give us a good look," Zip said. "You got a worse police
record than we do, nigga."

I was living day to day then. By now I was tired of all the bullshit
surrounding me. I didn't feel like there was anyone in my camp I
could trust and I got tired of all the Machiavellian power grabs, so I
got rid of my whole management team.

So now I had Shelly handling what was left of my career. I had a
rematch clause in my contract with Lennox Lewis and he wanted to
fight me again to get another big payday. But I didn't want to get my
ass kicked twice. If I was motivated and got in top shape I had no
doubt that I could have kicked his ass. But I wasn't interested in boxing; I was interested in drugs.

So Shelly and Lewis's people came up with the idea of me fighting
on the undercard of Lennox's next fight. I would be billed as a co-
headliner. I declined to fight on the undercard because it was a dis to
me. So we turned down Lewis's offer and they turned around and
sued me and Don King for $385 million, claiming that King was entic-
ing me to neglect the contract so he could promote my next fights.

My only real asset left was my suit against Don. By then, Jeff Wald
knew that I was meeting with Don and he was furious at me. He told
me that Don would keep delaying lawsuits that were filed against him
until the last minute before the trial was about to start and then he
would settle. Jeff and Dale Kinsella were telling me that we could
settle for as much as $60 million out of the $100 million we had sued
for and that I might even be able to get my fight film library back,
which would be money in the bank for me for years to come. All I had
to do was hold on until our court date in September.

But my financial predicament was so bad that the people who were
around me on a day-to-day basis were telling me to file for bank-

ruptcy. Jackie and I had been hanging around Jimmy Henchman at that time, the rap entrepreneur who managed the Game and was CEO of Czar Entertainment. Jimmy brought in Barry Hankerson, a record producer who had managed Toni Braxton and R. Kelly. They were all pushing for me to file for bankruptcy. Hankerson had told Jackie that I should file a Chapter 11 bankruptcy, so Jackie actually went online and Googled "Chapter 11 Bankruptcy." That was what I was dealing with at the time. Jackie was a good person but she was in way over her head. None of us knew anything about high finance or bankruptcy; we were just having fun and spending money.

So I called Jeff Wald and told him that all these people were suggesting that I go bankrupt.

"Do not file for bankruptcy because the minute you do, we don't control the lawsuit anymore, the bankruptcy judge does. Then the suit is out of our hands," he told me.

"Well, what if I lose?" I asked.

"You're not going to lose. It's black and white," he said.

I wasn't so sure. In my first deposition against Don I had picked up a pitcher of water and poured it on his lap. And now Don had that Florida stomping to hold over my head.

Wald was convinced that Don was working all my friends, including Jackie, to influence me to file for bankruptcy. He started calling me a few times a day, begging me not to file. But I didn't believe that my friends were taking kickbacks.

But when I looked at the mountains and mountains of bills that I couldn't pay, I decided to file. Hankerson got me a bankruptcy lawyer and we filed on August first. That same day, I went shopping on Rodeo Drive with Hankerson, Henchman, and my bodyguard Rick. Hey, just because I filed for bankruptcy didn't mean I had zero money. I just didn't have $100 million to pay off my debts. I was still hustling deals. The media made a big deal of me shopping on Rodeo Drive, but they didn't go into the stores with me. I was talking to Muslim guys who ran some of these high-end clothes stores and I pulled out my Muslim card in hopes they would cut me a deal.

"How about if I give you fifteen hundred dollars for this three-thousand-dollar suit, my brother. You know the golden rule of Islam. Want for your brother what you want for yourself."

The next day all the newspapers had every little detail of my finances splashed across their pages. I owed about $27 million, $17 million of which was for back taxes I owed the IRS and the English tax people. The other $10 million was for personal expenses, which included the money I owed Monica from the divorce, what I owed the banks for my mortgages, and my huge legal fees.

I was so overwhelmed and pissed off by the whole bankruptcy thing that I just gave up my house.

"Fuck it, take the fucking house," I told my lawyers and they auctioned it off. I was so high I couldn't get anything done. I was just working out. I had no fight scheduled, but I worked out anyway and got high.

I was a real adaptable kind of guy. I could live in the gutter or in an elevated state. I knew all the hustles and I was gambling with life. Even when I was in the gutter, I had my $2,000 pants and shoes on. I didn't have a nickel in my pocket, but I was still talking shit, hitting on chicks.

I spent some time in Phoenix with Shelley, the mother of my child. Dave Malone came down and hung out with me for a while. I was so poor that we were eating Frosted Flakes and Twizzlers for dinner. We had no money to do anything, so we used to sit in the backyard and watch my pigeons fly. Every once in a while, I'd set up an autograph signing somewhere and I'd charge twenty-five bucks for an autograph, just to get over the hump. I was so poor that a guy who had stolen my credit card account number went online to complain that I was so broke he couldn't even pay for a dinner with my credit card.

But there were some benefits. I went back east and I was hanging out with my friend Mario Costa who had some of my pigeons behind the Ringside Lounge, his restaurant and bar in Jersey City. It was a beautiful Indian summer day and we were sitting in the back where the pigeons were. I fell asleep and Mario left me alone. Two hours later I woke up and started shouting, "I'm rich! I'm rich!" Mario came running out back.

"You okay, champ?" he said.

"I'm rich, Mario," I said. "I don't have no watch, no money, no phone, but I feel so peaceful. No one's telling me to 'go here,' 'go there,' 'do this.' I used to have cars that I never drove and I wouldn't even know where the keys for them were. I had houses I didn't live in. I had everybody robbing me. Now I have nothing. Nobody calls me, nobody bothers me, nobody is after me. It's so peaceful. This is rich, man."

Some of my friends stepped up to the plate for me. My friend Eric Brown and his brother gave me a $50,000 advance from their company CMX Productions. I would have done anything for them, but I never had to.

Meanwhile, in August, my friend Craig Boogie started negotiating a deal for me with the mixed martial arts K-1 people. I had nowhere to live so the K-1 people put me up in a suite in the Beverly Wilshire Hotel in L.A. and paid all my expenses. I needed that. I had already been kicked out of every big hotel on the Strip in Vegas. In return, I did promotional appearances for them.

"Mike, we need you to be in the audience at this event in Hawaii."

Boom, I flew down to Hawaii. The next month I went somewhere else. I was getting fifty grand for this, a hundred grand for that. I was making all this money by doing nothing. Instead of saving that money and paying off my bills, I bought an Aston Martin Vanquish and a Rolls convertible. I had all these cars and nowhere to go. I shopped on Rodeo Drive every fucking day. I was in these shops, looking in the mirror, deciding how I was going to project myself when I went out that night. I'd be wearing $3,000 pants, a $4,000 shirt, and a $10,000 blazer. Meanwhile, I didn't have a pot to piss in or a window to throw it out of.

Everybody in the Beverly Wilshire knew me. They'd have these exclusive dinner parties in one of the meeting rooms and I'd crash them. If there was a Palestinian-Israeli debate, I was going. I was a master schnorrer.

I'd have parties in my room and order steaks and lobsters and caviar and Cristal. I'd invite up the biggest dope dealers and hustlers and we'd shoot dice. I'd whoop their asses in the dice game and then talk shit to them.

"Is that all the money you got, nigga? I thought you were a big-time motherfucking player out here in L.A. This is what happens when you fuck with the Iron One. You think I'm just a fighter? I'm a hard stone-cutter nigga, man. You may as well go play Lotto; you ain't gonna win nothing from me."

I lived it up in that suite for two years. Partying my ass off, getting high on weed and coke, having my girls come up. I ballooned up in weight from all the late-night eating.

Right after I signed up with K-1 that August, they put out a press release that I was going to fight Bob Sapp, a 6'5", 390-pound ex-NFL player who was one of the K-1 stars. But I was never going to fight no kickboxer.

"It might be nice," I told the *New York Times* when they called me. "But under the Marquis of Queensberry rules. I don't really feel like getting kicked in the head, you know?"

Then I showed up at the big K-1 fights at the Bellagio in Vegas on August fifteenth. Right after Bob Sapp won his match, he called me into the ring and challenged me.

"I'll do it right here," I told the crowd. "Get me a pair of shorts and I'll fight him tonight with the Marquis of Queensberry. Sign the contract, big boy."

This was wrestling shit talk. I loved doing these appearances.

A few weeks after I moved into the Beverly Wilshire, I went to Neverland to see Michael Jackson. It was nice hanging out with Michael. He was very low-key then. He asked me what I had been doing and I told him that I had been taking it easy.

"Rest is good. Rest is just real good, Mike," he told me. "Get as much as you can."

I didn't know then that he couldn't sleep at all.

It was weird, everyone was saying that he was molesting kids then, but when I went there he had some little kids there who were like thug kids. These were no little punk kids, these guys would have whooped his ass if he tried any shit.

In April 2004, I made a joint appearance with Ali at a big K-1 event. Again they announced that I had signed with them to fight and that I'd make my debut that summer. One of their stars had a press conference and said he looked forward to fighting me.

"I would accept a fight under boxing rules," Jerome Le Banner said. "But as soon as I am in the ring I'd do whatever the fuck I want . . . Western boxing or not, I will kick him . . . Tyson has already bit an ear, now he's gonna eat a size twelve foot."

I would have been crazy to fight those monsters. I'd rather go back to my hotel suite and just chill.

My bankruptcy was winding along. In June, Don finally settled the suit. The bankruptcy judge let him pay only $14 million. He had played everybody once again. I didn't get no film rights or anything. Monica was the first to get paid out of the settlement. The bankruptcy lawyers wound up costing $14 million. They got paid ahead of the IRS. I was still up shit's creek, so I had Shelly get me a fight. He chose an English boxer named Danny Williams and we signed to fight in Louisville on July thirtieth. Williams was the former British heavyweight champ who was on the comeback trail. He had knocked out his last two opponents, but he had lost to Julius Francis so I wasn't too worried about fighting him.

I had to do press again. A couple of weeks before the fight, I was my usual optimistic self when I met them.

"I guess the thing I am most curious about, Mike, is where you find serenity in your life?" I was asked.

"I don't know. I'm realizing that I am not the only person that has been in a situation. You have to understand I have lost everything and I mean everything. Anyone I ever cared about, anybody I ever loved, romantic, I've just lost everything. My money, home, I've lost everything. The people who love you, you just chase them away by being so belligerent and crazy. You have to lose it all. And I think at some point of your life you wish you could receive them back but I guess that is part of our growing pain. We lose people that we love and care about the most in order to start our life off fresh, with a brand-new start."

I was doing drugs right up to the fight. I went into the fight weighing 232, but I was in pretty good shape. My entourage was gone when I walked into the ring. I had made my security guy Rick one of my cornermen. I rocked Williams in the first round and almost had him out, but he was a smart fighter and he held on to me and got through the round. With thirty seconds to go, I felt something snap in my left knee after I threw a punch. I found out later that I had torn my meniscus, so I was fighting on one leg from the second round on. I still managed to rock him in the second round, but I couldn't move and be elusive and he started pounding me pretty good to the body. In the third round the ref deducted two points from him for low blows and a late punch.

By the fourth I was just out of gas and was a stationary target. He unleashed a barrage of punches and between my knee and my lack of conditioning I couldn't move. A final right hand sent me down. Then I was sitting up against the ropes, watching as the ref counted me out. That fight really killed my spirit.

I went back to Phoenix to Shelley's house and I had an operation on my knee. I was in a wheelchair for a while and then on crutches. Of course, that was another excuse to do drugs. I spent the next few months in a deep depression, just hanging out in the backyard and flying my birds.

I came out of seclusion in October when I went to New York to see the Trinidad-Mayorga fight at Madison Square Garden. I was there with my friend Zip and a new bodyguard from the Bronx. When we walked to our seats in the Garden, the people at the fight went nuts. They hadn't seen me for a long time and they were losing it. I got a standing ovation. I love Zip like a brother but Zip didn't understand that the people were just showing appreciation for me. He got so excited.

"We're back, Mike, we're back!" he said. "They'll be calling you for commercials soon. They'll get you in movies. We're going to have that big book deal. You're a hell of a man to overcome this, brother. We're back!!"

Forget the fact that I was a full-blown cokehead, we were back.

After the fight, we went to the after-party in a downtown club. I was sitting drinking with Zip when he pointed to the dance floor.

"Check your security out," he said.

I looked and saw my new bodyguard all hugged up dancing with a white girl while he was holding a champagne bottle. We stayed for a while and then me, Zip, the bodyguard, and the girl went back to the hotel.

Zip and I were chilling in the room, smoking some weed, when there was a knock on the door.

I answered. Some guy was standing there.

"Mike, your security is in the elevator and he's butt naked."

"What!!"

Zip and I rushed out to the elevator and we saw that the security guard was lying in the elevator and his pants were down around his ankles. I had Zip pull up his pants and put him back in his room. Then we went to our room.

A few minutes later the cops came. They told me that they had the whole incident on the surveillance cameras. The girl that my bodyguard had picked up had accused him of rape, but when they saw the footage, they saw her slipping him a Mickey and pulling his pants down. She was setting him up to rob him. So there wasn't going to be any charges or bad publicity.

I shut the door and we smoked some more weed. Then minutes later, there was another knock on the door. I looked through the peephole and saw four more cops.

"Hey, hey! Stop! Leave me alone, I'm finished talking to you guys! I didn't do nothing, I just talked to the cops! Please leave me alone."

Later that night I had the limo take Zip home and I went along for the ride. He was still bummed out from the bodyguard thing.

"Man, we were almost back, Mike," he said. "Almost back. We'd have been in the movies, we'd have been commentating fights. We were almost back and this dumb-assed motherfucking security guard fucked it up, Mike."

I got in trouble myself a month later. I was in Phoenix staying at a hotel with my regular security guy Rick. Some of my Arizona friends took me out, and Rick stayed back at the hotel. We went to the Pussycat Lounge in Scottsdale and got wasted on coke and booze. We were all fucked up when we were leaving the club and were walking across the street when we saw a car coming fast at us.

"I'm going to jump over the car," I told one of my friends. So I stopped in the middle of the street but the driver stopped too. I jumped up on his hood, got on my hands and knees, and started yelling and pounding the shit out of the car. The guy got out of his car to yell at me, but when he saw that it was me, he ran back into his car. My friends pulled me down and told the driver that he was okay. But the next day he looked at his Toyota and noticed there were dents all over the hood, so he called the police. I got charged with a misdemeanor criminal damage count but Darrow got involved and the guy got paid off.

I still had no money when the New Year rolled around. Shelley was pregnant again and in March we had a daughter we named Exodus. I called the other Shelly and told him I needed to make some quick money. He set up a fight with a palooka named Kevin McBride in Washington, D.C., on June eleventh. But he was a big palooka, 6'6" and 271 pounds.

A reporter from *USA Today* came out to my home in Phoenix after one of my sparring sessions and I unburdened myself on his ass.

"I'll never be happy. I believe I'll die alone. I would want it that way. I've been a loner all my life with my secrets and my pain. I'm really lost, but I'm trying to find myself. I'm really a sad, pathetic case. My whole life has been a waste—I've been a failure. I just want to escape. I'm really embarrassed with myself and my life. I want to be a missionary. I think I could do that while keeping my dignity without letting people know they chased me out of the country. I want to get this part of my life over as soon as possible. I want to develop my life into missionary work. I'm not going to be a Jesus freak. But that's what I'm going to give my life to. I love Jesus and I believe in Jesus too—and I'm a Muslim. Listen, I've got an imam, I got a rabbi, I got a priest, I got a reverend—I got 'em all. But I don't want to be holier than thou. I want to help everybody and still get some pussy.

"In this country, nothing good is going to come out of me. I'm so stigmatized there's no way I can elevate myself. I was depressed after my last fight. I was hanging out with a lot of prostitutes and stuff. I felt like scum, so I hung out with scum. I was getting high all the time. But you realize you've got to put all the drugs away and deal with reality."

I never should have been in that ring. I was missing wildly, I was standing still, I had no stamina. It was an ugly fight. At the end of the sixth round McBride just leaned on me when we were on the ropes and I went down on my ass. I just sat there with my legs sprawled out. The bell rang and I could hardly get up. McBride's corner was working on a cut that he got from a head butt. I sat in my corner and told my new trainer Jeff Fenech that it was over. I wasn't going out for the seventh round.

Jim Gray came over to me to do the interview.

"Mike, first let's start with you. Did you want to continue?"

"Well, I would like to have continued. But I saw that I was getting beat on. I realized, I don't think I have it anymore, because, um . . . I got the ability to stay in shape, but I don't got the fighting guts, I don't think, anymore."

"When did you recognize that, at what part of the fight?"

"I don't know, early into the fight. I'm just sorry I let everybody down. I just don't have this in my heart anymore."

"Did you feel as though you had it coming into the fight?"

"Um, no, I'm just fighting to take care of my bills, basically. I don't have the stomach for this no more. I'm more conscious of my children. I don't have that ferocity. I'm not an animal anymore."

"Does that mean we won't see you fight again?"

"Yes, most likely, I'm not gonna fight anymore. I'm not gonna dis-respect the sport anymore by losing to this caliber of fighters."

"Why did you come out so passive?"

"I'm not taking nothing away from Kevin. I don't love this no more.

I haven't loved fighting since 1990, but Kevin, congratulations on your career and good luck. And I wish you the best and make a lot of money."

I met the boxing reporters for the last time after a fight. I walked into the interview room and they gave me a standing ovation.

I told them to sit down and I repeated the same stuff I had told Jim Gray. I wasn't going to fight anymore because I didn't want to disgrace the sport.

And then I left the arena as a boxer for the last time. And I forgot about doing missionary work or contributing to society. I just said to myself, "Wow, this is over. Now I can go out and really have fun."

14

BACK WHEN I WAS TEN YEARS OLD, I WAS DOING A ROBBERY WITH THIS OLDER guy named Boo. He had me go through the window of this guy's house and we hit the mother lode—big-ass TV, nice stereo, some guns, and some money. Boo knew I was a good little hustler. He'd have me lure guys who wanted to fuck a little boy into a room and he and his friends would be there to smash him and take his money.

After this heist, Boo took me to the pad of this older black lady. She was an unscrupulous, evil-looking person, but when I got to know her she was really kind and considerate. There were a bunch of guys in the place lying around and nodding out. Boo gave her some money and she gave him an envelope with some white powder in it. I couldn't take my eyes off him as he put the powder into a spoon and heated it up with a lighter. When the shit started bubbling, he took out a syringe and sucked the liquid up through the needle. Then he tied off his arm and he was about to inject the shit into his vein when he turned to me.

"Turn around, baby, turn around, baby," he said to me.

He didn't want me to watch him shooting up heroin.

Later, when we left the shooting gallery, he slapped me on the head.

"I better not ever hear or see you doing this shit or I'm going to kill you dead, little motherfucker. Do you hear me?"

Of course, that made me want to do heroin even more. When an old heroin head would tell me not to fuck with dope, I'd be thinking, *Why is that? So that they can have it all to themselves?*

I tried heroin once when I was younger. I smoked it and it made me feel really bad. I had to throw up. Just looking at junkies was enough to put me off heroin. I could look at a heroin addict and see that his soul was gone. You figure that's what you have to look forward to.

I started buying and sniffing coke when I was eleven but I'd been drinking alcohol since I was a baby. I come from a long line of drunks. My mother used to give me Thunderbird or Gordon's gin to make me go to sleep. When I was ten, my friends and I would buy bottles of Mad Dog 20/20, Bacardi 151, Brass Monkey, the real cheap shit that kills your guts. We also started smoking weed and hash and even opium and angel dust. I even did some blotter acid once when I was young. We did some jostling when we were high on acid but that didn't work out so well. We'd be snatching shit and laughing and running.

"The cops, the cops, they're coming." We'd laugh and hide under a car.

Except for one two-year stretch and the time I was in prison, I always drank. Which was not surprising since all my role models who I had read about were raging drunks. Mickey Walker, Harry Greb. My heroes were these white, Irish drunks. They were the guys who would be in a bar drinking and laughing while their opponents were running and doing rope work.

Booze brought out the worst in me. When I got drunk, I'd become totally emotionless and careless about other people's feelings. I'd fight with anyone, even cops. Anybody that knew me would say, "Don't let Mike drink. Give him some pot, just don't let him drink." If I got high on pot, I was happy and I was ready to cry and give you all my fucking money. Just as long as you don't tell me not to get high, because if you tell me to stop getting high, then I'm mad at you. If you're okay with me getting high, then it's "You sure you don't need that nice Porsche out there?"

I really think that one reason that I started doing so much coke was because I was in a lot of physical pain from my boxing career. I know some hockey players who told me the same story. When you have that kind of pain, you can't be friendly with anybody. You're like a lion with a hurt paw. When an animal gets hurt, they know that the other animals will attack them. That's how I felt when I was in pain, vulnerable and scared. So you get some coke and then you're in the room alone with the coke and you want a woman in there, because you feel so bad about doing the drug that having a woman is going to kill the guilt.

I had no problem getting cocaine, even when I was totally broke. I knew a lot of the big drug dealers when they were little guys just coming up and I showed them some love. Now they're multimillionaires and they own big clubs, so when they see me they treat me real good. But I treat them as if they were still those little guys. I'd just say, "I'm going to go somewhere, run me some of those little packages." Or I might have just met an absolute stranger that knows the drug man and they'd say, "Give Mike two eight balls on me."

When you start doing coke, you can see that people who you've known all your life and you'd never suspect are doing coke also. I was once drinking with a major celebrity when he turned to me.

"You got any powder?" he asked me.

"What??"

I was trying to be discreet. How the fuck did he know I was doing blow?

"Yeah, I got some. But how did you know?" I asked him.

"People that do it know the people that do it, Mike," he said. "We have radar."

When you have cocaine, you could be in the Mojave Desert in the middle of the fucking night, snorting your blow, and out of nowhere a bitch pops up in a bathing suit. Coke radar. The women that I was around loved coke so much we even started naming it after them. If you wanted some coke, you'd say, "Where's that white bitch at? I want that ho." We'd also call it "blondie" or "white girl."

When I first started using coke heavily, I would carry half a brick with me. I was carrying sales weight but I didn't care, I just wanted to be able to share it and turn all my friends on. I would go around and ask people, "You want some?" People I never dreamed of were doing that shit. The interesting thing is that these motherfuckers would sniff my dope and then reprimand me while they were doing it.

Or all of a sudden some guy that you never snorted with before is now an expert. He does some lines, delicately wipes his nose clean, then he looks like he's deep in thought and says, "I can get you better stuff." All of a sudden, he's an aficionado.

Sometimes you get guys who can't wait to turn you onto their coke.

"Mike, are you ready for this shit? You sure you're ready for it," he'd say. "Welcome to fucking Dreamsville, buddy."

He laid out some lines and I snorted them.

"Pure Peruvian flake," he said proudly, like he had just opened a bottle of Lafite Rothschild.

But he was right. The shit was so good, it made my eyeballs freeze.

I WAS HANGING OUT WITH FRIENDS IN L.A. AFTER THE MCBRIDE FIGHT, feeling pretty depressed, when my phone rang. It was Jeff Greene, a new friend of mine. On the face of it, you'd think it was pretty improbable that Jeff and I would be friends. Jeff was a Jewish businessman who made a billion dollars playing the real estate market. I was a Muslim boxer who spent almost a billion dollars on bitches and cars and legal fees. I met him through a mutual friend and we just clicked. He started coming to my fights in Europe and I started traveling around the world with him on his yacht. He'd invite me over for dinner during Rosh Hashanah, shit I even got to read from the book during the Passover seder.

"Hey, Mike, why don't you come join me on my boat in Saint-Tropez? I'll charter a jet to take you to France and then I'll have my guy come pick you up and take you to the boat."

Jeff was worried that I'd get depressed just thinking about the way I went out of boxing, so he figured that hanging out with some of the most beautiful women in the world and partying might be just the remedy I needed.

Before I left, I called Zip to see if he wanted to come along.

"No, man, I can't go," he said. "Some nigga shot me and I want to find out why."

"Zip, come on. We're flying on a private jet, we'll be hanging out on a yacht all around the Mediterranean . . ."

"Shit, man. I got shot. Somebody else needs to get shot. A shot for a shot."

"We're going where the best pussy in the history of the world is and you're talking about someone getting shot? They don't care if you're toked or broke, if you're there, you're fucking," I said. But he was bent on getting revenge.

So I went there and it was cool. I didn't really feel out of place. I saw some people who I knew and they started taking me around. I would eat breakfast on Jeff's boat and then get on one of his Jet Skis and I'd be riding around and some Wall Street guy would see me and invite me over to his boat.

"Hey, my boat's bigger than Jeff's," they'd say. "Come over and party with us on our boat."

I don't know what these guys thought. I wasn't no nigga for rent. Jeff was a friend of mine. Besides, we had the most exciting boat. Jeff's boat was over 150 feet long but it wasn't big enough because there was too much fun happening.

I was a little nervous at first that I wouldn't fit in with Jeff's other friends.

"Jeff, this is white honky heaven. I don't know if Mr. As-salamu alaykum is gonna fit in here," I said. This was my introduction to real Jewish jubilance. All of a sudden Denise Rich saw me and she came over and introduced me to her friend, trying to get me comfortable. She's such a beautiful, elegant, sophisticated lady. And nobody's tripping out on me. Then I realized that I was the only one tripping in my head. So I'm sitting there getting comfortable with all my new Jewish friends and suddenly this rude, obnoxious rich Saudi Muslim comes up to us.

"My son was going to pay fifteen million dollars to get you out of jail when that girl said you raped her," he said. He didn't even say, "Mr. Tyson, so nice to meet you . . ."

"Oh, thank you, sir," I said.

Denise Rich looked sadly at me. "I am so sorry," she said.

What kind of guy does something like that? What arrogance. Suppose that my new friends here didn't know I was in prison for rape? Suppose they asked, "What were you in prison for, Mike? Did you embezzle money? Insider trading?" Thank you, Mr. Desert Jockey, for explaining this in minute detail to the whole Jewish jubilance. I didn't talk to that guy the whole rest of the night.

I had another more pleasant chance meeting while we were in Saint-Tropez. I was on another rich Jewish guy's yacht and I watched him checking out this other Jewish guy whose boat was moored nearby. They were looking at each other, just like black people do, you know how we look at each other? And then one guy said, "Harvard seventy-nine?"

"Yes, didn't you study macroeconomics?"

"Yeah. Didn't you date Cindy from Hyannis Port? I dated her too for a second."

So I'm on this boat and I see a big black guy. He's the bodyguard for a very well-known international arms dealer. And I'm looking at him and looking at him and I just can't place him. He came over to me.

"Spofford seventy-eight?" he asked.

"Shit, nigga, we met in lockdown," I remembered.

"Yeah, I got into that fight with the guy in the chow hall."

"All right, that's you!"

After Saint-Tropez we took that boat all over. We went up and down the coasts, and every time we stopped at another country, it was chaos when they found out I was on Jeff's boat. There's nothing like it. You could get off the plane anywhere and it's like you never left home. You get to meet kings, queens, and princes. Everything's carte blanche, people open doors for you. You never have to wait in line to go to a club, you always have a table at the finest restaurants in the world. It was just a wonderful world to live in. It seemed like one big blur. But one thing I did realize is that none of all that filled that big hole that I had in my soul. I never truly respected the championship; it all came very easy. I truly put in a lot of hard work to achieve what I did, but I took it for granted.

When we docked in Sicily, we went out to a party and about a hundred people followed us back onto the boat. They all wanted to see me and take pictures with me. All of a sudden, the whole boat started tilting and sinking. Everybody wanted to party with us. Which was ideal for my demons, no doubt about it.

We stopped in Sardinia and that was off the hook. I'm a history buff so when I think of Sardinia I think of the Punic Wars and Hannibal. I was vibing on the fact that great wars were fought here. Jeff and I stopped into a place called the Billionaire Club. That place lived up to its name. A bottle of champagne cost something like $100,000.

"You don't have to worry about me drinking tonight," I joked to Jeff. But they kept sending bottles over to us anyway. In Sardinia, we were hanging out with Cavalli and Victoria Beckham. He invited me on his boat that was so lavish that it changed colors. I would hop on one of Jeff's Jet Skis and go from boat to boat, eating some food, drinking some liquor.

We had one unpleasant incident in Sardinia. There was another guy on Jeff's boat who was an English friend of Jeff's. He brought these two French girls on the boat and we all got high. I took one of the girls to my room and had sex with her. Afterwards I went upstairs on the deck, and when I came down, I saw the girl I was with going through the staterooms. I was high as a kite but I got really pissed at her. I thought, *Holy shit. If anything comes up missing, they're gonna blame me. I'm the only nigga here.* So I grabbed the girl by her hair and said, "What the fuck are you doing?" I dragged her up onto the deck. I was so upset and paranoid from the coke that I was about to throw her overboard when a guy on the next boat saw me.

"No, Mike, stop, stop!" he yelled.

Now people were looking at us. So I grabbed the two girls and told the staff to kick them off the boat. This wasn't my boat. I felt responsible for whatever those girls did. We left Sardinia and we were about a hundred miles away near Capri when a police boat drove up. They looked a little scary because they had a machine gun mounted on the boat.

The coast guard police came onto our boat to investigate me for allegedly assaulting that girl. So they had to interview a bunch of people. When it was my turn to be interviewed I told the guy the truth.

"This girl was stealing stuff from the room, so I grabbed her . . ."

"Hold on," the cop said in halting English. "No, that is not what happened. Say it again, say what happened again."

I got it.

"She was in the room stealing and I didn't know what to do and she just ran off the boat and I couldn't catch her," I said.

"Yes, that is really what happened," he said and wrote it into the report.

I was really paranoid when those cops came aboard. I had a huge bag of weed and I didn't want them to search and find it so I had my friend Jenny, who was sunbathing butt naked, sit on the weed. The policemen kept staring at her but they never asked her to get up or anything.

We made a few more stops, including a stop in Turkey where I met and hung out with the prime minister, but I was looking forward to going to Moscow to see my therapist. Her name was Marilyn Murray and she was a kick-ass seventy-year-old psychologist who I had been seeing since 1999. I met her that summer when I had to do court-mandated anger management sessions because of the road rage incident. Monica went with me and we decided to try some marriage counseling at the same time. We went to this facility in Phoenix. I made an entrance like I was the President of the United States. A couple of big stretch limos, all the Secret Service–looking bodyguards in black suits. I came in sly with my expensive jewelry and diamonds and my Versace clothes and my $6,000 crocodile shoes. So we sat down with the therapist and started the session and I was convinced that Monica and this guy had colluded beforehand. They were both ripping me to shreds. He didn't say anything about Monica; he just kept beating up on me.

"Fuck both of you! Y'all set me up ahead of time," I said and stormed out.

Six months later I went back alone, in a cab, fucked up, broke, and broken.

"Can we try this again, please, sir?" I said humbly.

This time he assigned me to Marilyn. She had a really interesting background. She used to own an art gallery in Phoenix but she started getting sick and went into therapy to deal with some abuse from her childhood. When she was forty-five she went back to school and got her degree in psychology and became a psychotherapist. She volunteered for free for years in the Arizona prison system working with sex offenders, violent rapists, and child molesters. So she had a reputation for working with really hard cases, people who had suffered a lot of trauma in their lives.

They thought she'd be a good match for me. I'd been in therapy a lot over the years but the guys I had been seeing were all too white-bread for me. At first I thought she was just some foolish-ass white woman that thought she was going to change me. I was going to play the nice black man role and she'd never see Ike/Mike. But I didn't know that Marilyn was a beast. She didn't take any shit. She'd heard all the games before. I just never thought she had heard my international con game, the game I got over working with all those counselors since I was a kid.

In order to deal with me you had to have some kind of roaring ferocious animal in you to get my attention. Even if you go about it in a diplomatic way, even without expressing it to the naked eye, I have to know that that animal is in there. It might just be a subtle look in her eye. Well, Marilyn had it.

It was obvious to me after a while that Marilyn's job in life was to help people. Some people can't even conceive of that, a person whose whole goal is just to give her life energy to care about someone else. We're taught that people like that have ulterior motives. But she had a mission. Just like Cus said that "my boy's job is to put big strong scary men in their place," Marilyn's job was to take big strong scary men that society has rejected and make society accept them again and make them excel while they're being accepted.

Marilyn introduced me to a concept called "baseline normal." A healthy person might have a high baseline for normal but mine was way down in the gutter. My baseline normal was sex, alcohol, drugs, violence, more sex, more alcohol, more violence, and chaos. I told Marilyn that the scariest day of my life was when I won the championship belt and Cus wasn't there. I had all this money and I didn't have a clue how to comport myself. And then the vultures and the leeches came out.

I was a smuck with no self-esteem but everyone in the world was telling me how great I was so now I was a narcissistic smuck with no self-esteem and a big ego. Marilyn thought that I was still addicted to the chaos of my childhood so that anytime something good happened to me, I would do something to sabotage it. So I married a doctor and had two lovely children and I was running around screwing strippers and doing drugs and drinking my ass off. Marilyn wanted to break my addiction to chaos and to raise my baseline normal to a place that was healthy.

She was talking the right talk a hundred percent to me. I knew that my demons from my childhood were on my trail everywhere I went. So she wanted to deal with that little boy who was acting up my whole fight career, that little boy that had been bullied and brutalized and abused. I didn't know how to take care of him when I was the champion of the world and now I had to learn how to nurture him and give him the love he never received before.

Marilyn became more than a therapist, she became a mentor. She would take me to dinner, take me to movies. We'd go sightseeing and she taught me all about Phoenix. We really bonded. She has so much love and care and passion in her heart. She wasn't even tripping about making any money off me; she just wanted to see me improve. I don't know what she saw in my unrehabilitated ass.

Right after 9/11 Marilyn was invited to Russia to do some work, and from 2002 on she would go to Moscow and spend four months out of the year there. There was so much trauma and substance abuse in Russia that Marilyn was a godsend. So in 2002, she told me that she couldn't be my therapist anymore and that I needed someone who would be around full-time for me. I loved Marilyn. I didn't want to see her leave.

"Why you got to go? Stay here and be my mom," I pleaded with her. "Stay here and look after me, you don't work with nobody but me anyway." It was like she was my mother anyway. She was fighting like mad for me. She'd use any influence she had politically. She was on a crusade to save my ass. Funny thing was, back then I didn't want all that. I didn't know that I was that damaged. Marilyn had to show me how fucked up I was.

So I told Jeff Greene that I was going to go to Russia and he said we could take the boat around the Balkans and stop in the Ukraine. So every few days I'd call Marilyn and tell her that I was coming to see her. "Hey, Marilyn, I'm in Saint-Tropez." "Hey, Marilyn, I'm in Sardinia." "I'm in Istanbul, see you soon."

When we got to the Balkan states everything turned lawless. These gangsters really operated with impunity over there. All the stuff we do that people label "gangster" is nothing compared to these guys. They can walk the streets and you don't know who they are but the law is on their side. The next thing I knew, these guys were hanging with me. They pretty much kidnapped me and wined me and dined me and gave me whatever I wanted.

I was in Romania at one point and I was hanging with all these drug and gang figures, and they were trying to make me happy.

"What do you do?" they asked me.

"Do you have any cocaine?" I said.

These guys didn't do cocaine. But they made a call and a guy came in with a big brick and put it on the table.

"This is what you like?" they said.

I dug into it and then I told them that they all had to take a hit. So a couple of them joined me and then they started talking so much they couldn't believe it. I'm such a monster. I turned the Romanian Mafia onto coke.

We took the boat as far as the Ukraine. Jeff and I and our friend Muhammad were sitting at a restaurant eating and, out of nowhere, thousands of people rushed over to see me. It was so bad that the police had to escort us to our hotel. Later that night, Muhammad and I went to meet some local "businessmen." They were talking to me about doing an endorsement deal for their vodka. The guy running the show owned a mansion that was just massive. Everything was made out of marble. This was real tsar shit, in the immaculate robber baron arena. We were supposed to have a business dinner with some guys. So the owner came up to me before dinner.

"Come with me. I want to show you something."

We walked to the south side of the house, past a big balcony and down the hall to another room. He opened up the door and there were two beautiful women lounging on a bed.

"This is your dessert after dinner," he said.

So I went and got Muhammad to show him.

"We're going to skip dinner and go right to dessert," I said. And we just stayed in that room. The Ukrainian guys didn't think that was so cool. Who would skip an important dinner for some broads? They felt that was odd.

In all these countries, Ukraine, Russia, Bulgaria, everything was about sex and power. As soon as we got off the plane from the Ukraine to Moscow, people were coming up to me. "Are you okay? Do you need a woman? You're tired, you must want a woman."

Can you imagine a hound like me in Russia? If you're with the right people they will literally pull a girl off the street, pull her into the car next to you and say, "You go with him." That shit was crazy over there.

The vodka guys put me up at the Hyatt in a $5,000-a-night suite that was at least ten thousand square feet. If my doorbell rang, by the time I'd get to the door it was too late, the person had already left.

The guys who have the big bucks over there are first-, maybe second-generation wealth. Before that, their parents or grandparents were basically peasants, so these guys spent their money like crazy. I had guys shelling out $300,000 just to entertain me for one night. And that's not even going out and boogying, that was just to pay for chilling. They'd order a huge tin of caviar, sixty grand. Big bottles of Rémy Martin Louis XIII, thousands of dollars. Whatever I wanted, I had. Money was no object to them.

I got in late the first night and I called Marilyn and told her that I'd like to do some sightseeing before the whole country knew I was in Moscow. Only about three paparazzi had shown up at the airport when I arrived. My hotel was just a couple of blocks from Red Square. Back in 2005, Russia was pretty much like the old Wild West with kidnappings and terrorist bombings every other day. Marilyn and I were on the way to Red Square and we had just passed the big statue of Karl Marx near Revolution Square when suddenly two big black SUVs and two long Mercedes sedans pulled up. Out jumped four guys with Uzi machine guns. In the Mercedeses were big guys in leather jackets holding handguns. Marilyn looked panicked but they came up and told me they were our bodyguards sent by the Ukrainian businessmen.

"I don't think I've ever had security with Uzis before," I told Marilyn.

So now we were walking along in a procession—me, Marilyn, the bodyguards who were all in camo outfits, and the three paparazzi who were trailing me from the hotel. When people saw this entourage, they started spilling out of the stores or abandoning their cars. By the time we got to Red Square, there was a mob following us.

Despite the crowd tagging along, we managed to get in a little sightseeing. I really wanted to visit Tolstoy's house, and the translator who took us around was stunned that I knew the names of all of Tolstoy's kids and I was aware of the dynamics between Tolstoy and his wife. We went to the Pushkin museum too. But it was impossible to get near the Kremlin with all the people following us.

Marilyn and I had fun during the day and then she went home and the fun really began. You could get anything you wanted in Moscow. The city is like New York on steroids. One night I visited some Russian big shot who had a huge mansion. In one area of his house he had a massive steam room with wooden couches and towels. Next to the steam room was a room filled with nothing but women, at least fourteen of them. So you'd pick out a girl and take her into the steam room. And there was a phone in the room so if you wanted a different girl, you just called out and they'd send that girl in.

I met the real Russian mob through my interest in pigeons. After a few days, I wanted to see some Russian pigeons, so I asked my guide who the biggest pigeon fanciers in Moscow were. She took me to a Russian Mafia guy who lived on the outskirts of Moscow and who had the most deluxe home I'd ever seen. His pigeon coop alone was the size of my whole house in Vegas. He owned property as far as your eye could see.

I had the best time, though, with this Kazakhstani Muslim businessman I met one night. I was with a Serbian friend when we met this guy. I thought he was just in town from Kazakhstan for business. He was acting like a normal guy with some money, being generous and picking up our tabs. We went to a mosque and said our prayers together and then we smoked some weed and he said, "I have a dance club for girls in town. Do you want to go there?"

He led us into the club and we went to a private area and he pulled a screen down and, boom, there were twenty beautiful young Russian girls. The oldest was probably twenty. They started dancing for us and he said, "Which one do you want?"

I didn't want to pick anyone because I might pick someone who didn't like me and they'd still have to come. I was still insecure about all the women who'd protest me when I fought in their country.

"Listen, brother, just ask who wants to come home with me and that will be fine. Any one of them will do." My criteria at that moment was only that they were breathing.

He laughed.

"All right, who wants to go home with Mike?"

I heard screams echoing all over the place.

"Yeah, me, me, me!"

They all wanted to go back to my hotel with me.

"Now you have to pick because they'll all go with you," he said.

"Okay, how about her, she's pretty hot. And the brunette one with the short hair is nice too. And I liked that blonde when I first came in. And what about that girl on the end in the second row?"

"Mike, you can't take four girls. What are you going to do with four girls?" he said.

"I have to have them all, brother, or else I'll be thinking about the ones that I didn't have."

So I went back to the hotel with four girls. We were getting high on coke and liquor. We were having fun and one of the girls called her mother.

"Ma, I'm here with Mike Tyson!"

She was so excited. She told me her mother was really hot too. But four was enough.

Call girls in the States were a completely different breed than these Russian girls. The girls in the States didn't care to do anything but satisfy you sexually. That was their sole purpose. But these Russian girls all spoke four different languages. I called a friend in Belgium and one of them got on the phone and interpreted for the operator. Then I called Portugal and she was speaking fluently to them. We called Slovakia and she had the language down to a tee.

I was thinking, *How do I get these girls back to the States?* They could run a Fortune 500 company. They all had university degrees. I'm a smooth guy with the words I learned from the dictionary but I was being intellectually dwarfed like a motherfucker by these call girls. Oooh, how I wished I could have taken them home with me. Fuck that bankruptcy shit, I would have been out of Chapter 11 in a minute with these hos.

I only had them that one night. I was a pig back then so the next night it was onto other conquests. Those were great girls but it was time to go on to the next chapter of this story in Moscow.

We partied all night and then I was up bright and early to go to a museum with Marilyn. She knew what time it was. I didn't have to tell Marilyn anything. She took one look at me and said, "So when are we going to work on recovery?"

One day we were in Red Square having brunch and the guy who

owned the whole mall came up to us. He was a Jewish guy and he told me that he also made all the clothing for the Russian Olympic teams.

"Tonight we are having a special invitation-only event to debut the new 2006 Winter Olympics Russian uniforms. Every sports official in Russia will be there. Would you like to be our honored guest?"

Usually I charged big bucks for an appearance but meeting all these wonderful athletes was very exciting for me. I told him I'd be happy to attend, and then, in gratitude, he took me all around the mall to the finest Italian clothing stores, and he gave me all this incredible clothing.

That night we had dinner with him and he invited Viacheslav "Slava" Fetisov, the ex–hockey player who was the head of all sports in Russia then. They hadn't announced that I would be there, so when the event started and I was introduced and walked in, those athletes almost tore that building down. They had created a big podium to look like the Olympic torch, and they sat Marilyn and me up there, and she was blinded by all the flashbulbs from the press. When the event was over, all these athletes rushed us to get my autograph and I had some big security guys watch over Marilyn. She would have been trampled in that crush.

One day Jeff, Marilyn, and I were eating lunch at the New York Café, a downtown Moscow restaurant where all the players hung out. We were sitting there and we saw a Chechen politician who had been partying with us in Saint-Tropez. He was one of the senators from Chechnya in the Russian Parliament. In Saint-Tropez and Sardinia he was so humble and nice and respectful. He looked and acted like a true diplomat. So I started to say, "Hey, brother," but here in Moscow he wasn't the nice guy that he appeared to be back in Saint-Tropez.

"Mike, he's not as friendly as he was on the boat. What the fuck?" Jeff said.

This was not looking good for me. When we were hanging out on the boat, these Chechen guys pretty much kept me flush. I'd say, "I'm your Muslim brother. Please give me some money, I'm doing bad here." They had so much money they'd tip people enormous amounts. Well, I needed some money now. The deal with the Ukrainian vodka people had run its course and they were going to stop paying for my big hotel suite.

But things started looking up a bit when the senator came over to our table and sat down.

"I have someone with me that really, really wants to meet Mike," he told us. "This is a very special person."

I said "Sure" and we got up and left our food on the table and followed the senator to a private dining room to one side of the restaurant. There was a table set up in there and we all sat down. A few seconds later, the door opened and Ramzan Kadyrov, the Chechen leader, walked in. Now, I knew all about the Chechen wars from a few years before. Ramzan's father, Akhmad, was one of the most powerful warlords in Chechnya and one of the leaders of the independence movement to secede from Russia. It was a bloody, bloody struggle and the Russians made Akhmad president of Chechnya, hoping that would quell the rebellion. He was assassinated a year later and they made his son, Ramzan, the new leader. Ramzan was a big boxing fan and he wanted to meet me more than anything.

Ramzan sat down directly across the table from me. He was about twenty-eight years old but he looked much younger. After talking a bit, he pleaded with me to visit Chechnya. Now, the first thing that Americans were told when they entered Russia was "DO NOT GO TO CHECHNYA." Back in 2005 it was still a very violent and dangerous place to be.

While I was thinking about this, a young, tall, husky guy walked into the room. He looked like he pumped some serious iron. He was wearing a black leather jacket and he pulled the jacket open and revealed two large automatic handguns stuck in a huge ammunition belt around his waist. He was just one of Ramzan's bodyguards.

"Do you think anybody back in Arizona would believe any of this?" I whispered to Marilyn.

Ramzan kept pitching for me to come to his country, and we set up a lunch the following day at the Hyatt, my last day at the hotel. When I told them about my hotel situation, they offered to move me to the Rossiya, a huge non-touristy Russian hotel that was right near Red Square. The owner was a friend of Ramzan's. There must have been ten thousand rooms in this hotel. When Marilyn picked me up in the morning, it took her half an hour to get from the lobby to my room.

The third morning I was staying at the hotel, Marilyn came to get me but I wasn't there. She waited in the lobby for an hour and then she went home and frantically called Darryl, my assistant, back in Vegas and told him that she had lost me. He had no idea where I was. Later that night one of her friends called her.

"I just saw Mike on TV. He's in Chechnya."

I had left with Ramzan and his entourage that morning. I couldn't turn down all that money. Chechnya was an amazing place. As soon as I got there, they gave me a machine gun. I was nervous as hell. I didn't particularly want to shoot no goddamn gun but, hey, when in Rome do as the Romans do. Chechnya was predominately Muslim so they gave me a kufi to wear and they called me by my Muslim name, Malik Abdul Aziz, which meant "King and Servant of the Almighty" in Arabic. I only like to be called Abdul. If you don't call me Abdul then just call me Mike. I was being hailed to the whole country as a Muslim hero. Muslim hero, my ass—I was a raging cokehead.

It really was a primitive culture in Chechnya. Half of the country had been burnt down during the wars with Russia. There were hardly any stores where I was. Nothing but land, no buildings. Marilyn later told me that she was worried for my safety because some of the rebels were opposed to Ramzan's regime, but if anybody would have looked at me the wrong way while I was there those bodyguards would have taken their eyes out.

I made an appearance at their big soccer stadium. Their idea of excitement was to watch somebody do wheelies on a motorbike, Evel Knievel style. That was their culture. Look, if they're going to take me to watch something, I'm going to say, "This is magnificent." One thing I learned from that trip was to let people be in charge. I didn't want to be confrontational.

My main job there was to open a four-day national boxing tournament that was being held in the memory of Ramzan's dad.

"I am glad that I am in the Chechen Republic that I have read and heard so much about," I told the crowd. "And I'm glad that I am among Muslims. We have seen on television an unfair war being waged in the Chechen Republic for a long time. We in America prayed for it to end."

I went back to Moscow late that night. I didn't get a chance to meet any Chechen girls. This visit was all about spirituality, all about Allah and Islam.

Back in Moscow, I spent some more quality time with Marilyn. My purpose of going to Russia was to see her and get some therapy. And if I ever needed some help from the courts, I could tell them that I had put in time with Marilyn in Russia, so it was a good political move for me too.

One night Marilyn set up a dinner at a Georgian restaurant and I met some very prominent business leaders. The next day, I told Marilyn that I didn't want to meet any more big people. I wanted to hang out with some of her personal friends. So Marilyn invited me to lunch at her apartment. I was shocked when I saw the building she lived in. It reminded me of the tenement buildings I'd lived in as a kid. It even had the same stench of piss lingering in the halls. "Marilyn, what are you doing here?" I asked her. But that's where she wanted to be—with the people. After lunch, Marilyn invited over about seven of her close Russian friends. They were all psychologists and pastors, all professional people.

We sat around in a circle in Marilyn's living room and these people began to share their stories with me. Most of them had come from alcoholic homes. I knew just from living with Cus and Camille that Communism had some kind of ill backlash. So when they all started sharing I didn't want them to feel uncomfortable because I was there. They might think that I had it going on because I was famous and known around the world. They must have assumed that I had nothing in common with them until I started telling my story. That's what we all had in common, our stories. I was used to sharing like this just from being in all the institutions and group homes over the years. So I laid it all out for them. I told them about the violence in my childhood and the issues with my mother and being scared and bullied all the time. And they all felt more at ease.

There was a woman sitting next to me whose father had been a Russian military officer. Their home had been blown up by terrorists when she was a baby and her father died trying to save her life. She had been severely burnt in the attack and now her hands were just stubs and she had scars all over her body. She was now the head of the counseling psychology department for Moscow State University of Psychology and Education.

"Here I am, a psychologist, but nobody has ever been able to help me deal with my pain, all the psychological pain, the loss of my dad. I feel like I've waited my whole lifetime for Marilyn to come and to help me and know how to deal with this pain," she said.

She started crying as she talked and I slipped out of my seat and sat down on the floor at her feet and held what was left of her hand as she talked. When she finished, I stayed sitting on the floor.

All of us in the room really bonded. What was supposed to have been a two-hour session ended up running for six hours. When we were leaving, one of the people came up to me.

"We think you should either be a politician or a preacher," she said. "You could run for president of Russia and win."

But I knew that Russia was no place for me. In Russian they don't even have a word for "balance." There's no balance in Russia, only extremes. That's why I fit in so good there. That place was just too perfect for me and my demons. I loved being in Russia. I could do anything I wanted with impunity.

Jeff went back to the States and I went on to Portugal. I called my friend Mario to come meet me there the next day because he's Portuguese, but he couldn't just drop everything and come. I checked into a resort and I scored some coke and began doing it. I had been up for days without sleeping before that and the combination of that and the amount of coke I had done was enough to make me pass out. The lady I was with didn't think I was still breathing so she called for the hotel physician. By the time he arrived I was fine. He wanted me to go to the hospital to be checked out but I passed.

I didn't like where I was staying in Portugal very much. It was too stuffy for me. Everyone was too serious. The men all dressed up in suits. Everyone in the whole country was a workaholic. There was nobody to play with there. I got bored the second day and went to Amsterdam. Now, the Dutch knew how to party. I flew in a girl that I had met in Romania. She was a wonderful girl but she got nervous when I started doing a ton of cocaine and invited prostitutes up to our room. She told me she wasn't into drugs and went home. But I continued my orgies and partying. Two weeks later I couldn't take it anymore and I had Darryl come and get me. Even after he got there I partied for two more weeks before he could convince me to go home.

I flew back to Vegas and then I immediately left for L.A. I stayed there for a day and then I flew by myself to New York. I checked into the St. Regis hotel. It was my favorite hotel because they kept your butler on call by your door. I put down my suitcases and immediately got high on coke. Now I wanted to go out and party, so I opened one of my suitcases and I saw that my clothes were wrinkled. I panicked. My head started hurting, my heart started racing, and I freaked out. I was high as a kite when I called my butler.

"I NEED SOMEBODY UP HERE TO IRON MY PANTS, NOW!!! NOW, NOW!!"

The people on the phone were laughing because I was in a state of panic over my pants. I left the hotel and started walking while my pants were getting pressed. I wanted to eat something but the coke had killed my appetite so I figured that walking would wear down my high. I walked around Fifth Avenue, I walked over to Times Square, and then I walked back to the hotel.

When I got back to my room, the butler was just finishing up. He had ironed the contents of both of my suitcases. He was still laughing about my call. I gave the guy a huge tip and went out and partied.

The next day I flew down to Florida to see Roy Jones Jr. fight Antonio Tarver. I was high and I was tired but the whole time I was down there Tarver was chasing me around saying, "Me and you have got to fight, man." He was in my ear constantly.

"No, man," I finally told him. "I'm having a rough time. I don't even know if I want to be in America now. I'm really down now. I don't want to fight anybody."

I was still wired from coke, I'd been doing it nonstop since I went to Europe four months before. All I wanted to do was take a shit. When you've got all that cocaine in your system, you take these cocaine dumps because your guts are all wrapped up. But all that didn't stop me from driving over to the Overtown and Liberty City areas of Miami to score coke and some Cuban hookers. Of course, whenever I was in the ghettos, I'd get stopped by the police.

"Mike Tyson! What the hell are you doing here, man? This is a dangerous place, Mike," the cop said. "Get in the car, let us take you someplace safe."

"No, I'm fine, Officer. Please, you can just go. You're causing problems for me, sir."

"Mr. Tyson, please. They don't care that you're the champ, this is not the place to be," the cop insisted.

"Sir, I'll be in a lot of trouble if you keep hanging around. I'm fine."

I was trying to score some blow and some Cuban girls and these guys were making me hot. When I went to these neighborhoods, the people would see me and say, "What's up, champ, what are you looking for?"

They just saw it on me. They knew I wanted to get high.

I partied with drugs and alcohol nonstop from the time that I got out of the ring with McBride. After my trips around the world, I settled back into Vegas and established my drug routine. I'd try to wake up by ten p.m. and be out of the shower and all pretty and ready to go out by eleven p.m. By then, someone was on the way over here and I'd do a little coke before I left. We'd drive to the hood in North Vegas and hit the bars until about one a.m. unless there was something interesting going on there, like a new drug individual coming to town. Then I'd hit some clubs on the Strip. There it was all about knowing the maître d's, hanging out in the suites, and hustling girls. I'd hang out there until four or five a.m. when we'd hit the after-hours spots like Drai's. After staying there for an hour we'd go to the strip clubs like Seamless that had a crowd that came there to hang out. At these after-hours spots you'd see everyone from celebrities and beautiful models to hard-core hustlers.

These beautiful people were all drugpires. You never saw them in the daytime, going to a dentist's office or at a mall. Their life was just like mine; they'd be sleeping all day and partying all night. So we'd hang out with them one morning after the after-hours club and they all had beautiful homes. They were either drug dealers or rich, bad-seed kids. There were always tons of people hanging out with them at the clubs and they'd always get the bill.

I'd be out in the clubs and the next thing I knew, I was in a room in a big mansion with all these people. I don't even know how we got from the club to this house. By now I'd lost my woman. And I want to be the facilitator. When people do blow, for some reason they think I'm cute. And the women of these very scary guys decide that they want to touch me. I'm like, "Whoa, whoa, this is not what it's about right here. It's all about togetherness."

Now I get nervous. This guy is watching his woman touch me. I'm getting sober because the fear and the high just don't go together. Now I feel like a disgusting fat motherfucker. I can tell that this guy is a bad person. He's probably done time already and he's not afraid to kill someone. And he's got a crazy lady who's intent on touching me.

I've learned how to deal with women in these kinds of situations. I always put myself down, don't make myself important. I'm really good at that.

"Oh, baby, I'm a junkie. Please, girl, don't mess with me. I've caught so many diseases. I'm surprised you didn't get one just by being in my presence."

I know how to turn a woman off. And that's good for my health. Sometimes a woman is a man's whole life. A woman can invade a man's mind. She can take a pussy-whipped boyfriend and turn him into a gut-wrenching psychopath. So I never underestimate a guy like that.

One of the interesting people I met around then was a pimp I called Chance. I was at one of the strip club/after-hours clubs and he came over to me.

"Hey, Mr. Tyson. Wow, I always wanted to meet you because you always say you're the baddest man on the planet, and I'm always saying I'm the baddest pimp on the planet. The way you fight is the way I pimp."

"Is that true, nigga?" I said.

"Yeah, man, I ain't shitting. I know about your bankruptcy, I know about them stealing your money. Nigga, you're with me now, I've got nothing but money. You see all these men here? They're on the wagon until I come. I supply everything."

I started hanging out with Chance and he had all these pretty cars, Porsches, Ferraris, the Maseratis and Lamborghinis. I thought that he must like cocaine but this guy was a country pimp. He'd tell all these lies to make it seem like he was a man of the world but all he did was sissy drugs like ecstasy.

I was broke, so one night I said, "Get me some cocaine, nigga."

"Who got cocaine?" he said. "Let me call my man."

The next time I saw him, he had the coke. He called a weed dealer friend of his who had some. So I snorted some and then I passed it to him.

"Go ahead, man, do that shit, nigga," I said. "It's just like ecstasy but chopped up."

He did a couple of lines but he immediately had a bad reaction to the coke.

"Oh, my head!" he screamed and fell to the floor. "Oh shit, Mike! Pimp down! Pimp down!"

I was thinking, *Oh shit, this guy is about to die.* We were with his nephew so I got him to drive Chance home. I was in the front seat and Chance was lying down and moaning in the back of his four-door Maserati. Meanwhile, I was such a druggie, I was snorting the bad coke, I didn't care if it was killing Chance. We dropped him off at his house and I took the whole stash with me. Hey, bad coke is better than no coke. Chance recovered in a few days.

Around that time I started hanging out with this guy named Michael Politz. We had actually been in jail together in Maryland. He was in and out every once in a while because he said his crazy girlfriend at the time was slapping him with restraining orders that he kept violating so he could see his kid. Michael was totally plugged into the Vegas nightlife scene. He was straight, he didn't drink or do drugs, so he was a perfect sober companion for me. I was doing enough drugs for the two of us. One night he heard about this party that the strip club Scores was throwing in the bowling alley suite at the Palms Hotel. The adult video convention was in town and the party was packed full of beautiful porn stars. I was eyeing two of them, but they had their boyfriends with them. Meanwhile, Michael was hitting on a pretty waitress. I had a brief conversation with one of the girls out of earshot of the boyfriends and then I went back to Michael.

"Come here," I told him and I pulled him away from his waitress. We were whispering like little girls.

"Look behind me," I said. "That's the bathroom. I'm going to take these two girls into the bathroom and fuck them. Here's what I want you to do. See those two guys? Those are the girls' boyfriends. You're going to keep them busy."

"What!" Michael said.

"It's going to be fine, brother, don't worry," I said.

"And what if these guys fuck with me?"

"Don't worry, I'll be able to hear it. If I hear a commotion and they start to kick your ass, I'll be right out of the bathroom in seconds and help you out. It's going to be fine," I assured him.

My face was pressing against his ear, whispering all this shit. So to bust my balls, Michael blurted out all loud, "Mike, I'm not that comfortable right now with your mouth so close to my ear."

The whole room heard him. I started laughing hysterically. This was one crazy white boy.

"Now you really owe me, motherfucker," I said.

"All right, go," he told me.

I went into the bathroom with the one girl while Michael diverted the guys' attention. Then the other girl snuck in while he was telling them all these Mike Tyson stories. By the time the guys realized the girls were gone and asked where they went, Michael told them we all probably stepped outside for a second to smoke a joint.

That's just how I was back then. I was fucked up and attracting that kind of energy. I was gaining weight and I was starting to look like a fat rock star. But because of the blow, my confidence was sky-high.

I was getting more and more blatant with the coke while I was out in clubs. I was with my friend Mack the barber one night and we were hanging out at the bar at the Wynn Hotel. Between signing autographs and posing for pictures with people, I kept going to the bathroom. Finally, Security came up to Mack.

"You need to come get your friend," they told him. I had gotten caught doing blow in the bathroom and they were kicking me out of the hotel. That was the way it was then. I'd either get the royal treatment at the nightclubs or I'd be thrown out because people would report that I was doing coke in the bathroom or I was banging some broad in there. I was friendly with a lot of the doormen so they'd let me back in but some clubs totally barred me.

That's why I always liked going to strip clubs more.

"Why do we hang out at these dance clubs when we can go to the strip clubs?" I'd tell my friends. "These girls have their clothes on and they've got an attitude. At the strip clubs the girls are naked and they've got good attitudes. Let's get right to the nitty-gritty."

The strip club owners all worked with me. I had my own private bathroom in some of those clubs. I'd be in there for hours and then I'd come out and talk with the owner. I was such a prima donna that when the security guy would come up to me, I'd scream at him.

"Get away from me! Get away from me, I'm not bothering nobody."

It got so blatant that I'd be carrying my bag of coke openly with a straw coming out of it like it was a milkshake. I'd give a friend a hit and they'd think they'd be getting a little bump but then they'd squeal because so much coke was in the bag. They'd start coughing and spitting.

I started dating some of the strippers, and that was a volatile situation. I'd be high and I'd see one of my girls with a client, and I'd barge right over to her.

"Why are you not returning my calls?" I'd yell at her. She was doing a lap dance for some guy and I was in her face, harassing her.

"Hey, if there's a problem . . ." the scared customer would say to me.

"Just mind your business, I'm talking to her," I'd snarl.

Then the girls I was dating would get jealous and they'd start fighting with one another in the middle of the club. So I started getting banned from certain shifts.

The next thing you know, I started sleeping in the strip clubs. I'd get a box of fried chicken and I'd be eating it and then I'd just pass out from staying up for days on end. I'd be sleeping and the strippers were eating my chicken and going through my pockets. Then I'd wake up and start fighting with the G-string divas, not because they were going through my pockets but because they were eating my chicken and I was ravenously hungry. When you come down from coke, you're famished.

By November of 2005, I was really gone. I went to L.A. for the premiere of 50 Cent's *Get Rich or Die Tryin'*. I was really high on cocaine and Robin was there. She must have seen me running around before the movie started, hitting on girls and just being silly. When the movie was over, I got up from my seat and she was right there. She gave me a hug and I kissed her. I was hoping that I might get to fuck her again. But she just went "Whoa" and walked away. As soon as she walked away, I turned around and Naomi Campbell grabbed me and hugged me. She must have seen me hugging Robin and she was probably thinking, *He shouldn't be hugging that bitch. With all that shit he went through with her, he's hugging her?*

Naomi pulled out of the hug and looked me in the eyes.

"Mike, the word is out you're doing a lot of blow. You need to stop. You're fucking your life up."

She was mad and she was reading me a couple of paragraphs of the riot act. Nay Nay always cared deeply about me, and vice versa. She was a true friend.

But I didn't heed her advice. I kept right on doing blow. Now, if you get high on coke and you don't have girls around, that's not a good high. And if you have girls without the coke, that's not good either. You need both of them for the optimal experience. I used to say I needed "a ho and some blow." Now, you might think that doing a lot of cocaine was not conducive to having sex, but that's what Cialis and Viagra were for.

Around this time I started hanging out with Crocodile again. He would come back from training someone for a fight and he'd be in full party mode. One time, we were in my hotel room in Vegas with a famous porn star and her boyfriend. We had arranged for her to come to the room to have sex with us. As soon as they came into the room, Crocodile and I started taking off our clothes. Her boyfriend supposedly was okay with us both having sex with the porn star until he saw us naked.

"No, please don't do it," he cried to his girlfriend.

"What's the deal with homeboy here?" I asked her. "I thought he was cool with this."

"No, no! Just have oral sex with them," he pleaded.

"No, man, we want to step on this pussy," I told him.

He started crying so much that the porn star got up.

"I can't do this. I got to go with him," she said, and they both left.

Crocodile was too much. Every time he saw me with a girl, he automatically started taking his clothes off.

"Crocodile, this is my woman," I'd tell him. "Not this time."

"Oh, my bad, my bad," he'd apologize.

Croc and I were at a New Year's Eve 2006 party in Phoenix. Dennis Rodman and Charles Barkley were there too. At the end of the night I saw this beautiful, beautiful girl, one of the most exquisite women I had ever seen. She was an actress and she kept dropping names, like Charlie Sheen. The girl was in close proximity to Crocodile but I couldn't tell if she was really with him. I was looking at her and I said, "Who are you with?" And the next thing I knew, she said she was with Crocodile. *This is going to be interesting,* I thought.

We brought her back to a house that I had purchased in Phoenix and we started messing with the girl but we were both so high that we couldn't get an erection, even though we were kissing on her and licking her. So we went out to some twenty-four-hour porn shop and brought some dirty movies back. And that didn't even work. Man, it was so frustrating. This was the best-looking person I'd ever seen in my life and I couldn't do anything. Croc and I were like two little kids at Christmas who weren't strong enough to open the toy box. I was so pissed that I wasn't packing my Cialis that night. I was just out getting high, I didn't think I was going to run into any pussy.

I was able to buy that house in Phoenix because from time to time I'd make some money that didn't have to go right to the creditors. A company in Japan gave me $800,000 to do a Pachinko gambling machine and an extra $100,000 to allow them to put me in trunks that were not black.

So my partying shifted to Phoenix then. I had spent a lot of time with Shelly Finkel in Phoenix so I was pretty connected to some wealthy people there. If I needed a place to stay before I bought the house, they'd find me someplace. Phoenix is a smaller party scene than Vegas but in some ways it's much more intense. It looks like a quiet town, but at night it turned into a little animal. The partying there was really high end, everyone getting down in mansions or in great hotel suites.

I got into a party circle there that included a lot of doctors. One of the doctors was a plastic surgeon and he used to have me come to his office and he'd set me up in one of the examining rooms. I had my cocaine to one side, my weed to the other, Viagra out on the table.

"Hey, Doc, I'm coming down. I don't like the way I'm feeling," I told him one day.

"Don't worry, I'll set you up," he said and he went into the other room.

A few minutes later he wheeled in one of those intravenous drip things. He hooked me up to it.

"This'll take the edge right off," he said.

"What is it?" I asked him.

"A morphine drip," he said.

This plastic surgeon could party like crazy. One time, he was driving alone in his car, doing all this coke, and he rolled the car. He went through the window and his face got all scraped up by the trees and the brush he plowed through.

Shortly after this I went to his house. I was shocked when he opened the door.

"You better look at your face, man," I said. "You're fucked up."

All of the skin of his face had been peeled off by the brush and his whole face was one mask of blood. He was lucky he was a plastic surgeon.

I would get so fucked in Phoenix that I would start hallucinating. One time, I was in a car, and my assistant Darryl was driving. We were coming up to one of my friend's houses and I said to Darryl, "Look! There are all these people outside the house waving at us." There weren't no people, it was the trees' branches moving from the wind.

In July of 2006 I got another visit from the FBI. I had been partying the night before and when I saw an FBI SWAT team coming up the front steps of my house, I ran to the back door but they were right there too.

"Mr. Tyson? We need to talk to you, champ."

Oh shit, I thought. *Whose ass did I grab last night?*

"We'd like to know your association with this gentleman in the picture. His name is Dale Hausner," one of the agents said.

I looked at the picture. It showed this guy Dale and me shaking hands like we were buddies.

"Do you know this man? He's a boxing writer and a photographer," the agent said.

"I do remember this man. He came to visit me when I was working out in my gym. There were a few of the Mexican fighters there and they started hassling him.

"'Get out of here, you fucking fag,' one of the Mexican fighters said to him. 'The champ don't want to talk to you.'

"But it was Ramadan so I interceded and explained to the other fighters that this was a time of peace and that everybody had a place. So I let him interview me. I'm sorry if he was offended in any way. I didn't mean to cause him any discomfort."

"No, no, he liked you, Mr. Tyson," the FBI agent said. "He just didn't like the eight people that he murdered and the other nineteen people that he shot."

It turned out that the police were investigating Hausner and his friend for a string of drive-by shootings in Arizona from May 2005 through July 2006. It was a good thing that I stopped those guys and showed this guy some respect or he might have been waiting outside the gym to shoot me.

At the end of August, I got a gig doing boxing exhibitions at the Aladdin Hotel in Vegas. It was a sweet deal. They gave me a nice suite and paid me to work out in a room where they set up a boxing ring. Thousands of people coming through the hotel could see me sparring and hitting the heavy bag. I got free food, whatever I wanted, carte blanche. So I called all my friends.

"Come on over. I'm here for a month. You can order anything, it's on the bitch, nigga."

I called the hotel "the bitch" then. I was in that pimp mentality.

Bobby Brown was in town and I invited him and Karrine Steffans, aka Superhead, the girl he was currently seeing, to come up to see me. I had fooled around with her before too, so it was all good, so I thought. She was one of those girls who you couldn't get ahold of that often but when you did it was a great time.

Bobby didn't want to do that. I didn't realize that he was actually serious about her. So he brought his father and some other friends down. They came there first and I gave them the royal treatment. Then Bobby came. I was down in the lobby when he arrived and we went up the elevator together. People were going crazy when they saw the two of us. The wife in one couple said, "Oh shit! Mike Tyson and Bobby Brown. These two niggas together, it's on, baby, it is on." They knew that we were trouble.

I wanted Bobby to chill for a while with me. It was great to hang out with Bobby because when he was married to Whitney she would never let him hang out with me—although I couldn't blame her.

Around this time, I started to have difficulty acquiring my coke. It wasn't like there was any shortage of blow in Vegas; it was that the dealers didn't want to provide coke to my ass. Dealers were always notoriously late when they said they'd be by with the stuff, and I had no patience so sometimes I'd wind up copping in a burger joint. My drought began in the ghetto. First, they wouldn't let me in the bathroom of the bars on the Westside. Then the drug dealers started refusing to service me.

"Go train, Mike, we need you to train," they'd tell me. These guys had grown up with me in Vegas, seen me hanging around the barbershop for years, and they didn't want to contribute to my downfall. I used to hand out free turkeys to these guys when they were kids so they felt a real bond with me. So out of necessity I started fucking with the white people on the Strip. The casino greeters, the doormen at the clubs, they all had connections.

I was at the Aladdin during the time I was doing the exhibitions and I called up a guy to have an eight ball sent up to my suite. They sent this fucking country nigga with the blow. He was all excited, he thought that he was going to be partying with me and a bunch of girls. He was going to be the life of the party and hold everyone captive with that coke. I opened the door for him and let him in.

"You got the stuff?" I said.

"Yeah, but where the people at?"

"There ain't nobody. Just me here, nigga," I said. "You sell drugs, right? So just sell me the motherfucking drugs, okay?"

I grabbed the package from his hands.

"Fuck that shit, you don't need to do this stuff, Mike," he said. "You're the champ. We love you, Mike."

"As a matter of fact, I'll work out by escorting your ass to the door."

I opened the door and the fucker grabbed the bag of coke and ran out. "Go fucking train, Mike," he yelled back at me. I ran after him but I was fat and mad and I didn't have no clothes on. I was clutching a towel that was around my waist.

"You come back, motherfucker. I'm going to kill you!"

He was in shape and he got away. I really wanted to beat his ass. Who did he think he was, Florence Fucking Nightingale?

I started strong-arming the few dealers that would still sell to me when I was low on cash. One day a dealer came to me for help.

"Listen, Mike, can you help me out? Please tell Crocodile to pay me my money. I gave him all this coke."

Once he told me that, he was finished. I knew this guy was a pussy and I knew that I'd never have to pay him for drugs anymore if he couldn't get Crocodile to pay him.

"Sure, I'll talk to Crocodile, but give me that stuff you've got right now," and I snatched his coke right out of his hand.

"Oh, man, my boss is going to kill me. I need to bring back some money," he said.

"Your boss needs that money from that other nigga," I said.

"Nah, man, I got to get it from you."

"Well, you tell your boss to come and talk to me about the money then. Listen, you got me addicted, now you want to charge me money, motherfucker? I'm strung out on the coke, nigga."

Once when I had no money for coke I drove out to Summerlin where the big coke kings lived. I'd meet them in their big mansions and I'd hang with them for hours, taking pictures, doing lines with them. Then when it was time to get down to the negotiations, I'd play them. They'd tell me the price and I'd get indignant.

"Hey, what's this all about? You really want to sell me this shit, brother? You've been hanging out with me all day and you want to make me pay for this shit?"

"Here, take it," they'd finally say.

Cocaine is the devil, there's no doubt about it. I was always a chauvinist when it came to women. Even if I was broke, I'd never let them buy me dinner. But when I needed money for blow and I saw my girlfriend drop some money, I'd wait and then put it in my pocket. That was one of the worst feelings I ever felt. I didn't want to play with the devil any longer, but he still wanted to play and it wouldn't be over until he said it was over.

I was so destitute that I even went to Youngstown, Ohio, to put on a four-round boxing exhibition on October twentieth with my old sparring partner Corey Sanders. It was promoted by this ex-fighter named

Sterling McPherson. I didn't remember getting paid for the exhibition even though Sterling sold four thousand out of six thousand seats at prices from $25 to $200 and charged $29.95 for the pay-per-view of the event. But I thought that if I stayed busy I could get off drugs. McPherson was talking about touring this exhibition all over the world so maybe I'd get some gwap then.

The whole match was a fiasco. Corey came in at three hundred pounds, about fifty pounds bigger than me. He wore headgear and the crowd booed him for that. We began to spar and I got in a good shot and dropped Corey in the first round. I had him in trouble in the third and the fourth but I didn't press it. I didn't have any hurting in my heart back then.

As soon as the exhibition was over I went back to Vegas and got higher and higher. One night I was out on the town and I ran into the guy who had pulled a gun on me back at Bentley's years earlier in New York. He was still with his wife and they saw me in a club and I was looking so bad that they felt sorry for me.

"Are you all right, man?" he asked me.

He should have kicked my ass right there. I was vulnerable then.

By then, my nose was so fucked up from doing coke that I started smoking it. Not crack, I would take the regular powdered coke and take some tobacco out of one of my cigarettes and add it in. That's what we used to do when we were kids back in Brooklyn. All the sniffers, the people who sniff cocaine, they all hated me smoking coke. Burning cocaine is the worst smell in the world. It smells like burning plastic and rat poison combined. A friend of mine once told me that when you want to know something about anything, put some fire under it, the fire brings out everything. You want to know something about a motherfucker, but some fire under his ass. Well, when you put some fire under that cocaine, you know what it's made out of—all that poison, all that shit comes up out of there and it smells like hell.

I even smoked that shit in my favorite strip club in Vegas. The owner would let me go to the bathroom and smoke. He was helping me kill myself. In Phoenix they let me smoke my coke inside the club. Thank God the cops never walked in there when I was doing that. For me, doing coke was very ritualistic, so I re-created my rituals in the strip club. I had my Hennessy, my Cialis, my Marlboros all surrounding me. And, of course, the coke, which I would pass around to all my friends.

During this whole crazy period when I was doing all these drugs and bringing in hookers, I used to hear Cus in my head every day. But I didn't give a fuck because he wasn't there in the flesh. Living wasn't a big priority for me then. Now all I want to do is live, but back then, in the prime of my life, it meant nothing to me. By the time I was the champ at twenty, so many of my friends were dead or decimated. Some of them were sent away to prison for so long that when they came back out they were zombies, they didn't know what planet they were on. Some even did something intentionally to get back behind bars.

During those years, for me doing an eight ball a day, three and a half grams of coke, was just a good night. The more I did, the more I wanted to do it alone. Maybe I was just a pig or maybe I didn't want people to see me that sloppy. By then, there was nothing euphoric anymore about coke, it was just numbing. I wasn't even having sex with women with the coke anymore. Every now and then I had a girl with me but it was more to chill out with than to have sex.

I was living a crazy existence. One day I'd be in the sewage with some street hooker trying to get her to have sex without a condom, and the next night I'd be in Bel-Air with my rich friends with a happy face on, celebrating Rosh Hashanah. Right about then, I hit rock bottom. I was in a hotel suite in Phoenix. I had my morphine drip and my Cialis and my bottle of Hennessy. And seven hookers. All of a sudden, the coke made me paranoid and I thought that these women were trying to set me up and rob me. So I started beating them. That's when I realized that it wasn't just demons around me, it was the devil himself. And he had won. I kicked those hookers out of the room and did the rest of my coke.

Some of my lady friends, not lovers, just friends, would tell me that it was time that I found a woman to be with. They'd even say bullshit like "to die with."

"I'm going to do this to the end, baby. I'm going to play to a place I can't play anymore," I'd tell them. I was talking bullshit. I had to find myself before I could find somebody else. Jackie Rowe used to try to lecture me about drugs and I'd just tell her, "If you love me, you'd let me do this."

"Listen, Mike, I refuse to sit here and watch you go out like a loser. We're winners," she'd say. She used to actually go through all my pants and jackets before she'd send them down to the hotel cleaners to make sure there weren't drugs in them.

I knew that all my friends were concerned about my drug use but they knew better than to tell me to stop doing what I loved to my face. I began to isolate myself just so I didn't have to hear any of that shit. I had only one friend who could get away with telling me that. It was Zip. He did it in such a clever way too. He'd be with me chilling, smoking some weed, and then he'd turn serious on me.

"Don't worry, Mike, we are going to have a beautiful funeral for you. I've already put the money aside. We'll be smoking some weed and drinking that good Cristal and thinking about you. I'm going to get one of those carriages that the horses pull around and we'll have your casket behind it and we're going to flaunt your body through all the boroughs of the city, man. It's going to be beautiful, man."

At the end of October, I had lunch in Phoenix with my therapist Marilyn, who was back from Moscow. I was sitting in the restaurant and I saw a pretty young lady by herself at another table and I told the waiter that I would pay for her meal. Then the lady came over to our table and gave me her number.

When she left, Marilyn was quiet for a second. Then she spoke.

"I'll make you a bet that you couldn't last six weeks in a rehab."

That struck my macho nerves.

"Are you crazy? I could do six weeks like nothing, I'm disciplined."

The truth was, I was ready to do something like that. I had gotten tired of falling through the loopholes. I had a bad relationship with my kids, I had a bad relationship with the mothers of my kids, I had bad relationships with a lot of friends of mine. Some people were scared to be around me.

I was about to leave to do a meet-and-greet tour of England for six weeks so I decided that I would stop doing drugs, even weed, during that tour so that by the time I got back to Phoenix for the rehab, I'd be prepared. So I stopped. I didn't do coke or weed and I even stopped drinking.

That was when I knew that I really had a problem. The first couple of hours I was just losing my mind. I destroyed my hotel room, I was going crazy, but I didn't get high. I had a miserable trip but I didn't get high once. So when I got back to Phoenix, I was all clean and ready to go into rehab. I'd already gone through the severe withdrawals.

Marilyn took me to a place called The Meadows. We walked into that place and right off the bat it looked more like a prison than a rehabilitation center. The first thing they did there was to keep you high on medicine. Everybody in the place was fat and slow. If you'd get into a fight it would take them two hours to get there. So they banged me up on meds and then they took me for an interview with the counselors. I thought that rehab was a place where you just chilled and watched TV until your time was up. I didn't know I was going to have to talk about my deep past and my inner trauma. But these weird, intrusive motherfuckers were all over me with questions.

"How long have you been getting high?"

"What drugs have you used?"

"What external circumstances trigger your drug use?"

"What was your home life like as a child?"

"By any chance are you a homosexual?"

Holy shit, these guys wouldn't stop getting in my face. This guy that I didn't know from a can of paint expected me to answer all these intimate questions. I didn't want to deal with the reality of who I was and my relationship with my demons.

"Hey, get the fuck out of my head, motherfucker. Fuck all of you!" I said. "How dare you talk to me like this, you uppity piece of white trash."

And then I left the next day.

15

A WEEK LATER I CHECKED INTO ANOTHER REHAB IN TUCSON. MARILYN WAS
going to kill me if I didn't go back into treatment. She can give the
impression of being a nice, innocent, old grandmotherly white lady,
but she's not. She wouldn't let me quit. She gave me some real grimy
aggressive chastisement. She said, "No, no, you are going to finish
this bet." That's when I saw another side to her—that fire in her eyes.
She was nobody to play with, she meant business. So I tried another
place in Phoenix. I liked the people at this second place. I bonded with
this young wealthy girl who was going to school to be a fashion designer and was strung out on heroin. I got in trouble there because
someone hurt my feelings and said something about me to one of the
staff members and I ripped into them. Everybody got scared when I
was talking because they weren't used to a nigga talking to them that
way. The people running the place just said, "You have to go, everybody is scared," so I called this young girl I was dating and she came
and got me and I left.

Phoenix is a white-bread by-the-book-assed town. When you're in a drug rehabilitation program there, you can feel the superciliousness of racism there from these sophisticated doctors and the other people who were supposed to help you.

I was the token Negro there. The staff had a stereotypical preconceived notion of black men, and, in particular, black athletes. The head administrator even had the audacity to say to me, "We had other athletes here and they all had their jewelry on. I noticed you're not flashy like them."

"That's because I don't have any money," I responded curtly.

The undertone of his comments wasn't lost on me. He just omitted the word "black," although he was thinking it.

Marilyn saw that too and kept trying to find me a place that would work for me. But I had other things to do first. It was Christmas 2006 and I was determined to make it a white Christmas in Arizona. My assistant Darryl was sleeping in another room and I snuck out of the house and got into my BMW. I drove to the Pussycat Lounge, and when I got there, I looked for the manager, this hot Eastern European girl that I had been attracted to.

"Where's the white bitch at?" I asked her.

"I can get you some, one minute," she said.

She came back with three small plastic bags with a gram of coke in each one.

Then she shocked me.

"Can I have some?" she said.

I had never had any indication that this girl was interested in me. We went into the office and did a few lines each.

"You've been drinking, Mike," she observed. "Do you need me to drive you somewhere?"

"No, I'm okay," I said.

I couldn't believe I said that. Here was my chance to get that pussy that I had coveted for years. The devil was surely working on me then. I was thinking, *I'm not going to let her drive me, she just wants my cocaine. Fuck this bitch.* I wanted to be alone with my fantasy girl, the real white bitch. I was just being selfish about the cocaine. I could have gotten a ride home with the girl I was trying to get with for such a long time, but I didn't want to share any of the coke.

So I got in the car. I immediately dumped most of the coke from one of the baggies on the center console. Then I pulled out my Marlboros and took out half the tobacco from one cigarette and scooped up some coke and poured it into the cigarette. I took a few hits and then I started driving home.

Now, I'm not the best driver, even when I am stone-cold sober. So I was driving along, weaving between lanes, when I passed a police sobriety checkpoint. I didn't realize it but the cops saw the way I was driving so they started following me. After I blew past a stop sign and then nearly swerved into a sheriff's car, they pulled me over. When the cop approached my car, I frantically tried to brush all the coke off the console but the leather had pores in it and even if you spat and tried to wash it off, the pores would absorb some of the coke.

I rolled down my window and he asked for my license and registration. Then he realized it was me. And he saw the mess on the console.

"I can't believe this shit, Mike," he said.

He pulled me out of the car and did some field sobriety tests on me and I was too fucked up to pass. Then he searched me and found the other two baggies in my pants pocket. Then they brought the dope dog in and he sniffed the coke that was still in the car. So they took me in.

They had me in a holding cell before they interrogated me. I was really pissed. I had enough coke on me to warrant a felony. But whenever I was locked up, I'd always find a white guy in there that knows the system. This was no exception.

"Yo, champ, what are you in for?" the white kid asked me.

"Man, they caught me with some cocaine," I said.

"Have you ever been arrested for drugs before?" he asked.

"I've been arrested a lot of times but not for drugs."

His face brightened.

"Don't worry, bro. You're not going to jail," he said. "They can't lock you up for your first drug rap, they have to try to help you first."

Now that I knew what time it was, I was ready for my interrogation. The arresting officer brought me to a room.

"What drugs or medications have you been using?" he asked.

"Zoloft," I said.

"Anything else?"

"Marijuana and cocaine. I take one Zoloft pill a day."

"How much marijuana did you smoke?"

"Two joints, earlier in the day."

"When was the last time you used cocaine before now?" he asked me.

"Yesterday."

"How often do you use it?"

"Whenever I can get my hands on it. I had some this morning about nine a.m."

"Why do you use both marijuana and cocaine?"

"I'm an addict."

"Do you use them at the same time?"

"Yes. It makes me feel good when I use them together."

"What does the Zoloft do for you?" he asked.

"It regulates me. I'm fucked up."

"You don't appear to be fucked up," he said.

"I know, man, but I am fucked up," I said and then started laughing loudly like the guy in that movie *Reefer Madness* after he lit up a joint.

I told him that I smoked the coke in my Marlboros and he was intrigued how I did that so I took him through the whole process.

Another officer who was there asked me if I felt good because the drug was in my system while I was driving. I told him that I felt good earlier in the day.

"I want to thank you for being so cooperative, Mike," the first cop said.

"I'm a pretty cool guy," I said.

"In my town, people would start yelling at me if they knew I brought you in," he said.

I didn't know how to react so I just acted like a psycho. I looked down at the ground and spoke deeper than usual.

"Fuck you, I hate you. Fuck you, deadbeat. Fuck you."

"Does anyone ever give you shit, Mike?" the first cop asked.

"All the time. But I put it away and don't let it bother me," I said.

The cop turned off the tape recorder and walked me over to the Maricopa County Sheriff's Office mobile unit. They processed me in and set me up in a cell by myself. There was even a phone inside the cell. I spent most of the night making collect calls.

When I made bail the next morning, Darryl came to pick me up. I gave him a hug when I saw him. Darryl had been trying to keep me straight for years now, from Las Vegas to Amsterdam. It was a tough job.

"Yo, Mike, why did you bounce last night and not say anything to me?" he asked.

"Life's rough, brother. Life's rough," I said.

Darryl drove me to Shelley's house and I took a shower and saw my kids Miguel and Exodus, and had a nice meal. Then I got a lawyer. I called my contacts in Vegas and they came up with David Chesnoff, a really connected lawyer who was partners with Oscar Goodman, who represented me in my attempt to get my boxing license back. Even though it wasn't mandated, Chesnoff's strategy was to get me into rehab as soon as possible and for me to do meaningful community service to show the court that I was serious about straightening out my life.

So I went to my third rehab in Phoenix. It was in a small house where the guy who ran it lived. This guy was a real prick who kept trying to play me. I made one real friend there, though, an Italian guy from Brooklyn, one of those "Hey, let's get it going!" dudes. Great smile, great energy. I would have gotten kicked out a lot quicker if it wasn't for him. But the other people were afraid of me. The guy who ran the place used the fact that I forgot to lock up my medication as an excuse to boot my ass out.

I could have just said "Fuck you all, I ain't going back" at that point, but Marilyn and I had too strong a bond. So Marilyn and my lawyer did some research and they reached out to Dr. Sheila Balkan, a renowned criminologist who specialized in developing treatment options as an alternative to incarceration. She got me into my next rehab, a place in the Hollywood Hills called Wonderland. Sheila and Harold, one of her associates, came to pick me up and take me there. There was part of me that was so mad that I had to keep going back to these places and I got really high one more time before I left. A lot of junkies get high for the last ride. But these were really cool people, not judgmental at all. We got to Wonderland and I was a mess I was so high.

Wonderland was a universe apart from those other rehab places I had been to. This wasn't Arizona anymore; we had some liberal shit going on here. We were not dealing with judgmental people now, these are very interesting people who are not scared of difficult guys like me. Wonderland was one of those high-end rehabs that catered to the children of the elite—movie stars, bankers, you name it. This was mansion-style living, just like I had been accustomed to. It cost an arm and a leg, but I think they must have given me a break because I didn't have any money then.

I immediately fell in love with the place. I felt that this could be a life-saving deal. I had my own room and I was surrounded by all these cool young kids who didn't give a fuck. We were spitting distance from Marlon Brando's old house and the place where Jack Nicholson had lived for years. I settled in and started going to A.A. meetings. They let you go out into town on your own, you just had to be back at the house for curfew.

But a few weeks in, a wrench was thrown into the mix. Because I was a convicted level-three felon and I had the rape charge on my package, the administration was afraid of me being there with the other patients. If anything happened, everyone including the state of California could have been sued. I guess Sheila had called in a favor to get my ass in that place, but now it was touch and go whether I could stay. But I had become friends with all the kids there and they stepped up to the plate. Every night I would go and bring frozen yogurt back for everyone. At the meetings I brought cookies and milk. So we really had a family unit going on. Eventually they had a meeting and everyone was like, "Mike's got to stay. Don't let Mike go," and they voted and I was in.

I always prided myself on my discipline, but withdrawing from coke was a motherfucker. Every pain you ever got from boxing came back during the withdrawals. The coke and the liquor were like Novocaine for me. Once I stopped doing that, all my arthritis came roaring back. I was a cripple, I couldn't walk, my feet hurt so bad. Even today, I still have to get a cortisone shot every once in a while to get me through the pain.

I kept to the straight and narrow at Wonderland. There were temptations. A famous young actress was in there with me. She was going out every night with her friends. Four or five limos or Benzes would come pick them up. It was a whole convoy. She had a black guy who was running the show for her and he invited me to come along one night.

"Nah, I can't come. If there's even a picture of me hanging out with these guys, I'm going straight to prison," I told him.

I wanted to go so bad, it was still in me, but I resisted. But these kids were bending the rules right and left. One rich kid actually snuck a fifty-inch flat-screen TV into his room so that he could play his video games. They caught his ass and took it right out.

After a while, I got into a rhythm. I threw myself into my meetings. I did the 12-step work better than anyone. I was the poster boy for doing the work. Everybody was required to go to one meeting a day, I'd go to three or four. Marilyn came to visit me about three months after I got there and I took her to one of my meetings on the Sunset Strip. I passed the basket around to get donations for the coffee and tea. Then when the meeting was over, I put away the chairs and swept and mopped the floor. I wanted to feel good doing that stuff.

I still had conflicting feelings about all this. A lot of my heroes were losers when it came to managing their lives but were champions in their field. People wanted to get them off alcohol and drugs to save them, but sometimes without the alcohol and drugs, they'd lose their great qualities. The people in my life were happy when I was sober, but I was miserable. I just wanted to die.

But I always had Marilyn in my face when I thought like that.

"What are you talking about? You are going to be in the program," she'd yell. She'd go from a nice white-haired lady to a fucking demon. It was meant for that lady to be in my life. You're so caught up in your vice you don't even realize how sick you are. I equate sickness with blisters or dripping, not psychological illness.

Because of my celebrity they wanted me to go to the closed meetings. I went to a few of them and I was shocked. I saw some of the biggest names in the world in those rooms. And they liked me; they thought I was a badass. They would say, "Mike, you need money?" and they'd have someone put some cash in my account. One thing I found out in those meetings was everybody knows when you're getting high. One time, I saw this world-famous actor, one of the biggest, at a closed meeting. He greeted me and said, "Hey, we've been waiting for you here. I have a seat reserved for you."

How the hell did he know that I was using? I thought. But if you're using, everybody who is using knows you're using. We think no one sees us but we are more transparent than we believe.

But the closed-door meetings weren't my thing. I went about four times but I had to go back to the regular meetings. All the guys in the closed programs were elitists so they were going to run their own program. I had to do Bill W.'s program. I had to be in there with the masses.

I owe Marilyn a debt that can never be repaid for getting me into the recovery world. That is one fascinating world. You think cops got the biggest fraternity in the world? You think gangs are big? They're nothing compared to the recovery world. They got federal judges, marshals, and prosecutors. You be careful about what recovering alcoholic or addict you're fucking with, because this is one huge powerful family. Don't ever underestimate the power of recovery, because if you do, you're going down. They've got the ear of everyone, including the President.

They're a motley crew too. I saw ex–Hells Angels, ex-gangbangers, strange guys whose sole purpose in life is to get people to stop drinking and stop getting high. Do you feel me? Some of these guys have been in prison for most of their lives and their goal in life now is to save as many people as possible and get them to live life on life's terms and to face their fears sober. These are special people, Marilyn included. They are a different breed of people. All my intimidating, bullshit doesn't work with them. Big killers with knife scars on their face, mob hit men, these A.A. people don't get scared. It's almost impossible to scare an addict. Even if they say they're afraid of you, they're really not.

If anybody ever got out of place and said something disrespectful about Marilyn, I would have fucked their world up. I don't care if you're a billionaire, you don't have enough money to pay these people, you'd be slaving and indebted to them for the rest of your life. And they're at peace with themselves. They don't do this shit for money, they do it for moral accomplishment. A lot of these guys go through the motions and smile and they're cool until they have to go into action. We had a puny little Jewish kid who worked at Wonderland and would drive us around. One day we were going to get ice cream so a bunch of us got in the car. One patient came running up late and he got in the car and you could smell the alcohol on his breath. This puny staff guy got out of the car, threw the back door open, and dragged this drunk guy out of the car. "Oh shit," I said. I was the heavyweight champ, why didn't I do that? I had so much respect for that puny-assed kid. He didn't have a violent bone in his body until that switch went off and he did this thing. He's smiling "Beautiful day, huh?" until he smelled that liquor.

I got so much support when I was at Wonderland. A big rock star in the program called me right away when he heard I was having problems.

"Mike, come see me if you need anything."

He knew what my mind was doing. He was an incredible guy. One day a famous British actor came to visit me at Wonderland and shared about his bouts with alcoholism. What a beautiful man. People think addicts are bums and horrible people but they're the geniuses of our times.

It's not always a happy ending when you talk about recovery, but when endings are happy, they're almost godsent. People are going to die in our family, they're going to run away and get high and OD.

We're still going to get sick, we'll still get the short end of the stick in life, but now we have tools that are remarkable to help us deal with these problems. Getting involved with the recovery program was one of the greatest things that ever happened to me. These are great people and they never get enough credit from our society.

Going to Wonderland was really a turning point in my life. I could relate to the idea of improving myself, Cus had drilled that into me years earlier. But it was hard because all those drugs had suppressed all the good shit I had. But just to get back in a daily rhythm—go to work out, go to my meetings, and go out to dinner with my peers—was great. And when I saw all these other people who were supposed to be incurable addicts doing so well at meetings my competitive streak kicked in. I just jumped seeing that. If those guys could do it, I knew I could too. I wasn't going to let anyone outdo me. One guy had been sober for ten years. If you met this guy you would have thought he was a saint. But his parents still weren't talking to him. He had been a monster most of his life. But now he had a job, he was supporting his family, and his main goal in life was to get other people like him into recovery.

A lot of people relapse when they're in rehab but I couldn't even conceive of that. If I got high in that place then I would feel like the biggest loser. My whole purpose of being there was to not get high. When I'm around that positive energy I soak it up like a sponge. I'm the biggest cheerleader. "Hey, we're here to be sober. We're going to do it together. Yeah, let's do it!" But if I was by myself it would be, "Hey, you got a syringe?"

One of the scariest and most satisfying things was to go on 12-step calls. Guys who may have been sober for twenty years and you hear they're in the hospital, that they had a slip and had started drinking again. Some of the kids I was with at Wonderland snuck out and we had to go find them. I was just a patient and they were sending me out to look for those guys. So we drove down to Hollywood and Vine. You go right to the drug spot and that's where you'll find them. They were just sitting there on the street. They looked so bad they were hardly recognizable. They're white but the sun burned their skin so much that they looked dark. I saw a lot of bad stuff that year.

I was seeing all sorts of counselors when I was at Wonderland. Because of the road rage conviction, they sent me to anger management classes. The guy who ran the class was a tiny guy named Ian. I couldn't see what he could know about anger management. But after a while, I could see that Ian appeared as if he were ready to explode any minute. I guess they're the right people for the job. He taught me a Jewish proverb the first session we had.

"Bright light, dark shadows. The brighter the light, the darker the shadow." He told me that the biggest stars were the darkest ones, that was why I was here with him.

Marilyn suggested that I see a sex counselor too. She had sent me to one in Arizona but it wasn't until I got to Wonderland that I really got into that work. Whenever Marilyn and I hung out she saw how I reacted to women approaching me. I always felt that girls were coming on to me, that they were the ones with the problem.

"No, you're putting too much time into the conversation," Marilyn would lecture me. "You're not just saying 'Thank you' and giving them an autograph. You're asking them where they're from, how long they lived here, if they were single. We've been here thirty minutes and you have ten phone numbers already. Is there anybody you turn down?"

I was referred to Sean McFarland, an addictions therapist who specialized in sex addiction. He had an office in Venice. Sheila Balkan came along with me on my first visit. I was kind of skeptical about the whole sex addiction thing.

"Well, you're supposed to be the expert on sex addiction. How does that really work and what does that really mean?" I asked him.

Seano pointed to a picture of his son and his wife that was hanging on the wall of his office.

"Mike, that's a great question. I like to fuck street prostitutes and that beautiful boy and woman in that picture are my wife and kid. So when I drink and do blow and act out, I say 'Fuck you' to them because they're fucking my life up because I can't do what I want to do. That's sex addiction to me."

I signed right up with him. We spent a lot of time together. Seano was running a Sex Addicts Anonymous meeting and I started going to that one every Monday, Wednesday, and Saturday. That group was the most fun for me. I thought the guys were cool and it was interesting to hear about all that dysfunction. One day we had a guy show up who thought he was better than the rest of us guys because of his status.

"Hey, I don't think I belong here with you guys," he said. "I never chase a woman down the street and say I want to fuck her. The only reason I'm here is because my wife is frigid."

"Because you even said something like that shows that you belong here," I told him. "Don't try to figure it all out in one day. Just keep coming, okay?"

I was getting a lot of life skills from those meetings. I really changed my whole outlook on the way I relate to women. I never thought I was a sex addict. Being the champ, I thought that having sex with all those women was just a perk. You're supposed to have all those willing bodies around you. All the people I worshipped were sexual conquerors. I used to read about Errol Flynn, Jack Johnson, Jack Dempsey, all these great people, and what they all had in common was their conquests over women. So I always thought in order to be a great figure you had to have women in your life, and the more women you conquer, the greater the figure you were. I never knew that having sex with so many women takes so much from you, more than what it adds. I never really created my own self-image, so I read about a lot of people who I believed were great men and I took qualities from them. I was too young to know that these were great men that had bad qualities. Even Cus would have a "real man"–oriented mentality. But all that sex only brought me gonorrhea, chlamydia, and all those other scientific-named diseases.

Women were always available to me but I got too self-indulgent in sex. I'd have ten women in my room getting high and I'd have to do a press conference, so I'd bring a few with me and put them in a room for when I finished the interviews. Whenever a girl was willing, I'd do it. Either I'd hit on them or they'd hit on me. The problem was, I was trying to satisfy each and every one of them and be happy. That's sick. It's impossible to satisfy all of them, some of them were crazy, just as sick as I was, if not more. You'd lose your mind trying to do that.

I had my women in every city on the planet. You should have seen my Rolodex. Thank God they invented computers. I used to date a girl in Phoenix that saw me hanging around with my pigeons one day.

"Your birds are like your women. You have to have a lot of birds; just in case you lose one, you've got all those other ones. That's why you never have ten or twenty birds, you always have five hundred, because you're so emotionally attached that if you lose one you still have four hundred ninety-nine left. That's the same way you are with women."

She was just a young chick but she was right. I was so insecure, so scared of loss, so afraid to be alone. Towards the end of my career I was moving in with women and moving from one to the other. When I talked about this shit in the rooms, it evoked such painful feelings. That's all my mother ever did. Moving from man to man. No matter how much money I had, I still had my mother's traits. I was going from woman to woman. Right after one, boom, bow, right to the next one, boom, bow, right to the next one, boom, bow, right to the next one.

I may have said, "I'm crazy," kidding around from time to time, but something was wrong. The majority of people that I was attracting were violent, hot-blooded people always talking shit. Even the women were crazy. Most celebrities were afraid of their stalkers. I fucked mine. They'd be downstairs and the doorman wouldn't let them up.

"Oh, I'm godly to you? Come on up!"

They might be crazy but they looked great. I actually had one of those scrolling LED lights that you could program with your own message. I had mine read GOOD PUSSY, CRAZY BITCH. GOOD PUSSY, CRAZY BITCH. I had that in the bedroom and it looked great in the pitch-black dark.

Pussy was like a drug to me. When I was trying to get pussy, there was no one more desperate than me on the face of the planet. The only people that could outdo me were pedophiles or pansexuals. Pansexuals were people that could hit a deer, kill it, take it home, and fuck it. You only know that when you've been in the program.

I was so sex-crazed that I couldn't control myself even when I was getting an honorary doctorate from Ohio's Central State University in 1989.

"I don't know what kind of doctor I am, but watching all these beautiful sisters here, I'm debating whether I should be a gynecologist," I said in my speech. I was trying to compliment the women, but they didn't take it that way. But right after I said that there was a big line of women waiting at my door. It took me years to realize how bad that joke was. I only recently found out that my mother had gone to school right down the street from Central State. My mother and her family thought that education made them somebody. I could have said something awesome. But the first thing I thought about was my dick. I embarrassed five hundred years of our family that day.

What did all my sexual conquests amount to? When you're fucking all those girls it makes you feel like shit but you can't stop doing it. You hate yourself and you feel sorry for the girl. I never loved them. Everything I said was a fucking lie, even if I didn't realize that at the time. Being with all those women was the equivalent of masturbating. I had a lot of fun but it didn't produce anything. I thought I'd get emotional satisfaction out of sleeping with them but I was just a smuck. I was in love with love, not the actual individual.

I felt like I was in a hole and the more people I fucked the more despair I felt. It's a bad feeling when they're gone and you're alone in your bedroom and you can still feel some of their moisture on the bed. That was hell. I just felt so soulless. So then you just get more girls in so you don't have to think about that feeling. Now I needed someone else to hold me because I felt like a piece of shit. All that energy you'd get from those different people was torture. That's what made me feel hollow. At one point everything I did sexually consisted of orgies. Me and three, four, or five chicks. I didn't even know what the fuck was going on in there.

I never thought about it at the time but the pressure was enormous on me to be a great lover to all these people who were fucking "Mike Tyson." That was an encounter that they would talk about forever. I realized though that everybody doesn't fit with everybody else. Sex is a very complex situation. Everybody brings some kind of baggage to the arena. I still don't know what's important about sex. Is it the pleasure part or the actual intimacy? I've met people that deviate from the norm. I've met people that want to be held and people that want to be hurt or spit on. I knew this person who wanted to be with me and she said, "Oooh, I can take a good punch too." I just couldn't do that shit.

After putting in a lot of work in the program I realized that the reason that I always wanted to satisfy women was because I was hoping that they would satisfy me not with sex but with their love. I was using sex to get intimacy. In order for me to get that intimacy and that attachment, I had to have sex. You won't get it from her if you don't have the sex but it's really not about the sex itself. So I was a whore just like my mother. But it was different. This whore had the money. Hey, if I didn't make you happy and satisfy you sexually, how about this Mercedes-Benz? This car is really orgasmic, isn't it?

It sounds trite but I was probably looking for someone to mother me. My whole life I was looking for love from my mother. My mother never gave love to a man. She gave them headaches, she scalded them, she stabbed them. I never saw my mother kiss a man. I saw her in bed with them but I never heard "I love you" or saw someone kiss her forehead.

Even though I was on a pedestal at a young age, I was always attracted to street girls. That was from my mother. At least my mother had my back, but these girls had nobody's back but their baby's and I wasn't their baby. These women were horrible, miserable women for relationships. Just like my mother. They're great for compassion and loving children but a man was just to be used. I always liked that type of woman, that's why my life was so bad. An executive businesswoman wants to go out with me, forget it. I'm going to fuck the tramp.

When I was in rehab, I saw that film about Edith Piaf, *La Vie en*

Rose. That film reminded me so much of my life. Street people take a real liking to you and this bad person teaches you things. Someone kills him and no one cares because he's a bad guy, but to you he's great. You're benefiting by being in his company. You've got money, you've got clothes, you can buy your sister something. Just like they had that guy in the movie and he beat the shit out of her and they took her away from him. That was the same way with me. To everybody else they did her a favor, but to her, this was her life, she wanted to live with the prostitutes and the pimps, that was her family. It's so gut-wrenching to watch as they took her away and she was screaming for the prostitutes. That's when I lost it and just started bawling. That's one thing about happiness. You could be in hell and be happy there. Some people thrive in misery. You take away their misery and bring them into the light and they die emotionally and spiritually because pain and suffering has been their only comfort. The thought of someone loving them and helping them without wanting anything in return could never enter their minds.

Stopping your sexual addiction is in some ways different than stopping a drug or alcohol addiction, but you still have to just say no like you do with drugs. It's a lot of self-help work and even though you're a grown man, you have to conduct yourself like a child in a way. You're constantly analyzing what you're doing, how you're talking to a woman, the amount of time you can even look at them. My limit is three seconds.

One of the ways to break a sexual addiction, at least for me, was to be broke. If I didn't have any money, that shit wasn't fun anymore. If I'm broke I can't even think about fucking anyone because in my delusional mind I need that grandeur. I've got to be in a major suite or on some beautiful island. If I'm doing it in a seedy motel that's just me at my bottom.

It's really hard to control your sexual addiction. Any little thing can trigger it. I could be walking down the street and I would hear the click, click, click of a woman's high heels and I'm off. I could be walking down a dark alley at three in the morning and make a turn and see a beautiful woman and think that she's got to be a hooker or why would she be out that late at night?

I took a lot of trips back to Phoenix for various court appearances and I always traveled with Seano. He was originally from Phoenix. He was the best guy to be with. He knew what I was thinking, he knew I'd listen to those high heels clicking and get aroused. Hearing those high heels was like somebody knocking at my door. Seano and I would go out to eat and he'd know my demons so well. When we'd get back from lunch, he'd come over to me.

"Michael, what's wrong?"

"I walked into that restaurant and I felt like everyone in there was going, 'Look at that big, fat washed-up nigga.'" So we worked out some signals. When I got real scared, I'd very politely grab his arm. That was the signal for Seano to tell me, "It's okay, brother, we're cool."

Sometimes all of this work really got to me. The first time we went back to Arizona, Seano thought that I was such a high risk that he told me that he was going to stay with me in my hotel room.

"No, you're not," I said. "Nobody's going to stay with me in my room."

"Then let's get back on the plane. I know what you're up to. You're going to have somebody come over here and you are going to disappear on me and that ain't cool, so what do you want to do?"

I almost clocked him. But we slept side by side in that hotel room.

He could always pick up on my rage.

"What's going through your mind right now? You want to punch me, don't you?" Seano said.

"Yeah, I don't like it when you fucking look at me with those Irish eyes."

"I know, brother, I know, but let's just do this thing."

I had to laugh.

"You are fucking crazy, Seano."

"Yeah, you're crazy too, Michael, but let's just talk this thing out."

I knew that my life was on the line when I was in Wonderland. I was really trying to win. And in A.A. when you stay clean for a certain amount of time they gave you a token or a chip. I carried those tokens with me religiously. I'm a peacock and I always have to be proving that I'm achieving something. That was just the way I was wired. Those tokens were like my belts. In our community the tokens infer respect. You could have all the money in the world but no tokens, no time, and we don't respect you. I just loved it, I always looked forward to getting my chips.

As committed to my recovery as I was, I still managed to bend some rules. I had been in the program only a few weeks when I met this dynamite chick at one of the meetings. Her name was Paula and she was an awesome woman from Morocco. One day I went to a meeting and I saw her standing at the door welcoming people. She had this tight Adidas shirt on and she had big torpedo titties that were real!

Nobody really knew me in that room and I was the only black guy there and a pretty intimidating scary-looking figure. After seeing Paula a few times at the meetings I went up to her.

"Listen, I read the whole book. I'm up to my eighth step . . ."

"Mike, you don't remember me, do you?" she interrupted me.

She reminded me of an incident a few years earlier. I had been in L.A. driving down Sunset Boulevard and I had seen Paula walking down the street. I rolled down my window and slowed to a crawl and tried to get her to come in my car, like a pervert.

Hey, I can try again.

"Listen, I know we're not supposed to date in A.A. until after the first year but I'm working on my stuff. Do you think you can be my mentor? I want to be friends with you," I said.

Paula was four years older than me and she had been in recovery for eighteen years. She was a leading member of the program, a straight-to-the-book type of girl. If a crisis came up, she was going to bring out the A.A. book. Her life revolved around A.A. So she knew that us going out would be what they called "13-stepping," since I had only been in recovery a few weeks.

So at first we started hanging out as friends, but in a little while, we started dating. I'd get permission from Wonderland to spend the night with Paula. I got so much out of our relationship. I had a girl-friend who was sober for eighteen years and would help me stay clean. I'd never really been with a straight chick like her before. I liked straight women but I didn't seem to get along with them for long dura-tions. The dysfunctionist in me comes out and I put a crook into their straightness. But with Paula it was different and everything was going good.

I kind of bent some more rules when I shot a documentary about my life while I was in Wonderland. I was approached by my friend Jim Toback, a great filmmaker who I had worked with years earlier on an independent film called *Black and White*. I didn't really think I was an actor then. I was doing my part as a favor for Jim, I didn't get paid or anything. I was so high on weed the whole time we were shooting *Black and White*. My dialogue was all improvised because I couldn't even read a script, I was so blazed. I had a scene with Robert Downey Jr. and Jim wanted me to hit him and I couldn't even see him I was so high so I kept hitting him in the wrong place. Downey was on the floor kicking me. "Stop fucking hitting me! Stop hitting me!"

I wanted to do this documentary because I was getting some nice bucks for it and I needed that money desperately. I really undersold the whole project when I asked Seano if it was okay to do this. I made it sound like it was going to be a little interview and then it turned out to be hours and hours of shooting me in a rented house in Beverly Hills and by the ocean in Malibu. It's funny, watching that documen-tary now even though I wasn't drinking or doing drugs while we shot it, I see that I'm still in my addict character. I was basically doing a junkie documentary.

My rehab was going well and on September twenty-fourth, Seano and I flew to Arizona to appear in court where I pled guilty to posses-sion of coke. A month later I was back for my sentencing. While I was in rehab, I went all over the city to talk about addiction. I went to drug court, I went to neighborhood youth groups, I gave testimony to release programs and to prisons. I made the rounds and I put in hours and hours of work. It was the least I could do to give back. And it looked very impressive when we showed the judge all my community service. I got wonderful letters from my doctors and counselors in rehab and supportive letters from friends like Sugar Ray Leonard and the great lawyer Robert Shapiro. He had lost a son to drugs and he had started a foundation and he put on a boxing fund-raising exhibition where he fought Danny Bonaduce and I brought him into the ring as his trainer.

The fact that I had voluntarily entered rehab and had done so well impressed the judge who was a nice liberal lady. She could have put my ass away for years. Instead she sentenced me to twenty-four hours in jail, 360 hours of community service, and put me on probation for three years. Everything was looking rosy. Monica had been so supportive of me during this whole process. I would have been in the streets without her help. We were a horrible married couple but great friends. Monica had arranged a nice lunch for all my attorneys and me and Seano and then I was going to fly straight back to California and buy a house and continue my recovery work. Who knows, maybe I would have wound up marrying Paula or someone else in recovery and become one of those hard-core recovery people who would get irritated being around people that drank or smoked weed.

Everything was looking good until the D.A. decided to make one last example out of me. They found out that Wonderland was within a certain distance from a school and as a predator/offender I had to be registered with the state to be in a place in such close proximity. So they told us that if I flew back to California, the state of Arizona was going to have the LAPD arrest me at the airport. It was Wonderland's fault actually for not registering me. When we found out about this one of my lawyers told me that I could sue Wonderland. I couldn't believe that. These people had stuck their necks out and saved my life and now I was supposed to sue them? No way, I couldn't do that shit.

But I could start doing drugs again. My plan to go back to my nurturing community in California had been shot down. They should've sent me right back to California, but they brought me to Phoenix and without that support system, I got high six weeks later. And that was the end of my relationship with Paula. We visited each other a couple of times, but it just wasn't going to work. I was starting to go astray, getting back into the drug world, and she was on that straight path.

I wasn't back to being a full-blown cokehead though. I was on so many meds from the rehab people that I was pretty much zombied out. Now that I wasn't going to start a new life in California I decided to sell the house I had in Phoenix and buy a home in Las Vegas. I wanted to be where the real action was. So I bought a house in Henderson. In January, I invited one of my girlfriends out to stay with me and that turned out to be a momentous phone call.

I had known Kiki Spicer since she was thirteen. Her stepfather, Shamsud-din Ali, was a very well-respected and influential Muslim cleric who ran the biggest mosque in Philadelphia and had close ties to the Democratic political machinery there, including the mayor of Philadelphia and the governor of Pennsylvania. Her mother, Rita, was a journalist who had covered many of my fights. When I fought Buster Mathis in 1995, there was an issue with the venue at Atlantic City so Kiki's dad helped get the fight moved to Philadelphia. He brought Kiki to meet me at a press conference before the fight and she and her family hung out afterwards in my hotel room. I was so used to people offering their children to me that that's what I thought was happening. I was having a nice conversation about religion with her father the Imam and in my sick mind I was thinking he was offering me Kiki or one of her cousins. I was definitely attracted to Kiki but she looked so stiff and uncomfortable sitting there in front of her parents. She looked like she didn't want to be there.

It wasn't until a year later that I really got to know her. Her dad had to go on a business trip to the Pittsburgh area and he and her mom brought Kiki along. They called me to tell me that they were staying at a hotel just twenty minutes from my house in Ohio. When I heard that their daughter was with them, I pounced.

"No, no, don't stay at a hotel. Come stay at my house," I offered.

This was my opportunity to get this girl. When they got to my house, I insisted that the Imam and Rita take my bed. I'd just sleep in one of the many other bedrooms on the other side of the house. One of the bedrooms that was close to where Kiki would be sleeping. She went to bed and I was watching TV. A little later, Kiki came out of her room and showed me that there were some hairs on her pillow. So we searched for another pillowcase and then she asked if she could watch TV with me. We watched for a bit and then talked for what seemed like hours. Finally I made my move.

"You're so beautiful. You're so special. Can I kiss you?" Of course she fell for the bait. She was nineteen at the time so it was easy to make an impression on her.

We wound up sleeping in the same bed that night but she didn't give it up. I liked her, she made me laugh. We were like two kids acting silly, sneaking away from her parents for a chance to make out. We almost had sex during the four days they were there but it just didn't happen. When it was time for her mom and dad to leave, she asked me to ask her father if she could stay. There was no way in the world that was going to happen.

"I think it would be better if Kiki came with us this time." The Imam was diplomatic.

Before she left I gave her a chain with a nice Chopard diamond elephant pendant. It wasn't expensive, only $65,000 or so, I would give shit like that to a homeless person. I had a lot of them but Kiki really liked it so I was happy to make her happy. I was hoping that she'd give it up before she left, but it wasn't meant to be.

We spoke on the phone a few times and I couldn't stop thinking about her since that visit. I didn't know how I'd ever see her again; she was always with her parents everywhere they went. I guess my infatuation with Kiki became obvious to other people because Don King started warning me.

"Stay away from the Imam's daughter. That is trouble we can't handle. You hear what I'm saying?"

Don knew that he couldn't play games with Kiki's dad. He didn't want that kind of influence around me. But him saying that made me want to get Kiki even more. I invited Kiki and her brother Azheem and her cousin Asia to my thirtieth-birthday party but I had too many women there so I didn't make a play for her.

I had instituted a dress code for the party. Everyone had to dress up sharp, no jeans. Of course I made my entrance later wearing jeans and a nice pair of Cartier diamond bracelets. That was what Cus taught me. You always have to create an environment where you can be what others can't be. You set the rules. That was more of his psychological warfare. He was all about confusing the enemy.

Kiki's parents sent her to Italy for her junior year abroad and I got her number there from them and called her. I asked her for her address and told her that I would come out and visit her. But then I got into that motorcycle accident. I didn't see her again until the Vargas-Trinidad fight in Vegas on December 2, 2000. She had gotten credentials for the fight. I ran into her by the dressing rooms backstage. When I saw her, I picked her up and gave her a hug. The next day she came over to my place and the five-year wait was finally over.

"You're mine now," I told her. I had to leave later that day for Phoenix to train so I had her come along. She stayed with me for a few days and then went back to New York where she was living. I didn't want her to go, so I called her a few days later and flew her back to Phoenix. We did that for a while. Kiki was working as a stylist for music videos then so she had the flexibility to leave everything and come out.

We were having a lot of fun together until I acted like a cad and blew it. One night we were together in Vegas and we had gone to dinner at the Brown Derby and then caught the *Kings of Comedy* show. It was about 12:30 in the morning and on the way home I got a call from a stripper I was seeing. So when we got home I told her that I was going back out to meet up with my friend. Kiki was really hurt, although she didn't show it at the time. I just thought people were supposed to accept that behavior from me. All my life that is what they did. When I got back the next morning, her stuff was already packed and Darryl was about to drive her to the airport.

"Where are you going?" I asked her. "You gonna leave?"

"Yeah," she said.

"Oh, well, I'm an asshole. You knew that already," I said.

I called her and asked her to come see me a number of times in 2001, but she wouldn't talk to me. But we got together again in the summer of 2002. I invited Kiki to the Lennox Lewis fight. She came a week before the fight and stayed with me at a house I had rented. After the fight, Kiki stayed with me at the rented house for a week, tending to my wounds from the fight. Then we flew in a private jet to New York and I moved into her apartment in lower Manhattan. We were living together but not really living together. We were almost like roommates. I would go out at night and hang out. Sometimes she'd meet me at a club and then we'd go home together. Even if I scored with another girl, I'd come back to her house that night. And she never bitched about anything. She was so mellow.

I had been secretly seeing Liz at the same time. One night, I told her that I had a new girlfriend. She had a delayed response.

"Of course I don't like it, but I'm not going anywhere," she said.

But that feeling changed abruptly. I guess she didn't want to be a doormat. So after one phone argument we had, she decided she wasn't going to let me use her apartment as a storage facility so she boxed up all my stuff and FedExed it to my house in Vegas. In just a few months I had gone from living with Lisa to Kiki to Luz. That was my modus operandi then. And when I was living with Kiki, it was the first time ever that I realized that I could do this, I could commit to living with somebody for real.

After a little over a year, her anger had subsided and we'd hook up here and there. No matter who she was seeing at the time, she'd just take off to hang out with me for a few days. We'd have a lot of fun, and then not see each other for months or even a year. I saw her again in 2004 at that Trinidad fight at the Garden where my new bodyguard got slipped a Mickey from that hustler chick. I invited her to come hang out with me at an after-party at a club in the Meatpacking District. She came and sat at my booth. I was talking to some people, and when Kiki's back was turned for a second, this white girl who was in their party and who I had never seen before in my life came over to me and without even saying "Hi" just sat on my lap. A second later, boom, Kiki had punched me in the face.

Everyone just backed up then. Zip thought I might go crazy and beat her ass, but I loved her. I just started laughing. I knew that she had built up all that resentment for me doing her dirty with Luz when she was the one nursing me after the Lewis fight.

We didn't talk for a long time after that. I saw her again at the Magic Show convention in Las Vegas at the end of 2005. I bumped into her when I was with two lovely companions that I had just met that night. We hooked up when she was in Vegas and we had our usual good time.

After I moved into my new house in Vegas after my sentencing on the Phoenix coke bust, I was depressed. The doctors from Wonderland had me on so many meds I was totally lethargic. Darryl was really worried about me.

"You're not looking so good, Mike. You okay?" he asked me. "Listen, I got Kiki's number. I know she makes you happy every time you talk to her. Can I get her on the line?"

So we called her and I told her to come visit me. Kiki had just broken up with a guy and she was depressed. She later told me that she was finally getting over me and that she asked her mother if she should come visit.

"What do you have to lose? You always have such a good time with him," Rita said. "Just go for a pick-me-upper."

Kiki came out in January of 2008 to visit. The minute I laid eyes on her it was like my whole perception of her changed. *Wow, she's hot,* I thought. Maybe it was because I was seeing her when I was sober for the first time. She had blossomed into a beautiful woman. I really wanted to see if being committed to one person could work for me. But we were both pretty depressed at that time. I was trying to stay clean after my rehab and Kiki had been dealing with a family crisis for the past few years.

It seemed that the Bush administration was trying to crack down on the Democratic power structure in Philadelphia. They were wiretapping the mayor's office and the Imam's office. They went after the Imam and Rita and claimed that the Muslim school that they ran had been misappropriating federal funds. They even charged Kiki and her brother with conspiracy, mail fraud, and theft of federal funds, and slapped Kiki with an additional count of false statements to the grand jury. They were each facing over a hundred years. The case was bullshit to begin with, but Kiki and her mother, brother, and stepfather were convicted. The main issue was whether Kiki had taught the classes at the school that the government had subsidized. Kiki testified that she had, to the best of her knowledge. That wasn't good enough for the prosecutor.

"No, it's a yes or no question. Did you teach?"

"Yes, to the best of my knowledge," Kiki repeated. This went on over and over again. She wasn't going to let that prosecutor intimidate her. They eventually found her guilty of perjury because of that, but they just slapped her on the wrist and gave her six months of house arrest. But the feds weren't through harassing her, and they appealed her sentence. They won their appeal and she had to go back to be re-sentenced for the same crime that she already done the house arrest time for. When that hit the papers, she was laid off from her job. So she was bummed out too.

We were both watching a lot of *Law & Order* on TV all day long. I was hibernating on the couch, filling up on cookies and Dairy Queen. My meds made me quiet. I didn't have that usual swagger. At night, we'd go out to the clubs, but I was so out of it I hardly recognized my club friends.

I wasn't the only one who had a shift of perception. Kiki thought she had known me over the years. One day she came into the room while I was eating Cap'n Crunch and playing a video game.

"Wow, it's interesting how you think you know somebody, but you don't know them at all. You think they are one way and they're not that way at all. You conduct yourself totally different than what you really are, Mike," she said.

After hanging out with me a few days, Kiki started doing research into all the meds that the rehab doctors had me taking. Here's the list:

Depakote
Neurontin
Zyprexa

Abilify

Cymbalta

Wellbutrin XL

Tricor

Zocor

The last two were for my high cholesterol and triglycerides. But all the others were head drugs. One was a mood stabilizer. Two were antidepressants. Two were mood regulators for bipolar disorder. And one was used to treat epilepsy, something I never had. Kiki made up a whole list of the adverse side effects of these drugs and showed it to me. So I agreed that I should detox off them. She went out and got some Chinese herbal medicine to cleanse me.

I supplemented the herbs with my own regimen of cocaine. I was a zombie on these prescribed head pills but I could function in my dysfunction on coke. I would have preferred to smoke weed but I couldn't because I was still being tested by my probation officer once a month. Weed stays in your system and is detectable in your piss for over six months, more for me probably because I was getting morbidly obese and that THC from the grass binds right to your fat cells. But coke only stays in your system for three days and then it's gone. Definitely the drug of choice for those on probation.

Kiki went back to Philadelphia to be re-sentenced, so I was able to hide from her the fact that I was taking coke. On April Fools' Day, she got fooled when the judge ruled that she had to redo her six-month sentence, but this time she had to go to prison instead of just house arrest. Everyone was shocked. I didn't want her to go away for six months. She was ready to go right in that day, but they gave her thirty days to put her affairs in order, so she didn't have to report to jail until May first.

While Kiki was gone, I decided to try to go to an A.A. meeting in Henderson. It's a new, sleek-looking town, but the meetings were held in the creepiest section. I went to one meeting and I couldn't take it. After the meeting, I went out and got high. I was a relapse artist. If you read anything about A.A., you find that relapse is part of recovery. You can't have recovery without relapse. You've still got those demons that you have to struggle with. The devil fucks with me all the time. He knows I'm a relapse artist, that's why he comes to me. If he thought I was strong he wouldn't go near me. The devil is aware that I know God doesn't like me that much, so he wants me to rebel.

Kiki came back to stay with me before she had to turn herself in on May first. About a week before she was going to leave, I was watching TV downstairs when Kiki came over.

"Baby, we need to talk," she told me all dramatically.

I remembered that Johnny Depp movie *Blow* where the girl comes in to tell him that she's dying. I was high and when Kiki gave me that look, I freaked out. I just knew she had the Big C.

"No, baby, no," I said. "Are you sick?"

"No, you dumbass, I'm pregnant."

I felt like the weight of the world came off me. I had just been dumped into hell and pulled back out. But I had to read her the riot act.

"This shit might not work, you know. I'm horrible with marriages. I adore you but I'm not monogamous. I'm never going to have money again. I'm bankrupt now. It won't be like all your fancy boyfriends before, you ain't stepping out in limos. You might not have to wait in line in a restaurant but you're not going to wear any designer stuff unless you go to the discount shop. I'm going to be the brokest boyfriend you've ever had in your dating career."

"Well, listen, you don't have to be in the baby's life," she said.

Yeah, that same old bullshit—until the baby comes and hard times come and then I get hit with the fucking subpoena. That's how that shit goes.

"Listen," I said. "What do you want me to do? I'll help you. We'll do this together. I will give you the best that I can be."

Which I knew would be disastrous.

"But there won't be any glory in this. No cameras or nothing. The only cameras will be at my funeral. We're going to live life on life's terms. If you're willing to do this with me, maybe it'll be okay."

I didn't talk much to Kiki while she was in jail. I was starting to party pretty hard with cocaine again and Kiki refused to call me because she didn't want to find out that I was in a strip club and listen to all those bitches laughing in the background. I wasn't responsible for what she wanted to hear. As far as I was concerned, I made my commitment.

"You're going to be my girl when you come out. It's just going to be me and you," I told her right before she went in. "When you come out, I'm going to be there for you and the baby. I ain't gonna get nobody pregnant and I'm going to let all these women know that my woman is away and when she gets back home, this is all over."

I was basically going to have a six-month bachelor party. Thank God I didn't catch AIDS or something. Kiki got upset because while she was in prison she saw some photos of me with other women, but she had to take that on the chin. I had to take some stuff on the chin too, that's just what happens in relationships, you have to eat your partner's baggage. I wasn't ashamed of anything I did, because we were living in two different worlds. I don't know who called or visited her, that wasn't my concern.

On May eighteenth my documentary opened at Cannes. I was high on the plane going into Cannes. I brought some girl from D.C. and we partied the whole time I was there. She would get girls and we'd both sleep with them. We had reasons to party too; the film got rave reviews from the critics at Cannes. I gave my own little capsule review to the press.

"It's like a Greek tragedy. The only problem is that I'm the subject."

When I got back to Vegas, I kept on partying nonstop. My friend Martin and I had a friend named Paris who was a cool old motherfucker. He was at least eighty years old and he was a big drug dealer. He used to work as a pit boss at one of the casinos on the Strip and he was always a sharp dresser. Martin had been friends with Paris for forty years, but he didn't like it when I started hanging out with him because Martin thought he was a bad influence on me with the drugs. Martin is a country-assed Mississipi guy. He would see me high on coke and say, "You supposed to be some player from the Himalaya? Nigga, you ain't shit. You get on that cocaine, you can't do shit. You can't get no money, you can't get no bitch, you can't get nothing, nigga."

Even Paris tried to avoid me. I'd call him to come hang out and at first he was cool but then he saw how I was acting with the cocaine, because he had pure cocaine.

"Mike, you don't need none of this," he told me. He was such an arrogant motherfucker. "Go be with your big-time white friends, use that dirty dope they got. You're not good enough for this shit, you need that white-folk dope, Mike."

So Paris died and at his funeral they read his will.

"Martin and Mike Tyson are my only two friends. I want them to inherit my worldly possessions," they read. What are among a drug dealer's worldly possessions? His stash. So after the funeral, Martin took possession of Paris drug stash. Martin kept telling me that Paris wanted me to have his coke. But when I asked Martin for it, he'd say, "Mike, you're not doing good now. I can't in good conscience give you the stuff now."

"But that's my shit, Martin. How can you not give me something that belongs to me? You're not my father."

"Boy, I just can't do that."

Martin is one of those Southern Baptist Christians to the bone. He'd committed every sin in the Book but he was going to die for Jesus and he'd kill you for Jesus. I was convinced that the shit was at Martin's house and I was so hard up for it that I invited myself to sleep over at Martin.

"Kiki is locked up. I'm staying with you," I told Martin.

As soon as Martin left to go to work, I started ransacking his whole house. He had at least a hundred Stacy Adams suits in the closets and I was frantically going through each of the pockets to find the stash.

Whoa, let's calm down, Mike, I told myself. I was sweating like a pig I was so agitated. *All right, ghetto survival tactics. Go back to the hood. If you were in the ghetto where would you hide your drugs?*

So I looked into the barrels of Martin's guns. I looked into each one of his shoes. I looked under the bed and on top of the bed and under the mattress. At one point I was looking through all of Martin's tin cans and I found a little rock of coke that someone had given to him twenty years earlier. It was literally a rock by then. All of the bacteria and dirt from the last twenty years had singed down on the coke. It wasn't even white anymore; it was a sickly grayish-greenish color.

After a couple of hours the cleaning lady came in.

"GET OUT! GET OUT!" I screamed at her.

She was a Spanish lady and she didn't know what was going on with this crazy guy yelling at her, so she called Martin and he told her to come back the next day.

At the end of the day, Martin came home. He left the house sober but he drank all day at work so he was soused. He saw a do-rag that was lying on the living room table and he picked it up and slammed it down.

"Motherfucker, you had a woman in here," he said.

"No, Martin, I didn't," I said.

Martin had a young kid from the neighborhood with him because he always gave the kid some cash to do chores.

"Yeah, you had a bitch back there," he said.

I held up the do-rag and addressed the kid.

"Young man, as you are aware, this is not a woman's stocking, it's a do-rag."

"I know what it is," the kid said.

"Well, explain it to him."

Martin was so drunk that he didn't even recognize the do-rag that he would put over his hair every night before he went to sleep.

When Martin went into his bedroom, he was shocked.

"What the fuck happened to my room?" he said sadly.

I had actually disassembled the frame of his bed. Then, because I thought the coke might be in the legs of the frame, I broke them off. All the drawers of the dresser were out and ransacked. His closet was in a shambles. I had destroyed this man's house.

"Why the fuck did you do this, Mike?" he said.

"Because I was looking for the coke," I told him.

"I left it in the safe in my office. It's not in here."

"Martin, why didn't you just tell me? Why don't you just give me the fucking shit, man? It's mine."

"Hell no! I ain't giving you shit after what you done did."

And he never gave me the coke.

By then, I was so fat, I was almost 360 pounds. In my right frame of mind, I wouldn't even look at girl when I was that disgusting, but get some of that coke in me and I got the courage to approach anyone. The next thing you know, I was hanging around with a bunch of strangers thinking that I was beautiful.

I started having orgies at my house again. There'd be twenty naked people in my living room, all high on coke, and nobody saying a damn word. All the girls would walk by me and touch me and rub and kiss me.

One day we had been partying all night at my house. There were people all over the house having sex. I was in my bedroom with two women. I hadn't slept in two days and all of a sudden another chick ran into my room.

"Mike, your probation officer is outside knocking on the door."

My dick shrank right down. As soon as the word got out that there was a probation officer at the front door, one of the guys who was on parole threw his clothes on and ran right out the back door and jumped over the fence and split. I kept looking out the window at the front gate, sneaking peeks to see if he was still there. I was scared shitless but after a few minutes he just left.

Things really got weird when I started dating a couple of call girls in Vegas. When we partied late at night on the Strip, we'd get a hotel room to keep getting high instead of going back to Henderson. Once, I was in the room while my girl was turning a trick. Instead of smoking it, I snorted my good coke and my whole nose froze up. I called up my girlfriend. She answered it and I could hear the john fucking her in the background.

"You all right, baby?" she said.

"Oh, my nose is froze. I'm in the hotel room. I'm dying, baby."

"Take another hit," she said.

I followed her advice.

"Hey, I'm good. That's all I had to do?"

I took another snort.

"Now I'm really good," I said.

"Okay, if you need me, call," she said and went back to banging her john.

A lot of times we'd party in the after-hours clubs and then go back to someone's house to continue the party. One time, I was with one of my prostitute girlfriends and we went over to my friend Brian's house. I went right in the back room with my girl and got high on coke and some mushrooms. I came out and there was a whole new crew of people that had come to the party. They were a happy white-boy crew, nice guys who just wanted to do some lines. I went back to the room and chilled out with my girl and then I went out and the white boys had been replaced by a Mexican crew. Everybody was cool and humble and I partied with them for a while and then went back. When me and my girl came back out, now there was a black crew there. I was still in my happy white mood so I didn't think anything about this rainbow coalition that was rotating in front of my eyes. I was sure some of these guys wanted to date my girl, but I wasn't tripping about that, because if they were going to do that, they'd pay her, that was just what it was.

I went up to them.

"Hi, guys, you guys need anything?" I'm doing my best Uncle Tom nonthreatening shit, right? They just looked at me and shook their heads dismissively without responding. Once they did that, my ego started getting caught up.

Whoa, these niggas don't know who I am? They got to know who I am, I thought. *I'm Mike Tyson. How could they not worship me?* I'm tripping on the mushrooms now and the coke was propelling it forward.

These motherfuckers are acting like I was the help here, I was thinking. *They didn't even say "No, thank you" or nothing.*

I went to the bathroom and when I got back I saw that these guys had slipped my girl a Mickey. Now I was pissed. Why the fuck would they do that with me sitting right there?

These niggas must think I don't exist. They think I'm a fat nothing, not the guy I used to be, I thought.

I watched one of the guys and he was looking at my girl, soaking in her body. And then he started to laugh and he tapped me on the arm.

"You're crazy, Mike," he said.

Something just clicked then in my mind.

I'm going to have to kill these niggas, I thought.

I went into war mode. All the cocaine and the mushrooms and the Hennessy were telling me that these motherfuckers had to bow down to me. So I got up and grabbed a golf club that belonged to the owner of the place and I started swinging at these guys. I was screaming so much that my girl woke up out of her stupor. One guy ran right to the window and jumped out. One guy locked himself in the bathroom. I caught one guy who was cowering behind a sofa.

"Listen, nigga, I'm the motherfucking slaughterhouse here, man, I'm the killer. You all want anything, you ask me nicely. You say, 'Yes, sir, no sir, Mr. Tyson.'"

Meanwhile, my girl was begging me.

"No, baby, baby, baby, no, no, no, baby. Please come with me, baby, let's leave."

Fuck, this ho didn't know I was like this, huh? I thought.

While this was going on, the guy ran out the front door to join his pals. So we kept partying for about three more hours. Then we heard a voice coming from the bathroom.

"I'm calling the cops right now. I'm calling the cops, if you don't let me out of here."

"What the fuck, this nigga is still locked up in the bathroom?" I said. We had forgotten all about him.

I tried to convince myself that I didn't care that my girl was selling her body but I'm too emotional a guy to truly accept that concept. One night I was hanging at a guy's house that we were manipulating for drugs and money. My girl came in looking all nice from turning a trick.

"Are you ready to go home?" I asked her.

"You go home, baby. I'm going to stay here with this guy for a while. I'll see you back at the house later."

"Okay, baby," I said and gave her a kiss. As I was walking to my car, I started getting this weird feeling.

Hey, what the fuck just happened? I thought. *Did I just get played by that creepy white guy in there?*

I went home. When my girl came home she came right over to me.

"I know you're not tripping about that shit," she said. "If that motherfucker ever said something disrespectful about you when I was riding him, I would have slit his fucking throat."

She was one tough Italian chick.

"Baby, this is how we eat," she said. "You ain't fighting anymore. That shit don't mean nothing to me. I'm coming home to you, baby."

These girls were feeding me because I was broke but I didn't want them to give their pussy away. I was the only guy that made his prostitute girlfriends leave him because I didn't want them to work. I guess my father and Iceberg were right. I was never good with women. I wasn't the pimp type. People reacted to my violent image and thought I was some King Pimp, but I was more the trick than the pimp. I was Mr. Trickarooey.

I WAS RIGHT BACK IN COCAINE HELL DURING MY SIX-MONTH SABBATICAL from Kiki. And Marilyn tried to keep on my ass. She'd call me when I was getting high.

"Where is your A.A. book, Mike? Let's read it together right now. Read fifty-two."

I'd be high with her on the speakerphone and I'd look up the page she mentioned and started reading it out loud to her.

"On awakening let us think about the twenty-four hours ahead. We consider our plans for the day. Before we begin, we ask God to direct our thinking, especially asking that it be divorced from self-pity, dishonest or, self-seeking motives."

I'm reading this and Marilyn's yelling, "READ IT LOUDER!! LOUDER!!"

I never hung up on her or told her I was busy, because I wanted to be helped.

"Working with others, practical experience shows that nothing will so much ensure immunity from drinking as intensive work with other alcoholics."

The reading reminded me that I thought I was just a cokehead but no, I was an alcoholic. The only time I'd do coke was after a drink. And once I took a drink, everyone was in danger, even me.

I wanted to party in New York but that plan got derailed when I was accused of putting up $50,000 for a hit on the guys who had allegedly killed my buddy Darryl "Homicide" Baum back in 2000. This came out at a trial of one of the Cash Money Brothers organization that controlled the drug traffic in some of the projects in Brooklyn. Supposedly one of the guys who murdered Homicide heard about the bounty and then he put out a hit on my head and that it was almost carried out in the summer of 2000 when I was in Brooklyn. I had been spotted in one of my Range Rovers on Atlantic Avenue but some of the Cash Money guys objected to killing me because I was a Muslim.

All of this was bullshit, of course, but just mentioning my name in connection with hits on drug dealers helped perpetuate the idea that I was some crazy, hard-core guy. I was on probation then too, so now they were telling me that I can't even go to my hometown.

That was the world I grew up in. All my friends killed people, robbed their drugs. I went one direction and they went the other, but we kept in touch. Now I was getting dragged back into that world and it was a nightmare. I felt like the whole world was caving in on me.

So I stayed out in the west and kept getting fucked up. I took one of my call-girl girlfriends to the premiere of Will Smith's new film *Seven Pounds* in December. Kiki saw a picture of me and the girl on the red carpet while she was in jail and flipped out. I was flipping out too but it was because I was feeling like shit. I called my old friend Hope right before the after-party was going to begin and asked her to come and get me. She drove up to the place and I ran out got into her car and left my girl and my bodyguards back in the party.

I just had to get away. My bodyguards were calling, all freaked out, and I put Hope on the phone.

"He'll be fine. Let me just give him some space. I'll bring him back," she told them.

But I didn't want to go back; I just wanted to disappear. Hope took me back and she came to the party with us. I was walking around, just completely out of it.

Later that month, I went to one of my clubs in Vegas. I was going to my usual spot in the VIP area when I saw that there was a big crowd around the rope. Some of the big drug guys who normally sat in the VIP section were being refused admittance by the bouncer. But when he saw me he let me right in. So I took up my normal spot at my table and started drinking my Hennessy. There were a bunch of people at the next table drinking and having fun and I looked over at them, thinking to myself, *Who the fuck do they think they are sitting over here? This is our spot.* Then I saw one of the Olsen twins. So now I was figuring that this was a showbiz crowd. All these white people were looking over at me, the black interloper in the corner. But this was my place. In my mind I was some cool Las Vegas big shot. Then all of a sudden that comic actor Zach Galifianakis came over to me.

"Hey, we're shooting a movie with you in two weeks," he said.

"Fuck you are. For real?"

Zach laughed. He must have thought I was putting him on but it was news to me. I didn't know anything about any movie. I was doing my normal meet and greets to pick up enough money to keep me in drugs. Hey, if I had a movie, cool, let's go do a movie. I had no idea what the hell I was getting myself into.

"Come sit with us and have a drink," Zach said. He was a great guy.

In a couple of weeks I was on the set of *The Hangover.* I was fat, out of shape, and moody. But Todd Phillips, the director, and those actors were just so awesome. I don't know if they thought I was going to be some psycho on the set but Todd and the producers were all over me all the time.

"Is everything okay? Do you want to take a break?" Todd said. "Can you do one more take now? You don't have to do it now if you don't want to."

I was just so happy to work. I had been asking God to just give me another chance and I would never get high again, even though I couldn't stop using coke. I was high on coke the entire time we shot *The Hangover.* I had one of my hooker girlfriends with me on the set. And then Seano stopped in to see the filming. He took one look at my girl's ass and shook his head.

"I can see that me and the brothers are not on your mind too often these days, huh, Mike?" he said.

But I loved being on the set. They put up these craft services tables just stocked with the best cookies, cake, and food. I was stopping scenes to go get me some more of those cookies.

I didn't expect much from this film. But Todd kept telling me how this was going to be a huge movie and that I'd be on top again after it came out. That was cool, but it was more exciting for me just to be able to entertain people again. I realized that even when I was a fighter, entertaining the people was more paramount than winning the fights. Cus always had me around all these charismatic show-business and media people with magnetic personalities. I realized that Cus was all about the arts. When Cus talked about putting his thoughts in other people's minds, that was an art too, even if it was a dark art. The art of war, the art of survival, we always looked at everything as art. I'm not a good artist but I know the arts. It was like I said that I wasn't a good fighter, but I knew how to fight real good.

Kiki gave birth to our daughter Milan on December 24, 2008. She had just been released from jail and she went to a hospital in Philadelphia where Milan was induced because she was a couple of weeks late. Kiki called to tell me and I was stunned. That was my mother's birthday. I had gotten a small apartment for Kiki near my house in Vegas and had fixed it up for her and the baby. She was about to come out when fate intervened. I had a dirty urine test and the Phoenix people were thinking about putting me back in jail. But my lawyer convinced them that rehab would be better for me so in January, I checked myself into a posh rehab in Malibu called Promises.

Promises was awesome. I was in this mansion. It was just like doing rehab at home. Here we would go to meetings and also see our therapists. They were working me from all angles so I could get a good report and get off my drug case. Everything was going good until four weeks in. My time was up. I didn't want to leave but they already had booked someone else for my room. I really wasn't well yet. So I called my friend Jeff Greene and told him to come get me.

Jeff picked me up and took me to a friend's house, a guy who owned one of those energy drink companies. Jeff didn't know it but there was a full-fledged party going on at the house, complete with lots of pretty, young girls.

"Sit right here, Mike. Don't move," Jeff said. But of course, the party came to us and I was soon surrounded by beautiful women in their bathing suits.

Jeff was going to take me to another rehab the next day so I was going to stay at his house that night. So Jeff put the clamps on me. I couldn't move, I couldn't flirt with the girls, I was his prisoner. Eventually we went home and then the next day Jeff drove me to a branch of Promises that was in West L.A.

"Hey, Jeff, I'm flat broke. You're gonna have to pay for this shit, man. I want to get well. Okay?" I said.

We sat down to talk to the administration lady who would check me in. I saw that she had a Star of David on. She left to get some forms to fill out and I pounced on Jeff.

"Look, Jeff, she's one of your people. This is going to be good, we're going to get a good deal. They know the protocol. Talk to her, Jeff."

She came back and sat down but she was playing hardball—she wasn't giving nobody no play. Every time she said another aspect of treatment it was more money. Three grand for this, four grand for that, twenty-five grand for another thing. You take another pill that's another five grand.

Jeff was "plotzing," as he would say, as he heard how much money he was going to have to lay out.

"What the fuck, Mike? God, man, get sober," he said.

On January twenty-first, they let me out of rehab for a day to attend the U.S. premiere of my documentary film at Sundance. Seano came with me as a sober companion. And that was the first time that

I was going to see Milan. We met Kiki at the airport. She came off the plane with our little girl and she was all bummy-looking, like a homeless person. I was looking at Milan, saying "Hi," trying to see if she looked like me. Kiki was crying at the airport and I was still fucked up from the drugs in my system so I didn't really have much empathy for her. Even seeing Milan was strange. It was almost like, *Well, another out-of-wedlock baby again. I could do another one.* It wasn't the response we both anticipated. I don't even think I kissed Kiki when I saw her. It was just awkward.

We went to the movie premiere, and then afterwards we went back to the hotel. I couldn't have sex with Kiki because she was all stitched up from having Milan and also because Seano was there to block me from having sex with her anyway. I loved Milan, but all her crying just irritated me. I didn't feel like dealing with noise then. So we didn't get off to the best start, for sure.

The next morning, I went back to rehab in L.A. and Kiki and Milan went to the townhouse apartment I set up for them in Vegas. Kiki was all alone because her mom was still in a halfway house in Philly because of her bullshit conviction. I talked to Kiki from Promises and she was all depressed, but so was I. She didn't have much compassion for me then, she just saw me as some big spoiled brat moaning about things while I was in a country club for junkies. But the Promises branch I was in was nothing like the one in Malibu. It was in town, on the corner of some street where anybody could go in and kidnap you or something.

Kiki was really stressed about money then because I couldn't give her anything for the baby. She could barely afford diapers. She even threatened to take our child down to welfare and sign up for assistance. But I was really broke. I had something like $7,000 in my bank account and I owed over $8,000 a month in child support payments. Jeff was paying for my rehab. Whenever I could, I'd book an appearance for $10,000 to get some cash. So threatening to go on welfare didn't faze me. I told her she wasn't going to be living in the lap of luxury with me. Let her get her ass in the welfare line. I think she was actually in the line when Darryl came by and gave her $250 from my ATM for diapers and food.

In February, I got out of rehab and went back to Vegas. My plan was that I would live in my house and go visit Kiki and the baby, who were in the nearby townhouse. But I was so fucked up and fragile from rehab that I went over to the townhouse and just stayed there with Kiki for two weeks. I was literally afraid to leave the house because I didn't trust myself to stay clean. Kiki and I picked up where we left off before she went to prison. We laughed a lot and talked and watched TV and played with Milan. After two weeks Crocodile started coming around and we'd go out and go to Mack's barbershop and hang out for a couple of hours in the afternoon. But I was staying out of trouble.

When I had tested dirty, my probation went back to Phoenix from Vegas. But the probation officer in Phoenix was a great guy. Kiki and Milan and I drove down there and he saw that I was struggling and he knew about the new baby so he allowed me to live in Vegas and just report to him once a month in Phoenix. We drove back to Vegas after a day or two and I decided to stop by my house before dropping Kiki and Milan off at the townhouse. And fate intervened again. A pipe in my dishwasher had burst and the whole house was flooded. I don't know if it was divine intervention to get me and Kiki even closer, but it did inconvenience me like a motherfucker.

I moved in with them into the small townhouse. We were so broke that when we went shopping we would have to count the items in our cart as we went along, just to be certain that we didn't go over our budget. As we shopped I would keep taking things out of the cart even though Kiki had assured me she had counted correctly. I just didn't want to be embarrassed at the checkout counter. The last time I remember doing that was when my mother was on welfare. The checkout lady would have to put stuff aside that we wanted to purchase because we didn't have enough money. All that anxiety came back to me when Kiki and I would shop. My concept of buying things my whole adult life had been whatever I could see, I could buy. Now the sight of ordinary groceries intimidated me. Can you imagine that? I was the most vicious, feared fighter of my lifetime and the price of a fucking box of cereal was intimidating me.

Kiki and I continued bonding. We played a lot of trivia games, just for days on end, trivia, trivia, trivia. I was still too sick to go out and face the world. Kiki was probably secretly happy that she had me for herself. I think my old image was still weighing heavy on her.

A few weeks after Kiki and I moved in together, I left the house with Crocodile in the afternoon. We went to the gym to watch some fighters train. But this time after we did that I told Crocodile I wanted to get some blow. We got back to the townhouse at about ten, which was real late for me. Kiki was asleep upstairs and I went in the bedroom all happy, talking real hyper.

She popped out of bed like Linda Blair in *The Exorcist*.

"You did coke, didn't you!" she screamed.

"No, no, baby."

"Then why the fuck are you talking so fast? And fuck that Crocodile. He's supposed to be helping you and he's going off and doing drugs with you," she said.

"No, don't say anything to Crocodile. He doesn't know I did it," I lied.

"You really think I'm stupid and I'm supposed to believe that he doesn't know?"

She kicked my ass out of the house for doing coke. I saw it as her doing me a favor. I was happy to go. At that time, I'd rather be out doing coke than cooped up in that small apartment.

I binged on coke for two days and then I went back. Kiki was worried as hell. But I vowed not to slip up again and things returned to normal.

Until March, at least, when Kiki's mom Rita got out of the halfway house and moved in with us. Having four of us in that cramped apartment was not fun, especially when one of them was your girlfriend's mother. I couldn't even make love without the possibility of her mother hearing us because the walls were so thin.

Around then I began a series of relapses. I'd be good for a few weeks and then I'd go out and rage. I'd be gone a few days and then I'd come back all contrite.

"I'm a piece of shit. I just wish I was dead. I'm so sorry I'm doing this to you," I'd say.

I looked like a monster on these binges. When I'm fucked up on coke, I get spots all over my body, like a leper. I get dehydrated and break out in sores all over my face. I can't kiss anybody because the moisture from the other person's lips would burn me. I'd be bleeding from the nose. I couldn't talk, I was so congested.

Kiki would get so mad she would start screaming at me, calling me an asshole and a piece of shit.

"What's up? Why are you tripping?" I'd ask her.

Then she'd leave and I was so out of it, I didn't even know she was gone. That was how it was then. When I was high I felt great, but the people that I loved felt bad. And when they felt great, I felt bad because I was sober.

After these relapses I'd stay in for a week or two and then I'd get antsy again.

"You're going to do it, aren't you?" Kiki would say. "It's the time."

She got so sad because she saw that I really couldn't help myself. And she'd beg me to stay home and do the coke if I had to so I wouldn't be out somewhere getting in trouble. But there's no recovery without relapsing and I was trying my best to stay sober.

Crocodile left Vegas around then. He told me that he loved me too much to be around and help contribute to me poisoning myself. He moved to Arizona and flipped the script on us and went from being a hard-core Muslim to a born-again Christian. I told him that Jesus was cool but he shouldn't lose his whole personality. Jesus had savages with him. I told him if he wanted to evangelize, be the guy from *Buck and the Preacher,* have your Bible in one hand and your gun in the other. Croc cleaned up his act and he hasn't done any drugs since 2010.

Dealing with my drug problem was new for Kiki. One time, she went online and looked for a Narcotics Anonymous meeting near our house. She got the address and we went to the place. We were a couple of minutes late so we sat down and listened to the people share. The stories were all interesting, how they lost all their money by gambling it away. After a few minutes, I whispered in Kiki's ear, "We're in the wrong meeting." It was a Gamblers Anonymous meeting.

I didn't want to offend anybody by walking out while they were sharing with the group, but I didn't really want to be there. So after a half an hour I got up and addressed the room.

"Excuse me, guys, I'm very sorry but my girlfriend thought this was Narcotics Anonymous. I don't have a gambling problem, but God bless you guys."

During all this troubled time, Kiki kept her spirits up. She was always so optimistic. I was OD'ing right and left and she was talking about us starting our own production company and licensing my image for all sorts of things. She always had positive dreams for us. And I had some dreams too. Seeing Kiki and Milan on a daily basis and seeing the hopes she had for all of us seeped through that drug fog I was in. One day I woke up and said to myself, *I ain't going to do this shit no more.* I wanted to be awake, I want to be of service, I wanted to be a player in the game of life, functioning with all your marbles and responding to the best of your ability. That was the life that I wanted to live.

But then I got that phone call that no parent should ever have to get in their lifetime. It was Shelley, the mother of two of my children, calling from Phoenix.

"My baby's dead! My baby's dead!"

16

I WAS NUMB WHEN I HUNG UP THE PHONE. KIKI AND MA WERE CRYING THE
second they heard the news, like it was their kid. Darryl rushed over
and we drove to the airport. Kiki and Rita and Milan got in the car
and Zip drove them to Phoenix. When I got there I rushed to the
hospital.

To this day I don't understand what happened or why it happened.
All I knew was that the safety cord from the treadmill somehow got
tied around my four-year-old daughter's neck. My son found his sister
like that, he ran and got Shelley and she called 911. When I got to the
hospital, Exodus was on life support with no hope of recovering.

I was furious. I wanted to make someone pay. But then I was surrounded by the parents of other children who were in the hospital
dying. They were coming over to me to comfort me. Now I was a member of a club that nobody had ever wanted to join—the bereaved parents club.

I still had so many questions though. In my opinion, there was never a thorough investigation of her death. Losing Exodus was the most bitter and helpless feeling I ever had in my life. Now my son Miquel will never be the same. He will always have that image in his head of finding his sister hanging. How do we heal from a tragedy like this? How can someone deal with this kind of loss? It's not in the A.A. book. Just tell me what book it's in because that's a book I want to read. Losing Exodus is the only thing in my life that I can't find any gratitude for. Someone has to pay and take the pain, even if it's me. It's been four years now and I still don't know how I'm going to survive this. I often wonder that, if I was there, maybe things would have been different.

Kiki and the others had checked into the W Hotel. I went back there that night and I was shattered and drained. Everyone tried to console me but how the hell do you console somebody who just lost their child? I was trying to keep it together but I would just break down in tears and then I'd take these really deep breaths. The last thing I wanted to do was to get high then so Kiki gave me some Chinese herbal medicine to stay calm.

Exodus was taken off life support the next day. At her funeral, I didn't know what to do. You have to stand up and thank everyone for coming and be grateful for everyone's support, so I got up.

"Thank you very much for coming," I managed to get out. I didn't know what the hell I was supposed to do, so I sat down. But then my son Amir got up there and he began talking. Even though I was in grief I was still rational and I was checking him out and he was telling stories about his sister and he was doing it very calmly, very professionally. *What the hell is going on here?* I thought. Here was the big brother talking on behalf of his sister. He did such an awesome job. Once he was through, I felt much better.

Everyone was so supportive. Marilyn was there right by my side. She was a veteran of war, she knew death intimately. Monica was terrific. Amir and Rayna were always close to Miguel and Exodus and at times when I was broke, Monica would pay the rent and the bills for them. My oldest daughter Mikey was there as well as my stepdaughter Gena. I was so proud of all my children being there and standing strong and honoring their sister. Kiki and I agreed that it would be best if she and Milan stayed back at the hotel so she wouldn't unintentionally upset Shelley, who had just lost her own baby girl. In the face of tragedy we were all one big family.

Exodus had a funeral worthy of a dignitary. They used to listen to Spanish music in the house and her favorite artist was Nigga, a reggaeton star from Panama. I called up Luis de Cuba, who put me in touch with Roberto Duran. Roberto's son reached out and Nigga came and sang and played and he was wonderful. I didn't realize it until then but I suddenly knew the deep reason that I had always loved Duran. There is no way I can ever repay him for getting Nigga to perform to honor my daughter. I will always be indebted to both him and Nigga for their compassion. I would do anything for them. I was just so appreciative of everyone's support. Between the doctor's bill and the funeral it cost $200,000 and it was paid for by donations.

We stayed in Phoenix for a few days and then drove back to Vegas. I brought my son Miguel back with me because Shelley wasn't handling Exodus's death that well. My oldest daughter Mikey came back with us too. So now we had me, Kiki, Rita, and all the kids in that tiny townhouse.

THE OUTPOURING OF SUPPORT FOR ME FROM STRANGERS REALLY STARTLED me. It shook me into realizing that I wanted to be of service to society and not just be such a glutton caring about myself. I wanted to know how to stop being promiscuous and be loyal to one person. I wanted to know how to be a responsible adult, a responsible father. I didn't know how to do it, but I wanted it. And with all that money, with all that fame, and all those titles, the closest I had gotten to that was a divorce and a bunch of fatherless kids. But after Exodus's tragic death, my whole paradigm shifted. I realized that everything I always thought was the truth was a lie, so I had to start my life all over.

I wanted to create some sort of legacy for Exodus up there in heaven. I wanted her to know that her father was conducting himself in a dignified manner and that he was dealing with his fury and taking it to a whole other level of life. I lost Exodus but I had Milan. I wanted Milan to have a sister close in age so that they could grow up together. I really believe in my heart that Milan was a gift to help me through this tragedy even though she could never take Exodus's place. This was a chance for me to be a responsible dad with her. And then from being that guy with her I could work on re-creating my relationship with my other children. For years and years I had gone through the motions of going to A.A. meetings and reading the book and working my program. Then all of a sudden, my daughter died and that knowledge just kicked in without me even knowing it. Just autodrive, boom. It didn't happen overnight, and I'd have some slips down the road, but it was there in me. Mike, work on your lust. Mike, work on your conduct with women. Mike, put that blow away. Mike, lose that weight and get healthy. Mike, don't look at a woman longer than three seconds. I don't want to sound spooky, like I was possessed or anything, but the rehab teachings just clicked in my head.

I knew I had great discipline from my time with Cus, but everything I had done with him was from a posture of being superior to everyone else. Now I was using those same tools but from a different point of view, from humility not superiority. But I still had that megalomaniacal theory that I could do it. Even though it was going to be treacherous and hard, the megalomaniac in me said, "It will be done and you will suffer." That's what I had been used to all my life. Nothing mattered but the accomplishment of the deed.

But it was still a theory. A week after Exodus's death, all that pain just got to me. Kiki and Rita were out somewhere and I just told my daughter Mikey to lock the door behind me and I went out and scored some coke. I am a scourge from hell when I'm on my addiction. I started slipping for a few days. Kiki was so frustrated and worried that she couldn't help me anymore. Nobody could stop me from getting high. So Kiki reluctantly begged me to stay home and do the coke if I had to just so she would know something bad wouldn't happen to me. So one night I was up all night at home coked out and Kiki was up with me talking to me. First thing in the morning, she had to meet with her probation officer. We had some heavy talks that night and we decided that we were going to get married soon. So when she left, I was still emotional and I kissed and hugged her repeatedly. Then I went out to the balcony and waved good-bye.

"I love you," I said and blew her a kiss as she got in the car.

Kiki met with her probation officer and she gave Kiki her final random urine test. After a few minutes, the probation officer came back into the room.

"Cocaine came up in your system," she told Kiki.

"That's impossible. I don't do drugs," Kiki protested.

"This is a very serious matter, Kiki. You're breastfeeding your infant daughter. A positive coke test can start the process of removing your child from the home and placing her into protective custody with a foster parent."

"What?? I didn't do coke!" she said. "Wait. Can you get a positive test for coke from kissing someone?"

"I've never heard of that. But if you think that might be the way that the coke was introduced into your system, why don't you stay here for an hour and we'll retest your urine. If it was something as trivial as that, it should be out of your system by then," her probation officer said.

That was when my cell phone rang.

"You fucking motherfucker," Kiki screamed. "They're going to take my baby away because of your fucked-up addicted ass. I just tested positive for coke. Now your addictions are fucking with my family. I could lose my daughter! How could you do coke before you kissed me good-bye this morning?"

She had me there. I was a licker when it came to my blow. And I'm not talking about licking no little bit of residue off that folded sliver of paper that the coke might be in. I'm talking about a jar of coke. I stuck my tongue down that jar and I hit pure cocaine. So much that you don't even feel your tongue anymore.

I hung up the phone and told Mikey to lock the door again and I just started walking. I walked twenty miles from my place in Henderson to the ghetto in West Las Vegas. I was high and sweating like a motherfucker and people were pulling their cars over and offering me a ride.

"Mike, get in the car, man," they'd say.

"No, don't fuck with me, man. I'm going through some shit."

"Do you want me to call the cops?"

"No, no, I'm okay," I said.

Napoleon once said, "There is but one step from the sublime to the ridiculous." I was taking a hundred thousand steps. Kiki had waited an hour and taken her test and it had come back negative this time but I didn't know that. I just kept on walking and when I got home I got some coke and I binged for two days.

Then it was my turn to flunk a piss test. My piss came up dirty. I wasn't that worried because my lawyer's partner was close friends with my probation officer, but this time he didn't just let it slide. So between my test and Kiki's probation officer reporting the kiss incident, I was looking at possibly getting my ass sent back to prison or at the least having to go back to Arizona and be put under much more rigorous probation. That would have meant that Kiki and I would have been separated because she was under probation here in Vegas.

"Mike, if you go to prison, as your girlfriend I don't have any rights, I'm on probation too," Kiki told me one day. "I may not even be able to visit with you, even though we have a child together. That's why I want to be married too. We were planning to get married anyway."

"All right, when do you want to do it?" I said.

"Honestly? Tomorrow," she said.

"Why not tonight?"

It was about six p.m. on June sixth, just about ten days after Exodus had passed. Kiki Googled "wedding chapels" and made some calls and the person at the chapel at the Las Vegas Hilton said they could take us right away. Kiki was making it sound like it was a practical thing but I loved that crazy woman. I didn't want to marry her so she could visit me in prison with the baby, I wanted to marry her because I didn't want to live without her. We had been talking about it for a while and she had told me that she wasn't giving me an ultimatum but if I didn't lock her down, she wasn't going to wait years and years to get married. She might take another situation if it came along because she wanted to be married.

Right after I suggested that we get married that night, I got this Herculean pain from a pinched nerve or something in my neck. We were driving to the Hilton and I was writhing.

"You don't have to marry me. I don't want to force you into marrying me," Kiki said and started bawling.

"I want to marry you, but I'm just in such fucking pain, baby. Why does it always have to be about you? Why do I got to be happy and giggling like you? I'm in so much fucking pain."

I was a mess. I had cold sores all over my mouth from doing coke. I was grossly overweight and now I had this pinched nerve. Meanwhile, Kiki had done all the wedding bullshit. She was superstitious, so for something blue she put on a blue panties. For something borrowed, she was wearing her mom's bracelet. She had plenty of old stuff so that was no biggie. We got to the chapel and I couldn't believe that the guy that was marrying us looked just like Slick, the black pro-wrestling manager who managed Big Boss Man. We both looked so bad that we didn't even want pictures but then we broke down and got some. We started looking through the pictures and the guy that married us said, "That will be a donation of seventy-five dollars and up." How do you come off setting the price for a donation? I felt like he was getting ready to call the law on us like we were going to run off with the pictures.

We got home and Milan was crying so Kiki ran upstairs to breast-feed her. Rita was sitting there watching TV.

"Mom, we just got married," I told her.

"Get out of here! Who married you?" she said.

"Slick from the WWF," I said. Then I told her the truth and she was so excited.

But we didn't exchange rings or go on a honeymoon. We wouldn't get the rings for another year and the honeymoon was over in a couple of days. Kiki and I had never fought. We were cool until we said, "I do," and then we starting fighting like a motherfucker. When the reality hit me I thought, *What the fuck is going on here?* I was still in my addiction and I was just overstepping the boundaries a lot. I was fighting them about leaving the house. I was doing a good job; instead of doing coke every day I was doing it once a week now. Then it went from once a week to once every two weeks, then once every three weeks to once a month.

Every time I slipped I felt shame because now I was coming home to Kiki and her mom and our little baby. I'd come back sweating like a pig, burning up, and Rita would put the cold compresses on me while Kiki was running her mouth at me.

"Don't you see your mother? Don't fucking say nothing," I told Kiki. "Be like your mother."

"My mother is not married to you," she said.

A week after my birthday I went out with a friend and I stayed out all night doing coke. Kiki couldn't sleep because I hadn't come home so she started Googling my name to see if I had been arrested. Then she let out a scream and ran into Rita's room.

"Mike is dead! I just saw it on the Internet." They reported that I was out celebrating my birthday with friends and that I had succumbed to a massive heart attack.

Rita got on the phone immediately and called the coroner's office.

"Do you have a Mike Tyson there?" she asked.

"Why do you ask?" they answered.

"Because he's dead," she said.

"How do you know he's dead?"

"That's just the point. We don't know if he's dead, that's why we're calling," Rita said. "This is his mother-in-law and his wife. We're trying to find out if you have his body."

They put Rita on hold and then another guy picked up.

"No, we don't have anyone here by that name."

The next day, I walked jauntily into the house.

"Hey, guys," I said. I was high as a kite.

"You are such an asshole," Kiki said. "I was looking for you and I went online and it said that you died of a heart attack."

I started laughing.

"The reports of my death are greatly exaggerated," I paraphrased Mark Twain.

Kiki didn't think it was funny. She grabbed Milan.

"I'm getting out of here," she said and stormed down the stairs to the car.

"Where are you going?" Rita asked.

"I'm just leaving," Kiki said. "Are you staying with him?"

"Yeah, somebody needs to," Rita said.

"Don't worry, Momma. I'll take care of you," I offered. As if my high ass was in any condition to take care of anyone. I could barely stand up straight.

Kiki blew off some steam and came home. She was worried that she had forced me into marrying her and that's why we were fighting and I was slipping out.

"Do you feel like you settled with me?" she'd ask me.

"You know that no one can make me do anything I don't want to do," I reassured her.

I was getting sick of the slips myself. A few weeks earlier *The Hangover* had come out and it was a runaway smash. I was still getting high but I called up Todd Phillips, the director.

"When is the next fucking movie, Todd? Yo, I want in that movie, Todd. Don't play me, man."

In July we all went to L.A. to the Teen Choice Awards because *The Hangover* had been nominated. I brought Rayna, my daughter with Monica, and she was so excited to meet the Jonas Brothers. They were hosting it and they wanted to do a skit with me where I was a sadistic barber and I cut off one of the brothers' hair.

A few weeks later we were back in L.A. for the ESPY awards. That visit didn't go as well as the last one. We were so broke that we couldn't even afford to stay in the hotel room that ESPN put us up in for any additional days. When the show was over, Kiki and I had a fight on the way back to the hotel so when we got there she and Milan and Rita and Darryl went up to the rooms but I snuck off and went and got our car. I had brought some coke with me without them knowing it and I had snuck off periodically to do it and to have a few drinks so I was pretty high by now. I started the car and then remembered I had left my phone on the valet bench where I was waiting so I got out and got the phone but locked myself out of the car.

All the people from the show were spilling out and I saw this young Caucasian lady who I had had a one-night stand with a few years earlier. She was staying at the hotel too.

"Hey, what are you doing?" I said.

She took one look at my face and got scared. She could see I wasn't right.

"No, no, I'm just going back to my room," she said and scurried off.

Okay, I guess it was only a one-night stand for her too. So I called AAA and they came and opened the car and wouldn't even take any money. I got behind the wheel and I pulled out. A friend of mine was having a cocaine party at his house in Beverly Hills so I wasn't going to miss that, but I had no idea how to get to the freeway to Beverly Hills from this hotel in downtown L.A. I guess I was weaving a bit and then I made a weird turn. Then I saw lights in the rearview mirror and I heard a siren and then an amplified voice: "Pull over to the side of the road."

I not only pulled over, I pulled up onto the fucking curb I was so high. *Oh shit,* I thought. I was going straight back to jail. The cop got out of his car and approached my vehicle. I rolled down the window.

"Mike Tyson! Holy shit!" he said. "Hey, you were great in *The Hangover.* We've been following you for a while, Mike. You've been swerving all over the road."

I must have gotten this from Cus but in a tenth of a second, as soon as I detected any friendliness from him, I opened up all my love on him. I had to do something because my license was suspended and I had no documents in the car.

"Hey, guy, I'm sorry if I was driving erratically because I'm kind of lost. I'm trying to find my friend's house in Beverly Hills but I don't know how to get to the freeway. Can you help me with this address?"

I handed him my friend's address. He took the paper and he went back to his car. He was taking an awfully long time so I got paranoid that he was checking my record and would see my license suspension. I was sweating bullets when he came back to my car.

"Okay, Mike, we got it. Why don't you just follow us and we'll escort you there."

Yes! I had played my get-out-of-jail-free celebrity card tonight. I didn't think that officer was going to show me any love but he did. They got me to the party and then they actually escorted me to the front door!

My friend looked pretty shocked to see me and two LAPD police officers there.

"We're leaving Mike Tyson in your custody and you'd better make sure he gets home safely in the morning. If we hear that he was driving we have your address on file," the one cop said.

There's no bigger buzzkill than to show up at a coke party with two cops. So as soon as the cops pulled away, everybody left the party. So I went back into my car, high and drunk as hell, and somehow wound up at the Beverly Hilton Hotel. I dropped my car off and I went into the hotel to have a drink and make a call to score more coke. When I came back, the valet wouldn't give me my car keys.

"You cannot drive like that, man. I'm keeping your car," he said. So I called Kiki and told her to come pick me up. Before she got there I had changed my mind and I hailed a cab instead. I went down Sunset to my friend Mark's cigar bar. He wasn't in but his partner was there. As soon as he saw me, he looked so concerned that he immediately kicked everyone out and closed the place and called Mark. Mark came and picked me up and drove me to my friend Jeff Greene's house.

Meanwhile, Kiki had rushed over to the hotel and found the car but not me. But she was getting calls from friends of hers with Mike sightings. By the time she got to the cigar bar I was long gone. We eventually met up at the Andaz Hotel on Sunset and spent the night before returning to Vegas.

I had a few more relapses when we were back in Vegas and Kiki decided it was time to send me back to rehab. This time we had zero money and she certainly wasn't going to send me to a cushy summer camp for celebrities place like Wonderland or Promises. She thought I needed a real program. So she went online and found a program called Impact, about an hour outside of L.A. in Palm Springs. She read the online brochure and thought that all that discipline they were talking about would be good for me. I needed some no-frills, no-nonsense approach, not some bullshit celebrity pampering. She didn't know anything about rehabs so she had no idea that this place was looked at as the rehab place for lowlifes and dead-enders. She kept beating up on me until I finally agreed to go.

I copped a couple of eight balls of coke and packed a bag and off Darryl and I went to California. I was doing my last hurrah with the coke when we got to the place. I checked in and then one of the rehab counselors asked me if I had any drugs to surrender. So I gave him what I had left which was almost an eight ball.

"That's good," he said and disappeared in the back. When he came out again, he was acting strange. This motherfucker did my coke. And it was some good coke too. They had a junkie running the rehab! They showed me to my room and it was in a trailer. The whole place was basically a trailer park.

I was not a happy rehab camper. The place was crawling with violent meth heads and some court-sanctioned gangbangers who I really thought I might have to fight. I lasted the night and then at eight a.m. I told them I was leaving. They called Kiki and told her that I wasn't happy and wanted to leave. At eleven a.m. they called her back.

"Look, he's really not happy."

Then I called her.

"I can't believe you put me in this place. I can't stay here, I'm going to go."

"Try it for a little while," she begged.

A half hour later I broke one of the chairs, which was like lawn furniture, and they drove me to the nearest bus station. That place was way too hard-core for me. But I have to admit that when I was at Wonderland or Promises it took me eight to fourteen months to get my life together. I spent a half a day at this place and I came home and except for one small slip, I haven't had a drink or any coke since.

The success of *The Hangover* played a major role in getting me cleaned up. I remember the movie had just premiered and a small kid and his father walked by me on the street.

"Look, Daddy." The kid stopped and pointed at me. "That's the actor Mike Tyson."

"Hey, at one time I was the best fighter in the world too, kid," I said.

That began happening again and again. A whole generation of kids started knowing me as an actor, not a boxer. It just happened within a blink of an eye. I was drugged out on coke, almost suicidal, living the life of a loser and, BOOM. It happened so fast it was almost uncomfortable. But I knew I couldn't blow this opportunity to reinvent myself again. But before I could do that I had to do some serious reprogramming.

"I'm going to change, I'm going to win, I'm not going to end like this," I kept telling myself. I went back to my Cus shit. No one could stop me. My reign would be invincible. I had been on coke, I didn't even know what reign I was going to have. I knew it wasn't boxing but I had the same ideology and thrust and thirst and hunger to draw on.

But it was a different hunger and thirst. I wasn't hopeless back when I was a kid coming up. I still believed I was something back then. But now I had been in bed with some very bad spirits and I had annihilated all my dreams and hopes.

Prominent directors and actors were calling me and telling me that I had to do more film work.

"You have to keep doing comedic roles," they'd say. "Forget that tough-guy shit. You're a nice guy, Mike. Nobody sees that because it's been pushed down by all that dark shit that you've experienced in life. But you have to stay lit, because when you're in that light, you shine so brightly."

They were right. All that dark stuff was a pose, a persona that Cus had imposed on me. Cus wanted me to intimidate. He was using me to fulfill his own legacy. Don't get me wrong. It was a cool legacy to fulfill and if he asked me to do it again, I would do it but be even meaner and more vicious.

So I went from being hopeless to having a goal again. What happens now? My vanity kicks in. Everybody was telling me, "You're so good in movies, you have to pursue it." Then I looked in the mirror.

This body isn't good for the movies, I thought. *Who's going to want to hump this guy? Who's going to think I'm hot? I'm fucking Fat Albert. I weighed 380 pounds and the way the screen magnifies your ass, I'm going to look 680. Omar the Tentmaker is gonna have to make my suits.*

Now I had to get into serious shape. So for five weeks I ate nothing but tomato basil soup. My wife decided to go on a vegan diet for a week and I was right there next to her. Only I didn't stop. What's that? Vegan? Okay, I'm a full-on vegan.

I was sick of being a fat pig. I was embarrassed to have sex with my wife I was so fat. The narcissist with delusions of grandeur again! I come from a line of morbidly obese people. That's who I am. But I'm so vain, I'd rather literally work my ass off and do everything I hate to do rather than be the fat guy I truly am. Now my discipline kicked in. It has to be planned. I have to convene a little meeting of the committee in my head and give out the orders. "This is what we're going to do. These are the concrete steps we need to achieve this goal."

I didn't miss eating meat. I cheated one time and had the tiniest piece of beef and I was in pain and started throwing up. It was like poison to my body now. Eating all that meat just fueled my aggression. And dairy products made me bloat up. Now I was eating a lot of beans and Kiki was making me delicious fruit and vegetable shakes. Once I was in the full throes of my veganism all my ailments disappeared. My high blood pressure, my arthritis, my high glucose, poof, gone. I had been a walking dead man, eating like shit and smoking those Al Capone cigarillos. And now I was eating healthy and doing three hours of exercise and cardio a day. I'm just an extremist. It was either the yoga or the needle in my arm. One or the other.

In October, Oprah asked me to do her show. The DVD of my documentary had been released in August so everyone was telling me it was a great chance to promote that. But I had just started my serious diet and I was still as big as a house. But I had never been on Oprah before so I did it. We touched on everything in that interview—the death of Exodus, my rocky relationship with Robin—Oprah even brought out Kiki and baby Milan. But when we talked about the ear-biting incident with Evander, Oprah really got animated.

"When you apologized did you feel the apology?" she asked me.

"No, I did not. It wasn't sincere, it was insincere and stuff."

"Thank you for saying that because when I heard it, I didn't think it was," she said. "Why did you do it? Because you thought you had to do it?"

"Probably. Everybody on my crew was getting on my nerves. I said, 'Okay, I apologize.' Really I was more offended for apologizing then, because it was so insincere. I just always wanted to have a place to sit down and talk to him and shake his hand and just express myself to him."

"Have you talked to him?" she asked.

"No, I think when I see him sometimes he's a little leery of me, you know."

After the show aired, Oprah was inundated with letters and calls. Some people were irate because she had a convicted rapist on the show, but the majority of the e-mails and calls were positive and supportive. They felt me and understood where I had been coming from. And Evander called Oprah and asked her to set up a show where we could reunite. Oprah jumped all over that and a week later I was back in Chicago.

It was great seeing Evander. We both came from sewage and became established and esteemed fighters. I got a chance to truly apologize to him in public and we both were able to show young kids that if we could come together hopefully that could be an example for all of them to stop killing one another in senseless violence.

Oprah got feedback from one more person. Robin had been out of the limelight for a while, so she called to protest the portion of my first appearance where we discussed her. Oprah had shown a clip of Robin berating me while I stood by mute on *20/20*.

"Why did you sit there the whole time?" Oprah asked me.

"I don't know, I was just overwhelmed," I said.

"Were you surprised she was saying those things?"

"Yeah. I truly wanted to sock her at that particular moment, but I just didn't do it."

When I said that the whole audience laughed.

Robin was irate. She even got Oprah to put her on the show to rebut me and jump-start her career again. I was helping everyone out there.

All of our friends called to tell us how great the appearances with Oprah went. But I didn't have the heart to watch them. I was so self-conscious of my weight then it would have depressed me too much.

But I stayed on my vegan diet and kept working out and slowly but surely the pounds began melting away. Then in late January of 2010 I went out to a bar in the ghetto of Las Vegas and a friend of mine was there and one thing led to another and I did some blow. I hadn't slipped in six months by then. I don't know why I let my guard down and let the devil in but I did. I didn't do a lot, but it was still coke. I went home pretty early that night and Kiki was awake and she immediately could tell that I had gotten high. She didn't yell and scream and curse me out and threaten to leave the house with the baby like she had the previous times I slipped. She just went to sleep in Milan's room. I kept coming back there to talk to her, I felt so guilty. I didn't want to let her down and I especially didn't want Milan to ever see me fucked up.

"So you did coke tonight, didn't you?" Kiki asked.

"Yes," I said.

"Fuck. Dammit, Mike, come on. You've got to go back to rehab. We have to end this."

"No, please give me another chance," I said. There was no way I wanted to go back to that trailer park hell of a rehab.

"You've got to go in the morning," she insisted.

"I'll be okay. I'll be fine. Just give me one more chance."

She did. And I haven't had a drink or a line of coke since then.

We still had an income problem. In February we went to Europe where I did a talk in England and a meet and greet in France. In Switzerland I was paid to make an appearance at a big club and just hang out. But first we went to Italy, where I appeared on their version of *Dancing With the Stars*. I was hesitant to do it but they kept upping the ante and we needed the money. When Kiki saw my partner, she wasn't too pleased. She was an attractive Italian girl and she was all flirty with me. I was trying to get my cigarettes out of my pocket once and she said, "No, I'll get them," and I got nervous when she touched me. Kiki could watch our rehearsals from behind a two-way glass mirror and I could feel her looking at me through that glass. I started sweating and the girl tried to wipe my sweat off with her hand and I was, like, "Oh shit!" I wasn't interested in this young lady and I knew that things were boiling in Kiki's mind from my past behavior. But it all came out all right—we did our one number and made it through without embarrassing ourselves.

When I got back to the States, I did a guest appearance on *Entourage*. I had seen Jeremy Piven when I was talking to Jamie Foxx at a club in Vegas a while back but I was too high to approach him and shake his hand. A little while later I got a call that they wanted me to appear on the show as one of Ari Gold's clients, complaining that he wasn't getting me enough work. It was a fun cameo and two of my kids got to be in the scene, so that was great for them.

All of the cast and crew were awesome and we bonded with Doug Ellin, the creator. Kiki and her brother had created a TV show idea loosely based on a boxer like me and she pitched it to Doug and he loved it. *Entourage* was winding down and he was looking for another project. So he got another TV writer with a track record attached and they all worked on a pilot for HBO and Spike Lee came aboard to direct it. It was called *Da Brick*, and it got a lot of buzz, but in the end HBO passed.

In July I was hired to make an appearance at a film festival in Kazakhstan. Then we planned to make a pilgrimage to Mecca after that. Right before we left, Kiki found out that she was pregnant again. We had been discussing having a second child and I thought it would be nice for me to see Kiki go through her whole pregnancy since I didn't get to do that the last time because she had been in prison.

But things didn't work out so well at the festival. We were there for the premiere of a Weinstein brothers film, and they had brought a few celebrities out for this. Kiki and I got into a huge fight right before we did the red carpet, then another fight at the cocktail reception before the film. So when the screening was over Kiki went straight back to the hotel and went to her mother's room.

I came into the room a few minutes later.

"Look, I don't want to be married to you anymore, all right?" I told her.

"Fine, I agree," she said.

Kiki looked for a flight back to the States and there was one leaving in a few hours. We hadn't even been there for a full day but now she, Milan, and her mom flew back home. I really didn't think that this marriage was going to work out.

But I still had a religious pilgrimage to make. My old cellmate Farid was back working with me and he was a Muslim too, so we left the next day for Mecca. I was really looking forward to the hajj, although I was not your typical Muslim. I was born a Catholic, that's what my mother was. Even though he wasn't around much, my father was a Southern Baptist and he made sure that me and my brother and sister got baptized. I was ten when they took me for my baptism. It was one of those deals where they put their hands on you and praise God and then you're supposed to faint. I didn't want to faint.

"If you don't faint that means the devil is in you," my auntie said.

"I ain't gonna fucking faint," I insisted.

"Look, if you don't faint, that means the devil is in you and they're going to tie you to a burning stake," my sister added.

"What?" I said.

As soon as that reverend touched me, I fell down like I was shot.

My brother and my sister went to a rinky-dink little Catholic school. I think I even did too but I don't have much recollection of that other than the nuns whooping my ass. We weren't super Catholics but I basically did whatever my mother told me. Do the wrong thing and you'd burn in hell for eternity. Eat the body of Christ, drink the Kool-Aid. I was just a poor black bastard waiting for the Kool-Aid to come. I just knew that church was the place where you could go to pray to God that the other kids in the neighborhood wouldn't beat my ass.

It didn't take long for me to figure out that everything was a hustle. The preacher's I knew were the best-dressed guy in the poorest neighborhood with the flashiest car and he was fucking everyone's wives and sisters and daughters. And they all adored the preachers. The preacher was still the most respected man around. We would talk and laugh about him but when he told us to march somewhere to do something, everybody was doing it. That was the power he had. We knew he was a dirty motherfucker but when he said "March" we all did. Because we knew deep inside that if we had his power we would do the same thing.

People ask me if my faith in God was shaken by seeing so many of my friends getting killed but it wasn't like that. In most cases, if any of my friends got killed it was because they were looking to kill somebody too or violate someone in a different way. That was an unwritten rule of the game. Make a mistake that led to your death, that was the chance you took.

It's funny how I got to Islam. When I was younger, my friends and I used to beat and rob Muslims on the street. We hated Muslims.

"Fuck you, talking that bullshit like you a foreign nigga," we'd say.

So this is what God does to me now. We always become that which we mock. And now some day it'll be my turn. Somebody will come after a Muslim and beat my ass.

I became fascinated with Islam by watching the Muslim guys in jail. I wanted to grow in jail and I always enjoyed listening to people and getting educated. I loved learning the essence of Islam and becoming committed to it, loving the world and all of God's creatures. That's why I don't kill the hawk or the falcon no more. I used to shoot them out of the sky and make traps for them when they would come for my pigeons. But then I realized that they were God's creatures. This was the way God intended them to be. If you love Allah, you have to love all his creations. I guess most Muslims believe that Satan created the pig but I think even the pig is Allah's creation and you have to love it. (That don't mean you have to eat it.)

So I slowly embraced Islam. I wasn't any revelation guy. I just slowly realized that a Muslim was just who I was. I treat everybody the way that I want to be treated. What I want for myself, I want for everyone I like. When I first got involved with Islam in jail I was very hostile and I became too extreme a Muslim. I was too violent and I was projecting that violence on my religion. Islam is not about war, it's a religion of humanity. I didn't think that at first. I was hostile. If you didn't believe what I believed, you were the enemy. I was just bitter at the world. But then I had to go and do some research and some studying and I found out that wasn't the way to go. That's why I became more humble, more subservient, because that's what Islam is truly about. Islam is all love, peace, and submission. Because you submit in peace, it doesn't mean you're weak, but it's just being humble to God.

One thing that I learned from Islam is that we all have our own individual relationship with God. God is not going to send someone to hell for my mistakes. So God and I have to deal with my own salvation. When you get down to it, all religions say the same thing, that we should just love our fellow man. My little guys like Christmas. Do I tell them that that's bad, that it's a pagan holiday, that we don't celebrate Christian holidays? No, I don't say that. I say, "Hey, let's get some Christmas toys, then we can have Christmas every day." They know I'm Santa Claus. If they like listening to Christmas carols, it's fine. Besides my family and my mother, everyone I know is a Christian or a Jew. If I go to ten houses here in town, I don't think one of them would be a Muslim household. But when I go to pray, everyone is going to be a Muslim.

They say that only Muslims are going to be in heaven. If I go to heaven and there's only Muslims and I'm not with my friends that I know and love, I don't want to be there. I want to be in a place where I can laugh and fight with all my friends and loved ones, no matter what their religion is. I don't want to be in heaven with a bunch of guys who believe in the same God but who I don't know. I want to be with some people I can trust, even though we've got different Gods, the world is bigger than our religion. How am I going to do good if I am in heaven and I am praying all the time? My knees are messed up, my head is messed up and I don't see none of my friends and I've got to eat lamb and figs all the time in heaven. Do we have to have twenty billion Muslims in heaven, or a trillion Muslims? Bottom line, I don't want to go to heaven if it means I'm going to be alone. I'm serious, take me to hell where all my friends are, where the people I knew and respected when I was living are going to be.

Some people claim to have intimate knowledge of God but I certainly don't. To me, God is inconceivable. We were created in God's likeness? We can't even think that we're on his level. Is God a pig, a liar, a pervert? That's what we are. We're sex addicts, drug addicts, control freaks, manipulators, and narcissists. If this is what God is, we're fucked.

Sometimes I think that this life is just an illusion. Just think that I lost a child, and I think about that and it's like she never existed. I say, what about my baby? What about Cus? I think about him all the time. They're both a big part of my life, I think about them all the time. The more I think about these spiritual matters, the more I know that I know nothing.

The concept of God is too complicated for me. When I think of spirituality, I go from my Muslim perspective. I just don't understand religion and God. I want to, but I don't. I'm not going to go for "Oh, yes, let your mind believe and listen to the words in your heart," because people that lead blindly are blindly led. I'm just not going for that bullshit, I'm just not doing it. You can make it sound different, but it just boils down to the fact that you're following somebody that you don't know exists. Even if you say, "I don't believe in organized religion. I'm more into spirituality." Whose concept of the spiritual are you listening to? Your self-taught spirituality? If that's the case you've got a fool for both the student and the teacher. Look, people tell us who God is and we believe what they tell us.

I can't conceive what people tell me about God. It doesn't regulate to my piercing soul. But there must be some design to this universe. Chaos is overwhelming so there has to be some balance to allow us to focus in this maniacal atmosphere. But most religious people who go to church are exploited for business purposes. That's what I believe. So I have to have my own salvation with God. I love the concept of loving Allah. I don't know if it's a true reality, but it's a concept that I'm in love with and I think it's good.

Going to Mecca and Medina was an amazing experience. I got closer to my faith but in some ways I was put off by the actions of some of my brother Muslims. When I got there they immediately started broadcasting my visit to show off that Islam was a better religion than Christianity or the rest of the religions. It wasn't about me becoming a better person, it was more like, "We've got the Mighty Mike Tyson making hajj here." They didn't care about me as a person, they just cared about their publicity agenda. I was just a dumb nigga being used, that's all I've ever been in my life.

"We're going to make America know that you're a good Muslim," they actually told me.

In my mind I was saying, *Shit, I wasn't a good Christian, how am I going to be a good Muslim?*

Religion has to be in the man, a man can't be in the religion. It really was almost juvenile, seeing all these religious figures in Islam fronting like, "My prophet is better than yours."

But despite the political agendas, I felt good there. Anybody would feel like that there. Hundreds of thousands of people, all dressed the same, all there to worship and humble themselves. I was in a state of harmony, so I was harmonious.

BEING THERE HELPED ME GET MY HEAD TOGETHER AND PUT ME IN AN ISLAMIC frame of mind. It helped me focus on what I had to do when I got back home. How I had to lead my life. Not necessarily an Islamic life but a purer life, with no more drugs and no more drama. It was really a recharging of my spiritual batteries. I needed to go there.

At hajj, I realized that I could never be a good Muslim in the strictest pious sense. I brought a lot of baggage into the religion with me. But I could listen to the teachings of the Prophet and try to live my way on the same path. Judge people on the goodness of their hearts. It's hard for me to be that way. If you really practice Islam in its purest form you're a doormat. I don't like to live my life that way. That's beyond being pious, that's being humble. And none of us can truly be humble. If you mention the word "humble" that in itself tells us that you're not humble. Man is not meant to be humble, he's meant to be humbled.

I couldn't be humble when they pushed me to the front of the line to kiss the black stone. The stone itself is the eastern cornerstone of the Kaaba, the ancient stone building in Mecca towards which Muslims around the world pray. On the hajj you're supposed to circle the stone seven times and kiss it if you can. There are so many pilgrims though that some people who've been going to Mecca their whole lives have never kissed the black stone. I kissed it four times in thirty minutes. I'm there and they're splitting the people like the Red Sea and bringing me right up to kiss it. They're pushing these pious people to the side so I can put my dirty-assed, diseased coke-licking mouth on it. It made me feel horrible. They're trying to get us to feel better than everyone else and to love the religion. But when they do things like that to me, I'm saying, "You let us get in front of all these beautiful people? I don't want to be involved." Like Groucho Marx said, "I refuse to join any club that would have me as a member."

I felt bad that Kiki couldn't have come and made her hajj. We didn't talk for a couple of weeks after she had left Europe. We both felt that this might be the end of our marriage. I called her from Mecca and was all apologetic and we vowed to stick through it and work it out.

Kiki, deep down in her heart, is a Christian; she was raised that way. Her characteristics are Christian characteristics. Her mother married an Imam and they made a dramatic switch to being in a hijab. Kiki is free-loving. She wants to be involved with the world but she still has her conscience of Islam. But as a black female American she's not going to tolerate her husband having four wives as the Koran says you can have.

IN DECEMBER, I WENT TO ASIA WITH FARID. I WAS BEING NAMED CHINA'S boxing ambassador. I was on my best behavior in China. One guy came up to me and told me that he supplied all the stars that came over to China with weed.

"You can't be my friend," I told him. "You must be trying to set me up. You know that they're going to kill you for smoking a joint here."

After China, I went to Bangkok to film *The Hangover Part II*. There was controversy even before the film started shooting. Mel Gibson was signed to do a cameo as a Bangkok tattoo artist, but Zach and other cast members went to Todd and got him thrown off the picture. I wouldn't have gone that far. I met Mel Gibson once and he was a gentleman to me. Of course, his drunk anti-Semitic rant was deplorable, but I wasn't so quick to judge anyone. When they asked me for a reaction to his firing, all I could say was, "We all have that guy—a Mel Gibson—in us."

Kiki was too pregnant to come with me to the shoot and it was a shame because she would have loved Thailand. Everything was beautiful. We shot my scene on an island and I had a great room in the Four Seasons with a spectacular view of the water. On our way in from the airport, an elephant popped into the road out of nowhere. I had lost a hundred pounds by then, so I was excited to film my climactic scene where I sang "One Night in Bangkok." It was night and day from my first experience with Todd and the other actors. I was totally sober now and enjoying every minute on the set. Before, when I was high, I'd be telling people to run around and get me things. But now I didn't even come out of my room unless they needed me. Todd and them probably thought that I was just a motherfucker trying to kiss ass, but I was so grateful to them for what they had done for me. God, I owed those guys so much.

I got back to Vegas and I spent most of January with Kiki, waiting for the birth of our son. We had gotten through our rough patch and now we were really getting along. Kiki had gone into contractions at twenty-seven weeks, so they had her on bed rest with some medication and then she had to go in to get the baby's heart monitored once a week. I went to every appointment with her and rubbed her belly all the time. I really like being with Kiki. And I wanted to be a good parent. I didn't know if it was in me but I really had the desire. The baby had to be induced so we checked into the hospital on the night of January twenty-fourth, and our son Morocco arrived about noon the next day. I left the hospital the night we arrived at about four a.m. to go home and exercise and change. I got all dressed up nice and went back to the hospital.

"You look nice," Rita said.

"It's a big occasion. Today my son is being born," I told her.

I was in the room when he came out. I sat down at Kiki's side because both she and I didn't want me to be right up in her birth canal. I sat on the sidelines and whenever Kiki would look over I'd make funny faces. I couldn't believe how nervous I got. But he finally came out, all eight pounds, thirteen ounces. And he was a good-looking baby right from the get-go.

I had another great fortune that year. I was inducted into the International Boxing Hall of Fame in June. I never thought that I'd have been put in the Hall of Fame. No one in boxing liked me by then, I had such a bad reputation. There were guys who had started boxing after me and they were in the hall already so I just realized that I'd never get that honor. I knew how those old fighters must have felt. Down and out, broke, just waiting day by day for a call that might never come.

But my phone rang in February and the guy on the line said, "You've just been voted into the Hall of Fame." When the call was over, I just hung up the phone and started crying. I had been obsessed with boxing my whole life. I used to go to sleep cradling my boxing gloves. That's all I wanted to be. It feels so stupid now to think I would be this great fighter, one the world had never seen, another Achilles. My arrogance, my ego got so whacked out, that's why I just had to shut it down. It pushed me to accomplish so many things, but I shut it down, because I want to keep my family.

But to be honest, and not from an egotistical perspective, just from my understanding of the history of the game, it's going to be difficult to find a guy like me that could generate the money and income like I did in my time. Fighters today don't understand the sport, they don't understand how to entertain the people, they're not scholarly enough to examine the past, and not only to find out about the fighters, but who they hung out with. Gene Tunney and Benny Leonard hung out with George Bernard Shaw. Mickey Walker and Harry Greb were with Hemingway.

Regardless of what anybody said—"Mike Tyson is horrible, he's a bum"—I represented all the old-time fighters. I never let the people forget who they were. If I hit a guy with one of the punches I learned from Benny Leonard or Harry Greb, I'd always give them credit. Guys like Joe Gans and Leonard and John L. Sullivan were the first, and the first always have to be acknowledged. They made boxing an art.

I was happy to have been voted in, but I was uncertain whether I should go to the ceremony. I was probably a little bitter that I had been passed up before. But my friend Dave Malone was visiting me and he gave me a little speech.

"Listen, man, this is your fucking honor. But you're not only doing this for you, you're doing this for Brownsville, you're doing this for everyone in the hood. It's a great accomplishment. You came from the hood and you made it to the fucking Hall of Fame. Get out there and do this."

He was right. When I was up there getting introduced I thought about Cus. When I was fourteen, I used to always ask him, "Do you think I'll be in the Hall of Fame?" Cus marveled at my dedication to everything about boxing. He used to tell everyone, "I never saw anybody that had so much enthusiasm about boxing like this guy." I knew the history of the sport inside and out. I knew that most fighters that I had seen wound up broke and destitute or working a menial job. I knew that was going to happen, but I just wanted to be in that fraternity with those guys. Even though they were dead or senile, people still talk about these guys in the barbershop.

There is no sport in the world that is more passionate than fighting, when it is done correctly. You want to fight your brother or your father because the guy you're rooting for is you. He's representing your whole barometer about how you feel and think. Mixed martial arts are more popular than boxing now because you see so much passion in the cage. Boxers don't have that passion anymore. There's no guy that really has the heart to say "Not only do the gods deliver me and vex me, but one day I will reign with them." Today's guys don't say that shit, they don't have the balls, they spring from a milieu too meager to comprehend my kind of reality. They don't want to do that because they're afraid they will fail and people will laugh at them. That's why today's fighters don't get the total respect because they're afraid to really grab true greatness. They look at boxing as a check, they don't see it as something noble. They want money and adulation. I wanted adulation and immortality.

What makes an exciting fighter is his ability and willingness to want to hurt the other man. That makes for great fights and super-stars. When I was in the ring I projected myself as an animal. Like a dog in a pit, I was there to entertain the audience. The more I hurt someone, the quicker I hurt him, the more adulation I got from the crowd, and I fed off that. Today they don't dream about hurting their opponents. It's like the wussification of boxing. Sugar Ray Robinson, Rocky Marciano, those guys were going to die for that belt, you'd have to kill them to get it from them.

A lot of people have pronounced the death of boxing, but I think that's a little too premature. Boxing will come back, trust me. It's been around almost two hundred years, legally. It's not going to die easy. Just wait until we see the next really great heavyweight fighter. That will be a sight that we'll want to see again and again.

At the end of June, Kiki and I decided to renew our vows. It was my idea. We never had a proper wedding. My birthday was at the end of June and Kiki's was in the middle so I came up with the idea of inviting people to come to a joint birthday celebration. Then we'd sur-prise them with a wedding. At first we were going to have only about twenty-five people come but then it mushroomed to over 250. We rented a ballroom at the M Resort in Las Vegas, just minutes from our house. Kiki hired this great wedding planner. We had a cocktail reception that we both attended for about ten minutes and then we snuck off and changed into wedding attire and Rita made the an-nouncement to the crowd.

"I know you guys think you are here for a party, but actually Mike and Kiki are going to renew their vows," she said.

Then the curtain parted and you could see the beautiful aisleway for the wedding. The crowd went crazy. And right before we walked down the aisle, we got into a stupid fight.

We were in the back getting ready to come out and Kiki was going, "Shut the fuck up." And I was saying, "Fuck you. You shut the fuck up."

"I don't want to marry you," she said.

"I don't want to marry you either," I replied.

We were just nervous. You don't realize the nerves that are generated from reciting your vows in front of all those people. I'd been married twice before but this was the first official wedding for both of us.

But we went ahead with the ceremony and then we had a nice reception. And afterwards, Kiki and I got into another fight. So on our second wedding night, I wound up sleeping on the couch in the suite and Kiki was in the bed. We were always getting into these stupid little rifts, we were both so hotheaded. But in the morning everything was fine and we went home.

It was good that we made up, because Kiki and I had been working for a while on a new vehicle for me. After the HBO pilot wasn't picked up, we decided to try something else. In October of 2009, Kiki and I had gone to the Venetian to see Chazz Palminteri do his one-man show *A Bronx Tale*. We were both just blown away by the way he could captivate the entire audience for an hour and a half just by himself.

On the way home, I was inspired.

"Wow, this is almost like what I do when I go over to Europe or Asia," I told Kiki. "People would ask me questions and I'd go for so long on that one question that the other people would get mad because they couldn't get their questions in. It's funny, I hate looking at myself but I love talking about myself. I think I can do this. But, baby, my show is gonna be a little gut-wrenching."

Kiki was so excited. When she got home she immediately started writing down a few pages, the intro to the piece. The next day I read it and it was awesome. She wrote what I would have said if I had written it myself.

But it turned out to be a long arduous process, because Kiki would want to sit down and write and I would try to avoid her because it was painful talking about all the personal ups and downs of my life.

We used to get couples massages at the M Resort, and one day the masseuse gave us a card from this guy from New York named Adam Steck who was working out in Vegas. He told the attendant to tell us that he wanted to produce a one-man show with me. We called him and had him over to the house and he pitched us the idea. It was serendipity, because we had already started working on a one-man show. Adam had produced big hotel shows in town like *Thunder from Down Under* and a drag queen show called *Divas Las Vegas*. Adam brought in a director named Randy Johnson. Kiki wrote the whole script, but they gave Randy cowriting credit because he had a name already. By early 2012 we had a show ready to go.

We had a one-week run from April thirteenth to the eighteenth at the MGM Grand. I had so much fun on stage. The burden wasn't all on me. We had a jazz singer and a live rock band. They'd play the opening number and then I'd get introduced and the crowd went wild. I'd go into my monologue, but we had the piano player still there so I could play off him. The band played "Midnight at the Oasis" but we changed the lyrics to "Midnight at the Ho-asis," and everyone danced around. I was a party boy on stage, a real black Wayne Newton up there. I was talking about sad things in my life but it was delivered with a devil-may-care attitude. It was Vegas, I had my band, and I was busting off.

The show got great reviews. We had a dream that maybe we could tour it around the country and just maybe we could even get to Broadway with it. The day after the show closed Kiki and I flew to the U.K. for one of my meet and greets. Then we went to Poland because I had an endorsement deal with an energy drink company. While we were in Poland, I got a call from Spike Lee. One of his people had seen the show and loved it. So Spike had called the producer Jimmy Nederlander, and he wanted to bring it to Broadway with Spike directing it. By June we were rehearsing, and in August we had a ten-day run on Broadway.

Spike's version was a lot darker than the Vegas show. Spike wanted it to be gritty, a true one-man show, just me up there with some slides on a big screen behind me and some recorded musical segues. I actually preferred the Vegas version but people seemed to enjoy Spike's direction as well. We took Spike's show on the road, touring all over the country in 2013.

Getting on stage to bare my soul is a lot like going into the ring to box. I can't wait to get on stage but I'm also frightened to death. I'm like a racehorse just ready to burst out of the starting gate. I get out on the stage and I'm in control but also out of control. I have to rein myself in so I don't talk too fast. I wasn't born to do this but I learned to love it. Like almost everything else in my life, Cus was a big influence on the one-man show. I inherited Cus's ability to tell stories. I'm not nearly as good as he was but I have that ability because Cus would regale me with classic boxing stories that were epic in scope, legendary tales of adventure and betrayal.

I've always had the profoundest veneration for great accomplishments. Money never meant anything to me but stories of great accomplishments always inspired me to rise to the highest occasions. Entertaining people doesn't come as easy for me as boxing did. I hate what acting makes me do but I love how it makes me feel. I would do almost anything to achieve the accomplishment of entertaining someone.

I approached doing my one-man show the same way Cus taught me to approach boxing. I don't get involved emotionally with that person up on the stage. You have to be emotionless but you also have to do it with all the passion you possess. All my problems in life came when I was Mike Tyson and thought I deserved shit—a beautiful woman, a cool car, a mansion. That's when I got in trouble. I was always too impressed with my emotions. And soon the emotions became delusions. So I've spent my whole life since I met Cus trying to transcend myself.

But it was impossible to maintain that façade when it came time in the show to talk about Exodus. I had spent more time alone with Exodus than with any of my other children. I really knew her well. She was a true free spirit. A day doesn't go by when I don't break down and cry about my angel. I wear an earpiece during the show and Kiki sits backstage and gives me verbal cues when I need them. When it would come time to talk about Exodus, a beautiful picture of her would come up on the giant screen. Kiki would always say, "Look back at the picture." But I couldn't do that and still be able to get through the show.

In early 2013, I made two guest appearances on highly rated TV shows. On February sixth they aired my appearance on *Law & Order: Special Victims Unit*. I played Reggie Rhodes, a murderer on death row who gets a reprieve when he reluctantly testifies that the man he killed had sexually abused him when he was a child. I was so psyched for that role. For once I wasn't playing myself. They had to spend an hour putting makeup on my face to erase my tattoo. It was such a privilege to work with such great actors on that set. But then, before the show aired, more controversy got stirred up.

A woman started an online petition to force NBC to cancel that showing or boot me off the episode because I was a convicted rapist. She got a lot of publicity for this and her petition was signed by more than six thousand protestors, including *NCIS* star Pauley Perrette. My publicist suggested that I respond.

"I'm sorry that she has a difference of opinion, but she's entitled to it. I'm sorry she's not happy, but I didn't rape nobody or do anything like that and this lady wasn't there to know if I did or not. I don't trip on that stuff, I'm not trying to get rich and famous, I'm just trying to feed my family. Why should they care? Since I am clean and sober five years, I haven't broken any laws or did any crimes. I'm just trying to live my life."

That was my Uncle Tom response. What I really felt was that I had been broke for ten years. I had a family to feed and support. I'm not going to get rich from doing special-guest appearances on TV shows. What do these people want, for me to die? How am I going to make a living? If I can't work mainstream, do they want me to do porn?

Luckily, the creator of the show didn't buckle down to pressure. Dick Wolf issued a statement.

"I invite you to watch Ed Asner, Andre Braugher and Mike Tyson guest star in The Monster's Legacy episode of *Law and Order SVU* Wednesday, February 6th, at 9 o'clock on NBC. In my opinion one of our strongest episodes in the last five years as it focuses on what can happen when there is an emotionally charged rush to judgment."

I was also gratified that my friends, the ladies on *The View*, defended my right to work.

My other appearance wasn't at all controversial. I played myself on an episode of *How I Met Your Mother*. That experience was amazing. The show was run by these awesome ladies who created a totally family-type experience. All the writers, the producers, even the security guards and cleaning people had been working together for years. Women can put a touch on things that no men can. Working there was like being in a big puzzle and everybody had their piece and it went off flawlessly. I had a great time. Listen, I don't know if I am a good actor, but I know I love to act, and I know just from the love of acting something good will come out of it.

The national tour of *Mike Tyson—The Undisputed Truth*, my one-man show, began on February 13, 2013. By some weird coincidence, the opening night was in Indianapolis. I was really scared about going back to the place where I had been incarcerated for three years. I felt like I was in the house of hate. Driving from the airport to my hotel, checking in, I felt something heavy over my head, a distinct feeling of discomfort. The day before my show, I went out to the prison. It was something that I just had to do. Part of my A.A. contract is to make amends with people for my past bad behavior and when I was in that prison I was just an animal and a jerk.

I was shocked to find that Warden Slaven was still working there. When I was in, he was an assistant warden but now he had worked his way to the top. He's been there for forty-four years. Slaven was always such a wonderful guy. He would come in the hole for hours and hang out and talk to me. When I saw him again, we just bonded. He explained to me that he couldn't keep in contact with me because he still worked there but he was going to retire shortly and he was going to look me up. He didn't look the same. He had white hair now. He was a bit slimmer. But his energy was still so awesome. He's a real Christian; when he comes into a room you can palpably feel his spirituality.

When I left the prison, I just started to cry. I didn't think I'd do that but I felt like a weight had lifted off me. I realized that I had no problems with the city, I had issues with the prison. It was like I had been purified after seeing Slaven. It was incredible, I didn't think at this stage of my life I would feel that kind of feeling.

One thing I learned after completing my tour was that all I know how to do is entertain people. I don't care if it's ten thousand people or five, I love to perform. It's not easy because I'm basically shy. Even when I was a kid, I had the urge to perform. But when I would try to talk, some big guy would kick me and say, "Shut the fuck up, nigga." But Cus promoted the idea that I was there to entertain. "If you listen to me, every time you walk in the room, people won't be able to take their eyes off you. You'll suck all the air out of the room," he'd tell me. I'd feel like a peacock.

I know that I'll never again be able to turn on the Action News and hear, "Mike Tyson just signed a multimillion-dollar deal . . ." Those days are over. But I can continue to entertain people. I won't make much money, but I can do what I love to do. And just by doing what you love to do, out of love, good things happen.

WHEN I LOOK BACK ON MY LIFE, IT'S HARD TO BELIEVE HOW BIG AN ENTITY I was at the height of my fame. I was different than the rest of the big stars because I was flamboyant too. And I was just an immature child, really in over my head. I felt like I was part of a freak show for most of my career as a boxer. Later, I just felt like a freak. I'm truly grateful I don't have to live that way anymore. I'm reinventing myself, as they say. Now instead of filling up seventy-thousand-seat stadiums I'm doing more intimate venues. Maybe God is giving me what I can handle now.

All I wanted back then was to be glamorous and glorious. That's why I fucked all my money away. I just wanted glory, glory, glory. Your whole objective is to win honor, but as time goes on in life, I realize that honor cannot be won, it can only be lost. Then I got that epiphany that everything I knew was a lie and that I had to start over. I had to be respectful to my wife. I couldn't refer to women as bitches and guys as niggas anymore. I couldn't have forty-five girlfriends and be married. How the hell did I ever do that? Maybe you can do that when you're a low-key guy but I did that when I was champion of the world. Do you have any idea what that was like? I was constantly dealing with pregnancies, abortions, diseases. One gave me gonorrhea. Another one gave me mono. I was living in a big West Nile virus swamp.

When you've never had anything, you tend to want to accumulate a lot when you can. But as you get older, you realize that life is not about accumulation, life is about loss. The older you get, the more loss you experience. We lose our hair, we lose our teeth, we lose our loved ones. Hopefully we learn to be strong from those losses and we can pass on our wisdom to the people we care about.

I've caused many bad things to happen to people. I was so selfish when I was young. I was the first one to say, "Shoot that motherfucker, that nigga needs to die." Then I'd see guys bleeding on the floor and I'd laugh about it. When I'm with my old friends from Brooklyn I'll say, "Remember when we fucked up that guy who tried to kill us that day?"

My friends will say, "Fuck that shit, Mike, we out here now."

Maybe they thought I was wired. They don't like to talk about the things we did. My friend Dave Malone would always say, "Mike, by the grace of God we're here."

I'm so glad that I'm not that guy anymore. Now I'm totally compassionate. And this is no religious rap. I don't believe in confessing your sins to get into heaven. I don't believe in an afterlife. This world is it. And it makes sense to do good in this world for your own moral existence. Doing good feels better than doing bad. Believe me, I should know. I've gotten away with doing a lot of bad things. There's no satisfaction in that, only in doing good.

I've really come to a place of forgiveness. I'm not mad at anybody like I used to be. Back then, I never understood what a waste of time that was. I don't hate Bill Cayton or Jimmy Jacobs for what they did to me. We all had a lot of good times, they gave me my start and I should be very grateful to them. I'm more bitter about myself than anyone else.

I've had an extraordinary life—the good, the bad, the ugly, the not so ugly, the very ugly. I don't even harbor ill will towards Don King. I hear he's not doing very well healthwise. And I'm writing a book. Those guys thought I would be dead or be a loony-tune by now. They never in a million years thought that I could be telling the truth about them now. They thought their lies would die with them.

I still have a lot of work to do. I have to try to really love myself. Not on a superficial "I'm great" level but to really examine who I am. That's going to take a whole bunch of struggle, a whole bunch of thinking, and a whole bunch of therapy. I can't underestimate how much therapy has played a role in changing my life. I think of Marilyn and all my doctors and counselors in my various rehabs and I'm eternally grateful to them. Marilyn took me to a place that I could never have been able to go. I might not be totally there, but she took me to a place where I could live, I could survive, in my confusion. I've still got some mental and emotional issues but I'm learning to live in this world, be happy in this world, where before I could never have been happy with a hundred million dollars. I could give it away, but I couldn't get shit done. I don't even have one percent of that now and I'm getting shit done. Marilyn visualized me being a respectable man with my family, staying in the house. Before, you could never keep me in the house.

When you're a young kid with a ton of money and girls, God is not really paramount in your life. As you get older, you realize that from a spiritual perspective your life has been a waste. You never did anything to help people collectively. I need to be of service rather than just going around doing meet and greets and collecting money. I feel dirty after my appearances. People come up to me and say, "You were great. You were my hero!" No, I'm not. I'm filthy and I'm wretched. But I want to make up for it now, pay back in some way. I don't want to offend you if you have any veneration for me, but it's just that I'm very shallow and simple and I just want to do something good and help people.

Kiki and I started a charity called Mike Tyson Cares. We're providing resources for kids from broken homes but I want to concentrate now on the mental condition of these children. You can't give kids a fighting chance if you don't give them a fighting mind. I know what it's like to be misdiagnosed at an early age and be put on medication that's capable of killing you. It's not just kids. Do you know how many people are in prison right now who need to be in a mental hospital and not behind bars? We've got to reform that.

People often ask me what I regret in my life. I regret sleeping with all those women. I used to brag about that but now I'm so embarrassed by my conquests. I'm so happy to be with one woman. I still enjoy looking at girls but I never ever think of crossing the line and saying something out of line. You aren't going to see me on Page Six in a nightclub with a table full of gold diggers.

I finally realized that I had to look for a different type of woman than my mother. All her relationships were dysfunctional. The more my mother fought back the more these men loved her. The more she'd scald them with boiling water or stab them, the more they bought her presents. That was the power structure in my household. Women that fought men. But Kiki is not that kind. I'm so happy I broke that cycle.

Kiki dug me out of the gutter and cleaned me up. I owe a great deal of my blossoming as a functional human being to her. I never thought that after boxing I would be famous, still living my life, making a career out of my life. I figured that I'd be dead or at best owning a bar. I could see myself off the cocaine but I never thought that I'd give up alcohol. I thought I'd be overweight for the rest of my life. And here I am being responsible, working, taking my kids to school. I owe all that to Kiki.

I'm a Cancer and I always tried to rescue women. But I don't look at Kiki as a damsel in distress who I have to take care of. I see her as an equal in life with me. She's capable of doing everything that I'm capable of doing. If someone gives me a job to do, I'm great at that. It's only when I have nothing to do that my mind tempts me to fuck up. I haven't gotten arrested since being with Kiki because I've got something to do. We make this stuff go well. Even if it doesn't look well from anybody else's eyes, it is going well for us.

I never thought I'd say something like this but I'm really happy being married to my wife. She's the best thing that ever happened to me. I'm safe here. Some interviewer once asked me where I felt most comfortable—hanging out in Cannes or on the streets of Brooklyn. And I told him that I'm most comfortable in the presence of all my family members and we're safe. I can wake up in the morning and everybody is there. I can see them.

Sometimes I think that I switched my addiction from drugs and alcohol to getting involved with my family. I know how much trouble and humiliation I can bring down on them with just one hit of blow or one drink of Hennessy. I don't want to let them down in any kind of fashion. Like I did with boxing, I want to put all my energy into living with my family. I know there's an empty hole in me and I spent a lot of years trying to fill it with drugs and booze and sex. I think it all goes back to our mortality. We know that all this is temporary. I'm going to grow old and die tomorrow or ten years from now or forty years if I'm lucky. But when you're with your family, it makes you feel like you'll last forever.

You get to this age and you just thank God for letting you live another day. He didn't owe us that day. So you have to live every day like it's your last. And you have to take personal responsibility. You can't blame things on society. If you want to be a better person you have to look within and overcome that. You are your own worst enemy. I know I am my own worst enemy. The only guy who wants to kill me is me. If anybody else treated me the way I treat myself, I would blow their fucking brains out.

I DON'T MEAN TO PREACH. I'M THE LAST ONE TO TELL ANYBODY HOW TO LIVE their life. I'm not in control of my own life. I'm just following a map. Do you feel me? I'm following the sound of a fucking flute. Living life on life's terms. I hate that phrase but I use it a lot to keep myself in check. Sometimes I still think I'm in control, even after all that time in rehab and my burning through hundreds of millions of dollars. That is my grand delusion. I think I'm a hell of a motherfucker but I'm just a bum.

I've always sought comfort from my pigeons. No matter where I lived, I had them with me. And I collect a special breed of pigeon. They're called roller pigeons. Sir Anthony Hopkins played Hannibal Lecter in that great movie and he talked about them.

Do you know what a roller pigeon is, Barney? They climb high and fast, then roll over and fall just as fast towards the earth. There are shallow rollers and deep rollers. You can't breed two deep rollers, or their young will roll all the way down, hit, and die.

IT'S NO SURPRISE THAT I HAVE AN AFFINITY FOR ROLLERS. IT'S REALLY SOME-thing to watch them fly higher than all the other birds, way up to the top of the sky and the clouds and then just roll and roll and roll down and if they're lucky, pull out in time before they crash headfirst into the ground. Rollers who are the offspring of a pair of deep rollers can't do that. They roll so fast that they create a suction and they can't open their wings and they just explode on impact. It looks horrific to us but if we put ourselves into the heart of that bird there's nothing like that feeling of plummeting down and rolling. It's a smorgasbord of endorphins and dopamine and adrenaline. A little like snorting coke and drinking Hennessy while being hooked up to a morphine drip.

Both of my parents were deep rollers. I was bred to climb to the top of the sky and tumble down. And I'm truly grateful that I found my wings before I hit the ground.

EPILOGUE

SOMETIMES I WAKE UP AND I JUST KNOW IT'S GOING TO BE A BAD DAY.
*I think that no one loves me and how I'm not going to have the life I
had planned to have when I first started out, and then I think that
I might hurt someone. Then I wish that I was under a rock somewhere.
I don't know how to live every day. I try. I do everything I can to thwart
any forms of violence. I'd let somebody kick my ass to prevent me from
fighting back. I thought you're supposed to get more mellow as you age
but I'm getting more irritable and bitter.*

*Even though I have a loving wife and children, I feel like I threw my
life away. Don't get me wrong, I love my family. I would die or kill for
them. That's part of the problem. I want my children to have a better
life when I'm dead and I don't know if that will happen. I don't know
if they'll have a much better life than I had in Brownsville. They might
be middle-class kids. These days I drive an Escalade. Some people
might think that's great but in my mind an Escalade isn't good enough
to give to a prostitute. I still owe money to the IRS. I'll probably die*

before I pay them off. I'm not making much money now. I'm looking good but I'm making nothing. I'm a bum. I can't believe my wife is still married to me. I feel like a dog.

I just don't have a good psychological opinion of myself. I hate myself sometimes. I feel like I don't deserve anything. Sometimes I just fantasize about blowing somebody's brains out so I can go to prison for the rest of my life. Working on this book makes me think that my whole life has been a joke. I'm a dark and jaded motherfucker. I hate living like a peasant now. I don't know if I'll survive to the next day. I might just say "Fuck it" and jump and leave.

Sometimes I can't sleep. I think that the reason I get so emotional is because of all the drugs I've fucked with for some many years. Your emotions get out of whack. I have a lot of pain and I don't know how to let it go. I used to be the toughest guy on the planet, and now I cry at the slightest provocation. I don't know what's wrong with me. I think I'm falling to pieces sometimes.

I'm a waste. The only thing I did was fight, fuck, and bring in kids. Boxing, bitches, and babies. My baseline normal is to destroy myself. And when I don't do that I think I should get rewarded. I'm the quintessential addict. I'm a piece of shit who thinks that the world revolves around them. I have the lowest self-esteem in the world but the biggest ego God could ever create. I'm such a glory junkie that I'll have to die in front of a crowd. I can't die in isolation. I'd say shit like, "How many people are there on the planet? Five billion? I could beat every one of them in a fair fight." Who would say crazy stuff like that? A lot of people have money, a lot of people have fame, but nobody had the gall like I did. Most famous people allow their fame to be bigger than them and their fame rules them. I wanted to be bigger than the fame.

I've been betrayed so much in my life that I don't trust people now. When people make you feel like you're incapable of being loved, you keep those feelings and they never go away. And when you feel incapable of being loved, then you want to hurt people and do bad things. What's the purpose of doing good things in a situation like that?

I think about where my mother and father came from. We're street people. I did things that they never dreamed I could do. I know it doesn't mean anything to anybody but when you come from sewage it means a lot. Even my kids don't know who I am. I know they have their childhood issues they deal with but they've never lived with rats and dogs in the sewage. They don't know how to hide in shit-infested sewage water so someone doesn't kill them. And I'm proud to be from that world. It's nothing to be proud of, but I'm very proud. My kids can read and write better than me but they can never surpass me in the hard knocks of life. And I don't want them ever to have to.

And I still hang out in the ghetto. I'm just a ghetto rug rat. Sometimes I'll look over at Farid and say, "Why are we here, Farid, when we could be on a yacht in Saint-Tropez? Why are we with these broke-assed niggas?" Because those broke-assed niggas are our people. They're struggling day and night. I love those rotten, dirty motherfuckers even though I can't trust them as far as I can throw them.

I can take anything. I think about Nietzsche a lot. I know what the Overman is. I know I can endure without killing anybody, because I'm always close. Some people don't have any decency or respect. When we're out and we see a guy like that, I'm thinking, I wish he would say something to my wife, I'd blow his brains out. Those people are out there but I've got to stop that way of thinking. I'm trying to restrain that, to be this new guy. But how much of my balls do I have to cut off to be this new guy?

Why am I not worried about fucking other people since this is going to be my last time around? All my life that's all I thought about. But now I'm not thinking about fucking nobody else. Am I grown up now? What am I doing being married with two kids? I'm a street dog, I'm not a house dog. If I still thought in my mind that I was this hoe-entangling motherfucker with the big schlong I wouldn't live like this. So either I'm suppressing my ego or I'm just losing my spirit. I'd like to think that I'm with my wife and not fucking around because I'm ready to be down and I love her. Or is it that I'm just broken down and I don't have any balls anymore?

All that rage and energy that propelled me to fuck all those women, where did it all go? Why have I lost that sexual growl? Is it just a function of getting older and losing hormones? I might see a girl and think

"Wow" but I don't have the desire to say "Hey, baby." And don't tell me about Viagra or Cialis. That shit ain't the same thing as natural desire. It doesn't make the mind function. It's like having a gun with no bullets. It doesn't give you the fantasy you need in your mind.

All my life all I could ever do was make money for people. My love was always under the circumstances of Mike Tyson providing stuff. Who would I be if I was never Mike Tyson? How would I form relationships? I don't know what it's like to go outside and initiate a conversation with someone. I've never had to do that. Sometimes I look at myself and I say, "Mike, you're a pussy. What the fuck are you doing? You're going to die soon. You're going to give all this pussy up and you are going to be with this woman that you've been sleeping with since she was twenty-four for the rest of your life?" I'm sure that my wife sometimes feels that I'm overbearing because I'm with her too much. I'm that way because I want her to know that the reason I don't go out much is to show her that I'm here with her. We've had those trust issues before. But then I become a burden to her, being home a lot.

I can't find a balance between the two. I'm not a balanced person. It's not like I can say, "Well, I'll just find another woman to be devoted to." If I'm not going to live this monogamous life with Kiki, then we're going to get in trouble now. I'm going to do drugs, I'm going to fuck a bunch of strippers and prostitutes, I might catch a disease, and I might make some guy jealous and he'll blow my brains out.

I'm not a relationship guy. I don't stand up for myself in a relationship. And I don't like that about me. If I'm not a pussy in a relationship, then I'm dominating them. Either I'm a henpecked bitch nigga or I'm going to start brutalizing the woman. One or the other, there's no middle ground. And I don't want to brutalize them, so I wind up being the wimp.

I'm insecure when it comes to being in a relationship. And why not? Growing up all I saw was men beating their women, women scalding their lovers, or a man killing another man over a woman or vice versa. That was my culture. Now I'm in a relationship where I'm suppressing my baseline normal to be in a normal relationship. And the selfish addict in me is saying, "Where's my reward? I think I deserve more for behaving this way." I want a reward for improving myself as a person. In a million years my wife would never understand what my baseline normal is. It would scare her to death. My baseline normal is having a bunch of girls in here, no matter if it's their mothers or their sisters, and fucking them. No female species allowed on the premises without fornication. It's that crude. I threw all that away. I spared my wife and the babies from all my diseases and all my filth. And I want something back.

I can't believe I'm even in a relationship. I don't think I'm a good catch. I'm ignorant, I have a lisp, I pronounce words the wrong way sometimes but still people want to give me pussy and be in my presence because I'm Mike Tyson. But I'm the worst catch. I'm a self-centered brat. I can't live with myself; why would anyone want to live with me? Whenever I've been in a relationship I'd always think, Bullshit, this can't be real. This woman doesn't love me. How can I be more special than any other people?

Sometimes I think that one of the reasons I got married was to stop women from setting my ass up. It's better to be married to one woman and be happy with what you have than to be a mark, a sucker to a whole fucking constellation of women.

For me life is a constant struggle for survival. I tell my wife that and she says, "No. The world is beautiful and positive." My wife is a facilitator. She takes care of people. She wants everybody to be in happy mode, satisfied and not angry. That's not a reality in life. Kiki wants to be a friend to everybody and when you are a friend of everybody, you are an enemy to yourself.

"Hey, try to put your arms around the world," I tell her.

She just calls me a miserable vegan. But you just can't make everyone happy. If you're not conscious, they're going to fuck you, hurt you, and take advantage of you. She doesn't see the evil in people that I do. I look at the world through the eyes of hell.

I'm starting to freak out now that my name is in the papers all the time and I'm constantly on television again. I'm worried that I can't deal with fame and that I'll get violent again. My wife keeps saying, "You can handle it now." But I just don't like it when I'm a target. Now that my wife is writing, maybe she'll get some more shows launched. Then she's in this whole writing world. I get very overprotective about her because she's all I have. I don't have forty-five other bitches anymore. I focus my whole energy on this family and all of that energy might be overbearing sometimes. I'm scared. And when I'm scared, that dickhead Iron Mike comes out.

Now I'm an entertainer and I'm entering a whole different world—the world of showbiz. I'm dreaming and thinking that one day we're going to hit the mother lode and things are going to be great again and I can take care of my kids and I can die with dignity, but that's not going to happen. Everybody knows how show business can be. And if I get screwed, that's just going to trigger all the times that I got played by Don and then I have to go into that mode where someone is going to get hurt. That's the world of show business? Then meet my world of violence. And then I'm back in the joint and my wife is married to somebody else and he's probably fucking my daughters. That's how it goes.

There's no doubt that I have some self-hatred issues. I've done some bad things to people. I can read any of the great books on morality—the Torah, the Koran, the New Testament, the Bhagavad Gita, whatever, and I just know I'm going to hell. And I was born in hell. And any time I came up in life it was one step out of hell. I think that part of the reason that I gave away so much money (and I'm not talking about buying prostitutes cars) was because I'm an ignorant child and I believe this was a way to cleanse my sins and buy my way back to heaven. I was kind and giving to people because my soul was so black from my earlier deeds.

What am I doing with my life? I love entertaining people but I'm only happy for that little time that I'm up on that stage. I was happy for a moment when I was boxing but a lot of it went away when Cus died. I never wanted to be Iron Mike. I hated that guy. That's the guy I had to be in order to survive. But I'm stupid for doing that.

Sometimes I don't know if I was even made for life. I think I'm an aberration of fucking nature. I've got to deal with people constantly shooting at me and throwing arrows at me. And nobody hears if I scream out in pain. I hate my life, I hate myself. If I had balls, I'd kill myself. That's it, that's how I feel. . . .

Then my little sweetheart Milan walks into the room and my cloud is lifted.

This is my reward for acting responsibly, right here. When she's away at school, I'm always grouchy and the minute she comes in, my whole life changes. This is where my ego stops, right here. I think about some of the crazy things I've done, like that road rage incident in Maryland. I'm so mad at myself. I had no hope back then. Even if those feelings came back I can't even fathom acting out now. I'd never want to disappoint the situation now like I did with my other kids. I could never be at the point of being so out of control that I would jeopardize Milan or Rocco. I'd have to be shot first. I've learned to bite my tongue because of my kids. A lot of times when I want to say things that are going to be nasty, I just bite it. It's my turn to embrace these responsibilities. This stuff is not as stressful as fighting. I might blow it up, but it's nowhere near as stressful.

I can't believe how my kids with Monica turned out. When I was younger I would have despised kids like them. They had it all, the nice house, the nice car, European trips since they were young. They had maids their whole life. The corners of the wall remind me of the beatings I got from my mother. My son doesn't have that fear. I always thought kids should sacrifice to get things. That was my upbringing with Cus. You win this fight, I'll give you this. If my son does something good or not, he's still going to get it.

I just didn't have any love or security growing up. I look at my children and tease them and say they're wimpy kids, but that's what would have happened to me if I grew up with love. I'd have been just as wimpy. Hey, this is how I am now getting love late in my life. I've done things like biting Evander's ear that have caused my kids to be teased. That's just something they have to deal with. They surely haven't been picked on and teased worse than I was. They haven't been snatched off the street and beaten. They all go to private schools and, on paper, they have cool friends. My friends were pimps and killers, robbers and thieves.

I don't have any parenting skills at all, not even to this day. I know my wife must think I'm a Neanderthal, but I'm doing my best. My older kids should be grateful that they didn't have my father as their father. He wouldn't be laid back waiting for a check every month. He'd tell the girls, "You don't need anything from me. You're sitting on your moneymaker." I never told anybody to sell her pussy. They'd see how bad bad is if my father had got their mothers pregnant.

Speaking of kids, I'm taking care of that fifteen-year-old boy that's still in me. I have the tools, I can do that now. He hasn't gone anywhere. He's still traumatized, but he's living a productive life now. It's awesome. I could never do this when I had $300 million. I'm out here raising kids, being a respectable husband, not having to worry about giving my wife a venereal disease. I've never been in this space in my life before, and this is just going to be so awesome. I never thought I was the settling type, I thought I deserved the world, but I feel safe here. This is where I want to be. I get to nurture my children and grow deeper with my wife and it feels good in my soul. That's why I'm here.

I could never go out at night again. That's just not going to happen. I could never be me again because a lot of people would be unhappy. I believe I keep the peace by being at home a lot, because people would never think I'm somewhere doing something I shouldn't be doing. Sometimes I think my wife would rather me go out sometimes. When you're around too much you can become overbearing. I don't care who you are. The real me probably wants to have some friends and shoot dice, have fun. I don't do that anymore. Now fun is hanging out with my little girl and getting to know her and Rocco. And hopefully developing a better relationship with all my other kids. My oldest daughter Mikey is living with me now in Vegas. That's been great. But I don't have any man cave where me and my friends could go to smoke cigars and watch football.

Another reason I stay in the house is to avoid getting involved with people outside. Before I went out on my *Undisputed Truth* national tour I stayed in so I wouldn't come into contact with strange people giving me bad vibes. I'd go outside for a minute or two and then come right back in. When I used to go out a lot it felt good but at the end of the day I was paying out of pocket to settle suits, apologizing to a bunch of people on television and maybe even doing time. So I don't go that route anymore. I stay in the fucking house because I don't want to get into an altercation. Can you believe that shit? But it's necessary. Cus had programmed my mind to be a switch. I could be an emotional wreck and in the blink of an eye, boom, it changed. Sometimes I'm uncomfortable to go outside because I don't know when that shit is going to click. I really don't. When I'm outside on the street, I'm so scared of myself—how I might perceive a situation to be something it's not. I have a lot more power over it than I did when I was younger. When I was younger I was programmed to attack all the time. That's why I got into so many street brawls when I was champ. My ego got attacked. Cus was an ego guy too.

"This guy said what to you? What did you do about it?"

I was a little fucking kid and he was going, "What did you do about it?" That's a part of me I always wanted to go away. I just never know what might trigger that shit, even an innocuous "Hey, guy" and then, boom, I was ferocious.

I have a pretty upside-down schedule now. I go to sleep at about six or seven, unless my wife gets me to watch a TV show with her, then it might be nine. I wake up at midnight or two a.m. Then I ride the stationary bike for an hour, do the Treadmaster, and then do squats. Today I did two hours with weights for my legs.

By then, Kiki is up. When I see her take both my babies and leave the house, I think they're never coming back. That's my biggest fear now. I'm in terror while she's gone. It's sad whenever my family isn't here and I'm alone. I used to love being alone but that was before I had this family situation. I never even think about doing anything wrong now. I would never want to go to jail. My whole job in life now is just to take care of my family and try to help people less fortunate than us. I can't believe I'm like this.

Because of the horrific things I've seen in my life, I get extra cautious. I'm always telling my wife to lock the doors, to keep her eyes on the place, to watch the workers. I tell her about my experiences where

I was in a house talking to some friends and then I left and I heard that a few hours later everybody in the house got killed. So these ugly stories play in my head. My wife thinks I'm absolutely insane. They've never met anybody like me. If a stranger comes into the house, I think, *Who is this guy? Who brought him in here?* Then, after he leaves, I may ask her to get out the sage and cleanse the energy in the house. My borderline normal was to go into someone's house and scope it out, then after I left, the thugs came in with the guns and screamed, "Everyone get down." That was my borderline normal.

When Kiki and the kids are gone I have plenty of time to think. I think about what a weird childhood I had, depending on my mother most of the time. How did I get out of that lowly, pathetic environment? How does a guy like me come out of Brownsville and become heavy-weight champ? When you go back in history you see that the only thing I had in common with most of the champs was our poverty. Jack Dempsey was a fucking hobo. I tried to draw on that to make sense of my story but it didn't click. How did I meet this guy Bobby Stewart who introduced me to Cus? How did Cus get me to think so gung ho? How did my mind just click and say, "Let's do it?" Where did that thinking come from? Was it just from the way I would follow people when I was young? And then I morphed into this boxing mentality.

Cus was telling everyone that lightning had struck him twice and he was going to have another heavyweight champion. But I was only thirteen. I never had an amateur fight in my life when he first saw me.

So how did he know when he died that I was going to be that guy? He never saw me really being mean to anybody. He didn't really see my confidence and arrogance grow in the ring. I wonder what he would have thought about who I became. He was a hard guy. He'd say stuff about other fighters like, "This guy is gutless. Leave him there to die." Cus believed that in the ring you should die on your shield, you don't quit. But now I realize that nothing is more important than life. There's no trophy, no belt, no glory more important than life and the people you love. I used to be the first to want to die with honor in the ring. Not anymore. That's a sucker's game. And I was probably the biggest sucker that ever came into this game.

I just knew that I was the champion of the world before I even had that belt. That was who I was. I still had this other entity Mike Tyson who I really didn't come to grips with. I didn't know who the fuck that guy was. I was this super champion–type guy and I never found out who I was in there. You'd think I was one of America's most wanted. Probation officers wanted detailed reports of where I was any time I went out. People were really afraid of me. I was such a little pussy kid but my image was so badass. That was pretty intoxicating. I always wanted to show people that I wasn't afraid so I overcompensated. I thought I had to be tough and mean because Cus escalated that mentality. "Superior," that was his favorite word. I was a superior fighter.

If Cus was around right now he'd say, "Mike, you should be fighting. Are you crazy?" But I don't regret a minute of it. All of the great fighters, Ray Robinson, Peter Jackson, Joe Gans, Tony Canzoneri, ended up in the gutter or working in some goddamn hotel lobby sweeping up. They were so extreme in their passion for fighting that they never thought about exit plans. But whatever they went through afterwards, it was worth it to have that championship. Just to have one year of living Mike Tyson, the champ's life, I would be a bum sucking rat piss in the gutter. Shit, yeah.

I don't want to make it sound like I'm a total hermit. I do go out of the house and do things. When we were writing this book, Ratso, my collaborator, and I went to the fourth Pacquiao-Marquez fight. Going to the fight with me was one of the auction items at my first Mike Tyson Cares fund-raiser. Two really nice young Mexican gentlemen won the bid and they sat with Ratso and me. That was also the first public appearance since the election for Mitt Romney. Ratso and I couldn't believe it when we saw him and his wife walk down to their ringside seats.

"Hey, Mitt, we're the forty-seven percent!" I screamed at him. Being in a household with a liberal woman who watches MSNBC twenty-four-seven must have rubbed off on me.

"Mitt, you're a little late courting the Mexican vote," I yelled. The audience was predominately Mexican fans of Marquez. The fight itself was amazing. It was one of the nights that reminded people how great boxing can be.

A month earlier, Kiki, Ratso, and I went to see Barbra Streisand at the MGM Grand. I always loved Barbra. When I was young, I read that her ego could have dwarfed Al Jolson's. I was always attracted to people with big egos because Cus used to say that the reason that people were the best was because they thought about themselves with the grandest of visions. The sun would always set upon their eyes. I had met Barbra when she came to my dressing room after my fight with Larry Holmes. She was what I'd consider a superstar. She's very soulful and I'm not saying this from a black or an ethnic perspective. She just makes you feel good in your soul with her singing. People get jealous and put down people like her because they can't give off that kind of energy and love, they can't woo people's hearts like Barbra can. I was enraptured the whole show. Afterwards, we went back to her dressing room and took a picture with her and Marie Osmond. The next day I was still emotionally drained. It was so exciting to be around her and to have seen her sing. She's meant so much to my mother and other people in my life. I'm just happy to be alive when she's performing.

But even going to that concert was a bit of an ordeal. As we were walking to the show through the casino, I saw some of my old pimp and drug dealer friends. They see me with my wife, they know enough not to talk to me. They know I'm constantly battling demons. When I'm walking in a place like that I just walk straight through. The three of us went to another show while I was working on the book. Mike Epps was doing stand-up at the Palms. My wife was behind us and she didn't see that when I came to the table a lady got up and tried to hug me.

"No, I can't hug you," I told her. Luckily some guy had gotten between us.

"See how I saved you just now," the guy winked at me.

Kiki would have had a heart attack. That's why I don't like to go out that much. I have more fun chilling at home. It's fun to be out if

I'm in a controlled environment but most of the time people are all drunk and they can confront you. I've become more, I want to say protective, but it's really possessive of my wife than when we were dating. I think I always have to protect her. but she's very capable of handling men that hit on her. I forget how she handled me when I hit on her all those years before we finally connected. Kiki's a very smart and sophisticated lady. She knows her way around. I may think of her as almost my child at times but in our relationship, I'm more her child than she is mine.

Whenever I go to see a great entertainer, I'm just so thrilled to be in the same fraternity as them. If I could live this way for the rest of my life and still be paying bills, I'd be happy with my destiny. Paying my bills, not getting caught, not getting thrown in jail, not getting in any drama. I don't care if I don't have anything to leave behind to the kids, just to live where nobody is hurting is enough. I never thought I'd be in such desperate, dire straits to survive. I'm a material nigga. Some bad habits die slow. I don't want to be that way, I don't want to care more about my clothes than I do about my health. When I die, I want to have the cheapest funeral of all time. Put me in the dirt, no casket or anything, just throw me in there. Don't come visit me or none of that bullshit. But I'm sure some boxers in the future would search out my grave, like I did to the old-time guys. I'd be happy that people would treat me the same way I did with my heroes. Maybe I would have a tombstone. It could read, "Now I'm at peace."

When I think about Kiki and me I'm still amazed. Our love blossomed during a time of real adversity. I am such a difficult person to live with. Cancers magnetize shit inwardly. It sounds cool to live with a person that's so in tune with his sensitivity but there's nothing actually cool about that. He's so in tune with his sensitivity he may be delusional. I commend my wife for going through the duration of waiting for me to not be like that anymore. Going through the process of me changing my ill-thought-out ideas about women in general was almost like going through the Spanish Inquisition for her.

I have so much admiration for my wife. She makes me love myself when I want to blow my brains out. I respect her so much for how much she wants this stuff between us to work. If back then she would have said "Fuck it" and taken the baby somewhere else, I would have been so happy. I really have no idea what made me stay loyal to this girl. I don't even know what gave me the strength to try to change my barometer of the past forty years. I never knew anything about commitment. I've been madly in love with girls before but I still always cheated on them and was disloyal emotionally and physically. Kiki made me strong enough to even attempt to go on that journey towards being a loyal man. It's greatness in itself, even though you don't accomplish that attempt, even though you fail. That's how complex a situation this is. Imagine what you'd reach if you were that individual. That's when you become a champion of moral accomplishments.

I am so appreciative of Kiki. I don't care if my wife was a prostitute with full-blown AIDS, I wouldn't deserve her. That's real talk. I don't deserve my wife. I got her probably because of who I am and what my accomplishments were and because basically I'm a decent person but no way in life do I deserve to be with my wife. I'm such a bum compared to her.

What do we really know about love? Love commands us, we don't command love. And when it commands you, you have to answer that call. No one ever refuses love's call even if the nature of love is ruthless. I don't know what love is but I suffer from its symptoms: insanity and total bondage at an unfathomable level. But it also can command you to rise to the highest of your potential. Love can be just an orgasm to some people. To others it can be the thought of love, a fantasy we strive to grasp and live out. I tell my wife that I love her every second of the day but my love is what? My love is jaded, my love is toxic sometimes, my love is romantic, my love is lustful, my love is celibate, my love is many things. Love sacrifices control on its altar. It's disastrous to give up control and still don't know what you are giving it up for, but you're willing to do that because love felt good. But you still don't know if it's going to feel better than giving up the control. So you've got one foot in hell and one foot in heaven. Sometimes we like to conceive of lust as love because we think it feels so good it has to be love. Love is sacrifice, love is worth dying and killing for, history proves that. But we must have some kind of moral compass in our journey through life. All enjoyment is not good enjoyment.

I have a favorite book that I try to read every day. It's called *The World's Greatest Letters: From Ancient Greece to the Twentieth Century.* I love connecting to the past this way. You learn so much about these people by reading their letters. Some of these people are so self-centered they don't think that anyone else is capable of loving the way they do. A lot of these guys are control freaks and they get frustrated because their love is not answered quickly enough. What these people are writing is so poetic, the way they express themselves in language is so breathtaking. And sometimes the person they're writing to doesn't give a shit about them.

I read these letters and I cry. You think about Napoleon, this great world leader, and you read a letter where he's begging to his love Josephine to come to him and she doesn't. Check it out:

April 4th, 1796

By what art have you become able to captivate all my faculties, to concentrate in your self my moral existence? It is a magic, my sweet love which will end only with me. To live for Josephine, that is the history of my life. I am trying to reach you, I am dying to be near you. Time was when I prided myself on my courage and sometimes when considering the evil which men might be able to do me, a fate which I have expected. I fixed my eyes most steadfastly on the most unheard-of misfortunes without frowning, without being surprised. But today the idea that my Josephine might be unwell, the idea that she might be ill and above all, the cruel, the fatal thought that she might love me less, it withers my soul, stops my blood, makes me sad cast down, and leaves me not even the courage of fury and despair. I have often used to say to myself that man could have no power over him who dies without regrets. But today, to die without being loved

by you, to die without that certainty is the torment of hell, is the
lifelike and striking image of absolute annihilation. I feel as if I will
be stifled, my only companion, you who fate has decreed to make
with me the painful journey of life, the day when I shall no longer
possess your heart, will be that when parched nature will be without
warmth and without vegetation. Love thee as your eyes, but that is
not enough, as yourself, more than yourself, as your thoughts, your
mind, your sight, your all. Sweet beloved, forgive me, I am worn out.
Nature is weak for him who feels keenly, for him whom you love.

Your illness, that is what occupies my mind night and day.
Without appetite, without sleep, without care for my friendships, for
glory, for fatherland, you, and the rest of the world exists no more for
me than if it were annihilated. I prize honor since you prize it, I
prize victory since that gave you pleasure, without which I shall
have left all to throw myself at your feet. In your letter, my darling,
be careful to tell me that you are convinced that I love you beyond all
imagination. That you are persuaded that every moment of my life is
consecrated to you; that never an hour passes without my thinking of
you, that never has the thought of thinking of another woman has
entered my head.

I love this guy's stuff! Napoleon is a nut. He's turned out! Josephine didn't care a damn about Napoleon. That was a Robin Givens
deal right there. Sometimes I take the book up to our bedroom and I
read these letters to Kiki. This is my favorite. It's a letter written by
the great German poet and dramatist Heinrich von Kleist. In the fall
of 1811 he fell in love with a housewife named Henriette Vogel. He
was thirty-four, she was thirty-one. They shared a passion for music.
But Henriette was dying of uterine cancer. Heinrich was a depressive
type and he was poor and was looking for immortality. Vogel wasn't
the first lady that he asked to enter into a double-suicide pact, but she
was the first to say yes. They spent the night at a small inn drinking
wine and coffee with rum. The next morning they seemed ecstatic as
they went down to the lake. First he shot Henriette and then he shot
himself. This is one of his last letters to her:

My Jeanette, my little heart, my dear thing, my devout, my love, my dear, my sweet, my life, my light, my all good, my shadow, my castle, my acre, my lawn, my vineyards, O sun, oh my life, sun, moon, the stars, the heavens, my past, my future, my bride, my girl, my dear friend, my innermost being, my heart blood, my internal star of my eyes, O dearest what should I call you? My golden child, my pearl, my precious stone, my crown, my queen, my empress. You dear darling of my life, my highest, my most precious, my baptism, my children. You are my tragic plays, you are my posthumous reputation, you are my second, a better self, you are my virtue, you are my merit, you are my hope, my heaven, my child of God, you are my intercessor, you are my guardian, my angel, my concubine. How I love you so.

I read that out loud and then Kiki and I cry together.
Ain't that something?

POSTSCRIPT TO THE EPILOGUE

THAT WAS THE WAY I INTENDED TO END THE BOOK. KIKI AND I ALL MISTY-eyed, reading the love letters of great people in bed—my darkness gone, my spirit soaring from the inspirational words of our giants of history. But you have to live life on life's terms, as I've said in the book. And I couldn't live with myself if I lied and tried to cover up what happened in the last few months.

Maybe part of it was searching my soul and digging into the darkest corners of my psyche to honestly answer Ratso's questions about my life. It also could have been the pressure of going back into the world of boxing and entering the ring once again, this time as a promoter and nurturer of young boxing talent. Of course, my chronic negative self-image doesn't need much ammunition to act out and sabotage whatever joy and happiness comes into my life.

But it happened and I have to tell you about it. About a month or so after I completed work on the book, in April of 2013, I had a slip, my first one since January of 2010. I went out one night and I had a drink. And then another. And another. I told you I'm a bad, bad drunk so I smoked some pot to make me mellow again. I felt horrible when I came back to Kiki and the kids that night. But not terrible enough to stop me from repeating my slip a few more times in June and July of this year. And then in August, a week before my first Iron Mike fight promotion, which was broadcast on ESPN, I fell off the wagon again.

Look, I'm a vicious addict and if I don't follow my steps, I'm going to die. So I started going to A.A. meetings again. One of the most important steps is to make amends. So right before the first fight on my first card as a promoter I walked over to Teddy Atlas, my old trainer, who was doing the color commentary for ESPN. I extended my hand and I apologized to him for my part in what happened back there in Catskill in the '80s. I hadn't talked to Teddy for almost twenty years. It felt good to make amends. I guess that gesture meant a lot to people because that was the first thing they wanted to talk about both during the fights and in the interview I did between fights.

I was already dealing with a lot of emotions of guilt and shame for my recent relapses so seeing Teddy and making amends to him seemed to put me over the top. I realized that I couldn't just keep on lying and pretending that I was still clean; that I hadn't had some drinks or smoked some pot. So when someone at the postfight press conference asked me what it was like seeing Teddy again, I had to unburden myself.

"I knew that there was a possibility that I would be here with Teddy and I didn't have a good thought in mind about that at first, because I'm negative and I'm dark. And I wanna do bad stuff. I wanna hang out in this neighborhood alone [I pointed to my head], that's dangerous to hang out in this neighborhood alone up here, right? It wants to kill everything. It wants to kill me too. So I went to my A.A. meeting and I explained to my fellow alcoholics and junkies that I was gonna deal with this certain situation here, and I explained the feelings that I evoked from it. Almost like, um, something like a Hatfields and McCoys, I kind of explained to them. I made the right decision. I made Cus proud of me. I made myself proud of me.

"I hate myself. I'm trying to kill myself. I hate myself a lot, but I made myself proud of myself, and I don't do that much. I was happy I did that. Maybe it was overwhelming to Teddy and he didn't get it yet. But he has to know this is sincere. I don't wanna fight you no more. I was wrong. I'm sorry. I was wrong. I just wanted to make my amends. If he accepted it or not, at least I could die and go to my grave and say I made my amends with everybody I hurt. It's all about love and forgiveness, and in order for those guys to forgive me—other guys—you know, I want people to forgive the things I've done.

"I'm a motherfucker. I did a lot of bad things, and I want to be forgiven. So in order for me to be forgiven, I hope they can forgive me. I wanna change my life; I wanna live a different life now. I wanna live my sober life. I don't wanna die. I'm on the verge of dying, because I'm a vicious alcoholic. Wow. God, this is some interesting stuff."

I choked up. And then I confessed.

"I haven't drank or took drugs in six days, and for me that's a miracle. I've been lying to everybody else that thinks I was sober. I'm not. This is my sixth day. I'm never gonna use again."

The press in the audience gave me a standing ovation but that meant nothing to me. No one gives you standing ovations when you share in the rooms.

That was on August twenty-third. I've added a few days to my total as I'm writing this now. I hope that I can keep clean and add more and more days and get more and more chips. I guess I was arrogant thinking that I could beat this thing without the help of my support team and my A.A. family, who belong to the only club that accepts people like me as members. I don't want to die. I want to continue my boxing career as a promoter. I want to do my one-man show again. I want to do more movies.

After my recent relapse I was no fun to be around. Kiki and I were having a lot of rough times. Part of me was even trying to blame the pressures of being married as the reason for my relapse. Then the galleys for the book came. In going over the book with Kiki I had a spiritual rebirth. When we got to the section about Exodus it was very difficult to get through. We both cried our eyes out. And I realized in that very moment why I was married to Kiki. I suddenly knew the answer to the question "Why would a guy like me be married?" I realized that our marriage was more than the union of Kiki and me. I had to be married to Kiki to fulfill Exodus's legacy. My marriage will allow me to do that and to bolster my ability to be a good father. I'm a better person now because Exodus was in my life and I vow to continue to be a better person now that she's gone. I truly want to deepen my relationship with Kiki and see my kids grow up to be healthy and happy. But I can't do any of those things if I don't have control over myself. I can't help anyone if I'm not well myself, and I desperately want to get well. I have a lot of pain and I just want to heal. And I'm going to do my best to do just that. One day at a time.

A NOTE ON LEXICON

THERE ARE TWO WORDS THAT I FREQUENTLY USE IN THIS BOOK THAT DESERVE a bit of explanation. One of them is "nigga." This word gained widespread traction in the younger black community through its use by early hip hop and rap artists such as Grandmaster Flash, N.W.A., Tupac, and Ol' Dirty Bastard, as well as comedians such as Paul Mooney and Chris Rock. Whether I use the term pejoratively or endearingly depends on the context. I'm as apt to say "Fuck that nigga, I hate him" as I am to say "I love this nigga, I'd die for him." And I do not use the term exclusively to denote people of color. Back in Brownsville, we'd often say, "Man, those big old white stupid Italian niggas, they're trying to play me." Later in my life, after I'd meet with HBO or Showtime executives to discuss my fights, I'd say, "Fuck them niggas." "What the fuck are you talking about? Those are Jews," one of my friends would say. "No, they are niggas. A nigga is a state of mind."

While "nigga" can be used in both a positive and negative fashion, when you combine "nigga" with "shit" it can only be seen as a condemnation. For example, a friend of yours may have several fine ladies that he wishes to have fun with. He may ask a few of your friends to participate in the party but you are required by him to watch the door, effectively excluding you from the social intercourse. That is known as "nigga shit"—behavior characteristic of a selfish, no good motherfucker.

The other word that needs explanation is the term "smuck." My collaborator, Larry "Ratso" Sloman, is of the Jewish persuasion. After hearing me say "smuck" a few times, Ratso was quick to point out that I was mispronouncing the Yiddish word "schmuck." "Schmuck" originally meant penis, but its meaning was broadened to denote someone who was foolish or, in extreme cases, contemptible or detestable. In some Jewish homes, the word "schmuck" was thought to be so vulgar that it was actually taboo. After being corrected a few times, I informed Ratso that I had coined the term "smuck" quite properly. In my usage, a "smuck" is half a "schmuck." By preceding "smuck" with the "shhhh" you are, in fact, giving that contemptible person too much credit. A schmuck is a schmuck, but a smuck is not even worthy of schmuck status. In this book, I use both words advisedly.

ACKNOWLEDGMENTS

MIKE WOULD LIKE TO THANK:

Cus D'Amato, my mentor, friend, and general. Because of you, my life has reached heights I could never have imagined. Without you, I don't know where I would be today. My gratitude to you is immeasurable. As long as I am breathing, your legacy will continue to live on. Our names are forever synonymous. You can't mention my name without a reference to your legacy nor can people mention your name without a reference to my legacy.

I would like to give a very special thanks to my collaborator, Larry "Ratso" Sloman, for being such a cool "cat." (That's Larry's favorite word. I had to edit many of them out of the manuscript.) This entire process wasn't necessarily easy for me. At times it was very difficult to rehash some of the darker moments in my life. Larry, you have been the fly on the wall that at times I wanted to smash, but you knew how to buzz off and fly back around when the moment was better for me. I am grateful for your patience and diligence. You really know how to roll with the punches. I don't think there is another writer around that could have done a better job. When it comes to writing, you are "The Baddest Man on the Planet." You're more than just a writer to me, you're family. Looking forward to working on many other projects with you in the near future.

Thank you to David Vigliano at Vigliano Associates for coordinating everything. David, you are a great person. You're more than just a book agent. I consider you a friend.

Thank you to David Rosenthal, publisher of Blue Rider Press, for your patience and enthusiasm for this project. I'm really grateful that you believed in the vision and have supported it 100 percent.

I would also like to thank my legal team at Grubman Indursky Shire & Meiselas, P.C., in particular Kenny Meiselas for putting together such an incredible legal team. Thank you, Jonathan Ehrlich, for combing through the contracts with a fine-tooth comb.

Thank you to Damon Bingham and Harlan Werner for the initial introduction to Vigliano Associates.

My deepest love and gratitude to my friends, family, and supporters for taking time out of their busy lives to share stories with Ratso.

A very special acknowledgment to my children: Mikey, Gena, Rayna, Amir, Miguel, Milan, and Morocco. Everything I do is for you all. I love you, Exodus Sierra Tyson. You are my eternal Angel. There isn't a day that goes by that I don't think of you. The four years I shared with you on this planet were the best of my life. You will never be forgotten.

Finally, to my dear wife, Kiki—thank you for your unconditional love and support and putting up with me. I know it's not always easy, but I am very appreciative of everything you do. I love you.

LARRY WOULD LIKE TO THANK:

Michael Gerard Tyson. To say this project has been a labor of love would be an understatement. I've been wanting to work with Mike since 1994, right after *Private Parts*, my collaboration with Howard

Stern, was published. For me, Mike was one of the most interesting cultural figures on the scene and I felt that his story would be illuminating and moving. While Mike was incarcerated in Indiana, I sent him a copy of Nietzsche's autobiography, *Ecce Homo*, and proposed we work together on a memoir.

In 2008, thanks to the recommendation of his then-agent, Harlan Werner, and Dr. Monica Turner, his ex-wife, Mike chose me to be his collaborator. As you've read in this book, that time was not propitious for Mike to work on a book, and the project was postponed. Four years later, Mike was in a much better place, and we began.

Working with Mike was the most unusual and gratifying experience I'd had in my career as a celebrity chronicler. As the whole world knows, he's painfully honest and incredibly sensitive. When certain topics came up in our talks—his childhood or the role of Cus D'Amato, his mentor, are two prime examples—Mike would tear up and sometimes sob uncontrollably. On the other hand, in the middle of relating his favorite stories, he would jump up, do a little dance around the room, and then come back and slap me five. I've probably been slapped five more times by Mike Tyson than anybody else on the planet and lived to tell the tale. The man doesn't know his own strength.

Mike is not the kind of guy to sit down and calmly relate stories from his life. I taped conversations with him in his garage with his mating pigeons cooing in the background, in the back room of the barbershop he hangs out in in north Vegas, in the passenger seat of his Escalade on the way to picking up his daughter from school, and in the Salvatore Ferragamo shop at Caesars in Vegas while he tried on shirts. I carried around my Casio tape recorder 24/7 because I never knew when he would suddenly have an incredible insight into Cus or remember a story from his childhood that was spellbinding.

I spent months in Vegas at Mike's house, taping our talks, going over his massive legal files, and interviewing some of his closest associates. It's not easy and not always fun being away from home for so long, but I was adopted by two families in Vegas, both of whom made my life considerably more pleasant.

First, I have to give thanks to Mike's wonderful family. His wife, Kiki, is a spectacular helpmate to Mike, and you wouldn't be reading this book right now if not for her. Mike's mother-in-law, Rita; Kiki's brother Azheem and his wife, Jahira; and Mike's oldest daughter, Mikey, were always there to nurture me, feed me, and console me when Mike was more interested in shopping than talking. Mike's assistant, David Barnes, aka Wayno aka Farid, was always helpful and ready to go the extra mile. And Mike's two young children, Milan and Rocco, were always a source of much joy and mirth.

I had a second family in Vegas. While I was working with Mike, I stayed at the Slammer, the amazing home of my dear friend Penn Jillette. Penn; his wife, Emily Zolten; and his two children, his daughter, Moxie, and his son, Zolten, were the most gracious of hosts. At night, if I got bored, I went to see Penn and Teller perform. When I wanted to watch a grade-C movie, Penn and Emily's movie nights in the home theater were always a most welcome and riotous diversion.

I'm indebted to all of Mike's wonderful friends and colleagues who took the time out of their busy schedules to do interviews with me. Thanks to Brian Hamill, Craig Boogie, Calvin Hollins, Eric "EB" Brown, David Chesnoff, Steve "Crocodile" Fitch, David Malone, Frankie Mincieli, Jeff Greene, Hope Hundley, Jackie Rowe, Jay Bright, Lance Sherman, Latondia Lawson, Steve Lott, Mack Smith, Marilyn Murray, Mario Costa, Mark D'Attilio, Darryl Francis, Anthony Pitts, Michael Politz, Rick Bowers, Rodney Tyson, Sean MacFarland, Muhammad Siddeeq, Tom Patti, Tony Anderson, Damon Bingham, Jim Voyles, and Jeff Wald. We're also indebted to a man we never met but we heard. Early in the project Mike played me hours and hours of tapes of Cus and Cus's friends and colleagues talking to a young journalist in Catskill named Paul Zuckerman. These interviews were a great resource in getting into the head of Cus at the time when Mike had just come into his life. We tried to track down Zuckerman, to no avail. But hopefully his insights into Cus and his adroit interviews will someday see the light of day.

I owe a huge debt of gratitude to David Rosenthal, publisher extraordinaire, for his infinite patience and levelheaded wisdom. Thanks also to everyone up at Blue Rider Press, especially editor Vanessa Kehren. Also at Blue Rider, special thanks to Aileen Boyle, Sarah Hochman, Gregg Kulick, Phoebe Pickering, Brian Ulicky, Joe Benincase, Meredith Dros, Linda Rosenberg, Rob Sternitzky, and Eliza Rosenberry.

I'm always grateful to my wonderful agent, David Vigliano, for his persistence and counsel and to his associate Matthew Carlini for navigating all the foreign editions of this work.

It wouldn't be a Mike Tyson book without thanking some lawyers. My longtime lawyer, the late Laurie Rockett, carved out our initial agreement in 2008. Eric Rayman came on board in 2012 and worked his magic when the project was revived. And Linda Cowen did a fine job reviewing the manuscript for the publisher. And much thanks, as ever, to my attorney Charles DeStefano, who's always there for me.

Thanks always to the greatest transcriber around, Jill Matheson, for sacrificing body and soul to make the deadline. I'm also indebted to Zachary Zimmerman for his conscientious research work. No problem was too hard for him to surf the 'Net and solve.

And finally I'm always indebted to my number-one family, Christy Smith-Sloman and Lucy. They weathered Hurricane Sandy and ate peanut butter and jelly (or, in the case of Lucy, Newman's Own Peanut Butter Dog Treats) by candlelight while I was working thousands of miles away. Christy is always supportive of my works and my quirks and I'm eternally grateful for her love. And as long as those treats keep coming, Lucy's in my corner too.

PHOTO CREDITS

FIRST PHOTO INSERT
Page 1: (*top left*) courtesy of Mike and Kiki Tyson; (*top right*) courtesy of Mike and Kiki Tyson; (*bottom*) © Steve Lott/Boxing Hall of Fame Las Vegas
Page 2: (*top*) © Ken Regan; (*bottom*) © Steve Lott/Boxing Hall of Fame Las Vegas
Page 3: © Steve Lott/Boxing Hall of Fame Las Vegas
Page 4: © Steve Lott/Boxing Hall of Fame Las Vegas
Page 5: (*top*) © Ken Regan; (*bottom*) © Ken Regan
Page 6: © Lori Grinker/Contact Press Images
Page 7: (*top*) © Steve Lott/Boxing Hall of Fame Las Vegas; (*bottom*) © Lori Grinker/Contact Press Images
Page 8: (*top*) © Richard Harbus/Bettmann/Corbis; (*bottom right*) © Ken Regan; (*bottom left*) © AFP/Getty Images
Page 9: (*top*) © Charlie Blagdon/Bettmann/Corbis; (*bottom*) © Bettmann/Corbis
Page 10: (*top*) © Bettmann/Corbis; (*bottom*) © Bettmann/Corbis
Page 11: (*top*) © Lori Grinker/Contact Press Images; (*bottom*) © Bettmann/Corbis
Page 12: (*top*) © *The Ring* magazine/Getty Images; (*bottom*) © *The Ring* magazine/Getty Images
Page 13: (*top*) © Steve Lott/Boxing Hall of Fame Las Vegas; (*bottom*) © Steve Lott/Boxing Hall of Fame Las Vegas
Page 14: © Steve Lott/Boxing Hall of Fame Las Vegas
Page 15: (*top*) courtesy of Mike and Kiki Tyson; (*bottom*) © *The Ring* magazine/Getty Images
Page 16: (*top*) © Misha Erwitt/New York *Daily News* Archive via Getty Images; (*bottom*) © Anthony Barboza/Getty Images

SECOND PHOTO INSERT
Page 1: courtesy of Mike and Kiki Tyson
Page 2: (*top*) © Eugene Garcia/AFP/Getty Images; (*bottom*) © John Ruthroff/AFP/Getty Images
Page 3: © Lennox McLendon/Associated Press
Page 4: © Jeff Haynes/AFP/Getty Images
Page 5: © Mike Nelson/AFP/Getty Images
Page 6: (*top*) © Jeff Haynes/AFP/Getty Images; (*bottom*) © Jeff Haynes/AFP/Getty Images
Page 7: © Neil Leifer/*Sports Illustrated*/Getty Images
Page 8: (*top left*) courtesy of Mike and Kiki Tyson; (*top right*) courtesy of Mike and Kiki Tyson; (*bottom*) courtesy of Mike and Kiki Tyson
Page 9: © Trae Patton/NBCU Photo Bank
Page 10: © AFP/Getty Images
Page 11: (*top*) courtesy of Marilyn Murray; (*bottom*) courtesy of Mike and Kiki Tyson
Page 12: courtesy of Mike and Kiki Tyson
Page 13: courtesy of Mike and Kiki Tyson
Page 14: (*top*) courtesy of Mike and Kiki Tyson; (*bottom*) courtesy of Mike and Kiki Tyson
Page 15: courtesy of Mike and Kiki Tyson
Page 16: courtesy of Mike and Kiki Tyson

ABOUT THE AUTHORS

Mike Tyson is the former undisputed heavyweight champion of the world, and the first boxer to ever hold the three biggest belts in prizefighting—the WBC, WBA, and IBF world heavyweight titles—simultaneously. Tyson's enduring appeal has launched him into a career in entertainment: He was a standout in the blockbuster films *The Hangover* and *The Hangover Part II*, and recently he has earned tremendous acclaim for his one-man show *Tyson—The Undisputed Truth*. Tyson has launched a clothing company (Mike Tyson Collection) and Tyrrhanic Productions, which currently has several film projects in development. In 2011, Tyson was inducted into the Boxing Hall of Fame. He lives in Las Vegas with his wife, Kiki, and their children.

Larry "Ratso" Sloman is best known as Howard Stern's collaborator on *Private Parts* and *Miss America*. Sloman's recent collaborations include *The Secret Life of Houdini*, with magic theorist William Kalush; *Mysterious Stranger* with magician David Blaine; *Makeup to Breakup: My Life In and Out of Kiss* with drummer Peter Criss; and *Scar Tissue*, the memoir of Red Hot Chili Peppers lead singer Anthony Kiedis. All six books were *New York Times* best sellers.